ENCYCLOPEDIA OF
EMANCIPATION
AND ABOLITION
IN THE TRANSATLANTIC WORLD

VOLUME THREE

EDITED BY JUNIUS RODRIGUEZ

SHARPE REFERENCE
an imprint of M.E. Sharpe, Inc.

SHARPE REFERENCE

Sharpe Reference is an imprint of M.E. Sharpe, Inc.

M.E. Sharpe, Inc.
80 Business Park Drive
Armonk, NY 10504

Library of Congress Cataloging-in-Publication Data

Encyclopedia of emancipation and abolition in the transatlantic world / Junius Rodriguez, editor.
    p. cm.
Includes bibliographical references and index.
ISBN 978-0-7656-1257-1 (alk. paper)
    1. Slavery—History—Encyclopedias. 2. Liberty—History—Encyclopedias. I. Rodriguez, Junius P.

HT985.E53 2008
306.3′6203—dc22   2006035834

Cover images: Clockwise from top left corner, provided by Getty Images and the following:
English School/The Bridgeman Art Library; MPI/Stringer/Hulton Archive; FPG/Taxi; Stringer/
Hulton Archive; MPI/Stringer/Hulton Archive; Henry Guttmann/Stringer/Hulton Archive;
MPI/Stringer/Hulton Archive.

Printed and bound in the United States

Publisher: Myron E. Sharpe
Vice President and Editorial Director: Patricia Kolb
Vice President and Production Director: Carmen Chetti
Executive Editor and Manager of Reference: Todd Hallman
Senior Development Editor: Jeff Hacker
Development Editor: Gina Misiroglu
Project Editor: Laura Brengelman
Program Coordinator: Cathleen Prisco
Text Design: Carmen Chetti and Jesse Sanchez
Cover Design: Jesse Sanchez

Contents

Topic Finder

Abolitionists, American

Allen, Richard (African American bishop)
Allen, William G.
Anderson, Osborne Perry
Beecher, Henry Ward
Benezet, Anthony
Birkbeck, Morris
Birney, James Gillespie
Blanchard, Jonathan
Bowditch, Henry Ingersoll
Brown, John
Buffum, Arnold
Burleigh, Charles Calistus
Butler, Benjamin Franklin
Channing, William Ellery
Child, David Lee
Cornish, Samuel E.
Cuffe, Paul
Dawes, William
Day, William Howard
Delany, Martin Robison
Dillwyn, William
Downing, George Thomas
Du Bois, W.E.B.
Forten, James, Sr.
Foster, Stephen Symonds
Garnet, Henry Highland
Garrison, William Lloyd
Gatch, Philip
Gay, Sydney Howard
Gibbons, James Sloan
Gibbs, Mifflin Wistar
Grinnell, Josiah B.
Grosvenor, Cyrus Pitt
Hamilton, William
Hayden, Lewis
Hopkins, Samuel
Johnson, Oliver
Langston, John Mercer
Lay, Benjamin
Lovejoy, Elijah P.
Lovejoy, Owen
Lundy, Benjamin

May, Samuel Joseph
McKim, James Miller
Miller, Jonathan Peckham
Mott, James, and Lucretia Coffin Mott
Nell, William Cooper
Norton, John Treadwell
Olmsted, Frederick Law
Owen, Robert Dale
Paine, Thomas
Paul, Nathaniel
Pennington, James W.C.
Phillips, Wendell
Pillsbury, Parker
Purvis, Robert
Ray, Charles B.
Realf, Richard
Reason, Charles L.
Reason, Patrick H.
Rock, John Sweat
Rush, Benjamin
Smith, Gerrit
Spooner, Lysander
Steward, Austin
Stroyer, Jacob
Sunderland, La Roy
Tappan, Arthur
Tappan, Benjamin
Tappan, Lewis
Torrey, Charles Turner
Vaux, Roberts
Ward, Samuel Ringgold
Washington, Bushrod
Weld, Theodore Dwight
Whitting, William
Woolman, John
Wright, Elizur
Wright, Henry Clarke
Wright, Theodore Sedgwick

Abolitionists, Brazilian

Gama, Luís
Lacerda, Carlos de
Menezes, José Ferreira de

Historical Events, Periods, and Occasions

Laws, Decrees, and Governing Documents

Newspapers, Periodicals, Editors, and Publishers

Novels, Novelists, Playwrights, and Poets

Pamphlets, Tracts, Nonfiction Works, and Writers

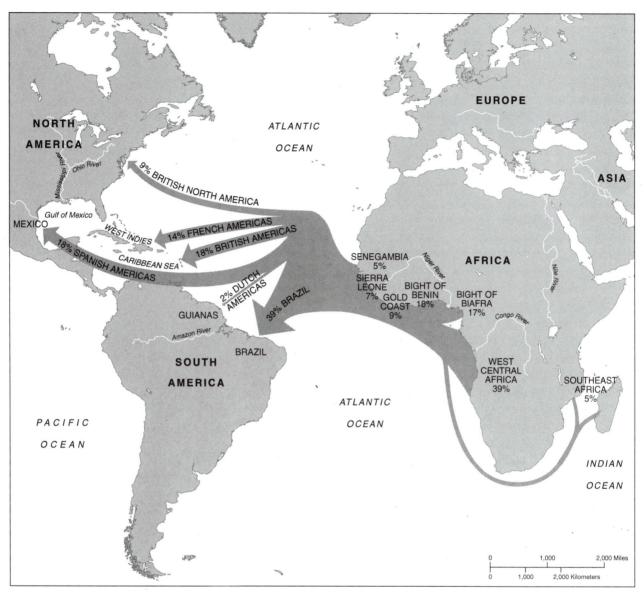

The transatlantic slave trade was a vast commercial enterprise that prospered for some 350 years, from the 1510s to the 1860s. Most of the slaves were captured in West and Central Africa, and transported by ship—the notorious Middle Passage—to South America and the Caribbean to work on plantations. Less than 10 percent were shipped directly from the African continent to the British colonies of North America or, after 1776, to the new United States. *(Cartographics)*

ENCYCLOPEDIA OF
EMANCIPATION
AND ABOLITION
IN THE TRANSATLANTIC WORLD

VOLUME THREE

Documents

Sermons and Religious Statements

For some, faith without deeds may constitute a form of spiritual emptiness, but this concern has not always clouded the conscience of people of goodwill. This dichotomous view is as old as the debate over salvation itself: Should we be concerned with individual salvation alone, or should the collective redemption of the larger community be our ultimate goal? For centuries, legions of sinners seeking grace have pondered such issues without finding solace or resolution in their struggle to give purposeful meaning to their beliefs.

Many of the early voices of the transatlantic abolitionist movement were motivated and inspired by an activist spirit of redemption that adherents found in the Christian gospels. These reformers fashioned a bold, new type of muscular Christianity that sought to remedy the social ills of their time through sustained campaigns to combat evil in all its forms. Whether they were combating slavery, challenging the social inequality afforded women, campaigning to end child labor, or lending support to a host of other causes that sought to remedy societal imperfections, the vital link between faith and action was real to these reformers, as they sought to proclaim a new social gospel that they believed would uplift the human community.

Utilizing one's faith to challenge the moral legitimacy of slavery might seem logical when viewed through the lens of modernity, but it was not always perceived as such. To charge that slavery was a spiritual shortcoming triggered a vociferous response from those in the proslavery camp, who could just as readily quote scriptural chapter and verse to prove that there was biblical support for slavery. Critics described social reformers as overzealous fanatics who sought to overturn the long-standing customs and traditions upon which their moral authority was founded. The pronouncements of faith-based abolitionists were reviled and discredited by those who believed with absolute certainty that the enslavement of their fellow human beings was somehow rooted in God's masterful plan for humanity.

Courage was a necessary attribute for those who joined the abolitionist movement and tried to compel their coreligionists to join the cause as well. Just as early Christians were persecuted for their beliefs, the proslavery forces hurled their animus at those who challenged the moral legitimacy of slavery; the ensuing violence produced a number of martyrs to the antislavery cause. Although the apostle Paul had described faith as "the essence of things hoped for, the evidence of things not seen," abolitionists who criticized slavery on the basis of their faith were certain that retribution would come their way. Still, they followed the dictates of conscience and spoke truth to power.

The following documents illustrate the methods and means by which faith-based criticism of slavery was articulated by abolitionists during the centuries of the transatlantic slave trade. Some of these documents demonstrate that criticism was occasionally slow in coming and condemnation was tempered at best. Others clearly show that critiques of slavery often were pointed and rooted in the essential articles of faith that were central to the worldviews of many people.

Far from ubiquitous in these critiques is the sense that slavery must end immediately—a number of individuals were satisfied with the gradual decline of the practice. Although slavery might be perceived as an undeniable evil and a manifestation of sin, there were different roads that one might follow to reach redemption.

Father Antonio Vieira's Sermon Condemning Indian Slavery (1653)

At what a different price the devil today buys souls compared to what he offered for them previously. There is no market in the world where the devil can get them more cheaply than right here in our own land. In the Gospel, he offered all the kingdoms of the world for one soul; in Maranhão the devil does not need to offer one-tenth as much for all the souls. It is not necessary to offer worlds, nor kingdoms; it is not necessary to offer cities, nor towns, nor villages.

All he has to do is offer a couple of Tapuya Indians and at once he is adored on both knees. What a cheap market! An Indian for a soul! That Indian will be your slave for the few days that he lives; and your soul will be a slave for eternity, as long as God is God. This is the contract that the devil makes with you. Not only do you accept it but you pay him money on top of it.

Christians, nobles, and people of Maranhão, do you know what God wants of you during this Lent? That you break the chains of injustice and let free those whom you have captive and oppressed. These are the sins of Maranhão; these are what God commanded me to denounce to you. Christians, God commanded me to clarify these matters to you and so I do it. All of you are in mortal sin; all of you live in a state of condemnation; and all of you are going directly to Hell. Indeed, many are there now and you will soon join them if you do not change your life.

Is it possible that an entire people live in sin, that an entire people will go to hell? Who questions thus does not understand the evil of unjust captivity. The sons of Israel went down into Egypt, and after the death of Joseph, the Pharaoh seized them and made slaves of them. God wanted to liberate those miserable people, and He sent Moses there with no other escort than a rod. God knew that in order to free the captives a rod was sufficient, even though He was dealing with a ruler as tyrannical as Pharaoh and with a people as cruel as the Egyptians. When Pharaoh refused to free the captives, the plagues rained down upon him. The land was covered with frogs and the air clouded with mosquitos; the rivers flowed with blood; the clouds poured forth thunder and lightning. All Egypt was dumbfounded and threatened with death. Do you know what brought those plagues to the earth? Unjust captivity. Who brought to Maranhão the plague of the Dutch? Who brought the smallpox? Who brought hunger and drought? These captives. Moses insisted and pressed the Pharaoh to free the people, and what did Pharaoh respond? He said one thing and he did another. What he said was, I do not know God and I do not have to free the captives. However, it appears to me proper and I do declare them free. Do you know why you do not give freedom to your illicitly gotten slaves? Because you do not know God. Lack of Faith is the cause of everything. If you possessed true faith, if you believed that there was an eternal Hell, then you would not take so lightly the captivity of a single Tapuya.

With what confidence can the devil today say to you: *Si cadens adoraveris me?* With all the confidence of having offered you the world. The devil made this speech: I offer to this man everything; if he is greedy and covetous, he must accept. If he accepts, then, he worships me because greed and covetousness are a form of idolatry. It is an idea expressed by St. Paul. Such was the greed of Pharaoh in wanting to keep and not to free the captive sons of Israel, confessing at the same time that he did not know God. This is what he said.

What he did was to take out after the fleeing Israelites with all the power of his kingdom in order to recapture them. And what happened? The Red Sea opened so that the captives could pass on dry land. It did not matter that the Hebrews did not merit this. They were worse than the Tapuyas. A few days later they worshiped a golden calf and of all the six hundred thousand men only two entered into the promised land, but God is so favorable to the cause of liberty that he grants it even to those who do not deserve it. When the Hebrews had reached the other side, Pharaoh entered between the walls of water which were still open, and as he crossed, the waters fell over his army and drowned them all. What impresses me is the way Moses tells this: that the waters enveloped them and the sea drowned them and the earth swallowed them up. Now, if the sea drowned them how could the earth swallow them? Those men, like his, had both a body and a soul. The waters drowned the bodies because they were at the bottom of the sea; the earth swallowed the souls because they descended to Hell. All went to Hell, without a single exception, because where all pursue and all capture, all are condemned. This is an excellent example. Now, let us look at the reasoning.

Any man who deprives others of their freedom and being able to restore that freedom does not do so is condemned. All or nearly all are therefore condemned. You will say to me that even if this were true they did not think about it or know it and that their good faith will save them. I deny that. They did think about it and know it just as you think of it and know it. If they did not think of it nor know it, they ought to have thought of it and to have known it. Some are condemned by their knowledge, others by their doubt, and still others by their ignorance. . . . If only the graves would open and some who died in that unhappy state could appear before you, and in the fire of their misery you could clearly read this truth. Do you know why God does not permit them to appear before you? It is exactly as Abraham said to the rich miser when he asked him to send Lazarus to this world: *Habent Moysen et Prophetas* (Luc. [Luke] 16.29). It is not necessary for one to appear on earth from Hell to tell you the truth because you already have Moses and the Law, you have the prophets and learned men. My brothers, if there are any among you who doubt this, here are the laws, here are the learned men, question them. There are in this State, three religious orders which have members of great virtue and learning. Ask them. Study the matter and inform yourselves. But it is not necessary to question the religious: go to Turkey, go to Hell, because there is no Turk so Turkish in Turkey nor no devil so devilish in Hell who will tell you that a free man can be a slave. Is there one among you with natural intelligence who can deny it? What do you doubt?

I know what you are going to tell me . . . our people, our country, our government cannot be sustained without Indians. Who will fetch a pail of water for us or carry a load of wood? Who will grind our manioc? Will our wives have to do it? Will our sons? In the first place, this is not the state into which I am placing you as you soon will see. But when necessity and conscience require such a thing, I answer yes and repeat again yes. You, your wives, your sons, all of us are able to sustain ourselves with our own labor. It is better to live from your own sweat than from the blood of others! . . .

You will tell me that your slaves are your very feet and hands. Also, you will say how much you love them because you raised them like children and took care of them as you would your very own. It may be so, but Christ said to this land: *Si oculus tuus scandalizat te, erue eum et si manus, vel pes tuus scandalizat te, amputa elum* (Math. [Matt.] 5–29; Marc. [Mark] 9.42.44). Christ did not mean to say that we should pull out our eyes nor that we ought to cut off our hands and feet. What he meant was that if that which we loved as our eyes harmed us, or that which was as necessary as our hands and feet harmed us, we should cast away from us that source of harm even if it hurts us as if we had cut it off from us. Who amongst you does not love his arm or his hand but should it become gangrenous would not permit its amputation in order to save his life. . . . If, in order to quiet your conscience or save your soul, it is necessary to lose everything and remain as miserable as Job, lose everything.

But take heart, my friends, it is not necessary to arrive at such a state, far from it. I have studied the matter carefully and in accordance with the most le-nient and favorable opinions and have come to a conclusion by which, with only minor worldly losses, all the inhabitants of this state can ease their consciences and build for a better future. Give me your attention.

All the Indians of this State are either those who serve as slaves or those who live as free inhabitants in the King's villages, or those who live in the hinterlands in their natural or free condition. These latter are the ones you go upriver to buy or "to rescue" (as they say), giving the pious verb "to rescue" to a sale so involuntary and violent that at times it is made at pistol point. These are held, owned, and bequeathed in bad faith: therefore they will be doing no small task if they forgive you for their past treatment. However, if after you have set them free, they, particularly those domestics whom you raised in your house and treated as your children, spontaneously and voluntarily wish to continue to serve you and remain in your home, no one will or can separate them from your service. And what will happen to those who do not wish to remain in your service? These will be obliged to live in the King's villages where they also will serve you in the manner which I shall mention. Each year you will be able to make your expeditions into the interior during which time you can really rescue those who are prisoners ready to be eaten. Those justly saved from death will remain your slaves. Also, all those captured in just wars will be made slaves. Upon this matter the proper judges will be the Governor of the State, the Chief Justice of the State, the Vicars of Maranhão or of Pará, and the Prelates of the four orders: Carmelite, Franciscan, Mercedarian, and the Company of Jesus. All of these who after judgment are qualified to be true captives, will be returned to the inhabitants. And what will happen to those captured in a war not classified as just? All of them will be placed in new villages or divided among the villages which exist today. There, along with the other village Indians they will be hired out to the inhabitants of this State to work for them for six months of every year alternating two months of hired work with two months devoted to their own labors and families. Thus, in this manner, all the Indians of this State will serve the Portuguese either as legitimate slaves, that is those rescued from death or captured in a just war, or those former slaves who freely and voluntarily wish to serve their old masters, or those from the King's villages who will work half the year for the good and growth of the State. It only remains to set the wages of those village Indians for their labor and service. It is a subject which would make any other nation of the world laugh and only in this land is not appreciated. The money of this land is cloth and cotton, and the ordinary price for which the Indians work and will work each month is seven feet of this cloth which has a market value of about twenty cents. An Indian will work for less than a penny a day. It is an insignificant amount and it is unworthy of a man of reason and of Christian faith not to pay such a slight price to save his soul and to avoid Hell.

Could there be anything more moderate? Could there be anything more reasonable than this? Whoever is dissatisfied or discontent with this proposal either is not a Christian or has no understanding. To conclude this point, let us look at the advantages and disadvantages of this proposal.

The single disadvantage is that some of you will lose a few Indians. I promise you they will be very few. But to you who question this, I ask: Do not some of your Indians die or flee? Many do. Will death do what reason will not? Will chance do what a good conscience will not? If smallpox strikes and carries off your Indians, what will you do? You will have to show patience. Well, is it not better to lose the Indians to the service of God than to lose them by a punishment of God? The answer is obvious.

Let us look at the advantages of which there are four principal ones. The first is that you will have a clear conscience. You will no longer live in a state of mortal sin. You will live like Christians, you will be confessed as Christians, you will die like Christians, you will bequeath your goods as Christians. In short, you will go to Heaven and not to Hell, which would certainly be a tragic ending.

The second advantage is that you will remove this curse from your homes. There is no greater curse on a home or a family than to be unjustly supported by the sweat and blood of others. . . .

The third advantage is that in this way more Indians will be rescued from cannibal practices. . . . It is important to invade the forest to save Indians from being killed and eaten.

The fourth and last advantage is that henceforth your proposals on the labor problem will be worthy of submission to His Majesty, and worthy of His Majesty's approval and confirmation. Whoever asks for the illegal and unjust deserves to have the legal and just denied him, and whoever petitions with justice, reason, and good conscience deserves the fulfillment of his request. You know the proposal which you made? It was a proposal which vassals could not make

in good conscience, nor could ministers consult it in good conscience. And even if the King might have permitted it, what good would it have done you? If the King permits me to steal falsely, will it mean that the false oath is no sin? If the King permits me to steal, will the theft be any less a sin? The same thing applies to the Indians. The King can command the slaves to be free, but his jurisdiction does not extend to the power to order the free to become slaves. If such a request went to Lisbon, the stones of the street would have to rise up against the men of Maranhão. On the other hand, if you submit a just, legal, and Christian request, those very same stones would take your part. . . .

Source: Father Antonio Vieira, "Vieira's Sermon Condemning Indian Slavery," in *A Documentary History of Brazil*, ed. E. Bradford Burns. New York: Alfred A. Knopf, 1966.

Pope Benedict XIV to the Bishops of Brazil (1741)

Men calling themselves Christians are so far forgetful of the sentiments of charity diffused in our hearts by the Holy Spirit as to reduce to slavery the unhappy Indians, the people of the Eastern and Western coasts of Brazil and other regions. . . .

Much more, they sell them as common herds of slaves, they despoil them of goods; and the inhumanity which they display towards them is the principal cause of turning them away from embracing the faith of Jesus Christ by making them look upon it with horror. . . .

All infractions of these regulations shall incur an excommunication "latae sententiae" . . . in order that in the future no one would dare to reduce the Indians to slavery, to sell, to exchange, or give them away, to separate them from their wives and children, to despoil them of their goods, to transport them from one place or country to another, in fine, in any way whatsoever to despoil them of their liberty and to retain them in servitude, or to assist those who act thus.

Source: Pope Benedict XIV, "Letter to Bishops of Brazil, 20 December 1741," in *Bullarium Benedicti XIV*. Rome: Prato, 1845.

An Antislavery Sermon (1788)

God hath made of one blood all the nations of men, to dwell on all the Face of the Earth. (Acts xvii.26)

There is no truth more obvious to the simple conceptions of man, than that the human race have natural rights, and common relations to each other; yet, there is no truth which may be more easily overlooked, or sooner perverted, when the principles of ambition, avarice, and cruelty, have blinded the understanding, and hardened the heart. Men's judgements are easily bribed by a vicious inclination; and they will soon persuade themselves to believe that to be true which they are unwilling to discover to be false.

This observation is strictly applicable to the case of Slavery; a case which now promises to undergo a thorough discussion: not, it is hoped, merely to please the speculations of the curious, or to interest the feelings of the humane; but to vindicate the wrongs of thousands; to restrain the hand of cruelty; and to let the oppressed go free.

The subject of Slavery has been examined in a moral, a historical, a political, and a commercial point of view, by authors of distinguished eminence; whose clearness of comprehension and powers of reasoning have honoured and advanced the cause of humanity in which they have warmly engaged.

It is my intention in this discourse to consider the subject in a religious point of view.

Slavery, or servitude, was indeed connived at by the Jewish Laws; but then it was restrained by wise and merciful regulations: and we know that GOD winked at the times of that ignorance, when men could not receive a purer law, or be influenced by better motives than those temporary rewards and punishments which were the sanctions of that dispensation.

But "GOD hath made of one blood all the natives of the earth." Creation is a comprehensive system of goodness; and the various parts thereof are so admirably connected together, that, if "one member suffer, all the members suffer with it." This goodness, discoverable in creation, is a communicative principle, flowing from the Author of all life and blessedness, and imparting itself to all his creatures; and his creatures are so far blessed, and rendered capable of superior enjoyments, as they are influenced by this communicative goodness; and, in consequence thereof, become instrumental in promoting each other's happiness.

All the relations of humanity, all the ties of kindred, are established for this benevolent purpose; that we may feel, reason, and act as members one of another. For "have we not all *one Father?* hath not One GOD created us? Why do we deal treacherously every man against his brother, by profaning the covenant of our fathers?" (Mal. xi.10) "The LORD He is the God; it is he who hath made us, and not we ourselves. We are his people, and the sheep of his pasture." (Ps. c.3)

"O LORD, thou art *our Father*; we are the clay, and thou art the potter; and we are all the work of thy hand." (Isa. lxiv.8) "Doubtless thou art *our Father*; thou, O LORD, art *our Father*, our Redeemer; thy name is from everlasting." (Isa. lxiii.16)

If then GOD be our Father, surely we are all brethren; and this sacred relationship, "this covenant of Brother," is not to be set aside by any distance of place, or by any accidental difference of appearances, or peculiarity of advantages. Wherever we see the human form, we see an image of GOD, and a brother according to the Flesh. Justly then might we call out to the African Trader, and the Indian Planter, if they had but hearts to hear, "Sirs, ye are brethren, why do you wrong one to another?" (Acts vii.26)

If this relationship be established by *Creation*, how much more important, more extensive, and more sacred, must it appear, when considered with a view to *Redemption*. "GOD was manifest in the flesh to reconcile a world of sinful creatures to himself, and to unite them in the bonds of eternal amity and love." He came to destroy the kingdom of darkness, evil, and misery; and to establish his everlasting kingdom of light and truth; of goodness and righteousness.

The extent of this great plan of mercy is as wide as the misery of sin, as universal as the empire of death. "Christ tasted death for *every man*; there is one Mediator between GOD and *man*, the man Christ Jesus, who gave himself a ransom for *all*, to be testified in due time." (1 Tim. ii.6) "We have an advocate with the Father, Jesus Christ the Righteous; and He is the propitiation for our sins; and not for ours only, but also for the sins of *the whole world*." (1 John ii.2) "For as in Adam *all* die, even so in Christ shall *all* be made alive." (1 Cor. xv.22)

All men, then, are heirs of the heavenly inheritance, and are capable of being translated from the kingdom of Satan into the kingdom of Christ. Gentiles and Jews, Heathens and Christians, on their belief of the Gospel, are fellow heirs together in a glorious immortality; for they are now the adopted children of one common parent, the purchased property of the same Saviour; and the same new and living way into the true holy of holies, even into Heaven itself, is open to all, through Jesus Christ our Lord.

The great and comprehensive mercy of the Gospel has united men more closely in the bonds of mutual charity. The endearing term of *brother*, as pointing out a special relationship between man and man, is there introduced. If I stand without excuse for injuring my brother after the flesh, how much more inexcusable am

I, if, to increase my wealth, to flatter my vanity, and to exercise a wanton cruelty, I injure and degrade my brother after the Spirit, for whom Christ died?

The mild and benevolent spirit of Christianity, in proportion as it prevailed among the nations which became converted to the gospel, abolished the servile condition, and taught mankind that the lowest as well as the highest, the ignorant as well as the wise, had rights which were sacred, and prospects which were eternal.

The happy revival of literature and religious knowledge at the time of the Reformation abolished all the remains of domestic slavery in our own country; but, about the same period, a more systematic and more horrid species of slavery was introduced; I mean, that of working the Western Islands, which the Spaniards had almost depopulated by their cruelties, by means of slaves imported from Africa. This evil is the more dreadful, because it is far removed from the observation of the wise and the good; it is practiced by the avaricious and the cruel, who are interested either to conceal their outrages by falsehood, or to defend them by sophistry. It is practiced in all the horrid luxuriance of iniquity by the English, a nation who boast that they are free, and profess that they are Christians. It is to this practice in particular that I wish to confine your present attention.

The evil consequences of the unnatural and degrading relation of Master and Slave are thus described by an able advocate. "It corrupts the morals of the master, by freeing him from those restraints with respect to his slave, so necessary for the control of the human passions, so beneficial in promoting the practice and confirming the habit of virtue.—It is dangerous to the master, because his oppression excited implacable resentment and hatred in the slave; and the extreme misery of his condition continually prompts him to risque the gratification of them; and his situation daily furnishes the opportunity.—To the slave it communicates all the afflictions of life, without leaving for him scarce any of its pleasures; and it depresses the excellency of his nature, by denying the ordinary means and motives of improvement. It is dangerous to the state, by its corruption of those citizens on whom its safety depends; and by admitting within it a multitude of persons who, being excluded from the common benefits of the constitution, are interested in scheming its destruction." (Hargrave's Argument in the Case of J. Somerset[t])

But how are these evils aggravated, when considered in a religious point of view—as affecting the slave and the master—the interests of the Gospel, and the welfare of the nation which tolerates such conduct!

In the extensive kingdoms of Africa, the most horrid wars, rapine, and desolation, have been encouraged for more than 200 years, to promote this trade in human blood. Some are entrapped by deceit, but the generality are seized by violence. Their fields are desolated; their houses are burnt with fire. The mild and peaceable Negro is driven from his comfortable home; torn from all the tender connections of social life; branded with a hot iron; confined on ship-board amidst chains and nakedness, filth and pestilence. There they are crowded in such numbers, and treated with such cruelty, that death brings a happy release unto thousands, who only experience "the beginning of sorrows." For those who escape the dangers of the sea, and endure the hardships of the voyage, new calamities are reserved in store when they arrive at the place of their destination.

Here the complicated evils of slavery properly begin: here they are exposed like cattle in a market; sent to the distant plantations; roused before the rising sun; and employed in the hardest labour; trembling under the tyranny of a master, who is exercised in scenes of blood, and knows scarce any restraint from the fear of unrighteous laws.

Here the sad remains of a wretched existence are dragged out; harassed by exhausted labour, surrounded with the view of the miseries of their countrymen; supported by the scanty pittance of the worst food; deprived of all the comforts of this life; and uninstructed in any hope of a better [life]. Their lives are not esteemed by their owners of so much value as the life of a beast; though even the life of his beast a merciful man will regard. Their misery is often so extreme that they seek for refuge in the arms of death. Some lay violent hands on themselves; and others refuse all sustenance, that they may find that rest in the grave which is denied them by men, by Englishmen, by Christians.

In the British Plantations it is no uncommon thing to behold the insolence of power and the wantonness of cruelty; to hear the groans of despair, and the cries of deserted infants. "The plowers plough upon their backs, and make long furrows." The fruits of the earth are produced amidst tears of blood, and groans of anguish. The prospect to them is hopeless: no industry can regain their freedom, no time can restore them to their native country. No distinction is made; no respect is paid to age or sex; but all are crowded together like a herd of brute beasts: and here we behold the wretched effects of this traffick in human blood, to degrade, to corrupt, to brutalize mankind.

Thus does our brother, for whom Christ died, become vile in our eyes.

Yet this most horrid traffick has continued for ages; in which, to speak within compass, not less than an hundred millions of the human race have most wretchedly perished, in hunger and in cold, in pestilence and in desolation, without a protector, without a comforter, without an avenger.

Yet the condition of the *Slaves*, though thus humiliating and severe, is infinitely preferable to that of their tyrants and oppressors, it being always better to suffer wrong than to inflict it.

But here I am happy to make some exceptions, though I fear they are but few; some Planters there are who treat their Slaves with mildness and compassion. These, although they have not an outward law to claim this, yet "they are a law unto themselves"; and they do not, in the actions of every day, "deny the LORD who bought them."

It will easily appear how much more deplorable is the state of the cruel Master than that of his suffering Slaves, if we consider his conduct here, as preparatory to an awful and eternal state hereafter.

There are but two Beings whom men worship and obey—these are GOD, who is Love; the Father of mercies and the GOD of all consolation, the Saviour of mankind, and the Devil or Satan, who was a murderer from the beginning, who is the destroyer, who delights in beholding acts of cruelty and bloodshed. The unrighteous Merchant, and the tyrannical Planter, "are of their Father the Devil, and the lusts of their Father they do." In his works of darkness they zealously engage, and "they shall in no wise lose their reward."

Of the peace and happiness resulting from benevolence, gentleness, meekness, and forbearance, they have no knowledge or experience: but, by the indulgence of every contrary temper, as cruelty, violence, and revenge; they exclude the Kingdom of Heaven from their souls; they fill up the measure of their iniquities; they lead a life of misery upon earth, which riches cannot console, nor intemperance enliven; and at death they pass into the eternal world, to meet their GOD and their Judge; to receive the fruit of their own doings; and to reap a full recompence of reward.

These infamous Traders, who have heaped up their riches, "the price of blood," and hardened themselves against their own flesh, will then lift up their eyes in torment, while they see Jesus afar off, and many of their once insulted, degraded, maimed, and murdered Slaves now happy in his bosom. Then perhaps they may beg that one of these may be sent with a drop of water to cool their tongues, because they are "tormented in that flame"; but even this request will then be denied by the Father of Mercies, for "as they shewed no mercy nor compassion on their poor slaves and dependents, so neither shall their Lord have pity on them."

But this unrighteous traffick in human blood is not more destructive to those concerned in it, than disgraceful to the religion they profess, and to the nation which tolerates their crimes. By their means the holy name of Jesus is blasphemed, and an invincible obstacle thrown in the way, to hinder the glorious Gospel of Christ from being received by these Heathens. Darkness is not more opposite to light than the principles of this traffick to the spirit of Christianity. That commands us "to preach good tidings unto the meek"; but these men deliberately withhold from their Slaves all rational instruction, and all religious improvement. The Prince of Peace sends us "to bind up the broken-hearted"; but these men bow down their fellow-creatures by oppression, and "regard not the cry of the poor destitute." The spirit of the Gospel "proclaims liberty to the captive, and the opening of the prison to them that are bound": but these men rivet the chains of slavery; "the iron enters into the Negro's soul," while his mind is left in all the darkness of ignorance, without one ray of those comforts which Christianity affords, to strengthen with patience, and to animate with hope, them that endure affliction, suffering wrongfully.

But these dreadful crimes are not only the crimes of individuals, but also of nations, which are conscious of these enormities, and do not interpose to restrain the fury of the tyrant, and to set the oppressed free. England is deeply stained with this guilt; she must answer for the blood of millions, for she knows, and yet she tolerates, this inhuman traffick. It was one of the sins of Tyre, that she "traded in the persons of men." (Ez[ek]. xxvii.13) And if we as a nation resemble her in our sins, we have reason to fear that we shall resemble her in our punishment. "Wherefore, O Nation greatly beloved, let my counsel be acceptable to thee, and break off thy sins by righteousness, and thine iniquities by shewing mercy to the poor (especially to captive Negros), if it may be a lengthening of thy tranquility." (Dan. iv.27)

May not the LORD of Heaven and Earth say unto this nation, as he did unto the Israelites of old,

"Your hands are defiled with blood, and your fingers with iniquity. None calleth for justice, nor any pleadeth for truth. Go to now, therefore, ye rich men; weep and howl for your miseries that shall come upon you; your heart goeth after your covetousness, and your land is defiled with blood. Behold the prayer of the needy, and the voice of the innocent blood which is shed, crieth and entereth the ears of the LORD of Sabbaoth, for a witness against us.—Shall I not visit for these things, saith the LORD, shall not my soul be avenged of such a nation as this? Behold, the LORD cometh out of his place, to punish the inhabitants of the earth for their iniquity; the earth also shall disclose her blood, and shall no more cover her slain. Vengeance is mine; I will repay, saith the LORD."

The Western Empire is gone from us, never to return; it is given to another more righteous than we; who consecrated the sword of resistance by declaring for the universal abolition of slavery. The West India islands have been visited with most tremendous hurricanes and earthquakes; by these, the cruel traders have been deprived of all their unrighteous gain, or have been involved with it in one common grave. "Verily, there is a reward for the righteous and for the wicked: doubtless there is a GOD who judgeth the earth."

As then the English have been most forward in promoting this abominable trade, "as the blood of the souls of the poor innocents is found in their skirts"; so let the English now stand forward to suppress this disgrace to their country.

Next in guilt to those who perpetrate these abominations are those who, knowing these enormities, do not interfere to prevent them. Every one may do something; he may declare his testimony against violence and wrong; he may appear on the side of humanity, equity, and religion.

Let every man then do what he is able against it, lest the guilt of innocent blood should lie at his door. As we value liberty ourselves, let us glory to make others free; as we have obtained mercy ourselves, so let us never rest, till this mercy be extended to others, and all tears be wiped from off all faces.

Then by all the glorious attributes of our GOD and Saviour, which are insulted by this inhuman traffick—by all the laws of divine love, which he has established; by all the glories of heaven which are displayed to the eye of Faith:—by the common blood which flows in all our veins; and by the blood of Christ which was shed for the sins of the whole world—by that freedom which is the common birth-right of all, and the distinguishing privilege of Englishmen—by

the right-aiming thunderbolts of the Almighty, prepared to execute vengeance on nations which deal in oppression—by the tender ties of domestic connections; by all the comforts we enjoy here; and, by all the happiness we expect hereafter;—let us unite with all our powers to vindicate the English name, to honour the Gospel of Peace, and to avert the judgements of Heaven, by the abolition of the Slave Trade, by "restraining the fury of the oppressor," and by the "letting the captive go free." The poor and afflicted slaves can never know their friends and benefactors; "they indeed cannot recompense us; but we shall be recompensed at the resurrection of the just."

Source: William Agutter, *The Abolition of the Slave Trade Considered in a Religious Point of View; A Sermon Preached Before the Corporation of the City of Oxford at St. Martin's Church, on Sunday, February 3, 1788.* London: J.F. & C. Rivington and G. Philips, 1788.

A Religious Defense of Slavery (1822)

Charleston, 24th December, 1822.

His Excellency GOVERNOR WILSON.

SIR,

When I had, lately, the honour of delivering to your Excellency an Address, from the Baptist Convention in this State, requesting that a Day of Public Humiliation and Thanksgiving might be appointed by you, as our Chief Magistrate, to be observed by the Citizens of the State at large, in reference to two important recent events, in which the interposition of Divine Providence has been conspicuous, and in which the interests and feelings of our Citizens have been greatly concerned,—viz: The protection afforded them from the horrors of an intended Insurrection; and the affliction they have suffered from the ravages of a dreadful Hurricane—I took the liberty to suggest, that I had a further communication to make on behalf of the Convention, in which their sentiments would be disclosed respecting the policy of the measure proposed; and on the lawfulness of holding slaves—the subject being considered in a moral and religious point of view.

You were pleased, sir, to signify, that it would be agreeable to you to receive such a communication. And as it is incumbent on me, in faithfulness to the trust reposed in me, to make it, I now take the liberty of laying it before you.

The Political propriety of bringing the intended Insurrection into view by publicly acknowledging its prevention to be an instance of the Divine Goodness, manifested by a providential, gracious interposition, is a subject, which has employed the serious attention of the Convention; and, if they have erred in the judgment they have formed upon it, the error is, at least, not owing to a want of consideration, or of serious concern. They cannot view the subject but as one of great magnitude, and intimately connected with the interests of the whole State. The Divine Interposition has been conspicuous; and our obligations to be thankful are unspeakably great. And, as principles of the wisest and best policy leads nations, as well as individuals, to consider and acknowledge the government of the Deity, to feel their dependency on him and trust in him, to be thankful for his mercies, and to be humbled under his chastening rod; so, not only moral and religious duty, but also a regard to the best interests of the community appear to require of us, on the present occasion, that humiliation and thanksgiving, which are proposed by the Convention in their request. For a sense of the Divine Government has a meliorating influence on the minds of men, restraining them from crime, and disposing them to virtuous action. To those also, who are humbled before the Heavenly Majesty for their sins, and learn to be thankful for his mercies, the Divine Favour is manifested. From them judgments are averted, and on them blessings are bestowed.

The Convention are aware that very respectable Citizens have been averse to the proposal under consideration; the proposal for appointing a Day of Public Thanksgiving for our preservation from the intended Insurrection, on account of the influence it might be supposed to have on the Black Population— by giving publicity to the subject in *their view*, and by affording them excitements to attempt something further of the same nature. These objections, however, the Convention view as either not substantial, or over-balanced by higher considerations. As to publicity, perhaps no fact is more generally known by the persons referred to; for the knowledge of it has been communicated by almost every channel of information, public and private, even by documents under the stamp of Public Authority; and has extended to every part of the State. But with the knowledge of the conspiracy is united the knowledge of its frustration; and of that, which Devotion and Gratitude should set in a strong light, *the merciful interposition of Providence,* which produced that frustration. The more rational among that class of men, as well as others, know also, that our preservation from the evil intended by the conspirators, is a subject, which should induce us to render thanksgivings to the Almighty; and it is hoped and believed, that the truly enlightened and religiously disposed among them, of which there appear to be many, are ready to unite in those thanksgivings, from a regard to their own true interests: if therefore it is apprehended, that an undue importance would be given to the subject in their view, by making it the matter of public thanksgiving; that this would induce the designing and wicked to infer our fear and sense of weakness from the fact, and thus induce them to form some other scheme of mischief: Would not our silence, and the omission of an important religious duty, under these circumstances, undergo, at least, as unfavorable a construction, and with more reason?

But the Convention are persuaded, that publicity, rather than secrecy is the true policy to be pursued on this occasion; especially, when the subject is taken into view, in connexion with other truths, of high importance and certainty, which relate to it, and is placed in a just light; the evidence and force of which truths, thousands of this people, when informed, can clearly discern and estimate. It is proper, the Convention conceives, that the Negroes should know, that however numerous they are in some parts of these Southern States, they, yet, are not, even including all descriptions, bond and free, in the United States, but little more than one sixth part of the whole number of inhabitants, estimating that number which it probably now is, at Ten Millions; and the Black and Coloured Population, according to returns made at 1,786,000: That their destitution in respect to arms, and the knowledge of using them, with other disabilities, would render their physical force, were they all united in a common effort, less than a tenth part of that, with which they would have to contend. That there are multitudes of the best informed and truly religious among them, who, from principle, as well as from prudence, would not unite with them, nor fail to disclose their machinations, when it should be in their power to do it: That, however in some parts of our Union there are Citizens, who favour the idea of general emancipation; yet, were they to see slaves in our Country, in arms, wading through blood and carnage to effect their purpose, they would do what both their duty and interest would require; unite under the government with their fellow citizens at large to suppress the rebellion, and bring the authors of it to condign punishment: That it may be expected, in every attempt to raise an insurrection (should other attempts be made) as well as it was in that defeated here, that the prime movers in such a nefarious scheme, will so form their plan, that in case of exigency, they may flee with their plunder and leave their deluded followers to suffer the punishment, which law and justice may inflict: And that therefore, there is reason to conclude, on the most rational and just principles, that whatever partial success might at any time attend such a measure at the onset, yet, in this country, it must finally result in the discomfiture and ruin of the perpetrators; and in many instances pull down on the heads of the innocent as well as the guilty, an undistinguishing ruin.

On the lawfulness of holding slaves, considering it in a moral and religious view, the Convention think it their duty to exhibit their sentiments, on the present occasion, before your Excellency, because they consider their duty to God, the peace of the State, the satisfaction of scrupulous consciences, and the welfare of the slaves themselves, as intimately connected with a right view of the subject. The rather, because certain writers on politics, morals and religion, and some of them highly respectable, have advanced positions, and inculcated sentiments, very unfriendly to the principle and practice of holding slaves; and by some these sentiments have been advanced among us, tending in their nature, *directly* to disturb the domestic peace of the State, to produce insubordination and rebellion among the slaves, and to infringe the rights of our citizens; and *indirectly*, to deprive the slaves of religious privileges, by awakening in the minds of their masters a fear, that acquaintance with the Scriptures, and the enjoyment of these privileges would naturally produce the aforementioned effects; because the sentiments in opposition to the holding of slaves have been attributed, by their advocates, to the Holy Scriptures, and to the genius of Christianity. These sentiments, the Convention, on whose behalf I address your Excellency, cannot think just, or well-founded: for the right of holding slaves is clearly established by the Holy Scriptures, both by precept and example. In the Old Testament, the Isrealites were directed to purchase their bond-men and bond-maids of the Heathen nations; except they were of the Canaanites, for these were to be destroyed. And it is declared, that the persons purchased were to be their "bond-men forever"; and an "inheritance for them and their children." They were not to go out free in the year of jubilee, as the Hebrews, who had been purchased, were: the line being clearly drawn between them. (See Leviticus xxv.44, 45, 46, &c) In example, they are presented to our view as existing in the fam-

ilies of the Hebrews as servants, or slaves, born in the house, or bought with money: so that the children born of slaves are here considered slaves as well as their parents. And to this well known state of things, as to its reason and order, as well as to special privileges, St. Paul appears to refer, when he says, "But I was free born."

In the New-Testament, the Gospel History, or representation of facts, presents us a view correspondent with that, which is furnished by other authentic ancient histories of the state of the world at the commencement of Christianity. The powerful Romans had succeeded, in empire, the polished Greeks; and under both empires, the countries they possessed and governed were full of slaves. Many of these with their masters, were converted to the Christian Faith, and received, together with them into the Christian Church, while it was yet under the ministry of the inspired Apostles. In things purely spiritual, they appear to have enjoyed equal privileges; but their relationship, as masters and slaves, was not dissolved. Their respective duties are strictly enjoined. The masters are not required to emancipate their slaves; but to give them the things that are just and equal, forbearing threatening; and to remember, they also have a master in Heaven. The "servants under the yoke" [*upo zugon Douloi:* bond-servants, or slaves. *Doulos* is the proper term for slaves; it is here in the plural and rendered more expressive by being connected with yoke—UNDER THE YOKE] mentioned by Paul to Timothy, as having "believing masters," are not authorized by him to demand of them emancipation, or to employ violent means to obtain it; but are directed to "account their masters worthy of all honour," and "not to despise them, because they were brethren" in religion; "but the rather to do them service, because they were faithful and beloved partakers of the Christian benefit." Similar directions are given by him in other places, and by other Apostles. And it gives great weight to the argument, that in this place, Paul follows his directions concerning servants with a charge to Timothy, as an Evangelist, to teach and exhort men to observe this doctrine.

Had the holding of slaves been a moral evil, it cannot be supposed, that the inspired Apostles, who feared not the faces of men, and were ready to lay down their lives in the cause of their God, would have tolerated it, for a moment, in the Christian Church. If they had done so on a principle of accommodation, in cases where the masters remained heathen, to avoid offences and civil commotion; yet, surely, where both master and servant were Christian, as in the case before us, they would have enforced the law of Christ, and required, that the master should liberate his slave in the first instance. But, instead of this, they let the relationship remain untouched, as being lawful and right, and insist on the relative duties.

In proving this subject justifiable by Scriptural authority, its morality is also proved; for the Divine Law never sanctions immoral actions.

The Christian golden rule, of doing to others, as we would they should do to us, has been urged as an unanswerable argument against holding slaves. But surely this rule is never to be urged against that order of things, which the Divine government has established; nor do our desires become a standard to us, under this rule, unless they have a due regard to justice, propriety and the general good.

A father may very naturally desire, that his son should be obedient to his orders: Is he, therefore, to obey the orders of his son? A man might be pleased to be exonerated from his debts by the generosity of his creditors; or that his rich neighbour should equally divide his property with him; and in certain circumstances might desire these to be done: Would the mere existence of this desire, oblige him to exonerate *his* debtors, and to make such a division of his property? Consistency and generosity, indeed, might require it of him, if he were in circumstances which would justify the act of generosity; but, otherwise, either action might be considered as the effect of folly and extravagance.

If the holding of slaves is lawful, or according to the Scriptures; then this Scriptural rule can be considered as requiring no more of the master, in respect of justice (whatever it may do in point of generosity) than what he, if a slave, could consistently, wish to be done to himself, while the relationship between master and servant should still be continued.

In this argument, the advocates for emancipation blend the ideas of injustice and cruelty with those, which respect the existence of slavery, and consider them as inseparable. But, surely, they may be separated. A bond-servant may be treated with justice and humanity as a servant; and a master may, in an important sense, be the guardian and even father of his slaves.

They become a part of his family, (the whole, forming under him a little community) and the care of ordering it and providing for its welfare, devolves on him. The children, the aged, the sick, the disabled, and the unruly, as well as those, who are capable of service and orderly, are the objects of his care: The labour of these, is applied to the benefit of those, and to their own support, as well as that of the master. Thus, what is effected, and often at a great public expense, in a free community, by taxes, benevolent institutions, bettering houses, and penitentiaries, lies here on the master, to be performed by him, whatever contingencies may happen; and often occasions much expense, care and trouble, from which the servants are free. Cruelty, is, certainly, inadmissible; but servitude may be consistent with such degrees of happiness as men usually attain in this imperfect state of things.

Some difficulties arise with respect to bringing a man, or class of men, into a state of bondage. For crime, it is generally agreed, a man may be deprived of his liberty. But, may he not be divested of it by his own consent, directly, or indirectly given: And, especially, when this assent, though indirect, is connected with an attempt to take away the liberty, if not the lives of others? The Jewish law favours the former idea: And if the inquiry on the latter be taken in the affirmative, which appears to be reasonable, it will establish a principle, by which it will appear, that the Africans brought to America were, slaves, by their own consent, before they came from their own country, or fell into the hands of white men. Their law of nations, or general usage, having, by common consent the force of law, justified them, while carrying on their petty wars, in killing their prisoners or reducing them to slavery; consequently, in selling them, and these ends they appear to have proposed to themselves; the nation, therefore, or individual, which was overcome, reduced to slavery, and sold would have done the same by the enemy, had victory declared on their, or his side. Consequently, the man made slave in this manner, might be said to be made so by his own consent, and by the indulgence of barbarous principles.

That Christian nations have not done all they might, or should have done, on a principle of Christian benevolence, for the civilization and conversion of the Africans: that much cruelty has been practised in the slave trade, as the benevolent Wilberforce, and others have shown; that much tyranny has been exercised by individuals, as masters over their slaves, and that the religious interests of the latter have been too much neglected by many cannot, will not be denied. But the fullest proof of these facts, will not also prove, that the holding men in subjection, as slaves, is a moral evil, and inconsistent with Christianity. Magistrates, husbands, and fathers, have proved tyrants. This does not prove, that magistracy, the husband's right to govern, and parental authority, are unlawful and wicked. The individual who abuses his authority, and acts with cruelty, must answer for it at the Divine tribunal; and civil authority should interpose to prevent or punish it; but neither civil nor ecclesiastical authority can consistently interfere with the possession and legitimate exercise of a right given by the Divine Law.

If the above representation of the Scriptural doctrine, and the manner of obtaining slaves from Africa is just; and if also purchasing them has been the means of saving human life, which there is great reason to believe it has; then, however the slave trade, in present circumstances, is justly censurable, yet might motives of humanity and even piety have been originally brought into operation in the purchase of slaves, when sold in the circumstances we have described. If, also, by their own confession, which has been made in manifold instances, their condition, when they have come into the hands of humane masters here, has been greatly bettered by the change; if it is, ordinarily, really better, as many assert, than that of thousands of the poorer classes in countries reputed civilized and free; and, if, in addition to all other considerations, the translation from their native country to this has been the means of their mental and religious improvement, and so of obtaining salvation, as many of themselves have joyfully and thankfully confessed—then may the just and humane master, who rules his slaves and provides for them, according to Christian principles, rest satisfied, that he is not, in holding them, chargeable with moral evil, nor with acting, in this respect, contrary to the genius of Christianity.—It appears to be equally clear, that those, who by reasoning on abstract principles, are induced to favour the scheme of general emancipation, and who ascribe their sentiments to Christianity, should be particularly careful, however benevolent their intentions may be, that they do not by a perversion of the Scriptural doctrine, through their wrong views of it, not only invade the domestic and religious peace and rights of our Citizens, on this subject; but, also by an intemperate zeal, prevent indirectly, the religious improvement of the people they design, professedly, to benefit; and, perhaps, become, evidently, the means of producing in our country, scenes of anarchy and blood; and all this in a vain attempt to bring about a state of things, which, if arrived at, would not probably better the state of that people; which is thought, by men of observation, to be generally true of the Negroes in the Northern states, who have been liberated.

To pious minds it has given pain to hear men, respectable for intelligence and morals, sometimes say, that holding slaves is indeed indefensible, but that to us it is necessary, and must be supported. On this principle, mere politicians, unmindful of morals, may act. But surely, in a moral and religious view of the subject, this principle is inadmissible. It cannot be said, that theft, falsehood, adultery and murder, are become necessary and must be supported. Yet there is reason to believe, that some of honest and pious intentions have found their minds embarrassed if not perverted on this subject, by this plausible but unsound argument. From such embarrassment the view exhibited above affords relief.

The Convention, Sir, are far from thinking that Christianity fails to inspire the minds of its subjects with benevolent and generous sentiments; or that liberty rightly understood, or enjoyed, is a blessing of little moment. The contrary of these positions they maintain. But they also consider benevolence as consulting the truest and best interests of its objects; and view the happiness of liberty as well as of religion, as consisting not in the name or form, but in the reality. While men remain in the chains of ignorance and error, and under the domination of tyrant lusts and passions, they cannot be free. And the more freedom of action they have in this state, they are but the more qualified by it to do injury, both to themselves and others. It is, therefore, firmly believed, that general emancipation to the Negroes in this country, would not, in present circumstances, be for their own happiness, as a body; while it would be extremely injurious to the community at large in various ways: And, if so, then it is not required even by benevolence. But acts of benevolence and generosity must be free and voluntary; no man has a right to compel another to the performance of them. This is a concern, which lies between a man and his God. If a man has obtained slaves by purchase, or inheritance, and the holding of them as such is justifiable by the law of God; why should he be required to liberate them, because it would be a generous action, rather than another on the same principle, to release his debtors, or sell his lands and houses, and distribute the proceeds among the poor? These also would be generous actions: Are they, therefore, obligatory? Or, if obligatory, in certain circumstances, as personal, voluntary acts of piety and benevolence, has any man or body of men, civil or ecclesiastic, a right to require them? Surely those, who are advocates for compulsory, or strenuous measures to bring about emancipation, should duly weigh this consideration.

Should, however, a time arrive, when the Africans in our country might be found qualified to enjoy freedom; and, when they might obtain it in a manner consistent with the interest and peace of the community at large, the Convention would be happy in seeing them free: And so they would, in seeing the state of the poor, the ignorant and the oppressed of every description, and of every country meliorated; so that the reputed free might be free indeed, and happy. But there seems to be just reason to conclude that a considerable part of the human race, whether they bear openly the character of slaves or are reputed freemen, will continue in such circumstances, with mere shades of variation, while the world continues. It is evident, that men are sinful creatures, subject to affliction and to death, as the consequences of their nature's pollution and guilt: That they are now in a state of probation; and that God as a Righteous, All-wise Sovereign, not only disposes of them as he pleases, and bestows upon them many unmerited blessings and comforts, but subjects them also to privations, afflictions and trials, with the merciful intention of making all their afflictions, as well as their blessings, work finally for their good; if they embrace his salvation, humble themselves before him, learn righteousness, and submit to his holy will. To have them brought to this happy state is the great object of Christian benevolence, and of Christian piety; for this state is not only connected with the truest happiness, which can be enjoyed at any time, but is introductory to eternal life and blessedness in the future world: And the salvation of men is intimately connected with the glory of their God and Redeemer.

And here I am brought to a part of the general subject, which, I confess to your Excellency, the Convention, from a sense of their duty, as a body of men, to whom important concerns of Religion are confided, have particularly at heart, and wish it may be seriously considered by all our Citizens: This is the religious interests of the Negroes. For though they are slaves, they are also men; and are with ourselves accountable creatures; having immortal souls, and being destined to future eternal reward. Their religious interests claim a regard from their masters of the most serious nature; and it is indispensible. Nor can the community at large, in a right estimate of their duty and happiness, be indifferent on this subject. To the truly benevolent it must be pleasing to know, that a number of masters, as well as ministers and pious individuals, of various Christian denominations among us, do conscientiously regard this duty;

but there is a great reason to believe, that it is neglected and disregarded by many.

The Convention are particularly unhappy in considering, that an idea of the Bible's teaching the doctrine of emancipation as necessary, and tending to make servants insubordinate to proper authority, has obtained access to any mind; both on account of its direct influence on those, who admit it; and the fear it excites in others, producing the effects before noticed. But it is hoped, it has been evinced, that the idea is an erroneous one; and, that it will be seen, that the influence of a right acquaintance with that Holy Book tends directly and powerfully, by promoting the fear and love of God, together with just and peaceful sentiments toward men, to produce one of the best securities to the public, for the internal and domestic peace of the State.

It is also a pleasing consideration, tending to confirm these sentiments, that in the late projected scheme for producing an insurrection among us, there were very few of those who were, as members attached to regular Churches, (even within the sphere of its operations) who appear to have taken a part in the wicked plot, or indeed to whom it was made known; of some Churches it does not appear, that there were any. It is true, that a considerable number of those who were found guilty and executed, laid claim to a religious character; yet several of these were grossly immoral, and, in general, they were members of an irregular body, which called itself the *African Church*, and had intimate connection and intercourse with a similar body of men in a Northern City, among whom the supposed right to emancipation is strenuously advocated.

The result of this inquiry and reasoning, on the subject of slavery, brings us, sir, if I mistake not, very regularly to the following conclusions:—That the holding of slaves is justifiable by the doctrine and example contained in Holy writ; and is; therefore consistent with Christian uprightness, both in sentiment and conduct. That all things considered, the Citizens of America have in general obtained the African slaves, which they possess, on principles, which can be justified; though much cruelty has indeed been exercised towards them by many, who have been concerned in the slave-trade, and by others who have held them here, as slaves in their service; for which the authors of this cruelty are accountable. That slavery, when tempered with humanity and justice, is a state of tolerable happiness; equal, if not superior, to that which many poor enjoy in countries reputed free. That a master has a scriptural right to govern his slaves so as to keep it in subjection; to demand and receive from them a reasonable service; and to correct them for the neglect of duty, for their vices and transgressions; but that to impose on them unreasonable, rigorous services, or to inflict on them cruel punishment, he has neither a scriptural nor a moral right. At the same time it must be remembered, that, while he is receiving from them their uniform and best services, he is required by the Divine Law, to afford them protection, and such necessaries and conveniencies of life as are proper to their condition as servants; so far as he is enabled by their services to afford them these comforts, on just and rational principles. That it is the positive duty of servants to reverence their master, to be obedient, industrious, faithful to him, and careful of his interests; and without being so, they can neither be the faithful servants of God, nor be held as regular members of the Christian Church. That as claims to freedom as a *right*, when that right is forfeited, or has been lost, in such a manner as has been represented, would be unjust; and as all attempts to obtain it by violence and fraud would be wicked; so all representations made to them by others, on such censurable principles, or in a manner tending to make them discontented; and finally, to produce such unhappy effects and consequences, as been before noticed, cannot be friendly to them (as they certainly are not to the community at large,) nor consistent with righteousness: Nor can the conduct be justified, however in some it may be palliated by pleading benevolence in intention, as the motive. That masters having the disposal of the persons, time and labour of their servants, and being the heads of families, are bound, on principles of moral and religious duty, to give these servants religious instruction; or at least, to afford them opportunities, under proper regulations to obtain it: And to grant religious privileges to those, who desire them, and furnish proper evidence of their sincerity and uprightness: Due care being at the same time taken, that they receive their instructions from right sources, and from their connexions, where they will not be in danger of having their minds corrupted by sentiments unfriendly to the domestic and civil peace of the community. That, where life, comfort, safety and religious interest of so large a number of human beings, as this class of persons is among us, are concerned; and, where they must necessarily, as slaves, be so much at the disposal of their masters; it appears to be a just and necessary concern of the Government, not only to provide laws to prevent or punish insurrections, and other violent and villanous conduct among them (which are indeed necessary) but, on the other hand, laws, also, to prevent their being oppressed and injured by unreasonable, cruel masters, and others; and to afford them, in respect of morality and religion, such privileges as may comport with the peace and safety of the State, and with those relative duties existing between masters and servants, which the word of God enjoins. It is, also, believed to be a just conclusion, that the interest and security of the State would be promoted, by allowing, under proper regulations, considerable religious privileges, to such of this class, as know how to estimate them aright, and have given suitable evidence of their own good principles, uprightness and fidelity; by attaching them, from principles of gratitude and love, to the interests of their masters and the State; and thus rendering their fidelity firm and constant. While on the other hand, to lay them under an interdict, as some have supposed necessary, in a case where reason, conscience, the genius of Christianity and salvation are concerned, on account of the bad conduct of others, would be felt as oppressive, tend to sour and alienate their minds from their masters and the public, and to make them vulnerable to temptation. All which is, with deference, submitted to the consideration of your Excellency.

With high respect, I remain, personally, and on behalf of the Convention, Sir, your very obedient and humble servant,

RICHARD FURMAN.
President of the Baptist State Convention.

Source: Richard Furman, *Exposition of the Views of the Baptists Relative to the Coloured Population of the United States, in a Communication to the Governor of South-Carolina.* Charleston, SC: A.E. Miller, 1823.

Pope Gregory XVI, In Supremo Apostolatus (1839)

Apostolic Letter condemning the slave trade, written by Pope Gregory XVI and read during the Fourth Provincial Council of Baltimore, December 3, 1839.

Placed at the summit of the Apostolic power and, although lacking in merits, holding the place of Jesus Christ, the Son of God, Who, being made Man through utmost Charity, deigned to die for the Redemption of the World, We have judged that it belonged to Our pastoral solicitude to exert Ourselves to turn away the Faithful from the inhuman slave trade in Negroes and all other men. Assuredly, since there was spread abroad, first of all amongst the Christians, the light of the Gospel, these miserable people, who in such great numbers, and chiefly through the effects of wars, fell into very cruel slavery, experienced an alleviation of their lot. Inspired in fact by the Divine Spirit, the Apostles, it is true, exhorted the slaves themselves to obey their masters, according to the flesh, as though obeying Christ, and sincerely to accomplish the Will of God; but they ordered the masters to act well towards slaves, to give them what was just and equitable, and to abstain from menaces, knowing that the common Master both of themselves and of the slaves is in Heaven, and that with Him there is no distinction of persons.

But as the law of the Gospel universally and earnestly enjoined a sincere charity towards all, and considering that Our Lord Jesus Christ had declared that He considered as done or refused to Himself everything kind and merciful done or refused to the small and needy, it naturally follows, not only that Christians should regard as their brothers their slaves and, above all, their Christian slaves, but that they should be more inclined to set free those who merited it; which it was the custom to do chiefly upon the occasion of the Easter Feast as Gregory of Nyssa tells us. There were not lacking Christians, who, moved by an ardent charity "cast themselves into bondage in order to redeem others," many instances of which our predecessor, Clement I, of very holy memory, declares to have come to his knowledge. In the process of time, the fog of pagan superstition being more completely dissipated and the manners of barbarous people having been softened, thanks to Faith operating by Charity, it at last comes about that, since several centuries, there are no more slaves in the greater number of Christian nations. But—We say with profound sorrow—there were to be found afterwards among the Faithful men who, shamefully blinded by the desire of sordid gain, in lonely and distant countries, did not hesitate to reduce to slavery Indians, Negroes and other wretched peoples, or else, by instituting or developing the trade in those who had been made slaves by others, to favour their unworthy practice. Certainly many Roman Pontiffs of glorious memory, Our Predecessors, did not fail, according to the duties of their charge, to blame severely this way of acting as dangerous for the spiritual welfare of those engaged in the traffic and a shame to the Christian name; they foresaw that as a result of this, the infidel peoples would be more and more strengthened in their hatred of the true Religion.

It is at these practices that are aimed the Letter Apostolic of Paul III, given on May 29, 1537, under the seal of the Fisherman, and addressed to the Cardinal Archbishop of Toledo, and afterwards another Letter, more detailed, addressed by Urban VIII on April 22, 1639 to the Collector Jurium of the Apostolic Chamber of Portugal. In the latter are severely and particularly condemned those who should dare "to reduce to slavery the Indians of the Eastern and Southern Indies," to sell them, buy them, exchange them or give them, separate them from their wives and children, despoil them of their goods and properties, conduct or transport them into other regions, or deprive them of liberty in any way whatsoever, retain them in servitude, or lend counsel, succour, favour and co-operation to those so acting, under no matter what pretext or excuse, or who proclaim and teach that this way of acting is allowable and co-operate in any manner whatever in the practices indicated.

Benedict XIV confirmed and renewed the penalties of the Popes above mentioned in a new Apostolic Letter addressed on December 20, 1741, to the Bishops of Brazil and some other regions, in which he stimulated, to the same end, the solicitude of the Governors themselves. Another of Our Predecessors, anterior to Benedict XIV, Pius II, as during his life the power of the Portuguese was extending itself over New Guinea, sent on October 7, 1462, to a Bishop who was leaving for that country, a Letter in which he not only gives the Bishop himself the means of exercising there the sacred ministry with more fruit, but on the same occasion, addresses grave warnings with regard to Christians who should reduce neophytes to slavery.

In our time Pius VII, moved by the same religious and charitable spirit as his Predecessors, intervened zealously with those in possession of power to secure that the slave trade should at least cease amongst the Christians. The penalties imposed and the care given by Our Predecessors contributed in no small measure, with the help of God, to protect the Indians and the other people mentioned against the cruelty of the invaders or the cupidity of Christian merchants, without however carrying success to such a point that the Holy See could rejoice over the complete success of its efforts in this direction; for the slave trade, although it has diminished in more than one district, is still practiced by numerous Christians. This is why, desiring to remove such a shame from all the Christian nations, having fully reflected over the whole question and having taken the advice of many of Our

Venerable Brothers the Cardinals of the Holy Roman Church, and walking in the footsteps of Our Predecessors, We warn and adjure earnestly in the Lord faithful Christians of every condition that no one in the future dare to vex anyone, despoil him of his possessions, reduce to servitude, or lend aid and favour to those who give themselves up to these practices, or exercise that inhuman traffic by which the Blacks, as if they were not men but rather animals, having been brought into servitude, in no matter what way, are, without any distinction, in contempt of the rights of justice and humanity, bought, sold, and devoted sometimes to the hardest labour. Further, in the hope of gain, propositions of purchase being made to the first owners of the Blacks, dissensions and almost perpetual conflicts are aroused in these regions.

We reprove, then, by virtue of Our Apostolic Authority, all the practices above-mentioned as absolutely unworthy of the Christian name. By the same Authority We prohibit and strictly forbid any Ecclesiastic or lay person from presuming to defend as permissible this traffic in Blacks under no matter what pretext or excuse, or from publishing or teaching in any manner whatsoever, in public or privately, opinions contrary to what We have set forth in this Apostolic Letter.

Source: Pope Gregory XVI, "Apostolic Letter of Our Most Holy Lord Gregory XVI, by Divine Providence, Pope: Concerning the Not Carrying on the Trade in Negroes," in *Letters of the Late Bishop England to the Hon. John Forsyth, on the Subject of Domestic Slavery: To Which Are Prefixed Copies, in Latin and English, of the Pope's Apostolic Letter, Concerning the African Slave Trade, With Some Introductory Remarks, etc.*, ed. John Murphy. New York: Negro Universities Press, 1969.

Speech of the Archbishop of Bahía, in the Brazilian Chamber of Deputies, on the Subject of the Treaty for the Abolition of the Slave-Trade (1852)

It will, perhaps, appear rash on my part, after hearing yesterday the erudite speech of an illustrious orator upon the treaty for the abolition of the commerce in slaves, in entering the field without being possessed of the same degree of intelligence and knowledge to combat the opinions he so learnedly expounded; but it is necessary that I should justify the discrepancy between our ideas in the report of the committee, whereof we both have the honour to be members.

The noble deputy commenced by making a profession of his political faith, declaring that he disap-

proved of the slave-trade, as being both unjust and criminal: but in the course of his speech he explained himself in such a manner, that, if I were not acquainted with his liberal and philanthropic sentiments, I should be persuaded that he is one of the most ardent and strenuous defenders and apologists of that trade. He said that the result of the abolition of this traffic would be the complete ruin of the Brazilian nation, and concluded by saying that the treaty was null, supporting his assertion by quoting the example of France in the time of Louis XII. I agree to the generally-admitted principle of the nullity of such treaties as are ruinous to a nation, as it never can be presumed that anyone would authorize its chief or leader to make compacts that could cause its ruin; but it appertained to the noble deputy to demonstrate that the treaty in question was one of such a nature; and this is what I think he has not done; but, on the contrary, that in confessing the prohibition by the treaty of an unjust and criminal proceeding, he manifestly contradicts himself, or supposes that injustice and crime can produce the happiness of a nation.

But who does not perceive the fallacy and danger of such a principle, and that policy, unaccompanied by justice, can only be a snare laid against the security and prosperity of nations, or that it is a ruinous foundation, which, sooner or later, will overturn the social edifice?

All nations are undoubtedly obliged to seek appropriate means for their preservation and welfare, and for avoiding their destruction; but it is necessary that those means be not unjust nor disallowed, nor prohibited by natural right.

This is what Vatel says, as well as all other writers who teach the first elements of natural right, and those of man. And is there any one who will say that the means furnished by the slave-trade are not unjust; or that this commerce is not illicit, shameful, degrading to man's dignity, anti-social, opposed to the spirit of Christianity, and only calculated to retard the progress of civilisation? I should most certainly wrong the noble sentiments of this august Chamber, if I were to undertake to demonstrate the injustice of a trade which is in contradiction to the intelligence of the age, and to the philanthropic principles loudly proclaimed and professed by the Brazilian nation. The illustrious orator afterwards presented a dismal view of the wars and hostilities reciprocally waged and committed by the African tribes, and showed that it was even an act of humanity to rescue the unfortunate

Negroes from the death or slavery to which they were condemned in their native country. But I believe, Mr. President, that not one of those Africans would be beholden to the illustrious deputy for this act of compassion and of humanity, which tears them away from their wives, their children, and from their country, in order to bring them over, with the most horrible degradation and contempt, to the whip of an implacable master; and the more so, it being well known by the testimony of all travelers, that those wars were never so frequent, nor so cruel, as since the fatal introduction of so abominable a traffic; that it was only since that evil period that slavery commenced, in African jurisprudence, to be the penalty of crime; that, since then, confidence and peace have deserted those regions, and that the appearance of a vessel upon the coast becomes the signal for the most barbarous persecution, for this stimulation of covetousness, and for the perfidy and act of vengeance displayed and exercised on the towns and villages within reach of their fatal influence. And who but the fitters-out of these vessels, or rather the Governments which consent to and authorize such expeditions, are the cause of these wars, hostilities, and effusion of blood, or suicides, and of so many horrors, at which nature revolts? To cover their crimes, they invoke the laws of humanity, atrociously supplanted, in the same manner that the sacred name of religion has been sacrilegiously invoked, under the pretext of converting the Africans, as if a celestial and divine religion, which proclaims the primitive rights of man, which restores to him his dignity, and engraves on his being the beautiful image of Divinity, a religion which forbids violence and force, which, in the phrase of the wise Fenelon, "cannot engender hypocrisy," could be propagated by measures so diametrically opposed to its prodigious establishment. The evangelical zeal of those dealers, and the extent to which their proceedings have contributed to alienate and to indispose the Africans against Christianity—of whose maxims they can only judge by the examples set by those who profess it—is, moreover, notorious; the zeal and care of the major part of the owners of Africans in the religious instruction of those miserable beings whom they look upon as mere beasts of burthen, only caring for the product of their labour, is also known. The intervention of the British Government is next declaimed against, whilst the Brazilian nation is demanding the abolition of the slave-trade.

I know, Mr. President, that no nation, however powerful it may be, has the right to interfere in the affairs of another nation, although it might be with the view to promote its improvement, and the perfection of its institutions, and much less to use measures of restraint, or threats; nor even to punish excesses or enormous faults against natural law; that is the doctrine of all writers excepting Grotius, who, in this last case, admits armed intervention. But let us see in what manner the English nation has proceeded. Every one knows that British intervention in this respect has the concurrence of all those Governments interested in the cessation of the slave-trade,—of France, Sweden, the United States, of the new Republics of the American Continent, and of the old Portuguese Government resident in Brazil, which solemnly bound itself to the gradual abolition of that trade; and if it be said that those treaties and promises cannot bind Brazil after the declaration of her independence, let me be allowed to assert, that this question has already become a completely Brazilian question, since the accession, as is well known, of the Constituent Assembly to the general vote for the abolition of slave-trading, and its having authorized the Executive to treat on this subject with the British Government. The slave-trade might, therefore, have long since been abolished; and there is no reason whatever for inveighing against the English Government, because it exacts compliance with such solemn promises; acting, as it does, in true accordance with the sentiments of all those civilised nations which so energetically pronounced themselves, through the organ of the Congress of Vienna, when it declared that the slave-trade desolated Africa, was degrading to Europe, and outraged humanity. But, even supposing the intervention of England to be illegal, and out of the sphere of the rights of man, it is necessary to take the nature of the thing into consideration. If the requisition of the British Government be founded upon universal justice, and conformable to the principles of religion and of nature, as is shown, we ought not to hesitate for one moment in conforming ourselves to it, even if such initiation were to have been promoted by our greatest enemy; "*fas est ab hoste doceri*"; and let us not imitate those Protestant nations which at first rejected the reform in the Calendar, notwithstanding its acknowledged utility, merely because it was the work of a Roman Pontiff.

From the accusations against the English, the noble orator went on depicting the unfortunate state to which Brazil will be reduced by the abolition of the slave-trade, and the fatal blow thereby given to the commerce, agriculture, industry, and navigation of the empire. Such are, Mr. President, the complaints and pretexts of covetousness and self-interest against wholesome and necessary reforms, but which interfere with the gains and advantages of some individuals. And what would be the term that could satisfy their insatiable desires? Let us undeceive them. If the treaty had stipulated that the traffic should last during a further term of twenty years, at the expiration of that period the same complaints would be renewed, and it would then be said that Brazil required the prolongation of this most execrable importation for twenty years more. Such was the case when the English colonies shook off the yoke of the metropolis; many persons in England, and even very able economists, considered the country as being ruined; that its mercantile marine, its commerce, and naval power would necessarily decay; but it was soon discovered that this was nothing more than a panic; and England has never prospered more, in population, in wealth, or in maritime preponderance, than since the emancipation of those colonies.

The same will happen to Brazil, when the want of slave labour will force her to resort to those more solid and durable measures which hitherto have been despised; some unavoidable inconvenience will be felt in such changes or mercantile alterations; but these will be only temporary, and will soon be counterbalanced by the better direction given to the capital now employed in the ruinous slave-trade. Although, during the term of three years, one-half of Africa may be transplanted to Brazil, the final abolition of this traffic will produce the good effect of improving the lot of the slaves now existing in this country, and of those who may still be imported, by promoting their marriages, and, consequently, their reproduction, and the education of their children; the frightful mortality of this unhappy race of beings will thus be avoided.

A liberal system of colonization, and above all, the soundness and stability of our political institutions, will attract to our fine country, not armed colonists, nor convicts released from prisons; for I do not think the means of subsistence are so abundant in Europe as to prevent many decent families and industrious men from coming to Brazil, when they shall be convinced that no country in the world offers them greater resources than this does, nor greater facilities for bettering their fortunes; and even in regard to such colonists as might come out of prisons, that sentence of Horace, "*Cælum non animum mutant, qui trans mare currunt,*" is not always made good, experience having shown that many of these have become

virtuous and useful to the State, founding great houses and establishments. The civilisation, finally, of the Indians. This great work, which has for a length of time been the object of solicitude to all good Brazilians and to this august chamber, will fill up the vacancy produced by the abolition of the slave-trade.

The forests of my native province alone (that of Para), present 200,000 aboriginals fit for all sorts of industry, whose labour has unfortunately been lost to the State, owing to the absence of a good system of instruction and colonisation, and perhaps, from the erroneous ideas ordinarily entertained of their indolence or intellectual capacity. I can affirm that they are exceedingly capable of being applied to commercial and navigating purposes; that many tribes, as for example the "Monducurus," are excellent hands for agriculture, and, in short, susceptible of all kinds of application—as is seen in the arsenal and in manufactories—almost without being taught, performing carpenter's work, and all other kinds of trades they are put to. Would it not, therefore, be possible to transform them into planters, artisans, seamen, &c., infinitely more useful than those unfortunate Negroes upon whose existence the prosperity of Brazilian commerce, industry, and navigation, is now made to depend?

The same illustrious orator, continuing his observations in regard to the slave-trade, stated that slavery did not product that degree of immorality which is generally supposed. I confess, Mr. President, that this is the first time I have heard such an argument as this advanced. I have always been persuaded that the word "slavery" awakens the idea of all sorts of vices and crimes, as well as that the sweet name of "liberty" stirs up sensations and ideas of all possible virtues and of all kinds of blessings. I have always considered that slavery is a state of violence, that it depresses the spirits, that it blunts the senses, perverts the heart, destroys elasticity and all emulation toward virtuous feelings; I have always, in short, pitied the lot of those tender Brazilian children, who, born and living among slaves, imbibe, from the earliest infancy, fatal impressions from the contagious examples set by those degenerate beings. Would to God I were mistaken! Would to God that the triumphs of seduction and the wreck of innocence were less frequent! Would to God that so many families had not to deplore the infamy and shame into which they have been precipitated by the immorality of their slaves! I agree with the illustrious deputy in his praise of the blacks and mulattoes, many of whom are deserving of the highest esteem. I do not set a value upon mankind from the colour of their skins, but according to their conduct and character: the slave, however, has no character, he is nothing more than a blind instrument of compliance with the will of his master; a virtuous slave is a prodigy in the order of morality.

It behoves me, finally, to reply to the wishes expressed by the noble orator, "that Brazil would make no treaties with European powers, and that it would become as incommunicable as China." If this idea could be admitted by a nation which has tasted the sweets of civilisation, it must at least be confessed that it is quite premature. China contains more than 200,000,000 of inhabitants, and Brazil scarcely 4,000,000, disseminated over an immense superficies of territory. Let us then wait until Brazil shall possess a superabundant population, and we will then build our wall of 500 leagues in length; we will publish severe laws against those Europeans who shall have the temerity to set foot upon our soil; we will adopt the beautiful institutions of the Chinese; we will have our lawyer mandarins, and the very paternal despotism of its emperor. Until the arrival of that period, let us continue to keep up our intercourse with those Europeans who have been our teachers and guides in the arts and sciences, and even in all liberal institutions. This sort of commerce is certainly more advantageous to us than that of the savage Africans.

I have now only to speak of the penalty of piracy imposed by the treaty in question, and I am truly sorry, after having paid the magnanimous British nation the just tribute of praise due to its philanthropy and to its efforts in behalf of humanity, that I should find myself forced to disapprove of its interference by imposing such a penalty. It is very painful to the Brazilian, who prizes the dignity of his country, that whilst the legislative bodies of other nations freely discuss and resolve upon matters of such importance, Brazil alone sees itself deprived of this unquestionable right, making the sacrifice of subjecting its citizens to the penalties inflicted by a foreign country.

I acknowledge, Mr. President, that if it be *bona fide* wished to put an end to the infamous slave-trade, a more efficacious measure could not be resorted to; for otherwise all precautions against the fruitful and unbridled cupidity of the fitters-out of vessels would be illusory; but it does not belong to the British Government to classify crimes and to establish penalties against the subjects of an independent nation. The committee withal, having duly considered all points of the case with the most serious attention and reflection, and being apprised by the Minister's note of the afflicting position of the government between two great evils—seeing, furthermore, that the treaty had been concluded and ratified, and only wanted the signature of the British Minister—did not object to sign the Report in the form in which it is couched, judging that under such circumstances nothing more could be expected from this Chamber, according to the 8th paragraph of Article 102 of the Constitution.

This is all I had to say upon the subject; protesting, with my usual candour and frankness, that even if the treaty had exacted the immediate abolition of the traffic, I would have subscribed to and have approved of so salutary a measure with infinite pleasure and gratitude.

Source: Anti-Slavery Reporter (New Series), 7:77 (May 1, 1852).

Pope Leo XIII, In Plurimis (1888)

Encyclical of Pope Leo XIII on the abolition of slavery in Brazil. Given at St. Peter's, in Rome, the fifth day of May, 1888, the eleventh of Our pontificate.

To the Bishops of Brazil,
Amid the many and great demonstrations of affection which from almost all the peoples of the earth have come to Us, and are still coming to Us, in congratulation upon the happy attainment of the fiftieth anniversary of Our priesthood, there is one which moves Us in a quite special way. We mean one which comes from Brazil, where, upon the occasion of this happy event, large numbers of those who in that vast empire groan beneath the yoke of slavery, have been legally set free. And this work, so full of the spirit of Christian mercy, has been offered up in cooperation with the clergy, by charitable members of the laity of both sexes, to God, the Author and Giver of all good things, in testimony of their gratitude for the favor of the health and the years which have been granted to Us. But this was specially acceptable and sweet to Us because it lent confirmation to the belief, which is so welcome to Us, that the great majority of the people of Brazil desire to see the cruelty of slavery ended, and rooted out from the land. This popular feeling has been strongly seconded by the emperor and his August daughter, and also by the ministers, by means of various laws which, with this end in view, have been introduced and sanctioned. We told the Brazilian ambassador last January what a consolation these things were to Us, and We also assured him that We

would address letters to the bishops of Brazil in behalf of these unhappy slaves.

We, indeed, to all men are the Vicar of Christ, the Son of God, who so loved the human race that not only did He not refuse, taking our nature to Himself, to live among men, but delighted in bearing the name of the Son of Man, openly proclaiming that He had come upon earth "to preach deliverance to the captives" in order that, rescuing mankind from the worst slavery, which is the slavery of sin, "he might re-establish all things that are in heaven and on earth," and so bring back all the children of Adam from the depths of the ruin of the common fall to their original dignity. The words of St. Gregory the Great are very applicable here: "Since our Redeemer, the Author of all life, deigned to take human flesh, that by the power of His Godhood the chains by which we were held in bondage being broken, He might restore us to our first state of liberty, it is most fitting that men by the concession of manumission should restore to the freedom in which they were born those whom nature sent free into the world, but who have been condemned to the yoke of slavery by the law of nations." It is right, therefore, and obviously in keeping with Our apostolic office, that We should favor and advance by every means in Our power whatever helps to secure for men, whether as individuals or as communities, safeguards against the many miseries, which, like the fruits of an evil tree, have sprung from the sin of our first parents; and such safeguards, of whatever kind they may be, help not only to promote civilization and the amenities of life, but lead on to that universal restitution of all things which our Redeemer Jesus Christ contemplated and desired.

In the presence of so much suffering, the condition of slavery, in which a considerable part of the great human family has been sunk in squalor and affliction now for many centuries, is deeply to be deplored; for the system is one which is wholly opposed to that which was originally ordained by God and by nature. The Supreme Author of all things so decreed that man should exercise a sort of royal dominion over beasts and cattle and fish and fowl, but never that men should exercise a like dominion over their fellow men. As St. Augustine puts it: "Having created man a reasonable being, and after His own likeness, God wished that he should rule only over the brute creation; that he should be the master, not of men, but of beasts." From this it follows that "the state of slavery is rightly regarded as a penalty upon the sinner; thus, the word slave does not occur in the

Bible until the just man Noah branded with it the sin of his son. It was sin, therefore, which deserved this name; it was not natural."

From the first sin came all evils, and specially this perversity that there were men who, forgetful of the original brotherhood of the race, instead of seeking, as they should naturally have done, to promote mutual kindness and mutual respect, following their evil desires began to think of other men as their inferiors, and to hold them as cattle born for the yoke. In this way, through an absolute forgetfulness of our common nature, and of human dignity, and the likeness of God stamped upon us all, it came to pass that in the contentions and wars which then broke out, those who were the stronger reduced the conquered into slavery; so that mankind, though of the same race, became divided into two sections, the conquered slaves and their victorious masters. The history of the ancient world presents us with this miserable spectacle down to the time of the coming of our Lord, when the calamity of slavery had fallen heavily upon all the peoples, and the number of freemen had become so reduced that the poet was able to put this atrocious phrase into the mouth of Caesar: "The human race exists for the sake of a few."

The system flourished even among the most civilized peoples, among the Greeks and among the Romans, with whom the few imposed their will upon the many; and this power was exercised so unjustly and with such haughtiness that a crowd of slaves was regarded merely as so many chattels—not as persons, but as things. They were held to be outside the sphere of law, and without even the claim to retain and enjoy life. "Slaves are in the power of their masters, and this power is derived from the law of nations; for we find that among all nations masters have the power of life and death over their slaves, and whatever a slave earns belongs to his master." Owing to this state of moral confusion it became lawful for men to sell their slaves, to give them in exchange, to dispose of them by will, to beat them, to kill them, to abuse them by forcing them to serve for the gratification of evil passions and cruel superstitions; these things could be done, legally, with impunity, and in the light of heaven. Even those who were wisest in the pagan world, illustrious philosophers and learned jurisconsults, outraging the common feeling of mankind, succeeded in persuading themselves and others that slavery was simply a necessary condition of nature. Nor did they hesitate to assert that the slave class was very inferior to the freemen both in intelligence and perfection of bodily development, and therefore that slaves, as things wanting in reason and sense, ought in all things to be the instruments of the will, however rash and unworthy, of their masters. Such inhuman and wicked doctrines are to be specially detested; for, when once they are accepted, there is no form of oppression so wicked but that it will defend itself beneath some color of legality and justice. History is full of examples showing what a seedbed of crime, what a pest and calamity, this system has been for states. Hatreds are excited in the breasts of the slaves, and the masters are kept in a state of suspicion and perpetual dread; the slaves prepare to avenge themselves with the torches of the incendiary, and the masters continue the task of oppression with greater cruelty. States are disturbed alternately by the number of the slaves and by the violence of the masters, and so are easily overthrown; hence, in a word, come riots and seditions, pillage and fire.

The greater part of humanity were toiling in this abyss of misery, and were the more to be pitied because they were sunk in the darkness of superstition, when in the fullness of time and by the designs of God, light shone down upon the world, and the merits of Christ the Redeemer were poured out upon mankind. By that means they were lifted out of the slough and the distress of slavery, and recalled and brought back from the terrible bondage of sin to their high dignity as the sons of God. Thus, the Apostles, in the early days of the Church, among other precepts for a devout life taught and laid down the doctrine which more than once occurs in the Epistles of St. Paul addressed to those newly baptized: "For you are all the children of God by faith, in Jesus Christ. For as many of you as have been baptized in Christ, have put on Christ. There is neither Jew, nor Greek; there is neither bond, nor free; there is neither male nor female. For you are all one in Christ Jesus." "Where there is neither Gentile nor Jew, circumcision nor uncircumcision, barbarian nor Scythian, bond nor free. But Christ is all and in all." "For in one Spirit were we all baptized into one body, whether Jews or Gentiles, whether bond or free; and in one Spirit we have all been made to drink." Golden words, indeed, noble and wholesome lessons, whereby its old dignity is given back and with increase to the human race, and men of whatever land or tongue of class are bound together and joined in the strong bonds of brotherly kinship. Those things St. Paul, with that Christian charity with which he was filled, learned from the very heart of Him who, with much surpassing goodness, gave

Himself to be the brother of us all, and in His own person, without omitting or excepting any one, so ennobled men that they might become participators in the divine nature. Through this Christian charity the various races of men were drawn together under the divine guidance in such a wonderful way that they blossomed into a new state of hope and public happiness; as with the progress of time and events and the constant labor of the Church the various nations were able to gather together, Christian and free, organized anew after the manner of a family.

From the beginning the Church spared no pains to make the Christian people, in a matter of such high importance, accept and firmly hold the true teachings of Christ and the Apostles. And now through the new Adam, who is Christ, there is established a brotherly union between man and man, and people and people; just as in the order of nature they all have a common origin, so in the order which is above nature they all have one and the same origin in salvation and faith; all alike are called to be the adopted sons of God and the Father, who has paid the self-same ransom for us all; we are all members of the same body, all are allowed to partake of the same divine banquet, and offered to us all are the blessings of divine grace and of eternal life. Having established these principles as beginnings and foundations, the Church, like a tender mother, went on to try to find some alleviation for the sorrows and the disgrace of the life of the slave; with this end in view she clearly defined and strongly enforced the rights and mutual duties of masters and slaves as they are laid down in the letters of the Apostles. It was in these words that the Princes of the Apostles admonished the slaves they had admitted to the fold of Christ. "Servants, be subject to your masters with all fear, not only to the good and gentle, but also to the forward." "Servants, be obedient to them that are your lords according to the flesh, with fear and trembling in the simplicity of your heart, as to Christ. Not serving to the eye, but as the servants of Christ, doing the will of God from the heart. With a good will serving as to the Lord, and not to men. Knowing that whatsoever good thing any man shall do, the same shall he receive from the Lord, whether he be bond or free." St. Paul says the same to Timothy: "Whosoever are servants under the yoke, let them count their masters worthy of all honor; lest the name of the Lord and his doctrine be blasphemed. But they that have believing masters, let them not despise them because they are brethren, but serve them the rather, because they are faithful and beloved, who are partakers of the benefit. These things teach and exhort." In like manner he commanded Titus to teach servants "to be obedient to their masters, in all things pleasing, not gainsaying. Not defrauding, but in all things showing good fidelity, that they may adorn the doctrine of God our Savior in all things.

Those first disciples of the Christian faith very well understood that this brotherly equality of all men in Christ ought in no way to diminish or detract from the respect, honor, faithfulness, and other duties due to those placed above them. From this many good results followed, so that duties became at once more certain of being performed, and lighter and pleasanter to do, and at the same time more fruitful in obtaining the glory of heaven. Thus, they treated their masters with reverence and honor as men clothed in the authority of Him from whom comes all power. Among these disciples the motive of action was not the fear of punishment or any enlightened prudence or the promptings of utility, but a consciousness of duty and the force of charity. On the other hand, masters were wisely counseled by the Apostle to treat their slaves with consideration in return for their services: "And you, masters, do the same things unto them, forbearing threatenings; knowing that the Lord both of them and you is in heaven, and there is not respect of persons with Him." They were also told to remember that the slave had no reason to regret his lot, seeing that he is "the freeman of the Lord," nor the freeman, seeing that he is "the bondman of Christ," to feel proud, and to give his commands with haughtiness. It was impressed upon masters that they ought to recognize in their slaves their fellow men, and respect them accordingly, recognizing that by nature they were not different from themselves, that by religion and in relation to the majesty of their common Lord all were equal. These precepts, so well calculated to introduce harmony among the various parts of domestic society, were practiced by the Apostles themselves. Specially remarkable is the case of St. Paul when he exerted himself in behalf of Onesimus, the fugitive of Philemon, with whom, when he returned him to his master, he sent this loving recommendation: "And do thou receive him as my own bowels, not now as a servant, but instead of a servant a most dear brother . . . And if he have wronged thee in anything, or is in thy debt, put that to my account."

Whoever compare the pagan and the Christian attitude toward slavery will easily come to the conclusion that the one was marked by great cruelty and wickedness, and the other by great gentleness and humanity, nor will it be possible to deprive the Church of the credit due to her as the instrument of this happy change. And this becomes still more apparent when we consider carefully how tenderly and with what prudence the Church has cut out and destroyed this dreadful curse of slavery. She has deprecated any precipitate action in securing the manumission and liberation of the slaves, because that would have entailed tumults and wrought injury, as well to the slaves themselves as to the commonwealth, but with singular wisdom she has seen that the minds of the slaves should be instructed through her discipline in the Christian faith, and with baptism should acquire habits suitable to the Christian life. Therefore, when, amid the slave multitude whom she has numbered among her children, some, led astray by some hope of liberty, have had recourse to violence and sedition, the Church has always condemned these unlawful efforts and opposed them, and through her ministers has applied the remedy of patience. She taught the slaves to feel that, by virtue of the light of holy faith, and the character they received from Christ, they enjoyed a dignity which placed them above their heathen lords, but that they were bound the more strictly by the Author and Founder of their faith Himself never to set themselves against these, or even to be wanting in the reverence and obedience due to them. Knowing themselves as the chosen ones of the Kingdom of God, and endowed with the freedom of His children, and called to the good things that are not of this life, they were able to work on without being cast down by the sorrows and troubles of this passing world, but with eyes and hearts turned to heaven were consoled and strengthened in their holy resolutions. St. Peter was addressing himself specially to slaves when he wrote: "For this is thanksworthy, if for conscience towards God a man endure sorrows, suffering wrongfully. For unto this you are called; because Christ also suffered for us, leaving you an example that you should follow his steps."

The credit for this solicitude joined with moderation, which in such a wonderful way adorns the divine powers of the Church, is increased by the marvelous and unconquerable courage with which she was able to inspire and sustain so many poor slaves. It was a wonderful sight to behold those who, in their obedience and the patience with which they submitted to every task, were such an example to their masters, refusing to let themselves be persuaded to prefer the wicked commands of those above them to the holy law of God, and even giving up their lives in the most cruel tortures with unconquered hearts and unclouded brows. The pages of Eusebius keep alive for us the memory of the unshaken constancy of the virgin Potamiana, who, rather than consent to gratify the lusts of her master, fearlessly accepted death, and sealed her faithfulness to Jesus Christ with her blood. Many other admirable examples abound of slaves, who, for their souls' sake and to keep their faith with God, have resisted their masters to the death. History has no case to show of Christian slaves for any other cause setting themselves in opposition to their masters of joining in conspiracies against the State.

Thence, peace and quiet times having been restored to the Church, the holy Fathers made a wise and admirable exposition of the apostolic precepts concerning the fraternal unanimity which should exist between Christians, and with a like charity extended it to the advantage of slaves, striving to point out that the rights of masters extended lawfully indeed over the works of their slaves, but that their power did not extend to using horrible cruelties against their persons. St. Chrysostom stands pre-eminent among the Greeks, who often treats of this subject, and affirms with exulting mind and tongue that slavery, in the old meaning of the word, had at that time disappeared through the beneficence of the Christian faith, so that it both seemed, and was, a word without any meaning among the disciples of the Lord. For Christ indeed (so he sums up his argument), when in His great mercy to us He wiped away the sin contracted by our birth, at the same time healed the manifold corruptions of human society; so that, as death itself by His means has laid aside its terrors and become a peaceful passing away to a happy life, so also has slavery been banished. Do not, then, call any Christian man a slave, unless, indeed, he is in bondage again to sin; they are altogether brethren who are born again and received in Christ Jesus. Our advantages flow from the new birth and adoption into the household of God, not from the eminence of our race; our dignity arises from the praise of our truth, not of our blood. But in order that that kind of evangelical brotherhood may have more fruit, it is necessary that in the actions of our ordinary life there should appear a willing interchange of kindnesses and good offices, so that slaves should be esteemed of nearly equal account with the rest of our household and friends, and that the master of the house should supply them, not only with what is necessary for their life and food, but also all necessary safeguards of religious training. Finally, from the marked address of Paul to Philemon, bidding grace and peace "to the church which is in thy house," the precept should be held in respect equally by Christian masters and servants, that they who have an intercommunion of faith should also have an intercommunion of charity.

Of the Latin authors, we worthily and justly call to mind St. Ambrose, who so earnestly inquired into all that was necessary in this cause, and so clearly ascribes what is due to each kind of man according to the laws of Christianity, that no one has ever achieved it better, whose sentiments, it is unnecessary to say, fully and perfectly coincide with those of St. Chrysostom. These things were, as is evident, most justly and usefully laid down; but more, the chief point is that they have been observed wholly and religiously from the earliest times wherever the profession of the Christian faith has flourished. Unless this had been the case, that excellent defender of religion, Lactantius, could not have maintained it so confidently, as though a witness of it. "Should any one say: Are there not among you some poor, some rich, some slaves, some who are masters; is there no difference between different persons? I answer: There is none, nor is there any other cause why we call each other by the name of brother than that we consider ourselves to be equals; first, when we measure all human things, not by the body but by the spirit, although their corporal condition may be different from ours, yet in spirit they are not slaves to us, but we esteem and call them brethren, fellow workers in religion."

The care of the Church extended to the protection of slaves, and without interruption tended carefully to one object, that they should finally be restored to freedom, which would greatly conduce to their eternal welfare. That the event happily responded to these efforts, the annals of sacred antiquity afford abundant proof. Noble matrons, rendered illustrious by the praises of St. Jerome, themselves afforded great aid in carrying this matter into effect; so that as Salvian relates, in Christian families, even though not very rich, it often happened that the slaves were freed by a generous manumission. But, also, St. Clement long before praised that excellent work of charity by which some Christians became slaves, by an exchange of persons, because they could in no other way liberate those who were in bondage.

Wherefore, in addition to the fact that the act of manumission began to take place in churches as an act of piety, the Church ordered it to be proposed to the faithful when about to make their wills, as a work very pleasing to God and of great merit and value with Him. Therefore, those precepts of manumission to the heir were introduced with the words, "for the love of God, for the welfare or benefit of my soul." Neither was anything grudged as the price of the captives, gifts dedicated to God were sold, consecrated gold and silver melted down, the ornaments and gifts of the basilicas alienated, as, indeed, was done more than once by Ambrose, Augustine, Hilary, Eligius, Patrick, and many other holy men.

Moreover, the Roman Pontiffs, who have always acted, as history truly relates, as the protectors of the weak and helpers of the oppressed, have done their best for slaves. St. Gregory himself set at liberty as many as possible, and in the Roman Council of 597 desired those to receive their freedom who were anxious to enter the monastic state. Hadrian I maintained that slaves could freely enter into matrimony even without their masters' consent. It was clearly ordered by Alexander III in the year 1167 to the Moorish King of Valencia that he should not make a slave of any Christian, because no one was a slave by the law of nature, all men having been made free by God. Innocent III, in the year 1190, at the prayer of its founders, John de Matha and Felix of Valois, approved and established the Order of the Most Holy Trinity for Redeeming Christians who had fallen into the power of the Turks. At a later date, Honorius III, and, afterwards, Gregory IX, duly approved the Order of St. Mary of Help, founded for a similar purpose, which Peter Nolasco had established, and which included the severe rule that its religious should give themselves up as slaves in the place of Christians taken captive by tyrants, if it should be necessary in order to redeem them. The same St. Gregory passed a decree, which was a far greater support of liberty, that it was unlawful to sell slaves to the Church, and he further added an exhortation to the faithful that, as a punishment for their faults, they should give their slaves to God and His saints as an act of expiation.

There are also many other good deeds of the Church in the same behalf. For she, indeed, was accustomed by severe penalties to defend slaves from the savage anger and cruel injuries of their masters. To those upon whom the hand of violence had rested, she was accustomed to open her sacred temples as places of refuge to receive the free men into her good faith, and to restrain those by censure who dared by evil inducements to lead a man back again into slavery. In the same way she was still more favorable to the freedom of the slaves whom, by any means she held as her own, according to times and places; when she laid down either that those should be released by the bishops from every bond of slavery who had shown themselves during a certain time of trial of praiseworthy honesty of life, or when she easily permitted the bishops of their own will to declare those belonging to them free. It must also be ascribed to the compassion and virtue of the Church that somewhat of the pressure of civil law upon slaves was remitted, and, as far as it was brought about, that the milder alleviations of Gregory the Great, having been incorporated in the written law of nations, became of force. That, however, was done principally by the agency of Charlemagne, who included them in his "Capitularia," as Gratian afterwards did in his "Decretum." Finally, monuments, laws, institutions, through a continuous series of ages, teach and splendidly demonstrate the great love of the Church toward slaves, whose miserable condition she never left destitute of protection, and always to the best of her power alleviated. Therefore, sufficient praise or thanks can never be returned to the Catholic Church, the banisher of slavery and causer of true liberty, fraternity, and equality among men, since she has merited it by the prosperity of nations, through the very great beneficence of Christ our Redeemer.

Toward the end of the fifteenth century, at which time the base stain of slavery having been nearly blotted out from among Christian nations, States were anxious to stand firmly in evangelical liberty, and also to increase their empire, this apostolic see took the greatest care that the evil germs of such depravity should nowhere revive. She therefore directed her provident vigilance to the newly discovered regions of Africa, Asia, and America; for a report had reached her that the leaders of those expeditions, Christians though they were, were wickedly making use of their arms and ingenuity for establishing and imposing slavery on these innocent nations. Indeed, since the crude nature of the soil which they had to overcome, nor less the wealth of metals which had to be extracted by digging, required very hard work, unjust and inhuman plans were entered into. For a certain traffic was begun, slaves being transported for that purpose from Ethiopia, which, at that time, under the name of "La tratta dei Negri," too much occupied those colonies. An oppression of the indigenous inhabitants (who are collectively called Indians), much the same as slavery, followed with a like maltreatment.

When Pius II had become assured of these matters without delay, on October 7, 1462, he gave a letter to the bishop of the place in which he reproved and condemned such wickedness. Some time afterwards, Leo X lent, as far as he could, his good offices and authority to the kings of both Portugal and Spain, who took care to radically extirpate that abuse, opposed alike to religion, humanity, and justice. Nevertheless, that evil having grown strong, remained there, its impure cause, the unquenchable desire of gain, remaining. Then Paul III, anxious with a fatherly love as to the condition of the Indians and of the Moorish slaves, came to this last determination, that in open day, and, as it were, in the sight of all nations, he declared that they all had a just and natural right of a threefold character, namely, that each one of them was master of his own person, that they could live together under their own laws, and that they could acquire and hold property for themselves. More than this, having sent letters to the Cardinal Archbishop of Toledo, he pronounced an interdict and deprival of sacraments against those who acted contrary to the aforesaid decree, reserving to the Roman Pontiff the power of absolving them.

With the same forethought and constancy, other Pontiffs at a later period, as Urban VIII, Benedict XIV, and Pius VII, showed themselves strong asserters of liberty for the Indians and Moors and those who were even as yet not instructed in the Christian faith. The last, moreover, at the Council of the confederated Princes of Europe, held at Vienna, called their attention in common to this point, that that traffic in Negroes, of which We have spoken before, and which had now ceased in many places, should be thoroughly rooted out. Gregory XVI also severely censured those neglecting the duties of humanity and the laws, and restored the decrees and statutory penalties of the apostolic see, and left no means untried that foreign nations, also, following the kindliness of the Europeans, should cease from and abhor the disgrace and brutality of slavery. But it has turned out most fortunately for Us that We have received the congratulations of the chief princes and rulers of public affairs for having obtained, thanks to Our constant pleadings, some

satisfaction for the long-continued and most just complaints of nature and religion.

We have, however, in Our mind, in a matter of the same kind, another care which gives Us no light anxiety and presses upon Our solicitude. This shameful trading in men has, indeed, ceased to take place by sea, but on land is carried on to too great an extent and too barbarously, and that especially in some parts of Africa. For, it having been perversely laid down by the Mohammedans that Ethiopians and men of similar nations are very little superior to brute beasts, it is easy to see and shudder at the perfidy and cruelty of man. Suddenly, like plunderers making an attack, they invade the tribes of Ethiopians, fearing no such thing; they rush into their villages, houses, and huts; they lay waste, destroy, and seize everything; they lead away from thence the men, women, and children, easily captured and bound, so that they may drag them away by force for their shameful traffic. These hateful expeditions are made into Egypt, Zanzibar, and partly also into the Sudan, as though so many stations. Men, bound with chains are forced to take long journeys, ill supplied with food, under the frequent use of the lash; those who are too weak to undergo this are killed; those who are strong enough go like a flock with a crowd of others to be sold and to be passed over to a brutal and shameless purchaser. But whoever is thus sold and given up is exposed to what is a miserable rending asunder of wives, children, and parents, and is driven by him into whose power he falls into a hard and indescribable slavery; nor can he refuse to conform to the religious rites of Mahomet. These things We have received not long since with the greatest bitterness of feeling from some who have been eyewitnesses, though tearful ones, of that kind of infamy and misery; with these, moreover, what has been related lately by the explorers in equatorial Africa entirely coincides. It is indeed manifest, by their testimony and word, that each year 400,000 Africans are usually thus sold like cattle, about half of whom, wearied out by the roughness of the tracks, fall down and perish there, so that, sad to relate, those traveling through such places see the pathway strewn with the remains of bones.

Who would not be moved by the thought of such miseries. We, indeed, who are holding the place of Christ, the loving Liberator and Redeemer of all mankind, and who so rejoice in the many and glorious good deeds of the Church to all who are afflicted, can scarcely express how great is Our commiseration for those unhappy nations, with what fullness of charity We open Our arms to them, how ardently We desire to be able to afford them every alleviation and support, with the hope, that, having cast off the slavery of superstition as well as the slavery of man, they may at length serve the one true God under the gentle yoke of Christ, partakers with Us of the divine inheritance. Would that all who hold high positions in authority and power, or who desire the rights of nations and of humanity to be held sacred, or who earnestly devote themselves to the interests of the Catholic religion, would all, everywhere acting on Our exhortations and wishes, strive together to repress, forbid, and put an end to that kind of traffic, than which nothing is more base and wicked.

In the meantime, while by a more strenuous application of ingenuity and labor new roads are being made, and new commercial enterprises undertaken in the lands of Africa, let apostolic men endeavor to find out how they can best secure the safety and liberty of slaves. They will obtain success in this matter in no other way than if, strengthened by divine grace, they give themselves up to spreading our most holy faith and daily caring for it, whose distinguishing fruit is that it wonderfully flavors and develops the liberty "with which Christ made us free." We therefore advise them to look, as if into a mirror of apostolic virtue, at the life and works of St. Peter Claver, to whom We have lately added a crown of glory. Let them look at him who for fully forty years gave himself up to minister with the greatest constancy in his labors, to a most miserable assembly of Moorish slaves; truly he ought to be called the apostle of those whose constant servant he professed himself and gave himself up to be. If they endeavor to take to themselves and reflect the charity and patience of such a man, they will shine indeed as worthy ministers of salvation, authors of consolation, messengers of peace, who, by God's help, may turn solicitude, desolation, and fierceness into the most joyful fertility of religion and civilization.

And now, venerable brethren, Our thoughts and letters desire to turn to you that We may again announce to you and again share with you the exceeding joy which We feel on account of the determinations which have been publicly entered into in that empire with regard to slavery. If, indeed, it seemed to Us a good, happy, and propitious event, that it was provided and insisted upon by law that whoever were still in the condition of slaves ought to be admitted to the status and rights of free men, so also it conforms and increases Our hope of future acts which will be the cause of joy, both in civil and religious matters. Thus the name of the Empire of Brazil will be justly held in honor and praise among the most civilized nations, and the name of its August emperor will likewise be esteemed, whose excellent speech is on record, that he desired nothing more ardently than that every vestige of slavery should be speedily obliterated from his territories. But, truly, until those precepts of the laws are carried into effect, earnestly endeavor, We beseech you, by all means, and press on as much as possible the accomplishment of this affair, which no light difficulties hinder. Through your means let it be brought to pass that masters and slaves may mutually agree with the highest goodwill and best good faith, nor let there be any transgression of clemency or justice, but, whatever things have to be carried out, let all be done lawfully, temperately, and in a Christian manner. It is, however, chiefly to be wished that this may be prosperously accomplished, which all desire, that slavery may be banished and blotted out without any injury to divine or human rights, with no political agitation, and so with the solid benefit of the slaves themselves, for whose sake it is undertaken.

To each one of these, whether they have already been made free or are about to become so, We address with a pastoral intention and fatherly mind a few salutary cautions culled from the words of the great Apostle of the Gentiles. Let them, then, endeavor piously and constantly to retain grateful memory and feeling towards those by whose council and exertion they were set at liberty. Let them never show themselves unworthy of so great a gift nor ever confound liberty with license; but let them use it as becomes well ordered citizens for the industry of an active life, for the benefit and advantage both of their family and of the State. To respect and increase the dignity of their princes, to obey the magistrates, to be obedient to the laws, these and similar duties let them diligently fulfill, under the influence, not so much of fear as of religion; let them also restrain and keep in subjection envy of another's wealth or position, which unfortunately daily distresses so many of those in inferior positions, and present so many incitements of rebellion against security of order and peace. Content with their state and lot, let them think nothing dearer, let them desire nothing more ardently than the good things of the heavenly kingdom by whose grace they have been brought to the light and redeemed by Christ; let them feel piously towards God who is their Lord and Liberator; let them love Him, with all their power; let them keep His commandments with all their might; let them rejoice in being sons of His spouse, the Holy Church; let them labor to be as good as possible, and as much as they can let them carefully return His love.

Do you also, Venerable Brethren, be constant in showing and urging on the freedmen these same doctrines; that, that which is Our chief prayer, and at the same time ought to be yours and that of all good people, religion, amongst the first, may ever feel that she has gained the most ample fruits of that liberty which has been obtained wherever that empire extends.

But that that may happily take place, We beg and implore the full grace of God and motherly aid of the Immaculate Virgin. As a foretaste of heavenly gifts and witness of Our fatherly good will towards you, Venerable Brethren, your clergy, and all your people, We lovingly impart the apostolic blessing.

Source: The Great Encyclicals of Pope Leo XII, ed. Rev. John J. Wynne. New York: Benziger Brothers, 1903.

Letter from Ch. Cardinal Lavigerie Regarding Pope Leo XIII's Statement on Abolition (1888)

Rome, November 22, 1888.

MY LORD,—

I cannot but be delighted with your Lordship's idea of introducing to notice in Manchester the Anti-Slavery crusade of our Holy Father POPE LEO XIII. I have already had the pleasure of preaching in London, and I can truly say that nowhere has this great ideal of humanity and justice found so benevolent and, I venture to say, so enthusiastic a reception. England indeed recognised in this new enterprise her most glorious souvenirs. It must never be forgotten that it was she who at the close of the last century and the first half of the present had the chief share in the work of abolishing colonial Slavery in the West Indies. She it was who, by the burning eloquence of BUXTON, WILBERFORCE, and so many others, excited the indignation of the civilised world against such barbarities. She it was who, by her statesmen, decided Europe, first at the Congress of Vienna, afterwards at the Conference of Verona, to take in hand resolutely the cause of the poor blacks, and to treat as

pirates those who, in the midst of so many scenes of carnage, did not blush to carry away entire populations from their native lands, from their families and their liberty, in order to transport them in the holds of their horrible vessels into the plantations and beneath the lash of the planters of America. She it was, in fine, who often undertook to carry out the decisions of Europe, and who often went so far as to constrain foreign nations to execute international conventions. And nowadays it is still she who, by means of LIVINGSTONE and her other explorers, calls the attention of Christian nations to the revival, in the interior of Africa and on the East Coast, of the Slave-trade, no longer indeed by planters, but by the Mussulmans of Asia and Northern Africa. Without doubt the African trade had never been interrupted; but after the great victory won over colonial Slavery it had been so to say, forgotten. The intrepid courage, the devotedness, the high probity and truthfulness of LIVINGSTONE, his repeated testimony to the dreadful scourge, his last wishes, immortalised by the English people by inscribing them on his tomb in Westminster Abbey, and after LIVINGSTONE'S time the testimony of so many others—BURTON, SPEKE, CAMERON, &c.—have produced on the entire world the same impression as was created by those Anti-Slavery agitators who fifty years ago abolished the colonial Slave-trade. Missionaries have joined their voices to those of explorers and philanthropists. Our Catholic missionaries from Algiers, who little by little have spread themselves with heroic courage over the Mussulman regions of the Soudan and the table-lands of the great lakes, very soon made known to me personally the horrors which they had witnessed. The sovereign Pontiff could not fail to denounce these horrors to the entire world. Hence in the audience accorded to the African Pilgrimage at the end of last May, he uttered that strenuous appeal which has found so powerful an echo in England, without distinction of political opinion, or even religious confession. How much I should like, My Lord, to accept your invitation, and to repeat once more in Manchester the appeal of LEO XIII. It is a real disappointment to me to be so far from your Lordship on so important an occasion; but being in Rome I desired to at least make known to the Holy Father your noble intention, and to engage his sympathy for all the members of the meeting. He most gladly acceded to my wishes, and charges you to formally bestow in his name the Apostolic blessing upon all those who partake in this great work. He blesses them for their generous idea—those who belong to the Catholic Church, because they honour their religion by this act of faith and charity; those who do not, in order that He who is the Infinite Charity may, in return for their charity, pour upon them the most abundant graces of light and unity. I could prolong this letter by giving your Lordship interesting details of the constitution and character of the Anti-Slavery work, but I prefer to forward several printed documents. You will be able to select from them better than I could what is most appropriate to your meeting.

Your Lordship's obedient and devoted brother in our Lord.
(Signed) Ch. Cardinal LAVIGERIE, Archbishop of Carthage and Algiers.

Source: Anti-Slavery Reporter, 4:7 (November/December 1888).

Personal Accounts, Papers, Journals, and Poetry

From the sixteenth through the nineteenth century, slavery was such a pervasive institution in the transatlantic world that few who encountered it could help but notice the social and economic implications of the practice. For many, however, slavery was an alien practice that took place in far-flung settings. Those who were not regularly exposed to the flesh trade seldom voiced their disapproval of the buying and selling of human beings on which much of colonial economic prosperity was based. "Out of sight, out of mind" was a fitting mantra for many who knew only of the benefits of slavery and who failed, perhaps purposefully, to recognize its demons.

Yet for those who did not allow themselves to be shielded by the oceanic buffer of the Atlantic Ocean, which kept images separated from imagination, slavery, with its sensory and moral revulsion, scarred the conscience of all but the most callous individuals. Many who witnessed the horrors of slavery firsthand were moved to speak against the practice, because they believed it not only violated that which they held most sacred but it also diminished the intrinsic value of human life. For these men and women of conscience, to remain silent about the greatest moral calamity of their time was a restriction they could not endure. As Baron de Montesquieu observed, "If they [African slaves] are, indeed, human, then we [whites] are not Christian."

Individual critiques of the practice of slavery varied greatly and not all antislavery texts were written with abolitionist consumption as their primary focus. Diaries, journals, letters, and other forms of correspondence from colonial outposts often revealed more about the system of slavery than some authors intended. Such narratives were seldom produced in a vacuum—authors' observations often are replete with social commentary about the nature of enslavement and slaveholders' apparent indifference to the humanity of the enslaved victims of the practice.

Stark realism flowed from the pen of casual visitors and poets, who tried to express what slavery did to both the slave and the slave owner. There was a recognized, omnipresent burden that weighed heavily on both the enslaved and the enslaver, as the necessities of social control constrained the freedom of all. Slavery's chains were that powerful.

Before organized societies of abolitionists ever began to call for an end to the slave trade and argue the merits of emancipation, it was the singular voices of the observers of slavery that piqued interest in the condition of those who were enslaved and the societal costs of their extended confinement. Even when large-scale movements began to agitate for an end to the system of slavery, writers continued to recognize that the powerful voice of the independent observer could have more power than the collective clamor that organized campaigning might produce.

Antislavery authors appealed to common sense, to reason, and to justice; they sought to persuade others through their social critiques, which analyzed the place that slavery held in the transatlantic world. The effectiveness of these techniques was evidenced in the growing antislavery sentiment that emerged during the late eighteenth and early nineteenth centuries. Those so inspired adopted activist methods to combat the existence and expansion of an inhumane system of exploitation that was effectively designed to crush the human spirit.

Powerful words can move people to action. As the following documents suggest, the nature of slavery's manifold injustices was made apparent to many who had the economic means and the capacity to act effectively to bring an end to this vast social injustice.

A Description of Brazil's Sugar Industry (1654)

I will return to speak of the Riches of the Country, chiefly consisting in their Sugar, which when I have named, I have named all; not that it wants others, but that it can want no others, having that, since that country which abounds with that commodity which all others have need of, can never want any commodity which others abound withall. . . . Now for their Sugar thus it grows, and thus 'tis made; Their Sugar canes are prun'd to the heighth of standing corn: nor need they other culture, but every second year to cut them close by the roots, as we do Osiers, when against the next year they never fail to spring up agen, the flaggs of which Canes are of a pleasant green, and shew a far off just like in a Field of Corn, which being ripe about the month of June, they joint them in pieces some foot long, and carry them to the Mill, turn'd by Oxen, or Water, consisting of two round Cylinders, about the bignesse of Mil-posts, plated with Iron, which turning inwards, and joyning as close together as they can meet, so squeez the canes in passing through them, as they come out on th'other side all bruzed, and dry as keques, which were all liquid before; which Liquor is conveyed by Troughs to certain Caldrons, where 'tis boyl'd, still retaining its amber colour, till pour'd out at last into their forms or coolers, with a certain Lee 'tis rendered white; And in these Mills they work both day and night, the work of immediately applying the canes into the Mill being so perillous as if through drousinesse or heedlessnesse a fingers end be but engag'd betwixt the posts, their whole body inevitably follows, to prevent which, the next Negro has always a Hatchet readie to chop off his Arm, if any such Misfortune should arrive.

Source: Richard Flecknoe, "A Description of the Sugar Industry," in *A Documentary History of Brazil,* ed. E. Bradford Burns. New York: Alfred A. Knopf, 1966.

John Woolman's Journal (1757)

Feeling the exercise in relation to a visit to the Southern Provinces to increase upon me, I acquainted our Monthly Meeting therewith, and obtained their certificate. Expecting to go alone, one of my brothers who lived in Philadelphia, having some business in North Carolina, proposed going with me part of the way; but as he had a view of some outward affairs, to accept of him as a companion was some difficulty with me, whereupon I had conversation with him at sundry times. At length feeling easy in my mind, I had conversation with several elderly Friends of Philadelphia on the subject, and he obtaining a certificate suitable to the occasion, we set off in the Fifth Month, 1757. Coming to Nottingham week-day meeting, we lodged at John Churchman's, where I met with our friend, Benjamin Buffington, from New England, who was returning from a visit to the Southern Provinces. Thence we crossed the river Susquehanna, and lodged at William Cox's in Maryland.

Soon after I entered this province, a deep and painful exercise came upon me, which I often had some feeling of since my mind was drawn toward these parts, and with which I had acquainted my brother before we agreed to join as companions. As the people in this and the Southern Provinces live much on the labour of slaves, many of whom are used hardly, my concern was that I might attend with singleness of heart to the voice of the true Shepherd, and be so supported as to remain unmoved at the faces of men.

As it is common for Friends on such a visit to have entertainment free of cost, a difficulty arose in my mind with respect to saving my money by kindness received from what appeared to me to be the gain of oppression. Receiving a gift, considered as a gift, brings the receiver under obligations to the benefactor, and has a natural tendency to draw the obliged into a party with the giver. To prevent difficulties of this kind, and to preserve the minds of judges from any bias, was that divine prohibition: "Thou shalt not receive any gift; for a gift blindeth the wise, and perverteth the words of the righteous" (Exod. xxiii.8). As the disciples were sent forth without any provision for their journey, and our Lord said the workman is worthy of his meat, their labour in the gospel was considered as a reward for their entertainment, and therefore not received as a gift; yet, in regard to my present journey, I could not see my way clear in that respect. The difference appeared thus: the entertainment the disciples met with was from them whose hearts God had opened to receive them, from a love to them and the truth they published; but we, considered as members of the same religious society, look upon it as a piece of civility to receive each other in such visits; and such receptions, at times, is partly in regard to reputation, and not from an inward unity of heart and spirit. Conduct is more convincing than language, and where people, by their actions, manifest that the slave-trade is not so disagreeable to their principles but that it may be encouraged, there is not a sound uniting with some Friends who visit them.

The prospect of so weighty a work, and of being so distinguished from many whom I esteemed before myself, brought me very low, and such were the conflicts of my soul that I had a near sympathy with the prophet, in the time of his weakness, when he said: "If thou deal thus with me, kill me, I pray thee, if I have found favour in thy sight" (Num. xi.15). But I soon saw that this proceeded from the want of a full resignation to the divine will. Many were the afflictions which attended me, and in great abasement, with many tears, my cries were to the Almighty for His gracious and Fatherly assistance, and after a time of deep trial I was favoured to understand the state mentioned by the Psalmist more clearly than ever I had done before; to wit: "My soul is even as a weaned child" (Ps. cxxxi.2).

Being thus helped to sink down into resignation, I felt a deliverance from that tempest in which I had been sorely exercised, and in calmness of mind went forward, trusting that the Lord Jesus Christ, as I faithfully attended to Him, would be a counsellor to me in all difficulties, and that by His strength I should be enabled even to leave money with the members of society where I had entertainment, when I found that omitting it would obstruct that work to which I believed He had called me. As I copy this after my return, I may here add that oftentimes I did so under a sense of duty. The way in which I did it was thus: When I expected soon to leave a Friend's house where I had entertainment, if I believed that I should not keep clear from the gain of oppression without leaving money, I spoke to one of the heads of the family privately, and desired them to accept of those pieces of silver, and give them to such of their negroes as they believed would make the best use of them; and at other times I gave them to the negroes myself, as the way looked clearest to me. Before I came out, I had provided a large number of small pieces for this purpose, and thus offering them to some who appeared to be wealthy people was a trial both to me and them. But the fear of the Lord so covered me at times that my way was made easier than I expected; and few, if any, manifested any resentment at the offer, and most of them, after some conversation, accepted of them.

Ninth of Fifth Month.—A Friend at whose house we breakfasted setting us a little on our way, I had conversation with him, in the fear of the Lord, concerning his slaves, in which my heart was tender; I used much plainness of speech with him, and he appeared to take it kindly. We pursued our journey without appointing meetings, being pressed in my mind to be at the Yearly Meeting in Virginia. In my travelling on the road, I often felt a cry rise from the centre of my mind, thus: "O Lord, I am a stranger on the earth, hide not thy face from me."

On the 11th, we crossed the rivers Patowmack and Rapahannock, and lodged at Port Royal. On the way we had the company of a colonel of the militia, who appeared to be a thoughtful man. I took occasion to remark on the difference in general betwixt a people used to labour moderately for their living, training up their children in frugality and business, and

those who live on the labour of slaves; the former, in my view, being the most happy life. He concurred in the remark, and mentioned the trouble arising from the untoward, slothful disposition of the negroes, adding that one of our labourers would do as much in a day as two of their slaves. I replied that free men, whose minds were properly on their business, found a satisfaction in improving, cultivating, and providing for their families; but negroes, labouring to support others who claim them as their property, and expecting nothing but slavery during life, had not the like inducement to be industrious.

After some further conversation I said, that men having power too often misapplied it; that though we made slaves of the negroes, and the Turks made slaves of the Christians, I believed that liberty was the natural right of all men equally. This he did not deny, but said the lives of the negroes were so wretched in their own country that many of them lived better here than there. I replied, "There is great odds in regard to us on what principle we act"; and so the conversation on that subject ended. I may here add that another person, some time afterwards, mentioned the wretchedness of the negroes, occasioned by their intestine wars, as an argument in favour of our fetching them away for slaves. To which I replied, if compassion for the Africans, on account of their domestic troubles, was the real motive of our purchasing them, that spirit of tenderness being attended to, would incite us to use them kindly, that, as strangers brought out of affliction, their lives might be happy among us. And as they are human creatures, whose souls are as precious as ours, and who may receive the same help and comfort from the Holy Scriptures as we do, we could not omit suitable endeavours to instruct them therein; but that while we manifest by our conduct that our views in purchasing them are to advance ourselves, and while our buying captives taken in war animates those parties to push on the war and increase desolation amongst them, to say they live unhappily in Africa is far from being an argument in our favour.

I further said, the present circumstances of these provinces to me appear difficult; the slaves look like a burdensome stone to such as burden themselves with them; and that, if the white people retain a resolution to prefer their outward prospects of gain to all other considerations, and do not act conscientiously toward them as fellow-creatures, I believe that burden will grow heavier and heavier, until times change in a way disagreeable to us. The person appeared very serious, and owned that in considering their condition and the manner of their treatment in these provinces he had sometimes thought it might be just in the Almighty so to order it.

Having travelled through Maryland, we came amongst Friends at Cedar Creek in Virginia, on the 12th; and the next day rode, in company with several of them, a day's journey to Camp Creek. As I was riding along in the morning, my mind was deeply affected in a sense I had of the need of divine aid to support me in the various difficulties which attended me, and in uncommon distress of mind I cried in secret to the Most High, "O Lord, be merciful, I beseech Thee, to Thy poor afflicted creature!" After some time I felt inward relief, and soon after a Friend in company began to talk in support of the slave-trade, and said the negroes were understood to be the offspring of Cain, their blackness being the mark which God set upon him after he murdered Abel, his brother; that it was the design of Providence they should be slaves, as a condition proper to the race of so wicked a man as Cain was. Then another spake in support of what had been said.

To all which I replied in substance as follows: that Noah and his family were all who survived the flood, according to Scripture; and as Noah was of Seth's race, the family of Cain was wholly destroyed. One of them said that after the flood Ham went to the land of Nod and took a wife; that Nod was a land far distant, inhabited by Cain's race, and that the flood did not reach it; and as Ham was sentenced to be a servant of servants to his brethren, these two families, being thus joined, were undoubtedly fit only for slaves. I replied, the flood was a judgment upon the world for their abominations, and it was granted that Cain's stock was the most wicked, and therefore unreasonable to suppose that they were spared. As to Ham's going to the land of Nod for a wife, no time being fixed, Nod might be inhabited by some of Noah's family before Ham married a second time; moreover the text saith "That all flesh died that moved upon the earth" (Gen. vii.21). I further reminded them how the prophets repeatedly declare "that the son shall not suffer for the iniquity of the father, but every one be answerable for his own sins."

I was troubled to perceive the darkness of their imaginations, and in some pressure of spirit said, "The love of ease and gain are the motives in general of keeping slaves, and men are wont to take hold of weak arguments to support a cause which is unreasonable. I have no interest on either side, save only the interest which I desire to have in the truth. I believe liberty is

their right, and as I see they are not only deprived of it, but treated in other respects with inhumanity in many places, I believe He who is a refuge for the oppressed will, in His own time, plead their cause, and happy will it be for such as walk in uprightness before Him." And thus our conversation ended.

Source: John Woolman, *The Journal and Other Writings of John Woolman.* London: J.M. Dent & Sons, 1910.

John Newton's Thoughts Upon the African Slave Trade *(1788)*

With our ships, the great object is, to be full. When the ship is there, it is thought desirable she should take as many as possible. The cargo of a vessel of a hundred tons, or little more, is calculated to purchase from two hundred and twenty to two hundred and fifty slaves. Their lodging-rooms below the deck, which are three (for the men, the boys, and the women), besides a place for the sick, are sometimes more than five feet high, and sometimes less; and this height is divided towards the middle, for the slaves lie in two rows, one above the other, on each side of the ship, close to each other, like books upon a shelf. I have known them so close that the shelf would not, easily, contain one more. And I have known a white man sent down, among the men, to lay them in these rows to the greatest advantage, so that as little space as possible might be lost.

Let it be observed, that the poor creatures, thus cramped for want of room, are likewise in irons, for the most part both hands and feet, and two together, which makes it difficult for them to turn or move, to attempt either to rise or to lie down, without hurting themselves, or each other. Nor is the motion of the ship, especially her heeling, or stoop on one side, when under sail, to be omitted; for this, as they lie athwart, or cross the ship, adds to the uncomfortableness of their lodging, especially to those who lie on the leeward or leaning side of the vessel. Dire is the tossing, deep the groans.—

The heat and smell of these rooms, when the weather will not admit of the slaves being brought upon deck, and of having their rooms cleaned every day, would be almost insupportable to a person not accustomed to them. If the slaves and their rooms can be constantly aired, and they are not detained too long on board, perhaps there are not many who die; but the contrary is often their lot. They are kept down, by the weather, to breathe a hot and corrupted air, sometimes for a week: this added to the galling of their irons, and the despondency which seizes their spirits when thus confined, soon becomes fatal. And every morning, perhaps, more instances than one are found, of the living and the dead, like the captives of Mezentius, fastened together.

Epidemical fevers and fluxes, which fill the ship with noisome and noxious effluvia, often break out, and infect the seamen likewise, and thus the oppressors, and the oppressed, fall by the same stroke. I believe, nearly one-half of the slaves on board, have, sometimes, died; and that the loss of a third part, in these circumstances, is not unusual. The ship, in which I was mate, left the coast with two hundred and eighteen slaves on board; and though we were not much affected by epidemical disorders, I find by my journal of that voyage (now before me), that we buried sixty-two on our passage to South Carolina, exclusive of those which died before we left the coast, of which I have no account.

I believe, upon an average between the more healthy, and the more sickly voyages, and including all contingencies, one fourth of the whole purchase may be allotted to the article of mortality: that is, if the English ships purchase *sixty thousand* slaves annually, upon the whole extent of the coast, the annual loss of lives cannot be much less than *fifteen thousand.*

Source: John Newton, *Thoughts Upon the African Slave Trade.* London: J. Buckland, 1788.

George Washington Frees His Slaves (1799)

The Last Will and Testament of George Washington {Excerpt}.

July 9, 1799.

In the name of God, amen!

I, George Washington of Mount Vernon, a citizen of the United States and lately President of the same, do make, ordain and declare this instrument, which is written with my own hand and every page thereof subscribed with my name, to be my last Will and Testament, revoking all others.

Imprimus. All my debts, of which there are but few, and none of magnitude, are to be punctually and speedily paid, and the legacies hereinafter bequeathed are to be discharged as soon as circumstances will permit, and in the manner directed.

Item. To my dearly beloved wife, Martha Washington, I give and bequeath the use, profit and benefit of my whole estate, real and personal, for the term of her natural life, except such parts thereof as are specially disposed of hereafter—my improved lot in the town of Alexandria, situated on Pitt and Cameron Streets, I give to her and her heirs forever, as I also do my household and kitchen furniture of every sort and kind with the liquors and groceries which may be on hand at the time of my decease, to be used and disposed of as she may think proper.

Item. Upon the decease of my wife, it is my will and desire, that all the slaves which I hold in my own right shall receive their freedom. To emancipate them during her life, would, tho' earnestly wished by me, be attended with such insuperable difficulties, on account of their intermixture by marriages with the dower negroes as to excite the most painful sensations—if not disagreeable consequences from the latter while both descriptions are in the occupancy of the same proprietor, it not being in my power under the tenure by which the dower Negroes are held to manumit them. And whereas among those who will receive freedom according to this devise there may be some who from old age, or bodily infirmities and others who on account of their infancy, that will be unable to support themselves, it is my will and desire that all who come under the first and second description shall be comfortably clothed and fed by my heirs while they live and that such of the latter description as have no parents living, or if living are unable, or unwilling to provide for them, shall be bound by the Court until they shall arrive at the age of twenty-five years, and in cases where no record can be produced whereby their ages can be ascertained, the judgment of the Court upon its own view of the subject shall be adequate and final. The negroes thus bound are (by their masters and mistresses) to be taught to read and write and to be brought up to some useful occupation, agreeably to the laws of the Commonwealth of Virginia, providing for the support of orphans and other poor children—and I do hereby expressly forbid the sale or transportation out of the said Commonwealth of any slave I may die possessed of, under any pretense, whatsoever—and I do moreover most positively, and most solemnly enjoin it upon my executors hereafter named, or the survivors of them to see that this clause respecting slaves and every part thereof be religiously fulfilled at the epoch at which it is directed to take place without evasion, neglect or delay after the crops which may then be on the ground are harvested, particularly as it respects the aged and infirm, seeing that a regular and permanent fund be established for their support so long as there are subjects requiring it, not trusting to the uncertain provisions to be made by individuals. And to my mulatto man, William (calling himself William Lee) I give immediate freedom or if he should prefer it (on account of the accidents which have befallen him and which have rendered him incapable of walking or of any active employment) to remain in the situation he now is, it shall be optional in him to do so. In either case, however, I allow him an annuity of thirty dollars during his natural life which shall be independent of the victuals and clothes he has been accustomed to receive; if he chooses the last alternative, but in full with his freedom, if he prefers the first, and this I give him as a testimony of my sense of his attachment to me and for his faithful services during the Revolutionary War.

Source: W.W. Abbot, ed., *The Papers of George Washington, Retirement Series*, vol. 4 (April–December 1799). Charlottesville: University Press of Virginia, 1999.

A British Antislavery Poem (1809)

Africa Delivered; or, the Slave Trade Abolished
By James Grahame

PART IV.
And they shall build houses and inhabit them; and they shall plant vineyards and eat the fruit of them. They shall not build and another inhabit; they shall not plant and another eat. (Isa. lxv.21, 22)

Hail! Africa, restored to human rights!
Blest be the hand benign of him who stretched
The royal sceptre forth, and, with the touch
Electric of Britannia's will, consumed
The tyrant's chain, yet left the slave unscathed!
And blest, Columbia, be thy distant shores!
For they peal with joy and freedom fraught
Re-echoed, till it reached the coast of blood,
And with redoubled thunder stunned the ear
Of Murder as he aimed the fatal blow.

Hail! Africa, to human rights restored!
Glad tidings of great joy to all who feel
For human kind! to him who sits at ease
And looks upon his children sport around
In health and happiness, even him ye bring
Delight ne'er felt before: the dying saint,
Whose hymning voice of joy is fainter heard
And fainter still, like the ascending lark,
As nearer heaven he draws, hears the glad words,
And bursts into a louder strain of praise:
The aged cottager, on sabbath eve,
Amid his children and their children ope[n]s

That portion of the sacred book, which tells,
How with a mighty and an outstretched arm
The Lord delivered Israel from his bonds;
Then kneeling blesses God that now the curse
Of guiltless blood lies on this land no more.
Even they who ne'er behold the light of heaven
But through the grated ir'on, forget awhile
Their mournful fate; and mark a gleam of joy
Pass o'er each fellow captive's clouded brow.

Nor was the sympathy of joy confined
Within this narrow sphere; the tidings flew
To heaven on angel wings; loud then the peal
Of choiring seraphim arose; and bright
A radiance from the throne of God diffused,
Its lustre shed upon th' assembled throng.
But still imperfect is the work of love.
Ye generous band, united in the cause
Of liberty to Africa restored,
O may your hands be strong, and hearts be firm
In that great cause! so may you reap the meed
Most grateful to your hearts, the glorious view
Of peace reviving, ignorance dispelled,
The arts improved, and, O most blessed thought!
That faith which trampled Slavery under foot,
And led captivity in captive chains,
Embraced by men in superstition sunk.
Already I behold the wicker dome,
To Jesus consecrated, humbly rise
Below the sycamore's wide spreading boughs:
Around the shapeless pillars twists the vine;
Flowers of all hues climb up the walls, and fill
The house of God with odours passing far
Sabean incense, while combined with notes
Most sweet, most artless, Zion's songs ascend,
And die in cadence soft; the preacher's voice
Succeeds; their native tongue the converts hear
In deep attention fixed, all but that child
Who eyes the hanging cluster, yet withholds,
In reverence profound, his little hand.

The faith of Jesus far and wide expands,
Till warfare, humanised, assumes the garb
Of mercy; captives now no more are slaves;
No more the negro dreads the white man's eye;
No more, from hatred to the teacher, spurns
Instruction: gladly he receives the boon
Of science and of art. What ecstasy
O'erpowers his faculties when first he sees
The wonders of the telescopic power;
The woody mountain side is brought so near,
He reaches forth to pull the loaded spray;—

But when, directed to the distant main,
The veering tube converts a little speck
Into a ship full sail, dashing the brine,
He recollecting shudders at the sight,
Till turning round he sees his teacher smile,
And reassured stoops to the magic glass.

Now will the triumph of thy plan benign
Be proved, O Lancaster: old age and youth,
The father and the child, will docile sit
And learn their common task, the glorious power
Of seeing thought, of seeing thought conceived
In distant ages and in distant climes;—
Of speaking through the storm athwart the deep.

Where scattered hovels lay, fair towns arise
With turrets, spires, and chiming bells that call
The crowding throngs to fill the house of prayer.
While erst the native plied the light canoe,
He steers the loaded ship, no longer deep
With human freight. Nor useful arts alone
Are cherished; music from afar is borne,
Wafte[d] by northern gales; and on the banks
Of Gambia's tide the Scottish seaman starts
To hear Lochaber's strain or Flodden field,
Then mounts the mast to hide the bursting tear.

The rugged accents, gradually refined,
Come forth a language, musical and full,
Sonorous, gentle, forceful, rapid, bold,
As suits the changes of the poet's lay,—
Nor yet unpliant to a foreign strain:—
Yes, Campbell, thy imperishable strains
Shall live in languages but now half formed,
And tell the slave-descended race the tale
Of Africa restored to human rights.

The intellectual powers emancipate,
Display an elasticity unknown
To men who pace the round of polished life:
Discovery, eagle-winged, to heaven ascends,
And sees, beyond the ocean that now bounds
The human ken, a world of nature's works
Unknown and unimagined yet by man.

And now, ye guardians of the sacred law
Which hails the sons of Africa as men,
Watch lest that law promulged by loud acclaim
All but unanimous of Britain's sons,
Be thwarted in its mild benignant course.
Or, if direct attempts should not be made,
May not connivance, with her half-shut eyes,
Permit the culprits to elude the law!

May not the secret hint be understood,
"Mark not the slave-ship; let her shape her course
Unhailed, unsearched": and may not some who hunt
Preferment through corruption's noisome sewers,
Obey the covert mandate? No, not one:
No British seaman owns a heart so base.
No, *Hearts of Oak*, by other ways pursue
Preferment's meed; the Sycophant's mean prayer
Ne'er soils their lips; they seek their high reward
In voice of thunder from their wooden walls.
But truce with censure's theme.

O that my voice,
To notes of praise unpractised and untuned,
I could but modulate to lofty strains
Of eulogy! then would I bear record
Of them who foremost stood in freedom's cause;
Of Benezet's enlightened early zeal;
The bold contempt with which the unfettered soul
Of Sharpe arraigned the pestilent response
Of law's high-priesthood, sanctioning an age
Of crimes, and paralyzing mercy's hand,
His dauntless arm that wielded nature's law,
And snatched the victim from the tyrant's gripe;
A Clarkson's every thought, and word, and deed,
Devoted in humanity's behalf,
His watchings, perils, toils by night and day,
His life one ceaseless act of doing good;
The eloquence pathetic and sublime,
And spirit undismayed, of Wilberforce,
Errect when foiled; the virtuous use of power
By Grenville on the side of Justice ranged;
The fervent beam of Gloucester's royal smile;
The hallowed wish of Fox's dying hour,—
Bequest most sacred to the freeman's heart,
Bequest, though faltered with his latest breath,
More powerful than the full careering storm
Of eloquence that thundered from his tongue.

Source: James Grahame, "Africa Delivered; or, the Slave Trade Abolished," in *Poems on the Abolition of the Slave Trade; Written by James Montgomery, James Grahame, and E. Benger.* London: T. Bensley, 1809.

Frederick Douglass Describes Slave Resistance (1834)

If at any one time of my life, more than another, I was made to drink the bitterest dregs of slavery, that time was during the first six months of my stay with this man Covey. We worked all weathers. It was never too hot, or too cold; it could never rain, blow, snow, or hail too hard for us to work in the field. Work, work, work, was scarcely more than the order of the day than of the night. The longest days were too short for him, and the shortest nights were too long for him. I was somewhat unmanageable at the first, but a few months of this discipline tamed me. Mr. Covey succeeded in *breaking* me—in body, soul, and spirit. My natural elasticity was crushed; my intellect languished; the disposition to read departed, the cheerful spark that lingered about my eye died out; the dark night of slavery closed in upon me, and behold a man transformed to a brute!

Sunday was my only leisure time. I spent this under some large tree, in a sort of beast-like stupor between sleeping and waking. At times I would rise up and a flash of energetic freedom would dart through my soul, accompanied with a faint beam of hope that flickered for a moment, and then vanished. I sank down again mourning over my wretched condition. I was sometimes tempted to take my life and that of Covey, but was prevented by a combination of hope and fear. My sufferings, as I remember them now, seem like a dream rather than like a stern reality.

Our house stood within a few rods of the Chesapeake bay, whose broad bosom was ever white with sails from every quarter of the habitable globe. Those beautiful vessels, robed in white, and so delightful to the eyes of free men, were to me so many shrouded ghosts, to terrify and torment me with thoughts of my wretched condition. I have often, in the deep stillness of a summer's Sabbath, stood all alone upon the banks of that noble bay, and traced, with saddened heart and tearful eye, the countless number of sails moving off to the mighty ocean. The sight of these always affected me powerfully. My thoughts would compel utterance; and there, with no audience but the Almighty, I would pour out my soul's complaint in my rude way with an apostrophe to the moving multitude of ships. . . .

I shall never be able to narrate half the mental experience through which it was my lot to pass, during my stay at Covey's. I was completely wrecked, changed, and bewildered; goaded almost to madness at one time, and at another reconciling myself to my wretched condition. All the kindness I had received at Baltimore, all my former hopes and aspirations for usefulness in the world, and even the happy moments spent in the exercises of religion, contrasted with my then present lot, served but to increase my anguish.

I suffered bodily as well as mentally. I had neither sufficient time in which to eat, or to sleep, except on Sundays. The overwork, and the brutal chastisements of which I was the victim, combined with that ever-gnawing and soul devouring thought—*"I am a slave—and a slave for life—a slave with no rational ground to hope for freedom"*—rendered me a living embodiment of mental and physical wretchedness.

Source: Frederick Douglass, "Frederick Douglass and the Slave-Breaker, 1834," in *A Documentary History of the Negro People in the United States,* vol. 1, *From Colonial Times Through the Civil War,* ed. Herbert Aptheker. New York: Citadel, 1951.

Solomon Northup Describes a Slave Auction (1841)

In the first place we were required to wash thoroughly, and those with beards to shave. We were then furnished with a new suit each, cheap, but clean. The men had hat, coat, shirt, pants and shoes; the women frocks of calico, and handkerchief to bind about their heads. We were now conducted into a large room in the front part of the building to which the yard was attached, in order to be properly trained, before the admission of customers. The men were arranged on one side of the room, the women at the other. The tallest was placed at the head of the row, then the next tallest, and so on in the order of their respective heights. Emily was at the foot of the line of women. Freeman {Theophilus Freeman, owner of the slave pen] charged us to remember our places; exhorted us to appear smart and lively,—sometimes threatening, and again, holding out various inducements. During the day he exercised us in the art of "looking smart," and of moving to our places with exact precision.

After being fed, in the afternoon, we were again paraded and made to dance. Bob, a colored boy, who had some time belonged to Freeman, played on the violin. Standing near him, I made bold to inquire if he could play the "Virginia Reel." He answered he could not, and asked me if I could play. Replying in the affirmative, he handed me the violin. I struck up a tune, and finished it. Freeman ordered me to continue playing, and seemed well pleased, telling Bob that I far excelled him—a remark that seemed to grieve my musical companion very much.

Next day many customers called to examine Freeman's "new lot." The latter gentleman was very loquacious, dwelling at much length upon our several good points and qualities. He would make us hold up our heads, walk briskly back and forth, while customers would feel of our hands and arms and bodies, turn us about, ask us what we could do, make us open our mouths and show our teeth, precisely as a jockey examines a horse which he is about to barter for or purchase. Sometimes a man or woman was taken back to the small house in the yard, stripped, and inspected more minutely. Scars upon a slave's back were considered evidence of a rebellious or unruly spirit, and hurt his sale.

An old gentleman, who said he wanted a coachman, appeared to take a fancy to me. From his conversation with Burch [Freeman's business associate], I learned he was a resident in the city. I very much desired that he would buy me, because I conceived it would not be difficult to make my escape from New Orleans on some northern vessel. Freeman asked him fifteen hundred dollars for me. The old gentleman insisted it was too much as times were very hard. Freeman, however, declared that I was sound of health, of a good constitution, and intelligent. He made it a point to enlarge upon my musical attainments. The old gentleman argued quite adroitly that there was nothing extraordinary about the Negro, and finally, to my regret, went out, saying he would call again.

During the day, however, a number of sales were made. David and Caroline were purchased together by a Natchez planter. They left us, grinning broadly, and in a most happy state of mind, caused by the fact of their not being separated. Sethe was sold to a planter of Baton Rouge, her eyes flashing with anger as she was led away.

The same man also purchased Randall. The little fellow was made to jump, and run across the floor, and perform many other feats, exhibiting his activity and condition. All the time the trade was going on, Eliza was crying aloud, and wringing her hands. She besought the man not to buy him, unless he also bought herself and Emily. She promised, in that case, to be the most faithful slave that ever lived. The man answered that he could not afford it, and then Eliza burst into a paroxysm of grief, weeping plaintively. Freeman turned round to her, savagely, with his whip in his uplifted hand, ordering her to stop her noise, or he would flog her. He would not have such work—such snivelling; and unless she ceased that minute, he would take her to the yard and give her a hundred lashes. Yes, he would take the nonsense out of her pretty quick—if he didn't, might he be d—d.

Eliza shrunk before him, and tried to wipe away her tears, but it was all in vain. She wanted to be with her children, she said, the little time she had to live. All the frowns and threats of Freeman, could not wholly silence the afflicted mother. She kept on begging and beseeching them, most piteously, not to separate the three. Over and over again she told them how she loved her boy. A great many times she repeated her former promises—how very faithful and obedient she would be; how hard she would labor day and night, to the last moment of her life, if he would only buy them all together. But it was of no avail; the man could not afford it. The bargain was agreed upon, and Randall must go alone. Then Eliza ran to him; embraced him passionately; kissed him again and again; told him to remember her—all the while her tears falling in the boy's face like rain.

Freeman damned her, calling her a blubbering, bawling wench, and ordered her to go to her place, and behave herself, and be somebody. He swore he wouldn't stand such stuff but a little longer. He would soon give her something to cry about, if she was not mighty careful, and that she might depend upon.

The planter from Baton Rouge, with his new purchase, was ready to depart.

"Don't cry, mama. I will be a good boy. Don't cry," said Randall, looking back, as they passed out of the door.

What has become of the lad, God knows. It was a mournful scene indeed. I would have cried myself if I had dared.

Source: Solomon Northup, *Twelve Years a Slave*, ed. Sue Eakin and Joseph Logsdon. Baton Rouge: Louisiana State University Press, 1975.

John Greenleaf Whittier to Joseph Sturge on the Fugitive Slave Law (1851)

Amesbury, January 7, 1851.

Since I last wrote, we have been greatly distressed by the operation of the wicked Fugitive Slave Law upon our poor coloured fellow-citizens. I have never felt so keenly the shame, and sin, and cruelty of slavery, as for the last few months; and in labouring to awaken the popular feeling against this terrible enactment, I have found it exceedingly difficult to speak and act with the moderation and prudence which should characterise the efforts of a Christian reformer. In my weak state of health the excitement has been very trying to me. I felt bound, in the interim, on the occasion of declining the nomination of Senator in the State by the democratic party, to declare that *I could not obey the law, that I should treat it as null and void, and open my door to the hunted fugitive in spite of its cruel provisions.* It cannot be obeyed by any man who professes to be a Christian or a friend of his kind; and it is a sad thing to have morality and justice on one side, and law on the other. But so it is; and while I deprecate with my whole heart any virulent resistance, I see no way left for us than to disobey the unrighteous act, and bear the penalty of fine and prison.

A case has just occurred in Philadelphia which shows, in a true light, the character of this law. A coloured man was seized by constables, under a false pretence, dragged before the slave commissioner, and although he produced two witnesses to prove him a free man, he was pronounced a slave, on the oath of a wretch who was then awaiting his trial for kidnapping, and hurried off to Maryland. Happily an officer of respectability accompanied the kidnappers and their victim to his pretended owner, who, on seeing him, had [the] honesty to declare *that the man was not his slave!*

Since writing the above, a poor young coloured man has been sent back into slavery from New York. Our noble friend, Lewis Tappan, made strenuous, but unavailing, efforts to save him; thou wilt doubtless get from him a full account of the case.

Our State legislature is now in session, and it is pretty certain that Charles Sumner—the true friend of peace and freedom, and every good word and work—will be chosen U.S. Senator, for six years from the 1st of 3d month next. He will, if elected, take the place which Daniel Webster has dishonoured.

Thou wilt be sorry to hear that the *Non-Slaveholder* has ceased to exist. Our dear friends, Samuel Richards and A.L. Pannock, sustained it a very long time, almost unaided. Nevertheless, the concern to avoid, as far as practicable, the use of slave products, is increasing, especially in our Society.

Source: Anti-Slavery Reporter (New Series), 6:62 (February 1, 1851).

An American Abolitionist Poem (1851)

The Fugitive Slave Law of America
By John Greenleaf Whittier

> The evil days have come: the poor
> Are made a prey;
> Bar up the hospitable door,
> Put out the fire-lights, point no more
> The wanderer's way.
>
> For pity now is crime: the claim
> Which binds our States
> Is melted at the hearth in twain,
> Is rusted by her tears' soft rain:
> Close up her gates.

> Our Union, like a glacier stirred
> By voice below,
> Or bell of kine, or wing of bird,
> A beggar's crust, or kindly word,
> May overthrow.
>
> Poor whispering tremblers!—yet we boast
> Our blood and name:
> Bursting its century-bolted frost,
> Each gray cairn of the Northman's coast
> Cries out for shame!
>
> Oh, for the open firmament,
> The prairie free,
> The desert hill-side, cavern-rent,
> The Pawnee's lodge, the Arab's tent,
> The Bushman's tree!
>
> Than web of Persian loom most rare,
> Or soft divan,
> Better the rough rock, bleak and bare,
> Or hollow tree, which man may share
> suffering man.
>
> I hear a voice: "Thus saith the law,
> Let Love be dumb:
> Clasping her liberal hands, in awe,
> Let sweet-lipped Charity withdraw
> From hearth and home."
>
> I hear another voice: "The poor
> Are thine to feed;
> Turn not the outcast from thy door,
> Nor give to bonds and wrong once more
> Whom God hath freed."
>
> Dear Lord! Between that law and Thee,
> No choice remains;
> Yet not untrue to man's decree,
> Though spurning its rewards, is he
> Who bears its pains.
>
> Not mine sedition's trumpet-blast
> And threatening word;
> I read the lesson of the past,
> That firm endurance wins at last
> More than the sword.
>
> Oh, clear-eyed Faith, and Patience, thou
> So calm and strong,
> Angels of God! Be near to show
> His glorious future shining through
> Our night of wrong!

Source: Anti-Slavery Reporter (New Series), 6:63 (March 1, 1851).

Henry Brown Escapes in a Box (1851)

I now began to get weary of my bonds; and earnestly panted after liberty. I felt convinced that I should be acting in accordance with the will of God, if I could snap in sunder those bonds by which I was held body and soul as the property of a fellow man. I looked forward to the good time which every day I more and more firmly believed would yet come, when I should walk the face of the earth in full possession of all that freedom which the finger of God had so clearly written on the constitutions of man, and which was common to the human race; but of which, by the cruel hand of tyranny, I, and millions of my fellow-men, had been robbed.

I was well acquainted with a storekeeper in the city of Richmond, from whom I used to purchase my provisions; and having formed a favourable opinion of his integrity, one day in the course of a little conversation with him, I said to him if I were free I would be able to do business such as he was doing; he then told me that my occupation was a money-making one, and if I were free I had no need to change for another. I then told him my circumstances in regard to my master, having to pay him 25 dollars per month, and yet that he refused to assist me in saving my wife from being sold and taken away to the South, where I should never see her again; and even refused to allow me to go and see her until my hours of labour were over. I told him this took place about five months ago, and I had been meditating my escape from slavery since, and asked him, as no person was near us, if he could give me any information about how I should proceed. I told him I had a little money and if he would assist me I would pay him for so doing. The man asked me if I was not afraid to speak that way to him; I said no, for I imagined he believed that every man had a right to liberty. He said I was quite right, and asked me how much money I would give him if he would assist me to get away. I told him that I had 166 dollars and that I would give him the half; so we ultimately agreed that I should have his service in the attempt for 86. Now I only wanted to fix upon a plan. He told me of several plans by which others had managed to effect their escape, but none of them exactly suited my taste. I then left him to think over what would be best to be done, and, in the mean time, went to consult my friend Dr. Smith, on the subject. I mentioned the plans which the storekeeper had suggested, and as he did not

approve either of them very much, I still looked for some plan which would be more certain and more safe, but I was determined that come what may, I should have my freedom or die in the attempt.

One day, while I was at work, and my thoughts were eagerly feasting upon the idea of freedom, I felt my soul called out to heaven to breathe a prayer to Almighty God. I prayed fervently that he who seeth in secret and knew the inmost desires of my heart, would lend me his aid in bursting my fetters asunder, and in restoring me to the possession of those rights, of which men had robbed me; when the idea suddenly flashed across my mind of shutting myself *up in a box,* and getting myself conveyed as dry goods to a free state.

Being now satisfied that this was the plan for me, I went to my friend Dr. Smith and, having aquainted him with it, we agreed to have it put at once into execution not however without calculating the chances of danger with which it was attended; but buoyed up by the prospect of freedom and increased hatred to slavery I was willing to dare even death itself rather than endure any longer the clanking of those galling chains. It being still necessary to have the assistance of the storekeeper, to see that the box was kept in its right position on its passage, I then went to let him know my intention, but he said although he was willing to serve me in any way he could, he did not think I could live in a box for so long a time as would be necessary to convey me to Philadelphia, but as I had already made up my mind, he consented to acompany me and keep the box right all the way.

My next object was to procure a box, and with the assistance of a carpenter that was very soon accomplished, and taken to the place where the packing was to be performed. In the mean time the storekeeper had written to a friend in Philadelphia, but as no answer had arrived, we resolved to carry out our purpose as best we could. It was deemed necessary that I should get permission to be absent from my work for a few days, in order to keep down suspicion until I had once fairly started on the road to liberty; and as I had then a gathered finger I thought that would form a very good excuse for obtaining leave of absence; but when I showed it to one overseer, Mr. Allen, he told me it was not so bad as to prevent me from working, so with a view of making it bad enough, I got Dr. Smith to procure for me some oil of vitriol in order to drop a little of this on it, but in my hurry I dropped rather much and made it worse than there was any occasion for, in fact it was very soon eaten in to the bone, and on presenting it again to

Mr. Allen I obtained the permission required, with the advice that I should go home and get a poultice of flax-meal to it, and keep it well poulticed until it got better. I took him instantly at his word and went off directly to the storekeeper who had by this time received an answer from his friend in Philadelphia, and had obtained permission to address the box to him, this friend in that city, arranging to call for it as soon as it should arrive.

There being no time to be lost, the store-keeper, Dr. Smith, and myself, agreed to meet next morning at four o'clock, in order to get the box ready for the express train. The box which I had procured was three feet one inch wide, two feet six inches high, and two feet wide: and on the morning of the 29th day of March, 1849, I went into the box—having previously bored three gimlet holes opposite my face, for air, and provided myself with a bladder of water, both for the purpose of quenching my thirst and for wetting my face, should I feel getting faint. I took the gimlet also with me, in order that I might bore more holes if I found I had not sufficient air. Being thus equipped for the battle of liberty, my friends nailed down the lid and had me conveyed to the Express Office, which was about a mile distant from the place where I was packed. I had no sooner arrived at the office than I was turned heels up, while some person nailed something on the end of the box. I was then put upon a waggon and driven off to the depot with my head down, and I had no sooner arrived at the depot, than the man who drove the waggon tumbled me roughly into the baggage car, where, however, I happened to fall on my right side.

The next place we arrived at was Potomac Creek, where the baggage had to be removed from the cars, to be put on board the steamer; where I was again placed with my head down, and in this dreadful position had to remain nearly an hour and a half, which, from the sufferings I had thus to endure, seemed like an age to me, but I was forgetting the battle of liberty, and I was resolved to conquer or die. I felt my eyes swelling as if they would burst from their sockets; and the veins on my temples were dreadfully distended with pressure of blood upon my head. In this position I attempted to lift my hand to my face but I had no power to move it; I felt a cold sweat coming over me which seemed to be a warning that death was about to terminate my earthly miseries, but as I feared even that, less than slavery, I resolved to submit to the will of God, and,

under the influence of that impression, I lifted up my soul in prayer to God, who alone, was able to deliver me. My cry was soon heard, for I could hear a man saying to another, that he had travelled a long way and had been standing there two hours, and he would like to get somewhat to sit down; so perceiving my box, standing on end, he threw it down and then two sat upon it. I was thus relieved from a state of agony which may be more easily imagined than described. I could now listen to the men talking, and heard one of them asking the other what he supposed *the box contained*; his companion replied he guessed it was "THE MAIL." I too thought it was a mail but not such a mail as he supposed it to be.

The next place at which we arrived was the city of Washington, where I was taken from the steamboat, and again placed upon a waggon and carried to the depot right side up with care; but when the driver arrived at the depot I heard him call for some person to help to take the box off the waggon, and some one answered him to the effect that he might throw it off; but, says the driver, it is marked "this side up with care;" so if I throw it off I might break something, the other answered him that it did not matter if he broke all that was in it, the railway company were able enough to pay for it. No sooner were these words spoken than I began to tumble from the waggon, and falling on the end where my head was, I could hear my neck give a crack, as if it had been snapped asunder and I was knocked completely insensible. The first thing I heard, after that, was some person saying, "there is no room for the box, it will have to remain and be sent through to-morrow with the luggage train;" but the Lord had not quite forsaken me, for in answer to my earnest prayer He so ordered affairs that I should not be left behind; and I now heard a man say that the box had come with the express, and it must be sent on. I was then tumbled into the car with my head downwards again, but the car had not proceeded far before, more luggage having to be taken in, my box got shifted about and so happened to turn upon its right side; and in this position I remained till I got to Philadelphia, of our arrival in which place I was informed by hearing some person say, "We are in port and at Philadelphia." My heart then leaped for joy, and I wondered if any person knew that such a box was there.

Here it may be proper to observe that the man who had promised to accompany my box failed to do what he promised; but, to prevent it remaining long at the station after its arrival, he sent a telegraphic message to his friend, and I was only twenty seven hours in the box, though travelling a distance of three hundred and fifty miles.

I was now placed in the depot amongst the other luggage, where I lay till seven o'clock, P.M., at which time a waggon drove up, and I heard a person inquire for such a box as that in which I was. I was then placed on a waggon and conveyed to the house where my friend in Richmond had arranged I should be received. A number of persons soon collected round the box after it was taken in to the house, but as I did not know what was going on I kept myself quiet. I heard a man say "let us rap upon the box and see if he is alive;" and immediately a rap ensued and a voice said, tremblingly, "Is all right within?" to which I replied—"all right." The joy of the friends was very great; when they heard that I was alive they soon managed to break open the box, and then came my resurrection from the grave of slavery.

I rose a free-man, but I was too weak, by reason of long confinement in that box, to be able to stand, so I immediately swooned away. After my recovery from the swoon the first thing, which arrested my attention, was the presence of a number of friends, every one seeming more anxious than another, to have an opportunity of rendering me their assistance, and of bidding me a hearty welcome to the possession of my natural rights. I had risen as it were from the dead; I felt much more than I could readily express; but as the kindness of Almighty God had been so conspicuously shown in my deliverance, I burst forth into the following him of thanksgiving.

> I waited patiently, I waited patiently for the Lord,
>   for the Lord;
> And he inclined unto me, and heard my calling:
> I waited patiently, I waited patiently for the Lord,
> And he inclined unto me, and heard my calling:
> And he hath put a new song in my mouth,
> Even a thanksgiving, even a thanksgiving, even a
>   thanksgiving unto our God.
> Blessed, Blessed, Blessed, Blessed is the man,
> Blessed is the man,
> Blessed is the man that hath set his hope, his hope
>   in the Lord;
> O Lord my God, Great, Great, Great.

Source: Henry Brown, "Henry Brown Escapes in a Box," in *A Documentary History of Slavery in North America*, ed. Willie Lee Rose. New York: Oxford University Press, 1976.

A Letter on Contrabands (1862)

Estanaula, Tennesee, August 17.

MESSRS. EDITORS:

The contraband question has engrossed, and is still likely to engross, a large share of public attention. The recent act of Congress authorizing the employment of blacks as teamsters, cooks and officer's servants, gives immense satisfaction to the army. It is a noteworthy fact, that a very large number of officers who came into the service decidedly opposed to "meddling" with the negro question, or with negroes in any manner, are now among the most determined of slavery-destroyers. Some such Captains in my regiment make it most uncomfortable for the negro hunters who come into our camps. And this feeling is constantly growing among us.

In going about in the country and conversing with the people, I find a general expectation among all classes that slavery is soon to be destroyed. Some of the slaveholders tell me that they are willing to give up their "chattels," with or without compensation, if peace can be restored again; while others exhibit great indignation at the "shadows of coming events."

One week ago last Sabbath, I was out about eight miles from Jackson, to spend the day with those of our companions who were there on picket duty. We were encamped on the grounds of an aged slaveholder, the owner of eighty men, women and children. I preached in the forenoon to our men, and a few negroes were present, who came and requested me to preach to them in the afternoon. I told them I would, if they would get their master's consent to have preaching in the dooryard. But this he refused. I then appointed a meeting in our camp for them, and half an hour before the time they had collected in large numbers from all the neighboring plantations. I then asked all who could read to hold up their right hands. Only three could read a little.

Then I asked all who thought they loved the Savior to raise their right hands. Some ten or fifteen responded. I then attempted to preach to the simple-minded and confiding creatures. I told them of Christ and his great love for all men in that he died for sinners such as we all are. I also told them that Christians up in the North have been praying for them for many years, that they might be Christians and also free men, and that now their Jubilee was coming. God was working for them, but that they must wait a little patiently, and give God thanks and praise. And, O, with what eagerness they drank in my words, as the tears streamed down their sable cheeks. One old man, the Patriarch of the number, could not restrain himself, but as we closed the services, he went about and shook hands with all, and sung the coming Jubilee. I felt that day that it was better to preach Jesus to those ignorant sons and daughters of oppression, sitting on the ground amid the forest trees, than to occupy the proudest pulpit in the most magnificent church in the land.

I will now just sketch another scene I witnessed in the city of Jackson, on the 14th "touching" a contraband. As I passed by the headquarters of Gen. John A. Logan, I heard the sharpest cracks of a whip, interspersed with screeches and screams, as of one in dying agonies. I with some others hastened to the spot, and found it was a negro-whipping operation, directed by Mrs. Benj. Long, and inflicted upon a boy fourteen years of age. The boy was the property of Mrs. Long, she said, and had been saucy to her and she ordered a large, stout negro man to whip him, and stood by to see that it was well done. When I arrived, I found several surgeons, captains, lieutenants, one colonel and many privates, present. One of the captains had ordered the whipping to cease, at which the "refined southern lady" was discharging a volley of abuse at him, charging him with being a black abolitionist for interfering in the chastisement of constitutional property. He stoutly denied being an abolitionist, but said he could never stand and see even a dumb beast abused as she was abusing the negro boy. I examined the boy and never saw such a sight before. His head and back were all a gore of blood, being all cut to pieces. The captain and the colonel presented the boy to Gen. Logan, but he refused to look at him and ordered him away, and then in a most profane manner cursed the officers for not attending to their own business, and for interfering in the chastisement of the slave. Every man present seemed to be filled with rage at the whipping and at the conduct of the General.

But I hear that the General has resigned his commission, and if so, many will be gratified.

The slaves all appear to think that the time for their deliverance is at hand, and they are willing to do anything for the army.

As slavery was the origin of this war, and continues to be the strength of the rebels, all in the army are hoping for its speedy downfall.

Yours, truly,
CHAS. BUTTON,
Chaplain 20th Ill. Inft.

Source: Christian Times and Illinois Baptist, September 3, 1862.

The Poet Whittier Celebrates Emancipation in Brazil (1867)

Freedom in Brazil
By John Greenleaf Whittier

With clearer light, Cross of the South,
   shine forth
     In blue Brazilian skies;
And thou, O river, cleaving half the earth
     From sunset to sunrise,
From the great mountains to the Atlantic waves
     Thy joy's long anthem pour;
Yet a few days (God make them less!) and slaves
     Shall shame thy pride no more.
No fettered feet thy shaded margins press;
     But all men shall walk free
Where thou, the high-priest of the wilderness,
     Hast wedded sea to sea.

And thou, great-hearted ruler, through
   whose mouth
     The Word of God is said,
Once more, "Let there be light!"—Son of
   the South,
     Lift up thy honored head,
Wear unashamed a crown by thy desert
     More than by birth thy own,
Careless of watch and ward; thou art begirt
     By grateful hearts alone.
The moated wall and battle-ship may fail,
     But safe shall justice prove;
Stronger than greaves of brass or iron mail
     The panoply of love.

Crowned doubly by man's blessing, and
   God's grace,
     The future is secure;
Who frees a people makes his statue's place
     In Time's Valhalla sure.
Lo! from his Neva's banks the Scythian Czar
   {Alexander}
     Stretches to thee his hand
Who, with the pencil of the Northern star,
     Wrote freedom on his land.
And he whose grave is holy, by our calm
   {Abraham Lincoln}
     And prairied Sangamon,
From his gaunt hand shall drop the martyr's palm
     To greet thee with "Well done!"

And thou, O earth, with smiles thy face
   make sweet,

And let thy wail be stilled,
To hear the Muse of prophecy repeat
    Her promise half fulfilled.
The voice that spake at Nazareth speaks still,
    No sound thereof hath died;
Alike thy hope and Heaven's eternal will,
    Shall yet be satisfied.
The years are slow, the vision tarrieth long,
    And far the end may be;
But, one by one, the fiends of ancient wrong
    Go out, and leave thee free.

Source: Atlantic Monthly, 20:117 (July 1867).

Correspondence Between Spanish and American Officials on the Merits of Abolition (1871)

Letter from the Spanish Consul
to Governor Harrison Reed of Florida
New Orleans, March 14, 1871.

Governor,—

The undersigned, Consul of Spain in New Orleans, has the honour to submit to your consideration the following request:—

It ranks prominent among the official duties of the undersigned to have his Government faithfully and reliably informed of the general condition of the country to which he has had the honour to be accredited as consular representative.

The abolition of Slavery decreed by the Spanish Government for Cuba and Porto Rico will, undoubtedly, give rise to questions of great moment, which should be met and decided with the utmost care and impartial spirit; it is, therefore, very desirable that the opinion of his government be enlightened with such reliable data upon the subject as can be compiled in the country; and with such suggestions as experience may point out as just and proper.

To attain this end in the part allotted to him by virtue of his office, the undersigned begs leave to ask you to kindly consent in furnishing him at your earliest convenience, with such official and private information, recent statistics, &c., as will impartially show the results of abolition in your State, from an economical as well as a social point of view.

Your valuable opinion in the matter shall be gratefully received; and the undersigned shall take great pleasure in informing his Government of your kind compliance with his request.

The undersigned, finally, begs leave to tender the assurance of his highest personal regard, and to remain, very respectfully,

Your most obedient servant,
CARLOS VIE.

Governor Reed's Reply
Tallahassee, March 29, 1871.

Sir,—

Your favour of the 14th instant, referring to the decree of the Spanish Government abolishing Slavery in Cuba and Porto Rico, and inviting information in relation to the results and practical effects of the abolition of Slavery in this country, is received, and I have the honour to reply. It affords me great satisfaction to be able to say that the results in this State are decidedly beneficial to the people and the State.

The fact that freedom was accomplished by violence, and in opposition to the will of the slaveholder, instead of being inaugurated through concession and by his consent, has occasioned much embarrassment and prevented many advantages which would otherwise have been realised; but enough has been developed to show that it is highly conducive to the progress, wealth and prosperity of the State, as well as to the advancement of civilisation.

Before and for some time after the abolition of Slavery the theory of the South was, that the negroes would not work except under compulsion, and that cotton, the great staple of the South, could not be produced by free labour. The fallacy of this has been demonstrated by the cotton crop of 1870, which is equal to the average of the last four years before the war of undisturbed Slave labour.

It was also contended that, in freedom and deprived of the protection and care of their owners, the slaves would become vagrant and dissolute, and subject to disease and death, and soon the race would be exterminated.

It was confidently asserted that the reduction through this demoralisation would, in 1870, equal one-half the population of 1860. But what is the fact?

Though thousands perished during the war, and thousands more from being suddenly thrust out without subsistence or resource, destitute of medical attendance, and frequently subjected to vindictive opposition from their disappointed and enraged late owners, who still possessed the soil, still, from the census just completed, it is found that the negro population of the cotton States has increased since 1860 eight and three-fourths per cent.

In the State of Florida the increase in wealth and population, during the three years of Republican government just past, has been unparalleled in her previous history.

Her increase in population has been at least fifty per cent, and in industrial resources more than two hundred per cent.

The inevitable effect of Slavery is to concentrate the wealth in the hands of a few, while the effect of freedom is directly the opposite—to diffuse that wealth among the masses. Slavery degrades labour to a mere brute standard, while freedom ennobles it and makes it a fit associate with intellectual and moral cultivation.

In an educational and moral point of view the results of the abolition of Slavery are equally satisfactory, notwithstanding prejudice and intolerance have cheated the emancipated race of half its possible attainments. This branch of the subject opens a wide and interesting field of discussion and enquiry, which time will not permit me here to enter. The barbarism of Slavery and the beneficence of Freedom have been fully attested in the conduct and progress of the coloured race, even under all the adverse circumstances which have attended the country since emancipation, and I cannot but congratulate you and the nation which you represent on the recent decree of emancipation in Cuba and Porto Rico.

I have the honor to be, Sir,
With high respect,
Your obedient servant,
HARRISON REED,
Governor of Florida.

Source: Anti-Slavery Reporter, 17:7 (October 2, 1871).

A Spaniard on the State of Things in Cuba (1874)

16th December, 1874.

DEAR FRIEND,
The address of General Grant is of great importance, as he declares himself in favour of intervention in Cuba, aided by other nations. This nation must be England, and I hope you are working to rouse public opinion in favour of intervention. I am sure that, under the guarantee of the United States and England, the insurrectionists would lay down their arms immediately if Abolition is proclaimed, and a Constitution,

like the one in Canada is *given* not *offered.* The Cubans have reason not to put any faith in the promises of Spain. They are tired of having promises that are never fulfilled. The Spanish government promised, on different occasions, many things in our favour, and these promises were made *to other nations.* Still Spain has not fulfilled her promises.

More yet, a law (Moret's) was published, declaring free the old men, children, &c, and abolishing the lash, and reducing the hours of work. Nothing of this is respected in Cuba. Slavery there is just the same as it was before. Since the fall of the Republic the prices of slaves have gone up.

In Porto Rico our poor freedmen are turned back into slavery, for they have not liberty to work where they choose, neither obtain just wages.

My only hope is now in intervention, and a settlement under the guarantee of the United States and England.

The revolution in Cuba not only gains ground, but is stronger every day. I have seen some of the persons just come from the mountains of Cuba, where they have been fighting from the beginning; they tell me that not only they are sure that Spain never will put down the insurrection, but they affirm that they are strong enough to conquer.

I am, yours truly,

——————.

Source: Anti-Slavery Reporter, 19:6 (March 1, 1875).

Charles Darwin on Slavery (1882)

On the 19th of August we finally left the shores of Brazil. I thank God, I shall never again visit a slave-country. To this day, if I hear a distant scream, it recalls with painful vividness my feelings, when passing a house near Pernambuco, I heard the most pitiable moans, and could not but suspect that some poor slave was being tortured, yet knew that I was as powerless as a child even to remonstrate. I suspected that these moans were from a tortured slave, for I was told that this was the case in another instance. Near Rio de Janeiro I lived opposite to an old lady, who kept screws to crush the fingers of her female slaves. I have stayed in a house where a young household mulatto, daily and hourly, was reviled, beaten, and persecuted enough to break the spirit of the lowest animal. I have seen a little boy six or seven years old, struck thrice with a horse-whip (before I could interfere) on his naked head, for having handed me a glass of water not quite clean; I saw his father tremble at a mere glance from his master's eye.

These latter cruelties were witnessed by me in a Spanish colony, in which it has always been said, that slaves are better treated than by the Portuguese, English, or other European nations. I have seen at Rio Janeiro a powerful negro afraid to ward off a blow directed, as he thought, at his face. I was present when a kind-hearted man was on the point of separating for ever the men, women, and little children of a large number of families who had long lived together.

I will not even allude to the many heart-sickening atrocities which I authentically heard of; nor would I have mentioned the above revolting details, had I not met with several people, so blinded by the constitutional gaiety of the negro as to speak of slavery as a tolerable evil. Such people have generally visited at the houses of the upper classes, where the domestic slaves are usually well treated; and they have not, like myself, lived amongst the lower classes. Such enquirers will ask slaves about their condition; they forget that the slave must, indeed be dull, who does not calculate on the chance of his answer reaching his master's ears.

It is argued that self-interest will prevent excessive cruelty; as if self-interest protected our domestic animals, which are far less likely than degraded slaves, to stir up the rage of their savage masters. It is an argument long since protested against with noble feelings, and strikingly exemplified, by the ever-illustrious Humboldt. It is often attempted to palliate slavery by comparing the state of slaves with our poorer countrymen: if the misery of our poor be caused not by the laws of nature, but by our institutions, great is our sin; but how this bears on slavery, I cannot see; as well might the use of the thumb-screw be defended in one land, by showing that men in another land suffered from some dreadful disease. Those who look tenderly at the slave owner, and with a cold heart at the slave, never seem to put themselves into the position of the latter; what a cheerless prospect, with not even a hope of change! Picture to yourself the chance, ever hanging over you, of your wife and your little children—those objects which nature urges even the slave to call his own—being torn from you and sold like beasts to the first bidder! And these deeds are done and palliated by men who profess to love their neighbours as themselves, who believe in God, and pray that His Will be done on earth! It makes one's blood boil, yet heart tremble, to think that we Englishmen and our American descendants, with their boastful cry of liberty, have been and are so guilty: but it is a consolation to reflect, that we at least have made a greater sacrifice, than ever made by any nation, to expiate our sin.

Source: Charles Darwin, *The Voyage of the Beagle.* Harvard Classics, vol. XXIX, ed. Charles W. Eliot. New York: P.F. Collier and Sons, 1909.

Collective Calls for Abolition and Emancipation

In the late eighteenth and early nineteenth centuries, a sense of agency on behalf of the marginalized and the oppressed attracted like-minded individuals to organize themselves into antislavery societies. Sensing that there was strength in numbers and that their collective voice would be greater than the sum of its parts, abolitionists came together first to advocate an end to the transatlantic slave trade and then to call for the emancipation of all who were enslaved.

Those who joined this movement in Great Britain, the United States, and elsewhere recognized they were attacking one of the fundamental institutions on which much of the contemporary economy was based. They rightly anticipated vehement opposition from the well-entrenched powers that profited immensely from the slave trade and slavery. Nonetheless, the abolitionists were willing to organize for collective action.

Although slavery was the focus of their interest, no single, unifying motivation urged the abolitionists toward their antislavery stance. Some were inspired to join the movement because they believed slavery was a moral transgression that violated the Judeo-Christian ethic on which Western society and thought was structured. Others opposed slavery because they believed it effectively diminished the value and relative position of "free" labor—essentially arguing that the economic position of wage laborers was weakened as long as slavery persisted and that cheap sources of labor remained an essential component of the marketplace.

A smaller number of abolitionists were drawn to the movement by intellectual notions rooted in the natural rights theory of the eighteenth-century Enlightenment. These antislavery advocates called for emancipation of the enslaved because they believed in the inherent freedom of all persons, and they maintained that slavery infringed on the inviolable natural right of all humans.

Other abolitionists melded ideologies and motives. The abolitionist-driven Free Soil political party in the United States, for example, was formed on a platform that opposed the expansion of slavery into new territories. Its members took the stance that free men who lived on free soil form a system morally and economically preferable to slavery, the institution that bound the Southern states.

Abolitionists were the social revolutionaries of their time: They challenged the authority of long-standing practices by decrying the legitimacy of slavery. To be an abolitionist meant the self-centered promotion of one's own understanding of righteousness, while discrediting the lofty authority of history, tradition, organized religion, and the law—all of which seemed to recognize the rightful place of slavery in human society. In an age when drawing undue attention to oneself was considered an act of imprudence, the abolitionist organizations shattered the social conventions of their time by asserting that their truth was greater than the collective wisdom of previous generations. Such heady rhetoric was not well received by a society that was rooted in tradition and looked upon radical notions of so-called progress with tremendous skepticism.

The members of these antislavery societies were quickly demonized by those who denied their accusations and defended the rightful maintenance of a slave-based society. These arguments had the unanticipated effect of polarizing society on the question of slavery, as extreme supporters on both sides strove to gain adherents to their cause by becoming more strident in their rhetoric. The battle lines became increasingly clear, and there was little room for ambivalence. The result, "a house divided against itself," as Abraham Lincoln would later call it, became self-evident in the generation leading up to the U.S. Civil War.

For the abolitionists, direct political action through the efforts of petitions, memorials, public addresses, and sustained efforts at noncooperation with slaveholding interests were perceived as the only effective means to purge the sin of slavery, which they believed sullied national honor and diminished the inherent value of the human being. In spite of the opposition that their views and approach engendered, the following treatises, petitions, protests, and addresses demonstrate that the abolitionists were not willing to remain silent when faced with what they believed was the greatest single moral transgression in history.

The Germantown Protest (1688)

Resolutions of the Germantown Mennonites,
February 18, 1688.

This is to the monthly meeting held at Richard Worrell's:

These are the reasons why we are against the traffic of men-body, as followeth: Is there any that would be done or handled at this manner? viz., to be sold or made a slave for all the time of his life? How fearful and faint-hearted are many at sea, when they see a strange vessel, being afraid it should be a Turk, and they should be taken, and sold for slaves into Turkey. Now, what is *this* better done, than Turks do? Yea, rather it is worse for them, which say they are Christians; for we hear that the most part of such negers are brought hither against their will and consent, and that many of them are stolen. Now, though they are black, we cannot conceive there is more liberty to have them slaves, as it is to have other white ones. There is a saying, that we should do to all men like as we will be done ourselves; making no difference of what generation, descent, or colour they are. And those who steal or rob men, and those who buy or purchase them, are they not all alike? Here is liberty of conscience, which is right and reasonable; here ought to be likewise liberty of the body, except of evil-doers, which is another case. But to bring men hither, or to rob and sell them against their will, we stand against. In Europe there are many oppressed for conscience-sake; and here there are those oppressed which are of a black colour. And we who know that men must not commit adultery—some do commit adultery *in* others, separating wives from their husbands, and giving them to others: and some sell the children of these poor creatures to other men. Ah! do consider well this thing, you who do it, if you would be done at this manner—and if it is done according to Christianity! You surpass Holland and Germany in this thing, This makes an ill report in all those countries of Europe, where they hear of [it], that the Quakers do here handel men as they handel there the cattle. And for that reason some have no mind or inclination to come hither. And who shall maintain this your cause, or plead for it? Truly, we cannot do so, except you shall inform us better hereof, viz.: that Christians have liberty to practice these things. Pray, what thing in the world can be done worse towards us, than if men should rob or steal us away, and sell us for slaves to strange countries; separating husbands from their wives and children. Being now this is not done in the manner we would be done at; therefore, we contradict, and are against this traffic of men-body. And we who profess that it is not lawful to steal, must, likewise, avoid to purchase such things as are stolen, but rather help to stop this robbing and stealing, if possible. And such men ought to be delivered out of the hands of the robbers, and set free as in Europe. Then is Pennsylvania to have a good report, instead, it hath now a bad one, for this sake, in other countries; Especially whereas the Europeans are desirous to know in what manner *the Quakers* do rule in *their* province; and most of them do look upon us with an envious eye. But if this is done well, what shall we say is done evil?

If once these slaves (which they say are so wicked and stubborn men,) should join themselves—fight for their freedom, and handel their masters and mistresses, as they did handel them before; will these masters and mistresses take the sword at hand and war against these poor slaves, like, as we are able to believe, some will not refuse to do? Or, have these poor negers not as much right to fight for their freedom, as you have to keep them slaves?

Now consider well this thing, if it is good or bad. And in case you find it to be good to handel these blacks in that manner, we desire and require you hereby lovingly, that you may inform us herein, which at this time never was done, viz., that Christians have such a liberty to do so. To the end we shall be satisfied on this point, and satisfy likewise our good friends and acquaintances in our native country, to whom it is a terror, or fearful thing, that men should be handelled so in Pennsylvania.

This is from our meeting at Germantown held ye 18th of the 2d month, 1688, to be delivered to the monthly meeting at Richard Worrell's.

Garret Henderich,
Derick op de Graeff,
Francis Daniel Pastorius,
Abram op de Graeff.

Source: "The Earliest Protest Against Slavery," in *Documents of American History*, 7th ed., ed. Henry Steele Commager. New York: Appleton-Century-Crofts, 1963.

Slaves Petition for Freedom During the American Revolution (1773)

Province of the Massachusetts Bay To His Excellency Thomas Hutchinson, Esq; Governor; To The Honorable His Majesty's Council, and To the Honorable House of Representatives in General Court assembled at Boston, the 6th Day of January, 1773.

The humble PETITION of many Slaves, living in the Town of Boston, and other Towns in the Province is this, namely

That your Excellency and Honors, and the Honorable the Representatives would be pleased to take their unhappy State and Condition under your wise and just Consideration.

We desire to bless God, who loves Mankind, who sent his Son to die for their Salvation, and who is no respecter of Persons; that he hath lately put it into the Hearts of Multitudes on both Sides of the Water, to bear our Burthens, some of whom are Men of great Note and Influence; who have pleaded our Cause with Arguments which we hope will have their weight with this Honorable Court.

We presume not to dictate to your Excellency and Honors, being willing to rest our Cause on your Humanity and Justice; yet would beg Leave to say a Word or two on the Subject.

Although some of the Negroes are vicious, (who doubtless may be punished and restrained by the same Laws which are in Force against other of the King's Subjects) there are many others of a quite different Character, and who, if made free, would soon be able as well as willing to bear a Part in the Public Charges; many of them of good natural Parts, are discreet, sober, honest, and industrious; and may it not be said of many, that they are virtuous and religious, although their Condition is in itself so unfriendly to Religion, and every moral Virtue except *Patience.* How many of that Number have there been, and now are in this Province, who have had every Day of their Lives embittered with this most intollerable Reflection, That, let their Behaviour be what it will, neither they, nor their Children to all Generations, shall ever be able to do, or to possess and enjoy any Thing, no, not even *Life itself,* but in a Manner as the *Beasts that perish.*

We have no Property! We have no Wives! No Children! We have no City! No Country! But we have a Father in Heaven, and we are determined, as far as his Grace shall enable us, and as far as our degraded contemptuous Life will admit, to keep all his Commandments: Especially will we be obedient to our Masters, so long as God in his sovereign Providence shall suffer us to be holden in Bondage.

It would be impudent, if not presumptuous in us, to suggest to your Excellency and Honors any Law or Laws proper to be made, in relation to our unhappy State, which, although our greatest Unhappiness, is not our *Fault*; and this gives us great Encouragement

to pray and hope for such Relief as is consistent with your Wisdom, Justice, and Goodness.

We think Ourselves very happy, that we may thus address the Great and General Court of this Province, which great and good Court is to us, the best judge, under God, of what is wise, just and good.

We humbly beg Leave to add but this one Thing more: We pray for such Relief only, which by no Possibility can ever be productive of the least Wrong or Injury to our Masters; but to us will be as Life from the dead.

Signed,
FELIX

Source: "Slaves Petition for Freedom During the Revolution," in *A Documentary History of the Negro People,* vol. 1, *From Colonial Times Through the Civil War,* ed. Herbert Aptheker. New York: Citadel, 1951.

William Wilberforce's Twelve Propositions (1789)

Correct Copies of the twelve Propositions submitted on Tuesday evening by Mr. WILBERFORCE, to the consideration of the Committee, to whom the Report of the Privy Council, various Petitions for the Abolition of the SLAVE TRADE, and other Papers relative thereto, had been referred; which Propositions were by consent ordered to lie on the Table.

I. That the number of Slaves annually carried from the coast of Africa in British vessels, is supposed to amount to about 38,000.

That the number annually carried to the British West India islands has amounted to about 22,500, on an average of four years, to the year 1787 inclusive.

That the number annually retained in the said islands, as far as appears by the Custom-House Accounts, has amounted on the same average, to about 17,500.

II. That much the greater number of the Negroes carried away by European vessels are brought from the interior parts of the continent of Africa, and many of them from a very great distance.

That no precise information appears to have been obtained of the manner in which these persons have been made Slaves.

But that from the accounts, as far as any have been procured on this subject, with respect to the Slaves brought from the interior parts of Africa, and from the information which has been received respecting the countries nearer to the Coast, the Slaves may in general be classed under some of the following descriptions:

    1st. Prisoners taken in war.

    2d. Free persons sold for debt, or on account of real or imputed crimes, particularly adultery and witchcraft, in which cases they are frequently sold with their whole families, and sometimes for the profit of those by whom they are condemned.

    3d. Domestic Slaves sold for the profit of their masters, in some places at the will of the masters, and in some places on being condemned by them, for real or imputed crimes.

    4th. Persons made Slaves by various acts of oppression, violence, or fraud, committed either by the princes and chiefs of those countries on their subjects, or by private individuals on each other, or lastly by Europeans, engaged in this traffic.

III. That the trade carried on by European nations on the coast of Africa for the purchase of Slaves, has necessarily a tendency to occasion frequent and cruel wars among the natives, to produce unjust convictions and punishments for pretended or aggravated crimes, to encourage acts of oppression, violence and fraud, and to obstruct the natural course of civilization and improvement in those countries.

IV. That the continent of Africa, in its present state, furnishes several valuable articles of commerce, highly important to the trade and manufactures of this kingdom, and which are in a great measure peculiar to that quarter of the globe: And that the soil and climate have been found by experience well adapted to the production of other articles, with which we are now either wholly or in great part supplied by foreign nations.

    That an extensive commerce with Africa in these commodities might probably be substituted in the place of that which is now carried on in Slaves, so as at least to afford a return for the same quantity of goods as has annually been carried thither in British vessels: And lastly, that such a commerce might reasonably be expected to increase in proportion to the progress of civilization and improvement on that continent.

V. That the Slave Trade has been found by experience to be peculiarly injurious and destructive to the British seamen, who have been employed therein. And that the mortality among them has been much greater than his majesty's ships stationed on the coast of Africa, or than has been usual in British vessels employed in any other trade.

VI. That the mode of transporting the Slaves from Africa to the West Indies, necessarily exposes them to many and grievous sufferings, for which no regulations can provide an adequate remedy; and that in consequence thereof, a large proportion of them has annually perished during the voyage.

VII. That a large proportion of the Slaves so transported has also perished in the harbours in the West Indies, previous to their being sold; That this loss is stated by the Assembly of the island of Jamaica at about four and a half per cent, of the number imported; and is by medical persons of experience in that island ascribed in great measure to diseases contacted during the voyage; and to the mode of treatment on board the ships, by which those diseases have been suppressed for a time, in order to render the Slaves fit for immediate sale.

VIII. That the loss of newly imported Negroes within the first three years after their importation, bears a large proportion to the whole number imported.

IX. That the natural increase of population among the Slaves in the islands appears to have been impeded principally by the following causes.

    1st. The inequality of the sexes in the importations from Africa.

    2d. The general dissoluteness of manners among the Slaves, and the want of proper regulations for the encouragement of marriages, and of rearing children.

    3d. The particular diseases which are prevalent among them, and which are in some instances attributed to too severe labour, or rigorous treatment, and in others to insufficient or improper food.

    4th. Those diseases which affect a large proportion of Negro children in their infancy, and those to which the Negroes newly imported from Africa have been found to be particularly liable.

X. That the whole number of Slaves in the Island of Jamaica in 1768, was about 167,000. That the number in 1774 was, as stated by Governor Keith, about 193,000. And that the number in December, 1787, as stated by Lieut. Governor Clerke, was about 256,000.

    That by comparing these numbers with the numbers imported into and retained in the island in the several years from 1768 to 1774 inclusive, as appearing from the accounts delivered to the Committee of Trade by Mr. Fuller, and in the several years from 1775 inclusive, to 1787 also inclusive, as appearing by the accounts delivered in by the Inspector General, and allowing for a loss of about 1–22d part by deaths on ship-board after entry, as stated in the report of the Assembly of the said Island of Jamaica, it appears, that the annual excess of deaths above births in the Island, in the whole period of 19 years, has been in the proportion of about 7–8ths per cent, computing on the medium number of Slaves in the Island during that period. That in the first six years of the said nineteen, the excess of deaths was in the proportion of rather more than one on every hundred on the medium number. That in the last thirteen years of the said nineteen, the excess of deaths was in the proportion of about three fifths on every hundred on the medium number: and that a number of Slaves, amounting to 15,000 is stated by the Report of the Island of Jamaica to have perished during the latter period in consequence of repeated hurricanes, and of the want of foreign supplies of provisions.

XI. That the whole number of Slaves in the Island of Barbadoes was in the year 1764, according to the account given to the Committee of Trade by Mr. Braithwaite[,] 70,706. That in 1774 the number was, by the same account[,] 74,874. In 1780, by ditto 68,270. In 1781, after the hurricane, according to the same account[,] 63,248. In 1786, by ditto 62,115.

That by comparing these numbers with the number imported into this Island, according to the same account (not allowing for any re-exportation) that the annual excess of deaths above births in the 10 years from 1764 to 1774, was in the proportion of about five on every hundred, computing on the medium number of Slaves in the Island during that period.

That in the seven years from 1774 to 1780, both inclusive, the excess of deaths was in the proportion of about one and one-third on every hundred on the medium number.

That between the year 1780 and 1781, there appears to have been a decrease in the number of Slaves of about 5000.

That in the six years from 1781 to 1786, both inclusive, the excess of deaths was in the proportion of rather less than seven-eighths in every hundred on the medium number.

And that in the four years from 1783 to 1786, both inclusive, the excess of deaths was in the proportion of rather less than one-third in every hundred on the medium number.

And that during the whole period there is no doubt that some were exported from the island, but considerably more in the first part of this period than in the last.

XII. That the accounts from the Leeward Islands and from Dominica, Grenada, and St. Vincents, do not furnish sufficient grounds for comparing the state of population in the said Islands at different periods, with the number of Slaves which have been from time to time imported into the said Islands, and exported therefrom. But that from the evidence which has been received respecting the present state of these Islands, as well as of Jamaica and Barbadoes, and from a consideration of the means of obviating the causes which have hitherto operated to impede the natural increase of the Slaves, and of lessening the demand of manual labour, without diminishing the profit of the Planter, it appears that no considerable or permanent inconvenience would result from discontinuing the farther importation of African Slaves.

Source: The Speech of William Wilberforce, Esq., Representative for the County of York, on Wednesday the 13th of May, 1789, on the Question of the Abolition of the Slave Trade. London: Logographic Press, 1789.

Letter Written by La Société des Amis des Noirs (1789)

Translation of a letter written by the Society of the Friends of the Negroes, in France, to the Different Bailliages, or districts, that are entitled to send delegates to the Estates-General.

GENTLEMEN,
At the very time in which America shook off her servitude, the generous friends of liberty conceived that their cause would be degraded, if the slavery of the negroes received the sanction of law. A free man who holds slaves, or who approves of his countrymen holding them, either acknowledges himself guilty of injustice, or must assume as a principle, that liberty is only an advantage procured by force, not a right received from nature. The abolition, therefore, of negro slavery, was esteemed by the General United States, and by the convention in which they were represented, not only a measure dictated by sound policy, but an act of justice required by humanity and honour. And indeed, how could they claim, without blushing, those declarations of right—those inviolable bulwarks of the liberty and security of the people, if they indulged

themselves in the continual violation of their most sacred principles?—With what propriety could they talk of those rights, had they debased them into arbitrary conditions of mutual agreement, by shewing, in their conduct, that they did not think them intended for all mankind?

As the French nation is now busy in recovering rights, the exercise of which she has neglected, she will doubtless shew a spirit similar to that of the people whose cause she has espoused, to whom probably she owes a great part of her knowledge, and whose cool and steady wisdom (notwithstanding the difference of circumstances, of obstacles, and the proposed end) it were to be wished she would imitate. How can the nation protest against abuses, sanctioned by time, and established by legal forms, and urge against them the natural and unprescriptive rights of mankind, and the authority of reason, if she tolerates, by silence on the subject, so glaring a violation of reason and natural right, as the slavery of the negroes?

The Society of the Friends of the Negroes therefore trusts, that the nation will consider the trade in slaves and slavery among the evils, the destruction of which they must resolve on, and prepare for; and they address themselves confidently to their countrymen, met to choose their representatives, to bring to their view these criminal customs, established by violence, sanctioned by law, and pleaded for by prejudice.

We know that there are abuses which cannot be remedied in a day, which being connected with political interest, or seeming to be so, are only to be done away with the precaution requisite to insure the desirable object, and are not to be bought at too dear a rate; and we do not request you to vote for the instant overthrow of such evils.

We now beseech you only to turn your attention to the sufferings of 400,000 men, consigned to slavery by treachery or force, condemned with their families to labour, without hope of release, exposed to the rigorous and arbitrary treatment of their masters, deprived of all the rights of nature, and of society, and reduced to the condition of domestic animals; having only, like them, the interest of their owners for a pledge of their life and happiness.

We lay at your feet the cause of twenty nations, and of millions of mankind, whose liberty, peace, manners, and virtues, have been these two hundred years sacrificed to the interests of commerce, and those interests probably ill understood.

We request you to insert in your instructions a special one, enjoining your deputies to require of the General States, to consider the means of *putting an end* to the Slave Trade, and of *preparing* for the abolition of Slavery; for it is too degrading to human nature to suppose, that such abuses can be necessary to the political existence and prosperity of a great nation—that the welfare of twenty-four millions of Frenchmen must be necessarily supported by the misery of 400,000 Africans;—or that nature has provided for no means of happiness uncorrupted with the tears of men like themselves, and undefiled with blood. And we must be permitted also to wish, that France may have the honour of setting an example to the nations, which interest will soon oblige them to follow.

You may be told that this business is foreign to your purpose; but can any of the rights of justice and humanity be so to noble and feeling minds? The assertion, however, is deceitful.—What is opposed to those who wish to soften the hard lot of slaves?—Necessity—Policy—Custom. And are not necessity, policy, and custom, opposed to your own wishes when you demand justice for yourselves? Is it not your dearest interest to maintain that no custom, no prerogative, should stand against rights which have their foundation in nature itself?—If you will condescend to look into books tending to apologize for slavery, or setting forth the difficulty of subverting it, you will perceive that the principles and concessions they contain, will equally justify every kind of tyranny, and every inroad on the rights of humanity.

We are not content with declaring slavery to be unjust, and the Slave Trade a source of crimes; but we desire you to consider, whether in this question (as in many others) sound policy and justice do not go hand in hand;—whether the very pecuniary interest of the nation does not require a change of principles and conduct, as much as the interests of humanity;—and whether, as far as regards the abolition of the Slave Trade, this pecuniary interest does not require speedy and efficacious exertions, which it may be imprudent to delay.

We are accused of being enemies to the planters—we are enemies only of injustice—but we do say, that no man can by any means become another man's property:—We do not want to injure their possessions; but we want to purify the source of their riches, and to render them innocent and lawful. In short, whilst we thus plead on behalf of the negroes, we speak the language of many planters, who are sufficiently well informed to perceive that our views are not contrary to their permanent interest, and sufficiently candid to assist us in a work, which has for one object the giving them the liberty to be humane and just.—

We are, Gentlemen, your very humble, and most obedient servants,
The MARQUIS DE CONDORCET, *Pres{ident}.*
BREBAN, *Treas{urer}.*
GRAMAGNAC, *Secr{etary}.*

Resolved unanimously, at a General Assembly of the Society of the Friends of the Negroes, held at Paris, at the Hotel de Sussan, Rue Croix des petits Champs, the 3d February, 1789.

Source: Speeches in Parliament Respecting the Abolition of the African Slave Trade. Edinburgh: D. Willison, 1789.

Prospectus of the Society for the Mitigation and Gradual Abolition of Slavery Throughout the British Dominions (1823)

Among the manifold evils to which man is liable, there is not perhaps one more extensively productive of wretchedness than PERSONAL SLAVERY.

Slavery may, without exaggeration, be described as inflicting on the unhappy subjects of it almost every injury which law, even in its rudest state, was intended to prevent. Is property an object of solicitude? The Slave, generally speaking, can neither acquire nor securely enjoy it. Is exemption from personal wrong indispensable to comfort? The Slave is liable to indignity and insult, to restraint and punishment, at the mere caprice of another. He may be harassed and rendered miserable in a thousand ways which, so far from admitting the proof that would be requisite to obtain legal redress (even where any legal redress is ostensibly provided), can perhaps with difficulty be distinguished from such exercise of a master's power as admits of no regulation or controul. Even life itself may, with impunity, be wantonly sported with; it may be abridged by insufficient sustenance; it may be wasted by excessive labour; nay, it may be sacrificed by brutal violence, without any proportionate risk of adequate punishment.

In short, the Slave can have no security for property, comfort, or life; because he himself is not *his own:* he belongs to another, who, with or without the offer of a reason or pretence, can at once separate all from him and him from all which gives value to existence.

Again: What sense of moral obligation can he be expected to possess who is shackled with respect to every action and purpose, and is scarcely dealt with as an accountable being? Will the man, for example, whose testimony is rejected with scorn, be solicitous to establish a character for veracity? Will those who are treated as cattle, be taught thereby to restrain those natural appetites which they possess in common with their fellow-labourers in the team? Or will women be prepared for the due performance of domestic and maternal duties by being refused the connubial tie, or by being led to regard prostitution to their owner, or his representative, as the most honourable distinction to which they can aspire?

From this source of Slavery, then flows every species of personal suffering and moral degradation, until its wretched victim is sunk almost to the level of the brute; with this farther disadvantage, that, not being wholly irrational, he is capable of inspiring greater degrees of terror, resentment, and aversion, and will therefore seem to his owner to require and to justify severer measures of coercion.

And let it not be forgotten, that Slavery is itself not merely the effect, it is also the very cause, of the Slave Trade—of that system of fraud and violence by which Slaves are procured. If Slavery were extinct, the Slave Trade must [c]ease. But while it is suffered to exist, that murderous traffic will still find a fatal incentive in the solicitude of the Slaveholder to supply the waste of life which his cupidity and cruelty have occasioned. Thus, in every point of view, is Slavery productive of the worst consequences to all the parties concerned. Besides all the direct and wide-wasting injuries which it inflicts on its immediate victims, it substitutes for the otherwise peaceful merchant a blood-thirsty pirate trading in human flesh; and, by ministering to pride, avarice, and sensuality, by exciting the angry passions, and hardening the heart against the best feelings of our nature, it tends to convert the owner of Slaves into a merciless tyrant.

The Society, be it remembered, are not now endeavouring to rouse indignation against particular acts of extraordinary cruelty, or to hold up to merited reprehension individuals notorious for their crimes. They are only exhibiting a just picture of the nature and obvious tendencies of Slavery itself, wheresoever and by whomsoever practised. They are very far from asserting, or supposing, that every one of the enormities to which they have alluded will be found to co-exist in all their horrors in every place where Slaves may be found; but they know that in such places they have existed, at one time or other, in a greater or less degree; that in many places they are even now in full and fearful force; and that they are liable to be revived in all. Should this picture appear to some persons to be overcharged, they would refer them to the most decisive and unquestionable authorities. The felon Slave-trader, indeed, they consign to the laws of England, and to the recorded reprobation of Europe. But for the accuracy of their delineation of the wretchedness and degradation connected with the condition of Personal Slavery, (most willing as they are to admit the humanity of many of the owners of Slaves, and the praiseworthy efforts which some of them have made to mitigate, on their own estates, the evils of colonial bondage,) they appeal to ancient and to modern history, and to every traveller worthy of credit who has visited the regions where that condition of society prevails. Three thousand years ago, a heathen poet could tell us,

Jove fixed it certain, that whatever day
Makes man a Slave takes half his worth away.

And this might be shewn to be the concurrent testimony of all ages.

The enemies of Negro freedom, in our own age and country, were so sensible of this truth, that with great shrewdness they disputed the claim of the Negro race to be regarded as men. They doubtless felt with Montesquieu, that if "Negroes were allowed to be men, a doubt might arise whether their masters could be Christians." This position, however, has been abandoned as untenable; and we may therefore indulge a sanguine hope of at length recovering from them the indubitable rights of humanity, so long and so cruelly withheld by the strong arm of oppression.

Some persons, however, may here be disposed to ask, how it is possible, if slavery is an evil so enormous as it has now been represented to be, that it should not only have been tolerated, but recognized and established as a legal condition of society, by so many polished and even Christian nations, up to this very day? The Society admit, that, to a humane and considerate mind, nothing can seem more extraordinary, than that this and other enormities, the removal of which lies obviously within the compass of human ability,

should yet continue to torment mankind from age to age. But our past supineness in no degree weakens the obligation we are under to attempt their removal, when their real nature has been detected and exposed. Nor will the plea of prescription and antiquity, or of previous connivance, justify the prolongation of practices which both religion and natural justice condemn as crimes. The African Slave Trade, with all the abominations accompanying its every stage, had been carried on for centuries, without attracting observation; and, even after it had excited the attention of a few benevolent individuals, it cost many a laborious effort and many a painful disappointment, before a conviction of its inherent turpitude and criminality became general, and its condemnation was sealed in this country. In the exultation produced by this victory, it was perhaps too readily believed that the Colonial Slavery, which had been fed by the Slave Trade, would, when all foreign supply was stopped, undergo a gradual, but rapid mitigation, until it had ceased to reproach our free institutions and our Christian profession, and was no longer known but as a foul blot in our past history. It was this hope, joined to a liberal confidence in the enlarged and benevolent purposes of the colonial proprietary, which prevented the immediate prosecution of such further parliamentary measures as should have at once placed the unhappy Slave under the protection of the law, and have prepared the way for his restoration to those sacred and inalienable rights of humanity of which he had been unjustly dispossessed. But if, as is the fact, these hopes have proved illusory, and have only served to render the disappointment more bitter and mortifying, shall the friends of the African race be now reproached for waiting no longer, when the real ground of reproach is, that they should have waited so long? They place themselves then on the immoveable ground of Christian principle, while they invoke the interference of Parliament, and of the country at large, to effect the immediate mitigation, with a view to the gradual and final extinction, in all parts of the British Dominions, of a system which is at war with every principle of religion and morality, and outrages every benevolent feeling. And they entertain the fullest conviction that the same spirit of justice and humanity which has already achieved so signal a victory will again display itself in all its energy, nor relax its efforts until it shall have consummated its triumphs.

The *objects* of this Society cannot be more clearly and comprehensively defined than in the following

Resolutions, which were unanimously adopted at its first meeting.

"That the individuals composing the present meeting are deeply impressed with the magnitude and number of the evils attached to the system of Slavery which prevails in many of the Colonies of Great Britain; a system which appears to them to be opposed to the spirit and precepts of Christianity, as well as repugnant to every dictate of natural humanity and justice.

That they long indulged a hope, that the great measure of the Abolition of the Slave Trade, for which an Act of the Legislature was passed in 1807, after a struggle of twenty years, would have tended rapidly to the mitigation and gradual extinction of Negro bondage in the British Colonies; but that in this hope they have been painfully disappointed; and, after a lapse of sixteen years, they have still to deplore the almost undiminished prevalence of the very evils which it was one great object of the abolition to remedy.

That under these circumstances they feel themselves called upon, by the most binding considerations of their duty as Christians, by their best sympathies as men, and by their solicitude to maintain unimpaired the high reputation and the solid prosperity of their country, to exert themselves, in their separate and collective capacities, in furthering this most important object, and in endeavouring by all prudent and lawful means to mitigate, and eventually to abolish, the Slavery existing in our Colonial possessions.

That an Association be now formed, to be called 'The Society for mitigating and gradually abolishing the State of Slavery throughout the British Dominions;' [also known as the Society for the Mitigation and Gradual Abolition of Slavery Throughout the British Dominions] and that a Subscription be entered into for that purpose."

With respect to the *means* of carrying these objects into effect, they must, in some measure, depend on circumstances. For such as are more obvious, particularly the obtaining and diffusing of information, considerable funds will be required; and it will therefore be necessary to promote subscriptions, not only in the metropolis, but in all parts of the kingdom.

Source: Society for the Mitigation and Gradual Abolition of Slavery Throughout the British Dominions, *Substance of the Debate in the House of Commons 1823: On the 15th May, 1823 on a Motion for the Mitigation and Gradual Abolition of Slavery Throughout the British Dominions.* London: Ellerton and Henderson, 1823.

Prospectus of the Society for the Extinction of the Slave Trade and for the Civilization of Africa (1839)

Instituted June, 1839.

In the year 1807 Great Britain prohibited all her subjects from engaging in the Slave Trade, and the Legislature of this country, in accordance with the voice of the people, repudiated a commerce which had produced more crime and misery than, perhaps, any other single cause of guilt and iniquity; but neither the Government nor the Legislature, nor the subjects of this realm, were satisfied with a mere cessation from crime.

Remembering how deeply, in times of comparative ignorance, we had sustained and augmented this trade, so repugnant to every Christian principle and feeling, the nation determined to use its utmost influence, and expend its resources, in the noble attempt to extinguish it for ever.

The compass of this address will not allow even of the most compendious statement of the measures resorted to, of the treaties concluded with foreign powers, of the monies expended, and the various other efforts made to effect this object; suffice it to say that, since the year 1807, all the great Powers of Europe have been induced by Great Britain to unite in expressing their abhorrence of this traffic; and, with all, treaties more or less stringent have been made for its extinction.

The United States of America, though from political reasons they have declined any actual co-operation, have not the less denounced and prohibited all traffic in slaves from Africa. Great Britain has expended, in bounties alone, upwards of £940,000, and, in the maintenance of the courts established for the adjudication of captured slaves, above £330,000, besides a very large sum annually in supporting a considerable force of cruizers in various parts of the globe, to intercept and destroy the traffic. An infinitely more important sacrifice has been made in the loss of British life, which has been necessarily incurred in pursuing this object. The result, the melancholy result, remains to be stated. The traffic has not been extinguished, has not been diminished, but by the latest accounts from which any estimate can be correctly formed, the numbers exported have increased—the destruction of human life, and all the guilt and misery consequent thereon, have been fearfully augmented; and at the same time it may be stated, that the numbers exported from Africa are, as compared with the year

1807, as two to one, and that the annual loss of life has risen from seventeen to twenty-five per cent.

Let no man, however, say that these efforts have been thrown away. Who can tell how fearful might not have been the amount of enormity, if those exertions had not been made? Who would presume to say that the very assertion of the great principles of justice and truth has not accelerated in the final extirpation of those detested practices? Who could venture to assert that a criminal inaction on the part of Great Britain might not have caused an indefinite continuance of the guilt on the part of other nations?

But the people of England have not succeeded to the extent of their wishes:—Assuming it to be so, what remains to be done?—but led on by the same Christian principles, the same devotion to truth, justice, and humanity, to continue our efforts, and to apply, if possible, other and more efficient remedies in accordance with these great principles.

Animated by these feelings, a number of noblemen and gentlemen of all political opinions, and of Christian persuasions of divers kinds, have formed themselves into a Society for the purpose of effecting the extinction of the Slave Trade; and they now call on the public to unite their exertions for the accomplishment of this great end.

That the British public, apprised of the extent of the enormity, and deeply feeling the guilt and misery now prevailing, will receive with favour the announcement of the formation of this Society, no doubt is entertained; but various opinions do and will exist as to the most fitting means to be adopted for the establishment of peace and tranquillity in Africa.

It is expedient, therefore, to state the leading principles on which this Society is formed, and the measures intended to be pursued.

It is the unanimous opinion of this Society, that the only complete cure of all these evils is the introduction of Christianity into Africa. They do not believe that any less powerful remedy will entirely extinguish the present inducements to trade in human beings, or will afford to the inhabitants of those extensive regions a sure foundation for repose and happiness.

But they are aware that a great variety of views may exist as to the manner in which religious instruction should be introduced. Distinctly avowing, therefore, that the substitution of our pure and holy faith for the false religion, idolatry, and superstitions of Africa, is, in their firm conviction, the true ultimate remedy for the calamities that afflict her, they

are most anxious to adopt every measure which may eventually lead to the establishment of Christianity throughout that continent; and hoping to secure the cordial co-operation of all, they proceed to declare that the grand object of their association is *the extinction of the Slave Trade.*

The primary object of this Society will be constantly kept in view under all circumstances of difficulty or discouragement, as the grand end to which their efforts, of whatever character, should be resolutely and unchangeably directed.

As one of the principal means, they have cordially co-operated with Mr. Buxton in inducing Her Majesty's Government to undertake an expedition to the River Niger, with the view of obtaining the most accurate information as to the state of the countries bordering on its mighty waters.

The immense importance of this object alone, as opening a highway into the interior of Africa, and bringing the efforts of British philanthropy into immediate contact with the numerous and populous nations it contains, will be at once perceived and acknowledged.

It will be one of the first duties then of this Society to watch over the proceedings of this expedition, to record its progress, and to digest and circulate the valuable information which it may be confidently expected to communicate.

When this leading step has been taken, it is anticipated that a large field for exertions of a different description will then be opened; but desirable as such exertions may be, it must be clearly understood that this Society, associated solely for benevolent purposes, can bear no part whatever in them: still, in order that a comprehensive view may be taken of the whole, though each part must be accomplished by agencies entirely distinct, it may be expedient to state some of the expectations which are entertained.

One most important department must entirely rest with Her Majesty's Government,—the formation of Treaties with the native rulers of Africa for the suppression of the Slave Trade. Such Treaties, however, will not be carried into execution, unless those wants, which have hitherto been supplied from the profits arising from the sale of the natives, should be satisfied through the means of legitimate Commerce. It may appear expedient to the Government to obtain from the Chiefs the possession of some convenient districts which may be best adapted to carrying on trade with safety and success; and when this is effected, another and wholly distinct Society may perhaps be formed, for the purpose of aiding in the cultivation of those districts, and of promoting the growth of those valuable products for which the soil of those countries is peculiarly fitted.

The present Society can take part in no plan of Colonization or of Trade. Its objects are, and must be, exclusively pacific and benevolent; but it may, by encouragement and by the diffusion of information, most materially aid in the civilization of Africa, and so pave the way for the successful exertions of others, whether they be directed to colonization and the cultivation of the soil, or to commercial intercourse, or to that which is immeasurably superior to them all, the establishment of the Christian faith on the Continent of Africa.

At home, this Society will direct its vigilant attention to all which may arise with respect to the traffic in slaves, and give publicity to whatever may be deemed most essential to produce its suppression.

In Africa, there are various means whereby it may effectually work to the same end. One of the great impediments at present existing to the advancement of knowledge, is the state of the native languages of Western and Central Africa.

Amongst the many nations which inhabit those regions, there are certainly many different dialects, and not improbably several leading languages. A few only of those languages have yet been reduced into writing, and consequently the difficulty of holding intercourse with the natives, and imparting knowledge to them, is greatly increased. By the adoption of effectual measures for reducing the principal languages of Western and Central Africa into writing, a great obstacle to the diffusion of information will be removed, and facility afforded for the introduction of the truths of Christianity.

There is another subject, of no light importance, which would legitimately fall within the views of this Institution. In Africa, medical science can scarcely be said to exist, yet in no part of the world is it more profoundly respected. As at present understood by the natives, it is intimately connected with the most inveterate and barbarous superstitions; and its artful practitioners, owing their superiority to this popular ignorance, may be expected to interpose the most powerful obstacles to the diffusion of Christianity and of Science.

To encourage, therefore, the *introduction* of more enlightened views on this subject, to prevent or mitigate the prevalence of disease and suffering among the people of Africa, and to secure the aid of medical science generally to the beneficent objects of African civilization, must be considered of immense importance; nor would its benefits be confined to the native population. It is equally applicable to the investigation of the climate and localities of that country. To render Africa a salubrious residence for European constitutions may be a hopeless task; but to diminish the danger, to point out the means whereby persons proceeding thither may most effectually guard against its perils, may perhaps be effected; nor must it be forgotten that, in however humble a degree this advantage can be attained, its value cannot be too highly appreciated.

Various other measures may come within the legitimate scope of this Institution. It may be sufficient to recapitulate a few:—the encouragement of practical science in all its various branches,—the system of drainage best calculated to succeed in a climate so humid and so hot, would be an invaluable boon to all who frequent that great Continent, whatever might be their purpose. Though this Society would not embark in agriculture, it might afford essential assistance to the natives, by furnishing them with useful information as to the best mode of cultivation; as to the productions which command a steady market, and by introducing the most approved agricultural implements and seeds. The time may come when the knowledge and practice of the mighty powers of steam might contribute rapidly to promote the improvement and prosperity of that Country.

Even matters of comparatively less moment may engage the attention of the Society. It may assist in promoting the formation of roads and canals. The manufacture of paper, and the use of the printing press, if once established in Africa, will be amongst the most powerful auxiliaries in the dispersion of ignorance and the destruction of barbarism.

It is hoped that enough has now been stated to justify the Society in calling for the aid and co-operation of all who hold in just abhorrence the iniquitous traffic in human beings—of all who deeply deplore the awful crimes which have so long afflicted, and still continue to devastate, Africa—of all who remember with deep sorrow and contrition that share which Great Britain so long continued to have in producing those scenes of bloodshed and of guilt. A variety of collateral means has thus been suggested sufficiently important and interesting to demonstrate the necessity of a distinct Society, and to entitle it to the best wishes and firmest support of every sincere friend of Africa.

To its success, cordial and united co-operation is indispensable. It proposes to act by means in which the whole community, without regard to religious or political opinions, may concur; and though it does not embrace the establishment, by its own agency, of schools for the spread of religious instruction, it abstains from such an undertaking, not because it does not value the introduction of Christian knowledge, as the greatest blessing which can be bestowed on that idolatrous land, but because a diversity of opinion as to the mode of proceeding must of necessity interfere with the unity of action so essential for the common prosecution of such an important object, and thus impede instead of facilitate the objects of this Institution.

It is impossible, however, to close this address without again expressing, in the most emphatic terms, the conviction and earnest hope of all who have already attached themselves as members of this Institution, that the measures to be adopted by them for the suppression of the traffic in Slaves—for securing the peace and tranquility of Africa—for the encouragement of agriculture and commerce—will facilitate the propagation and triumph of that faith which one and all feel to be indispensable for the happiness of the inhabitant of that Continent. Howsoever the extension of the Christian religion may be attempted, it is far more likely to take root and flourish where peace prevails, and crime is diminished, than where murder and bloodshed, and the violation of every righteous principle, continue to pollute the land.

Office of the Society
15, Parliament Street,
14th February, 1840

Source: Proceedings at the First Public Meeting of the Society for the Extinction of the Slave Trade and for the Civilization of Africa, Held at Exeter Hall, on Monday, 1st June, 1840. London: W. Clowes and Sons, 1840.

Henry Highland Garnet's Address to the Slaves of the United States of America (1843)

Delivered before the National Convention of Colored Citizens, Buffalo, New York, August 16, 1843.

Brethren and Fellow Citizens,
Your brethren of the North, East, and West have been accustomed to meet together in National Conventions, to sympathize with each other, and to weep over your unhappy condition. In these meetings we have addressed all classes of the free, but we have never, until this time, sent a word of consolation and advice to you. We have been contented in sitting still and mourning over your sorrows, earnestly hoping that before this day your sacred liberty would have been restored. But, we have hoped in vain. Years have rolled on, and tens of thousands have been borne on streams of blood and tears, to the shores of eternity. While you have been oppressed, we have also been partakers with you; nor can we be free while you are enslaved. We, therefore, write to you as being bound with you.

Many of you are bound to us, not only by the ties of a common humanity, but we are connected by the more tender relations of parents, wives, husbands, children, brothers, and sisters, and friends. As such we most affectionately address you.

Slavery has fixed a deep gulf between you and us, and while it shuts out from you the relief and consolation which your friends would willingly render, it affects and persecutes you with a fierceness which we might not expect to see in the fiends of hell. But still the Almighty Father of mercies has left to us a glimmering ray of hope, which shines out like a lone star in a cloudy sky. Mankind are becoming wiser, and better—the oppressor's power is fading, and you, every day, are becoming better informed, and more numerous. Your grievances, brethren, are many. We shall not attempt, in this short address, to present to the world all the dark catalogue of this nation's sins, which have been committed upon an innocent people. Nor is it indeed necessary, for you feel them from day to day, and all the civilized world look upon them with amazement.

Two hundred and twenty-seven years ago, the first of our injured race were brought to the shores of America. They came not with glad spirits to select their homes in the New World. They came not with their own consent, to find an unmolested enjoyment of the blessings of this fruitful soil. The first dealings they had with men calling themselves Christians, exhibited to them the worst features of corrupt and sordid hearts; and convinced them that no cruelty is too great, no villainy and no robbery too abhorrent for even enlightened men to perform, when influenced by avarice and lust. Neither did they come flying upon the wings of Liberty, to a land of freedom. But they came with broken hearts, from their beloved native land, and were doomed to unrequited toil and deep degradation. Nor did the evil of their bondage end at their emancipation by death. Succeeding generations inherited their chains, and millions have come from eternity into time, and have returned again to the world of spirits, cursed and ruined by American slavery.

The propagators of the system, or their immediate ancestors, very soon discovered its growing evil, and its tremendous wickedness, and secret promises were made to destroy it. The gross inconsistency of a people holding slaves, who had themselves "ferried o'er the wave" for freedom's sake, was too apparent to be entirely overlooked. The voice of Freedom cried, "Emancipate yourselves." Humanity supplicated with tears for the deliverance of the children of Africa. Wisdom urged her solemn plea. The bleeding captive plead his innocence, and pointed to Christianity who stood weeping at the cross. Jehovah frowned upon the nefarious institution, and thunderbolts, red with vengeance, struggled to leap forth to blast the guilty wretches who maintained it. But all was in vain. Slavery had stretched its dark wings of death over the land, the Church stood silently by—the priests prophesied falsely, and the people loved to have it so. Its throne is established, and now it reigns triumphant.

Nearly three millions of your fellow-citizens are prohibited by law and public opinion, (which in this country is stronger than law,) from reading the Book of Life. Your intellect has been destroyed as much as possible, and every ray of light they have attempted to shut out from your minds. The oppressors themselves have become involved in the ruin. They have become weak, sensual, and rapacious—they have cursed you—they have cursed themselves—they have cursed the earth which they have trod.

The colonists threw the blame upon England. They said that the mother country entailed the evil upon them, and that they would rid themselves of it if they could. The world thought they were sincere, and the philanthropic pitied them. But time soon tested their sincerity.

In a few years the colonists grew strong, and severed themselves from the British Government. Their independence was declared, and they took their station among the sovereign powers of the earth. The declaration was a glorious document. Sages admired it, and the patriotic of every nation reverenced the God-like sentiments which it contained. When the power of Government returned to their hands, did they emancipate the slaves? No; they rather added new links to our chains. Were they ignorant of the principles of Liberty? Certainly they were not. The sentiments of their revolutionary orators fell in burning eloquence upon their hearts, and with one voice they cried, *Liberty or death.* Oh what a sentence was that! It ran from soul to soul like electric fire, and nerved the arm of thousands to fight in the holy cause

of Freedom. Among the diversity of opinions that are entertained in regard to physical resistance, there are but a few found to gainsay that stem declaration. We are among those who do not. Slavery! How much misery is comprehended in that single word. What mind is there that does not shrink from its direful effects? Unless the image of God be obliterated from the soul, all men cherish the love of Liberty. The nice discerning political economist does not regard the sacred right more than the untutored African who roams in the wilds of Congo. Nor has the one more right to the full enjoyment of his freedom than the other. In every man's mind the good seeds of liberty are planted, and he who brings his fellow down so low, as to make him contented with a condition of slavery, commits the highest crime against God and man. Brethren, your oppressors aim to do this. They endeavor to make you as much like brutes as possible. When they have blinded the eyes of your mind—when they have embittered the sweet waters of life—then, and not till then, has American slavery done its perfect work.

To SUCH DEGRADATION IT IS SINFUL IN THE EXTREME FOR YOU TO MAKE VOLUNTARY SUBMISSION. The divine commandments you are in duty bound to reverence and obey. If you do not obey them, you will surely meet with the displeasure of the Almighty. He requires you to love him supremely, and your neighbor as yourself—to keep the Sabbath day holy—to search the Scriptures—and bring up your children with respect for his laws, and to worship no other God but him. But slavery sets all these at nought, and hurls defiance in the face of Jehovah. The forlorn condition in which you are placed, does not destroy your moral obligation to God. You are not certain of heaven, because you suffer yourselves to remain in a state of slavery, where you cannot obey the commandments of the Sovereign of the universe. If the ignorance of slavery is a passport to heaven, then it is a blessing, and no curse, and you should rather desire its perpetuity than its abolition. God will not receive slavery, nor ignorance, nor any other state of mind, for love and obedience to him. Your condition does not absolve you from your moral obligation. The diabolical injustice by which your liberties are cloven down, NEITHER GOD, NOR ANGELS, OR JUST MEN, COMMAND YOU TO SUFFER FOR A SINGLE MOMENT. THEREFORE IT IS YOUR SOLEMN AND IMPERATIVE DUTY TO USE EVERY MEANS, BOTH MORAL, INTELLECTUAL, AND PHYSICAL

THAT PROMISES SUCCESS. If a band of heathen men should attempt to enslave a race of Christians, and to place their children under the influence of some false religion, surely Heaven would frown upon the men who would not resist such aggression, even to death. If, on the other hand, a band of Christians should attempt to enslave a race of heathen men, and to entail slavery upon them, and to keep them in heathenism in the midst of Christianity, the God of heaven would smile upon every effort which the injured might make to disenthral themselves.

Brethren, it is as wrong for your lordly oppressors to keep you in slavery, as it was for the man thief to steal our ancestors from the coast of Africa. You should therefore now use the same manner of resistance, as would have been just in our ancestors when the bloody foot-prints of the first remorseless soul-thief was placed upon the shores of our fatherland. The humblest peasant is as free in the sight of God as the proudest monarch that ever swayed a sceptre. Liberty is a spirit sent out from God. and like its great Author, is no respecter of persons.

Brethren, the time has come when you must act for yourselves. It is an old and true saying that, "if hereditary bondmen would be free, they must themselves strike the blow." You can plead your own cause, and do the work of emancipation better than any others. The nations of the world are moving in the great cause of universal freedom, and some of them at least will, ere long, do you justice. The combined powers of Europe have placed their broad seal of disapprobation upon the African slave-trade. But in the slaveholding parts of the United States, the trade is as brisk as ever. They buy and sell you as though you were brute beasts. The North has done much—her opinion of slavery in the abstract is known. But in regard to the South, we adopt the opinion of the *New York Evangelist*—We have advanced so far, that the cause apparently waits for a more effectual door to be thrown open than has been yet. We are about to point out that more effectual door. Look around you, and behold the bosoms of your loving wives heaving with untold agonies! Hear the cries of your poor children! Remember the stripes your fathers bore. Think of the torture and disgrace of your noble mothers. Think of your wretched sisters, loving virtue and purity, as they are driven into concubinage and are exposed to the unbridled lusts of incarnate devils. Think of the undying glory that hangs around the ancient name of Africa—and forget not that you are native born American citizens, and as such, you are justly entitled

to all the rights that are granted to the freest. Think how many tears you have poured out upon the soil which you have cultivated with unrequited toil and enriched with your blood; and then go to your lordly enslavers and tell them plainly, that you *are determined to be free.* Appeal to their sense of justice, and tell them that they have no more right to oppress you, than you have to enslave them. Entreat them to remove the grievous burdens which they have imposed upon you, and to remunerate you for your labor. Promise them renewed diligence in the cultivation of the soil, if they will render to you an equivalent for your services. Point them to the increase of happiness and prosperity in the British West Indies since the Act of Emancipation.

Tell them in language which they cannot misunderstand, of the exceeding sinfulness of slavery, and of a future judgment, and of the righteous retributions of an indignant God. Inform them that all you desire is FREEDOM, and that nothing else will suffice. Do this, and for ever after cease to toil for the heartless tyrants, who give you no other reward but stripes and abuse. If they then commence the work of death, they, and not you, will be responsible for the consequences. You had better all *die—die immediately,* than live slaves and entail your wretchedness upon your posterity. If you would be free in this generation, here is your only hope. However much you and all of us may desire it, there is not much hope of redemption without the shedding of blood. If you must bleed, let it all come at once—rather *die freemen, than live to be slaves.* It is impossible like the children of Israel, to make a grand exodus from the land of bondage. The Pharaohs are on both sides of the blood-red waters! You cannot move *en masse,* to the dominions of the British Queen—nor can you pass through Florida and overrun Texas, and at last find peace in Mexico. The propagators of American slavery are spending their blood and treasure, that they may plant the black flag in the heart of Mexico and riot in the halls of the Montezeumas. In the language of the Rev. Robert Hall, when addressing the volunteers of Bristol, who were rushing forth to repel the invasion of Napoleon, who threatened to lay waste the fair homes of England, "Religion is too much interested in your behalf, not to shed over you her most gracious influences."

You will not be compelled to spend much time in order to become inured to hardships. From the first moment that you breathed the air of heaven, you have been accustomed to nothing else but hardships. The heroes of the American Revolution were never put upon harder fare than a peck of corn and a few herrings per week. You have not become enervated by the luxuries of life. Your sternest energies have been beaten out upon the anvil of severe trial. Slavery has done this, to make you subservient, to its own purposes; but it has done more than this, it has prepared you for any emergency. If you receive good treatment, it is what you could hardly expect; If you meet with pain, sorrow, and even death, these are the common lot of slaves.

Fellow men! Patient sufferers! behold your dearest rights crushed to the earth! See your sons murdered, and your wives, mothers and sisters doomed to prostitution. In the name of the merciful God, and by all that life is worth, let it no longer be a debatable question whether it is better to choose *Liberty or death.*

In 1822, Denmark Veazie [Vesey], of South Carolina, formed a plan for the liberation of his fellow men. In the whole history of human efforts to overthrow slavery, a more complicated and tremendous plan was never formed. He was betrayed by the treachery of his own people, and died a martyr to freedom. Many a brave hero fell, but history, faithful to her high trust, will transcribe his name on the same monument with Moses, Hampden, Tell, Bruce and Wallace, Toussaint L'Ouverture, Lafayette and Washington. That tremendous movement shook the whole empire of slavery. The guilty soul-thieves were overwhelmed with fear. It is a matter of fact, that at that time, and in consequence of the threatened revolution, the slave States talked strongly of emancipation. But they blew but one blast of the trumpet of freedom and then laid it aside. As these men became quiet, the slaveholders ceased to talk about emancipation; and now behold your condition today! Angels sigh over it, and humanity has long since exhausted her tears in weeping on your account!

The patriotic Nathaniel Turner followed Denmark Veazie [Vesey]. He was goaded to desperation by wrong and injustice. By despotism, his name has been recorded on the list of infamy, and future generations will remember him among the noble and brave.

Next arose the immortal Joseph Cinque, the hero of the *Amistad.* He was a native African, and by the help of God he emancipated a whole shipload of his fellow men on the high seas. And he now sings of liberty on the sunny hills of Africa and beneath his native palm-trees, where he hears the lion roar and feels himself as free as that king of the forest.

Next arose Madison Washington that bright star of freedom, and took his station in the constellation of true heroism. He was a slave on board the brig *Creole,* of Richmond, bound to New Orleans, that great slave mart, with a hundred and four others. Nineteen struck for liberty or death. But one life was taken, and the whole were emancipated, and the vessel was carried into Nassau, New Providence.

Noble men! Those who have fallen in freedom's conflict, their memories will be cherished by the true-hearted and the God-fearing in all future generations; those who are living, their names are surrounded by a halo of glory.

Brethren, arise, arise! Strike for your lives and liberties. Now is the day and the hour. Let every slave throughout the land do this, and the days of slavery are numbered. You cannot be more oppressed than you have been—you cannot suffer greater cruelties than you have already. *Rather die freemen than live to be slaves.* Remember that you are FOUR MILLIONS!

It is in your power so to torment the God-cursed slaveholders that they will be glad to let you go free. If the scale was turned, and black men were the masters and white men the slaves, every destructive agent and element would be employed to lay the oppressor low. Danger and death would hang over their heads day and night. Yes, the tyrants would meet with plagues more terrible than those of Pharaoh. But you are a patient people. You act as though you were made for the special use of these devils. You act as though your daughters were born to pamper the lusts of your masters and overseers. And worse than all, you tamely submit while your lords tear your wives from your embraces and defile them before your eyes. In the name of God, we ask, are you men? Where is the blood of your fathers? Has it all run out of your veins? Awake, awake; millions of voices are calling you! Your dead fathers speak to you from their graves. Heaven, as with a voice of thunder, calls on you to arise from the dust.

Let your motto be resistance! *resistance!* Resistance! No oppressed people have ever secured their liberty without resistance. What kind of resistance you had better make, you must decide by the circumstances that surround you, and according to the suggestion of expediency. Brethren, adieu! Trust in the living God. Labor for the peace of the human race, and remember that you are FOUR MILLIONS.

Source: David Walker and Henry Highland Garnet, *Walker's Appeal: With a Brief Sketch of His Life by Henry Highland Garnet; And Also Garnet's Address to the Slaves of the United States of America.* New York: J.H. Tobitt, 1848.

The Free Soil Party's Platform of Principles (1852)

Having assembled in National Convention as the delegates of the Free Democracy of the United States, united by a common resolve to maintain rights against wrongs, and freedom against slavery—confiding in the intelligence, the patriotism, and the discriminating justice of the American people—putting our trust in God for the triumph of our cause, and invoking His guidance in our endeavours to advance it—we now submit, for the candid judgment of all men, the following declaration of principles and measures:—

First.—That Governments, deriving their just powers from the consent of the governed, are instituted among men to secure to all those inalienable rights of life, liberty, and the pursuit of happiness, with which they are endowed by their Creator, and of which none can be deprived by valid legislation, except for crime.

Second.—That the true mission of Democracy is to maintain the liberties of the people, the sovereignty of the States, and the perpetuity of the Union, by the impartial application to public affairs, without sectional discrimination, of the fundamental principles of equal rights, strict justice, and economical administration.

Third.—That the Federal Government is one of limited powers, derived solely from the Constitution, and the grants of power therein ought to be strictly construed by all the departments and agents of the Government; and it is inexpedient and dangerous to exercise doubtful constitutional powers.

Fourth.—That the early history of the Government clearly shows the settled policy to have been, not to extend, nationalise, and encourage, but to limit, localise, and discourage slavery; and to this policy, which should never have been departed from, the Government ought forthwith to return.

Fifth.—That the Constitution of the United States, ordained to form a more perfect union, to establish justice, and secure the blessings of liberty, expressly denies to the General Government any power to deprive any person of life, liberty, or property, without due process of law; and therefore the Government, having no more power to make a slave than to make a king, and no more power to establish slavery than to establish monarchy, should at once proceed to relieve itself from all responsibilities for the extension of slavery, wherever it possesses constitutional power to legislate for its extenstion.

Sixth.—That to the preserving and importunate demands of the slave power for more slave States, new slave territories, and the nationalisation of slavery, our distinct and final answer is—No more slave states, no slave territories, no nationalised slavery, and no national legislation for the extradition of slaves.

Seventh.—That the Act of Congress, known as the Compromise measures of 1850—by making the admission of a sovereign State contingent upon the adoption of other measures, demanded by the special interest of slavery—by their omission to guarantee freedom in free territories—by their attempt to impose unconstitutional limitations of the power of Congress and the people to admit new States—by their provisions for the assumption of five millions of the State debt of Texas, and for the payment of five millions more and the cession of a large territory to the same State under menace, as an inducement to the relinquishment of a groundless claim—and by their invasion of the sovereignty of the States and the liberties of the people, through the enactments of an unjust, oppressive, and unconstitutional Fugitive Slave Law, are proved to be incompatible with all the principles and maxims of Democracy, and wholly inadequate to the settlement of the questions of which they are claimed to be an adjustment.

Eighth.—That no permanent settlement of the slavery question can be looked for, except in the practical recognition of the truth that slavery is sectional and freedom national—by the total separation of the General Government from slavery, and the exercise of its legitimate and constitutional influence on the side of freedom—and by leaving to the States the whole subject of slavery and the extradition of fugitives from service.

[The next five resolutions have reference to the general politics of the country; we, therefore, pass them over, and proceed to others having reference to the anti-slavery cause.]

Fourteenth.—That slavery is a sin against God and a crime against man, the enormity of which no law nor usage can sanction or mitigate, and that Christianity and humanity alike demand its abolition.

Fifteenth.—That the Fugitive Slave Act of 1850 is repugnant to the Constitution, to the principles of the common law, to the spirit of Christianity, and to the sentiments of the civilised world—we therefore deny its binding force upon the American people, and demand its immediate and total repeal.

Sixteenth.—That the doctrine that any human law is a finality, and not subject to modification or repeal, is not in accordance with the creed of the founders of our Government, and is dangerous to the liberties of our people.

Seventeenth.—That the independence of Hayti ought to be recognised by our Government, and our commercial relations with it placed on the footing of the most favoured nations.

Eighteenth.—That it is the imperative duty of the General Government to protect all persons, of whatever colour, visiting any of the United States, from unjust and illegal imprisonment, or any other infringement of their rights.

Nineteenth.—That we recommend the introduction into all treaties hereafter to be negotiated between the United States and foreign nations of some provision for the amicable settlement of difficulties by a resort to decisive arbitration.

Twentieth.—That the Free Democratic party is not organised to aid either the Whig or the Democratic section of the great slave Compromise party of the nation, but to defeat them both; and that, repudiating and renouncing both as hopelessly corrupt, and utterly unworthy of confidence, the purpose of the Free Democracy is to take possession of the Federal Government, and administer it for the better protection of the rights and interests of the whole people.

Twenty-first.—That we inscribe on our banner, Free Soil, Free Speech, Free Labour, and Free Men, and under it will fight on, and fight ever, until a triumphant victory shall reward our exertions.

Source: Anti-Slavery Reporter (New Series), 7:81 (September 1, 1852).

The Free Produce Movement (1857)

The following excerpt is taken from Elihu Burritt's Citizen of the World:

It is certainly the fact, that movements involving political excitement and fervid speech-making present an attraction to the great majority of anti-slavery men of this country, which the quiet free-labour enterprise does not offer them. In seeking to introduce into the Southern States the enriching industry of free sinews, and to shew here and there, by repeated demonstrations, that cotton, sugar, rice, &c., may be grown by those unbought sinews more profitably than by slave-labour, although we undermine powerfully the system of Slavery, we do not array against the slaveholders that sharp and wordy antagonism which is the chief characteristic of political action. We would not insti-

tute any comparison between these two forms of effort. There is plenty of room and occasion for both. The noiseless free-labor movement has this particular merit at least: it is designed to operate in the very heart of the old Slave States, and directly upon those interests interwoven with their "peculiar institution." It is an agency calculated to make the most salutary impression upon the planter, and the poor unfortunate white man whom slavery has degraded and oppressed. We are persuaded that it is the necessary complement to all other efforts for the extinction of the cruel system of human bondage. As such, we would earnestly solicit for it the co-operation of all the friends of freedom and humanity. Let them glance at all the other operations, political, religious, and philanthropic, directed against that system at this moment, and they will find that they are almost entirely confined to the Free States, or to the Territories, and designed to affect public sentiment on action north of Mason and Dixon's line. What other effort has been set on foot for the express purpose of enlightening the people south of that line, in regard to the wrong, and waste, and wretchedness of the iniquitous system they uphold? Are there any agents, missionaries, tracts, or other instrumentalities employed to this end in those States? No. All the influences put forth upon them on this subject by the North are merely indirect and incidental. The free-labour enterprise, on the other hand, makes the South its especial field of exertion. It penetrates to the very citadel of the slave-power. It makes every acre tilled by free sinews over against the planter's estate a mute but most intelligible anti-slavery lecture, illustrated with cuts, contrasting his wasteful economy with the productive and fertilizing industry of well-paid toil. It presents a simple picture-book to the slave, with the alphabet of freedom reduced to his understanding. It comes in as a valuable auxiliary to the poor white man, to inspire him with self-respect, and to make him feel that he belongs to the great democracy of free-labour, which shall triumph gloriously in the end. For each of these three parties composing the population of the South, it works in the spirit of good-will, aiming to promote their best interests. And good-will is the most energetic sentiment wherewith to work for humanity. It works without flagging, through good and evil report. All its implements are shaped and pointed for constructions. It displaces, supplants, supersedes. It does not aim at mere demolition or uprooting. It does not seek to create a blank; but is ever erecting something. This sentiment is the motive force of the free-labour enterprise; and we hope this fact will commend it to the hearty and generous support of all the friends of freedom and righteousness who may become acquainted with its operations.

Source: Anti-Slavery Reporter (New Series), 5:3 (March 2, 1857).

British Advocacy Against the Power of "King Cotton" (1863)

England AND SLAVERY.

The Present Crisis and our Duty.

Two hundred thousand of our fellow-countrymen are on the very brink of starvation! The cause of this disaster is undeniably the failure of supply of one single article of commerce—cotton. But that cotton has a history attached to it. Every single bale of it which reached our shores was produced by a system which all English hearts abhor—a social system in which men and women work without wages under the constraint of the lash, possess no legal rights, are prohibited from learning to read God's own work, are debarred from lawful wedlock, may be separated the husband from the wife, at the caprice of a master, or to settle an account. All this is true of the system at its best, and we have driven it away as an accursed thing from our possessions.

And yet 200,000 of our manufacturing poor are starving because we have not the power of obtaining the product of slave-labour. We have fostered Slavery in America by the purchase of American cotton. Slavery only exists in South Carolina because cotton is required in Manchester; the sin would long ago have ceased to exist if we had dissolved our connection with it.

God has dissolved the connection for us which we would not dissolve for ourselves and we have at this time to feed 200,000 persons for an indefinite period, whom, for fear of this very result, we were contented to see engaged in manufacturing slave produce, and thus maintaining Slavery.

And yet, notwithstanding, some are looking forward to the conclusion of the war in America as the end of our troubles, which it can only be by a continuance of the sin both in America and in England. If the war should issue in the emancipation of the slaves, American cotton will not compete with Indian; and if Slavery remains in America, we can only find relief in that quarter by entering afresh into the unlawful traffic which the hand of God has for the time extinguished.

Large quantities of free-grown cotton from India, and Africa, and Australia, are at this time in England, and an increased demand will insure a continual supply. And India is capable of producing cotton as good and as cheap as New Orleans.

God, in his providence, is in the most marvellous way giving this country the choice between right and wrong. Here is the cotton, but the risk of having soon a large quantity of slave-grown cotton suddenly thrown into the market prevents it from being used. He, in whose hands are the tides of commerce as really as those of ocean, has so ordained that we cannot use this free-grown cotton for our own convenience unless prepared to use it in obedience to his will. We cannot have both; one must be sacrificed to the other. If we are not willing to renounce slave-grown cotton for the future, we cannot have that which is free-grown. It is a crisis in the history of our country. God grant us the grace to act in it aright!

Do English Christians think it sinful to have slaves, but not sinful to maintain Slavery? Do they think that this crushing disaster has fallen on our country without some voice of God in it? Are they willing to stake the very existence of our manufacturing population on the hope that the curse of Slavery will outlive the American war? Because, if not, let them say so. Let them say, unmistakeably, slave-grown cotton goods we will not have any more. The manufacturer who can stamp the word "free-grown" on his goods, and whose name will vouch for his honesty, will sell the only goods that will meet our wants. If Manchester will not make them, we must go to Stockport. If Stockport cannot produce them, we shall try Preston. The goods we must have. And it will be strange indeed if such a demand for an article worn all over India, free-grown cotton fabric, should fail of meeting a supply.

Such a course holds out the best hope of ultimate relief to our starving myriads, as well as of the emancipation of the negroes in America. It also tends to bring the war to a close, by diminishing the commercial value of slave-labour. But, whatever the result, it is the path of duty, and God's blessing will rest upon it. English Christians must not be partakers in other men's sins.

DECLARATION

"We the undersigned, wish to express our conviction that our country has incurred guilt in the sight of God by its maintenance of American Slavery, through the past use of slave-grown cotton, and earnestly beseech our sisters, the women of Great Britain and Ireland, to join with us in discountenancing its use in future."

(signed) _____

Source: Anti-Slavery Reporter (New Series), 2:10 (October 1, 1863).

Address to King Amadeus I of Spain (1870)

TO HIS MOST GRACIOUS MAJESTY KING AMADEUS I OF SPAIN.

May it please Your Majesty:—
The Committee of the British and Foreign Anti-Slavery Society, established many years since for the purpose of promoting, by pacific means, the total abolition of Slavery and the Slave-trade throughout the world, ask leave to present to your Majesty their respectful plea on behalf of the slaves in the Spanish possessions of Cuba and Porto Rico.

They rejoice in the conviction that the people of Spain earnestly desire the entire abolition of Slavery, and that they unite with the people of every civilised and Christian nation in the utter condemnation of the sin and injustice of holding man in forced bondage.

We cannot doubt but that the sympathies of your Majesty are strongly in favour of justice and freedom to all, and especially towards that class which has been in time past the most injured and oppressed among mankind.

Slavery derives no countenance from Christianity—on the contrary, it was condemned by its Divine Author in those memorable words, "All things whatsoever ye would that men should do to you, do ye even so to them."

It has been condemned from its origin by the Roman Catholic Church:—Pius the Second, Paul the Third, Urban the Sixth, Benedict the Fourteenth, Leo the Tenth, and Gregory the Sixteenth, have all borne emphatic testimony against the Slave-trade and Negro Slavery.

England, France, Denmark, Sweden, Holland, and the United States of America, have abolished Slavery.

We rejoice that the Spanish Cortes has given some attention to the subject, and especially that, at the proposal of the present Spanish Cabinet, it has pledged itself to an act of complete abolition in the present session.

We trust, for the sake of all parties, for the master no less than the slave, that no further delay will be allowed to take place, and that the Cortes may see the wisdom of adopting a measure of entire and immediate emancipation. Between slavery and freedom there is no safe resting-place.

It is well known that England in the first instance tried a system of apprenticeship, but its working was found so injurious, that the masters themselves were glad to displace that gradual system, and adopt immediate emancipation.

Without dwelling upon the fact at the present moment, faithfulness requires that we should state that, by virtue of existing treaties, Great Britain has a right to claim the immediate freedom of a very large proportion of those now held in slavery in Cuba and Porto Rico.

Had the claims of justice to the Slave, so urgently demanded by the people of Spain in the Autumn of 1868, been met, all the blood and treasure which has been sacrificed in Cuba since that time might have been spared.

It cannot be overlooked that a fatal persistence in maintaining Slavery brought about that tremendous civil war which recently desolated the United States of America. Although the immediate and entire emancipation of nearly four millions of Slaves in that country was effected under all the disadvantages of that fearful struggle, yet it has been attended with the most beneficial consequences—for it is a striking fact that the production of cotton and sugar in the former Slave States of America has, in the year 1869–70, been one of the largest ever known.

For the sake, therefore, of all parties in Cuba and Porto Rico—for the sake of the great people of Spain—for the honour of your Royal House, which has not been wont to rule over slaves; in the name of humanity and of the sacred religion of Christ, we respectfully, but earnestly, entreat your Majesty to inaugurate your reign by insisting on the restoration of liberty to the Slave, in depriving him of which no human power could ever be justified.

It is righteousness which exalteth a nation, and proves the stability of governments.

May the reign of your Majesty be established by righteousness and justice, that so the blessing of the Most High may rest upon you, upon your august Queen, and upon the people of Spain.

We are,
Your Majesty's humble, obedient servants,

Signed on behalf of the Committee,
JOSEPH COOPER,
EDMUND STURGE, *Hon. Secs.*
ROBERT ALSOP.

27, New Broad Street, London,
December 31st, 1870.

Source: Anti-Slavery Reporter, 17:5 (April 1, 1871).

Address of the Spanish Abolition Society to the Senate in Madrid (1872)

Madrid, September 22, 1872.

The undersigned, President, Vice-President, Secretaries, and members of the Sociedad Abolicionista Española, approach the Senate respectfully, representing:—

First. That the definite Law of Abolition, promised in Moret's Preparatory Law of 4th July, 1870, and which has also been repeatedly and solemnly promised by the Spanish Government, both before the Chambers and to Foreign Cabinets, is not yet introduced or promulgated.

Secondly. That Moret's Preparatory Law of 1870, itself, in spite of professed urgency has in its principal articles, been in suspense till the publication, in the *Gazette* of Aug. 19, of the Rules (*Reglamento*) for its working.

Thirdly. That the Reglamento referred to not only omits completely the grave matter consulted upon with the Capt.-General of Cuba, respecting the fulfilment of Article 5 of the said Preparatory Law, but by the nature of many of its dispositions renders necessary another new Reglamento, creating institutions, respecting whose significance there cannot be the least doubt.

Fourthly. That the slaves who are free by right, through the insurgents having renounced dominion over them, and who, according to Article 5 of the Law of 1870, cannot be held by the State, as it is forbidden to the State to possess slaves, are nevertheless retained in slavery. The state holding them by confiscation, but contrary to law.

Fifthly. That to the non-fulfilment of the Preparatory Law has been added the non-fulfilment of the promises made by many slave-owners in Cuba, to send to the Government a project of Abolition, according to official telegrams of the 2nd and 15th of July, 1870.

Sixthly. That there constantly appear in the official *Gazette* of Porto Rico concessions of freedom made by masters to their slaves in that Island. The number of slaves existing there in 1868 was 43,361, but has now been reduced by voluntary manumission to 31,041.

Seventhly. That the insurrection of Cuba has produced the dispersion or death of two-thirds of the slaves of the Central and Eastern Departments of the Island, who in 1862 amounted to nearly 180,000 persons.

Eighthly. That, according to official declarations, the base of the Cuban insurrection at present is formed of slaves and Chinese vagabonds.

Considering, therefore,—

1. That "Slavery is an outrage on human nature, and a stain on the only nation in the civilised world which retains it," according to the eloquent and manly declaration of the Revolutionary Junta of Madrid, on the 15th of October, 1868.

2. That Slavery is utterly incomprehensible in the dominions of a people who, like the Spaniards, procuring for themselves and by themselves the Constitution of 1869, have recognised the existence of the natural and inherent rights of man.

3. That as often as our Antilles have been consulted on the subject, numerous Spaniards there have proposed to the mother country the Abolition of Slavery, as is proved by the Reports of the Commissioners of 1866, and the projects presented and sustained by the Porto Rico Deputies in all the Cortes to which they have been called.

4. That the question of Slavery being a question of the Rights of Man, the Ministers and representatives of the great free peoples of the world have protested against it, and against the conduct of the Spanish Government; and there has at this moment been initiated abroad a grand movement of public opinion against our attitude, the results of which we ought to foresee, and the disgrace of which we ought not to incur.

5. That the ill-result of the Preparatory Law of 1870 does not cause surprise to those who know the history of Emancipation, where it has proved that measures of that nature have always failed, and the Legislators have had to accord new and radical ones, like that of immediate Abolition, as happened in Jamaica, in St. Thomas, in the French Colonies, and as at this moment happening in Brazil.

6. THAT THE ABOLITION OF SLAVERY AT THIS PRESENT TIME WILL BE A Measure HIGHLY Political TO END THE INSURRECTION IN CUBA, WHILE ITS DELAY MAY HELP THE

Resistance, AS HAPPENED IN 1793 AND 1804 IN THE ISLAND OF SANTO DOMINGO.

THE UNDERSIGNED THEREFORE PRAY THE SENATE TO PROCEED TO THE DISCUSSION AND VOTATION OF A DEFINITE LAW FOR THE IMMEDIATE ABOLITION OF SLAVERY IN CUBA AND PORTO RICO.

FERNANDO DE CASTRO.
FRANCISCO PI Y MARGALL.
JOAQUIN M. SANROMA.
GABRIEL RODRIGUEZ.
RAFAEL M. DE LABRA.
EMILIO CASTELAR.
MANUEL RUIZ DE QUEVEDO.
FRANCISCO GINER.
ESTANISLAO FIGUERAS.
FRANCISCO DIAZ QUINTERO.
JOSE FRENANDO GONZALES.
LUIS PADIAL.
MANUEL REGIDOR.
RAFAEL CERVERA.
EDUARDO CHAO.
BERNARDO GARCIA.
LUIS VIDART.
NICOLAS SALMERON.
FELIX DE BONA.
FRANCISCO DELGADO JUGO.
JULIO VIZCARRONDO.
RICARDO LOPEZ VAZQUEZ.
F. FACUNDO CINTRON.

Source: Anti-Slavery Reporter, 18:4 (January 1, 1873).

Memorial to the Marquis of Salisbury on the Slave Trade and Slavery in Afghanistan (1874)

TO THE RIGHT HONOURABLE THE MARQUIS OF SALISBURY, HER MAJESTY'S PRINCIPAL SECRETARY OF STATE FOR INDIA.

My Lord,—

The Committee of the British and Foreign Anti-Slavery Society beg respectfully to call your Lordship's attention to the slave-trade and slavery, as existing very extensively throughout the Affghan territories, the Ameer of which receives annually a large subsidy from the British Indian Government.

Your Memorialists are informed that slave-marts, some of which are very large, are found in most of the principal cities, where the slaves are bought and sold like cattle, while at times the most revolting cruelties are practised.

To meet the demand for slaves, raids are made by the Ameer's soldiers on adjacent territory, and by merchants and traders on the weaker tribes near Chitral, the hindu Kush, and other localities. These slave-hunts are carried out on a very extensive scale, as may be instanced in the case of a late Governor of Faizabad, Mir Ghulam Bey, who had eight thousand horse in his employ, whose only occupation was to scour the country for the purpose of kidnapping. The sunni merchants of Badakhshan also capture all whom they can seize, and not only sell the shiahs, who are considered infidels, and therefore legitimate subjects for sale, but also compel their Sunni co-religionists to undergo the severest torments to induce them to avow themselves shiahs and so become liable for sale.

Your Memorialists would especially and earnestly solicit your Lordship's attention to the slave-hunts by the Affghans against the Siah Posh Kafirs, supposed to be a colony of about three hundred thousand white persons planted in the Hindu Kush mountains by Alexander the Great, and to possess some knowledge of the Christian religion, in which they have been further instructed by native Christian evangelists. These people have had to suffer lamentably from the kidnapping expeditions of the Affghans.

Your Memorialists learn that, so long as their invaders possessed only the ordinary weapons of the country, the Siah Posh Kafirs resisted the forces of the Affghan chiefs. Since, however, the Ameer has become a feudatory of the Indian Government, and received yearly large sums of money, and several thousands of the latest improved fire-arms, it is feared the colony will eventually be subdued and enslaved; a calamity the more to be deplored, as it will thus be brought about by the aid afforded to a Mahommedan ruler from a Christian nation whose policy has been to exterminate the slave-trade and slavery wherever found.

Your Memorialists would also observe, that the said raid against the Siah Posh Kafirs, and their consequent retaliation on Mahommedan travelers, renders the roads in the direct route between Turkistan and the Punjab so insecure as to stop commercial intercourse altogether, or to compel merchants and traders to make a long detour, either *via* Yarkand or Kabul, in their journeys, involving a serious loss of time and property.

Your Memorialists learn with much satisfaction that since His Imperial majesty the Emperor of Russia has been pleased to induce the Khans of Khiva and Bokhara to suppress the slave-trade and slavery in their territories, a very great check has been given to the slave-hunts in the exposed districts.

Your Memorialists respectfully submit that as the Ameer, Sheer Ali, is a feudatory of, and is in the receipt annually of a considerable subsidy of money and arms from Her Majesty's Government in India, that his attention should be called to the subject, and that her Majesty's Government should use their influence, as promptly as practicable, with the Sovereign of Affghanistan for the extinction of slavery in his dominions.

In thus respectfully urging this important subject on the attention of your Lordship, the Committee feel assured that the object they have in view will meet with your Lordship's sympathy and interest, and with that of the British nation at large.

On behalf of the Committee of the British and Foreign Anti-Slavery Society,
We are, very respectfully,
JOSEPH COOPER,
EDMUND STURGE, *Hon. Secs.*
ROBERT ALSOP,
BENJAMIN MILLARD, *Sec.*

27, New Broad Street, London,
12th March, 1874

Source: *Anti-Slavery Reporter*, 19:2 (April 1, 1874)

The Anti-Slavery Jubilee (1884)

An interview with C.H. Allen, the Secretary of the Anti-Slavery Society.

August 1, 1834, was a great day for England and for humanity, . . . and the popular rejoicings which took place on that occasion are among the most vivid recollections of my boyhood. Slavery was a terrible reality to us in those days, a monster, the horror and the shame of which was keenly felt by the nation. Half a century has rolled by, since then; in fifty years a new generation has grown up, which finds it difficult, not to say impossible, to recall the enthusiasm that animated our fathers. Slavery is to Englishmen a thing with which they have no personal concern. Its moral leprosy does not cleave to our garments, and we are therefore supposed to be free from any necessity to bestir ourselves in the matter. We paid £20,000,000. We liberated our slaves. That was our share. Let other nations follow our example. We have done enough. That in a rough way represents the feeling of En-

glishmen to-day. There is no longer among us a Clarkson or a Wilberforce, nor do we support the cause for which they laboured with anything approaching to the liberality and devotion which enabled them to carry their cause to victory in spite of almost insurmountable obstacles.

The work of abolition was perhaps always more or less the work of a few. There was no doubt a very widespread sympathy for the cause in the abstract, but its chief promoters and sustainers were from the first a mere handful of public-spirited men, largely recruited from the Society of Friends; and although some of them are still with us they have not bequeathed their zeal to their successors. Were it not so our society would not be left to carry on the crusade against the sum of all villanies with an annual revenue of £200 a year, which has to be supplemented by liberal donations from a few generous supporters.

There is a prejudice existing against our society in some quarters owing to the mistaken belief that we advocate war as a means of suppressing slavery. It is a total mistake. Quakers are not wont to found societies for waging war even against slavery, and as a matter of fact our constitution strictly provides that the extinction of slavery is to be sought by "the employment of those means which are of a moral, religious, and pacific character." The only basis for the popular calumny is that we have maintained, and as long as we continue to exist will continue to maintain, that wherever the British flag flies no slave shall breathe, and that the rights and interests of all emancipated slaves shall be cared for as sedulously as the property of their former owners. We do not seek to extend the sovereignty of England in the hope that the conqueror will prove an emancipator. We only insist that when the soldier has made his conquests the legislator shall not forget his responsibilities. In other words, that when England has exerted her power she shall not neglect her duty. Our society has been a sort of conscience to the empire, and it will be an evil day for the coloured man when England allows that conscience to be silenced by their neglect.

Another delusion not less mischievous is the idea prevailing in some quarters that our work is done, that slavery is extinct, and that there is therefore no need of any further sacrifices to carry "the civilizing torch of freedom" among the nations of the earth. Would that it were the case! No one would rejoice more than I if our society had attained that supreme object of its existence, and could cease to exist because there was no longer a slave to free. But surely the most careless cannot have forgotten Africa. That is one of the most populous of continents; but it is, from the Mediterranean to the Indian Ocean, a continent of slaves. A great reservoir of slaves—a vast arena of slave raids; the hunting ground of slave traders, whose map is threaded by slave routes, and whose roads are marked by the bleaching skulls of the victims of the slaver. A dark continent truly, the mere overflow of which fills Moslem Asia with slaves. There is work in Africa alone for a dozen societies such as ours. But Africa is not the only continent where there is great and urgent need for the exertions of the Argus eye of organized philanthropy. Turn where we will, one can hardly fail to see some territory blighted by some form of slavery.

Before passing in review the field yet to be won for freedom, I would like just to say a word upon the triumphs already attained. Briefly stated; we may say that all European Powers but Spain have recognized that the owning of slaves is an offence against humanity, not to be tolerated by any of their subjects. That is a great gain. Russia has emancipated all her serfs; slavery has ceased to be legal in British India; the legal status of slavery has been suppressed in West Africa; and the American Union has purged itself from the guilt of slavery in one of the most tremendous wars of modern times. Nor is it only civilized nations that have placed slavery outside the pale of the law. The Bey of Tunis abolished slavery before his dominions were absorbed by France. Emancipation follows the wake of Russian conquest in Central Asia. In Brazil and Cuba gradual emancipation offers a prospect of the entire extinction of slavery before many years are past. So that we may say with truth that civilization is now almost entirely free from the older forms of slavery and the slave trade.

That is a great deal to be thankful for. But the world is not half civilised, and even in the civilised regions new forms of servitude are continually springing up which recall the worst horrors of the old Slavery. Look at China. There are probably at this moment fifty million Slaves in that great empire. We can do nothing for them, but at Hong Kong, at our treaty ports, and elsewhere we might do much more than we do to enforce the sound principle of personal freedom. We cannot hinder the Chinese having Slaves, but we might more vigorously punish British subjects who keep Slaves, and above all, we should repress the horrible custom, largely prevailing in Hong Kong, of importing female Slaves for immoral purposes. It is a veritable Slave-trade of the worst kind. The girls are bought and sold like sheep, and their fate is unspeak-

able infamy. Yet this goes on every day under the British flag. At the Straits settlements, also, there prevails an elaborate system of domestic Slavery with which it is most difficult to deal. If a man gets into debt he can pawn himself, his wife, and all his children to his creditor, who becomes to all intents and purposes his owner. It is a bad system, and it is one of the many reasons for the necessity for constant vigilance. Another illustration of the need for watchfulness is afforded by the labour traffic of the Southern Seas. There under the British flag Englishmen have established a system of labour-recruiting which in many respects is identical with the Slave-trade. Efforts have been made to regulate it, but hitherto they have failed. Its total abolition seems the only way out of the difficulty. Whenever you have coloured men employed by whites you have a great temptation that the latter will reduce the former to a condition of vassalage indistinguishable from Slavery. Take the case of Queensland. We look with the gravest suspicion upon the attempts to import Cinghalese coolies to work the sugar plantations on the coast. Malabar blacks might do, but Cinghalese, who at home never work on their own coffee plantations, have been carried off to Brisbane and set to work which must be fatal. The whole of the coolie traffic requires the most vigorous overhauling. The regulations that have been framed in order to ensure that the coolie labourer knows where he is going and the terms of his engagement are much too laxly enforced; but we greatly doubt whether any system of coolie immigration can be framed which would not lead to gross abuse.

In India we believe that male slavery has practically ceased since 1843 by the simple operation of abolishing the legal status of the slave. But among women in the secret recesses of the harem, into which no man can penetrate, a good deal of slavery lingers, to await exposure and extinction at the hands of some future Mrs. Fry. Traveling further west we come to the French colony of Réunion, where a form of slavery still exists under the euphemism of the *engagée* system. Thanks largely to the attention called to it by this society, Lord Hartington, when Secretary for India, entirely suppressed the emigration of coolies from India to the French colonies. We could get no security for their good treatment, and it was the right thing to do. But the immediate result was to precipitate the French upon Madagascar, where they hope to find a fresh recruiting ground for their planters.

We have now come to Africa, the continent of the slave. The utmost that we can do seems less than nothing compared with the magnitude of the evil with which we are struggling. Our only hope of suppressing the slave trade in Africa is by stopping the demand for slaves in Egypt and outside the borders. No cruisers will be able to prevent swift Arab dhows slipping across the Red Sea, laden to the gunwale with the wretched victims of slave traders in the Soudan. The law governing the seizure of slavers is shamefully lax. If a slaver can run his dhow ashore he can land his cargo beneath the guns of our cruisers, who can only make seizures on the high seas. Then, again, the slaver has only to secure a French flag, and he is free from all danger. If a captain make a technical mistake, although morally he may have been right, he is compelled to pay heavy damages to the rascally owner of the disguised slaver. Altogether it is a bad business. We do not believe in cruisers; but if you have a squadron detailed for the suppression of the slave trade, it should not be compelled to work under impossible conditions. Something might be done by holding the Red Sea ports, but our great reliance must always be on diminishing the demand. So far as one great slave market is concerned, it is not difficult. Egypt lies in the hollow of our hand. Why can we not do there as we do in India, and induce the Khedive to issue a decree declaring that the legal status of slavery is abolished, and thereby allowing all slaves to free themselves, if, and when they pleased? Sir Evelyn Baring objects to this, but if we wield supreme power in Egypt I hardly see how we can continue to evade our responsibilities. Pressure brought to bear on Turkey to increase the severity of the regulations against the slave trade might do something in Arabia; but so long as these regions remain Mahommedan, so long is it to be feared they will drain the life-blood of Africa, in spite of all that we can do. In Northern Africa slavery exist[s] unabashed in Morocco, and our British Resident seldom lifts a finger to induce his Imperial protégé to suppress the slave markets which disgrace Tangiers. On the western coast the slave trade has ceased to exist in the cessation of the demand for slaves from the New World. Further south there is reason to fear that the Portuguese have established a system differing little from slavery—a strong reason for rejoicing that the recent attempt to extend her dominion to the Congo has been promptly checked.

Across the Atlantic the emancipation of the slaves in the Southern States, although effected in the worst way, has been a great economical success. The free South raises more cotton than ever was raised by slave labour; and although the negro citizen is by no means perfect, he is, with all his faults, higher in the scale of manhood than when he was a slave. In Cuba we have one of the black spots of the world. It is cursed by slavery to this day, and the half-hearted attempts of the Spanish Government to rid the Pearl of the Antilles from this dark stain have met with a very partial success. In our own West Indian possessions the chief complaint is that the emancipated negro is too comfortable to work. He is not too comfortable to work for himself, nor would he refuse to work for others at a reasonable wage. That he is not reluctant to labour may be seen from the fact that thousands have flocked to the Panama Canal to work as navvies under m. de Lesseps. In South America slow but steady progress is being made in Brazil, the only slave State left in the New World. There are nearly 1,500,000 slaves still to be emancipated, and only one province in the empire is entirely free.

To sum up, we have still to uproot slavery of the old kind from Cuba and Brazil. We have to suppress domestic slavery in the Straits Settlements and in Egypt; we have to put down the labour traffic in the Pacific, and to discountenance in every way the importation of coolie traffic to the Mauritius, Queensland, and the West Indies. We have to bring pressure to bear upon the French and Portuguese to prevent the re-establishment of slavery under a nominal apprenticeship, and we have to seek a modification of the laws which at present cripple the efficiency of our squadron on the East Coast of Africa. And, above all, we have to keep our eyes fixed on that open sore of the world, the African slave trade, and compel the civilised world to realise the horrors that are ceaselessly enacted on the Dark Continent.

These things are beyond the strength of a society inadequately supported as ours. We do what we can; but if the work is to be kept up in a proper style, it will have to be properly supported. We sadly want a few hundred fresh annual subscribers of one guinea each. Surely rich anti-slavery England might furnish these.

Source: Anti-Slavery Reporter (Series IV), 4 (October 1884).

Legislation and Court Cases and Decisions

Throughout history, individuals have questioned the extent to which morality can be legislated upon a populace that is unwilling to accept such an imposed change. In similar fashion, many have questioned the wisdom of judicial pronouncements promulgated by so-called "activist" judges who seek to impose their will through selective interpretation of the law. Efforts to legislate and decree public policy in this way sometimes have been considered a form of social engineering, whereby controversial policies are given the force of law, despite widespread public opposition.

Many abolitionists of the late eighteenth and early nineteenth centuries based their antislavery rhetoric on the premise that moral suasion could effectively dismantle the apparatus of slavery that had been built over the course of several centuries. They believed that those who supported slavery could be persuaded—through logical reasoning and moral arguments—to see the error of their ways and be swayed to support the abolitionist cause. Such notions of transformation and atonement were appealing to many abolitionists who believed that civil dialogue and powerful testimony of faith were the only prompts needed to redeem the nation. In reality, however, the majority of proslavery supporters were well entrenched in their views and not inclined to change their ways.

The issue was complicated by the position of abolitionists such as William Lloyd Garrison, who urged his supporters to disavow the U.S. Constitution, which he viewed as a proslavery document. By dismissing any constitutional means to effect change, these radical abolitionists severely limited the courses of action that antislavery advocates could pursue.

Moral suasion alone might have ended slavery—if it were possible for society to recognize and accept a code of universally sanctioned ethics and agree that such a code proscribed slavery as an unacceptable practice. Unfortunately, the persistence of some forms of slavery even into the twenty-first century indicates that such a noble gesture has not prevailed. As a result, positive action through legislative bodies and the courts has been the most effective means of transforming antislavery thought into public policy.

No one should imagine that legislative action and court decrees alone can provide a perfect remedy to slavery or deliver emancipation to those held in bondage. Effective enforcement mechanisms are necessary to guarantee that public policy decisions are honored within the political community, and the success of those enforcement efforts depends on the level of commitment of political authorities. Government-sanctioned noncompliance can render laws and court rulings useless and maintain the status quo of the old order.

Although some of the more radical abolitionists advocated violence as a means of overthrowing the slaveholding regime and supported slave insurrections, such methods did not find widespread support within the antislavery community. Most abolitionists recognized that a solution to the slavery question had to be found within the political order of the day. Instead of violence, they sought to use constitutional prerogatives—executive, legislative, and judicial—to hasten the demise of slavery. Laws alone might not transform the hearts and minds of proslavery advocates, but antislavery legislation was far more effective than any extralegal action could ever be.

Although some individuals resisted legal efforts to abolish slavery, the governments of the transatlantic world generally dedicated themselves to enforcing the law, as the following documents illustrate. Though enforcement was sometimes lax, societal transformation began to occur. As the social and economic structures that supported slavery were dismantled, former slave owners found new means to operate in a world that was profoundly transformed.

The Yorke-Talbot Slavery Opinion (1729)

We are of Opinion, That a slave by coming from the West Indies to Great Britain or Ireland, either with or without his master, doth not become free, and that his Master's Property or Right in him is not thereby determined or varied: And that Baptism doth not bestow freedom on him, or make any Alteration in his Temporal Condition in these kingdoms. We are also of Opinion, that His Majesty may legally compel him to return again to the Plantations.

Source: Gentleman's Magazine, 1740, 126–27.

Lord Mansfield's Decision in Knowles v. Somersett (1772)

We pay due attention to the opinion of *Sir Philip Yorke* and Mr. *Talbot*, in the year 1729, by which they pledged themselves to the British planters for the legal consequences of bringing Negroe-slaves into this kingdom, or their being baptized; which opinion was repeated and recognized by lord Hardwicke, sitting as chancellor, on the 19th of October, 1749, to the following effect: he said: "that trover would lay for a negroe-slave: that a notion prevailed, that if a slave came into England, or became a Christian, he thereby became emancipated; but there was no foundation in law for such a notion: that when he and Lord Talbot were attorney and solicitor general, this notion of a slave becoming free by being baptized prevailed so strongly, that the planters industriously prevented their becoming Christians: upon which their opinion was taken; and *upon their best consideration they were both clearly of opinion,* that a slave did not in the least alter his situation or state towards his master or *owner,* either by being christened, or coming to England: that though the statute of Charles II. Had abolished tenure so far, that no man could be a *Villein regardant*; yet if he would acknowledge himself a *Villein* engrossed in any court of record, he knew of no way by which he could be entitled to his freedom, without the consent of his master." We feel the force of the inconveniences and consequences that will follow the decision of this question: yet all of us are so clearly of one opinion upon the *only* question before us, that we think we ought to give judgment without adjourning the matter to be argued before all the judges, as usual in the habeas corpus, and as we at first intimated an intention of doing in this case. The only question then is, *Is the cause returned sufficient for the remanding him? If not,* he must be discharged. The cause returned is, the *slave* absented himself and departed from his master's service, and refused to return and serve him during his stay in *England*; whereupon, by his master's orders, he was put on board the ship by force, and there detained in secure custody, to be carried out of the kingdom and sold. So high an act of dominion must derive its authority, if any such it has, from the law of the kingdom *where* executed. A foreigner cannot be imprisoned *here* on the authority of any law existing in his own country. The power of a master over his servant is different in all countries, more or less limited or extensive, the exercise of it therefore must always be regulated by the laws of the place where exercised. The state of slavery is of such a nature, that it is incapable of being now introduced by courts of justice upon mere reasoning, or inferences from any principles natural or political; it must take its rise from *positive law*; the origin of it can in no country or age be traced back to any other source. Immemorial usage preserves the memory of *positive law* long after all traces of the occasion, reason, authority, and time of its introduction, are lost, and IN A CASE SO ODIOUS AS THE CONDITION OF SLAVES MUST BE TAKEN STRICTLY. (*Tracing the subject to natural principles, the claim of slavery can never be supported.*) THE POWER CLAIMED BY THIS RETURN WAS NEVER IN USE Here: (*or acknowledged by the law.*) No master ever was allowed here to take a slave by force to be sold abroad because he had deserted from his service, or for any other reason whatever; WE CANNOT SAY, *the cause set forth by this return* IS ALLOWED OR APPROVED OF BY THE LAWS OF THIS KINGDOM, *and therefore the man must be discharged.*

Source: Granville Sharp, The Just Limitation of Slavery in the Laws of God, Compared With the Unbounded Claims of the African Traders and British American Slaveholders. London, 1776.

Pennsylvania Abolishes Slavery (1780)

An Act for the Gradual Abolition of Slavery.

[Section] I. When we contemplate our abhorrence of that condition to which the arms and tyranny of Great Britain were exerted to reduce us, when we look back on the variety of dangers to which we have been exposed, and how miraculously our wants in many instances have been supplied, and our deliverances wrought, when even hope and human fortitude have become unequal to the conflict, we are unavoidably led to a serious and grateful sense of the manifold blessings, which we have undeservedly received from the hand of that Being from whom every good and perfect gift cometh. Impressed with these ideas, we conceive that it is our duty, and we rejoice that it is in our power to extend a portion of that freedom to others which hath been extended to us, and release from that state of thraldom to which we ourselves were tyrannically doomed, and from which we now have every prospect of being delivered. It is not for us to inquire why in the creation of mankind the inhabitants of several parts of the earth were distinguished by a difference in feature or complexion. It is sufficient to know that all are the work of an Almighty Hand. We find in the distribution of the human species that the most fertile as well as the most barren parts of the earth are inhabited by Men of complexions different from ours and from each other; from whence we may reasonably as well as religiously infer that He who placed them in their various situations, hath extended equally His care and protection to all, and that it becometh not us to counteract His mercies.

We esteem it a peculiar blessing granted to us, that we are enabled this day to add one more step to universal civilization, by removing as much as possible the sorrows of those who have lived in undeserved bondage, and from which by the assumed authority of the Kings of Great Britain no effectual legal relief could be obtained. Weaned, by a long course of experience, from those narrow prejudices and partialities we have imbibed, we find our hearts enlarged with kindness and benevolence toward men of all conditions and nations, and we perceive ourselves at this particular period extraordinarily called upon by the blessings which we have received, to manifest the sincerity of our profession to give substantial proof of our gratitude.

[Section] II. And, whereas, the condition of those persons who have heretofore been denominated Negro and Mulatto slaves, has been attended with circumstances which not only deprived them of the common blessings that they were by nature entitled to, but has cast them into the deepest afflictions by an unnatural separation and sale of husband and wife from each other and from their children, an injury the greatness of which can only be conceived by supposing that we were in the same unhappy case. In justice, therefore, to persons so unhappily circumstanced, and who, having no prospect before them whereon they may rest their sorrows and hopes, have no reasonable inducement to render their services to society, which they

otherwise might, and also in grateful commemoration of our own happy deliverance from that state of unconditional submission to which we were doomed by the tyranny of Britain.

[Section] III. *Be it enacted, and it is hereby enacted,* That all persons as well Negroes and Mulattoes, as others, who shall be born within this State from and after the passing of this act shall not be deemed and considered as servants for life, or slaves; and that all servitude for life, or slavery of children in consequence of the slavery of their mothers, in the case of all children born within this State from and after the passing of this act, as aforesaid, shall be, and hereby is, utterly taken away, extinguished, and forever abolished.

[Section] IV. *Provided always, and be it further enacted,* That every Negro and Mulatto child, born within this State after the passing of this act as aforesaid (who would, in case this act had not been made, have been born a servant for years, or life, or a slave) shall be deemed to be, and shall be, by virtue of this act, the servant of such person, or his or her assigns, who would in such case have been entitled to the service of such child, until such child shall attain the age of twenty-eight years, in the manner, and on the conditions, whereon servants bound, by indenture for four years are or may be retained and holden; and shall be liable to like corrections and punishment, and entitled to like relief, in case he or she be evilly treated by his or her master or mistress, and to like freedom dues and other privileges, as servants bound by indenture for four years are or may be entitled, unless the person, to whom the service of any such child shall belong, shall abandon his or her claim to the same; in which case the Overseers of the Poor of the city, township, or district, respectively, where such child shall be abandoned, shall, by indenture, bind out every child so abandoned, as an apprentice, for a time not exceeding the age herein before limited for the service of such children.

[Section] V. *And be it further enacted,* That every person, who is or shall be the owner of any Negro or Mulatto slave or servant for life, or till the age of thirty-one years, now within this State, or his lawful attorney, shall, on or before the said first day of November next, deliver, or cause to be delivered, in writing, to the Clerk of the peace of the county, or to Clerk of the court of record of the city of Philadelphia, in which he or she shall respectively inhabit, the name and surname, and occupation or profession of such owner, and the name of the county and township, district or ward, wherein he or she resideth; and also the name and names of such slave and slaves, and servant and servants for life, or till the age of thirty-one years, together with their ages and sexes, severally and respectively set forth and annexed, by such persons owned or statedly employed, and then being within this State, in order to ascertain and distinguish the slaves and servants for life, and till the age of thirty-one years, within this State, who shall be such on the said first day of November next, from all other persons; which particulars shall, by said Clerk of the sessions and Clerk of the said city court, be entered in books to be provided for that purpose by the said Clerks; and that no Negro or Mulatto, now within this State, shall, from and after the said first day of November, be deemed a slave or servant for life, or till the age of thirty-one years, unless his or her name shall be entered as aforesaid on such record, except such Negro and Mulatto slaves and servants as herein excepted; the said Clerk to be entitled to a fee of two dollars for each slave or servant so entered as aforesaid, from the Treasurer of the county to be allowed to him in his accounts.

[Section] VI. *Provided always,* That any person, in whom the ownership or right to the service of any Negro or Mulatto shall be vested at the passing of this act, other than such as are hereinbefore accepted, his or her heirs, executors, administrators, and assigns, and all and every of them, severally, shall be liable to the Overseers of the city, township, or district, to which any such Negro or Mulatto shall become chargeable, for such necessary expense, with costs of suit thereon, as such Overseers may be put to through the neglect of the owner, master, or mistress of such Negro or Mulatto, notwithstanding the name and other descriptions of such Negro or Mulatto shall not be entered as aforesaid, unless his or her master or owner shall, before such slave or servant attain his or her twenty-eighth year, execute and record in the proper county, a deed or instrument, securing to such slave or servant his or her freedom.

[Section] VII. *And be it further enacted,* That the offences and crimes of Negroes and Mulattoes, as well slaves and servants as freemen, shall be enquired of, adjudged, corrected, and punished, in like manner as the offences and crimes of the other inhabitants of this State are, and shall be enquired of, adjudged, corrected, and punished, and not otherwise, except that a slave shall not be admitted to bear witness against a freeman.

[Section] VIII. *And be it further enacted,* That in all cases wherein sentence of death shall be pronounced against a slave, the jury before whom he or she shall be tried shall appraise and declare the value of such slave; and in such case sentence be executed, the court shall make an order on the State Treasurer, payable to the owner for the same, and for the costs of prosecution, but in case of remission or mitigation, for costs only.

[Section] IX. *And be it further enacted,* That the reward for taking up runaway and absconding Negro and Mulatto slaves and servants, and the penalties for enticing away, dealing with or harboring, concealing or employing Negro and Mulatto slaves and servants, shall be the same, and shall be recovered in like manner, as in case of servants bound for four years.

[Section] X. *And be it further enacted,* That no man or woman of any nation, or color, except the Negroes or Mulattoes who shall be registered as aforesaid, shall, at any time, be deemed, adjudged, and holden within the territories of this commonwealth as slaves and servants for life, but as free men and free women; except the domestic slaves attending upon Delegates in Congress from other American States, foreign Ministers and Consuls, and persons passing through or sojourning in this State, and not becoming resident therein, and seamen employed in ships not belonging to any inhabitant of this State, nor employed in any ship owned by such inhabitants; provided such domestic slaves be not aliened or sold to any inhabitant, nor (except in the case of Members of Congress, foreign Ministers and Consuls) retained in this State longer than six months.

[Section] XI. *Provided always, and be it further enacted,* That this act, or anything in it contained, shall not give any relief or shelter to any absconding or runaway Negro or Mulatto slave or servant, who has absented himself or shall absent himself, from his or her owner, master or mistress, residing in any other State or country, but such owner, master or mistress, shall have like right and aid to demand, claim, and take away his slave or servant, as he might have had in case this act had not been made; and that all Negro and Mulatto slaves now owned and heretofore resident in this State, who have absented themselves, or been clandestinely carried away, or who may be employed abroad as seamen, and have not returned or been brought back to their owner, masters or mistresses, before the passing of this act, may, within five years, be registered, as effectually as is ordered by this act concerning those who are now within the State, on producing such slave before any two Justices of the Peace, and satisfying the said Justices, by due proof, of the former residence, absconding, taking away, or absence of such slaves as aforesaid, who thereupon shall direct and order the said slave to be entered on the record as aforesaid.

[Section] XII. And whereas attempts may be made to evade this act, by introducing into this State Negroes and Mulattoes bound by covenant to serve for long and unreasonable terms of years, if the same be not prevented.

[Section] XIII. *Be it therefore enacted,* That no covenant of personal servitude or apprenticeship whatsoever shall be valid or binding on a Negro or Mulatto for a longer time than seven years, unless such servant or apprentice were, at the commencement of such servitude or apprenticeship, under the age of twenty-one years, in which case such Negro or Mulatto may be holden as a servant or apprentice, respectively, according to the covenant, as the case shall be, until he or she shall attain the age of twenty-eight years, but no longer.

[Section] XIV. *And be it further enacted,* That an act of Assembly of the Province of Pennsylvania, passed in the year one thousand seven hundred and five, entitled *An Act for the trial of Negroes*; and another act of Assembly of the said Province, passed in the year one thousand seven hundred and twenty-five, entitled *An Act for the better regulating of Negroes in this Province*; and another act of Assembly of the said Province, passed in the year one thousand seven hundred and sixty-one, entitled *An Act for laying a duty on Negro and Mulatto slaves imported into this Province*; and also another act of Assembly of the said Province, passed in the year one thousand seven hundred and seventy-three, entitled *An Act for making perpetual an act for laying a duty on Negro and Mulatto slaves imported into this Province, and for laying an additional duty on said slaves*, shall be, and are hereby, repealed, annulled, and made void.

John Bayard, Speaker
Enacted into a Law at Philadelphia on
Wednesday the first day of March, A.D. 1780
Thomas Paine, Clerk of the General Assembly.

Source: Pennsylvania Law Book, vol. I; text from William Henry Egle, *History of the Counties of Dauphin and Lebanon, in the Commonwealth of Pennsylvania: Biographical and Genealogical.* Philadelphia: Everts & Peck, 1883.

The Northwest Ordinance (1787)

An Ordinance for the government of the Territory of the United States northwest of the River Ohio,
July 13, 1787.

Be it ordained by the United States in Congress assembled, That the said territory, for the purposes of temporary government, be one district, subject, however, to be divided into two districts, as future circumstances may, in the opinion of Congress, make it expedient.

Be it ordained by the authority aforesaid, That the estates, both of resident and nonresident proprietors in the said territory, dying intestate, shall descent to, and be distributed among their children, and the descendants of a deceased child, in equal parts; the descendants of a deceased child or grandchild to take the share of their deceased parent in equal parts among them: And where there shall be no children or descendants, then in equal parts to the next of kin in equal degree; and among collaterals, the children of a deceased brother or sister of the intestate shall have, in equal parts among them, their deceased parents' share; and there shall in no case be a distinction between kindred of the whole and half blood; saving, in all cases, to the widow of the intestate her third part of the real estate for life, and one third part of the personal estate; and this law relative to descents and dower, shall remain in full force until altered by the legislature of the district. And until the governor and judges shall adopt laws as hereinafter mentioned, estates in the said territory may be devised or bequeathed by wills in writing, signed and sealed by him or her in whom the estate may be (being of full age), and attested by three witnesses; and real estates may be conveyed by lease and release, or bargain and sale, signed, sealed and delivered by the person being of full age, in whom the estate may be, and attested by two witnesses, provided such wills be duly proved, and such conveyances be acknowledged, or the execution thereof duly proved, and be recorded within one year after proper magistrates, courts, and registers shall be appointed for that purpose; and personal property may be transferred by delivery; saving, however to the French and Canadian inhabitants, and other settlers of the Kaskaskies, St. Vincents and the neighboring villages who have heretofore professed themselves citizens of Virginia, their laws and customs now in force among them, relative to the descent and conveyance, of property.

Be it ordained by the authority aforesaid, That there shall be appointed from time to time by Congress, a governor, whose commission shall continue in force for the term of three years, unless sooner revoked by Congress; he shall reside in the district, and have a freehold estate therein in 1,000 acres of land, while in the exercise of his office.

There shall be appointed from time to time by Congress, a secretary, whose commission shall continue in force for four years unless sooner revoked; he shall reside in the district, and have a freehold estate therein in 500 acres of land, while in the exercise of his office. It shall be his duty to keep and preserve the acts and laws passed by the legislature, and the public records of the district, and the proceedings of the governor in his executive department, and transmit authentic copies of such acts and proceedings, every six months, to the Secretary of Congress: There shall also be appointed a court to consist of three judges, any two of whom to form a court, who shall have a common law jurisdiction, and reside in the district, and have each therein a freehold estate in 500 acres of land while in the exercise of their offices; and their commissions shall continue in force during good behavior.

The governor and judges, or a majority of them, shall adopt and publish in the district such laws of the original States, criminal and civil, as may be necessary and best suited to the circumstances of the district, and report them to Congress from time to time: which laws shall be in force in the district until the organization of the General Assembly therein, unless disapproved of by Congress; but afterwards the Legislature shall have authority to alter them as they shall think fit.

The governor, for the time being, shall be commander in chief of the militia, appoint and commission all officers in the same below the rank of general officers; all general officers shall be appointed and commissioned by Congress.

Previous to the organization of the general assembly, the governor shall appoint such magistrates and other civil officers in each county or township, as he shall find necessary for the preservation of the peace and good order in the same: After the general assembly shall be organized, the powers and duties of the magistrates and other civil officers shall be regulated and defined by the said assembly; but all magistrates and other civil officers not herein otherwise directed, shall during the continuance of this temporary government, be appointed by the governor.

For the prevention of crimes and injuries, the laws to be adopted or made shall have force in all parts of the district, and for the execution of process, criminal and civil, the governor shall make proper divisions thereof; and he shall proceed from time to time as circumstances may require, to lay out the parts of the district in which the Indian titles shall have been extinguished, into counties and townships, subject, however, to such alterations as may thereafter be made by the legislature.

So soon as there shall be five thousand free male inhabitants of full age in the district, upon giving proof thereof to the governor, they shall receive authority, with time and place, to elect a representative from their counties or townships to represent them in the general assembly: *Provided,* That, for every five hundred free male inhabitants, there shall be one representative, and so on progressively with the number of free male inhabitants shall the right of representation increase, until the number of representatives shall amount to twenty five; after which, the number and proportion of representatives shall be regulated by the legislature: *Provided,* That no person be eligible or qualified to act as a representative unless he shall have been a citizen of one of the United States three years, and be a resident in the district, or unless he shall have resided in the district three years; and, in either case, shall likewise hold in his own right, in fee simple, two hundred acres of land within the same; *Provided, also,* That a freehold in fifty acres of land in the district, having been a citizen of one of the states, and being resident in the district, or the like freehold and two years residence in the district, shall be necessary to qualify a man as an elector of a representative.

The representatives thus elected, shall serve for the term of two years; and, in case of the death of a representative, or removal from office, the governor shall issue a writ to the county or township for which he was a member, to elect another in his stead, to serve for the residue of the term.

The general assembly or legislature shall consist of the governor, legislative council, and a house of representatives. The Legislative Council shall consist of five members, to continue in office five years, unless sooner removed by Congress; any three of whom to be a quorum: and the members of the Council shall be nominated and appointed in the following manner, to wit: As soon as representatives shall be elected, the Governor shall appoint a time and place for them to meet together; and, when met, they shall nominate ten persons, residents in the district, and each possessed of a freehold in five hundred acres of land, and return their names to Congress; five of whom

Congress shall appoint and commission to serve as aforesaid; and, whenever a vacancy shall happen in the council, by death or removal from office, the house of representatives shall nominate two persons, qualified as aforesaid, for each vacancy, and return their names to Congress; one of whom Congress shall appoint and commission for the residue of the term. And every five years, four months at least before the expiration of the time of service of the members of council, the said house shall nominate ten persons, qualified as aforesaid, and return their names to Congress; five of whom Congress shall appoint and commission to serve as members of the council five years, unless sooner removed. And the governor, legislative council, and house of representatives, shall have authority to make laws in all cases, for the good government of the district, not repugnant to the principles and articles in this ordinance established and declared. And all bills, having passed by a majority in the house, and by a majority in the council, shall be referred to the governor for his assent; but no bill, or legislative act whatever, shall be of any force without his assent. The governor shall have power to convene, prorogue, and dissolve the general assembly, when, in his opinion, it shall be expedient.

The governor, judges, legislative council, secretary, and such other officers as Congress shall appoint in the district, shall take an oath or affirmation of fidelity and of office; the governor before the president of Congress, and all other officers before the Governor. As soon as a legislature shall be formed in the district, the council and house assembled in one room, shall have authority, by joint ballot, to elect a delegate to Congress, who shall have a seat in Congress, with a right of debating but not voting during this temporary government.

And, for extending the fundamental principles of civil and religious liberty, which form the basis whereon these republics, their laws and constitutions are erected; to fix and establish those principles as the basis of all laws, constitutions, and governments, which forever hereafter shall be formed in the said territory: to provide also for the establishment of States, and permanent government therein, and for their admission to a share in the federal councils on an equal footing with the original States, at as early periods as may be consistent with the general interest:

It is hereby ordained and declared by the authority aforesaid, That the following articles shall be considered as articles of compact between the original States and the people and States in the said territory and forever remain unalterable, unless by common consent, to wit:

Art[icle] 1. No person, demeaning himself in a peaceable and orderly manner, shall ever be molested on account of his mode of worship or religious sentiments, in the said territory.

Art[icle] 2. The inhabitants of the said territory shall always be entitled to the benefits of the writ of *habeas corpus,* and of the trial by jury; of a proportionate representation of the people in the legislature; and of judicial proceedings according to the course of the common law. All persons shall be bailable, unless for capital offenses, where the proof shall be evident or the presumption great. All fines shall be moderate; and no cruel or unusual punishments shall be inflicted. No man shall be deprived of his liberty or property, but by the judgment of his peers or the law of the land; and, should the public exigencies make it necessary, for the common preservation, to take any person's property, or to demand his particular services, full compensation shall be made for the same. And, in the just preservation of rights and property, it is understood and declared, that no law ought ever to be made, or have force in the said territory, that shall, in any manner whatever, interfere with or affect private contracts or engagements, *bona fide,* and without fraud, previously formed.

Art[icle] 3. Religion, morality, and knowledge, being necessary to good government and the happiness of mankind, schools and the means of education shall forever be encouraged. The utmost good faith shall always be observed towards the Indians; their lands and property shall never be taken from them without their consent; and, in their property, rights, and liberty, they shall never be invaded or disturbed, unless in just and lawful wars authorized by Congress; but laws founded in justice and humanity, shall from time to time be made for preventing wrongs being done to them, and for preserving peace and friendship with them.

Art[icle] 4. The said territory, and the States which may be formed therein, shall forever remain a part of this Confederacy of the United States of America, subject to the Articles of Confederation, and to such alterations therein as shall be constitutionally made; and to all the acts and ordinances of the United States in Congress assembled, conformable thereto. The inhabitants and settlers in the said territory shall be subject to pay a part of the federal debts contracted or to be contracted, and a proportional part of the expenses of government, to be apportioned on them by Congress according to the same common rule and measure by which apportionments thereof shall be made on the other States; and the taxes for paying their proportion shall be laid and levied by the authority and direction of the legislatures of the district or districts, or new States, as in the original States, within the time agreed upon by the United States in Congress assembled. The legislatures of those districts or new States, shall never interfere with the primary disposal of the soil by the United States in Congress assembled, nor with any regulations Congress may find necessary for securing the title in such soil to the *bona fide* purchasers. No tax shall be imposed on lands the property of the United States; and, in no case, shall nonresident proprietors be taxed higher than residents. The navigable waters leading into the Mississippi and St. Lawrence, and the carrying places between the same, shall be common highways and forever free, as well to the inhabitants of the said territory as to the citizens of the United States, and those of any other States that may be admitted into the confederacy, without any tax, impost, or duty therefor.

Art[icle] 5. There shall be formed in the said territory, not less than three nor more than five States; and the boundaries of the States, as soon as Virginia shall alter her act of cession, and consent to the same, shall become fixed and established as follows, to wit: The western State in the said territory, shall be bounded by the Mississippi, the Ohio, and Wabash Rivers; a direct line drawn from the Wabash and Post Vincents, due North, to the territorial line between the United States and Canada; and, by the said territorial line, to the Lake of the Woods and Mississippi. The middle State shall be bounded by the said direct line, the Wabash from Post Vincents to the Ohio, by the Ohio, by a direct line, drawn due north from the mouth of the Great Miami, to the said territorial line, and by the said territorial line. The eastern State shall be bounded by the last mentioned direct line, the Ohio, Pennsylvania, and the said territorial line: *Provided, however,* and it is further understood and declared, that the boundaries of these three States shall be subject so far to be altered, that, if Congress shall hereafter find it expedient, they shall have authority to form one or two States in that part of the said territory which lies north of an east and west line drawn through the southerly bend or extreme of Lake Michigan. And, whenever any of the said States shall have sixty thousand free inhabitants therein, such State shall be admitted, by its delegates, into the Congress of the

United States, on an equal footing with the original States in all respects whatever, and shall be at liberty to form a permanent constitution and State government: *Provided,* the constitution and government so to be formed, shall be republican, and in conformity to the principles contained in these articles; and, so far as it can be consistent with the general interest of the confederacy, such admission shall be allowed at an earlier period, and when there may be a less number of free inhabitants in the State than sixty thousand.

Art[icle] 6. There shall be neither slavery nor involuntary servitude in the said territory, otherwise than in the punishment of crimes whereof the party shall have been duly convicted: *Provided, always,* That any person escaping into the same, from whom labor or service is lawfully claimed in any one of the original States, such fugitive may be lawfully reclaimed and conveyed to the person claiming his or her labor or service as aforesaid.

Be it ordained by the authority aforesaid, That the resolutions of the 23rd of April, 1784, relative to the subject of this ordinance, be, and the same are hereby repealed and declared null and void.

Source: "The Northwest Ordinance," in *Documents of American History,* 7th ed., ed. Henry Steele Commager. New York: Appleton-Century-Crofts, 1963.

Declaration of the Rights of Man and of the Citizen (1789)

The representatives of the French people, organized as a National Assembly, believing that the ignorance, neglect, or contempt of the rights of man are the sole cause of public calamities and of the corruption of governments, have determined to set forth in a solemn declaration the natural, unalienable, and sacred rights of man, in order that this declaration, being constantly before all the members of the Social body, shall remind them continually of their rights and duties; in order that the acts of the legislative power, as well as those of the executive power, may be compared at any moment with the objects and purposes of all political institutions and may thus be more respected, and, lastly, in order that the grievances of the citizens, based hereafter upon simple and incontestable principles, shall tend to the maintenance of the constitution and redound to the happiness of all.

Therefore the National Assembly recognizes and proclaims, in the presence and under the auspices of the Supreme Being, the following rights of man and of the citizen:

Articles:

1. Men are born and remain free and equal in rights. Social distinctions may be founded only upon the general good.
2. The aim of all political association is the preservation of the natural and imprescriptible rights of man. These rights are liberty, property, security, and resistance to oppression.
3. The principle of all sovereignty resides essentially in the nation. No body nor individual may exercise any authority which does not proceed directly from the nation.
4. Liberty consists in the freedom to do everything which injures no one else; hence the exercise of the natural rights of each man has no limits except those which assure to the other members of the society the enjoyment of the same rights. These limits can only be determined by law.
5. Law can only prohibit such actions as are hurtful to society. Nothing may be prevented which is not forbidden by law, and no one may be forced to do anything not provided for by law.
6. Law is the expression of the general will. Every citizen has a right to participate personally, or through his representative, in its foundation. It must be the same for all, whether it protects or punishes. All citizens, being equal in the eyes of the law, are equally eligible to all dignities and to all public positions and occupations, according to their abilities, and without distinction except that of their virtues and talents.
7. No person shall be accused, arrested, or imprisoned except in the cases and according to the forms prescribed by law. Any one soliciting, transmitting, executing, or causing to be executed, any arbitrary order, shall be punished. But any citizen summoned or arrested in virtue of the law shall submit without delay, as resistance constitutes an offense.
8. The law shall provide for such punishments only as are strictly and obviously necessary, and no one shall suffer punishment except it be legally inflicted in virtue of a law passed and promulgated before the commission of the offense.
9. As all persons are held innocent until they shall have been declared guilty, if arrest shall be deemed indispensable, all harshness not essential to the securing of the prisoner's person shall be severely repressed by law.
10. No one shall be disquieted on account of his opinions, including his religious views, provided their manifestation does not disturb the public order established by law.
11. The free communication of ideas and opinions is one of the most precious of the rights of man. Every citizen may, accordingly, speak, write, and print with freedom, but shall be responsible for such abuses of this freedom as shall be defined by law.
12. The security of the rights of man and of the citizen requires public military forces. These forces are, therefore, established for the good of all and not for the personal advantage of those to whom they shall be intrusted.
13. A common contribution is essential for the maintenance of the public forces and for the cost of administration. This should be equitably distributed among all the citizens in proportion to their means.
14. All the citizens have a right to decide, either personally or by their representatives, as to the necessity of the public contribution; to grant this freely; to know to what uses it is put; and to fix the proportion, the mode of assessment and of collection and the duration of the taxes.
15. Society has the right to require of every public agent an account of his administration.
16. A society in which the observance of the law is not assured, nor the separation of powers defined, has no constitution at all.
17. Since property is an inviolable and sacred right, no one shall be deprived thereof except where public necessity, legally determined, shall clearly demand it, and then only on condition that the owner shall have been previously and equitably indemnified.

Approved by the National Assembly of France, August 26, 1789

Source: French National Assembly, "Declaration of the Rights of Man—1798." Avalon Project at Yale Law School, http://www.yale.edu/lawweb/avalon/rightsof.htm.

The Fugitive Slave Act (1793)

An Act respecting fugitives from justice, and persons escaping from the service of their masters.

Section 1. *Be it enacted by the Senate and House of Representatives of the United States of America in Congress assem-*

bled, That whenever the executive authority of any state in the Union, or of either of the territories northwest or south of the river Ohio, shall demand any person as a fugitive from justice, of the executive authority of any such state or territory to which such person shall have fled, and shall moreover produce the copy of an indictment found, or an affidavit made before a magistrate of any state or territory as aforesaid, charging the person so demanded, with having committed treason, felony or other crime, certified as authentic by the governor or chief magistrate of the state or territory from whence the person so charged fled, it shall be the duty of the executive authority of the state or territory to which such person shall have fled, to cause him or her to be arrested and secured, and notice of the arrest to be given to the executive authority making such demand, or to the agent of such authority appointed to receive the fugitive, and to cause the fugitive to be delivered to such agent when he shall appear: But if no such agent shall appear within six months from the time of the arrest, the prisoner may be discharged. And all costs or expenses incurred in the apprehending, securing, and transmitting such a fugitive to the state or territory making such demand, shall be paid by such state or territory.

Sec[tion] 2. *And be it further enacted*, That any agent, appointed as aforesaid, who shall receive the fugitive into his custody, shall be empowered to transport him or her to the state or territory from which he or she shall have fled. And if any person or persons shall by force set at liberty, or rescue the fugitive from such agent while transporting, as aforesaid, the person or persons so offending shall, on conviction, be fined not exceeding five hundred dollars, and be imprisoned not exceeding one year.

Sec[tion] 3. *And be it also enacted*, That when a person held to labour in any of the United States, or in either of the territories on the northwest or south of the river Ohio, under the laws thereof, shall escape into any other of the said states or territory, the person to whom such labour or service may be due, his agent or attorney, is hereby empowered to seize or arrest such fugitive from labour, and to take him or her before any judge of the circuit or district courts of the United States, residing or being within the state, or before any magistrate of a county, city or town corporate, wherein such seizure or arrest shall be made, and upon proof to the satisfaction of such judge or magistrate, either by oral testimony or affidavit taken before and certified

by a magistrate of any such state or territory, that the person so seized or arrested, doth, under the laws of the state or territory from which he or she fled, owe service or labour to the person claiming him or her, it shall be the duty of such judge or magistrate to give a certificate thereof to such claimant, his agent or attorney, which shall be sufficient warrant for removing the said fugitive from labour, to the state or territory from which he or she fled.

Sec[tion] 4. *And be it further enacted*, That any person who shall knowingly and willingly obstruct or hinder such claimant, his agent or attorney in so seizing or arresting such fugitive from labour, or shall rescue such fugitive from such claimant, his agent or attorney when so arrested pursuant to the authority herein given or declared; or shall harbor or conceal such person after notice that he or she was a fugitive from labour, as aforesaid, shall, for either of the said offences, forfeit and pay the sum of five hundred dollars. Which penalty may be recovered by and for the benefit of such claimant, by action of debt, in any court proper to try the same; saving moreover to the person claiming such labour or service, his right of action for or on account of the said injuries or either of them.

APPROVED, February 12, 1793.

Source: Laws of the United States, vol. 2 (2nd Cong., 1st and 2nd sess., 1791–1793). Philadelphia: Richard Folwell, 1796.

An Act Prohibiting Entry of Slaves into Non-Slave States (1803)

An Act to Prevent the Importation of Certain Persons Into Certain States, Where, by the Laws Thereof, Their Admission Is Prohibited.

[Section 1.] *Be it enacted by the Senate and House of Representatives of the United States of America in Congress assembled,* That from and after the first day of April next, no master or captain of any ship or vessel, or any other person, shall import or bring, or cause to be imported or brought, any negro, mulatto, or other person of colour, not being a native, a citizen, or registered seaman of the United States, or seamen natives of countries beyond the Cape of Good Hope, into any port or place of the United States, which port or place shall be situated in any state which by law has prohibited or shall prohibit the admission or importation of such negro, mulatto, or other person of colour, and if any captain or master aforesaid, or any other person, shall import or bring, or cause to be imported or brought into any of the ports or places aforesaid, any of the persons whose admission or importation is prohibited, as aforesaid, he shall forfeit and pay the sum of one thousand dollars for each and every negro, mulatto, or other person of colour aforesaid, brought or imported as aforesaid, to be sued for and recovered by action of debt, in any court of the United States; one half thereof to the use of the United States, the other half to any person or persons prosecuting for the penalty; and in any action instituted for the recovery of the penalty aforesaid, the person or persons sued may be held to special bail: Provided always, that nothing contained in this act shall be construed to prohibit the admission of Indians.

Section 2. *And be it further enacted,* That no ship or vessel arriving in any of the said ports or places of the United States, and having on board any negro, mulatto, or other person of colour, not being a native, a citizen, or registered seaman of the United States, or seamen natives of countries beyond the Cape of Good Hope as aforesaid, shall be admitted to an entry. And if any such negro, mulatto, or other person of colour, shall be landed from on board any ship or vessel, in any of the ports or places aforesaid, or on the coast of any state prohibiting the admission or importation, as aforesaid, the said ship or vessel, together with her tackle, apparel, and furniture, shall be forfeited to the United States, and one half of the nett proceeds of the sales on such forfeiture shall inure and be paid over to such person or persons on whose information the seizure on such forfeiture shall be made.

Section 3. *And be it further enacted,* That it shall be the duty of the collectors and other officers of the customs, and all other officers of the revenue of the United States, in the several ports or places situated as aforesaid, to notice and be governed by the provisions of the laws now existing, of the several states prohibiting the admission or importation of any negro, mulatto, or other person of colour, as aforesaid. And they are hereby enjoined vigilantly to carry into effect the said laws of said states, conformably to the provisions of this act; any law of the United States to the contrary notwithstanding.

APPROVED, February 28, 1803.

Source: Laws of the United States, vol. 6 (7th Cong., 1st and 2nd sess., 1801–1803). Philadelphia: Matthew Cary, 1804.

Great Britain's Slave Trade Act (1807)

An Act for the Abolition of the Slave Trade.

[I.] Whereas the Two Houses of Parliament did, by their Resolutions of the Tenth and Twenty-fourth Days of June One thousand eight hundred and six, severally resolve, upon certain Grounds therein mentioned, that they would, with all practicable Expedition, take effectual Measures for the Abolition of the African Slave Trade, in such Manner, and at such Period as might be deemed adviseable: And Whereas it is fit upon all and each of the Grounds mentioned in the said Resolutions, that the same should be forthwith abolished and prohibited, and declared to be unlawful;

[B]e it therefore enacted by the King's most Excellent Majesty, by and with the Advice and Consent of the Lords Spiritual and Temporal, and Commons, in this present Parliament assembled, and by the Authority of the same, That from and after the First Day of May One thousand eight hundred and seven, the African Slave Trade, and all and all manner of dealing and trading in the Purchase, Sale, Barter, or Transfer of Slaves, or of Persons intended to be sold, transferred, used, or dealt with as Slaves, practised and carried on, in, at, to or from any Part of the Coast or Countries of Africa, shall be, and the same is hereby utterly abolished, prohibited, and declared to be unlawful; and also that all and all manner of dealing, either by way of Purchase, Sale, Barter, or Transfer, or by means of any other Contract or Agreement whatever, relating to any Slaves, or to any Persons intended to be used or dealt with as Slaves, for the Purpose of such Slaves or Persons being removed and transported either immediately or by Transhipment at Sea or otherwise, directly or indirectly from Africa, or from any Island, Country, Territory, or Place whatever, in the West Indies, or in any other Part of America, not being in the Dominion, Possession, or Occupation of His Majesty, to any other Island, Country, Territory or Place whatever, is hereby in like Manner utterly abolished, prohibited, and declared to be unlawful; and if any of His Majesty's Subjects, or any Person or Persons resident within this United Kingdom, or any of the Islands, Colonies, Dominions, or Territories thereto belonging, or in His Majesty's Occupation or Possession, shall from and after the Day aforesaid, by him or themselves, or by his or their Factors or Agents or otherwise howsoever, deal or trade in, purchase, sell, barter, or transfer, or contract or agree for the dealing or trading in, purchasing, selling, bartering, or transferring of any Slave or Slaves, or any Person or Persons intended to be sold, transferred, used, or dealt with as a Slave or Slaves contrary to the Prohibitions of this Act, he or they so offending shall forfeit and pay for every such Offence the Sum of One hundred Pounds of lawful Money of Great Britain for each and every Slave so purchased, sold, bartered, or transferred, or contracted or agreed for as aforesaid, the One Moiety thereof to the Use of His Majesty, His Heirs and Successors, and the other Moiety to the Use of any Person who shall inform, sue, and prosecute for the same.

II. And be it further enacted, That from and after the said First Day of May One thousand eight hundred and seven, it shall be unlawful for any of His Majesty's Subjects, or any Person or Persons resident within this United Kingdom, or any of the Islands, Colonies, Dominions or Territories thereto belonging, or in His Majesty's Possession or Occupation, to fit out, man, or navigate, or to procure to be fitted out, manned, or navigated, or to be concerned in the fitting out, manning, or navigating, or in the procuring to be fitted out, manned, or navigated, any Ship or vessel for the Purpose of assisting in, or being employed in the carrying on of the African Slave Trade, or in any other the Dealing, Trading, or Concerns hereby prohibited and declared to be unlawful, and every Ship or Vessel which shall, from and after the Day aforesaid, be fitted out, manned, navigated, used, or employed by any such Subject or Subjects, Person or Persons, or on his or their Account, or by his or their Assistance or Procurement for any of the Purposes aforesaid, and by this Act prohibited, together with all her Boats, Guns, Tackle, Apparel, and Furniture, shall become forfeited, and may and shall be seized and prosecuted as hereinafter is mentioned and provided.

III. And be it further enacted, That from and after the said First Day of May One thousand eight hundred and seven, it shall be unlawful for any of His Majesty's Subjects, or any Person or Persons resident in this United Kingdom, or in any of the Colonies, Territories, or Dominions thereunto belonging, or in His Majesty's Possession or Occupation, to carry away or remove, or knowingly and wilfully to procure, aid, or assist in the carrying away or removing, as Slaves, or for the Purpose of being sold, transferred, used, or dealt with as Slaves, any of the Subjects or Inhabitants of Africa, or of any Island, Country, Territory, or Place in the West Indies, or any other Part of America, whatso-

ever, not being in the Dominion, Possession, or Occupation of His Majesty, either immediately or by Transhipment at Sea or otherwise, directly or indirectly from Africa, or from any such Island, Country, Territory, or Place as aforesaid, to any other Island, Country, Territory, or Place whatever, and that it shall also be unlawful for any of His Majesty's Subjects, or any Person or Persons resident in this United Kingdom, or in any of the Colonies, Territories, or Dominions thereunto belonging, or in His Majesty's Possession or Occupation, knowingly and wilfully to receive, detain, or confine on board, or to be aiding, assisting, or concerned in the receiving, detaining, or confining on board of any Ship or Vessel whatever, any such Subject or Inhabitant as aforesaid, for the purpose of his or her being so carried away or removed as aforesaid, or of his or her being sold, transferred, used, or dealt with as a Slave in any, Place or Country whatever; and if any Subject or Inhabitant, Subjects or Inhabitants of Africa, or of any Island, Country, Territory, or Place in the West Indies or America, not being in the Dominion, Possession or Occupation of His Majesty, shall from and after the Day aforesaid, be so unlawfully carried away or removed, detained, confined, transhipped, or received on board of any Ship or Vessel belonging in the Whole or in Part to, or employed by any Subject of His Majesty, or Person residing in His Majesty's Dominions or Colonies, or any Territory belonging to or in the Occupation of His Majesty, for any of the unlawful Purposes aforesaid, contrary to the Force and Effect, true Intent and Meaning of the Prohibitions in this Act contained, every such Ship or Vessel in which any such Person or Persons shall be so unlawfully carried away or removed, detained, confined, transhipped, or received on board for any of the said unlawful Purposes together with all her Boats, Guns, Tackle, Apparel, and Furniture, shall be forfeited, and all Property or pretended Property in any Natives of Africa so unlawfully carried away or removed, detained, confined, transhipped or received on board, shall also be forfeited and the same respectively shall and may be seized and prosecuted as herein-after is mentioned and provided; and every Subject of His Majesty, or Person resident within this United Kingdom, or any of the Islands, Colonies, Dominions, or Territories thereto belonging, or in His Majesty's Possession or Occupation, who shall, as Owner, Part Owner, Freighter or Shipper, Factor or Agent, Captain, Mate, Supercargo, or Surgeon, so unlawfully carry away, or remove, detain, confine, tranship, or receive on board, for any of the unlawful

Purposes aforesaid, any such Subject or Inhabitant of Africa, or of any Island, Country, Territory, or Place, not being in the Dominion, Possession, or Occupation of His Majesty, shall forfeit and pay for each and every Slave or Person so unlawfully carried away, removed, detained, confined, transhipped, or received on board, the Sum of One hundred Pounds of lawful Money of Great Britain, One Moiety thereof to the Use of His Majesty, and the other Moiety to the Use of any Person who shall inform, sue, and prosecute for the same.

IV. And be it further enacted, That if any Subject or Inhabitant, Subjects or Inhabitants of Africa, or of any Island, Country, Territory, or Place, not being in the Dominion, Possession, or Occupation of His Majesty, who shall, at any Time from and after the Day aforesaid, have been unlawfully carried away or removed from Africa, or from any Island, Country, Territory, or Place in the West Indies or America, not being in the Dominion, Possession, or Occupation of His Majesty, contrary to any of the Prohibitions or Provisions in this Act contained, shall be imported or brought into any Island, Colony, Plantation, or Territory, in the Dominion, Possession, or Occupation of His Majesty, and there sold or disposed of as a Slave or Slaves, or placed, detained, or kept in a State of Slavery, such Subject or Inhabitant, Subjects or Inhabitants, so unlawfully carried away, or removed and imported, shall and may be seized and prosecuted as forfeited to His Majesty, by such Person or Persons, in such Courts, and in such Manner and Form, as any Goods or Merchandize unlawfully imported into the same Island, Colony, Plantation, or Territory, may now be seized and prosecuted therein by virtue of any Act or Acts of Parliament now in force for regulating the Navigation and Trade of His Majesty's Colonies and Plantations and shall and may, after his or their Condemnation, be disposed of in Manner herein-after mentioned and provided.

V. And be it further enacted, That from and after the said First Day of May One thousand eight hundred and seven, all Insurances whatsoever to be effected upon or in respect to any of the trading, dealing, carrying, removing, transhipping, or other Transactions by this Act prohibited, shall be also prohibited and declared to be unlawful; and if any of His Majesty's Subjects, or any Person or Persons resident within this United Kingdom, or within any of the Islands, Colonies, Dominions, or Territories thereunto belonging, or in His Majesty's Possession or Occupation, shall knowingly and wilfully subscribe, effect, or make, or

cause or procure to be subscribed, effected, or made, any such unlawful Insurances or Insurance, he or they shall forfeit and pay for every such Offence the Sum of One hundred Pounds for every such Insurance, and also Treble the Amount paid or agreed to be paid as the Premium of any such Insurance, the One Moiety thereof to the Use of His Majesty, His Heirs and Successors, and the other Moiety to the Use of any Person who shall inform, sue, and prosecute for the same.

VI. Provided always, That nothing herein contained shall extend, or be deemed or construed to extend, to prohibit or render unlawful the dealing or trading in the Purchase, Sale, Barter, or Transfer, or the carrying away or removing for the Purpose of being sold, transferred, used, or dealt with as Slaves, or the detaining or confining for the Purpose of being so carried away or removed, of any Slaves which shall be exported, carried, or removed from Africa, in any Ship or Vessel which, on or before the said First Day of May One thousand eight hundred and seven, shall have been lawfully cleared out from Great Britain according to the Law now in force for regulating the carrying of Slaves from Africa, or to prohibit or render unlawful the manning or navigating any such Ship or Vessel, or to make void any Insurance thereon, so as the Slaves to be carried therein shall be finally landed in the West Indies on or before the First Day of March One thousand eight hundred and eight, unless prevented by Capture, the Loss of the Vessel, by the Appearance of an Enemy upon the Coast, or other unavoidable Necessity, the Proof whereof shall lie upon the Party charged; any Thing herein-before contained to the contrary notwithstanding.

VII. And Whereas it may happen, That during the present or future Wars, Ships or Vessels may be seized or detained as Prize, on board whereof Slaves or Natives of Africa, carried and detained as Slaves, being the Property of His Majesty's Enemies, or otherwise liable to Condemnation as Prize of War, may be taken or found, and it is necessary to direct in what Manner such Slaves or Natives of Africa shall be hereafter treated and disposed of: And Whereas it is also necessary to direct and provide for the Treatment and Disposal of any Slaves or Natives of Africa carried, removed, treated or dealt with as Slaves, who shall be unlawfully carried away or removed contrary to the Prohibitions aforesaid, or any of them, and shall be afterwards found on board any Ship or Vessel liable to Seizure under this Act, or any other Act of Parliament made for restraining or prohibiting the African

Slave Trade, or shall be elsewhere lawfully seized as forfeited under this or any other such Act of Parliament as aforesaid; and it is expedient to encourage the Captors, Seizors and Prosecutors thereof; Be it therefore further enacted, That all Slaves and all Natives of Africa, treated, dealt with, carried, kept or detained as Slaves, which shall at any Time from and after the said First Day of May next be seized or taken as Prize of War, or liable to Forfeiture, under this or any other Act of Parliament made for restraining or prohibiting the African Slave Trade, shall and may for the Purposes only of Seizure, Prosecution, and Condemnation as Prize or as Forfeitures, be considered, treated, taken, and adjudged as Slaves and Property, in the same Manner as Negro Slaves have been heretofore considered, treated, taken, and adjudged, when seized as Prize of War, or as forfeited for any Offence against the Laws of Trade and Navigation respectively; but the same shall be condemned as Prize of War, or as forfeited to the sole Use of His Majesty, His Heirs and Successors, for the Purpose only of divesting and barring all other Property, Right, Title, or Interest whatever, which before existed, or might afterwards be set up or claimed in or to such Slaves or Natives of Africa so seized, prosecuted and condemned; and the same nevertheless shall in no case be liable to be sold, disposed of, treated or dealt with as Slaves, by or on the Part of His Majesty, His Heirs or Successors, or by or on the Part of any Person or Persons claiming or to claim from, by or under His Majesty, His Heirs and Successors, or under or by force of any such Sentence of Condemnation: Provided always, that it shall be lawful for His Majesty, His Heirs and Successors, and such Officers, Civil or Military, as shall, by any general or special Order of the King in Council, be from Time to Time appointed and empowered to receive, protect, and provide for such Natives of Africa as shall be so condemned, either to enter and enlist the same, or any of them, into His Majesty's Land or Sea Service as Soldiers, Seamen or Marines, or to bind the same, or any of them, whether of full Age or not, as Apprentices, for any Term not exceeding Fourteen Years, to Such Person or Persons, in such Place or Places, and upon such Terms and Conditions, and subject to such Regulations, as to His Majesty shall seem meet, and shall by any general or special Order of His Majesty in Council be in that Behalf directed and appointed; and any Indenture of Apprenticeship duly made and executed, by any Person or Persons to be for that Purpose appointed by any such Order in Council, for any Term not exceeding Fourteen Years,

shall be of the same Force and Effect as if the Party thereby bound as an Apprentice had himself or herself, when of full Age upon good Consideration, duly executed the same; and every such Native of Africa who shall be so enlisted or entered as aforesaid into any of His Majesty's Land or Sea Forces as a Soldier, Seaman, or Marine, shall be considered, treated, and dealt with in all Respects as if he had voluntarily so enlisted or entered himself.

VIII. Provided also, and be it further enacted, That where any Slaves or Natives of Africa, taken as Prize of War by any of His Majesty's Ships of War, or Privateers duly commissioned, shall be finally condemned as such to His Majesty's Use as aforesaid, there shall be paid to the Captors thereof by the Treasurer of His Majesty's Navy, in like Manner as the Bounty called Head Money is now paid by virtue of an Act of Parliament, made in the Forty-fifth Year of His Majesty's Reign, intituled, *An Act for the Encouragement of Seamen, and for the better and more effectually manning His Majesty's Navy during the present War,* such Bounty as His Majesty, His Heirs and Successors, shall have directed by any Order in Council, so as the same shall not exceed the Sum of Forty Pounds lawful Money of Great Britain for every Man, or Thirty Pounds of like Money for every Woman, or Ten Pounds of like Money for every Child or Person not above Fourteen Years old, that shall be so taken and condemned, and shall be delivered over in good Health to the proper Officer or Officers, Civil or Military, so appointed as aforesaid to receive, protect, and provide for the same; which Bounties shall be divided amongst the Officers, Seamen, Marines, and Soldiers on board His Majesty's Ships of War, or hired armed Ships, in Manner, Form, and Proportion, as by His Majesty's Proclamation for granting the Distribution of Prizes already issued, or to be issued for that Purpose is or shall be directed and appointed, and amongst the Owners, Officers, and Seamen of any private Ship or Vessel of War, in such Manner and Proportion as, by an Agreement in Writing that they shall have entered into for that Purpose, shall be directed.

IX. Provided always, and be it further enacted, That in order to entitle the Captors to receive the said Bounty Money, the Numbers of Men, Women, and Children, so taken, condemned, and delivered over, shall be proved to the Commissioners of His Majesty's Navy, by producing, instead of the Oaths and Certificates prescribed by the said Act as to Head Money, a Copy, duly certified, of the Sentence or Decree of

Condemnation whereby the Numbers of Men, Women, and Children, so taken and condemned, shall appear to have been distinctly proved; and also, by producing a Certificate under the Hand of the said Officer or Officers, Military or Civil, so appointed, as aforesaid, and to whom the same shall have been delivered, acknowledging that he or they hath or have received the same, to be disposed of according to His Majesty's Instructions and Regulations as aforesaid.

X. Provided also, and be it further enacted, That in any Cases in which Doubts shall arise whether the Party or Parties claiming such Bounty Money is or are entitled thereto, the same shall be summarily determined by the Judge of the High Court of Admiralty, or by the Judge of any Court of Admiralty in which the Prize shall have been adjudged, subject nevertheless to an Appeal to the Lords Commissioners of Appeals in Prize Causes.

XI. Provided also, and be it further enacted, That on the Condemnation to the Use of His Majesty, His Heirs and Successors, in Manner aforesaid, of any Slaves or Natives of Africa, seized and prosecuted as forfeited for any Offence against this Act, or any other Act of Parliament made for restraining or prohibiting the African Slave Trade (except in the Case of Seizures made at Sea by the Commanders or Officers of His Majesty's Ships or Vessels of War) there shall be paid to and to the Use of the Person who shall have sued, informed, and prosecuted the same to Condemnation, the Sums of Thirteen Pounds lawful Money aforesaid for every Man, of Ten Pounds like Money for every Woman, and of Three Pounds like Money for every Child or Person under the Age of Fourteen Years, that shall be so condemned and delivered over in good Health to the said Civil or Military Officer so to be appointed to receive, protect, and provide for the same, and also the like Sums to and to the Use of the Governor or Commander in Chief of any Colony or Plantation wherein such Seizure shall have been made; but in Cases of any such Seizures made at Sea by the Commanders or Officers of His Majesty's Ships or Vessels of War, for Forfeiture under this Act, or any other Act of Parliament made for restraining or prohibiting the African Slave Trade, there shall be paid to the Commander or Officer who shall so seize, inform, and prosecute, for every Man so condemned and delivered over, the Sum of Twenty Pounds like Money, for every Woman the Sum of Fifteen Pounds like Money, and for every Child or Person under the Age of Fourteen Years the Sum of Five Pounds like

Money, subject nevertheless to such Distribution of the said Bounties or Rewards for the said Seizures made at Sea as His Majesty, His Heirs and Successors, shall think fit to order and direct by any Order in Council made for that Purpose; for all which Payments so to be made as Bounties or Rewards upon Seizures and Prosecutions for Offences against this Act, or any other Act of Parliament made for restraining or abolishing the African Slave Trade, the Officer or Officers, Civil or Military, so to be appointed as aforesaid to receive, protect, and provide for such Slaves or Natives of Africa so to be condemned and delivered over, shall, after the Condemnation and Receipt thereof as aforesaid, grant Certificates in favour of the Governor and Party seizing, informing, and prosecuting as aforesaid respectively, or the latter alone (as the Case may be) addressed to the Lords Commissioners of His Majesty's Treasury; who, upon the Production to them of any such Certificate, and of an authentic Copy, duly certified, of the Sentence of Condemnation of the said Slaves or Africans to His Majesty's Use as aforesaid, and also of a Receipt under the Hand of such Officer or Officers so appointed as aforesaid, specifying that such Slaves or Africans have by him or them been received in good Health as aforesaid, shall direct Payment to be made from and out of the Consolidated Fund of Great Britain of the Amount of the Monies specified in such Certificate, to the lawful Holders of the same, or the Persons entitled to the Benefit thereof respectively.

XII. And be it further enacted, That if any Person shall wilfully and fraudulently forge or counterfeit any such Certificate, Copy of Sentence of Condemnation, or Receipt as aforesaid, or any Part thereof, or shall knowingly and wilfully utter or publish the same, knowing it to be forged or counterfeited, with Intent to defraud His Majesty, His Heirs and Successors, or any other Person or Persons whatever, the Party so offending shall, on Conviction, suffer Death as in Cases of Felony, without Benefit of Clergy.

XIII. And be it further enacted, That the several Pecuniary Penalties or Forfeitures imposed and inflicted by this Act, shall and may be sued for, prosecuted, and recovered in any Court of Record in Great Britain, or in any Court of Record or Vice Admiralty in any Part of His Majesty's Dominions wherein the Offence was committed, or where the Offender may be found after the Commission of such Offence; and that in all Cases of Seizure of any Ships, Vessels, Slaves or pretended Slaves, Goods or Effects, for any Forfeiture under this

Act, the same shall and may respectively be sued for, prosecuted and recovered in any Court of Record in Great Britain, or in any Court of Record or Vice Admiralty in any Part of His Majesty's Dominions in or nearest to which such Seizures may be made, or to which such Ships or Vessels, Slaves or pretended Slaves, Goods or Effects (if seized at Sea or without the Limits of any British Jurisdiction) may most conveniently be carried for Trial; and all the said Penalties and Forfeitures, whether pecuniary or specific (unless where it is expressly otherwise provided for by this Act) shall go and belong to such Person and Persons in such Shares and Proportions, and shall and may be sued for and prosecuted, tried, recovered, distributed, and applied in such and the like Manner and by the same Ways and Means, and subject to the same Rules and Directions, as any Penalties or Forfeitures incurred in Great Britain, and in the British Colonies or Plantations in America respectively, by force of any Act of Parliament relating to the Trade and Revenues of the said British Colonies or Plantations in America, now go and belong to, and may now be sued for, prosecuted, tried, recovered, distributed and applied respectively in Great Britain or in the said Colonies or Plantations respectively, under and by virtue of a certain Act of Parliament made in the Fourth Year of His present Majesty, intituled, *An Act for granting certain Duties in the British Colonies and Plantations in America; for continuing, amending, and making perpetual an Act passed in the Sixth Year of the Reign of his late Majesty, King George the Second, intituled, An Act for the better securing and encouraging the Trade of His Majesty's Sugar Colonies in America; for applying the Produce of such Duties to arise by virtue of the said Act towards defraying the Expences of defending, protecting, and securing the said Colonies and Plantations; for explaining an Act made in the Twenty-fifth Year of the Reign of King Charles the Second, intituled, An Act for the Encouragement of the Greenland and Eastland Trades, and for the better securing the Plantation Trade, and for altering and disallowing several Drawbacks on Exports from this Kingdom, and more effectually preventing the clandestine Conveyance of Goods to and from the Colonies and Plantations, and improving and securing the Trade between the same and Great Britain.*

XIV. And be it further enacted, That all Ships and Vessels, Slaves or Natives of Africa, carried, conveyed, or dealt with as Slaves, and all other Goods and Effects that shall or may become forfeited for any Offence committed against this Act, shall and may be

any Officer of His Majesty's Customs or Excise, or by Commanders or Officers of any of His Majesty's Ships or Vessels of War, who, in making and prosecuting any such Seizures, shall have the Benefit of all the Provisions made by the said Act of the Fourth Year of His present Majesty, or any other Act of Parliament made for the Protection of Officers seizing and prosecuting for any Offence against the said Act or any other Act of Parliament relating to the Trade and Revenues of the British Colonies or Plantations in America.

XV. And be it further enacted, That all Offences committed against this Act may be inquired of, tried, determined, and dealt with as Misdemeanors, as if the same had been respectively committed within the Body of the County of Middlesex.

XVI. Provided also, and be it further enacted, That it shall and may be lawful for His Majesty in Council from Time to Time to make such Orders and Regulations for the future Disposal and Support of such Negroes as shall have been bound Apprentices under this Act, after the Term of their Apprenticeship shall have expired, as to His Majesty shall seem meet, and as may prevent such Negroes from becoming at any time chargeable upon the Island in which they shall have been so bound Apprentices as aforesaid.

XVII. Provided always, and be it further enacted, That none of the Provisions of any Act as to enlisting for any limited Period of Service, or as to any Rules or Regulations for the granting any Pensions or Allowances to any Soldiers discharged after certain Periods of Service, shall extend, or be deemed or construed in any Manner to extend, to any Negroes so enlisting and serving in any of His Majesty's Forces.

XVIII. And be it further enacted, That if any Action or Suit shall be commenced either in Great Britain or elsewhere, against any Person or Persons for any Thing done in pursuance of this Act, the Defendant or Defendants in such Action or Suit may plead the General Issue, and give this Act and the Special Matter in Evidence at any Trial to be had thereupon, and that the same was done in pursuance and by the Authority of this Act; and if it shall appear so to have been done, the jury shall find for the Defendant or Defendants; and if the Plaintiff shall be nonsuited or discontinue his Action after the Defendant or Defendants shall have appeared, or if judgement shall be given upon any Verdict or Demurrer against the Plaintiff, the Defendant or Defendants shall recover Treble Costs and have the like Remedy for the same, as Defendants have in other Cases by Law.

Source: "An Act for the Abolition of the Slave Trade," in *Documents Illustrative of the History of the Slave Trade to America*, vol. II, *The Eighteenth Century*, ed. Elizabeth Donnan. Washington, DC: Carnegie Institution of Washington, 1931.

The Closing of the African Slave Trade in the United States (1807)

An Act to Prohibit the Importation of Slaves into any Port or Place Within the Jurisdiction of the United States.

[Section 1.] *Be it enacted by the Senate and House of Representatives of the United States of America in Congress assembled,* That from and after the first day of January, one thousand eight hundred and eight, it shall not be lawful to import or bring into the United States or the territories thereof from any foreign kingdom, place, or country, any negro, mulatto, or person of colour, with intent to hold, sell, or dispose of such negro, mulatto, or person of colour, as a slave, or to be held to service or labour.

Section 2. *And be it further enacted,* That no citizen or citizens of the United States, or any other person, shall, from [and] after the first day of January, in the year of our Lord one thousand eight hundred and eight, for himself, or themselves, or any other person whatsoever, either as master, factor, or owner, build, fit, equip, load or otherwise prepare any ship or vessel, in any port or place within the jurisdiction of the United States, nor shall cause any ship or vessel to sail from any port or place within the same, for the purpose of procuring any negro, mulatto, or person of colour, from any foreign kingdom, place, or country, to be transported to any port or place whatsoever, within the jurisdiction of the United States, to be held, sold, or disposed of as slaves, or to be held to service or labour: and if any ship or vessel shall be so fitted out for the purpose aforesaid, or shall be caused to sail so as aforesaid, every such ship or vessel, her tackle, apparel, and furniture, shall be forfeited to the United States, and shall be liable to be seized, prosecuted, and condemned in any of the circuit courts or district courts, for the district where the said ship or vessel may be found or seized.

Section 3. *And be it further enacted,* That all and every person so building, fitting out, equipping, loading, or otherwise preparing or sending away, any ship or vessel, knowing or intending that the same shall be employed in such trade or business, from and after

the first day of January, one thousand eight hundred and eight, contrary to the true intent and meaning of this act, or any ways aiding or abetting therein, shall severally forfeit and pay twenty thousand dollars, one moiety thereof to the use of the United States, and the other moiety to the use of any person or persons who shall sue for and prosecute the same to effect.

Section 4. *And be it further enacted,* If any citizen or citizens of the United States, or any person resident within the jurisdiction of the same, shall, from and after the first day of January, one thousand eight hundred and eight, take on board, receive or transport from any of the coasts or kingdoms of Africa, or from any other foreign kingdom, place, or country, any negro, mulatto, or person of colour, in any ship or vessel, for the purpose of selling them in any port or place within the jurisdiction of the United States as slaves, or to be held to service or labour, or shall be in any ways aiding or abetting therein, such citizen or citizens, or person, shall severally forfeit and pay five thousand dollars, one moiety thereof to the use of any person or persons who shall sue for and prosecute the same to effect; and every such ship or vessel in which such negro, mulatto, or person of colour, shall have been taken on board, received, or transported as aforesaid, her tackle, apparel, and furniture, and the goods and effects which shall be found on board the same, shall be forfeited to the United States, and shall be liable to be seized, prosecuted, and condemned in any of the circuit courts or district courts in the district where the said ship or vessel may be found or seized. And neither the importer, nor any person or persons claiming from or under him, shall hold any right or title whatsoever to any negro, mulatto, or person of colour, nor to the service or labour thereof, who may be imported or brought within the United States, or territories thereof, in violation of this law, but the same shall remain subject to any regulations not contravening the provisions of this act, which the legislatures of the several states or territories at any time hereafter may make, for disposing of any such negro, mulatto, or person of colour.

Section 5. *And be it further enacted,* That if any citizen or citizens of the United States, or any other person resident within the jurisdiction of the same, shall, from and after the first day of January, one thousand eight hundred and eight, contrary to the true intent and meaning of this act, take on board any ship or vessel from any of the coasts or kingdoms of Africa, or from any other foreign kingdom, place, or country, any negro, mulatto, or person of colour, with intent to sell him, her, or them, for a slave, or slaves, or to be held to service or labour, and shall transport the same to any port or place within the jurisdiction of the United States, and there sell such negro, mulatto, or person of colour, so transported as aforesaid, for a slave, or to be held to service or labour, every such offender shall be deemed guilty of a high misdemeanor, and being thereof convicted before any court having competent jurisdiction, shall suffer imprisonment for not more than ten years nor less than five years, and be fined not exceeding ten thousand dollars, nor less than one thousand dollars.

Section 6. *And be it further enacted,* That if any person or persons whatsoever, shall, from and after the first day of January, one thousand eight hundred and eight, purchase or sell any negro, mulatto, or person of colour, for a slave, or to be held to service or labour, who shall have been imported, or brought from any foreign kingdom, place, or country, or from the dominions of any foreign state, immediately adjoining to the United States, into any port or place within the jurisdiction of the United States, after the last day of December, one thousand eight hundred and seven, knowing at the time of such purchase or sale, such negro, mulatto or person of colour, was so brought within the jurisdiction of the Unified States, as aforesaid, such purchaser and seller shall severally forfeit and pay for every negro, mulatto, or person of colour, so purchased or sold as aforesaid, eight hundred dollars; one moiety thereof to the United States, and the other moiety to the use of any person or persons who shall sue for and prosecute the same to effect: Provided, that the aforesaid forfeiture shall not extend to the seller or purchaser of any negro, mulatto, or person of colour, who may be sold or disposed of in virtue of any regulation which may hereafter be made by any of the legislatures of the several states in that respect, in pursuance of this act, and the constitution of the United States.

Section 7. *And be it further enacted,* That if any ship or vessel shall be found, from and after the first day of January, one thousand eight hundred and eight, in any river, port, bay, or harbor, or on the high seas, within the jurisdictional limits of the United States, or hovering on the coast thereof, having on board any negro, mulatto, or person of colour, for the purpose of selling them as slaves, or with intent to land the same, in any port or place within the jurisdiction of the United States, contrary to the prohibition of this act,

every such ship or vessel, together with her tackle, apparel, and furniture, and the goods or effects which shall be found on board the same, shall be forfeited to the use of the United States, and may be seized, prosecuted, and condemned, in any court of the United States, having jurisdiction thereof[.] And it shall be lawful for the President of the United States, and he is hereby authorized, should he deem it expedient, to cause any of the armed vessels of the United States to be manned and employed to cruise on any part of the coast of the United States, or territories thereof, where he may judge attempts will be made to violate the provisions of this act, and to instruct and direct the commanders of armed vessels of the United States, to seize, take, and bring into any port of the United States all such ships or vessels, and moreover to seize, take, and bring into any port of the United States all ships or vessels of the United States, wheresoever found on the high seas, contravening the provisions of this act, to be proceeded against according to law, and the captain, master, or commander of every such ship or vessel, so found and seized as aforesaid, shall be deemed guilty of a high misdemeanor, and shall be liable to be prosecuted before any court of the United States, having jurisdiction thereof; and being thereof convicted, shall be fined not exceeding ten thousand dollars, and be imprisoned not less than two years, and not exceeding four years. And the proceeds of all ships and vessels, their tackle, apparel, and furniture, and the goods and effects on board of them, which shall be so seized, prosecuted and condemned, shall be divided equally between the United States and the officers and men who shall make such seizure, take, or bring the same into port for condemnation, whether such seizure be made by an armed vessel of the United States, or revenue cutters [t]hereof, and the same shall be distributed in like manner, as is provided by law, for the distribution of prizes taken from an enemy: Provided, that the officers and men, to be entitled to one half of the proceeds aforesaid, shall safe keep every negro, mulatto, or person of colour, found on board of any ship or vessel so by them seized, taken, or brought into port for condemnation, and shall deliver every such negro, mulatto, or person of colour, to such person or persons as shall be appointed by the respective states, to receive the same, and if no such person or persons shall be appointed by the respective states, they shall deliver every such negro, mulatto, or person of colour, to the overseers of the poor of the port or place where such ship or vessel may be brought or found, and shall immediately transmit to the governor or chief magistrate of the state, an account of their proceedings, together with the number of such Negroes, mulattoes, or persons of colour, and a descriptive list of the same, that he may give directions respecting such Negroes, mulattoes, or persons of colour.

Section 8. *And be it further enacted,* That no captain, master or commander of any ship or vessel, of less burthen than forty tons, shall, from and after the first day of January, one thousand eight hundred and eight, take on board and transport any negro, mulatto, or person of colour, to any port or place whatsoever, for the purpose of selling or disposing of the same as a slave, or with intent that the same may be sold or disposed of to be held to service or labour, on penalty of forfeiting for every such negro, mulatto, or person of colour, so taken on board and transported, as aforesaid, the sum of eight hundred dollars; one moiety thereof to the use of the United States, and the other moiety to any person or persons who shall sue for, and prosecute the same to effect: Provided[,] however, That nothing in this section shall extend to prohibit the taking on board or transporting on any river, or inland bay of the sea, within the jurisdiction of the United States, any negro, mulatto, or person of colour, (not imported contrary to the provisions of this act) in any vessel or species of craft whatever.

Section 9. *And be it further enacted,* That the captain, master, or commander of any ship or vessel of the burthen of forty tons or more, from and after the first day of January, one thousand eight hundred and eight, sailing coastwise, from any port in the United States, to any port or place within the jurisdiction of the same, having on board any negro, mulatto, or person of colour, for the purpose of transporting them to be sold or disposed of as slaves, or to be held to service or labour, shall, previous to the departure of such ship or vessel, make out and subscribe duplicate manifests of every such negro, mulatto, or person of colour, on board such ship or vessel, therein specifying the name and sex of each person, their age and stature, as near as may be, and the class to which they respectively belong, whether negro, mulatto, or person of colour, with the name and place of residence of every owner or shipper of the same, and shall deliver such manifests to the collector of the port, if there be one, otherwise to the surveyor, before whom the captain, master, or commander, together with the owner or shipper, shall severally swear or affirm to the best of their knowledge and belief, that the persons therein speci-

fied were not imported or brought into the United States, from and after the first day of January, one thousand eight hundred and eight, and that under the laws of the state, they are held to service or labour; whereupon the said collector or surveyor shall certify the same on the said manifests, one of which he shall return to the said captain, master, or commander, with a permit, specifying thereon the number, names, and general description of such persons, and authorizing him to proceed to the port of his destination. And if any ship or vessel, being laden and destined as aforesaid, shall depart from the port where she may then be, without the captain, master, or commander having first made out and subscribed duplicate manifests, of every negro, mulatto, and person of colour, on board such ship or vessel, as aforesaid, and without having previously delivered the same to the said collector or surveyor, and obtained a permit, in manner as herein required, or shall, previous to her arrival at the port of her destination, take on board any negro, mulatto, or person of colour, other than those specified in the manifests, as aforesaid, every such ship or vessel, together with her tackle, apparel and furniture, shall be forfeited to the use of the United States, and may be seized, prosecuted and condemned in any court of the United States having jurisdiction thereof; and the captain, master, or commander of every such ship or vessel, shall moreover forfeit, for every such negro, mulatto, or person of colour, so transported, or taken on board, contrary to the provisions of this act, the sum of one thousand dollars, one moiety thereof to the United States, and the other moiety to the use of any person or persons who shall sue for and prosecute the same to effect.

Section 10. *And be it further enacted,* That the captain, master, or commander of every ship or vessel, of the burthen of forty tons or more, from and after the first day of January, one thousand eight hundred and eight, sailing coastwise, and having on board any negro, mulatto, or person of colour, to sell or dispose of as slaves, or to be held to service or labour, and arriving in any port within the jurisdiction of the United States, from any other port within the same, shall, previous to the unlading or putting on shore any of the persons aforesaid, or suffering them to go on shore, deliver to the collector, if there be one, or if not, to the surveyor residing at the port of her arrival, the manifest certified by the collector or surveyor of the port from whence she sailed, as is herein before directed, to the truth of which, before such officer, he shall swear or affirm, and if the collector or surveyor shall be satisfied therewith, he shall thereupon grant a permit for unlading or suffering such negro, mulatto, or person of colour, to be put on shore, and if the captain, master, or commander of any such ship or vessel being laden as aforesaid, shall neglect or refuse to deliver the manifest at the time and in the manner herein directed, or shall land or put on shore any negro, mulatto, or person of colour, for the purpose aforesaid, before he shall have delivered his manifest as aforesaid, and obtained a permit for that purpose, every such captain, master, or commander, shall forfeit and pay ten thousand dollars, one moiety thereof to the United States, the other moiety to the use of any person or persons who shall sue for and prosecute the same to effect.

APPROVED, March 2, 1807.

Source: Laws of the United States, vol. 8 (9th Cong., 1st and 2nd sess., 1805–1807). Washington City: R.C. Weightman, 1807.

The Abolition of Slavery in Mexico (1829)

Given in the federal palace of Mexico, on the 15th of September, 1829.

Desiring to signalize the year 1829, the anniversary of our independence, by an act of national justice and beneficence that may turn to the benefit and support of such a valuable good; that may consolidate more and more public tranquility; that may cooperate to the aggrandizement of the republic, and return to an unfortunate portion of its inhabitants those rights which they hold from nature, and that the people protect by wise and equitable laws, in conformity with the 30th article of the constitutive act,

Making use of the extraordinary faculties which have been granted to the executive, I thus decree:

1st. Slavery is forever abolished in the republic.

2d. Consequently all those individuals who until this day look upon themselves as slaves, are free.

3d. When the financial situation of the republic admits, the proprietors of slaves shall be indemnified, and the indemnification regulated by a law.

And in order that the present decree may have its full and entire execution, I order it to be printed, published and circulated to all those whose obligation it is to have it fulfilled.

Source: W.O. Blake, ed., The History of Slavery and the Slave Trade, Ancient and Modern. Columbus, OH: H. Miller, 1861.

The British Emancipation Act (1833)

An Act for the Abolition of Slavery throughout the British Colonies; for Promoting the Industry of the Manumitted Slaves; and for Compensating the Persons hitherto Entitled to the Services of such Slaves, 28th August, 1833.

[I.] Whereas divers persons are holden in slavery within divers of His Majesty's colonies, and it is just and expedient that all such persons should be manumitted and set free, and that a reasonable compensation should be made to the persons hitherto entitled to the services of such slaves for the loss which they will incur by being deprived of their right to such services: And whereas it is also expedient that provision should be made for promoting the industry and securing the good conduct of the persons so to be manumitted, for a limited period after such their manumission: And whereas it is necessary that the laws now in force in the said several colonies should forthwith be adapted to the new state and relations of society therein which will follow upon such general manumission as aforesaid of the said slaves; and that, in order to afford the necessary time for such adaptation of the said laws, a short interval should elapse before such manumission should take effect; Be it therefore enacted by the King's most Excellent Majesty, by and with the advice and consent of the Lords spiritual and temporal, and Commons, in this present Parliament assembled, and by the authority of the same, That from and after the first day of *August* one thousand eight hundred and thirty-four all persons who in conformity with the laws now in force in the said colonies respectively shall on or before the first day of *August* one thousand eight hundred and thirty-four have been duly registered as slaves in any such colony, and who on the said first day of *August* one thousand eight hundred and thirty-four shall be actually within any such colony, and who shall by such registries appear to be on the said first day of *August* one thousand eight hundred and thirty-four of the full age of six years or upwards, shall by force and virtue of this act, and without the previous Execution of any Indenture of Apprenticeship, or other Deed or Instrument for that purpose, become and be apprenticed labourers; provided that, for the purposes aforesaid, every slave engaged in his ordinary occupation on the seas shall be deemed and taken to be within the colony to which such slave shall belong.

II. And be it further enacted, That during the continuance of the apprenticeship of any such apprenticed labourer such person or persons shall be entitled to the services of such apprenticed labourer as would for the time being have been entitled to his or her services as a slave if this act had not been made.

III. Provided also, and be it further enacted, That all slaves who may at any time previous to the passing of this act have been brought with the consent of their possessors, and all apprenticed labourers who may hereafter with the like consent be brought, into any part of the United Kingdom of *Great Britain* and *Ireland*, shall from and after the passing of this act be absolutely and entirely free to all intents and purposes whatsoever.

IV. And whereas it is expedient that all such apprenticed labourers should, for the purposes herein-after mentioned, be divided into three distinct classes, the first of such classes consisting of praedial apprenticed labourers attached to the soil, and comprising all persons who in their state of slavery were usually employed in agriculture, or in the manufacture of colonial produce or otherwise, upon lands belonging to their owners; the second of such classes consisting of praedial apprenticed labourers not attached to the soil, and comprising all persons who in their state of slavery were usually employed in agriculture, or in the manufacture of colonial produce or otherwise, upon lands not belonging to their owners; and the third of such classes consisting of non praedial apprenticed labourers and comprising all apprenticed labourers not included within either of the two preceding classes: Be it therefore enacted, that such division as aforesaid of the said apprenticed labourers into such classes as aforesaid shall be carried into effect in such manner and form and subject to such rules and regulations as shall for that purpose be established under such authority, and in and by such acts of assembly, ordinances, or Orders in Council, as herein after mentioned: Provided always, that no person of the age of twelve years and upwards shall by or by virtue of any such act of assembly, ordinance, or Order in Council be included in either of the said two classes of praedial apprenticed labourers unless such person shall for twelve calendar months at the least next before the passing of this present act have been habitually employed in agriculture or in the manufacture of colonial produce.

V. And be it further enacted, That no person who by virtue of this act, or of any such act of assembly, ordinance, or Order in Council as aforesaid, shall become a praedial apprenticed labourer, whether attached or not attached to the soil, shall continue in such apprenticeship beyond the first day of *August* one thousand eight hundred and forty; and that during such his or her apprenticeship no such praedial apprenticed labourer, whether attached or not attached to the soil, shall be bound or liable, by virtue of such apprenticeship, to perform any labour in the service of his or her employer or employers for more than forty-five hours in the whole in any one week.

VI. And be it further enacted, That no person who by virtue of this act or of any such act of assembly, ordinance, or Order in Council as aforesaid, shall become a non-praedial apprenticed labourer, shall continue in such apprenticeship beyond the first day of August one thousand eight hundred and thirty-eight.

VII. And be it further enacted, That if before any such apprenticeship shall have expired the person or persons entitled for and during the remainder of any such term to the services of such apprenticed labourer shall be desirous to discharge him or her from such apprenticeship, it shall be lawful for such person or persons so to do by any deed or instrument to be by him, her, or them for that purpose made and executed; which deed or instrument shall be in such form, and shall be executed and recorded in such manner and with such solemnities, as shall for that purpose be prescribed under such authority, and in and by such acts of assembly, ordinances, or Orders in Council, as herein-after mentioned: Provided nevertheless, that if any person so discharged from any such apprenticeship by any such voluntary act as aforesaid shall at that time be of the age of fifty years or upwards, or shall be then labouring under any such disease or mental or bodily infirmity as may render him or her incapable of earning his or her subsistence, then and in every such case the person or persons so discharging any such apprenticed labourer as aforesaid shall continue and be liable to provide for the support and maintenance of such apprenticed labourer during the remaining term of such original apprenticeship, as fully as if such apprenticed labourer had not been discharged therefrom.

VIII. And be it further enacted, That it shall be lawful for any such apprenticed labourer to purchase his or her discharge from such apprenticeship, even without the consent, or in opposition, if necessary, to the will of the person or persons entitled to his or her services, upon payment to such person or persons of the appraised value of such services; which appraisement shall be effected, and which purchase money shall be paid and applied, and which discharge shall be given and executed, in such manner and form, and upon, under, and subject to such conditions, as shall be prescribed under such authority, and by such acts of assembly ordinances, or Orders in Council, as are herein-after mentioned.

IX. And be it further enacted, That no apprenticed labourer shall be subject or liable to be removed from the colony to which he or she may belong; and that no praedial apprenticed labourer who may in manner aforesaid become attached to the soil shall be subject or liable to perform any labour in the service of his or her employer or employers except upon or in or about the works and business of the plantations or estates to which such praedial apprenticed labourer shall have been attached or on which he or she shall have been usually employed on or previously to the said first day of *August* one thousand eight hundred and thirty-four: Provided nevertheless, that with the consent in writing of any two or more justices of the peace holding such special commission as herein-after mentioned, it shall be lawful for the person or persons entitled to the services of any such attached praedial apprenticed labourer or labourers to transfer his or their services to any other estate or plantation within the same colony to such person or persons belonging; which written consent shall in no case be given, or be of any validity, unless any such justices of the peace shall first have ascertained that such transfer would not have the effect of separating any such attached praedial apprenticed labourer from his or her wife or husband, parent or child, or from any person or persons reputed to bear any such relation to him or her, and that such transfer would not probably be injurious to the health or welfare of such attached praedial apprenticed labourer; and such written consent to any such removal shall be expressed in such terms, and shall be in each case given, attested, and recorded in such manner, as shall for that purpose be prescribed under such authority, and by such acts of assembly, ordinances, and Orders in Council, as herein-after mentioned.

X. And be it further enacted and declared, That the right or interest of any employer or employers to and in the services of any such apprenticed labourers as aforesaid shall pass and be transferable by bargain and sale, contract, deed, conveyance, will, or descent, according to such rules and in such manner as shall for

that purpose be provided by any such acts of assembly, ordinances, or Orders in Council as herein-after mentioned; provided that no such apprenticed labourer shall, by virtue of any such bargain and sale, contract, deed, conveyance, will, or descent, be subject or liable to be separated from his or her wife or husband, parent or child, or from any person or persons reputed to bear any such relation to him or her.

XI. And be it further enacted, That during the continuance of any such apprenticeship as aforesaid the person or persons for the time being entitled to the services of every such apprenticed labourer shall be and is and are hereby required to supply him or her with such food, clothing, lodging, medicine, medical attendance, and such other maintenance and allowances as by any law now in force in the colony to which such apprenticed labourer may belong an owner is required to supply to and for any slave being of the same age and sex as such apprenticed labourer shall be; and in cases in which the food of any such praedial apprenticed labourer shall be supplied, not by the delivery to him or her of provisions, but by the cultivation by such praedial apprenticed labourer of ground set apart for the growth of provisions, the person or persons entitled to his or her services shall and is or are hereby required to provide such praedial apprenticed labourer with ground adequate, both in quantity and quality, for his or her support, and within a reasonable distance of his or her usual place of abode, and to allow to such praedial apprenticed labourer, from and out of the annual time during which he or she may be required to labour, after the rate of forty-five hours *per* week as aforesaid, in the service of such his or her employer or employers, such a portion of time as shall be adequate for the proper cultivation of such ground, and for the raising and securing the crops thereon grown; the actual extent of which ground and the distance thereof from the place of residence of the praedial apprenticed labourer for whose use it may be so allotted, and the length of time to be deducted for the cultivation of the said ground from the said annual time, shall and may, in each of the colonies aforesaid, be regulated under such authorities, and by such acts of assembly, ordinances, or Orders in Council as herein-after mentioned.

XII. And be it further enacted, That subject to the obligations imposed by this act, or to be imposed by any such act of general assembly, ordinance, or Order in Council as herein-after mentioned, upon such apprenticed labourers as aforesaid, all and every the persons who on the said first day of *August* one thousand eight hundred and thirty-four shall be holden in slavery within any such *British* colony as aforesaid shall upon and from and after the said first day of *August* one thousand eight hundred and thirty-four become and be to all intents and purposes free and discharged of and from all manner of slavery, and shall be absolutely and for ever manumitted; and that the children thereafter to be born to any such persons, and the offspring of such children shall in like manner be free from their birth; and that from, and after the said first day of *August* one thousand eight hundred and thirty-four slavery shall be and is hereby utterly and for ever abolished and declared unlawful throughout the *British* colonies, plantations, and possessions abroad.

XIII. And whereas it may happen that children who have not attained the age of six years on the said first day of *August* one thousand eight hundred and thirty-four, or that children who after that day may be born to any female apprenticed labourers, may not be properly supported by their parents, and that no other person may be disposed voluntarily to undertake the support of such children; and it is necessary that provision should be made for the maintenance of such children in any such contingency; Be it therefore enacted, That if any child who on the said first day of *August* one thousand eight hundred and thirty-four had not completed his or her sixth year, or if any child to which any female apprenticed labourer may give birth on or after the said first day of *August* one thousand eight hundred and thirty-four, shall be brought before any justice of the peace holding any such special commission as herein-after mentioned, and if it shall be made to appear to the satisfaction of such justice that any such child is unprovided with an adequate maintenance, and that such child hath not completed his or her age of twelve years, it shall be lawful for such justice, and he is hereby required on behalf of any such child to execute an indenture of apprenticeship, thereby binding such child as an apprenticed labourer to the person or persons entitled to the services of the mother of such child, or who had been last entitled to the services of such mother; but in case it shall be made to appear to any such justice that such person or persons aforesaid is or are unable or unfit to enter into such indenture, and properly to perform the conditions thereof, then it shall be lawful for such justice and he is hereby required by such indenture to bind any such child to any other person or persons to be by him for that purpose approved, and

who may be willing and able properly to perform such conditions; and it shall by every such indenture of apprenticeship be declared whether such child shall thenceforward belong to the class of attached praedial apprenticed labourers, or to the class of unattached praedial apprenticed labourers, or to the class of non-praedial apprenticed labourers; and the term of such apprenticeship of any such child shall by such indenture be limited and made to continue in force until such child shall have completed his or her twenty-first year, and no longer; and every child so apprenticed as aforesaid by the order of any such justice of the peace as aforesaid shall during his or her apprenticeship be subject to all such and the same rules and regulations respecting the work or labour to be by them done or performed, and respecting the food [and] other supplies to be to him or her furnished, as any other such apprenticed labourers as aforesaid: provided always that the said indenture of apprenticeship shall contain sufficient words of obligation upon the employer to allow reasonable time and opportunity for the education and religious instruction of such child.

XIV. And for ensuring the effectual superintendence of the said apprenticed labourers, and the execution of this act, Be it enacted, That it shall and may be lawful for His Majesty to issue, or to authorize the governor of any such colony as aforesaid, in the name and on the behalf of His Majesty, to issue under the public seal of any such colony, one or more special commission or commissions to any one or more person or persons, constituting him or them a justice or justices of the peace for the whole of any such colony, or for any parish, precinct, quarter, or other district within the same, for the special purpose of giving effect to this present act, and to any laws which may, in manner herein-after mentioned, be made for giving more complete effect to the same; and every person to or in favour of whom any such commission may be issued shall by force and virtue thereof, and without any other qualification, be entitled and competent to act as a justice of the peace within the limits prescribed by such his commission for such special purposes aforesaid, but for no other purposes: provided nevertheless, that nothing herein contained shall prevent or be construed to prevent any person commissioned as a justice of the peace for such special purpose as aforesaid from being included in the general commission of the peace for any such colony, or for any parish, precinct, quarter or other district thereof, in case it shall seem fit to His Majesty, or to the governor of any such colony acting by His Majesty's authority, to address both such special commission and such general commission as aforesaid in any case to the same person or persons.

XV. And be it further enacted, That His Majesty shall be and he is hereby authorized to grant to any person or persons, not exceeding one hundred in the whole, holding any such special commission or commissions as aforesaid, and so from time to time as vacancies may occur, salaries at and after a rate not exceeding in any case the sum of three hundred pounds sterling *per annum*, which salary shall be payable so long only as any such justice of the peace shall retain any such special commission, and shall be actually resident in such colony, and engaged in the discharge of the duties of such his office; provided that no person receiving or entitled to receive any half pay, pension, or allowance for or in respect of any past services in His Majesty's naval or land forces shall, by the acceptance of any such special commission or salary as aforesaid, forfeit or become incapable of receiving or lose his right to receive such half pay, pension, or allowance, or any part thereof, any law, statute, or usage to the contrary in anywise notwithstanding: provided also, that there be annually laid before both houses of Parliament a list of the names of all persons to whom any such salary shall be so granted, specifying the date of every such commission, and the amount of the salary assigned to every such justice of the peace.

XVI. And whereas it is necessary that various rules and regulations should be framed and established for ascertaining, with reference to each apprenticed labourer within the said colonies respectively, whether he or she belongs to the class of attached praedial apprenticed labourers, or to the class of unattached apprenticed labourers, or to the class of non-praedial apprenticed labourers, and for determining the manner and form in which and the solemnities with which the voluntary discharge of any apprenticed labourer from such his or her apprenticeship may be effected, and for prescribing the form and manner in which and the solemnities with which the purchase by any such apprenticed labourer [of] his or her discharge from such apprenticeship without, or in opposition, if necessary, to, the consent of the person or persons entitled to his or her services, shall be effected, and how the necessary appraisement of the future value of such services shall be made, and how and to whom the amount of such appraisement shall in each case be paid and applied, and in what manner and form and by whom the discharge from any such apprenticeship

shall thereupon be given, executed, and recorded; and it is also necessary, for the preservation of peace throughout the said colonies, that proper regulations should be framed and established for the maintenance of order and good discipline amongst the said apprenticed labourers, and for ensuring the punctual discharge of the services due by them to their respective employers, and for the prevention and punishment of indolence, or the neglect or improper performance of work by any such apprenticed labourer, and for enforcing the due performance by any such apprenticed labourer of any contract into which he or she may voluntarily enter for any hired service during the time in which he or she may not be bound to labour for his or her employer, and for the prevention and punishment of insolence and insubordination on the part of any such apprenticed labourers towards their employers, and for the prevention or punishment of vagrancy or of any conduct on the part of any such apprenticed labourers injuring or tending to the injury of the property of any such employer, and for, the suppression and punishment of any riot or combined resistance of the laws on the part of any such apprenticed labourers, and for preventing the escape of any such apprenticed labourers, during their term of apprenticeship, from the colonies to which they may respectively belong: and whereas, it will also be necessary for the protection of such apprenticed labourers as aforesaid that various regulations should be framed and established in the said respective colonies for securing punctuality and method in the supply to them of such food, clothing, lodging, medicines, medical attendance, and such other maintenance and allowances as they are herein-before declared entitled to receive, and for regulating the amount and quality of all such articles in cases where the laws at present existing in any such colony may not in the case of slaves have made any regulation or any adequate regulation for that purpose; and it is also necessary that proper rules should be established for the prevention and punishment of any frauds which might be practiced, or of any omissions or neglects which might occur, respecting the quantity or the quality of the supplies so to be furnished, or respecting the periods for the delivery of the same: and whereas it is necessary, in those cases in which the food of any such praedial apprenticed labourers as aforesaid may either wholly or in part be raised by themselves by the cultivation of ground to be set apart and allotted for that purpose, that proper regulations should be made and established as to the extent of such grounds, and as to the distance at which such grounds may be so allotted from the ordinary place of abode of such praedial apprenticed labourers, and respecting the deductions to be made from the cultivation of such grounds, from the annual time during which such praedial apprenticed labourers are herein-before declared liable to labour: and whereas it may also be necessary, by such regulations as aforesaid, to secure to the said praedial apprenticed labourers the enjoyment for their own benefit of that portion of their time during which they are not hereby required to labour in the service of their respective employers, and for securing exactness in the computation of the time during which such praedial apprenticed labourers are hereby required to labour in the service of such their respective employers; and it is also necessary that provision should be made for preventing the imposition of task-work on any such apprenticed labourer without his or her free consent to undertake the same; but it may be necessary by such regulations in certain cases to require and provide for the acquiescence of the minority of the praedial apprenticed labourers attached to any plantation or estate in the distribution and apportionment amongst the whole body of such labourers of any task-work which the majority of such body shall be willing and desirous collectively to undertake; and it is also necessary that regulations should be made respecting any voluntary contracts into which any apprenticed labourers may enter with their respective employers or with any other person for hired service for any future period, and for limiting the greatest period of time to which such voluntary contract may extend, and for enforcing the punctual and effectual performance of such voluntary contracts on the part both of such apprenticed labourers and of the person or persons engaging for their employment and hire; and it is also necessary that regulations should be made for the prevention or punishment of any cruelty, injustice, or other wrong or injury which may be done to or inflicted upon any such apprenticed labourers by the persons entitled to their services; and it is also necessary that proper regulations should be made respecting the manner and form in which such indentures of apprenticeship as aforesaid shall be made on behalf of such children as aforesaid, and respecting the registering and preservation of all such indentures: and whereas it is also necessary that provision should be made for ensuring promptitude and dispatch, and for preventing all unnecessary expence, in the discharge by the justices of the peace holding such special commissions as aforesaid of the jurisdiction and authorities thereby committed to them, and for enabling such justices to decide in a summary way such questions as may be brought before them in that capacity, and for the division of the said respective colonies into districts for the purposes of such jurisdiction, and for the frequent and punctual visitation by such justices of the peace of the apprenticed labourers within such their respective districts; and it is also necessary that regulations should be made for indemnifying and protecting such justices of the peace in the upright execution and discharge of their duties: and whereas such regulations as aforesaid could not without great inconvenience be made except by the respective governors, councils, and assemblies, or other local legislatures of the said respective colonies, or by his majesty, with the advice of his Privy Council, in reference to those colonies to which the legislative authority of His Majesty in council extends; Be it therefore enacted and declared, that nothing in this act contained extends or shall be construed to extend to prevent the enactment by the respective governors, councils, and assemblies, or by such other local legislatures as aforesaid, or by His Majesty, with the advice of his Privy Council, of any such acts of general assembly, or ordinances, or Orders in Council as may be requisite for making and establishing such several rules and regulations as aforesaid, or any of them, or for carrying the same or any of them into full and complete effect: provided nevertheless, that it shall not be lawful for any such governor, council, and assembly, or for any such local legislature, or for His Majesty in council, by any such acts of assembly, ordinances, or Orders in Council as aforesaid, to make or establish any enactment, regulation, provision, rule, or order which shall be in anywise repugnant or contradictory to this present act or any part thereof, but that every such enactment, regulation, provision, rule, or order shall be and is hereby declared to be absolutely null and void and of no effect.

XVII. Provided also, and be it further enacted, That it shall not be lawful for any such governor, council, and assembly, or other colonial legislature, or for His Majesty in council, by any such act, ordinance, or order in council, to authorize any person or persons entitled to the services of any such apprenticed labourer, or any other person or persons other than such justices of the peace holding such special commissions as aforesaid, to punish any such apprenticed labourer for any offence by him or her committed or alleged to have been committed by the whipping, beating, or imprisonment of his or her person, or by any other personal or other correction or punishment whatsoever, or by any addition to the hours of labour hereinbefore limited; nor to authorize any court, judge, or justice of the peace to punish any such apprenticed labourer, being a female, for any offence by her committed, by whipping or beating her person; and that every enactment, regulation, provision, rule, or order for any such purpose in any such act, ordinance, or order in council contained shall be and is hereby declared to be absolutely null and void and of no effect: provided always, that nothing in this act contained doth or shall extend to exempt any apprenticed labourer in any of the said colonies from the operation of any law or police regulation which is or shall be in force therein for the prevention or punishment of any offence, such law or police regulation being in force against and applicable to all other persons of free condition.

XVIII. Provided also, and be it further enacted, That it shall not be lawful for any such governor, council, and assembly, or for any such local legislature, or for His Majesty in council, by any such acts of general assembly, ordinances, or Orders in Council as aforesaid, to authorize any magistrate or justice of the peace, other than and except the justices of the peace holding such special commissions as aforesaid, to take cognizance of any offence committed or alleged to have been committed by any such apprenticed labourer, or by his or her employer, in such their relation to each other, or of the breach, violation, or neglect of any of the obligations owed by them to each other, or of any question, matter or thing incident to or arising out of the relations subsisting between such apprenticed labourers and the persons respectively entitled to their services; and every enactment, regulation, provision, rule, or order in any such acts, ordinances, and Orders in Council to the contrary contained shall be and is hereby declared to be null and void and of no effect.

XIX. And it is hereby further declared and enacted, That the several justices of the peace having special commissions as aforesaid shall, within the respective colonies to which they shall be respectively appointed, have, exercise, and enjoy a sole and exclusive jurisdiction over, and shall solely and exclusively take cognizance of, all such offences or alleged offences as last aforesaid, and of every such breach, violation, or neglect of any of the aforesaid obligations, and of every such question, matter, or thing as aforesaid, any law,

custom, or usage in any of the said colonies to the contrary in anywise notwithstanding: provided nevertheless, that nothing herein contained shall extend, or be construed to extend to abrogate or take away the powers by law vested in the supreme courts of record, or the superior courts of civil and criminal justice in any of the said respective colonies.

XX. Provided also, and be it further enacted, That no apprenticed labourer shall, by any such act of assembly, ordinance, or order in council as aforesaid, be declared or rendered liable for and in respect of any offence by him or her committed, or for any cause or upon any ground or pretext whatsoever, except as hereafter is mentioned, to any prolongation of his or her term of apprenticeship, or to any new or additional apprenticeship, or to any such additional labour as shall impose upon any such apprenticed labourer the obligation of working in the service or for the benefit of the person or persons entitled to his or her services for more than fifteen extra hours in the whole in any one week, but every such enactment, regulation, provision, rule, or order shall be and is hereby declared null and void and of no effect: provided nevertheless, that any such act of assembly, ordinance, or order in council as aforesaid may contain provisions for compelling any such apprenticed labourer who shall, during his or her apprenticeship, wilfully absent himself or herself from the service of his or her employer, either to serve his or her employer after the expiration of his or her apprenticeship for so long a time as he or she shall have so absented himself or herself from such service, or to make satisfaction to his or her employer for the loss sustained by such absence, (except so far as he or she shall have made satisfaction for such absence, either out of such extra hours as aforesaid, or otherwise,) but nevertheless so that such extra service or compensation shall not be compellable after the expiration of seven years next after the termination of the apprenticeship of such apprentice.

XXI. Provided always, and be it hereby further enacted, That neither under the provisions of this act, nor under the obligations imposed by this act, or to be imposed by any act of any general assembly, ordnance, or order in council, shall any apprenticed labourer be compelled or compellable to labour on *Sundays*, except in works of necessity or in domestic services, or in the protection of property, or in tending of cattle, nor shall any apprenticed labourer be liable to be hindered or prevented from attending anywhere on *Sundays* for religious worship, at his or her free will or pleasure, but shall be at full liberty so to do without any let, denial, or interruption whatsoever.

XXII. And whereas it may be expedient that persons in the condition of apprenticed labourers should, during the continuance of such their apprenticeship be exempted from the performance of certain civil and military services, and be disqualified from holding certain civil and military offices, and from the enjoyment of certain political franchises, within the said colonies, and be exempted from being arrested or imprisoned for debt; Be it therefore enacted, That nothing in this act contained extends or shall be construed to extend to interfere with or prevent the enactment by the respective governors, councils, and assemblies, or by such other local legislature as aforesaid of any such colonies, or by His Majesty in council in reference to such of the said colonies as are subject to the legislative authority of His Majesty in council, of any acts, ordinances, or Orders in Council for exempting any such apprenticed labourers as aforesaid, during the continuance of such their apprenticeship, from any such civil or military service as aforesaid, or for disqualifying them or any of them during the continuance of any such apprenticeships from the enjoyment or discharge of any such political franchise as aforesaid, or for exempting them during the continuance of such apprenticeships from being arrested or imprisoned for debt.

XXIII. And whereas it would be desirable that such of the provisions of this act as relate to the internal concerns of the said respective colonies should be enacted in such respective colonies so far as may be possible by the authority of the several local legislatures of such colonies respectively; Be it therefore enacted, That in case the governor, council, and assembly of any one or more of His Majesty's colonies aforesaid shall, by any act or acts of general assembly for that purpose made, substitute for the several enactments herein-before contained, or any of them, any enactments accomplishing the several objects in such herein-before contained enactments respectively contemplated as fully and to the like effect, but in a manner and form better adapted to the local circumstances of any such colonies or colony, and in case His Majesty shall by any order or orders to be by him made, by the advice of his Privy Council, confirm and allow any such act or acts of assembly, and shall in and by any such order or Orders in Council recite and set forth at length the several provisions and enact-

ments of this present act for which such other enactments as aforesaid shall have been substituted by any such act or acts of general assembly, then and in such case so much and such parts of this present act as shall be so recited and set forth at length in any such order or orders of His Majesty in council shall be suspended and cease to be of any force or effect in any such colony from and after the arrival and proclamation therein of any such order or orders of His Majesty in council, and shall continue to be so suspended so long as any such substituted enactments shall continue in force and unrepealed, and no longer.

XXIV. And whereas, towards compensating the persons at present entitled to the services of the slaves to be manumitted and set free by virtue of this act for the loss of such services, His Majesty's most dutiful and loyal subjects the commons of *Great Britain* and *Ireland* in Parliament assembled have resolved to give and grant to His Majesty the sum of twenty millions pounds sterling; Be it enacted, That the lords commissioners of His Majesty's treasury of the United Kingdom of *Great Britain* and *Ireland* may raise such sum or sums of money as shall be required from time to time under the provisions of this act, and may grant as the consideration for such sum or sums of money redeemable perpetual annuities or annuities for terms of years (which said annuities reflectively shall be transferable and payable at the *Bank of England*), upon such terms and conditions and under such regulations as to the time or times of paying the said sums of money agreed to be raised as may be determined upon by the said commissioners of the treasury, not exceeding in the whole the sum of twenty millions pounds sterling: provided nevertheless, that the rate of interest at which the said sums of money shall be from time to time raised shall be regulated and governed by the price of the respective redeemable perpetual annuities or annuities for terms of years on the day preceding (or on the nearest preceding day if it shall so happen that there shall be no price of such said annuities respectively on the day immediately preceding) the day of giving notice for raising such sum or sums of money, and that the rate of interest to be allowed to the contributors for such sum or sums of money [may] in no case exceed five shillings *per centum per annum* above the current rate of interest produced by the market price of any such redeemable perpetual annuities or annuities for terms of years existing at the time, and in which such contracts shall be made.

XXV. Provided always, and be it further enacted, That before raising any such sum or sums by redeemable perpetual annuities or annuities for terms of years (unless the same shall be subscribed or contributed as herein-after mentioned by the commissioners for the reduction of the national debt,) the said commissioners of the treasury are hereby required to give public notice of the intention to raise such sum, or such part thereof as shall not be subscribed or contributed as aforesaid, through the governor and deputy governor of the *Bank of England*, of their desire to receive biddings for any such annuities, which said biddings and the mode of raising such annuities shall be conducted in such and the like manner as has usually been practiced with respect to the raising of money by way of annuities for the service of the public: provided also, that no contract or agreement for raising any sum or sums by annuities as aforesaid shall be entered into except during the sitting of Parliament, and when the same shall have been entered into all proceedings, tenders, and contracts respecting the same shall be forthwith laid before Parliament.

XXVI. And be it further enacted, That whatever redeemable annuities or annuities for any term of years which shall be created from time to time by the sums of money raised by virtue of this act (which said redeemable annuities and annuities for terms of years so created shall be of the like description of some redeemable annuities or annuities for terms of years existing at the time of raising such sum or sums of money,) shall be deemed and taken to be redeemable annuities or annuities for terms of years of the like description then existing, in which such sum or sums shall be agreed to be raised.

XXVII. And be it further enacted, That all the several redeemable annuities and annuities for terms of years which shall be created from time to time by virtue of this act shall be deemed and taken to be and shall be added to and form part of the like redeemable annuities or annuities for terms of years in which such sums of money shall be raised, and shall be subject to all the clauses, conditions, provisions, directions, regulations, and periods of payment as fully and effectually to all intents and purposes, except as altered and varied by virtue of this act, as if the said clauses, conditions, provisions, directions, regulations, and periods of payment were severally repeated and re-enacted in this act.

XXVIII. And be it enacted, That the commissioners for the reduction of the national debt may subscribe and contribute from time to time towards the raising any sum or sums of money to be raised under the provisions of this act any part of the monies which shall be at any time handing in their names in the books of the governor and company of the *Bank of England* under and by virtue of an act passed in the ninth year of the reign of King *George* the fourth, intituled *An Act to consolidate and amend the laws relating to savings banks*, and of another act passed in the tenth year of the reign of King *George* the fourth, intituled *An Act to consolidate and amend the laws relating to friendly societies*, and also to sell and dispose of the bank annuities and exchequer bills, or any part thereof, which may be now standing or may hereafter stand in their names in the books of the said bank in pursuance of the said respective acts, and with the proceeds thereof may subscribe and contribute such monies from time to time, or any part thereof, towards the raising the sums of money which may be required from time to time under the provisions of this act.

XXIX. And be it enacted, That all sums of money which shall be raised from time to time by virtue of this act shall be paid into the *Bank of England* to the account of the commissioners for the reduction of the national debt, under the title of "the *West India* compensation account," and the cashiers of the *Bank of England* are hereby required to receive all such sums of money, and to place the same from time to time to the said account.

XXX. And be it enacted, That the cashier or cashiers of the governor and company of the *Bank of England*, who shall have received or shall receive any part of any contribution towards any sum or sums of money raised or to be raised under the provisions of this act, shall give a receipt or receipts in writing to every such contributor for all such sums; and that the said receipts so to be given shall be assignable at any time for and during such period as shall and may be determined upon by the said commissioners of the treasury; and the said receipts shall be in such form and words and under such regulations as shall be approved by the said commissioners of His Majesty's Treasury: provided always, that in case any such contributors who have already deposited with or shall hereafter pay to the said cashier or cashiers any sum or sums of money, at the time and in the manner specified in the proposals of the several loans, in part of the sum or sums so by them respectively subscribed, or their respective executors, administrators, successors, or assigns, shall not advance and pay so the said cashier or cashiers the residue of the sum or sums so subscribed at the times and in the manner stated in the proposals, then and in every such case so much of the respective sum or sums so subscribed as shall have been actually paid in part thereof to the said cashier or cashiers shall be forfeited for the benefit of the public, and all right and title to the said redeemable annuities or annuities for terms of years in respect thereof shall be extinguished; any thing in this act contained to the contrary thereof in anywise not withstanding.

XXXI. And be it further enacted, That all the said annuities, interest, dividends, and charges for management which shall become payable in respect of the said sum of twenty millions, or any part thereof, shall be charged and chargeable upon and the same is hereby charged upon and made payable out of the consolidated fund of the United Kingdom of *Great Britain* and *Ireland.*

XXXII. And be it further enacted, That so much money shall from time to time be set apart and issued at the receipt of the exchequer in *England* out of the consolidated fund of the United Kingdom of *Great Britain* and *Ireland* to the said cashier or cashiers of the governor and company of the *Bank of England* as shall be sufficient to satisfy and pay the respective annuities to be created in respect of the said sum of twenty millions, or any part thereof, together with the charges attending the same.

XXXIII. And for the distribution of the said compensation fund and the apportionment thereof amongst the several persons who may prefer claims thereon, be it enacted, That it shall and may be lawful for His Majesty from time to time, by a commission under the great seal of the United Kingdom, to constitute and appoint such persons, not being less than five, as to His Majesty shall seem meet, to be commissioners of arbitration for inquiring into and deciding upon the claims to compensation, which may be preferred to them under this act.

XXXIV. And be it further enacted, That the said commissioners to be appointed by virtue of this act shall each of them, previously to his entering upon the execution of such commission, take an oath before the chancellor of the exchequer or the master of the rolls for the time being, which oath they are hereby respectively authorized to administer, the tenor thereof shall be as follows; (that is to say,)

'I, A B. do swear, that according to the best of my judgment I will faithfully and impartially execute the several powers and trusts vested in me by an act,' intituled [*here set forth the title of this act*].

XXXV. And be it further enacted, That the said commissioners may meet and sit from time to time in such place or places as they shall find it most convenient, with or without adjournment, and with the consent and approbation of the commissioners of the treasury for the time being, or any three of them, in writing; and shall and may employ a secretary, and clerks, messengers, and officers, and shall and may allow such secretary, clerks, messengers, and officers, with the like consent and approbation, reasonable salaries, and shall and may employ a solicitor, and allow to such solicitor a reasonable salary or reward, and shall and may give and administer to such solicitor or solicitors, secretary, clerks, and officers respectively an oath for their faithful demeanor in all things relating to the due performance of the trusts reposed in them by the said commissioners, and in all other things touching the premises; and the said commissioners shall and may from time, to time, at their discretion, dismiss and discharge such solicitor or solicitors, secretary, clerks, messengers, and other officers, and appoint others in their place; and the said solicitor or solicitors, secretary, clerks, and other officers are hereby required faithfully to execute and perform the said trusts in them severally and respectively reposed, without taking any thing for such service other than such salaries or rewards as the said commissioners, with such approbation as aforesaid shall direct or appoint in manner aforesaid.

XXXVI. And be it further enacted, That all acts, matters, and things which the said commissioners for the execution of this act are by this act authorized so to do or execute may be done and executed by any three or more of such commissioners.

XXXVII. And be it further enacted, That no remuneration shall be given for and in respect of the execution of the said commission to such of the said commissioners as shall be members of either house of Parliament, nor to any number exceeding three of the said commissioners.

XXXVIII. And whereas it may be necessary that assistant commissioners should be appointed to act in aid of and under the directions of the commissioners appointed by this act in the said several colonies; Be it therefore enacted, That the governor and the attorney general or other chief law adviser of the government of the said colonies respectively shall, with any two or more resident inhabitants for each of such colonies, to be nominated during pleasure by the governor thereof, be commissioners for the colony to which they respectively belong, to assist in aid of the commissioners under this act in all such cases and in relation to all matters and things which shall be referred to them by the said commissioners, and for all such purposes shall have and use and exercise all the powers and authorities of the said commissioners; and such assistant commissioners shall take an oath, to be administered to the governor by the chief justice or any judge of the said colonies respectively, and to the other assistant commissioners by the governor thereof, that they will well and truly and impartially execute the powers and authorities given to them as such assistant commissioners in the several matters and things which shall be referred or submitted to them under the provisions of this act; and the said assistant commissioners shall, in all matters which shall be referred to them by the commissioners, transmit to the said commissioners a full statement of the several matters which shall have been given in evidence before them, and true copies of such written evidence as shall have been received by them, and thereupon the said commissioners shall proceed to adjudicate upon the same, and upon such other evidence, if any, as may be laid before them.

XXXIX. And be it further enacted, That the lords commissioners of the treasury, or any three or more of them, or the lord high treasurer for the time being, shall be and they are hereby respectively authorized and required to issue and cause to be advanced all such sums of money to such person or persons, in such manner, and in such proportion as the said commissioners appointed by this act shall, by writing under their hands, from time to time require, out of the said sum of twenty millions, which sums so to be issued and advanced shall be employed for the payment of allowances, and in defraying all other necessary charges and expences, in or about the execution of the said commission, without other account than that before the lords commissioners of His Majesty's Treasury; and which money so to be issued shall not be subject to any tax, duty, rate, or assessment whatsoever imposed by authority of Parliament; but that an account of the said charges and expences shall be laid before both houses of Parliament within two months after the commencement of the then next ensuing session of Parliament.

XL. And be it further enacted, That the said commissioners shall be and are hereby authorised, by a summons under their hands, or under the hands of any three of them to require the attendence before them, by a time to be in such summons for that purpose limited, of any person or persons competent, or whom such commissioners may have reason to believe to be competent, to give evidence upon any question depending before them; and if any person upon whom any such summons shall be served by the actual delivery thereof to him or her, or by the leaving thereof at his or her usual place of abode, shall, without reasonable cause to be allowed by such commissioners, fail to appear before them at the time and place in such summons for that purpose mentioned, or so appearing shall refuse to be sworn or to make his or her solemn affirmation, as the case may be, or having been so sworn or having made such affirmation shall not make answer to any such questions as may by the said commissioners be proposed to him or her touching any matter or thing depending before them, or shall refuse or fail to produce and exhibit to the said commissioners any such papers and documents relating to any question, matter, or thing depending before such commissioners as shall by them be called for or required, every such person shall, for such his default, refusal, or neglect as aforesaid, incur and become liable to all such fines and penalties, prosecutions, civil suits, or actions as any person may by law incur or become liable to for default of appearance or for refusing to be sworn or to give evidence upon any issue joined in any action depending in His Majesty's court of king's bench; and the said commissioners shall have all such and the same powers, jurisdiction, and authority for imposing and causing to be levied and recovered any such fines and penalties as aforesaid as are by law vested in any of the judges of the said court for imposing or causing to be levied and recovered any fines or penalties incurred by any person failing to appear as a witness or refusing to be sworn and to give evidence in the trial of any action before any such judges or judge.

XLI. And be it further enacted, That the said commissioners may examine upon oath or affirmation (which oath or affirmation they or any one or two of them are and is hereby authorized to administer) all persons who shall appear before them to be examined as witnesses touching any matters or things which may be depending, or touching any questions which may arise, in the execution of the powers vested in the said commissioners by this act, and may also receive any affidavits or depositions in writing, upon oath or affirmation, touching such matters or things as aforesaid, which shall be made before any justice of the peace of any county or shire, or any magistrate of any borough or town corporations, in *Great Britain* or *Ireland*, where or near which the person making such affidavit or deposition shall reside, or before any chief justice or any other judge of any of the courts of record or any supreme courts of judicature in any of the said colonies respectively, and certified and transmitted to the said commissioners under the hand and seal of such justice or magistrate, chief justice or judge (and which oath or affirmation every such justice or magistrate shall be and is hereby authorized and empowered to administer); provided that in every such affidavit or deposition there shall be expressed the addition of the party making such affirmation or deposition, and the particular place of his or her abode.

XLII. And be it further enacted, That if any person or persons upon examination on oath or affirmation before the said commissioners respectively, or if any person or persons making any such affirmation or deposition as before mentioned, shall wilfully and corruptly give false evidence, or shall in such affirmation, affidavit or deposition wilfully or corruptly swear, affirm, or allege any matter or thing which shall be false or untrue, every such person or persons so offending, and being thereof duly convicted, shall be and is and are hereby declared to be subject and liable to the pains and penalties of persons convicted of wilful and corrupt perjury by any law in force at the time of such perjury being committed.

XLIII. And be it further enacted, That the said commissioners shall and may receive and send by the general post, from and to places within the United Kingdom, all letters and packets relating solely and exclusively to the execution of this act free from the duty of postage, provided that such letters and packets as shall be sent to the said commissioners be directed to the "commissioners of compensation," at their office in *London*, and that all such letters and packets as shall be sent by the said commissioners shall be in covers, with the words "compensation office, pursuant to act of Parliament passed in the third and fourth years of the reign of His Majesty King *William* the fourth," printed on the same, and be signed on the outside thereof, under such words, with the name of such person as the said commissioners, with the consent of the lords commissioners of the treasury or any three or more of them, shall authorize and appoint, in his own handwriting (such name to

be from time to time transmitted to the secretaries of the general post office in *London* and *Dublin*), and be sealed with the seal of the said commissioners, and under such other regulations and restrictions as the said lords commissioners, of any three or more of them, shall think proper and direct; and the person so to be authorized is hereby strictly forbidden so to subscribe or seal any letter or packet whatever except such only concerning which he shall receive the special direction of his superior officer, or which he shall himself know to relate solely and exclusively to the execution of this act; and if the person so to be authorised, or any other person, shall send, or cause or permit to be sent, under any such cover, any letter, paper, or writing, or any enclosure, other than what shall relate to the execution of this act, every person so offending shall forfeit and pay the sum of one hundred pounds, and be dismissed from his office; one moiety of the said penalty to the use of His Majesty, his heirs and successors, and the other moiety to the use of the person who shall inform or sue for the same, to be sued for and recovered in any of His Majesty's courts of record at *Westminster* for offences committed in *England*, and in any of His Majesty's courts of record in *Dublin* for offences committed in *Ireland*, and before the sheriff or stewartry court of the shire or stewartry within which the party offending shall reside or the offence shall be committed for offences committed in *Scotland*.

XLIV. And be it further enacted, That no part of the said sum of twenty millions of pounds sterling shall be applied or shall be applicable to the purposes aforesaid, for the benefit of any person now entitled to the services of any slave in any of the colonies aforesaid, unless an order shall have been first made by His Majesty, with the advice of his Privy Council, declaring that adequate and satisfactory provision hath been made by law in such colony for giving effect to this present act by such further and supplementary enactments as aforesaid, nor unless a copy of such order in council, duly certified by one of the clerks in ordinary of His Majesty's Privy Council, shall by the lord president of the council have been transmitted to the lords commissioners of His Majesty's Treasury or to the lord high treasurer for the time being for their or his guidance or information; and every such order shall be published three several times in the *London Gazette*, and shall be laid before both houses of Parliament within six weeks next after the date thereof if Parliament shall be then in session, and if not within six weeks from the then next ensuing session of Parliament.

XLV. And be it further enacted, That the said commissioners shall proceed to apportion the said sum into nineteen different shares, which shall be respectively assigned to the several *British* colonies or possessions herein-after mentioned: (that is to say,) the *Bermuda Islands*, the *Bahama Islands*, *Jamaica*, *Honduras*, the *Virgin Islands*, *Antigua*, *Montserrat*, *Nevis*, *Saint Christopher's*, *Dominica*, *Barbados*, *Grenada*, *Saint Vincent's*, *Tobago*, *Saint Lucia*, *Trinidad*, *British Guiana*, the *Cape of Good Hope*, and *Mauritius*; and in making such apportionment of the said funds between the said several colonies the said commissioners shall and are hereby required to have regard to the number of slaves belonging to or settled in each of such colonies as the same may appear and are stated according to the latest returns made in the office of the registrar of slaves in *England*, appointed in pursuance and under the authority of an act passed in the fifty-ninth year of His late Majesty King *George* the Third, intituled *An Act for establishing a Registry of Colonial Slaves in* Great Britain, *and for making further provision with respect to the removal of slaves from* British *colonies*; and the said commissioners shall and they are hereby further required, in making such apportionment as aforesaid, to have regard to the prices for which, on an average of eight years ending on the thirty-first day of *December* one thousand eight hundred and thirty, slaves have been sold in each of the colonies aforesaid respectively, excluding from consideration any such sales in which they shall have sufficient reason to suppose that such slaves were sold or purchased under any reservation, or subject to any express or tacit condition affecting the price thereof; and the said commissioners shall then proceed to ascertain in reference to each colony, what amount of sterling money will represent the average value of a slave therein for the said period of eight years; and the total number of the slaves in each colony being multiplied into the amount of sterling money so representing such average value as aforesaid of a slave therein, the product of such multiplication shall be ascertained for each such colony separately; and the said twenty millions of pounds sterling shall then be assigned to and apportioned amongst the said several colonies rateably and in proportion to the product so ascertained for each respectively.

XLVI. And be it further enacted, That in case it shall appear to the said commissioners that any persons in respect of whom claims for compensation under the provisions of this act shall have been made have been registered and held in slavery in any of the said colonies in this act mentioned contrary to law, then and in every such case the said commissioners shall deduct from the sum to be appropriated as compensation to the proprietors in such colony such sums as shall correspond with the estimated value and number of the said persons so illegally registered and held in slavery; and all such sum or sums which may be deducted as herein-before provided shall be applied towards defraying the general expences of the commission to be hereby appointed: provided always that for the purpose of ascertaining in what cases such deductions shall be made, every question which shall arise in any such colony respecting the servile condition of any persons therein registered as slaves shall be inquired of and determined by the commissioners to be appointed under this act according to such rules of legal presumption and evidence as are or shall be established by any law in force or which shall be in force in any such colony.

XLVII. And whereas it is necessary that provision should be made for the apportionment amongst the proprietors of the slaves to be manumitted by virtue of this act, in each of the said colonies respectively, of that part of the said compensation fund which shall be so assigned as aforesaid to each of the respective colonies: and whereas the necessary rules for that purpose cannot be properly or safely established until after full inquiry shall have been made into the several circumstances which ought to be taken into consideration in making such apportionment; Be it therefore enacted, That it shall be the duty of the said commissioners, and they are hereby authorized and required, to institute a full and exact inquiry into all the circumstances connected with each of the said several colonies which in the judgment of the said commissioners ought, in justice and equity, to regulate or affect the apportionment within the same of that part of the said general compensation fund which shall in manner aforesaid be assigned to each of the said colonies respectively; and especially such commissioners shall have regard to the relative value of praedial slaves and of unattached slaves in every such colony; and such commissioners shall distinguish such slaves, whether praedial or unattached, into as many distinct classes as, regard being had to the circumstances of each colony, shall appear just; and such commissioners shall, with all practicable precision, ascertain and fix the average value of a slave in each of the classes into which the slaves in any such colony shall be so divided; and the said commissioners shall also proceed to inquire and consider of the principles according to which the compensation to be allotted in respect to any slave or body of slaves ought, according to the rules of law and equity, to be distributed amongst persons who, as owners or creditors, legatees or annuitants, may have any joint or common interest in any such slave or slaves, or may be entitled to or interested in such slave or slaves, either in possession, remainder, reversion, or expectancy; and the said commissioners shall also proceed to inquire and consider of the principles upon which and the manner in which provision might be most effectually made for the protection of any interest in any such compensation money which may belong to or be vested in any married women, infants, lunatics, or persons of insane or unsound mind, or persons beyond the seas, or labouring under any other legal or natural disability or incapacity, and according to what rules, and in what manner, and under what authority trustees should, when necessary, be appointed for the safe custody, for the benefit of any person or persons, of any such compensation fund or of any part thereof, and for regulating the duties of such trustees, and providing them with a fair and reasonable indemnity; and the said commissioners shall also inquire and consider upon what principles, according to the established rules of law and equity in similar cases, the succession to such funds should be regulated upon the death of any person entitled thereto who may die intestate; and the said commissioners shall and they are also authorized and required to consider of any other question which it may be necessary to investigate in order to establish just and equitable rules for the apportionment of such compensation money amongst the persons seized of, or entitled to, or having any mortgage, charge, incumbrance, judgment, or lien upon, or any claim to, or right or interest in, any slave or slaves so to be manumitted as aforesaid, at the time of such their manumission; and having made all such inquiries, and having taken all such matters and things as aforesaid into their consideration, the said commissioners shall and are hereby required to proceed to draw up and frame all such general rules, regard being had to the laws and usages in force in each colony respectively, as to them may seem best adapted in each colony respectively for securing the just and equitable distribution of the said funds amongst or for the benefit of such several persons as aforesaid, and for the protection of such funds, and for the appointment and indemnification of such trustees as aforesaid; and

such general rules when so framed, and when agreed upon by the said commissioners, shall by them be subscribed with their respective hands and seals, and transmitted to the lord president of His Majesty's council, to be by him laid before His Majesty in council; and so from time to time as often as any further general rules should be so framed and agreed to for the purposes aforesaid or any of them.

XLVIII. And be it further enacted, That the general rules to be transmitted as aforesaid to the said lord president shall be forthwith published in the *London Gazette* on three several occasions at least, together with a notice that all persons interested in or affected by any such general rules may, by a time to be in such notice limited, appeal against any such rules to His Majesty in council; and it shall be lawful for the lords and others of His Majesty's Privy Council, or for any three or more of them, by any further notice or notices to be for that purpose published in the *London Gazette*, to enlarge, as to them may seem meet, the time for receiving any such appeals.

XLIX. And be it further enacted, That if within the time so to be limited for receiving such appeals any person or persons shall prefer any petition of appeal to His Majesty in council against any such general rule so published as aforesaid in the *London Gazette*, it shall be lawful for His Majesty in council, or for any committee of Privy Council, to hear such appeal, and to cause notice thereof to be served upon the said commissioners, who shall thereupon undertake the defence of such appeal; and upon hearing any such appeal it shall be lawful for His Majesty in council to confirm and annul or to rescind and disallow any such general rule as aforesaid, or thereupon to alter, amend, or vary any such rule in such manner as to His Majesty may seem just, or to remit the same to the said commissioners for further consideration and revision.

L. And be it further enacted, That at the expiration of the time limited for receiving such appeals as aforesaid it shall be lawful for His Majesty in council to confirm and allow, or to rescind and disallow, in the whole or in part, or to amend, alter, or vary, any such general rule or rules, though not so appealed against, as to His Majesty may seem just, or to remit such rules to the said commissioners for further consideration and revision.

LI. And be it further enacted, That when and so often as any such general rule or rules as aforesaid shall by His Majesty in council have been confirmed and allowed, an order shall be made by His Majesty in council, reciting at length any such rule or rules, with any alterations or amendments which may have been therein made as aforesaid; and a copy of every such order in council shall be duly certified by the lord president of His Majesty's council for the time being to the lord high chancellor or keeper of the great seal, or to the master of the rolls, for the time being, and shall be duly inrolled among the records of the high court of chancery, and shall there remain and be of record.

LII. And be it further enacted, That it shall be lawful, by any rules so to be framed, published, confirmed, allowed, and inrolled as aforesaid, to revoke, amend, alter, and again renew, as occasion may require, and as may be thought just, any former or preceding rule or rules.

LIII. And be it further enacted, That every such general rule as aforesaid, when so inrolled as aforesaid, shall be of the same validity, force, virtue, and effect as if the same had been made and enacted by His Majesty, by and with the advice and consent of Parliament: provided nevertheless, that no such rule shall be in anywise repugnant to or at variance with this act or any part thereof, or with the laws and usages in force in the several colonies respectively to which such rules may relate, so far as any such laws or usages may not be repugnant to or at variance with the provisions of this act.

LIV. And be it further enacted, That the said general rules, when so framed, confirmed, allowed, and inrolled as aforesaid, shall be observed and followed by the said commissioners, and shall be binding upon them in the further execution of the said commission, and in the exercise of the powers and authorities hereby committed to them, and shall in all cases be taken, observed, and followed as the rules for the decision of and adjudication upon all claims which may be preferred to them by any person or persons having or claiming to have any interest in the said compensation fund or in any part thereof.

LV. And be it further enacted, That any person having or claiming to have had any right, title, or interest in or to, or any mortgage, judgment, charge, incumbrance, or other lien upon, any slave or slaves so to be manumitted as aforesaid, at the time of such their manumission, shall and may prefer such claims before the said commissioners; and for ensuring method, regularity, and dispatch in the mode of preferring and of proceeding upon such claims, the said commissioners shall and are hereby authorized by general rules, to be framed and published, confirmed, allowed, and inrolled as aforesaid, to prescribe the form and manner of proceeding to be observed by any claimant or claimants preferring any such claims, and to authorize the assistant commissioners so to be appointed in the said several colonies to receive and report upon the same or any of them in such manner and form and under such regulations as to the commissioners so to be appointed by His Majesty as aforesaid shall seem meet, and to prescribe the manner, the time or times, the place or places, and the form or forms in which notices of such claims shall be published for general information, or especially communicated to or served upon any person or persons interested therein or affected thereby, and to prescribe the form and manner of proceeding to be observed upon the prosecution of such claims, or in making any opposition to the same, and to make all such regulations as to them may seem best adapted for promoting method, economy, and dispatch in the investigation of such claims, and respecting the evidence to be taken and admitted for or against the same, and respecting the manner and form of adjudicating thereupon, and otherwise however respecting the method, form, and manner of proceeding to be observed either by them the said assistant commissioners, or by the parties to any proceedings before them, their agents or witnesses, and which rules shall from time to time be liable to be amended, altered, varied, or renewed as occasion may require, in such manner as is herein-before directed.

LVI. And be it further enacted, That the said commissioners shall proceed, in the manner to be prescribed by any such general rules as last aforesaid, to inquire into and adjudicate upon any such claims as may be so preferred to them, and shall upon each such claim make their adjudication and award in such manner and form as shall be prescribed by any such last-mentioned general rules; and if any person interested in or affected by any such adjudication or award shall be dissatisfied therewith, it shall be lawful for such person to appeal therefrom to His Majesty in council, and notice of any such appeal shall be served upon the said commissioners, who shall thereupon undertake the defence thereof; and it shall be competent to His Majesty in council to make and establish all such rules and regulations as to His Majesty shall seem meet respecting the time and manner of preferring and proceeding upon such appeals, and respecting the course to be observed in defending the same, which rules shall be so framed as to promote as far as may be consistent with justice, all practicable economy and dispatch in the proceeding upon the decision thereof; and in cases in which any two or more persons shall have preferred before the said commissioners adverse or opposing claims, and in which any or either of such persons shall be interested to sustain the adjudications or award of such commissioners thereupon, then and in every such case it shall be lawful for any person or persons so interested, to undertake the defence of any such appeal in lieu and instead of the said commissioners.

LVII. And be it further enacted, That it shall be lawful for His Majesty in council, upon hearing any such appeal as aforesaid, either to confirm and allow or to reverse or to amend or alter any such adjudication or award as to His Majesty in council shall seem fit, or to remit any such adjudication and award to the said commissioners for further consideration and revision, or for the admission of further evidence; but it shall not be lawful for His Majesty in council, upon the hearing of any such appeal, to admit any new evidence which was not admitted by or tendered to the said commissioners before the making of such their adjudication and award.

LVIII. And be it further enacted, That the several adjudications and awards of the said commissioners, unless duly appealed from within the respective times to be limited by His Majesty in council for that purpose, shall be final and conclusive and binding upon all persons interested therein or affected thereby; and that the decisions of His Majesty in council upon any such appeal shall in like manner be final, binding, and conclusive.

LIX. And be it further enacted, That the lord high treasurer or the commissioners of His Majesty's Treasury, or any three or more of them, for the time being, may order and direct to be issued and paid out of the said sum of twenty millions of pounds sterling any sum or sums of money for the payment of salaries to commissioners, officers, clerks, and other persons acting in relation to such compensation in the execution of this act, and for discharging such incidental expences as shall necessarily attend the same, in such manner as the lord high treasurer, or commissioners of the treasury, or any three or more of them, shall from time to time think fit and reasonable; and an account of such expence shall be annually laid before Parliament.

LX. And be it enacted, That a certificate containing a list of the names and designation of the several persons in whose favour any sum or sums of money shall be awarded from time to time under the provisions of this act by the commissioners, as herein-before mentioned, shall be signed by three or more of the said commissioners, who shall forthwith transmit the same to His Majesty's principal secretary of state then having charge of the affairs of the said colonies, for his approbation and signature, who shall, when he shall have signed the same, transmit it to the commissioners of His Majesty's Treasury; and the said commissioners of the treasury, or any three of such commissioners, shall thereupon, by warrant under their hands, authorize the commissioners for the reduction of the national debt to pay the said sums, out of the monies standing upon their account in the books of the said bank under the title of "the *West India* compensation account," to the persons named in such certificate; and the said commissioners for the reduction of the national debt, or the comptroller general or assistant comptroller general acting under the said commissioners, are hereby required to pay all such sums of money to the persons named therein under such forms and regulations as the said commissioners for the reduction of the national debt shall think sit to adopt for that purpose.

LXI. And whereas in some of the colonies aforesaid a certain statute, made in the thirteenth and fourteenth years of King *Charles* the second, intituled *An Act for preventing the mischiefs and dangers that may arise by certain persons called Quakers and others refusing to take lawful oaths*; and a certain other statute made in the seventeenth year of King *Charles* the second, intituled *An Act for restraining Nonconformists from inhabiting in corporations*; and a certain other statute, made in the twenty-second year of King *Charles* the second, intituled *An Act to prevent and suppress seditious conventicles*; and a certain other statute, made in the first and second year of King *William* and Queen *Mary*, intituled *An Act for exempting Their Majesties Protestant subjects dissenting from the church of England from the penalties of certain laws*; and a certain other statute, made in the tenth year of Queen *Anne*, intituled *An Act for prefering the Protestant religion by better securing the church of* England *as by law established; and for confirming the toleration granted to Protestant Dissenters by an act intituled 'An Act for exempting Their Majesties Protestant subjects dissenting from the church of*

England *from the penalties of certain laws,' and for supplying the defects thereof; and for the further securing the Protestant succession by requiring the practicers of the law in* North Briton *to take the oaths and subscribe the declaration therein mentioned*; or some or one of those statutes, or some parts thereof or of some of them, have and hath been adopted, and are or is in force; be it further enacted, That in such of the colonies aforesaid in which the said several statutes or any of them, or any parts thereof or any of them, have or hath been adopted, and are or is in force, a certain statute made in the fifty-second year of his late majesty King *George* the third, intituled *An Act to repeal certain acts and amend other acts relating to religious worship and assemblies, and persons teaching or preaching therein,* shall be and is hereby declared to be in force as fully and effectually as [if] such colonies had been expressly named and enumerated for that purpose in such last-recited statute: provided nevertheless, that in the said several colonies to which the said act of his late majesty King *George* the third is so extended and declared applicable as aforesaid any two or more justices of the peace holding any such special commission as aforesaid shall have, exercise, and enjoy all and every the jurisdiction, powers, and authorities whatsoever which by force and virtue of the said act are within the realm of *England* had, exercised, and enjoyed by the several justices of the peace, and by the general and quarter sessions therein mentioned.

LXII. And whereas in the settlements in the occupation of His Majesty and of His Majesty's subjects in *Honduras,* no law is in force for the registration of slaves, and doubts might be entertained respecting the authority of His Majesty, with the advice of his Privy Council, to make laws binding on His Majesty's subjects therein; Be it therefore declared and enacted that it is and shall be lawful for His Majesty, by any order or orders to be by him for that purpose made with the advice of his Privy Council, to establish a registry of slaves for the purposes of this act within the settlement; and all laws made by His Majesty for the government of his said subjects shall, for the purposes of this act, be as valid and effectual as any laws made by His Majesty in council for the government of any colonies subject to the legislative authority of His Majesty in council are or can be.

LXIII. And be it further enacted, That within the meaning and for the purposes of this act every person who for the time being shall be in the lawful administration of the government of any of the said colonies shall be taken to be the governor thereof.

LXIV. And be it further enacted, That nothing in this act contained doth or shall extend to any of the territories in the possession of the *East India* company, or to the island of *Ceylon,* or to the island of *Saint Helena.*

LXV. And be it further enacted, That in the colonies of the *Cape of Good Hope* and *Mauritius* the several parts of this act shall take effect and come into operation, or shall cease to operate and to be in force, as the case may be, at periods more remote than the respective periods herein-before for such purposes limited by the following intervals of time: *videlicet*, by four calendar months in the colony of the *Cape of Good Hope,* and by six calendar months in the colony of the *Mauritius.*

LXVI. And be it further enacted and declared, That within the meaning and for the purposes of this act all islands and territories dependent upon any of the colonies aforesaid, and constituting parts of the same colonial government, shall respectively be taken to be parts of such respective colonies.

Source: Anti-Slavery Reporter, 6:6 (December 26, 1833).

The Gag Rule (1836)

The main question was then stated, viz: that the House do agree to the resolutions reported by the committee, which are as follows:

1. *Resolved,* That Congress possesses no constitutional authority to interfere, in any way, with the institution of slavery in any of the States of this confederacy.

2. *Resolved,* That Congress ought not to interfere, in any way, with slavery in the District of Columbia.

And whereas, it is extremely important and desirable that the agitation of this subject should be finally arrested, for the purpose of restoring tranquillity to the public mind, your committee respectfully recommend the adoption of the following additional resolution, viz:

3. *Resolved,* That all petitions, memorials, resolutions, propositions, or papers, relating in any way or to any extent whatever to the subject of slavery, or the abolition of slavery, shall, without being either printed or referred, be laid upon the table, and that no further action whatever shall be had thereon.

Source: U.S. House Journal, 24th Cong., 1st sess., May 25, 1836.

The Cuban Slave Code (1843)

Article I. It shall be the duty of every owner of slaves to instruct them in the principles of the Roman catholic Apostolical Religion, in order that they may be baptized, if they have not already been so; and, in the case of necessity, he shall baptize them himself, it being certain that under such circumstances any one may do so.

Article II. The instruction to which the preceding article refers, is to be given at night after the hours of labour, and he (the owner) shall every evening oblige them to repeat to him the Rosary, or some other devout prayers.

Article III. On Sundays and festivals, after the slaves shall have fulfilled their religious duties, the master or manager may employ them for the space of two hours, and no longer, in cleaning out the houses and offices; but he shall not employ them in the labours of the field unless it be in the time of crop, or in other duties which do not admit of delay; in which cases they shall labour as on ordinary days.

Article IV. They (the masters or managers) shall, on their responsibility, take care that the slaves who have been baptized, and who may be of sufficient age, shall have the sacrament of the mass administered to them, at such time as the Holy Mother Church directs, or it may be necessary.

Article V. They shall use the utmost pains, and all possible diligence, to make them comprehend the obedience which they owe to the constituted authorities; the obligation to reverence the priests; to respect white persons; to comport themselves properly with people of colour; and to live in harmony among themselves.

Article VI. The masters shall give to their field slaves two or three meals daily, as may appear best to the master, provided that they be sufficient to maintain and to reinvigorate them after their fatigues; it being understood, as of absolute necessity, that the daily nourishment for each individual shall be six or eight plantains, or its equivalent in sweet potatoes, yams, cassava, or other esculent roots; eight ounces of beef or salt fish; and four ounces of rice, meal, or flour.

Article VII. The masters shall be obliged to provide the slaves with two dresses annually, in the months of December and May. Each one composed of a shirt and trowsers of duck or osnaburgh, a cap or hat, and a handkerchief. To these in December he shall add, alternately, one year a shirt or jacket of flannel, and another year a blanket, to protect themselves during the winter.

Article VIII. New-born or infant negroes, whose mothers are employed in the labours of the field, shall be nourished with easily digestible things, as soups, *atoles* (a liquor made of Indian corn in its milky state), milk, &c., until they have passed the time of weaning and dentition.

Article IX. Whilst the mothers are at work, all the children shall remain in a house or apartment, which should be provided for the purpose on every sugar and coffee estate, and which shall be under the care of one or more negresses, as the master or manager may deem requisite, according to their number.

Article X. If the infants should be sick during their lactation, they shall then be nourished at the breasts of their own mothers; the latter being, for that purpose, separated from the ordinary labours of the field, and employed in domestic occupations.

Article XI. Until they arrive at the age of three years, the children shall be provided with short check shirts; from three to six they shall be of duck; to the females, from six to twelve years, shall be given petticoats or large shifts; and the males, from six to fourteen, shall also be provided with trowsers,—after this age they shall have the ordinary clothing.

Article XII. On ordinary occasions, the slaves shall labour from nine to ten hours daily, the master regulating them in the way which may appear to him best. On sugar estates, during the time of crop, the hours of labour shall be sixteen daily, divided in such manner as to leave two hours rest during the day, and six hours at night for sleep.

Article XIII. On Sundays and festivals, and during the hours appropriated to rest on working days, the slaves shall be permitted to employ themselves, within the estate, in manufactures or occupations, which shall result in their personal benefit, in order that they may acquire *peculium* with a view of redeeming themselves.

Article XIV. No male slaves above seventy years of age or under seventeen, nor any female, shall be forced to perform task-work; and neither of these classes shall be employed in labours which are unsuitable to their sex, age, health, and strength.

Article XV. The slaves who through advanced age or infirmity are no longer fit for labour, should be supported by the owners; and they shall not grant them their liberty in order to get rid of them, unless they are provided with a sufficient *peculium*, to the satisfaction of the constituted authorities, the Syndic being first heard, in order that they may be maintained without the need of other assistance.

Source: Anti-Slavery Reporter, 4:4 (February 22, 1843).

The French Colonial Act of Emancipation (1848)

The French National Assembly, April 27, 1848.

PROCLAMATION.

In the name of the French people, the Provisional Government, Considering that slavery is an attack against human dignity; that by destroying man's free will, it removes the natural principles of the right and the duty; that it is a flagrant violation of the republican dogma:

Liberty, Equality, Fraternity, decrees:—

Art[icle] 1. Slavery is completely abolished in the French colonies and possessions.

Art[icle] 2. The system of engagement currently established in Senegal, is suppressed.

Art[icle] 3. Governors and general commissioners of the Republic are charged with applying all the measures, appropriate to ensure liberty in Martinique, Guadeloupe and its dependencies, Reunion, French Guiana, Senegal and other French settlements of African's eastern coast, Mayotte and the dependencies, and Algeria.

Art[icle] 4. Old slaves who were charged with misdemeanors or personally entailed this punishment for facts which, ascribed to free people, should not have entailed punishment, are freed. People who were deported by administrative measures are recalled.

Art[icle] 5. The National Assembly will settle the quota of the indemnity which will be granted to the colonists.

Art[icle] 6. The colonies cleansed from bondage and the Indian possession will be represented at the National Assembly.

Art[icle] 7. The principle that the French soil liberates the slave who reaches it applies to the Republic's colonies and possessions.

Art[icle] 8. In the future, even in foreign countries, it is prohibited for French people to possess, buy or sell slaves or participate either directly or indirectly in all that kind of traffic or exploitation. All infractions of these decisions will entail the loss of French citizenship.

Art[icle] 9. The Minister of the Navy and the colonies and the Minister of the War are charged with the execution of the terms of the present decree.

Source: Anti-Slavery Reporter (New Series), 3:30 (June 1, 1848).

Emancipation Decrees for the French Colonies (1848)

Liberty, Equality, Fraternity.

PROVISION FOR THE AGED, INFIRM, AND ORPHANS.

In the name of the French people.—The Provisional Government, considering that aid and assistance are due by society to all its members in case of need, and that the principle of brotherhood imposes the like duty upon all men one to another, decrees—

Art[icle] 1. In the colonies where slavery is abolished by the decree of this day, the aged and infirm shall be kept upon those plantations where the labourers are willing to give the proprietors an amount of labour equivalent to their maintenance, with board and lodging.

Art[icle] 2. The sacrifices consented to by the generosity of the emancipated shall be regulated by the local authority.

Art[icle] 3. The aged and infirm without help, until the establishment of asylums for their reception, shall be placed under the care of decent families, with an equitable allowance.

Art[icle] 4. Helpless orphans shall be placed in agricultural schools, or other establishments of public instruction, to receive an intellectual and professional education.

Eating-houses and asylums shall be opened in all the villages whenever judged necessary by the authority. Fines collected on decisions of the justices of the peace and district juries, shall be lodged in the municipal chests, and exclusively appropriated to the support of the aged and infirm, orphans, and children of labourers.

EDUCATION.

The Provisional Government, considering that the preparation of youth for a moral, civil, and political life, is one of the first duties which society owes to itself; that the more there are of enlightened men in a nation, the more are the law and justice respected; and that society owes a gratuitous education to all its members; decrees—

Art[icle] 1. In the colonies where slavery is abolished by the decree of this day, there shall be founded, in each district, a free elementary school for girls, and one for boys.

Art[icle] 2. Such schools, placed in localities chosen with a view to facilitating the attendance of the children, shall be increased in number according to the wants of the population.

Art[icle] 3. None shall be suffered to evade the duty of sending to school his child, whether boy or girl, of between six and ten years of age, unless he provides the means for their instruction under the paternal roof.

Art[icle] 4. Every father, mother, or guardian, who without good reason, and after being thrice warned by the mayor of the district, shall neglect to send his or her children to school, shall be liable to fifteen days' imprisonment.

Art[icle] 5. The absence of the child from school shall be noted by the teacher in a weekly report to be addressed by him to the mayor of the district; the justice of the peace to decide on view of such report, and after hearing the delinquent.

Art[icle] 6. The classes shall not be held during less than six hours per day.

Art[icle] 7. The Government will cause to be made, for the colonial schools, elementary books, wherein shall be prominently set forth the advantages and respectability of agricultural pursuits.

Art[icle] 8. The school-rooms may be placed at the disposal of the persons accepted by the Government, for the holding of evening and Sunday classes, for the benefit of adults of both sexes.

Art[icle] 9. The establishment of public schools not to prevent private schools, which should be opened conformably to the existing laws.

Art[icle] 10. A normal school of arts and trades shall be established in each colony.

An academy, designed for the introduction into the colonies of secondary instruction, shall be founded in Guadaloupe, without prejudice to district colleges that should be established.

Art[icle] 11. An institution of a superior degree shall be established in Martinique for young females.

COMPOSITION OF DISTRICT JURIES.

Art[icle] 1. There shall be established in each district, a jury composed of six members, sitting in public court, at the principal place of the district, under the presidency of the justice of the peace. This jury to be renewed every month one-third.

Art[icle] 2. The jurors to be balloted for out of the electoral lists of the district. The names borne upon these lists shall be placed in an urn, and the justice of the peace will cause them to be drawn in open court. This drawing must designate six incumbent jurors, and afterwards three supernumeraries, residing at the principal place of the district. There shall be no challenges but such as are authorized by the general law against the judges. The registrar will prepare the *process-verbal* of the operation. The citizens drawn in the ballot shall be apprized thereof by administrative notification at least eight days prior to the 1st of each month.

Art[icle] 3. Three citizens possessing or exercising a trade (*industrie*), and three others, industrial or agricultural labourers, shall be qualified to form such jury. The magistrate, who is chief of the jury, to decide all questions of impediment, exclusion, or disqualification.

Art[icle] 4. Such of the incumbent jurors as may be declared excluded, shall be replaced out of the three supernumeraries.

The jury to sit at least twice a week, and the days of its sessions shall be announced by placards throughout all the district.

POWERS OF THE DISTRICT JURIES IN CIVIL MATTERS.

Art[icle] 5. The jury shall conciliate, if possible, of its own accord, or on presentation of the parties, or upon notice to appear free of cost, all disputes upon the performance of engagements; whether between proprietors and managers, masters, workmen, labourers, or domestics; or between the heads of industry, manufacturers or tradesmen, and their clerks, overseers, workmen, or apprentices. In default of conciliation, the jury shall decide upon a simple citation, and without costs. The judgments shall be signed by the magistrate who is foreman of the jury, and by his registrar. There shall be no appeal where the judgment does not exceed 300 francs; above that sum, the appeal may be taken before the tribunal of the arrondissement. The provisional execution shall take place in all cases, but security must be given when the judgment does not exceed 300 francs.

Art[icle] 6. [Article] 1781 of the Code Civil, enacting that the master shall be believed on his affirmation, in the cases set forth in the said article, is repealed.

POWERS OF THE JURIES IN PENAL MATTERS.

Art[icle] 7. Everything tending to the interruption of order or work upon the estates, workshops, manufactories, or stores; all serious offences of the proprietors, managers, workmen, or labourers, towards one another, may be punished by the district juries with a fine of 5 to 100 francs, without prejudice to such higher pains as the offender may be liable to under the Penal Code; the condemnation to be without appeal.

Art[icle] 8. All combinations among the superintendents of workmen, or among the labourers, tending unjustly or abusively to lower or raise wages, to interrupt work in an establishment, to prevent attendance or continuance thereat before or after certain hours, and every combination generally which may be prejudicial to the general maintenance of work, shall be punished by a fine of 20 fr[ancs] to 3,000 fr[ancs].

Art[icle] 9. The same punishment shall be inflicted on all individuals employing people to work and on all working people, who shall have imposed penalties, prohibitions, interdictions, or proscriptions one against the other.

Art[icle] 10. The Articles 414, 415, and 416, of the Penal Code, are repealed, and Articles 8 and 9 of the present decree substituted for them.

Art[icle]. 11. In the cases provided for by the foregoing Articles, 7, 8, and 9, the proceedings to be instituted by the public prosecutor before the courts of simple police, and according to the established forms of such courts. In the cases of Articles 8 and 9, the convicted shall have the right of appealing to the correctional jurisdictions established in the colonies.

Art[icle] 12. The jurors shall be entitled, if they require it, to an indemnity of two francs for each day of the sessions.

Art[icle] 13. The attributions of the justices of the peace, whether in civil cases or police matters, as determined by existing legislation in the colonies, are retained wherever they are not repugnant to the requirements of the present decree.

WORKING ESTABLISHMENTS.

The Provisional Government of the Republic, considering that the right of work should be secured to all, decrees—

That under the denomination of National Establishments (*ateliers nationaux*), there shall be instituted in the colonies working establishments, the organization of which shall be regulated under instructions of the Minister of Marine and the Colonies. Any individual out of work may there find employment, on agreeing to the terms prescribed by ministerial instructions.

MENDACITY AND VAGABONDAGE.

The Provisional Government of the Republic, considering work to be the first guarantee of morality in order to liberty; and that the general safety is interested in the repressing of mendacity and vagabondage, decrees—

Art[icle] 1. In the colonies where slavery is abolished by the decree of this day, mendacity and vagabondage shall be punished correctionally, as follows:—All beggars, persons of no known profession, or vagabonds, shall be placed at the disposition of the Government for a determinate period between three and six months, according to the gravity of the case. They shall during that time be employed, to the benefit of the state, on public works, in disciplinary establishments, the organization and system of which shall be regulated by an order of the Minister of Marine and the Colonies. They may either be kept within doors at the establishment, or conducted out to work in charge of agents of the public force.

Art[icle] 2. The houses and grounds now appropriated to the slaves, as also the fruit trees of which they have the enjoyment, shall remain the property of the masters, unless otherwise agreed. Nevertheless, the proprietors shall not have the power of depriving the emancipated of the fruits and crops, whether pending by the branch or by the root.

Art[icle] 3. Any person who shall occupy lands belonging to the State or to private parties, without being allowed the usufruct, or without the title of lessee, tenant, or otherwise, shall be ejected by authority of the administrative police, and be liable to the penalties set forth in Article 1.

Art[icle] 4. There shall be organized a corps of rural inspectors invested with the judiciary powers of police, and especially appointed to detect the offences set forth in the preceding articles. The rural inspectors shall wear a distinguishing uniform, but shall not go armed.

Art[icle] 5. All the provisions of the *Code Penal* are held in force, except where they may be repugnant to the present decree.

SAVINGS' BANKS.

The Provisional Government decrees—

That Savings' Banks, in imitation of those of France, be established in the colonies, under the auspices of the Republic, and under the direction of the administration.

TAXATION.

The Provisional Government decrees—

Art[icle] 1. There shall be provided by order of the Commissaries-General of the Republic, a new apportionment of personal taxes after emancipation in the colonies.

Art[icle] 2. The tax-payer may be authorized, without being thereto constrained, to pay this tax by three days' labour.

The tax upon the manufacture and consumption of rum, *tafia*, wine, and other spirituous liquors, shall be imposed or raised by order of the Commissaries-General of the Republic, in conformity with the decree of this day regulating their powers.

Art[icle] 3. There shall be made an augmentation of the price of licences of grog-shop keepers and other retailers of spirits.

REWARDS OF INDUSTRY.

The Provisional Government, considering slavery to have dishonoured labour in the colonies; that it becomes necessary to efface by all possible means the character of degradation which has been imparted by servitude to agriculture; and that remunerations given to the best working-hands would still increase the happy influence of freedom upon the manners; decrees—

That there shall be celebrated each year, a festival of work, with all its paraphernalia and all the pomp wherewith it may be possible to surround it. It shall be presided over, in the principal town, by the Commissary-General of the Republic; in the second-rate town, by the Procureur-General; and in each canton, by the justice of the peace. There shall be publicly awarded at such festival, in each principal place of the canton, a prize to the labourer (male or female) most distinguished for good conduct: the prize to be 200 francs, or thirty acres of good arable land. Besides this prize, there shall be given six distinguishing eulogiums in honour of the most meritorious. At the seat of government, the Commissary-General of the Republic will award a superior prize to the labourer (man or woman) meriting that distinction: this superior prize to be of 600 francs, or of a *hectare* of good arable land, besides a place in the Colonial Academy of Guadaloupe, of which the laureate, if without a child of his or her own, may dispose to the benefit of any child of his or her choice; if the election should fall upon a female, she shall be brought up in the institution established by Art[icle] 11 of the decree on public instruction. The Colonial Council of each commune will name a candidate for the district prize. The mayors of each canton, meeting at the principal place of such canton, under the presidency of the justice of the peace, will select amongst the candidates so presented the one worthy of the district prize. The justices of the peace, assembled under the presidency of the Director of the Interior, will select amongst the district laureates the one meriting the superior prize. No one shall obtain a prize or distinguishing honour who shall have been seen at any time during the year in a state of drunkenness. All labourers who shall have gained a superior prize, and who shall not have subsequently proved unworthy, shall obtain a place of honour in all national fetes and ceremonies. The festival of work shall be celebrated every year on the anniversary of emancipation.

SUPPRESSION OF THE COLONIAL COUNCILS.

Whereas Art[icle] 3, of the decree of the 5th March, admits the French Colonies into the National Representation, the Provisional Government decrees—

That the Colonial Councils of Martinique, Guadaloupe, French Guiana, and the Ile de la Reunion, and the General Councils of Senegal and the French Settlements in India, are suppressed. The functions of the Colonial Delegates are likewise suppressed from this date.

POWER OF REALIZING CHARGES ON ESTATES.

The Provisional Government, considering the necessity of restoring prosperity in the French colonies by the re-establishment of credit, and of maintaining work in securing a just remuneration to the labourers freed from slavery; that the impossibility of realizing mortgages by means of auction sales, outbiddings, or levies on immoveable property (*saisie reelle*), is the principal cause of the sufferings of colonial agriculture and industry, and that the case should be provided for; but that, nevertheless, in re-establishing to this effect a general law in the colonies, it is necessary temporarily to admit of certain modifications; decrees—

That the requirements of the 18th and 19th sections of the 3rd book of the *Code Civil*, concerning mortgages and compulsory expropriation, shall continue to be executed, or shall come into effect under certain specified modifications, in the colonies of Martinique, Guadaloupe and its dependencies, French Guiana, and the Ile de la Reunion, so soon as the present decree shall have been promulgated in those colonies.

LIBERTY OF THE PRESS.

The Provisional Government, considering that the liberty of the press is the first business of a free country; that the colonies are from henceforth called to enjoy all the public rights of the nation; and that if colonial communities, in times of slavery, stood in dread of free discussion, they should be now equally unfettered in mind, as they are in servitude; decrees—

Art[icle] 1. That censorship over newspapers and other writings, invested in the administrative authority by the Articles 44 and 49 of the ordinance of 9th February 1837, is abolished. In future all journals may be printed and published without previous authorization, and are not liable to be suspended or disallowed by the administration. All writings not condemned by the tribunals may be freely introduced into the colonies.

Art[icle] 2. The laws and ordinances regarding the press and printing, the repression and prosecution of crimes, offences, or contravention committed through the medium of the press or other means of publication of newspapers or periodical writings, are in force in the colonies, until determined by the National Assembly, and under the modifications decreed by the Provisional Government.

Art[icle] 3. Nevertheless, the provisions of laws incompatible with the existing judicial system of the colonies shall remain ineffective. The courts of appeal acting correctionally shall take cognizance of simple contraventions; all crimes and offences committed through the press, or other means of publication, shall be judged by the court of assizes, composed in conformity with Art[icle]. 67 of the ordinance of 24th September, 1838. Article 176 of that ordinance is abrogated.

Source: Anti-Slavery Reporter (New Series), 3:32 (August 1, 1848).

Brazil's Queiros Law (1850)

Given at the Palace of Rio de Janeiro, this 4th of September, 1850, 29th of the Independence and of the Empire.

We, Dom Pedro, by the Grace of God, and the unanimous acclamation of the people, Constitutional Emperor and Perpetual Defender of Brazil, make known to all our subjects, that the General Legislative Assembly has decreed, and we have approved, the following Law:

Art[icle] 1. All Brazilian vessels encountered in any parts whatever, and all foreign vessels found in the ports, bays, anchorages, or territorial waters of Brazil, with slaves on board, (whose importation is prohibited by the law of the 7th of November, 1831,) or having landed any slaves, shall be seized by the public authorities, or vessels of war of Brazil, and considered as importers of slaves. Those vessels which have no slaves on board, nor recently landed any, but which may be found with appearances of being engaged in the slave-trade, shall be seized in like manner, and considered as intending to import slaves.

Art[icle] 2. The Imperial Government shall designate, by regulations what circumstances shall be considered a legal presumption that such vessels were intended for the slave-trade.

Art[icle] 3. The owners, captain or master, mate, and boatswain of the vessel, as likewise the supercargo, shall be considered as principals in the crime of importation. The crew shall be considered accomplices, as also those who shall assist at the landing of any slaves within the Brazilian territories, or shall aid in concealing them from the knowledge of the authorities, or in preventing their capture at sea, or in the act of being landed, when chased.

Art[icle] 4. The importing of slaves into the territories of the empire shall be considered "piracy," and shall be punished by its tribunals with the penalties set forth in the 2nd Article of the law of the 7th of November, 1831. The attempt to import, and complicity, shall be punished agreeably to the rules laid down in the 34th and 35th Articles of the Criminal Code.

Art[icle] 5. All vessels described in the 1st and 2nd Articles, and all craft employed in landing, concealing, or escaping of slaves, shall be sold together with the cargoes found on board them; and the proceeds shall belong to the captors, deducing one-fourth part for the informers, should there be any.

The Government, on any vessel being condemned as a good prize, shall award the officers and crew of the vessel making the capture, the sum of 40 milreis for each slave taken, to be distributed amongst them according to the laws in force on that subject.

Art[icle] 6. All slaves captured shall be sent back, at the expense of the Government, to the ports whence they came, or to any port or place out of the empire, which the Government may consider more convenient. Until such re-exportation shall take place, they shall be employed under the protection of the Government, but in no case shall their services be granted to individuals.

Art[icle] 7. No passport shall be granted to merchant vessels for the ports on the coast of Africa, without the owners and captains, or masters, entering into a bond, not to receive on board any slave whatever, the owner giving security equivalent to the value of the ship and cargo; which security shall not be given up, unless within eighteen months he shall prove that the conditions of the bond have been fully complied with.

Art[icle] 8. The seizure of all vessels, by virtue of the first and second Articles, and likewise the liberation of all slaves taken on the high seas, or on the coast, previous to being landed, in the act of landing, or immediately afterwards, in warehouses, or depots situated on the coast, or in the harbour, shall be prosecuted and adjudicated, on the first hearing, in the *auditorias* of the navy (the Judge Advocate's Court), and on the second hearing, in the Council of State.

The Government shall determine, by regulations, the mode of proceeding on the first and second hearings, and may appoint *auditores* (Judge Advocates) in such ports as may be required. The *Juizes de Direito* (magistrates) serving as auditors in the respective districts which may be selected for that purpose.

Art[icle] 9. The *auditores* of the navy shall also be competent to prosecute and adjudicate the culprits mentioned in the 3rd Article of the present law; from their decisions there shall be the same appeal—*relação*—as in the "*Crimes de responsibilidade.*"

Those included in the 3rd Article of the law of the 7th of November, 1831, which are not included in the 3rd Article of the present law, shall be prosecuted and adjudicated as heretofore, in the common law courts.

Art[icle] 10. All provisions to the contrary are hereby revoked.

We command, therefore, all the authorities to whom a knowledge and the execution of the said Law belongs to execute the same, and to cause it to be executed, and thoroughly to observe that which is contained in it. Let the Department of Justice cause this to be printed, published, and distributed.

Source: Anti-Slavery Reporter (New Series), 5:60 (December 2, 1850).

The Fugitive Slave Act (1850)

Sec[tion] 1. *Be it enacted by the Senate and House of Representatives of the United States of America in Congress assembled,* That the persons who have been, or may hereafter be, appointed commissioners, in virtue of any act of Congress, by the Circuit Courts of the United States, and Who, in consequence of such appointment, are authorized to exercise the powers that any justice of the peace, or other magistrate of any of the United States, may exercise in respect to offenders for any crime or offense against the United States, by arresting, imprisoning, or bailing the same under and by the virtue of the thirty-third section of the act of the twenty-fourth of September seventeen hundred and eighty-nine, entitled "An Act to establish the judicial courts of the United States" shall be, and are hereby, authorized and required to exercise and discharge all the powers and duties conferred by this act.

Sec[tion] 2. *And be it further enacted,* That the Superior Court of each organized Territory of the United States shall have the same power to appoint commissioners to take acknowledgments of bail and affidavits, and to take depositions of witnesses in civil causes, which is now possessed by the Circuit Court of the United States; and all commissioners who shall hereafter be appointed for such purposes by the Superior Court of any organized Territory of the United States, shall possess all the powers, and exercise all the duties, conferred by law upon the commissioners appointed by the Circuit Courts of the United States for similar purposes, and shall moreover exercise and discharge all the powers and duties conferred by this act.

Sec[tion] 3. *And be it further enacted,* That the Circuit Courts of the United States shall from time to time enlarge the number of the commissioners, with a view to afford reasonable facilities to reclaim fugitives from labor, and to the prompt discharge of the duties imposed by this act.

Sec[tion] 4. *And be it further enacted,* That the commissioners above named shall have concurrent jurisdiction with the judges of the Circuit and District Courts of the United States, in their respective circuits and districts within the several States, and the judges of the Superior Courts of the Territories, severally and collectively, in term-time and vacation; shall grant certificates to such claimants, upon satisfactory proof being made, with authority to take and remove such fugitives from service or labor, under the restrictions herein contained, to the State or Territory from which such persons may have escaped or fled.

Sec[tion] 5. *And be it further enacted,* That it shall be the duty of all marshals and deputy marshals to obey and execute all warrants and precepts issued under the provisions of this act, when to them directed; and should any marshal or deputy marshal refuse to receive such warrant, or other process, when tendered, or to use all proper means diligently to execute the same, he shall, on conviction thereof, be fined in the sum of one thousand dollars, to the use of such claimant, on the motion of such claimant, by the Circuit or District Court for the district of such marshal; and after arrest of such fugitive, by such marshal or his deputy, or whilst at any time in his custody under the provisions of this act, should such fugitive escape, whether with or without the assent of such marshal or his deputy, such marshal shall be liable, on his official bond, to be prosecuted for the benefit of such claimant, for the full value of the service or labor of said fugitive in the State, Territory, or District whence he escaped: and the better to enable the said commissioners, when thus appointed, to execute their duties faithfully and efficiently, in conformity with the requirements of the Constitution of the United States and of this act, they are hereby authorized and empowered, within their counties respectively, to appoint, in writing under their hands, any one or more suitable persons, from time to time, to execute all such warrants and other process as may be issued by them in the lawful performance of their respective duties; with authority to such commissioners, or the persons to be appointed by them, to execute process as aforesaid, to summon and call to their aid the bystanders, or posse comitatus of the proper county, when necessary to ensure a faithful observance of the clause of the Constitution referred to, in conformity with the provisions of this act; and all good citizens are hereby commanded to aid and assist in the prompt and efficient execution of this law, whenever their services may be required, as aforesaid, for that purpose; and said warrants shall run, and be executed by said officers, any where in the State within which they are issued.

Sec[tion] 6. *And be it further enacted,* That when a person held to service or labor in any State or Territory of the United States, has heretofore or shall hereafter escape into another State or Territory of the United States, the person or persons to whom such service or labor may be due, or his, her, or their agent or attorney, duly authorized, by power of attorney, in writing, acknowledged and certified under the seal of some legal officer or court of the State or Territory in which the same may be executed, may pursue and reclaim such fugitive person, either by procuring a warrant from some one of the courts, judges, or commissioners aforesaid, of the proper circuit, district, or county, for the apprehension of such fugitive from service or la-

bor, or by seizing and arresting such fugitive, where the same can be done without process, and by taking, or causing such person to be taken, forthwith before such court, judge, or commissioner, whose duty it shall be to hear and determine the case of such claimant in a summary manner; and upon satisfactory proof being made, by deposition or affidavit, in writing, to be taken and certified by such court, judge, or commissioner, or by other satisfactory testimony, duly taken and certified by some court, magistrate, justice of the peace, or other legal officer authorized to administer an oath and take depositions under the laws of the State or Territory from which such person owing service or labor may have escaped, with a certificate of such magistracy or other authority, as aforesaid, with the seal of the proper court or officer thereto attached, which seal shall be sufficient to establish the competency of the proof, and with proof, also by affidavit, of the identity of the person whose service or labor is claimed to be due as aforesaid, that the person so arrested does in fact owe service or labor to the person or persons claiming him or her, in the State or Territory from which such fugitive may have escaped as aforesaid, and that said person escaped, to make out and deliver to such claimant, his or her agent or attorney, a certificate setting forth the substantial facts as to the service or labor due from such fugitive to the claimant, and of his or her escape from the State or Territory in which he or she was arrested, with authority to such claimant, or his or her agent or attorney, to use such reasonable force and restraint as may be necessary, under the circumstances of the case, to take and remove such fugitive person back to the State or Territory whence he or she may have escaped as aforesaid. In no trial or hearing under this act shall the testimony of such alleged fugitive be admitted in evidence; and the certificates in this and the first [fourth] section mentioned, shall be conclusive of the right of the person or persons in whose favor granted, to remove such fugitive to the State or Territory from which he escaped, and shall prevent all molestation of such person or persons by any process issued by any court, judge, magistrate, or other person whomsoever.

Sec[tion] 7. *And be it further enacted,* That any person who shall knowingly and willingly obstruct, hinder, or prevent such claimant, his agent or attorney, or any person or persons lawfully assisting him, her, or them, from arresting such a fugitive from service or labor, either with or without process as aforesaid, or shall rescue, or attempt to rescue, such fugitive from service or labor, from the custody of such claimant, his or her agent or attorney, or other person or persons lawfully assisting as aforesaid, when so arrested, pursuant to the authority herein given and declared; or shall aid, abet, or assist such person so owing service or labor as aforesaid, directly or indirectly, to escape from such claimant, his agent or attorney, or other person or persons legally authorized as aforesaid; or shall harbor or conceal such fugitive, so as to prevent the discovery and arrest of such person, after notice or knowledge of the fact that such person was a fugitive from service or labor as aforesaid, shall, for either of said offences, be subject to a fine not exceeding one thousand dollars, and imprisonment not exceeding six months, by indictment and conviction before the District Court of the United States for the district in which such offence may have been committed, or before the proper court of criminal jurisdiction, if committed within any one of the organized Territories of the United States; and shall moreover forfeit and pay, by way of civil damages to the party injured by such illegal conduct, the sum of one thousand dollars for each fugitive so lost as aforesaid, to be recovered by action of debt, in any of the District or Territorial Courts aforesaid, within whose jurisdiction the said offence may have been committed.

Sec[tion] 8. *And be it further enacted,* That the marshals, their deputies, and the clerks of the said District and Territorial Courts, shall be paid, for their services, the like fees as may be allowed for similar services in other cases; and where such services are rendered exclusively in the arrest, custody, and delivery of the fugitive to the claimant, his or her agent or attorney, or where such supposed fugitive may be discharged out of custody for the want of sufficient proof as aforesaid, then such fees are to be paid in whole by such claimant, his or her agent or attorney; and in all cases where the proceedings are before a commissioner, he shall be entitled to a fee of ten dollars in full for his services in each case, upon the delivery of the said certificate to the claimant, his agent or attorney; or a fee of five dollars in cases where the proof shall not, in the opinion of such commissioner, warrant such certificate and delivery, inclusive of all services incident to such arrest and examination, to be paid, in either case, by the claimant, his or her agent or attorney. The person or persons authorized to execute the process to be issued by such commissioner for the arrest and detention of fugitives from service or labor as aforesaid, shall also be entitled to a fee of five dollars each for

each person he or they may arrest, and take before any commissioner as aforesaid, at the instance and request of such claimant, with such other fees as may be deemed reasonable by such commissioner for such other additional services as may be necessarily performed by him or them; such as attending at the examination, keeping the fugitive in custody, and providing him with food and lodging during his detention, and until the final determination of such commissioners; and, in general, for performing such other duties as may be required by such claimant, his or her attorney or agent, or commissioner in the premises, such fees to be made up in conformity with the fees usually charged by the officers of the courts of justice within the proper district or county, as near as may be practicable, and paid by such claimants, their agents or attorneys, whether such supposed fugitives from service or labor be ordered to be delivered to such claimant by the final determination of such commissioner or not.

Sec[tion] 9. *And be it further enacted,* That, upon affidavit made by the claimant of such fugitive, his agent or attorney, after such certificate has been issued, that he has reason to apprehend that such fugitive will be rescued by force from his or their possession before he can be taken beyond the limits of the State in which the arrest is made, it shall be the duty of the officer making the arrest to retain such fugitive in his custody, and to remove him to the State whence he fled, and there to deliver him to said claimant, his agent, or attorney. And to this end, the officer aforesaid is hereby authorized and required to employ so many persons as he may deem necessary to overcome such force, and to retain them in his service so long as circumstances may require. The said officer and his assistants, while so employed, to receive the same compensation, and to be allowed the same expenses, as are now allowed by law for transportation of criminals, to be certified by the judge of the district within which the arrest is made, and paid out of the treasury of the United States.

Sec[tion] 10. *And be it further enacted,* That when any person held to service or labor in any State or Territory, or in the District of Columbia, shall escape therefrom, the party to whom such service or labor shall be due, his, her, or their agent or attorney, may apply to any court of record therein, or judge thereof in vacation, and make satisfactory proof to such court, or judge in vacation, of the escape aforesaid, and that the person escaping owed service or labor to such party.

Whereupon the court shall cause a record to be made of the matters so proved, and also a general description of the person so escaping, with such convenient certainty as may be; and a transcript of such record, authenticated by the attestation of the clerk and of the seal of the said court, being produced in any other State, Territory, or district in which the person so escaping may be found, and being exhibited to any judge, commissioner, or other office, authorized by the law of the United States to cause persons escaping from service or labor to be delivered up, shall be held and taken to be full and conclusive evidence of the fact of escape, and that the service or labor of the person escaping is due to the party in such record mentioned. And upon the production by the said party of other and further evidence if necessary, either oral or by affidavit, in addition to what is contained in the said record of the identity of the person escaping, he or she shall be delivered up to the claimant, And the said court, commissioner, judge, or other person authorized by this act to grant certificates to claimants or fugitives, shall, upon the production of the record and other evidences aforesaid, grant to such claimant a certificate of his right to take any such person identified and proved to be owing service or labor as aforesaid, which certificate shall authorize such claimant to seize or arrest and transport such person to the State or Territory from which he escaped: Provided, That nothing herein contained shall be construed as requiring the production of a transcript of such record as evidence as aforesaid. But in its absence the claim shall be heard and determined upon other satisfactory proofs, competent in law.

Approved, September 18, 1850.

Source: "Fugitive Slave Act of 1850," Avalon Project at Yale Law School, www.yale.edu/lawweb/avalon/fugitive.htm.

The Kansas-Nebraska Act (1854)

An Act to Organize the Territories of Nebraska and Kansas.

[Section 1.] *Be it enacted by the Senate and House of Representatives of the United States of America in Congress assembled,* That all that part of the territory of the United States included within the following limits, except such portions thereof as are hereinafter expressly exempted from the operations of this act, to wit: beginning at a point in the Missouri River where the fortieth parallel of north latitude crosses the same; then west on said parallel to the east boundary of the

Territory of Utah, the summit of the Rocky Mountains; thence on said summit northwest to the forty-ninth parallel of north latitude; thence east on said parallel to the western boundary of the territory of Minnesota; thence southward on said boundary to the Missouri River; thence down the main channel of said river to the place of beginning, be, and the same is hereby, created into a temporary government by the name of the Territory Nebraska; and when admitted as a State or States, the said Territory or any portion of the same, shall be received into the Union with or without slavery, as their constitution may prescribe at the time of the admission: *Provided,* That nothing in this act contained shall be construed to inhibit the government of the United States from dividing said Territory into two or more Territories, in such manner and at such time as Congress shall deem convenient and proper, or from attaching a portion of said Territory to any other State or Territory of the United States: *Provided further,* That nothing in this act contained shall be construed to impair the rights of person or property now pertaining the Indians in said Territory so long as such rights shall remain unextinguished by treaty between the United States and such Indians, or include any territory which, by treaty with any Indian tribe, is not, without the consent of said tribe, to be included within the territorial line or jurisdiction of any State or Territory; but all such territory shall [be] excepted out of the boundaries, and constitute no part of the Territory of Nebraska, until said tribe shall signify their assent to the President of the United States to be included within the said Territory of Nebraska or to affect the authority of the government of the United States [to] make any regulations respecting such Indians, their lands, property, or other rights, by treaty, law, or otherwise, which it would have been competent to the government to make if this act had never passed.

Sec[tion] 2. *And Be it further enacted,* That the executive power and authority in and over said Territory of Nebraska shall be vested in a Governor who shall hold his office for four years, and until his successor shall be appointed and qualified, unless sooner removed by the President of the United States. The Governor shall reside within said Territory, and shall be commander-in-chief of the militia thereof. He may grant pardons and respites for offences against the laws of said Territory, and reprieves for offences against the laws of the United States, until the decision of the President can be made known thereon; he shall commission all officers who shall be appointed to office under the laws of the [s]aid Territory, and shall take care that the laws be faithfully executed.

Sec[tion] 3. *And Be it further enacted,* That there shall be a Secretary of said Territory, who shall reside therein, and hold his office for five years, unless sooner removed by the President of the United States; he shall record and preserve all the laws and proceedings of the Legislative Assembly hereinafter constituted, and all the acts and proceedings of the Governor in his executive department; he shall transmit one copy of the laws and journals of the Legislative Assembly within thirty days after the end of each session, and one copy of the executive proceedings and official correspondence semi-annually, on the first days of January and July in each year to the President of the United States, and two copies of the laws to the President of the Senate and to the Speaker of the House of Representatives, to be deposited in the libraries of Congress, and in or case of the death, removal, resignation, or absence of the Governor from the Territory, the Secretary shall be, and he is hereby, authorized and required to execute and perform all the powers and duties of the Governor during such vacancy or absence, or until another Governor shall be duly appointed and qualified to fill such vacancy.

Sec[tion] 4. *And be it further enacted,* That the legislative power and authority of said Territory shall be vested in the Governor and a Legislative Assembly. The Legislative Assembly shall consist of a Council and House of Representatives. The Council shall consist of thirteen members, having the qualifications of voters, as hereinafter prescribed, whose term of service shall continue two years. The House of Representatives shall, at its first session, consist of twenty-six members, possessing the same qualifications as prescribed for members of the Council, and whose term of service shall continue one year. The number of representatives may be increased by the Legislative Assembly, from time to time, in proportion to the increase of qualified voters: *Provided,* That the whole number shall never exceed thirty-nine. An apportionment shall be made, as nearly equal as practicable, among the several counties or districts, for the election of the council and representatives, giving to each section of the Territory representation in the ratio of its qualified voters as nearly as may be. And the members of the Council and of the House of Representatives shall reside in, and be inhabitants of, the district or county, or counties for which they may be elected,

respectively. Previous to the first election, the Governor shall cause a census, or enumeration of the inhabitants and qualified voters of the several counties and districts of the Territory, to be taken by such persons and in such mode as the Governor shall designate and appoint; and the persons so appointed shall receive a reasonable compensation therefor. And the first election shall be held at such time and places, and be conducted in such manner, both as to the persons who shall superintend such election and the returns thereof, as the Governor shall appoint and direct; and he shall at the same time declare the number of members of the Council and House of Representatives to which each of the counties or districts shall be entitled under this act. The persons having the highest number of legal votes in each of said council districts for members of the Council, shall be declared by the Governor to be duly elected to the Council; and the persons having the highest number of legal votes for the House of Representatives, shall be declared by the Governor to be duly elected members of said house: *Provided,* That in case two or more persons voted for shall have an equal number of votes, and in case a vacancy shall otherwise occur in either branch of the Legislative Assembly, the Governor shall order a new election; and the persons thus elected to the Legislative Assembly shall meet at such place and on such day as the Governor shall appoint; but thereafter, the time, place, and manner of holding and conducting all elections by the people, and the apportioning the representation in the several counties or districts to the Council and House of Representatives, according to the number of qualified voters, shall be prescribed by law, as well as the day of the commencement of the regular sessions of the Legislative Assembly: *Provided,* That no session in any one year shall exceed the term of forty days, except the first session, which may continue sixty days.

Sec[tion] 5. *And be it further enacted,* That every free white male inhabitant above the age of twenty-one years who shall be an actual resident of said Territory, and shall possess the qualifications hereinafter prescribed, shall be entitled to vote at the first election, and shall be eligible to any office within the said Territory; but the qualifications of voters, and of holding office, at all subsequent elections, shall be such as shall be prescribed by the Legislative Assembly: *Provided,* That the right of suffrage and of holding office shall be exercised only by citizens of the United States and those who shall have declared on oath their intention to become such, and shall have taken an oath to support the Constitution of the United States and the provisions of this act: And provided further, That no officer, soldier, seaman, or marine, or other person in the army or navy of the United States, or attached to troops in the service of the United States, shall be allowed to vote or hold office in said Territory, by reason of being on service therein.

Sec[tion] 6. *And Be it further enacted,* That the legislative power of the Territory shall extend to all rightful subjects of legislation consistent with the Constitution of the United States and the provisions of this act; but no law shall be passed interfering with the primary disposal of the soil; no tax shall be imposed upon the property of the United States; nor shall the lands or other property of non-residents be taxed higher than the lands or other property of residents. Every bill which shall have passed the Council and House of Representatives of the said Territory shall, before it become a law, be presented to the Governor of the Territory; if he approve, he shall sign it; but if not, he shall return it with his objections to the house in which it originated, who shall enter the objections at large on their journal, and proceed to reconsider it. If, after such reconsideration two thirds of that house shall agree to pass the bill, it shall be sent, together with the objections, to the other house, by which it shall likewise be reconsidered, and if approved by two thirds of that house, it shall become a law. But in all such cases the votes of both houses shall be determined by yeas and nays, to be entered on the journal of each house respectively. If any bill shall not be returned by the Governor within three days (Sundays excepted) after it shall have been presented to him, the same shall be a law in like manner as if he had signed it, unless the Assembly, by adjournment, prevents its return, in which case it shall not be a law.

Sec[tion] 7. *And be it further enacted,* That all township, district, and county officers, not herein otherwise provided for, shall be appointed or elected, as the case may be, in such manner as shall be provided by the Governor and Legislative Assembly of the Territory of Nebraska. The Governor shall nominate, and, by and with the advice and consent of the Legislative Council, appoint all officers not herein otherwise provided for; and in the first instance the Governor alone may appoint all said officers, who shall hold their offices until the end of the first session of the Legislative Assembly; and shall lay off the necessary districts for members of the Council and House of Representatives, and all other officers.

Sec[tion] 8. *And be it further enacted,* That no member of the Legislative Assembly shall hold, or be appointed to, any office which shall have been created, or the salary or emoluments of which shall have been increased, while he was a member, during the term for which he was elected, and for one year after the expiration of such term; but this restriction shall not be applicable to members of the first Legislative Assembly; and no person holding a commission or appointment under the United States, except Postmasters, shall be a member of the Legislative Assembly, or hold any office under the government of said Territory.

Sec[tion] 9. *And be it further enacted,* That the judicial power of said Territory shall be vested in a Supreme Court, District Courts, Probate Courts, and in Justices of the Peace. The Supreme Court shall consist of a chief justice and two associate justices, any two of whom shall constitute a quorum, and who shall hold a term at the seat of government of said Territory annually, and they shall hold their offices during the period of four years, and until their successor shall be appointed and qualified. The said Territory shall be divided into three judicial districts, and a district court shall be held in each of said districts by one of the justices of the Supreme Court, at such times and places as may be prescribed by of law; and the said judges shall, after their appointments, respectively, reside in the districts which shall be assigned them. The jurisdiction of the several courts herein provided for, both appellate and original, and that of the probate courts and of justices of the peace, shall be as limited by law: *Provided,* That justices of the peace shall not have jurisdiction of any matter in controversy when the title or boundaries of land may be in dispute, or where the debt or sum claimed shall exceed one hundred dollars; and the said supreme and districts courts, respectively, shall possess chancery as well as common law jurisdiction. Each District Court, or the judge thereof, shall appoint its clerk, who shall also be the register in chancery, and shall keep his office at the place where the court may, be held. Writs of error, bills of exception, and appeals, shall be allowed in all cases from the final decisions of said district courts to the Supreme Court, under such regulations as may be prescribed by law; but in no case removed to the Supreme Court shall trial by jury be allowed in said court. The Supreme Court, or the justices thereof, shall appoint its own clerk, and every clerk shall hold his office at the pleasure of the court for which he shall have been appointed. Writs of error, and appeals from the final decisions of said Supreme Court, shall be allowed, and may be taken to the Supreme Court of the United States, in the same manner and under the same regulations as from the circuit courts of the United States, where the value of the property, or the amount in controversy, to be ascertained by the oath or affirmation of either party, or other competent witness, shall exceed one thousand dollars; except only that in all cases involving title to slaves, the said writs of error, or appeals shall be allowed and decided by the said Supreme Court, without regard to the value of the matter, property, or title in controversy; and except also that a writ of error or appeal shall also be allowed to the Supreme Court of the United States, from the decision of the said Supreme Court created by this act, or of any judge thereof, or of the district courts created by this act, or of any judge thereof, upon any writ of habeas corpus, involving the question of personal freedom: *Provided,* that nothing herein contained shall be construed to apply to or affect the provisions to the "act respecting fugitives from justice, and persons escaping from the service of their masters," approved February twelfth, seventeen hundred and ninety-three, and the "act to amend and supplementary to the aforesaid act," approved September eighteen, eighteen hundred and fifty; and each of the said district courts shall have and exercise the same jurisdiction in all cases arising under the Constitution and Laws of the United States as is vested in the Circuit and District Courts of the United States; and the said Supreme and District Courts of the said Territory, and the respective judges thereof, shall and may grant writs of habeas corpus in all cases in which the same are granted by the judges of the United States in the District of Columbia; and the first six days of every term of said courts, or so much thereof as shall be necessary, shall be appropriated to the trial of causes arising under the said constitution and laws, and writs of error and appeal in all such cases shall be made to the Supreme Court of said Territory, the same as in other cases. The said clerk shall receive in all such cases the same fees which the clerks of the district courts of Utah Territory now receive for similar services.

Sec[tion] 10. *And Be it further enacted,* That the provisions of an act entitled "An act respecting fugitives from justice, and persons escaping from the service of their masters," approved February twelve, seventeen

hundred and ninety-three, and the provisions of the act entitled "An act to amend, and supplementary to, the aforesaid act, approved September eighteen, eighteen hundred and fifty, be, and the same are hereby, declared to extend to and be in full force within the limits of said Territory of Nebraska.

Sec[tion] 11. *And be it further enacted,* That there shall be appointed an Attorney for said Territory, who shall continue in office for four years, and until his successor shall be appointed and qualified, unless sooner removed by the President, and who shall receive the same fees and salary as the Attorney of the United States for the present Territory of Utah. There shall also be a Marshal for the Territory appointed, who shall hold his office for four years, and until his successor shall be appointed and qualified, unless sooner removed by the President, and who shall execute all processes issuing from the said courts when exercising their jurisdiction as Circuit and District Courts of the United States; he shall perform the duties, be subject to the same regulation and penalties, and be entitled to the same fees, as the Marshal of the District Court of the United States for the present Territory of Utah, and shall, in addition, be paid two hundred dollars annually as a compensation for extra services.

Sec[tion] 12. *And be it further enacted,* That the Governor, Secretary, Chief Justice, and Associate Justices, Attorney and Marshal, shall be nominated, and, by and with the advice and consent of the Senate, appointed by the President of the United States. The Governor and a Secretary to be appointed as aforesaid, shall, before they act as such, respectively take an oath or affirmation before the District Judge or some Justice of the Peace in the limits of said Territory, duly authorized to administer oaths and affirmations by the laws now in force therein, or before the Chief Justice, or some Associate Justice of the Supreme Court of the United States, to support the Constitution of the United States, and faithfully to discharge the duties of their respective offices, which said oaths, when so taken, shall be certified by the person by whom the same shall have been taken; and such certificates shall be received and recorded by the said Secretary among the Executive proceedings; and the Chief Justice and Associate Justices, and all other civil officers in said Territory, before they act as such, shall take a like oath or affirmation before the said Governor or Secretary, or some Judge or Justice of the Peace of the Territory, who may be duly commissioned and qualified, which said oath or affirmation shall be certified and transmitted by the person taking the same to the Secretary, to be by him recorded as aforesaid; and, afterwards, the like oath or affirmation shall be taken, certified, and recorded, in such manner and form as may be prescribed by law. The Governor shall receive an annual salary of two thousand five hundred dollars. The Chief Justice and Associate Justices shall each receive an annual salary of two thousand dollars. The Secretary shall receive an annual salary of two thousand dollars. The said salaries shall be paid quarter-yearly, from the dates of the respective appointments, at the Treasury of the United States; but no such payment shall be made until said officers shall have entered upon the duties of their respective appointments. The members of the Legislative Assembly shall be entitled to receive three dollars each per day during their attendance at the sessions thereof, and three dollars each for every twenty miles' travel in going to and returning from the said sessions, estimated according to the nearest usually travelled route; and an additional allowance of three dollars shall be paid to the presiding officer of each house for each day he shall so preside. And a chief clerk, one assistant clerk, a sergeant-at-arms, and doorkeeper, may be chosen for each house; and the chief clerk shall receive four dollars per day, and the said other officers three dollars per day, during the session of the Legislative Assembly; but no other officers shall be paid by the United States: *Provided,* That there shall be but one session of the legislature annually, unless, on an extraordinary occasion, the Governor shall think proper to call the legislature together. There shall be appropriated, annually, the usual sum, to be expended by the Governor, to defray the contingent expenses of the Territory, including the salary of a clerk of the Executive Department; and there shall also be appropriated, annually, a sufficient sum, to be expended by the Secretary of the Territory, and upon an estimate to be made by the Secretary of the Treasury of the United States, to defray the expenses of the Legislative Assembly, the printing of the laws, and other incidental expenses; and the Governor and Secretary of the Territory shall, in the disbursement of all moneys intrusted to them, be governed solely by the instructions of the Secretary of the Treasury of the United States, and shall, semi-annually, account to the said Secretary for the manner in which the aforesaid moneys shall have been expended; and no expenditure shall be made by said Legislative Assembly for objects not specially authorized by the acts of Congress, making the appropriations, nor beyond the sums thus appropriated for such objects.

Sec[tion] 13. *And be it further enacted,* That the Legislative Assembly of the Territory of Nebraska shall hold its first session at such time and place in said Territory as the Governor thereof shall appoint and direct; and at said first session, or as soon thereafter as they shall deem expedient, the Governor and Legislative Assembly shall proceed to locate and establish the seat of government for said Territory at such place as they may deem eligible; which place, however, shall thereafter be subject to be changed by the said Governor and Legislative Assembly.

Sec[tion] 14. *And be it further enacted,* That a delegate to the House of Representatives of the United States, to serve for the term of two years, who shall be a citizen of the United States, may be elected by the voters qualified to elect members of the Legislative Assembly, who shall be entitled to the same rights and privileges as are exercised and enjoyed by the delegates from the several other Territories of the United States to the said House of Representatives, but the delegate first elected shall hold his seat only during the term of the Congress to which he shall be elected. The first election shall be held at such time and places, and be conducted in such manner, as the Governor shall appoint and direct; and at all subsequent elections the times, places, and manner of holding the elections, shall be prescribed by law. The person having the greatest number of votes shall be declared by the Governor to be duly elected; and a certificate thereof shall be given accordingly. That the Constitution, and all Laws of the United States which are not locally inapplicable, shall have the same force and effect within the said Territory of Nebraska as elsewhere within the United States, except the eighth section of the act preparatory to the admission of Missouri into the Union approved March sixth, eighteen hundred and twenty, which, being inconsistent with the principle of non-intervention by Congress with slaves in the States and Territories, as recognized by the legislation of eighteen hundred and fifty, commonly called the Compromise Measures, is hereby declared inoperative and void; it being the true intent and meaning of this act not to legislate slavery into any Territory or State, nor to exclude it therefrom, but to leave the people thereof perfectly free to form and regulate their domestic institutions in their own way, subject only to the Constitution of the United States: *Provided,* That nothing herein contained shall be construed to revive or put in force any law or regulation which may have existed prior to the act of sixth March, eighteen hundred and twenty, either protecting, establishing, prohibiting, or abolishing slavery.

Sec[tion] 15. *And Be it further enacted,* That there shall hereafter be appropriated, as has been customary for the Territorial governments, sufficient amount, to be expended under the direction of the said Governor of the Territory of Nebraska, not exceeding the sums heretofore appropriated for similar objects, for the erection of suitable public buildings at the seat of government, and for the purchase of a library, to be kept at the seat of government for the use of the Governor, Legislative Assembly, Judges of the Supreme Court, Secretary, Marshal, and Attorney of said Territory, and such other persons, and under such regulations as shall be prescribed by law.

Sec[tion] 16. *And be it further enacted,* That when the lands in the said Territory shall be surveyed under the direction of the government of the United States, preparatory to bringing the same into market, sections numbered sixteen and thirty-six in each township in said Territory shall be, and the same are hereby, reserved for the purpose of being applied to schools in said Territory, and in the States and Territories hereafter to be erected out of the same.

Sec[tion] 17. *And be it further enacted,* That, until otherwise provided by law, the Governor of said Territory may define the Judicial Districts of said Territory, and assign the judges who may be appointed for said Territory to the several districts; and also appoint the times and places for holding courts in the several counties or subdivisions in each of said Judicial Districts by proclamation, to be issued by him; but the Legislative Assembly, at their first or any subsequent session, may organize, alter, or modify such Judicial Districts, and assign the judges, and alter the times and places of holding the courts, as to them shall seem proper and convenient.

Sec[tion] 18. *And be it further enacted,* That all officers to be appointed by the President, by and with the advice and consent of the Senate, for the Territory of Nebraska, who, by virtue of the provisions of any law now existing, or which may be enacted during the present Congress, are required to give security for moneys that may be intrusted with them for disbursement, shall give such security, at such time and place, and in such manner, as the Secretary of the Treasury may prescribe.

Sec[tion] 19. *And be it further enacted,* That all that part of the Territory of the United States included within the following limits, except such portions thereof as are hereinafter expressly exempted from the operations of this act, to wit, beginning at a point on the western boundary of the State of Missouri, where the thirty-seventh parallel of north latitude crosses the same; thence west on said parallel to the eastern boundary of New Mexico; thence north on said boundary to latitude thirty-eight; thence following said boundary westward to the east boundary of the Territory of Utah, on the summit of the Rocky Mountains; thence northward on said summit to the fortieth parallel of latitude, thence east on said parallel to the western boundary of the State of Missouri; thence south with the western boundary of said State to the place of beginning, be, and the same is hereby, created into a temporary government by the name of the Territory of Kansas; and when admitted as a State or States, the said Territory, or any portion of the same, shall be received into the Union with or without slavery, as their Constitution may prescribe at the time of their admission: *Provided,* That nothing in this act contained shall be construed to inhibit the government of the United States from dividing said Territory into two or more Territories, in such manner and at such times as Congress shall deem convenient and proper, or from attaching any portion of said Territory to any other State or Territory of the United States: *Provided* further, That nothing in this act contained shall be construed to impair the rights of person or property now pertaining to the Indians in said Territory, so long as such rights shall remain unextinguished by treaty between the United States and such Indians, or to include any territory which, by treaty with any Indian tribe, is not, without the consent of said tribe, to be included within the territorial limits or jurisdiction of any State or Territory; but all such territory shall be excepted out of the boundaries, and constitute no part of the Territory of Kansas, until said tribe shall signify their assent to the President of the United States to be included within the said Territory of Kansas, or to affect the authority of the government of the United States to make any regulation respecting such Indians, their lands, property, or other rights, by treaty, law, or otherwise, which it would have been competent to the government to make if this act had never passed.

Sec[tion] 20. *And be it further enacted,* That the executive power and authority in and over said Territory of Kansas shall be vested in a Governor, who shall hold his office for four years, and until his successor shall be appointed and qualified, unless sooner removed by the President of the United States. The Governor shall reside within said Territory, and shall be commander-in-chief of the militia thereof. He may grant pardons and respites for offences against the laws of said Territory, and reprieves for offences against the laws of the United States, until the decision of the President can be made known thereon; he shall commission all officers who shall be appointed to office under the laws of the said Territory, and shall take care that the laws be faithfully executed.

Sec[tion] 21. *And be it further enacted,* That there shall be a Secretary of said Territory, who shall reside therein, and hold his office for five years, unless sooner removed by the President of the United States; he shall record and preserve all the laws and proceedings of the Legislative Assembly hereinafter constituted, and all the acts and proceedings of the Governor in his Executive Department; he shall transmit one copy of the laws and journals of the Legislative Assembly within thirty days after the end of each session, and one copy of the executive proceedings and official correspondence semi-annually, on the first days of January and July in each year, to the President of the United States, and two copies of the laws to the President of the Senate and to the Speaker of the House of Representatives, to be deposited in the libraries of Congress; and, in case of the death, removal, resignation, or absence of the Governor from the Territory, the Secretary shall be, and he is hereby, authorized and required to execute and perform all the powers and duties of the Governor during such vacancy or absence, or until another Governor shall be duly appointed and qualified to fill such vacancy.

Sec[tion] 22. *And be it further enacted,* That the legislative power and authority of said Territory shall be vested in the Governor and a Legislative Assembly. The Legislative Assembly shall consist of a Council and House of Representatives. The Council shall consist of thirteen members, having the qualifications of voters, as hereinafter prescribed, whose term of service shall continue two years. The House of Representatives shall, at its first session, consist of twenty-six members possessing the same qualifications as prescribed for members of the Council, and whose term of service shall continue one year. The number of representatives may be increased by the Legislative Assembly, from time to time, in proportion to the increase of qualified voters: *Provided,* That the whole number shall never exceed thirty-nine. An apportionment shall be made, as nearly equal as practicable, among the several counties or districts, for the election of the Council and Representatives, giving to each section of the Territory representation in the ratio of its qualified voters as nearly as may be. And the members of the Council and of the House of Representatives shall reside in, and be inhabitants of, the district or county, or counties, for which they may be elected, respectively. Previous to the first election, the Governor shall cause a census, or enumeration of the inhabitants and qualified voters of the several counties and districts of the Territory, to be taken by such persons and in such mode as the Governor shall designate and appoint; and the persons so appointed shall receive a reasonable compensation therefor. And the first election shall be held at such time and places, and be conducted in such manner, both as to the persons who shall superintend such election and the returns thereof, as the Governor shall appoint and direct; and he shall at the same time declare the number of members of the Council and House of Representatives to which each of the counties or districts shall be entitled under this act. The persons having the highest number of legal votes in each of said Council Districts for members of the Council, shall be declared by the Governor to be duly elected to the Council; and the persons having the highest number of legal votes for the House of Representatives, shall be declared by the Governor to be duly elected members of said house: *Provided,* That in case two or more persons voted for shall have an equal number of votes, and in case a vacancy shall otherwise occur in either branch of the Legislative Assembly, the Governor shall order a new election; and the persons thus elected to the Legislative Assembly shall meet at such place and on such day as the Governor shall appoint; but thereafter, the time, place, and manner of holding and conducting all elections by the people, and the apportioning the representation in the several counties or districts to the·Council and House of Representatives, according to the number of qualified voters, shall be prescribed by law, as well as the day of the commencement of the regular sessions of the Legislative Assembly: *Provided,* That no session in any one year shall exceed the term of forty days, except the first session, which may continue sixty days.

Sec[tion] 23. *And be it further enacted,* That every free white male inhabitant above the age of twenty-one years, who shall be an actual resident of said Territory, and shall possess the qualifications hereinafter prescribed, shall be entitled to vote at the first election, and shall be eligible to any office within the said Territory; but the qualifications of voters, and of holding office, at all subsequent elections, shall be such as shall be prescribed by the Legislative Assembly: *Provided,* That the right of suffrage and of holding office shall be exercised only by citizens of the United States, and those who shall have declared, on oath, their intention to become such, and shall have taken an oath to support the Constitution of the United States and the provisions of this act: And, provided further, That no officer, soldier, seaman, or marine, or other person in the army or navy of the United States, or attached to troops in the service of the United States, shall be allowed to vote or hold office in said Territory by reason of being on service therein.

Sec[tion] 24. *And be it further enacted,* That the legislative power of the Territory shall extend to all rightful subjects of legislation consistent with the Constitution of the United States and the provisions of this act; but no law shall be passed interfering with the primary disposal of the soil; no tax shall be imposed upon the property of the United States; nor shall the lands or other property of non-residents be taxed higher than the lands or other property of residents. Every bill which shall have passed the Council and House of Representatives of the said Territory shall, before it become a law, be presented to the Governor of the Territory; if he approve, he shall sign it; but if not, he shall return it with his objections to the house in which it originated, who shall enter the objections at large on their journal, and proceed to reconsider it. If, after such reconsideration, two thirds of that house shall agree to pass the bill, it shall be sent, together with the objections, to the other house, by which, it shall likewise be reconsidered, and, if approved by two thirds of that house, it shall become a law. But in all such cases the votes of both houses shall be determined by yeas and nays, to be entered on the journal of each house, respectively. If any bill shall not be returned by the Governor within three days (Sundays excepted) after it shall have been presented to him, the same shall be a law in like manner as if he had signed it, unless the Assembly, by adjournment, prevent its return, in which case it shall not be a law.

Sec[tion] 25. *And be it further enacted,* That all township, district, and county officers, not herein otherwise provided for, shall be appointed or elected as the case may be, in such manner as shall be provided by the Governor and Legislative Assembly of the Territory of Kansas. The Governor shall nominate, and, by and with the advice and consent of the Legislative Council, appoint all officers not herein otherwise provided for; and, in the first instance, the Governor alone may appoint all said officers, who shall hold their offices until the end of the first session of the Legislative Assembly; and shall lay off the necessary districts for members of the Council and House of Representatives, and all other officers.

Sec[tion] 26. *And be it further enacted,* That no member of the Legislative Assembly shall hold, or be appointed to, any office which shall have been created, or the salary or emoluments of which shall have been increased, while he was a member, during the term for which he was elected, and for one year after the expiration of such term; but this restriction shall not be applicable to members of the first Legislative Assembly; and no person holding a commission or appointment under the United States, except postmasters, shall be a member of the Legislative Assembly, or shall hold any office under the government of said Territory.

Sec[tion] 27. *And be it further enacted,* That the judicial power of said Territory shall be vested in a supreme court, district courts, probate courts, and in justices of the peace. The Supreme Court shall Consist of [a] chief justice and two associate justices, any two of whom shall constitute a quorum, and who shall hold a term at the seat of government of said Territory annually; and they shall hold their offices during the period of four years, and until their successors shall be appointed and qualified. The said Territory shall be divided into three judicial districts, and a district court shall be held in each of said districts by one of the justices of the Supreme Court, at such times and places as may be prescribed by law; and the said judges shall, after their appointments, respectively, reside in the districts which shall be assigned them. The jurisdiction of the several courts herein provided for, both appellate and original, and that of the probate courts and of justices of the peace, shall be as limited by law: *Provided,* That justices of the peace shall not have jurisdiction of any matter in controversy when the title or boundaries of land may be in dispute, or where the debt or sum claimed shall exceed one hundred dollars; and the said supreme and district courts, respectively, shall possess chancery as well as common law jurisdiction. Said District Court, or the judge thereof, shall appoint its clerk, who shall also be the register in chancery, and shall keep his office at the place where the court may be held. Writs of error, bills of exception, and appeals shall be allowed in all cases from the final decisions of said district courts to the Supreme Court, under such regulations as may be prescribed by law; but in no case removed to the Supreme Court shall trial by jury be allowed in said court. The Supreme Court, or the justices thereof, shall appoint its own clerk, and every clerk shall hold his office at the pleasure of the court for which he shall have been appointed. Writs of error, and appeals from the final decisions of said supreme court, shall be allowed, and may be taken to the Supreme Court of the United States, in the same manner and under the same regulations as from the Circuit Courts of the United States, where the value of the property, or the amount in controversy, to be ascertained by the oath or affirmation of either party, or other competent witness, shall exceed one thousand dollars; except only that in all cases involving title to slaves, the said writ of error or appeals shall be allowed and decided by said supreme court, without regard to the value of the matter, property, or title in controversy; and except also that a writ of error or appeal shall also be allowed to the Supreme Court of the United States, from the decision of the said supreme court created by this act, or of any judge thereof, or of the district courts created by this act, or of any judge thereof, upon any writ of habeas corpus, involving the question of personal freedom: *Provided,* That nothing herein contained shall be construed to apply to or affect the provisions of the "act respecting fugitives from justice, and persons escaping from the service of their masters," approved February twelfth, seventeen hundred and ninety-three, and the "act to amend and supplementary to the aforesaid act," approved September eighteenth, eighteen hundred and fifty; and each of the said district courts shall have and exercise the same jurisdiction in all cases arising under the Constitution and laws of the United States as is vested in the Circuit and District Courts of the United States; and the said supreme and district courts of the said Territory, and the respective judges thereof, shall and may grant writs of habeas corpus in all cases in which the same are granted by the judges of the United States in the District of Columbia; and the first six days of every term of said courts, or so much thereof as may be necessary, shall be appropriated to the trial of causes arising under the said Constitution and laws, and writs of error and appeal in all such cases shall be made to the Supreme Court of said Territory, the same as in other cases. The said clerk shall

receive the same fees in all such cases, which the clerks of the district courts of Utah Territory now receive for similar services.

Sec[tion] 28. *And be it further enacted,* That the provisions of the act entitled "An act respecting fugitives from justice, and persons escaping from, the service of their masters," approved February twelfth, seventeen hundred and ninety-three, and the provisions of the act entitled "An act to amend, and supplementary to, the aforesaid act," approved September eighteenth, eighteen hundred and fifty, be, and the same are hereby, declared to extend to and be in full force within the limits of the said Territory of Kansas.

Sec[tion] 29. *And be it further enacted,* That there shall be appointed an attorney for said Territory, who shall continue in office for four years, and until his successor shall be appointed and qualified, unless sooner removed by the President, and who shall receive the same fees and salary as the Attorney of the United States for the present Territory of Utah. There shall also be a marshal for the Territory appointed, who shall hold his office for four years, and until his successor shall be appointed and qualified, unless sooner removed by the President, and who shall execute all processes issuing from the said courts where exercising their jurisdiction as Circuit and District Courts of the United States; he shall perform the duties, be subject to the same regulations and penalties, and be entitled to the same fees, as the Marshal of the District Court of the United States for the present Territory of Utah, and shall, in addition, be paid two hundred dollars annually as a compensation for extra services.

Sec[tion] 30. *And be it further enacted,* That the Governor, Secretary, Chief Justice, and Associate Justices, Attorney, and Marshal, shall be nominated, and, by and with the advice and consent of the Senate, appointed by the President of the United States. The Governor and Secretary to be appointed as aforesaid shall, before they act as such, respectively take an oath or affirmation before the district judge or some justice of the peace in the limits of said Territory, duly authorized to administer oaths and affirmations by the laws now in force therein, or before the Chief Justice or some Associate Justice of the Supreme Court of the United States, to support the Constitution of the United States, and faithfully to discharge the duties of their respective offices, which said oaths, when so taken, shall be certified by the person by whom the same shall have been taken; and such certificates shall be received and recorded by the said secretary among the executive proceedings; and the Chief Justice and Associate Justices, and all other civil officers in said Territory, before they act as such, shall take a like oath or affirmation before the said Governor or Secretary, or some Judge or Justice of the Peace of the Territory who may be duly commissioned and qualified, which said oath or affirmation shall be certified and transmitted by the person taking the same to the Secretary, to be by him recorded as aforesaid; and, afterwards, the like oath or affirmation shall be taken, certified, and recorded, in such manner and form as may be prescribed by law. The Governor shall receive an annual salary of two thousand five hundred dollars. The Chief Justice and Associate Justices shall receive as an annual salary of two thousand dollars. The Secretary shall receive an annual salary of two thousand dollars. The said salaries shall be paid quarter-yearly, from the dates of the respective appointments, at the Treasury of the United States; but no such payment shall be made until said officers shall have entered upon the duties of their respective appointments. The members of the Legislative Assembly shall be entitled to receive three dollars each per day during their attendance at the sessions thereof, and three dollars each for every twenty miles' travel in going to and returning from the said sessions, estimated according to the nearest usually travelled route; and an additional allowance of three dollars shall be paid to the presiding officer of each house for each day he shall so preside. And a chief clerk, one assistant clerk, a sergeant at-arms, and door-keeper, may be chosen for each house; and the chief clerk shall receive four dollars per day, and the said other officers three dollars per day, during the session of the Legislative Assembly; but no other officers shall be paid by the United States: *Provided,* That there shall be but one session of the Legislature annually, unless, on an extraordinary occasion, the Governor shall think proper to call the Legislature together. There shall be appropriated, annually, the usual sum, to be expended by the Governor, to defray the contingent expenses of the Territory, including the salary of a clerk of the Executive Department and there shall also be appropriated, annually, a sufficient sum, to be expended by the Secretary of the Territory, and upon an estimate to be made by the Secretary of the Treasury of the United States, to defray the expenses of the Legislative Assembly, the printing of the laws, and other incidental expenses; and the Governor and Secretary of the Territory shall, in the disbursement of all moneys intrusted to them, be governed solely by the instructions of the secretary of the Treasury of the United States, and shall, semi-annually, account to the said secretary for lit the manner in which the aforesaid moneys shall have been expended; and no expenditure shall be made by said Legislative Assembly for objects not specially authorized by the acts of Congress making the appropriations, nor beyond the sums thus appropriated for such objects.

Sec[tion] 31. *And be it further enacted,* That the seat of government of said Territory is hereby located temporarily at Fort Leavenworth; and that such portions of the public buildings as may not be actually used and needed for military purposes, may be occupied and used, under the direction of the Governor and Legislative Assembly, for such public purposes as may be required under the provisions of this act.

Sec[tion] 32. *And be it further enacted,* That a delegate to the House of Representatives of the United States, to serve for the term of two years, who shall be a citizen of the United States, may be elected by the voters qualified to elect members of the Legislative Assembly, who shall be entitled to the same rights and privileges as are exercised and enjoyed by the delegates from the several other Territories of the United States to the said House of Representatives, but the delegate first elected shall hold his seat only during the term of the Congress to which he shall be elected. The first election shall be held at such time and places, and be conducted in such manner, as the Governor shall appoint and direct; and at all subsequent elections, the times, places, and manner of holding the elections shall be prescribed by law. The person having the greatest number of votes shall be declared by the Governor to be duly elected, and a certificate thereof shall be given accordingly. That the Constitution, and all laws of the United States which are not locally inapplicable, shall have the same force and effect within the said Territory of Kansas as elsewhere within the United States, except the eighth section of the act preparatory to the admission of Missouri into the Union, approved March sixth, eighteen hundred and twenty, which, being inconsistent with the principle of non-intervention by Congress with slavery in the States and Territories, as recognized by the legislation of eighteen hundred and fifty, commonly called the Compromise Measures, is hereby declared inoperative and void; it being the true intent and meaning of this act not to legislate slavery into any Territory or State, nor to exclude it therefrom, but to leave the people thereof perfectly free to form and regulate their domestic institutions in their own way, subject only to the Constitution of the United States: *Provided,* That nothing herein contained shall be construed to revive or put in force any law or regulation which may have existed prior to the act of sixth of March, eighteen hundred and twenty, either protecting, establishing, prohibiting, or abolishing slavery.

Sec[tion] 33. *And be it further enacted;* That there shall hereafter be appropriated, as has been customary for the territorial governments, a sufficient amount, to be expended under the direction of the said Governor of the Territory of Kansas, not exceeding the sums heretofore appropriated for similar objects, for the erection of suitable public buildings at the seat of government, and for the purchase of a library, to be kept at the seat of government for the use of the Governor, Legislative Assembly, Judges of the Supreme Court, Secretary, Marshal, and Attorney of said Territory, and such other persons, and under such regulations, as shall be prescribed by law.

Sec[tion] 34. *And be it further enacted,* That when the lands in the said Territory shall be surveyed under the direction of the government of the United States, preparatory to bringing the same into market, sections numbered sixteen and thirty-six in each township in said Territory shall be, and the same are hereby, reserved for the purpose of being applied to schools in said Territory, and in the States and Territories hereafter to be erected out of the same.

Sec[tion] 35. *And be it further enacted,* That, until otherwise provided by law, the Governor of said Territory may define the Judicial Districts of said Territory, and assign the judges who may be appointed for said Territory to the several districts; and also appoint the times and places for holding courts in the several counties or subdivisions in each of said judicial districts by proclamation, to be issued by him; but the Legislative Assembly, at their first or any subsequent session, may organize, alter, or modify such judicial districts, and assign the judges, and alter the times and places of holding the courts as to them shall seem proper and convenient.

Sec[tion] 36. *And be it further enacted,* That all officers to be appointed by the President, by and with the advice and consent of the Senate, for the Territory of Kansas, who, by virtue of the provisions of any law now existing, or which may be enacted during the present Congress, are required to give security for moneys that may be intrusted with them for disbursement, shall give such security, at such time and place, and in such manner as the Secretary of the Treasury may prescribe.

Sec[tion] 37. *And be it further enacted,* That all treaties, laws, and other engagements made by the government of the United States with the Indian tribes inhabiting the territories embraced within this act, shall be faithfully and rigidly observed, notwithstanding any thing contained in this act; and that the existing agencies and superintendencies of said Indians be continued with the same powers and duties which are now prescribed by law, except that the President of the United States may, at his discretion, change the location of the office of superintendent.

Approved, May 30, 1854

Source: U.S. Statutes at Large, vol. 10, ed. George Minot. Boston: Little, Brown, 1855.

The Ostend Manifesto (1854)

Communication addressed to U.S. Secretary of State
William L. Marcy,
Aix-la-Chapelle, October 18, 1854.

Sir:—

The undersigned, in compliance with the wish expressed by the President in the several confidential despatches you have addressed to us, respectively, to that effect, have met in conference, first at Ostend, in Belgium, on the 8th, 10th, and 11th instant, and then at Aix la Chapelle in Prussia, on the days next following, up to the date hereof.

There has been a full and unresolved interchange of views and sentiments between us, which we are most happy to inform you has resulted in a cordial coincidence of opinion on the grave and important subjects submitted to our consideration.

We have arrived at the conclusion, and are thoroughly convinced, that an immediate and earnest effort ought to be made by the government of the United States to purchase Cuba from Spain at any price for which it can be obtained, not exceeding the sum of $—

The proposal should, in our opinion, be made in such a manner as to be presented through the necessary diplomatic forms to the Supreme Constituent Cortes about to assemble. On this momentous question, in which the people both of Spain and the United States are so deeply interested, all our proceedings ought to be open, frank, and public. They should be of such a character as to challenge the approbation of the world.

We firmly believe that, in the progress of human events, the time has arrived when the vital interests of Spain are as seriously involved in the sale, as those of the United States in the purchase, of the island and that the transaction will prove equally honorable to both nations.

Under these circumstances we cannot anticipate a failure, unless possibly through the malign influence of foreign powers who possess no right whatever to interfere in the matter.

We proceed to state some of the reasons which have brought us to this conclusion, and, for the sake of clearness, we shall specify them under two distinct heads:

1. The United States ought, if practicable, to purchase Cuba with as little delay as possible.
2. The probability is great that the government and Cortes of Spain will prove willing to sell it, because this would essentially promote the highest and best interests of the Spanish people.

Then, 1. It must be clear to every reflecting mind that, from the peculiarity of its geographical position, and the considerations attendant on it, Cuba is as necessary to the North American republic as any of its present members, and that it belongs naturally to that great family of States of which the Union is the providential nursery.

From its locality it commands the mouth of the Mississippi and the immense and annually increasing trade which must seek this avenue to the ocean.

On the numerous navigable streams, measuring an aggregate course of some thirty thousand miles, which disembogue themselves through this magnificent river into the Gulf of Mexico, the increase of the population within the last ten years amounts to more than that of the entire Union at the time Louisiana was annexed to it.

The natural and main outlet to the products of this entire population, the highway of their direct intercourse with the Atlantic and the Pacific States, can never be secure, but must ever be endangered whilst Cuba is a dependency of a distant power in whose possession it has proved to be a source of constant annoyance and embarrassment to their interests.

Indeed, the Union can never enjoy repose, nor possess reliable security, as long as Cuba is not embraced within its boundaries.

Its immediate acquisition by our government is of paramount importance, and we cannot doubt but that it is a consummation devoutly wished for by its inhabitants.

The intercourse which its proximity to our coasts begets and encourages between them and the citizens of the United States, has, in the progress of time, so united their interests and blended their fortunes that they now look upon each other as if they were one people and had but one destiny.

Considerations exist which render delay in the acquisition of this island exceedingly dangerous to the United States.

The system of immigration and labor lately organized within its limits, and the tyranny and oppression which characterize its immediate rulers, threaten an insurrection at every moment which may result in direful consequences to the American people.

Cuba has thus become to us an unceasing danger, and a permanent cause of anxiety and alarm.

But we need not enlarge on these topics. It can scarcely be apprehended that foreign powers, in violation of international law, would interpose their influence with Spain to prevent our acquisition of the island. Its inhabitants are now suffering under the worst of all possible governments, that of absolute despotism, delegated by a distant power to irresponsible agents, who are changed at short intervals, and who are tempted to improve the brief opportunity thus afforded to accumulate fortunes by the basest means.

As long as this system shall endure, humanity may in vain demand the suppression of the African slave trade in the island. This is rendered impossible whilst that infamous traffic remains an irresistible temptation and a source of immense profit to needy and avaricious officials, who, to attain their ends, scruple not to trample the most sacred principles under foot. The Spanish government at home may be well disposed, but experience has proved that it cannot control these remote depositories of its power.

Besides, the commercial nations of the world cannot fail to perceive and appreciate the great advantages which would result to their people from a dissolution of the forced and unnatural connection between Spain and Cuba, and the annexation of the latter to the United States. The trade of England and France with Cuba would, in that event, assume at once an important and profitable character, and rapidly extend with the increasing population and prosperity of the island.

2. But if the United States and every commercial nation would be benefited by this transfer, the interests of Spain would also be greatly and essentially promoted.

She cannot but see what such a sum of money as we are willing to pay for the island would effect in the development of her vast natural resources.

Two-thirds of this sum, if employed in the construction of a system of railroads, would ultimately prove a source of greater wealth to the Spanish people than that opened to their vision by Cortez. Their prosperity would date from the ratification of that treaty of cession.

France has already constructed continuous lines of railways from Havre, Marseilles, Valenciennes, and Strasbourg, *via* Paris, to the Spanish frontier, and anxiously awaits the day when Spain shall find herself in a condition to extend these roads through her northern provinces to Madrid, Seville, Cadiz, Malaga, and the frontiers of Portugal.

This object once accomplished, Spain would become a centre of attraction for the travelling world, and secure a permanent and profitable market for her various productions. Her fields, under the stimulus given to industry by remunerating prices, would teem with cereal grain, and her vineyards would bring forth a vastly increased quantity of choice wines. Spain would speedily become, what a bountiful Providence intended she should be, one of the first nations of Continental Europe—rich, powerful, and contented.

Whilst two-thirds of the price of the island would be ample for the completion of her most important public improvements, she might, with the remaining forty millions, satisfy the demands now pressing so heavily upon her credit, and create a sinking fund which would gradually relieve her from the overwhelming debt now paralyzing her energies.

Such is her present wretched financial condition, that her best bonds are sold upon her own Bourse at about one-third of their par value; whilst another class, on which she pays no interest, have but a nominal value, and are quoted at about one-sixth of the amount for which they were issued.

Besides, these latter are held principally by British creditors who may, from day to day, obtain the effective interposition of their own government for the purpose of coercing payment. Intimations to that effect have been already thrown out from high quarters, and unless some new source of revenue shall enable Spain to provide for such exigencies, it is not improbable that they may be realized.

Should Spain reject the present golden opportunity for developing her resources, and removing her financial embarrassments, it may never again return.

Cuba, in its palmiest days, never yielded her exchequer after deducting the expenses of its government a clear annual income of more than a million and a half of dollars. These expenses have increased to such a degree as to leave a deficit chargeable on the treasury of Spain to the amount of six hundred thousand dollars.

In a pecuniary point of view, therefore, the island is an incumbrance, instead of a source of profit, to the mother country.

Under no probable circumstances can Cuba ever yield to Spain one per cent on the large amount which the United States are willing to pay for its acquisition. But Spain is in imminent danger of losing Cuba, without remuneration.

Extreme oppression, it is now universally admitted, justifies any people in endeavoring to relieve themselves from the yoke of their oppressors. The sufferings which the corrupt, arbitrary, and unrelenting local administration necessarily entails upon the inhabitants of Cuba, cannot fail to stimulate and keep alive that spirit of resistance and revolution against Spain, which has, of late years, been so often manifested. In this condition of affairs it is vain to expect that the sympathies of the people of the United States will not be warmly enlisted in favor of their oppressed neighbors.

We know that the President is justly inflexible in his determination to execute the neutrality laws; but should the Cubans themselves rise in revolt against the oppression which they suffer, no human power could prevent citizens of the United States and liberal minded men of other countries from rushing to their assistance. Besides, the present is an age of adventure, in which restless and daring spirits abound in every portion of the world.

It is not improbable, therefore, that Cuba may be wrested from Spain by a successful revolution; and in that event she will lose both the island and the price which we are now willing to pay for it—a price far beyond what was ever paid by one people to another for any province.

It may also be remarked that the settlement of this vexed question, by the cession of Cuba to the United States, would forever prevent the dangerous complications between nations to which it may otherwise give birth.

It is certain that, should the Cubans themselves organize an insurrection against the Spanish government, and should other independent nations come to the aid of Spain in the contest, no human power could, in our opinion, prevent the people and government of the United States from taking part in such a civil war in support of their neighbors and friends.

But if Spain, dead to the voice of her own interest, and actuated by stubborn pride and a false sense of honor, should refuse to sell Cuba to the United States, then the question will arise, What ought to be the course of the American government under such circumstances? Self-preservation is the first law of nature, with States as well as with individuals. All nations have, at different periods, acted upon this maxim. Although it has been made the pretext for committing flagrant injustice, as in the partition of Poland and other similar cases which history records, yet the principle itself, though often abused, has always been recognized.

The United States have never acquired a foot of territory except by fair purchase, or, as in the case of Texas, upon the free and voluntary application of the people of that independent State, who desired to blend their destinies with our own.

Even our acquisitions from Mexico are no exception to this rule, because, although we might have claimed them by the right of conquest in a just war, yet we purchased them for what was then considered by both parties a full and ample equivalent.

Our past history forbids that we should acquire the island of Cuba without the consent of Spain, unless justified by the great law of self-preservation. We must, in any event, preserve our own conscious rectitude and our own self-respect.

Whilst pursuing this course we can afford to disregard the censures of the world, to which we have been so often and so unjustly exposed.

After we shall have offered Spain a price for Cuba far beyond its present value, and this shall have been refused, it will then be time to consider the question, does Cuba, in the possession of Spain, seriously endanger our internal peace and the existence of our cherished Union?

Should this question be answered in the affirmative, then, by every law, human und divine, we shall be justified in wresting it from Spain if we possess the power, and this upon the very same principle that would justify an individual in tearing down the burning house of his neighbor if there were no other means of preventing the flames from destroying his own home.

Under such circumstances we ought neither to count the cost nor regard the odds which Spain might enlist against us. We forbear to enter into the question, whether the present condition of the island would justify such a measure? We should, however, be recreant to our duty, be unworthy of our gallant forefathers, and commit base treason against our posterity, should we permit Cuba to be Africanized and become a second St. Domingo, with all its attendant horrors to the white race, and suffer the flames to extend to our own neighboring shores, seriously to endanger or actually to consume the fair fabric of our Union.

We fear that the course and current of events are rapidly tending towards such a catastrophe. We, however, hope for the best, though we ought certainly to be prepared for the worst.

We also forbear to investigate the present condition of the questions at issue between the United States and Spain. A long series of injuries to our people have been committed in Cuba by Spanish officials and are unredressed. But recently a most flagrant outrage on the rights of American citizens and on the flag of the United States was perpetrated in the harbor of Havana under circumstances which, without immediate redress, would have justified a resort to measures of war in vindication of national honor. That outrage is not only unatoned, but the Spanish government has deliberately sanctioned the acts of its subordinates and assumed the responsibility attaching to them.

Nothing could more impressively teach us the danger to which those peaceful relations it has ever been the policy of the United States to cherish with foreign nations are constantly exposed than the circumstances of that case. Situated as Spain and the United States are, the latter have forborne to resort to extreme measures.

But this course cannot, with due regard to their own dignity as an independent nation, continue; and our recommendations, now submitted, are dictated by the firm belief that the cession of Cuba to the United States, with stipulations as beneficial to Spain as those suggested, is the only effective mode of settling all past differences and of securing the two countries against future collisions.

We have already witnessed the happy results for both countries which followed a similar arrangement in regard to Florida.

Yours, very respectfully,
JAMES BUCHANAN
J. Y. MASON
PIERRE SOULÉ

Source: U.S. *House Executive Documents*, 33rd Cong., 2nd sess., vol. 10.

Emancipation Is Declared in Peru (1854)

Given in the House of Supreme Government in Huancayo, December 3, 1854.

Considering—That it is due to justice to restore to man his freedom: that one of the chief objects of the revolution of 1854 was to recognize and guarantee the rights of humanity, oppressed, denied, and scorned by the tribute of the Indian, and Slavery of the Negro:

[T]hat this obligation being satisfied, in part, by the Decree of July 5, which released the natives from the burden of tribute, it still remains to complete it, by restoring their personal liberty to the slaves and serving-freed men:

[T]hat if the provisory government delayed decreeing liberty to the slaves till after it had destroyed the tyranny, it was because it desired not to excite distrust respecting the indemnification due to the masters, nor would it sully that act of justice to humanity, by inducing the slave to offer his life as the price of his liberty, in a civil war which he could not comprehend, even though he had not let alone political ideas while in a state of Slavery:

[T]hat the ex-President Echenique having, in his Decree of November last, demanded the blood of the slaves for two years, and disturbed the right of property, by the vague indemnity he offered, being only for those who would sell themselves to fight against the people, in his extremity—it would be a stain on the name of Peru if the provisory government did not declare immediately the national principles, and condemn that new and horrible traffic in human blood:—

Decrees—The men and women held until the present time in Peru as slaves, or servant-freedmen, whether in that condition by sale or birth, and in whichever mode held in servitude, perpetual or temporary—all, without distinction of age, are from this day wholly and for ever free.

Declares—1st. That the provisory government created by the people restores, unconditionally, liberty to the slaves and servant-freedmen; thus fulfilling in a solemn manner a duty of national justice, proclaimed by the revolution of 1854.

2d. The old and infirm, and those unfitted for labour by any physical cause, at the time of regaining their liberty, shall be supported in a house of charity, which the government must provide.

3d. Only those slaves or servants shall be debarred from freedom who take up arms to sustain the tyranny of Don José Rufino Echenique, who made war against the liberties of the people.

Guarantees the rights of property—By assuming that fair prices shall be paid to the owners of slaves and patrons of serving-freedmen, on the following terms:

1st. Debts to be paid in five years.

2d. Bears interest at six percent.

3d. and 4th. Relate to form, &c., of notes issued.

5th. Speaks of aiding the proprietors in obtaining a European emigration for reviving agriculture along the coast.

6th. Debt secured by national dues and customs.

7th. Urges the assistance of the proprietors in executing the Decree.

RAMON CASTILLA

Source: Anti-Slavery Reporter (New Series), 3:7 (July 2, 1855).

Law Abolishing Slavery in Certain Territories of the Province of Angola (1856)

Given at the Palace of Necessidades, on 5th July, 1856.

Dom Peter, by the grace of God King of Portugal and the Algarves, &c.

We hereby make known to all our subjects that the General Cortes have decreed, and we confirm, the following Law:

Article 1. The condition of slavery is hereby abolished in the following territories of the Province of Angola—(1.) In the district of Ambriz, from the River Lifune to the River Zaire. (2.) In the territories of Cabinda and Molembo.

Article 2. This law shall come into execution, in the district of Ambriz, at the expiration of six months from the date of this publication in the "Boletini Official" of Angola; and in the other territories mentioned in the preceding Article, six months from the establishment in each, by the Government of administrative and military authorities.

Article 3. All legislative enactments to the contrary are hereby revoked.

We therefore command all the authorities to whom the knowledge and execution of the above Law appertains, to carry it out, and cause it to be carried out and observed fully, as therein contained. The Minister and Secretary of State for Marine and Colonial Affairs shall cause it to be printed, published, and circulated.

(Signed) KING
(Countersigned) VISCOUNT SA DA BANDEIRA

Source: Anti-Slavery Reporter (New Series), 6:7 (July 1, 1858).

Law Liberating Slaves Upon Entering Into the Kingdom of Portugal (1856)

Given at the Palace of Cintra, August 18th, 1856.

Dom Peter, by the grace of God King of Portugal and the Algarves, &c.

We hereby make known to all our subjects that the General Cortes have decreed, and we confirm, the following Law:

Article 1. All slaves embarked on board of Portuguese vessels become free on entering any port or anchorage of the Kingdom of Portugal, or of the Archipelagoes of Madeira and the Azores.

Article 2. All slaves belonging to foreigners shall become equally free on landing in any of the Portuguese territories above-mentioned.

&. With regard to such slaves as, although they have become free by virtue of the provisions of the preceding Articles, will have to be given up to the commanders of the vessels to which they belong, the provisions of treaties entered into with foreign nations shall be observed.

Article 3. The provisions of the preceding Articles are applicable to slaves entering the Kingdom of Portugal by the frontier.

Article 4. The stipulations contained in the two first Articles shall come into execution six months from the date of the publication of the Law in the "Diario do Governo."

Article 5. The stipulations of Articles 1 and 2 of this Law shall be observed in the territories forming the States of India, and in the city of Macao and its dependencies. The period treated of in Article 4 shall be extended to one year from these territories.

Article 6. The Alvara of the 10th March, 1800, and all other legislative enactments to the contrary, are hereby revoked.

We therefore command all the authorities, &c.
(Signed) KING
(Countersigned)
MARQUIS DE LOULE.
JULIO GOMES DE SILVA SANCHEZ.
VISCONDE DE SA DA BANDEIRA.

Source: Anti-Slavery Reporter (New Series), 6:7 (July 1, 1858).

Vermont's Personal Liberty Law (1858)

An Act to Secure Freedom to All Persons Within this State.

It is hereby enacted, &c.:
Section 1. No person within this State shall be considered as property, or subject, as such, to sale, purchase, or delivery; nor shall any person, within the limits of this State, at this time, be deprived of liberty or property without due process of law.

Section 2. Due process of law, mentioned in the preceding section of this Act shall, in all cases, be defined to mean the usual process and forms in force by the laws of this State, and issued by the courts thereof; and under such process, such person shall be entitled to a trial by jury.

Section 3. Whenever any person in this State shall be deprived of liberty, arrested, or detained, on the ground that such person owes service or labor to another person, not an inhabitant of this State, either party may claim a trial by jury; and, in such case, challenges shall be allowed to the defendant agreeably to sections four and five of chapter one hundred and eleven of the compiled statutes.

Section 4. Every person who shall deprive or attempt to deprive any other person of his or her liberty, contrary to the preceding sections of this Act, shall, on conviction thereof, forfeit and pay a fine not exceeding two thousand dollars nor less than five hundred dollars, or be punished by imprisonment in the State

Prison for a term not exceeding ten years: Provided, that nothing in said preceding sections shall apply to, or affect the right to arrest or imprison under existing laws for contempt of court.

Section 5. Neither descent near or remote from an African, whether such African is or may have been a slave or not, nor color of skin or complexion, shall disqualify any person from being, or prevent any person from becoming, a citizen of this State, nor deprive such person of the rights and privileges thereof.

Section 6. Every person who may have been held as a slave, who shall come, or be brought, or be in this State, with or without the consent of his or her master or mistress, or who shall come, or be brought, or be, involuntarily or in any way in this State, shall be free.

Section 7. Every person who shall hold, or attempt to hold, in this State, in slavery, or as a slave, any person mentioned as a slave in the sixth section of this act, or any free person, in any form, or for any time, however short, under pretence that such person is or has been a slave, shall, on conviction thereof, be imprisoned in the State Prison for a term not less than one year, nor more than fifteen years, and be fined not exceeding two thousand dollars.

Section 8. All Acts and parts of Acts inconsistent with the provisions of this Act are hereby repealed.

Section 9. This Act shall take effect from its passage.

Approved November 25, 1858.

Source: Lydia Maria Child, *The Duty of Civil Disobedience to the Fugitive Slave Act: An Appeal to the Legislators of Massachusetts.* Boston: American Anti-Slavery Society, 1860.

The Emancipation of the Serfs in Russia (1861)

Given at St. Petersburgh the 19th day of February (March 3), of the Year of Grace 1861, and the seventh of our reign.

MANIFESTO OF HIS MAJESTY THE EMPEROR.

By the grace of God, we, Alexander II, Emperor and Autocrat of all the Russias, King of Poland, Grand Duke of Finland, &c., to all our faithful subjects make known:

Called by Divine Providence and by the sacred right of inheritance to the throne of our ancestors, we took a vow in our innermost heart so to respond to the mission which is entrusted to us as to surround with our affection and our imperial solicitude all our faithful subjects of every rank and of every condition, from the warrior who nobly bears arms for the defence of the country, to the humble artisan devoted to the works of industry; from the official in the career of the high offices of the State to the labourer whose plough furrows the soil.

In considering the various classes and conditions of which the State is composed, we come to the conviction that the legislation of the empire having wisely provided for the organization of the upper and middle classes, and having defined with precision their obligations, their rights, and their privileges, has not attained the same degree of efficiency as regards the peasants attached to the soil (*krépostnyé*), thus designated because either from ancient laws or from custom, they have been hereditarily subjected to the authority of the proprietors, on whom it was incumbent at the same time to provide for their welfare. The rights of the proprietors have been hitherto very extended, and very imperfectly defined by the law, which has been supplied by tradition, custom, and the good pleasure of the proprietors. In the most favourable cases this state of things has established patriarchal relations founded upon a solicitude sincerely equitable and benevolent on the part of the proprietors, and on an affectionate submission on the part of the peasants; but in proportion as the simplicity of morals diminished, as the diversity of the mutual relations became complicated, as the paternal character of the relations between the proprietors and the peasants became weakened, and moreover, as the seigneurial authority fell sometimes into hands exclusively occupied with their personal interests, those bonds of mutual goodwill slackened, and a wide opening was made for an arbitrary sway, which weighed upon the peasants, was unfavourable to their welfare, and made them indifferent to all progress under the conditions of their existence.

These facts had already attracted the notice of our predecessors of glorious memory, and they had taken measures for improving the condition of the peasants; but among those measures some were not stringent enough, insomuch as they remained subordinate to the spontaneous initiative of such proprietors who shewed themselves animated with liberal intentions; and others, called forth by peculiar circumstances, have been restricted to certain localities, or simply adopted as an experiment. It was thus that Alexander I published the regulations for the free cultivators, and that the late Emperor Nicholas, our beloved father, promulgated that one which concerns the peasants *bound by contract.* In the Western Governments regulations called *"inventaires"* had fixed the territorial allotments due to the peasants, as well as the amount of their rent dues; but all these reforms have only been applied in a very restricted manner.

We thus came to the conviction that the work of a serious improvement of the condition of the peasants was a sacred inheritance bequeathed to us by our ancestors; a mission which, in the course of events, Divine Providence called upon us to fulfil.

We have commenced this work by an expression of our imperial confidence towards the nobility of Russia, which has given us so many proofs of its devotion to the throne, and of its constant readiness to make sacrifices for the welfare of the country.

It is to the nobles themselves, conformable to their own wishes, that we have reserved the task of drawing up the propositions for the new organization of the peasants; propositions which make it incumbent upon them to limit their rights over the peasants, and to accept the onus of a reform which could not be accomplished without some material losses. Our confidence has not been deceived. We have seen the nobles assembled in committees in the districts, through the medium of their confidential agents, making the voluntary sacrifice of their rights as regards the personal servitude of the peasants. These committees, after having collected the necessary data, have formulated their propositions concerning the new organization of the peasants attached to the soil (*krépostnyé*) in their relations with the proprietors.

These propositions having been found very diverse, as was to be expected from the nature of the question, they have been compared, collated, and reduced to a regular system, then rectified and completed in the superior committee instituted for that purpose; and these new dispositions, thus formulated relative to the peasants and domestics (*dvorovyé*) of the proprietors, have been examined in the Council of the Empire.

Having invoked the Divine assistance, we have resolved to carry this work into execution.

In virtue of the new dispositions above mentioned, the peasants attached to the soil (*attachés à la glèbe*) will be invested within a term fixed by the law, with all the rights of free cultivators.

The proprietors retaining their rights of property on all land belonging to them, grant to the peasants, for a fixed regulated rental, the full enjoyment of their close (*enclos*); and, moreover, to ensure their livelihood, and to guarantee the fulfillment of their obligations towards the Government, the quantity of arable land is fixed by the said dispositions, as well as other rural appurtenances (*ougodié*).

But, in the enjoyment of these territorial allotments, the peasants are obliged, in return, to acquit the rentals fixed by the same dispositions to the profit of the proprietors. In this state, which must be a transitory one, the peasants shall be designated as "temporarily bound" (*temporairement obligés*).

At the same time they are granted the right of purchasing their close (*enclos*), and, with the consent of the proprietors, they may acquire in full property the arable lands and other appurtenances which are allotted to them as a permanent holding (*jouissance*). By the acquisition in full property of the quantity of land fixed, the peasants are free from their obligations towards the proprietors for land thus purchased, and they enter definitively into the condition of free peasants—landholders (*paysans libres—propriétaires*).

By a special disposition concerning the domestics (*gens de la domesticité—dvorovyé*) a transitory state is fixed for them adapted to their occupations and the exigencies of their position. On the expiration of a term of two years, dating from the day of the promulgation of these dispositions, they shall receive their full enfranchisement and some temporary immunities.

It is according to these fundamental principles that the dispositions have been formulated which define the future organization of the peasants and of the domestics (*dvorovyé*), which establish the order of the general administration of this class, and specify in all their details the rights given to the peasants and to the domestics, as well as the obligations imposed upon them towards the Government and towards the proprietors.

Although these dispositions, general as well as local, and the special supplementary rules for some particular localities, for the lands of small proprietors, and for the peasants who work in the manufactories and establishments (*usines*) of the proprietors, have been, as far as was possible, adapted to economical necessities and local customs, nevertheless, to preserve the existing state where it presents reciprocal advantages, we leave it to the proprietors to come to amicable terms with the peasants, and to conclude transactions relative to the extent of the territorial allotment, and to the amount of rental to be fixed in consequence, observing at the same time the established rules to guarantee the inviolability of such agreements.

As the new organization, in consequence of the inevitable complexity of the changes which it necessitates, cannot be immediately put into execution; as a lapse of time is necessary, which cannot be less than two years or thereabouts, to avoid all misunderstanding, and to protect public and private interests during this interval, the system (*régime*) actually existing on the properties of landowners (*seigneurs*) will be maintained up to the moment when a new system shall have been instituted by the completion of the required preparatory measures.

For which end we have deemed it advisable to ordain:

1. To establish in each district (*gouvernement*) a special Court for the question of the peasants; it will have to investigate the affairs of the rural communes established on the land of the lords of the soil (*seigneurs*).
2. To appoint in each district justices of the peace to investigate on the spot all misunderstandings and disputes which may arise on the occasion of the introduction of the new regulation, and to form district assemblies with these justices of the peace.
3. To organize in the seigneurial properties communal administrations, and to this end to leave the rural communes in their actual composition, and to open in their large villages district administrations (provincial boards) by uniting the small communes under one of these district administrations.
4. To formulate, verify, and confirm, in each rural district or estate, a charter of rules (*une charte réglementaire—oustavnaía gramota*), in which shall be enumerated on the basis of the Local Statute, the amount of land reserved to the peasants in permanent enjoyment, and the extent of the charges which may be exacted from them for the benefit of the proprietor, as well for the land as for other advantages granted by him.
5. To put these charters of rules into execution as they are gradually confirmed in each estate, and to introduce their definitive execution within the term of two years, dating from the day of publication of the present manifesto.
6. Up to the expiration of this term the peasants and domestics (*gens de la domesticité*) are to remain in the same obedience towards their proprietors, and to fulfil their obligations without scruple.
7. The proprietors will continue to watch over the maintenance of order on their estates, with the right of jurisdiction and of police, until the organization of the districts (*volosti*) and of the district tribunals has been effected.

Aware of all the difficulties of the reform we have undertaken, we place, above all things, our confidence in the goodness of Divine Providence, who watches over the destinies of Russia.

We also count upon the generous devotion of our faithful nobility, and we are happy to testify to that body the gratitude it has deserved from us, as well as from the country, for the disinterested support it has given to the accomplishment of our designs. Russia will not forget that the nobility, acting solely upon its respect for the dignity of man, and its love for its neighbour, has spontaneously renounced rights given to it by serfdom actually abolished, and laid the foundation of a new future, which is thrown open to the peasants. We also entertain the firm hope that it will also nobly exert its ulterior efforts to carry out the new regulation by maintaining good order, in a spirit of peace and benevolence, and that each proprietor will complete within the limits of his property the great civic act accomplished by the whole body, by organizing the existence of the peasants domiciliated on his estates, and of his domestics, under mutual advantageous conditions, thereby giving to the country population the example of a faithful and conscientious execution of the regulations of the State.

The numerous examples of the generous solicitude of the proprietors for the welfare of their peasants, and of the gratitude of the latter for the benevolent solicitude of their lords, give us the hope that a mutual understanding will settle the majority of complications, in some cases inevitable, in the partial application of general rules to the different conditions under which isolated estates are placed; that in this manner the transition from the ancient order of things to the new will be facilitated; and that the future will strengthen definitively mutual confidence, a good understanding, and the unanimous impulsion towards public utility.

To render the transactions between the proprietors and the peasants more easy, in virtue of which the latter may acquire in full property their close (*enclos*—homestead) and the land they occupy, the Government will advance assistance according to a special regulation, by means of loans or a transfer of debts encumbering an estate.

We thus confidently rely upon the upright feeling of the nation.

When the first news of this great reform, meditated by the Government, became diffused among the rural populations, who were scarcely prepared for it, it gave rise in some instances to misunderstandings among individuals more intent upon liberty than mindful of the duties which it imposes. But generally the good sense of the country has not been wanting. It has not misunderstood either the inspirations of natural reason, which says that every man who accepts freely the benefits of society owes it in return the fulfillment of certain positive obligations; nor the teachings of the Christian law, which enjoins that "every one be subject unto the higher powers" (St. Paul to the Romans, xiii. 1); and to "render to all their dues," and, above all, to whomsoever it belongs, tribute, custom, respect, and honour, (*Ibid.*, 7 v.). It has understood that the proprietors would not be deprived of rights legally acquired, except for a fit and sufficient indemnity, or by a voluntary concession on their part; that it would be contrary to all equity to accept this enjoyment of the lands conceded by the proprietors without accepting also towards them equivalent charges.

And now we hope with confidence that the freed serfs, in the presence of the new future which is opened before them, will appreciate and recognize the considerable sacrifices which the nobility have made on their behalf. They will understand that the blessing of an existence supported upon the base of guaranteed property, as well as a greater liberty in the administration of their goods, entails upon them, with new duties towards society and themselves, the obligation of justifying the protecting designs of the law by a loyal and judicious use of the rights which are now accorded to them. For if men do not labour themselves to insure their own well-being under the shield of the laws, the best of those laws cannot guarantee it to them.

It is only by assiduous labour, a rational employment of their strength and their resources, a strict economy, and, above all, by an honest life, a life constantly inspired by the fear of the Lord, that they can arrive at prosperity, and insure its development.

The authorities intrusted with the duty of preparing by preliminary measures the execution of the new organization, and of presiding at its inauguration, will have to see that this work is accomplished with calmness and regularity, taking into account the requirements of the seasons, in order that the cultivator may not be drawn away from his agricultural labours. Let him apply himself with zeal to those labours, that he may be able to draw from an abundant granary the seed which he has to confide to that land which will be given him for permanent enjoyment, or which he has acquired for himself as his own property.

And now, pious and faithful people, make upon thy forehead the sacred sign of the cross, and join thy prayers to ours to call down the blessing of the Most high upon thy first free labourers, the sure pledge of thy personal well being and of the public prosperity.

ALEXANDER

Source: Anti-Slavery Reporter (New Series), 9:7 (July 1, 1861).

Emancipation in the Dutch Colonies (1862)

LAW OF AUGUST 8TH, 1862, RELATING TO THE ABOLITION OF SLAVERY IN THE COLONY OF SURINAM

William the Third, by the Grace of God King of the Netherlands, Prince of Orange and Nassau, Grand Duke of Luxemburg, &c. &c. &c.

To all, to whom these presents shall come, greeting:

Whereas for divers good causes to Us appearing, We have deemed it right that Slavery in the Colony of Surinam should be abolished;

And whereas We are desirous at the same time to provide the means of maintaining, and, as much as possible, extending the agriculture and the industry of the Colony;

Wherefore, We having consulted the Council of State, do hereby, with the advice and approval of the States' General, enact:

CHAPTER I. *General Principles.*

Art[icle] 1. That Slavery in the Colony of Surinam shall be abolished from and after the *first* of July 1863.

Art[icle] 2. That compensation shall be given to the owners of slaves.

Art[icle] 3. That those who are made free by virtue of Art[icle] 1, are to be, from the first of July, under particular surveillance of the State, for the term of *ten* years at the utmost.

Art[icle] 4. The colonization of Surinam, by free labourers, shall be encouraged by the State.

Premiums will be granted by the State, for the importation of free-labourers, during the term of five years at the utmost, from the promulgation of the present law.

The sum of these premiums shall not exceed *one million* of guilders.

The conditions, on the fulfillment of which the payment of these premiums shall depend, shall be determined by Us, and the Government shall regulate also the mode and manner of inspecting the immigrants when they are landed.

CHAPTER II. *Compensation.*

Art[icle] 5. Within *thirty* days after the promulgation of this law in the Colony of Surinam, all owners of slaves, or their representatives, shall deliver to the Secretary of the Government a return in duplicate, containing the names of the plantations to which the slaves belong; the names and residences of the owners, or their representatives; the name, the sex, the age, the profession or trade, and the religion of the slaves belonging to them, with a list of those who have a right to manumission, and of those who have been classed as infected with leprosy or elephantiasis. A receipt for such return shall be delivered to those who produce it.

Art[icle] 6. Owners of slaves, or their representative[s], neglecting to produce the return mentioned in Art[icle] 5, within the stated term, it will be made out by the Government, and the expenses thereof shall be paid by the defaulter.

Art[icle] 7. The returns mentioned in the two preceding Articles shall be checked by the Government, within a short term fixed by the Governor of Surinam, against the actual number of slaves, and, if need be, with the registers.

Art[icle] 8. The amount of compensation for slaves, belonging to plantations or to private estates, or for personal slaves, is fixed, without difference as to age or sex, at 300 guilders a head.

Art[icle] 9. Compensation will not be given for:

a. Slaves who are infected, or who must be removed on account of infection. With regard to those who, according to the decree published Sept. 7th, 1830 (*Royal Gazette*, No. 13), or those who, in consequence of the verification mentioned in Art[icle] 7, may be afterwards declared suspected of being infected with one of the therein specified maladies, the decision as to the adjudging of a compensation shall be suspended. No compensation shall be given if the infected individual is not declared healthy by the commission, mentioned in Art[icle]. 8 of the Decree of Sept. 7th, 1830, within a year after the promulgation of this law in the Colony of Surinam.

b. Slaves who have deserted or been lost longer than *one* month before the day of the verification mentioned in Art[icle] 7.

c. Slaves condemned to compulsory labour, whose term of punishment will not be fulfilled within *four* years after the first of July 1863.

d. Children born of women slaves after the promulgation of the present law in the Colony of Surinam.

Art[icle] 10. Compensation shall include not only the person of the slave, but also his clothes, cattle, and poultry, and all moveable possessions, these being considered, according to colonial custom, his own. These possessions then become his property absolutely.

Art[icle] 11. According to the verified returns (*vide* Art[icle] 7), a list will be made out, containing the amounts of compensations that are to be granted, which list will be, during *thirty* days after the expiration of the above-mentioned term, deposited with the Secretary of the Government for examination.

Art[icle] 12. If the owners, or their representative[s], are dissatisfied with that list, they may, within *fourteen* days after the term mentioned in the preceding article, declare opposition to the Government Secretary, through the public crier, mentioning the motives of their complaint.

Art[icle] 13. During the first fortnight after registration, all cases of opposition shall be submitted, on penalty of annulment, to the first assembly of the court of the colony of Surinam.

On the day of hearing, the evidence on each side shall be set forth verbally, without attorneys, and without written pleadings.

The court shall declare its decision as soon as possible, but may order a further inquiry within a term to be stated.

The decision of the court shall be without appeal.

Art[icle] 14. The compensation mentioned in Art[icle] 8, shall be paid within *three* months from the abolition of Slavery, to the owner or his representative.

The payment shall be made in Bills of Exchange, in guilders, to be drawn by the Governor on the Minister for the Colonies, payable one month after sight by the Bank of the Netherlands in Amsterdam; or, if desired, and if, in the opinion of the governor, the colonial treasury can meet the demand, at Paramaribo, and in coin of legal currency.

Art[icle] 15. In case of any difference as to the right to any slave, or if a third party claim the amount of the compensation, or a part of it, the payment of the whole sum shall be delayed till the parties are agreed, or till the question of right has been determined.

Art[icle] 16. The right to compensation, under the present law, shall be forfeited, with regard to all sums which are not claimed within *four* years after the abolition of Slavery.

Art[icle] 17. The returns, declarations, discharges, and all documents required, according to the stipulations of this chapter, shall be exempted from stamp duty.

CHAPTER III. *On the surveillance of the State.*
Art[icle] 18. The surveillance of the freed Negroes shall be performed by paid functionaries whose functions and competence shall be set forth and determined by a general ordinance.

These functionaries shall not be connected with the administration of the colonies, nor shall they have any pecuniary interest in any enterprise in Surinam.

Art[icle] 19. The surveillance of the State is for the protection of the emancipated, and with a view to instruct them in family and public life; to prevent idleness, to regulate labour, and also to promote secular and religious instruction; further, to prescribe the manner of aiding the indigent, and to make provision for nursing the sick; and, in general, to take whatever measures may be requisite in behalf of the emancipated negroes or for the preservation of public order.

Art[icle] 20. The Governor of Surinam is authorised to discharge from the surveillance of the State, those freed Negroes who may distinguish themselves by their morality and diligence.

CHAPTER IV.
Art[icle] 21. The slaves who are made free, shall adopt a family name, by which they are to be registered, and as much as possible, in family groups.

Such register shall be signed in some form by those who are registered, and it shall set forth their names and Christian names, the date of their birth, or their probable age.

The Governor of the colony shall see that the registration is made at the time of the abolition of Slavery.

Art[icle] 22. The common civil and penal law is to be applied to the freed Negroes, save to such as are excepted during their surveillance by the State.

Art[icle] 23. The freed slaves shall be considered as inhabitants of the colony, but until the expiration of the term of the State surveillance, they shall not come into the full enjoyment of the rights of citizenship, save such as are discharged from such surveillance.

Art[icle] 24. Labour shall be obligatory upon all who are placed under the surveillance of the State, subject to the following rules:

A. Respecting those who have been settled, or who have been ordinary labourers on plantations or estates.

1. All, from the age of fifteen to sixty shall be competent to enter into contracts, at their choice, with planters or employers of husbandmen, for the performance of plantation labour.

2. Such contracts shall be made before the functionary mentioned in Art[icle] 18, and according to the ordinances relating thereto, for not less than one year, and not for more than three years.

3. The Governor shall have the power, in so far as he may deem it necessary for the maintenance of peace and order, to restrict, during the two first years after the promulgation of this law, the choice of the freed Negroes to enter into contracts for labour, to the district where they may be settled on the *first* of July 1863.

4. Those who have not entered into contracts within *three* months after the abolition of slavery shall be set to work, under the care of the Government, in Government plantations, or on works of general utility.

5. Those who are above sixty years of age shall remain with the families to which they belong, likewise children under fifteen who, in every case, shall follow their mothers.

6. The aged and the children shall help, according to their strength and capacity, and shall be paid proportionate wages, by the tenant or the planter with whom the head of the family, or the mother of the children, shall have entered into a contract.

B. Respecting those who are not settled, or who have not been ordinary labourers on plantations or estates.

1. These, like the former plantation slaves, from the age of fifteen to sixty, shall enter into contracts with persons of their choice, to perform labour or service.

2. Such contracts, entered into before the functionary mentioned in Art[icle] 18, and according to the ordinances relating thereto, shall be made for not less than *three* months and for not longer than *one* year, for work or service in town. When the engagements are for plantation labourers, the rules of 2, 5, and 6 of subdivision A. shall be applied.

3. To those who can satisfactorily prove that they are able to practise some calling, profession, or trade,

and to provide for their own wants and those of their family, a license to exercise such calling shall be given, upon payment of a license duty, to be levied by general colonial ordinance in regard to the practice of such calling, profession, or trade. This profession or trade license shall be renewed yearly.

4. Those who do not enter into any contract within *three* months after the abolition of Slavery, and those who, by virtue of the license given to them, do not practise any calling, profession, or trade, shall be set to work, under the inspection of the Government, according to their strength and capacity, on Government plantations, or on works of general utility.

5. Those who are above *sixty* years of age, and children from *twelve* to *fifteen*, shall perform light labour, according to their strength and capacity.

6. Children shall not be separated from their mothers, unless they are above *twelve* years of age.

CHAPTER V. *General stipulations.*

Art[icle] 25. Religious and secular instruction shall be encouraged, and as much as possible supported by the State.

Art[icle] 26. Permission to possess or to bear weapons, shall be given only under peculiar circumstances, to those who are under the inspection of the State, and to field and plantation labourers.

Art[icle] 27. Except penal labour, all labour on Government plantations or on works of general utility shall be remunerated; the wages, as also the work itself, shall be regulated by the Government, according to a tariff.

The tariff shall fix the rate of wages for plantation labour contracted for by private individuals, unless the contract contain other conditions.

A working-day shall be calculated to consist of *eight* hours of labour in the fields, and of *ten* hours in buildings, and a working-year shall be *three hundred* working-days.

Art[icle] 28. When no volunteers can be obtained for reasonable hire, for military and other service, or for works of general utility, the Government shall have the right to employ those who are under State surveillance, from fifteen to sixty years of age, as also all other field and plantation labourers.

Art[icle] 29. Idleness and vagrancy shall be punishable according to ordinance, to be hereafter issued.

Art[icle] 30. Owners of slaves shall lodge, during *three* months at the utmost, after the abolition of Slavery, those of their former slaves who shall be at

that time without a domicile. They may, however, release themselves from this obligation, by paying the cost of lodging them elsewhere, to the satisfaction of the State Inspector.

On the other hand, the freed Negroes shall be bound to work at least *four* days a week, for the benefit of him who lodges them.

Art[icle] 31. Any one setting to work or holding any who are under State surveillance, without a written contract, shall be punished by fine, and be liable to arrest, according to a general ordinance to be made for that purpose.

Art[icle] 32. The Government shall take care that those who are under its surveillance obtain medical assistance and attendance when sick, by an ordinance to that effect; and that *on the plantations*, the owners shall provide suitable rooms for the sick, medical treatment and attendance; *and that for others, elsewhere*, hospitals shall be established. Those who, by virtue of existing ordinances, are removed on account of contagion, shall be treated in establishments specially set apart for this purpose.

Art[icle] 33. Those who hire freed Negroes, who are under State surveillance, shall provide them with suitable habitations; and, further, give them grounds for cultivating food for their own use. Ordinances, to this effect, will be enacted later.

Art[icle] 34. The freed Negroes who are not at work on plantations, shall provide themselves with lodging and medical treatment, as also their family, unless other conditions are made in their contract for labour or service.

Art[icle] 35. The Government shall undertake the lodging and care of orphans and other indigents.

Towards the expenses of such charge, all the freed negroes who are able to contract, all the field and plantation labourers, and those who, according to Art[icle] 24 B., 3, come under the conditions of the licence duty, are to be subjected to a yearly tax: the men 3f. (5s.), and the women 1.50f. (2s. 6d.). This tax shall be paid in the first instance, by the employer, into the State Treasury at the beginning of the year, and shall be deducted in the course of the year from the wages of the labourers; also by those who pay license duty, and by independent free Negroes, on the delivery of the licence mentioned in 3.

Art[icle] 36. The penalties for not fulfilling contracts are:

a. The employer shall be liable to arrest, with or without the annulment of his contract; in the first instance with indemnification, if the terms of the contact justify the same.

b. The labourer shall be liable to fine, and, in the case of non-payment, the amount shall be deducted from his wages.

c. He may also be put to hard labour on the public works.

These matters shall be regulated by ordinance to be hereafter made, and by which, at the same time, the judge shall be indicated, and the manner of proceeding prescribed.

Art[icle] 37. The Governor of Surinam shall retain, in certain cases, the power given to him by Art[icle]. 78 of the regulations for the management of the Government in the colony of Surinam, as set forth by Royal decree of August 9th, 1832, No. 69 (*Government Newspaper*, No. 13).

Art[icle] 38. Expenses, resulting from the application of the present law, shall not be incurred unless the sums required are previously sanctioned by the law.

Art[icle] 39. Every year, beginning with 1863, an account shall be sent by our minister of the Colonies to the States' General, relating to the execution of the present law.

It is ordered that this Law be published in the *Royal Gazette*, and that all the ministerial departments, authorities, colleges, and functionaries to whom it comes, shall see to its exact execution.

Done at Wiesbaden, this 8th day of August, 1862.

WILLIAM

The Minister for the Colonies,
G.H. UHLENBECK.

Source: Anti-Slavery Reporter (New Series), 2:3 (March 5, 1863).

The Emancipation Proclamation (1863)

BY THE PRESIDENT OF THE UNITED STATES OF AMERICA:
A Proclamation

Whereas on the 22d day of September, A.D. 1862, a proclamation was issued by the President of the United States, containing, among other things, the following, to wit:

"That on the 1st day of January, A.D. 1863, all persons held as slaves within any State or designated part of a State the people whereof shall then be in rebellion against the United States shall be then, thenceforward, and forever free; and the executive government of the United States, including the military and naval authority thereof, will recognize and maintain the freedom of such persons and will do no act or acts to repress such persons, or any of them, in any efforts they may make for their actual freedom.

That the executive will on the 1st day of January aforesaid, by proclamation, designate the States and parts of States, if any, in which the people thereof, respectively, shall then be in rebellion against the United States; and the fact that any State or the people thereof shall on that day be in good faith represented in the Congress of the United States by members chosen thereto at elections wherein a majority of the qualified voters of such States shall have participated shall, in the absence of strong countervailing testimony, be deemed conclusive evidence that such State and the people thereof are not then in rebellion against the United States."

Now, therefore, I, Abraham Lincoln, President of the United States, by virtue of the power in me vested as Commander-In-Chief of the Army and Navy of the United States in time of actual armed rebellion against the authority and government of the United States, and as a fit and necessary war measure for suppressing said rebellion, do, on this 1st day of January, A.D. 1863, and in accordance with my purpose so to do, publicly proclaimed for the full period of one hundred days from the first day above mentioned, order and designate as the States and parts of States wherein the people thereof, respectively, are this day in rebellion against the United States the following, to wit:

Arkansas, Texas, Louisiana (except the parishes of St. Bernard, Plaquemines, Jefferson, St. John, St. Charles, St. James, Ascension, Assumption, Terrebonne, Lafourche, St. Mary, St. Martin, and Orleans, including the city of New Orleans), Mississippi, Alabama, Florida, Georgia, South Carolina, North Carolina, and Virginia (except the forty-eight counties designated as West Virginia, and also the counties of Berkeley, Accomac, Northhampton, Elizabeth City, York, Princess Anne, and Norfolk, including the cities of Norfolk and Portsmouth), and which excepted parts are for the present left precisely as if this proclamation were not issued.

And by virtue of the power and for the purpose aforesaid, I do order and declare that all persons held as slaves within said designated States and parts of States are, and henceforward shall be, free; and that the Executive Government of the United States, including the military and naval authorities thereof, will recognize and maintain the freedom of said persons.

And I hereby enjoin upon the people so declared to be free to abstain from all violence, unless in necessary self-defense; and I recommend to them that, in all case[s] when allowed, they labor faithfully for reasonable wages.

And I further declare and make known that such persons of suitable condition will be received into the armed service of the United States to garrison forts, positions, stations, and other places, and to man vessels of all sorts in said service.

And upon this act, sincerely believed to be an act of justice, warranted by the Constitution upon military necessity, I invoke the considerate judgment of mankind and the gracious favor of Almighty God.

Source: "The Emancipation Proclamation," in *Documents of American History,* 7th ed., ed. Henry Steele Commanger. New York: Appleton-Century-Crofts, 1963.

The Reconstruction Amendments (1865, 1868, 1870)

AMENDMENT XIII
Passed by Congress January 31, 1865. Ratified December 6, 1865.

Section 1. Neither slavery nor involuntary servitude, except as a punishment for crime whereof the party shall have been duly convicted, shall exist within the United States, or any place subject to their jurisdiction.

Section 2. Congress shall have power to enforce this article by appropriate legislation.

AMENDMENT XIV
Passed by Congress June 13, 1866. Ratified July 9, 1868.

Section 1. All persons born or naturalized in the United States, and subject to the jurisdiction thereof, are citizens of the United States and of the State wherein they reside. No State shall make or enforce any law which shall abridge the privileges or immunities of citizens of the United States; nor shall any State deprive any person of life, liberty, or property, without due process of law; nor deny to any person within its jurisdiction the equal protection of the laws.

Section 2. Representatives shall be apportioned among the several States according to their respective numbers, counting the whole number of persons in each State, excluding Indians not taxed. But when the right to vote at any election for the choice of electors for President and Vice-President of the United States, Representatives in Congress, the Executive and Judicial officers of a State, or the members of the Legislature thereof, is denied to any of the male inhabitants of such State, being twenty-one years of age, and citizens of the United States, or in any way abridged, except for participation in rebellion, or other crime, the basis of representation therein shall be reduced in the proportion which the number of such male citizens shall bear to the whole number of male citizens twenty-one years of age in such State.

Section 3. No person shall be a Senator or Representative in Congress, or elector of President and Vice-President, or hold any office, civil or military, under the United States, or under any State, who, having previously taken an oath, as a member of Congress, or as an officer of the United States, or as a member of any State legislature, or as an executive or judicial officer of any State, to support the Constitution of the United States, shall have engaged in insurrection or rebellion against the same, or given aid or comfort to the enemies thereof. But Congress may by a vote of two-thirds of each House, remove such disability.

Section 4. The validity of the public debt of the United States, authorized by law, including debts incurred for payment of pensions and bounties for services in suppressing insurrection or rebellion, shall not be questioned. But neither the United States nor any State shall assume or pay any debt or obligation incurred in aid of insurrection or rebellion against the United States, or any claim for the loss or emancipation of any slave; but all such debts, obligations, and claims shall be held illegal and void.

Section 5. The Congress shall have the power to enforce, by appropriate legislation, the provisions of this article.

AMENDMENT XV
Passed by Congress February 26, 1869. Ratified February 3, 1870.

Section 1. The right of citizens of the United States to vote shall not be denied or abridged by the United States or by any State on account of race, color, or previous condition of servitude.—

Section 2. The Congress shall have power to enforce this article by appropriate legislation.

Source: Constitution of the United States.

Brazil's Free Birth Law (1871)

Given at the Palace of Rio de Janeiro, on the 28th September, 1871.

Princess Imperial, Regent, in the name of His Majesty the Emperor Senhor D. Pedro II, makes known to all the subjects of the Empire, that the General Assembly has decreed, and that she has sanctioned, the following Law:

I. The children of women slaves that may be born in the Empire from the date of this Law shall be considered to be free.

1. The said minors shall remain with and be under the dominion of the owners of the mother, who shall be obliged to rear and take care of them until such children shall have completed the age of eight years.

On the child of the slave attaining this age, the owner of its mother shall have the option either of receiving from the State the indemnification of 600 dollars, or of making use of the services of the minor until he shall have completed the age of twenty-one years.

In the former event the Government will receive the minor, and will dispose of him in conformity with the provisions of the present Law.

The pecuniary indemnification above fixed shall be paid in Government bonds, bearing interest at six per cent per annum, which will be considered extinct at the end of thirty years.

The declaration of the owner must be made within thirty days, counting from the day on which the minor shall complete the age of eight years; and should he not do so within that time it will be understood that he embraces the option of making use of the service of the minor.

2. Any one of those minors may ransom himself from the onus of servitude, by means of a previous pecuniary indemnification, offered by himself, or by any other person, to the owner of his mother, calculating the value of his services for the time which shall still remain unexpired to complete the period, should there be no agreement on the quantum of the said indemnification.

3. It is also incumbent on owners to rear and bring up the children which the daughters of their female slaves may have while they are serving the same owners.

Such obligation, however, will cease as soon as the service of the mother ceases. Should the latter die within the term of servitude the children may be placed at the disposal of the Government.

4. Should the female slave obtain her freedom, her children under eight years of age who may be under the dominion of her owners shall, by virtue of 1, be delivered up, unless she shall prefer leaving them with him, and he consents to their remaining.

5. In case of the female slave being made over to another owner her free children under twelve years of age shall accompany her, the new owner of the said slave being invested with the rights and obligations of his predecessor.

6. The services of the children of female slaves shall cease to be rendered before the term marked in 1, if by decision of the Criminal judge it be known that the owner of the mothers ill-treat the children, inflicting on them severe punishments.

7. The right conferred on owners by 1 shall be transferred in cases of direct succession; the child of a slave must render his services to the person to whose share in the division of property the said slave shall belong.

II. The Government may deliver over to associations which they shall have authorized, the children of the slaves [who] may be born from the date of this Law forward, and given up or abandoned by the owners of said slaves, or taken away from them by virtue of Article I, 6.

1. The said associations shall have a right to the gratuitous services of the minors, until they shall have completed the age of twenty-one years, and may hire out their services, but shall be bound—

1st. To rear and take care of the said minors.

2ndly. To save a sum for each of them, out of the amount of wages, which for this purpose is reserved in the respective statutes.

3rdly. To seek to place them in a proper situation when their term of service shall be ended.

2. The associations referred to in the previous paragraph shall be subject to the inspection of judges of the Orphans' Court, in as far as affects minors.

3. The disposition of this Article is applicable to foundling asylums, and to the persons whom the judges of the Orphans' Court charge with the education of the said minors, in default of associations or houses established for that purpose.

4. The Government has the free right of ordering the said minors to be taken into the public establishments, the obligations imposed by 1 on the authorised associations being in this case transferred to the State.

III. As many slaves as correspond in value to the annual disposable sum from the emancipation fund shall be freed in each province of the Empire.

1. The emancipation fund arises from—

1st. The tax on slaves.

2ndly. General tax on transfer of the slaves as property.

3rdly. The proceeds of six lotteries per annum, free of tax, and the tenth part of those which may be granted from this time forth, to be drawn in the capital of the Empire.

4thly. The fines imposed by virtue of this Law.

5thly. The sums which may be marked in the general budget, and in those of the provinces and municipalities.

6thly. Subscriptions, endowments, and legacies for that purpose.

2. The sums marked in the provincial and municipal budgets, as also the subscriptions, endowments, and legacies for the local purpose, shall be applied for the manumission of slaves in the provinces, districts, municipalities, and parishes designated.

IV. The slave is permitted to form a saving fund from what may come to him through gifts, legacies, and inheritances, and from what, by consent of his owner, he may obtain by his labor and economy. The Government will see to the regulations as to the placing and security of said savings.

1. By the death of the slave half of his savings shall belong to his surviving widow, if there be such, and the other half shall be transmitted to his heirs in conformity with civil law.

In default of heirs the savings shall be adjudged to the emancipation fund of which Article III treats.

2. The slave who, through his savings, may obtain means to pay his value has a right to freedom.

If the indemnification be not fixed by agreement it shall be settled by arbitration. In judicial sales or inventories the price of manumission shall be that of the valuation.

3. It is further permitted the slave, in furtherance of his liberty, to contract with a third party the hire of his future services, for a term not exceeding seven years, by obtaining the consent of his master, and approval of the judge of the Orphans' Court.

4. The slave that belongs to joint proprietors, and is freed by one of them, shall have a right to his freedom by indemnifying the other owners with the share of the amount which belongs to them. This indemnification may be paid by services rendered for a term not exceeding seven years, in conformity with the preceding paragraph.

5. The manumission, with the clause of services during a certain time, shall not become annulled by want of fulfilling the said clause, but the freed man shall be compelled to fulfil, by means of labour in the public establishments, or by contracting for his services with private persons.

6. Manumissions, whether gratuitous or by means of onus, shall be exempted from all duties, emoluments, or expenses.

7. In any case of alienation or transfer of slaves, the separation of husband and wife, and children under twelve years of age from father or mother, is prohibited under penalty of annulment.

8. If the division of property among heirs or partners does not permit the union of a family, and none of them prefers remaining with the family by replacing the amount of the share belonging to the other interested parties, the said family shall be sold and the proceeds shall be divided among the heirs.

9. The ordination, Book 4th, title 63, in the part which revokes freedom, on account of ingratitude, is set aside.

V. The Emancipation Societies which are formed, and those which may for the future be formed, shall be subject to the inspection of the Judges of the Orphans' Court.

The said societies shall have the privilege of commanding the services of the slaves whom they may have liberated, to indemnify themselves for the sum spent in their purchase.

VI. The following shall be declared free:

1. The slaves belonging to the State, the Government giving them such employment as they may deem fit.

2. The slave given in usufruct to the Crown.

3. The slaves of unclaimed inheritances.

4. The slaves who have been abandoned by their owners.

Should these have abandoned the slaves from the latter being invalids they shall be obliged to maintain them, except in case of their own penury, the maintenance being charged by the judge of the Orphans' Court.

5. In general the slaves liberated by virtue of this Law shall be under the inspection of Government during five years. They will be obliged to hire themselves under pain of compulsion; if they lead an idle life they shall be made to work in the public establishments.

The compulsory labour, however, shall cease so soon as the freed man shall exhibit an engagement of hire.

VII. In trials in favour of freedoms—

1. The process shall be summary.

2. There shall be appeal ex officio when the decisions shall be against the freedom.

VIII. The Government will order the special registration of all the slaves existing in the Empire to be proceeded with, containing a declaration of name, sex, age, state, aptitude for work, and filiation of each, if such should be known.

1. The date on which the registry ought to commence closing shall be announced beforehand, the longest time possible being given for preparation by means of edicts repeated, in which shall be inserted the dispositions of the following paragraph.

2. The slaves who, through the fault or omission of the parties interested, shall not have been registered up to one year after the closing of the register, shall, de facto, be considered as free.

3. For registering each slave the owner shall pay, once only, the emolument of 500 reis, if done within the term marked, and one dollar should that be exceeded. The produce of those emoluments shall go towards the expenses of registering, and the surplus to the emancipation fund.

4. The children of a slave mother, who by this Law became free, shall also be registered in a separate book.

Those persons who have become remiss shall incur a fine of 100 dollars to 200 dollars, repeated as many times as there may be individuals omitted: and for fraud, in the penalties of Article CLXXIX of the Criminal Code.

5. The parish priests shall be obliged to have special books for the registry of births and deaths of the children of slaves born from and after the date of this law. Each omission will subject the parish priest to a fine of 100 dollars.

IX. The Government, in its regulations, can impose fines of as much as 100 dollars, and the penalty of imprisonment up to one month.

X. All contrary dispositions are revoked.

Therefore, order all authorities to whom, &c.

PRINCESS IMPERIAL, REGENT.
THEODORO MACHADO FREIRE
PEREIRA DA SILVA.

Source: Dom Pedro II, "The Law of Free Birth," in *A Documentary History of Brazil*, ed. E. Bradford Burns. New York: Alfred A. Knopf, 1966.

The Reception of Fugitive Slaves Aboard British Ships (1875)

The Lord Commissioners of the Admiralty have been pleased to issue the following instructions with reference to the question, how far officers in command of Her Majesty's ships are justified in receiving on board fugitive slaves, who, escaping from their masters, may claim the protection of the British flag:—

1. Cases of this kind may be divided into three classes: where slaves come on board a ship or boat in harbour, or within territorial waters, either to escape from the alleged cruelty of their masters, or to avoid the consequences of their misdeeds; where the British ship or boat is on the high seas, and the refugee slave—escaping, perhaps, from a vessel also at sea—would be in danger of losing his life were he not received on board; where a person has been detained on shore in a state of slavery, and, escaping to a British ship or boat, claims British protection on the ground that he has been so detained contrary to treaties existing between Great Britain and the country from the shores of which he escapes, as in the case of territories which, like Oman, Madagascar, and Johanna, are partially free.

2. The broad rule to be observed is, that a fugitive slave should not be permanently received on board any description of ship under the British flag, unless his life would be endangered if he were not allowed to come on board. The reason for this rule is that, were it otherwise, the practical result would be, in the first instance, to encourage and assist a breach of the law of the country; and, next, to protect the person breaking that law. And a contrary rule would lead to endless disputes and difficulties with the legal masters of slaves; for it might happen—to take an extreme instance—that the whole slave portion of the crews of vessels engaged

in the pearl fishery in the Persian Gulf might take refuge on board British ships, and, if free there, their masters would be entirely ruined, and the mistrust and hatred caused in their minds would be greatly prejudicial to British interests.

3. Such being the general and broad rule, it remains to apply it, as far as possible, to the three classes of cases mentioned above. In the first class, the slave must not be allowed to remain on board after it has been proved to the satisfaction of the officer in command that he is legally a slave. In the second, the slave should be retained on board on the ground that on the high seas the British vessel is a part of the dominions of the Queen, but when the vessel returns within the territorial limits of the country from a vessel of which the slave has escaped, he will be liable to be surrendered on demand being made, supported by necessary proofs. In the third class, a negro might claim protection on the ground that being by the terms of a treaty free, he was nevertheless being detained as a slave. It would then become the duty of the commanding officer to satisfy himself as to the truth of this statement, and to be guided in his subsequent proceedings in regard to such person by the result of his inquiries, and the law which would then affect the case. Those interested in maintaining the slavery of the person claiming his freedom should assist at the inquiry, and in the event of his claim being established, the local authorities should be requested to take steps to ensure his not relapsing into slavery.

4. As a general principle, care should be taken that slaves are not misled into the belief that they will find their liberty by getting under the British Flag afloat, or induced by the presence of a British ship to leave their own ships, if at sea, or their employment, if on shore.

5. When surrendering fugitive slaves, commanding officers should exercise their discretion in endeavouring, according to the circumstances of each case, to obtain an assurance that the slaves will not be treated with undue severity.

6. A special report is to be made of every case of a fugitive slave seeking refuge on board one of Her Majesty's ships.

7. The above instructions are also to be considered part of the general Slave-Trade instructions, and to be inserted at page 29 of that volume, with a heading of "Receipt of Fugitive Slaves."

The following memorial was forwarded to the Admiralty:—

TO THE LORDS OF THE ADMIRALTY.
The members of the British and Foreign Anti-Slavery Society respectfully beg to convey to your Lordships the expression of their profound regret that certain instructions have been issued, requiring naval officers to surrender fugitive slaves to their masters.

They submit that these instructions constitute the entire abandonment of that noble and honourable policy, which has distinguished Great Britain for more than a hundred years.

Ever since the decision in the case of the slave Somerset, nobly defended by Granville Sharp in 1772, it has always been held that a slave on British soil, or on board a British vessel of war, was absolutely free, and the property of no man.

This is the cherished opinion of the people of this country, and we should feel alarmed for the cause of humanity, could we believe they would ever consent to allow the settled policy of the nation to be reversed, and fugitive slaves once on board Her Majesty's ships to be ever delivered back to the grasp of the slave owner. "Thou shalt not deliver unto his master the servant who escaped from his master unto thee," was the command of God under the Old Dispensation, and being in harmony with the spirit and principles of the New Testament, should be binding upon every Christian nation.

In addition to all the other objections to these instructions, we cannot shut our eyes to the fact that they afford a moral support and give the direct sanction of this country to slavery.

On all these grounds they therefore respectfully urge upon the Lords Commissioners the immediate repeal of these obnoxious regulations.

On behalf of the British and Foreign Anti-Slavery Society,
We are, very respectfully,
JOSEPH COOPER,
EDMUND STURGE, *Hon. Secs.*
ROBERT ALSOP,
AARON BUZACOTT, *Secretary.*

27, New Broad Street, London,
20th September, 1875.

Source: Anti-Slavery Reporter, 19:9 (November 1, 1875).

Resolutions Adopted by the Association for the Reform and Codification of the Law of Nations (1883)

Association for the Reform & Codification of the Law of Nations

Conference on International Law,
Held at Milan, September 11th to 14th, 1883

RESOLUTIONS

1. The Conference expresses the desire that the Slave-trade be assimilated in international law to piracy.

2. Slavery being contrary to natural law, every nation is justified according to international law in refusing in any way to recognise the institution, alike in the case of foreigners who are within its own territory as in the case of its own subjects who have refused to recognise the institution of Slavery within the territory of another State.

3. Every clause in any international treaty which binds a State to give up Slaves which have come within its territory is invalid with regard to international law.

4. Where the extradition of an accused person who was a slave in the country seeking his extradition is requested, such extradition should only be accorded if the extradition of a free man would be accorded in the same case, nor should such extradition be accorded if the former Slave would be judged by a different judge, or punished by other penalties than if he had always been a free man.

5. Every State should prohibit its subjects from possessing, buying, or selling Slaves in foreign countries, and from participating either directly or indirectly in any traffic of the same kind, or in any contract having Slaves for its object, and this prohibition should be enforced by such penalties as each State may enact.

TRAVERS TWISS, *President.*
CHARLES STUBBS, *Hon. Sec.*

Source: Anti-Slavery Reporter, 4:4 (March 1884).

The "Golden Law" Abolishing Slavery in Brazil (1888)

Given in the Palace of Rio de Janeiro, May 13, 1888, the 67th year of Independence and of the Empire.

The Princess Imperial Regent, in the name of His Majesty the Emperor Dom Pedro II, makes known to all subjects of the Empire that the General Assembly has decreed, and she has approved, the following Law:—

Art[icle]. 1. From the date of this Law slavery is declared abolished in Brazil.

[Article] 2. All contrary provisions are revoked.

She orders, therefore, all the authorities to whom belong the knowledge and execution of the said Law to execute it, and cause it to be fully and exactly executed and observed.

The Secretary of State for the Departments of Agriculture, Commerce, and Public Works, and ad interim for Foreign Affairs, Bachelor Rodrigo Augusto da Silva, of the Council of His Majesty the Emperor, will cause it to be printed, published, and circulated.

PRINCESS IMPERIAL REGENT
RODRIGO AUGUSTO DA SILVA

Source: Anti-Slavery Reporter (Series IV), 8 (May/June 1888).

Newspaper Editorials

The study of editorial opinion provides a unique view of the collective will of a community as it grapples with contentious issues. Though they may not express the conventional wisdom of the times in which they are written, editorial perspectives presented in newspapers do tend to be on target in reflecting what is tolerable in their day with respect to such controversial topics as antislavery agitation and other divisive national concerns. Thus, they represent a somewhat inexact social barometer that helps historians to assess why public policy initiatives succeeded or failed and to examine how the court of popular opinion regarded sustained campaigns aimed at influencing such initiatives.

When evaluating the merits of editorial opinion as an indicator of public values and mores, we must remember that a wide gulf has always separated the popular press, which aims to serve a mass audience, and the advocacy press, which addresses its message to a more narrowly defined community of shared interests. While generally broader in its appeal, the popular press often is affected by regional identification, its editorial views commonly affirming the values held most dear by its local community and readership. Likewise, the advocacy press often engages in the act of "microcasting" its message to an audience of true believers who are already attuned to the principles and values articulated in its pages. Although these two types of journalism might be poles apart in many respects, each hopes that its editorial views might reach and influence individuals beyond its subscription base, thus influencing national policy.

Both proslavery and antislavery editorial opinion often assumed a doomsday theme, as editors anticipated the worst-case scenario that might occur in their communities if a particular policy were pursued with respect to slavery. In this fashion, the views of the editorialists formulated a mental bulwark with which fellow advocates could construct a formidable defense to protect the views they considered sacrosanct. The war of words that proslavery and antislavery advocates waged in the press only served to ratchet up sectional animosity, as papers attacked opposing positions and belittled all who ascribed to such views.

Not surprisingly, the authors who published their opinions on slavery were often personally targeted by their adversaries, and some were physically attacked for the views they espoused. William Lloyd Garrison was physically assaulted on a number of occasions in response to editorials he published in the pages of *The Liberator,* one of the leading antislavery papers of the day. Elijah P. Lovejoy, editor of the *Alton Observer,* became a martyr to the abolitionist cause when he was murdered while defending his printing press and upholding his constitutional right to freedom of the press. These papers and their editors became not merely chroniclers of the antislavery movement but also vital participants in its history. The editorialists were actors in the unfolding drama that transpired on the national stage.

The editorials that follow also must be evaluated with the understanding that they reflect opinion and not necessarily fact. The arguments presented were literary efforts that were meant to persuade readers, and specific evidence and logical development seldom were required elements of such persuasive discourse.

Many editorialists sought to strike an emotional chord rather than an intellectual one. Their writings were designed to incite passions within supporters that would move them to action on a specific issue or policy proposal. As such, the proslavery and antislavery presses were extremely effective at motivating their audiences to sustain the cause and fight the good fight, as needed.

Inaugural Editorial of Freedom's Journal *(1827)*

TO OUR PATRONS

In presenting our first number to our Patrons, we feel all the diffidence of persons entering upon a new and untried line of business. But a moment's reflection upon the noble objects, which we have in view by the publication of this journal; the expediency of its appearance at this time, when so many schemes are in action concerning our people—encourage us to come boldly before an enlightened publick. For we believe, that a paper devoted to the dissimination of useful knowledge among our brethren, and to their moral and religious improvement, must meet with the cordial approbation of every friend to humanity.

The peculiarities of this Journal, render it important that we should advertise to the world the motives by which we are actuated, and the objects which we contemplate.

We wish to plead our own cause. Too long have others spoken for us. Too long has the publick been deceived by misrepresentations, in things which concern us dearly, though in the estimation of some mere trifles; for though there are many in society who exercise towards us benevolent feelings; still (with sorrow we confess it) there are others who make it their business to enlarge upon the least trifle, which tends to the discredit of any person of colour; and pronounce anathemas and denounce our whole body for the misconduct of this guilty one. We are aware that there are many instances of vice among us, but we avow that it is because no one has taught its subjects to be virtuous; many instances of poverty, because no sufficient efforts accommodated to minds contracted by slavery, and deprived of early education have been made, to teach them how to husband their hard earnings, and to secure to themselves comforts.

Education being an object of the highest importance to the welfare of society, we shall endeavour to present just and adequate views of it, and to urge upon our brethren the necessity and expediency of training their children, while young, to habits of industry, and thus forming them for becoming useful members of society. It is surely time that we should awake from this lethargy of years, and make a concentrated effort for the education of our youth. We form a spoke in the human wheel, and it is necessary that we should understand our pendence on the different parts, and theirs on us, in order to perform our part with propriety.

Though not desirous of dictating, we shall feel it our incumbent duty to dwell occasionally upon the general principles and rules of economy. The world has grown too enlightened, to estimate any man's character by his personal appearance. Though all men acknowledge the excellency of Franklin's maxims, yet comparatively few practise upon them. We may deplore when it is too late, the neglect of these self-evident truths, but it avails little to mourn. Ours will be the task of admonishing our brethren on these points.

The civil rights of a people being of the greatest value, it shall ever be our duty to vindicate our brethren, when oppressed; and to lay the case before the publick. We shall also urge upon our brethren, (who are qualified by the laws of the different states) the expediency of using their elective franchise; and of making an independent use of the same. We wish them not to become the tools of party.

And as much time is frequently lost, and wrong principles instilled, by the perusal of works of trivial importance, we shall consider it a part of our duty to recommend to our young readers, such authors as will not only enlarge their stock of useful knowledge, but such as will also serve to stimulate them to higher attainments in science.

We trust also, that through the columns of the FREEDOM'S JOURNAL, many practical pieces, having for their bases, the improvement of our brethren, will be presented to them, from the pens of many of our respected friends, who have kindly promised their assistance.

It is our earnest wish to make our Journal a medium of intercourse between our brethren in the different states of this great confederacy: that through its columns an expression of our sentiments, on many interesting subjects which concern us, may be offered to the publick: that plans which apparently are beneficial may be candidly discussed and properly weighed; if worthy, receive our cordial approbation; if not, our marked disapprobation.

Useful knowledge of every kind, and every thing that relates to Africa, shall find a ready admission into our columns; and as that vast continent becomes daily more known, we trust that many things will come to light, proving that the natives of it are neither so ignorant nor stupid as they have generally been supposed to be.

And while these important subjects shall occupy the columns of the FREEDOM'S JOURNAL, we would not be unmindful of our brethren who are still in the iron fetters of bondage. They are our kindred by all the ties of nature; and though but little can be effected by us, still let our sympathies be poured forth, and our prayers in their behalf, ascend to Him who is able to succour them.

From the press and the pulpit we have suffered much by being incorrectly represented. Men, whom we equally love and admire have not hesitated to represent us disadvantageously, without becoming personally acquainted with the true state of things, nor discerning between virtue and vice among us. The virtuous part of our people feel themselves sorely aggrieved under the existing state of things—they are not appreciated.

Our vices and our degradation are ever arrayed against us, but our virtues are passed by unnoticed. And what is still more lamentable, our friends, to whom we concede all the principles of humanity and religion, from these very causes seem to have fallen into the current of popular feeling and are imperceptibly floating on the stream—actually living in the practice of prejudice, while they abjure it in theory; and feel it not in their hearts. Is it not very desirable that such should know more of our actual condition, and of our efforts and feelings, that in forming or advocating plans for our amelioration, they may do it more understandingly? In the spirit of candor and humility we intend by a simple representation of facts to lay our case before the publick, with a view to arrest the progress of prejudice, and to shield ourselves against the consequent evils. We wish to conciliate all and to irritate none, yet we must be firm and unwavering in our principles, and persevering in our efforts.

If ignorance, poverty and degradation have hitherto been our unhappy lot; has the Eternal decree gone forth, that our race alone, are to remain in this state, while knowledge and civilization are shedding their enlivening rays over the rest of the human family? The recent travels of Denham and Clapperton in the interior of Africa, and the interesting narrative which they have published; the establishment of the republic of Hayti after years of sanguinary warfare; its subsequent progress in all the arts of civilization; and the advancement of liberal ideas in South America, where despotism has given place to free governments, and where many of our brethren now fill important civil and military stations, prove the contrary.

The interesting fact that there are FIVE HUNDRED THOUSAND free persons of colour, one half of whom might peruse, and the whole be benefitted by the publication of the Journal; that no publication, as yet, has been devoted exclusively to their improvement—that many selections from approved standard authors, which are within the reach of few, may occasionally be made—and more important still, that this large body of our citizens have no public channel—all serve to prove the real necessity, at present, for the appearance of the FREEDOM'S JOURNAL.

It shall ever be our desire so to conduct the editorial department of our paper as to give offence to none of our patrons; as nothing is farther from us than to make it the advocate of any partial views, either in politics or religion. What few days we can number, have been devoted to the improvement of our brethren; and it is our earnest wish that the remainder may be spent in the same delightful service.

In conclusion, whatever concerns us as a people, will ever find a ready admission into the FREEDOM'S JOURNAL, interwoven with all the principal news of the day.

And while every thing in our power shall be performed to support the character of our Journal, we would respectfully invite our numerous friends to assist by their communications, and our coloured brethren to strengthen our hands by their subscriptions, as our labour is one of common cause, and worthy of their consideration and support. And we most earnestly solicit the latter, that if at any time we should seem to be zealous, or too pointed in the inculcation of any important lesson, they will remember, that they are equally interested in the cause in which we are engaged, and attribute our zeal to the peculiarities of our situation; and our earnest engagedness in their well-being.

THE EDITORS.

Source: Freedom's Journal, March 16, 1827.

Inaugural Editorial of The Liberator (1831)

To the Public

In the month of August, I issued proposals for publishing "The Liberator" in Washington City; but the enterprise, though hailed in different sections of the country, was palsied by public indifference. Since that time, the removal of the *Genius of Universal Emancipation* to the Seat of Government has rendered less imperious the establishment of a similar periodical in that quarter.

During my recent tour for the purpose of exciting the minds of the people by a series of discourses on the subject of slavery, every place that I visited gave fresh evidence of the fact, that a greater revolution in public sentiment was to be effected in the free states—*and particularly in New-England*—than at the south. I found contempt more bitter, opposition more active, detraction more relentless, prejudice more stubborn, and apathy more frozen, than among slave owners themselves. Of course, there were individual exceptions to the contrary. This state of things afflicted, but did not dishearten me. I determined, at every hazard, to lift up the standard of emancipation in the eyes of the nation, *within sight of Bunker Hill and in the birth place of liberty.* That standard is now unfurled; and long may it float, unhurt by the spoliations of time or the missiles of a desperate foe—yea, till every chain be broken, and every bondman set free! Let southern oppressors tremble—let their secret abettors tremble—let their northern apologists tremble—let all the enemies of the persecuted blacks tremble.

I deem the publication of my original Prospectus unnecessary, as it has obtained a wide circulation. The principles therein inculcated will be steadily pursued in this paper, excepting that I shall not array myself as the political partisan of any man. In defending the great cause of human rights, I wish to derive the assistance of all religions and of all parties.

Assenting to the "self-evident truth" maintained in the American Declaration of Independence, "that all men are created equal, and endowed by their Creator with certain inalienable rights—among which are life, liberty and the pursuit of happiness," I shall strenuously contend for the immediate enfranchisement of our slave population. In Park-street Church, on the Fourth of July, 1829, in an address on slavery, I unreflectingly assented to the popular but pernicious doctrine of gradual abolition. I seize this opportunity to make a full and unequivocal recantation, and thus publicly to ask pardon of my God, of my country, and of my brethren the poor slaves, for having uttered a sentiment so full of timidity, injustice and absurdity. A similar recantation, from my pen, was published in the *Genius of Universal Emancipation* at Baltimore, in September, 1829. My confidence is now satisfied.

I am aware, that many object to the severity of my language; but is there not cause for severity? I *will* be as harsh as truth, and as uncompromising as justice. On this subject, I do not wish to think, or speak, or write, with moderation. No! no! Tell a man whose house is on fire, to give a moderate alarm; tell him to moderately rescue his wife from the hand of the ravisher; tell the mother to gradually extricate her babe from the fire into which it has fallen;—but urge me not to use moderation in a cause like the present. I am in earnest—I will not equivocate—I will not excuse—I will not retreat a single inch—AND I WILL BE HEARD. The apathy of the people is enough to make every statue leap from its pedestal, and to hasten the resurrection of the dead.

It is pretended, that I am retarding the cause of emancipation by the coarseness of my invective, and the precipitancy of my measures. The *charge is not true.* On this question my influence,—humble as it is,—is felt at this moment to a considerable extent, and shall be felt in coming years—not perniciously, but beneficially—not as a curse, but as a blessing; and posterity will bear testimony that I was right. I desire to thank God, that he enables me to disregard "the fear of man which bringeth a snare," and to speak his truth in its simplicity and power. And here I close with this fresh dedication:

Oppression! I have seen thee, face to face,
And met thy cruel eye and cloudy brow;
But thy soul-withering glance I fear not now—
For dread to prouder feelings doth give place
Of deep abhorrence! Scorning the disgrace
Of slavish knees that at thy footstool bow,
I also kneel—but with far other vow
Do hail thee and thy herd of hirelings base:—
I swear, while life-blood warms my throbbing veins,
Still to oppose and thwart, with heart and hand,
Thy brutalizing sway—till Afric's chains
Are burst, and Freedom rules the rescued land,—
Trampling Oppression and his iron rod:
Such is the vow I take—SO HELP ME GOD!

William Lloyd Garrison

Source: The Liberator, 1:1 (January 1, 1831).

To Readers of the Alton Observer (1837)

September 11, 1837.
To The Friends of the Redeemer in Alton

Dear Brethren,
It is at all times important that the friends of truth should be united. It is especially so at the present time, when iniquity is coming in like a flood. I should be false to my covenant vows, and false to every feeling in my heart, were I to refuse making any personal sacrifice to effect so desirable an object. Having learned

that there is a division of sentiments among the brethren, as it regards the propriety of my continuing long to fill the office of Editor of the "Alton Observer," I do not hesitate a moment to submit the question to your decision. Most cheerfully I will resign my post, if in your collective wisdom you think the cause we all profess to love will thereby be promoted. And in coming to a decision on this question, I beseech you as a favour—may I not enjoin it as a duty?—that you act without any regard to my personal feelings. I should be false to the Master I serve, and of whose gospel I am a minister, should I allow my own interests, (real or supposed,) to be placed in competition with his. Indeed, I have no interest, no wish, at least I think I have none; I know I wrought to have none other than such as are subordinate to his will. Be it yours, brethren, to decide what is best for the cause of truth, most for the glory of God, and the salvation of souls, and rest assured—whatever my own private judgment may be—of my cordial acquiescence in your decision.

I had, at first, intended to make an unconditional surrender of the editorship into your hands. But as such a course might be liable to misconstructions, I have, by the advice of a beloved brother, determined to leave the whole matter with you. I am ready to go forward if you say so, and equally ready to yield to a successor, if such be your opinion. Yet let me say, promptly, that in looking back over my past labours as Editor of the "Observer," while I see many imperfections, and many errors and mistakes, I have, nevertheless, done the best I could. This I say in the fear of God; so that if I am to continue [as] the Editor, you must not, on the whole, expect a much better paper than you have had.

Should you decide that I ought to give place to a successor, I shall expect the two following conditions to be fulfilled.

1. That you will assume in its behalf, all my obligations contracted in consequence of my connection with the "Observer." Some of them were contracted immediately on behalf of the "Observer," and some in supporting my family while its Editor.
2. As I have now spent four among the best years of my life in struggling to establish the "Observer," and place it on its present footing, I shall expect you will furnish me with a sum sufficient to enable me to remove myself and family to another field of labour. More I do not ask, and I trust this will not be thought unreasonable. I would not ask even this had I the means myself, but I have not.

On these conditions I surrender into your hands the "Observer's" subscription list, now amounting to more than two thousand one hundred names, and constantly increasing, together with all the dues coming to the establishment. A list of both of the debts and credits accompanies this communication.

May the spirit of wisdom, dear brethren, guide you to a wise and unanimous decision—to a decision which God will approve and ratify, and which shall redound to the glory of his name.

Yours affectionately,
Elijah P. Lovejoy

Source: Alton Observer, Alton, Illinois, September 11, 1837.

Frederick Douglass's Introduction to The North Star (1847)

We are now about to assume the management of the editorial department of a newspaper, devoted to the cause of Liberty, Humanity and Progress. The position is one which, with the purest motives, we have long desired to occupy. It has long been our anxious wish to see, in this slave-holding, slave-trading, and Negro-hating land, a printing-press and paper, permanently established, under the complete control and direction of the immediate victims of slavery and oppression.

Animated by this intense desire, we have pursued our object, till on the threshold of obtaining it. Our press and printing materials are bought, and paid for. Our office [is] secured, and is well situated, in the centre of business, in this enterprising city. Our office Agent, an industrious and amiable young man, thoroughly devoted to the interests of humanity, has already entered upon his duties. Printers well recommended have offered their services, and are ready to work as soon as we are prepared for the regular publication of our paper. Kind friends are rallying round us, with words and deeds of encouragement. Subscribers are steadily, if not rapidly coming in, and some of the best minds in the country are generously offering to lend us the powerful aid of their pens. The sincere wish of our heart, so long and so devoutly cherished seems now upon the eve of complete realization.

It is scarcely necessary for us to say that our desire to occupy our present position at the head of an Anti-Slavery Journal, has resulted from no unworthy distrust or ungrateful want of appreciation of the zeal, integrity, or ability of the noble band of white laborers in this department of our cause; but, from the sincere and settled conviction that such a Journal, if conducted with only moderate skill and ability, would do a most important and indispensable work, which it would be wholly impossible for our white friends to do for us.

It is neither a reflection on the fidelity, nor a disparagement of the ability of our friends and fellow-laborers, to assert what "common sense affirms and only folly denies," that the man who has *suffered the wrong* is the man to *demand redress*,—that the man STRUCK is the man to CRY OUT—and that he who has *endured the cruel pangs of Slavery* is the man to *advocate Liberty*. It is evident we must be our own representatives and advocates, not exclusively, but peculiarly—not distinct from, but in connection with our white friends. In the grand struggle for liberty and equality now waging, it is meet, right and essential that there should arise in our ranks authors and editors, as well as orators, for it is in these capacities that the most permanent good can be rendered to our cause.

Hitherto the immediate victims of slavery and prejudice, owing to various causes, have had little share in this department of effort: they have frequently undertaken, and almost as frequently failed. This latter fact has often been urged by our friends against our engaging in the present enterprise; but, so far from convincing us of the impolicy of our course, it serves to confirm us in the necessity, if not the wisdom of our undertaking. That others have failed, is a reason for OUR earnestly endeavoring to succeed. Our race must be vindicated from the embarrassing imputations resulting from former non-success. We believe that what *ought* to be done, *can* be done. We say this, in no self-confident or boastful spirit, but with a full sense of our weakness and unworthiness, relying upon the Most High for wisdom and strength to support us in our righteous undertaking. We are not wholly unaware of the duties, hardships and responsibilities of our position. We have easily imagined some, and friends have not hesitated to inform us of others. Many doubtless are yet to be revealed by that infallible teacher, experience. A view of them solemnize, but do not appal us. We have counted the cost. Our mind is made up, and we are resolved to go forward.

In aspiring to our present position, the aid of circumstances has been so strikingly apparent as to almost stamp our humble aspirations with the solemn sanctions of a Divine Providence. Nine years ago, as most of our readers are aware, we were held as a slave, shrouded in the midnight ignorance of that infernal system—sunken in the depths of senility and degradation—registered with four footed beasts and creeping things—regarded as property—compelled to toil without wages—with a heart swollen with bitter anguish—and a spirit crushed and broken. By a singular combination of circumstances we finally succeeded in escaping from the grasp of the man who claimed us as his property, and succeeded in safely reaching New Bedford, Mass[achusetts]. In this town we worked three years as a daily laborer on the wharves. Six years ago we became a Lecturer on Slavery. Under the apprehension of being re-taken into bondage, two years ago we embarked for England. During our stay in that country, kind friends, anxious for our safety, ransomed us from slavery, by the payment of a large sum. The same friends, as unexpectedly as generously, placed in our hands the necessary means of purchasing a printing press and printing materials. Finding ourself now in a favorable position for aiming an important blow at slavery and prejudice, we feel urged on in our enterprise by a sense of duty to God and man, firmly believing that our effort will be crowned with entire success.

Source: The North Star, December 3, 1847.

South Carolina Herald *Editorial* (1851)

We have been frequently charged with being hostile to the present Federal Government. We are so, and for the following very satisfactory reasons, among many others.

Because, for the last thirty years, it has proven a withering and unmitigated curse upon the South, having robbed us during this period of not less than one thousand millions, to build up Northern interests and institutions.

Because it has, by its late action, destroyed the sovereignty and equality of fifteen States of this Confederacy, and degraded them to the condition of colonial dependencies.

Because it has ceased to afford us protection in any particular, its whole aim being to break down and destroy the South.

Because it is an Abolition Government, striking directly at the institutions and domestic policy of the section in which we live, its whole legislation being shaped to this end, and having this only for its object.

Because in fine, it has most signally failed, as an experiment of the capacity of the people for self-government, inasmuch as the rights of one section has been trampled under foot, to gratify the fanaticism and lust for power of the other.

We are in favour of its dissolution or disunion—

Because it will bring wealth and greatness to the south, under a Southern Confederacy, which must inevitably arise from dissolution.

Because it will afford us protection in our persons, property, &c.

Because it will kill off the foul spirit of abolition, by taking away the food it feeds on.

Because it will put an end to kidnapping and border thieving, and restore peace and security to the frontier States.

Because it will promote the case of religion, morality, and civilisation, in the South.

Because it will build up a system of internal improvements, increase the number of schools, colleges, &c.

Because it will destroy entirely pauperism, by enabling every man, not physically diseased, to earn his daily bread, and accumulate, from the abundance of our prosperity, a fortune for himself in a short time.

Because it will renew and perpetuate the experiment of the capability of the people for self-government.

Because, even if the Slavery Question is settled, the seeds of discord have been too deeply sown by the North, ever to bring forth any other fruit than hostility, and constant wrangling between the two sections.

Because the Union is too large, and composed of too various interests, ever to harmonise together.

Because we honestly believe the Almighty never intended that the generous and noble Southerner should constitute one people, with the cold, calculating, plundering Yankee.

Source: Anti-Slavery Reporter (New Series), 6:61 (January 1, 1851).

Editorial Responses to the Brooks-Sumner Affair (1856)

By the news from Washington it will be seen that Senator Sumner has been savagely and brutally assaulted, while sitting in his seat in the Senate chamber, by the Hon. Mr. Brooks of South Carolina, the reason assigned therefore being that the Senator's remarks on Mr. Butler of South Carolina, who is uncle to the man who made the attack. The particulars show that Mr. Sumner was struck unawares over the head by a loaded cane and stunned, and then the ruffianly attack was continued with many blows, the Hon. Mr. Keitt of South Carolina keeping any of those around, who might be so disposed, from attempting a rescue. No meaner exhibition of Southern cowardice—generally miscalled Southern chivalry—was ever witnessed. It is not in the least a cause for wonder that a member of the national House of Representatives, assisted by another as a fender-off, should attack a member of the national Senate, because, in the course of a constitutional argument, the last had uttered words which the first chose to consider distasteful.

The reasons for the absence of collision between North and South—collision of sentiment and person—which existed a few years back, have ceased; and as the South has taken the oligarchic ground that Slavery ought to exist, irrespective of color—that there must be a governing class and a class governed—that Democracy is a delusion and a lie—we must expect that Northern men in Washington, whether members or not, will be assaulted, wounded or killed, as the case may be, so long as the North will bear it. The acts of violence during this session—including one murder—are simply overtures to the drama of which the persecutions, murders, robberies and war upon the Free-State men in Kansas, constitute the first act. We are either to have Liberty or Slavery. Failing to silence the North by threats, notwithstanding the dough-faced creatures who so long misrepresented the spirit of the Republic and of the age, the South now resorts to actual violence. It is reduced to a question whether there is to be any more liberty of speech south of Mason and Dixon's line, even in the ten miles square of the District of Columbia. South of that, liberty has long since departed; but whether the common ground where the national representatives meet is to be turned into a slave plantation where Northern members act under the lash, the bowie-knife and the pistol, is a question to be settled.

That Congress will take any action in view of this new event, we shall not be rash enough to surmise; but if the Northern people are not generally the poltroons they are taken for by the hostile slave-breeders and slavedrivers of the South, they will be heard from. As a beginning, they should express their sentiments upon this brutal and dastardly outrage in their popular assemblies. The Pulpit should not be silent.

If, indeed, we go on quietly to submit to such outrages, we deserve to have our names flattened, our skins blacked, and to be placed at work under task-masters; for we have lost the noblest attributes of freemen, and are virtually slaves.

Source: New York Tribune, May 23, 1856.

The outrage in the Senate, on Thursday last is without a parallel in the legislative history of the country. Nothing has heretofore seemed so bold, so bad, so alarming. There have been affrays, more or less serious, in the House, for the House is a popular, and therefore, a tumultuous body; there have been encounters in the streets, for the streets are arenas in which any assassin may display his prowess; but never before has the sanctity of the Senate Chamber been violated; never before has an intruder ventured to carry into those privileged precincts his private hostilities; never before has a Senator been struck down in his seat, and stretched, by the hand of a lawless bully, prostrate, bleeding, and insensible upon the floor. The wrong is full of public importance; and we almost forget the private injury of Mr. Sumner in the broad temerity of the insult which has been offered to the country, to Massachusetts, to the Senate. This first act of violence may pass into a precedent; what a single creature has done today, a hundred, equally barbarous, may attempt tomorrow; until a band of alien censors may crowd the galleries, and the lobbies, and even the floor of the Senate, and by the persuasive arguments of the bludgeon, the bowie knife, and the revolver, effectually refute and silence any member who may dare to utter, with some thing of force and freedom, his personal convictions. The privileges which we have fondly supposed were conferred with the Senatorial dignity; the right to characterize public measures and public men, with no responsibility, save to God and to conscience; the freedom of debate, without which its forms are a mere mockery—these will all disappear; and in their place we shall have the government of a self-constituted and revolutionary tribunal, overawing the Senate, as the Jacobins of Paris overawed the National Assembly of France, as the soldiers of Cromwell intimidated the Parliament of Great Britain. Shall we have, did we say? We have it already. There is freedom of speech in Washington, but it is only for the champions of slavery. There is freedom of the press, but only of the press which extenuates or defends political wrongs. Twice already the South, failed in the arguments of reason, has resorted to the argument of folly. Driven from every position, constantly refuted in its reasoning, met and repulsed when it has resorted to invective, by an invective more vigorous than its own, at first astonished and then crazed by the changing and bolder tone of Northern man, the South has taken to expedients with which long use has made it familiar, and in which years of daily practice have given it a nefarious skill. Thank God, we know little of these resources in New England! We have our differences, but they are differences controlled by decency. We have our controversies, but we do not permit their warmth to betray us into brutality; we do not think it necessary to shoot, to slash, or to stun the man with whom we may differ upon political points. The controversial ethics of the South are of another character, and they find their most repulsive illustration in the event of Thursday.

The barbarian who assaulted Mr. Sumner, and who sought in the head of his bludgeon for an argument which he could not find in his own, complained that South Carolina have been insulted by the Senator from Massachusetts, and that his venerable uncle had been spoken of in disrespectful terms! If every State, the public policy of which is assailed in the Senate, had been entitled to send to Washington a physical champion, we should long ago have despatched thither our brauniest athlete. If every nephew, whose uncle provokes criticism by public acts, is to rush into the Senate, the champion of his kinsman, we shall have a nepotism established quite unauthorized by the Constitution! The South complains of hard words, of plain speech, of licentious language! Have its members then been accustomed to bridle their tongues, to control their tempers, to moderate their ire, to abstain from personalities? What indeed have we had from that quarter, save one long stream of vituperation, one endless rain of fish-wife rhetoric, one continuous blast of feverish denunciation and passionate threat? Let the world judge between us. We have borne and forborne. We have been patient until patience has become ignominious. There are wrongs which no man of spirit will suffer tamely; there are topics which it is impossible to discuss with coldness; there are injuries which must lend fire to language, and arouse the temper of the most stolid. Mr. Sumner's speech is before the country and it is for the country to decide whether it does or does not justify the violence with which it has been met. Our Senator comments freely upon the character of the Kansas bill, upon the apologies which have been made for it, in Congress, upon the readiness of the Administration to promote the schemes of its supporters, upon the unparalleled injuries which have been inflicted upon the unfortunate people of Kansas. Others have spoken upon the same topics with equal plainness, although not perhaps with equal ability. Mr. Sumner is singularly well sustain[ed] in all his positions, in his opinions of the bill, and in his estimate of Douglas and Butler, by the mind and heart, not only of his constituents, but of the whole North. The time had come for plain and unmistakable language, and it has been uttered. There are those who profess to believe that Northern rhetoric should always be emasculated, and that Northern members should always take care to speak humbly and with "bated breath." They complain with nervous fastidiousness that Mr. Sumner was provoking. So were Mr. Burke and Mr. Sheridan, when in immoderate language they exposed the wrongs of India and the crimes of Hastings; so was Patrick Henry, when he plead against the parsons; so was Tristram Burges, when he silenced Randolph of Roanoke; so was Mr. Webster, when, in the most remarkable oration of modern times, he launched the lightning of his overwhelming invective, while every fibre of his great frame was full of indignation and reproach. Smooth speeches will answer for smooth times; but there is a species of oratory, classic since the days of Demosthenes, employed without a scruple upon fit occasions, in all deliberative assemblies, perfectly well recognized, and sometimes absolutely necessary. Who will say that Kansas, and Atchison, and Douglas together, were not enough to inspire and justify a new Philippic?

But we care not what Mr. Sumner said, nor in what behalf he was pleading. We know him only as the Senator of Massachusetts; we remember only that the commonwealth has been outraged. Had the Senator of any other State been subjected to a like indignity, we might have found words in which to express our abhorrence of the crime; but now we can only say, that every constituent of Mr. Sumner ought to feel that the injury is his own, and that it is for him to expect redress. A high-minded Senate, would vindicate its trampled dignity; a respectable House of Representatives would drive the wrong-doer from its benches; in a society unpolluted by barbarism, the assaulter of an unarmed man, would find himself the object of general contempt.

We can hardly hope that such a retribution will visit the offender; but Massachusetts, in other and better times, would have had a right confidently to anticipate the expulsion of Preston Brooks from the house of Representatives. We leave it to others to decide how far it may be fit and proper for her officially to express her sense of this indignity. For our own part, we think she can rely upon the generosity and the justice of her sister states, that an outrage so indefensible will meet with a fitting rebuke from the people, if not from the representatives of the people. And if in this age of civilization, brute force is to control the government of the country, striking down our senators, silencing debate, and leaving us only the name of Freedom, there are remedies with which Massachusetts has found it necessary to meet similar exigencies in the past, which she will not hesitate to employ in the future.

Source: Boston Daily Atlas, May 24, 1856.

The news of the cowardly attack on Mr. Sumner by a villainous South Carolinian, stirred up a deeper indignation among our citizens, yesterday, than we have ever before witnessed. It was an indignation that pervaded all classes and conditions of men. The assault was deliberately planned, being made in the presence and under the encouragement of a crowd of bullies, when Mr. Sumner was alone, unarmed and defenceless, and it was conducted so brutally—fifty blows being inflicted upon an unresisting victim, until the weapon of attack was used up, and not one hand raised among the bystanders to stay the fury of the perfidious wretch, that every feeling of human nature revolts at the exhibition. Barbarians and savages would not be guilty of such unmanliness; and even the vulgar blackguards who follow the business of bruisers and shoulder-hitters would have a far higher sense of fair play than was shown by these patterns of chivalry. A universal cry of "Shame!" would go up from the lips of the people, if, unfortunately, the people did not, in view of this and similar outrages, feel a bitter shamefacedness at their own degradation in having to submit to them.

It is time, now, to inaugurate a change. It can no longer be permitted that all the blows shall come from one side. If Southern men will resort to the fist to overawe and intimidate Northern men, blow must be given back for blow. Forbearance and kindly deportment are lost upon these Southern ruffians. It were as well to throw pearls before swine as turn one cheek to them when the other is smitten. Under the circumstances now prevailing, neither religion nor manhood requires submission to such outrages. Northern men must defend themselves; and if our present representatives will not fight, when attacked, let us find those who will. It is not enough, now, to have backbone; there must be strong right arms, and a determination to use them. The voters of the Free States, in vindication of their own manliness will, hereafter, in addition to inquiring of candidates. Will you vote so-and-so, have to enlarge the basis of interrogation, and demand an affirmative answer to the question, Will you fight? It has come to that, now, that Senators and Representatives cannot enjoy the right of free speech or free discussion, without being liable to brutal assaults; and they must, of necessity, arm themselves with sword-canes or revolvers. To think of enduring quietly such attacks as that upon Mr. SUMNER, is craven and pusillanimous.—

These cut-throat Southrons will never learn to respect Northern men until some one of their number has a rapier thrust through his ribs, or feels a bullet in his thorax. It is lamentable that such should be the case; but it is not in human nature to be trampled on.

Source: Pittsburgh Gazette, Pittsburgh, Pennsylvania, May 24, 1856.

Editorial Responses to the Dred Scott *Decision (1857)*

We do not know how other persons may feel in view of the recent *dicta* of the Supreme Court in the case of Dred Scott, an abstract of which was published in our telegraphic column on Saturday morning, but it appears to us that the almost diabolical spirit it evinces in going out of the way to Freedom at the expense of Slavery, ought to be sufficient to arouse to indignation the coolest and most torpid of northern men. The decision is a fitting crown to the aborted tyranny which has just submerged with Pierce; an iron clasp, well forged to link the dead with the living administration. It comes pat upon the recent inaugural, "rounds and caps it to the tyrant's eye" and just fills up the cup of inequity.

What matter is it that this decision upsets those we have on record? New lights have arisen with the progress of revolving years, and Story and Marshall, Jefferson, Madison, and Monroe hide their twinkling lights before the full-orbed glory of Douglas, Pierce and Davis. The Supreme Court has aimed a blow at State Sovereignty which is baser and more iniquitous than any thing we had before conceived of. The State of Illinois for example, under this decision in her legislative capacity, has no power to enact such a law as can make a slave coming there with the consent of his master a freeman! The decision that the Court has no jurisdiction in this case make[s] all the other remarks from the bench touching the ordinance of 1787, and the compromise of 1820, mere *obiter dicta*, it is true, but the fact that the Court has gone out of its way to

say what it has, shows its animus, and trumpets to the four corners of the earth the eager alacrity with which it echoes the mouthings of demagogues like Pierce and Douglas. We may henceforth throw to the winds the reasoning of Story and the decisions of Marshall, so far as this court is concerned, and submit to seeing the government surrendered, bound hand and foot to the same power which has given Kansas over to blood and desolation, elevated a weak old man to the executive chair, given the Treasury, the Post Office, the Army, the Navy and the Department of the Interior to be its willing servants and exhilarated and energized by its success, pressed on to the Supreme Court, made that the echo of its will and left no place for hope to rest upon, but the virtue of the masses of the people, to which we must henceforth appeal. Let them come in their might and at the ballot box root up the rotten fabric to its foundations which four years of misrule has served so much to weaken, and which the four years to come will doubtless not improve or strengthen.

Source: Pittsburgh Gazette, Pittsburgh, Pennsylvania, March 7, 1857.

It is impossible to exaggerate the importance of the recent decision of the Supreme Court. The grounds and methods of that decision we have exposed elsewhere; and we now turn from them to contemplate the great fact which it establishes—the fact that *Slavery is National*; and that, until that remote period when different Judges, sitting in this same Court, shall reverse this wicked and false judgment, the Constitution of the United States is nothing better than the bulwark of inhumanity and oppression.

It is most true that this decision is bad law; that it is based on false historical premises and wrong interpretations of the Constitution; that it does not at all represent the legal or judicial opinion of the Nation; that it is merely a Southern sophism clothed with the dignity of our highest Court. Nevertheless there it is; the final action of the National Judiciary, established by the founders of the Republic to interpret the Constitution, and to embody the ultimate legal conclusions of the whole people—an action proclaiming that in the view of the Constitution *slaves are property*. The inference is plain. If slaves are recognized as property by the Constitution, of course no local or State law can either prevent property being carried through an individual State or Territory, or forbid its being sold as such wherever its owner may choose to hold it. This is all involved in the present decision; but let a single case draw from the Court an official judgment that slaves can be held and protected under National law, and we shall see men buying slaves for the New York market. There will be no legal power to prevent it. At this moment, indeed, any wealthy New York jobber connected with the Southern trade can put in his next orders: "Send me a negro cook, at the lowest market value! Buy me a waiter! Balance my account with two chambermaids and a truckman!" Excepting the interference of the Underground Railroad and the chance of loss, there will be nothing to stop this. But then these underhanded efforts for stealing property must, of course, be checked by our Police. Mr. Matsell will have no more right to allow gentlemen's servants to be spirited away by burgarious Abolitionists than gentlemen's spoons. They are property under even stronger pledges of security than mere lifeless chattels. The whole power of the State—the military, the Courts and Governor of the State of New York—will necessarily be sworn to protect each New York slave-owner from the robbery or burglary of his negro. If they are not sufficient, why then the United States Army and Navy can be called upon to guard that singular species of property which alone of all property the Constitution of the United States has especially recognized. Slaves can be kept in Boston; Mr. Toombs can call the roll of his chattels on the slope of Bunker Hill; auctions of black men may be held in front of Faneuil Hall, and the slave-ship, protected by the guns of United States frigates, may land its dusky cargo at Plymouth Rock. The free hills of Vermont, the lakes of Maine, the valleys of Connecticut, the city where the ancient Oak of Liberty has wisely fallen, may be traversed by the gangs of the negro-driver, and enriched by the legitimate commerce of the slave-pen. Are we told that public opinion will prevent this? What can public opinion do against the Supreme Court and all the power of the United States? Shall not a citizen of this Union have the right to take and hold his property, his horses, his oxen, his dogs, his slaves, wherever it seems to him good? According to the law now established, the Free-State men of Kansas are robbers, for they attack the Constitutional and inalienable rights of property. The bogus laws of which they presume to complain, but which the mild and paternal punishment of death is not to protect from infractions, are just and necessary laws for the safety of those sacred rights. The number of Free Soil men in that Territory can make no difference hereafter, as it has made none hitherto. Slavery is

there, as the ownership of horses or land is there, by supreme national law. Of what use, then, to contend for such a shadow as the difference between a Free and a Slave Constitution? Or what sense in that old fiction of State Rights? The States have no rights as respects Freedom; their rights consist only in establishing and strengthening Slavery—nothing more.

Another most pregnant change is wrought by this decision, in respect of the Northern people. We have been accustomed to regard Slavery as a local matter for which we were in no wise responsible. As we have been used, to say, it belonged to the Southern States alone, and they must answer for it before the world. We can say this no more. Now, wherever the stars and stripes wave, they protect Slavery and represent Slavery. The black and cursed stain is thick on our hands also. From Maine to the Pacific, over all future conquests and annexations, wherever in the islands of western seas, or in the South American Continent, or in the Mexican Gulf, the flag of the Union, by just means or unjust, shall be planted, there it plants the curse, and tears, and blood, and unpaid toil of this "institution." The Star of Freedom and the stripes of bondage are henceforth one. American Republicanism and American Slavery are for the future synonymous. This, then, is the final fruit. In this all the labors of our statesmen, the blood of our heroes, the life-long cares and toils of our forefathers, the aspirations of our scholars, the prayers of good men, have finally ended! America the slavebreeder and slaveholder!

Source: New York Tribune, March 11, 1857.

Five of its nine silk gowns are worn by Slaveholders. More than half its long Bench is filled with Slaveholders. Its Chief Justice is a Slaveholder. The Free States with double the population of the Slave State, do not have half the Judges. The majority represent a minority of 350,000. The minority represent a majority of twenty Millions!

It has long been so. Originally there were three Northern and three Southern Judges. But the South soon got the bigger share of the black robes, and kept them. Of the thirty-eight who have sat there in judgment, twenty-two were nurtured "on plantation." The Slave States have been masters of the Court fifty-seven years, the Free States but eleven! The Free States have had the majority only seven years, this century. Even the Free State Judges are chosen from Slavery extending parties. Presidents nominate, and Senates confirm none other. Three times a new Judgeship has been created, and every time it has been filled with a Slave-holder. The advocate who pleads there against Slavery, wastes his voice in its vaulted roof, and upon ears stuffed sixty years with cotton. His case is judged before it is argued, and his client condemned before he is heard.

Source: Albany Evening Journal, Albany, New York, March 19, 1857.

Southern Editorial Responses to the Harpers Ferry Raid (1859)

Our despatches this morning give us some particulars of a serious outbreak among the employees on the government works at Harper's Ferry, Virginia, in which the negros, led on by some infuriated abolitionists, have been forced to co-operate. The trains were stopped and telegraphic wires cut, and, as the despatch informs us, the whole town was in possession of the insurgents. It will be seen, however, that the most active means have been put into execution to quell the disturbance; that several companies of artillery and infantry have proceeded to the scene, and, no doubt, before this reaches the eye of our readers, perfect quiet has been again established. We regret, however, that our telegraphic agent closed his reports so early, as it would have been exceedingly gratifying to learn that the miserable leaders of this unfortunate and disgraceful affair had received their just deserts.

Source: Charleston Mercury, Charleston, South Carolina, October 18, 1859.

The telegraphic despatches in another column, concerning the outbreak at Harper's Ferry, are stirring enough for ordinary purposes. We believe the affair, however, to be greatly exaggerated, as such occurrences usually are. There is at least no cause for uneasiness elsewhere in the State, notwithstanding the reports concerning the complicity of the negroes in the business.—Indeed, we rather incline to the belief that the entire report of the affair is pretty much of a humbug. That there is something of a riot there, on the part of a few of the operatives, we have no doubt; but the object of the rebels is to take possession of the public funds which were deposited there on Saturday.

Our goodly city was in a state of the liveliest excitement all yesterday evening. The military, particularly, were in great commotion. The Governor, we learn, has ordered the whole volunteer Regiment to the scene of disturbance. Company "F," under command of Col. Cary left at 8 o'clock last night—the

Fred[e]ricksburg mail train having been detained for their accommodation. The remainder of the Regiment, consisting of six or seven companies, will leave at 6 o'clock this morning. The Governor accompanied Col. Cary's company last night—and we slightly incline to the opinion that Harper's Ferry will be captured, and the rebels put down, especially as the military from the surrounding country and Old Point, Baltimore Washington, and Alexandria, have been ordered to the scene of action. We think these are almost enough to put an end to the "war" during the course of the week—provided all hands stand firm, as they no doubt will, with some exceptions.

The "soldiers" took leave of their wives and little ones last night amid such weeping and wailing, not expecting ever to see them more! It was a heart-rending scene, to be sure. We endeavored to procure a lock of the hair of several of the "soldiers," as a memento of them, in case they should fight, bleed and die in the service of their country; but they were too much afflicted by the parting scene to pay any attention to our request. We expect to see half of the "soldiers" back at least.—But good fortune to them all.

Source: Daily Richmond Whig, Richmond, Virginia, October 18, 1859.

We publish to-day full telegraphic particulars of the riot at Harper's Ferry, a briefer outline of which had heretofore appeared in our columns. The first report attributed the riot to the fact that a contractor on the Government works had absconded, leaving his employees unpaid, who had seized the arsenal with the purpose of securing Government funds and paying themselves. Later accounts seem conclusive that it was a concerted attempt at insurrection, aided by leading Northern Abolitionists. The papers of Brown, the leader, are said to have fallen into the hands of Gov. Wise, and to include among them letters from Gerrit Smith, Fred Douglass and others. We shall hear more in a few days, when, no doubt, the whole plot will be disclosed.

In the mean time, the facts already before us show that Abolitionism is working out its legitimate results, in encouraging fanatics to riot and revolution. The "harmless republicanism" out of which there is serious talk even here of making a national party, to defeat the Democracy, fosters and sustains, and is formidable only from the zeal of, the class within its ranks who incited this insurrection. Of the capacity of the South to defend and protect herself, we have no doubt. But when called on to do this, as at Harper's

Ferry, she must know who are her friends and who are her enemies. She can have no political association with men who are only watching a safe opportunity to cut the throats of her citizens. It will not do for Northern Republicans to attribute this outbreak to the fanaticism of a few zealots. The Republican party of the North is responsible for it. It is the legitimate result of Sewardism. It is the commencement of what Seward spoke of as the "irrepressible conflict." The South will hold the whole party of Republicans responsible for the blood-shed at Harper's Ferry. For the fanatics engaged there would never have dared the attempt at insurrection but for the inflammatory speeches and writings of Seward, Greeley, and the other Republican leaders. Waiting for the details before saying more, we refer the reader to the accounts of the insurrection published in another place in this paper.

Source: Nashville Union and American, Nashville, Tennessee, October 21, 1859.

"The Prayer of Twenty Millions" by Horace Greeley (1862)

August 19, 1862.

To Abraham Lincoln, President of the United States:

DEAR SIR:

I do not intrude to tell you—for you must know already—that a great proportion of those who triumphed in your election, and of all who desire the unqualified suppression of the rebellion now desolating our country, are sorely disappointed and deeply pained by the policy you seem to be pursuing with regard to the slaves of rebels. I write only to set succinctly and unmistakably before you what we require, what we think we have a right to expect, and of what we complain.

I. We require of you, as the first servant of the Republic, charged especially and preeminently with this duty, that you EXECUTE THE LAWS. Most emphatically do we demand that such laws as have been recently enacted, which therefore may fairly be presumed to embody the public will and to be dictated by the *present* needs of the republic, and which, after due consideration, have received your personal sanction, shall by you be carried into full effect and that you publicly and decisively instruct your subordinates that such laws exist, that they are binding on all functionaries and citizens, and that they are to be obeyed to the letter.

II. We think you are strangely and disastrously remiss in the discharge of your official and imperative duty with regard to the emancipating provisions of the new Confiscation Act. Those provisions were designed to fight Slavery with Liberty. They prescribe that men loyal to the Union, and willing to shed their blood in her behalf, shall no longer be held, with the nation's consent, in bondage to persistent, malignant traitors, who for twenty years have been plotting and for sixteen months have been fighting to divide and destroy our country. Why these traitors should be treated with tenderness by you, to the prejudice of the dearest rights of loyal men, we cannot conceive.

III. We think you are unduly influenced by the councils, the representations, the menaces, of certain fossil politicians hailing from the Border Slave States. Knowing well that the heartily, unconditionally loyal portion of the white citizens of those States do not expect nor desire that Slavery shall be upheld to the prejudice of the Union—(for the truth of which we appeal not only to every Republican residing in those States, but to such eminent loyalists as H. Winter Davis, Parson Brownlow, the Union Central Committee of Baltimore, and to *The Nashville Union*)—we ask you to consider that Slavery is everywhere the inciting cause and sustaining base of treason: the most slaveholding sections of Maryland and Delaware being this day, though under the Union flag, in full sympathy with the rebellion, while the free labor portions of Tennessee and of Texas, though writhing under the bloody heel of treason, are unconquerably loyal to the Union.

So emphatically is this the case that a most intelligent Union banker of Baltimore recently avowed his confident belief that a majority of the present legislature of Maryland, though elected as and all professing to be Unionists, are at heart desirous of the triumph of the Jeff Davis conspiracy, and when asked how they could be won back to loyalty, replied— "Only by the complete abolition of slavery."

It seems to us the most obvious truth, that whatever strengthens or fortifies Slavery in the Border States strengthens also treason, and drives home the wedge intended to divide the Union. Had you, from the first, refused to recognize in those States, as here, any other than unconditional loyalty—that which stands for the Union, whatever may become of Slavery—those States would have been, and would be, far more helpful and less troublesome to the defenders of the Union than they have been, or now are.

IV. We think timid counsels in such a crisis calculated to prove perilous, and probably disastrous. It is the duty of a Government so wantonly, wickedly assailed by rebellion as ours has been, to oppose force to force in a defiant, dauntless spirit. It cannot afford to temporize with traitors, nor with semi-traitors. It must not bribe them to behave themselves, nor make them fair promises in the hope of disarming their causeless hostility. Representing a brave and high-spirited people, it can afford to forfeit any thing else better than its own self-respect, or their admiring confidence, For our Government even to seek, after war has been made on it, to dispel the affected apprehensions of armed traitors that their cherished privileges may be assailed by it, is to invite insult and encourage hopes of its own downfall. The rush to arms of Ohio, Indiana, Illinois, is the true answer at once to the rebel raids of John Morgan and the traitorous sophistries of Beriah Magoffin.

V. We complain that the Union cause has suffered, and is now suffering immensely, from mistaken deference to rebel Slavery. Had you, sir, in your Inaugural Address, unmistakably given notice that, in case the rebellion already commenced, were persisted in, and your efforts to preserve the Union and enforce the laws should be resisted by armed force, *you would recognize no loyal person as rightfully held in Slavery by a traitor*, we believe the rebellion would therein have received a staggering if not fatal blow. At that moment, according to the returns of the most recent elections, the Unionists were a large majority of the voters of the slave States. But they were composed in good part of the aged, the feeble, the wealthy, the timid—the young, the reckless, the aspiring, the adventurous, had already been largely lured by the gamblers and negro-traders, the politicians by trade and the conspirators by instinct, into the toils of treason. Had you then proclaimed that rebellion would strike the shackles from the slaves of every traitor, the wealthy and the cautious would have been supplied with a powerful inducement to remain loyal.

As it was, every coward in the South soon became a traitor from fear; for loyalty was perilous, while treason seemed comparatively safe. Hence the boasted unanimity of the South—a unanimity based on Rebel terrorism and the fact that immunity and safety were found on that side, danger and probable death on ours. The Rebels, from the first, have been eager to confiscate, imprison, scourge, and kill; we have fought wolves with the devices of sheep. The result is just what might have been expected. Tens of thousands are fighting in the Rebel ranks today whose original bias and natural leanings would have led them into ours.

VI. We complain that the Confiscation Act which you approved is habitually disregarded by your Generals, and that no word of rebuke for them from you has yet reached the public ear. Frémont's Proclamation and Hunter's Order favoring Emancipation were promptly annulled by you; while Halleck's Number Three, forbidding fugitives from slavery to rebels to come within his lines—an order as unmilitary as inhuman, and which received the hearty approbation of every traitor in America—with scores of like tendency, have never provoked even your remonstrance.

We complain that the officers of your armies have habitually repelled rather than invited the approach of slaves who would have gladly taken the risks of escaping from their Rebel masters to our camps, bringing intelligence often of inestimable value to the Union cause. We complain that those who *have* thus escaped to us, avowing a willingness to do for us whatever might be required, have been brutally and madly repulsed, and often surrendered to be scourged, maimed, and tortured by the ruffian traitors who pretend to own them. We complain that a large proportion of our regular Army officers, with many of the volunteers, evince far more solicitude to uphold slavery than to put down the rebellion.

And finally, we complain that you, Mr. President, elected as a Republican, knowing well what an abomination Slavery is, and how emphatically it is the core and essence of this atrocious rebellion, seem never to interfere with these atrocities, and never give a direction to your military subordinates, which does not appear to have been conceived in the interest of Slavery rather than of Freedom.

VII. Let me call your attention to the recent tragedy in New Orleans, whereof the facts are obtained entirely through Pro-Slavery channels. A considerable body of resolute, able-bodied men, held in Slavery by two Rebel sugar-planters in defiance of the Confiscation Act which you have approved, left plantations thirty miles distant and made their way to the great mart of the South-West, which they knew to be in the disputed possession of the Union forces. They made their way safely and quietly through thirty miles of Rebel territory, expecting to find freedom under the protection of our flag. Whether they had or had not heard of the passage of the Confiscation Act, they reasoned logically that we could not kill them for deserting the service of their lifelong oppressors, who had through treason become our implacable enemies. They came to us for liberty and protection, for which they were willing [to] render their best service:

they met with hostility, captivity, and murder. The barking of the base curs[e] of Slavery in this quarter deceives no one—not even themselves. They say, indeed, that the negroes had no right to appear in New Orleans armed (with their implements of daily labor in the cane-field); but no one doubts that they would gladly have laid these down if assured that they should be free. They were set upon and maimed, captured and killed, because they sought the benefit of that act of Congress which they may not specifically have heard of, but which was none the less the law of the land which they had a clear right to the benefit of—which it was somebody's duty to publish far and wide, in order that so many as possible should be impelled to desist from serving Rebels and the Rebellion and come over to the side of the Union. They sought their liberty in strict accordance with the law of the land—they were butchered or re-enslaved for so doing by the help of Union soldiers enlisted to fight against slaveholding Treason. It was somebody's fault that they were so murdered—if others shall hereafter suffer in like manner, in default of explicit and public directions to your generals that they are to recognize and obey the Confiscation Act, the world will lay the blame on you. Whether you will choose to hear it through future History and at the bar of God, I will not judge. I can only hope.

VIII. On the face of this wide earth, Mr. President, there is not one disinterested, determined, intelligent champion of the Union cause who does not feel that all attempts to put down the rebellion and at the same time uphold its inciting cause are preposterous and futile—that the rebellion, if crushed out tomorrow, would be renewed within a year if Slavery were left in full vigor—that army officers who remain to this day devoted to Slavery can at best be but halfway loyal to the Union—and that every hour of deference to Slavery is an hour of added and deepened peril to the Union. I appeal to the testimony of your ambassadors in Europe. It is freely at your service, not at mine. Ask them to tell you candidly whether the seeming subserviency of your policy to the slaveholding, slavery-upholding interest, is not the perplexity, the despair of statesmen of all parties, and be admonished by the general answer!

IX. I close as I began with the statement that what an immense majority of the loyal millions of your countrymen require of you is a frank, declared, unqualified, ungrudging execution of the laws of the land, more especially of the Confiscation Act. That act gives freedom to the slaves of rebels coming within our lines, or whom those lines may at any time inclose—we ask you to render it due obedience by publicly requiring all your subordinates to recognize and obey it. The rebels are everywhere using the late anti-negro riots in the North, as they have long used your officers' treatment of negroes in the South, to convince the slaves that they have nothing to hope from a Union success—that we mean in that case to sell them into a bitter bondage to defray the cost of the war.

Let them impress this as a truth on the great mass of their ignorant and credulous bondmen, and the Union will never be restored—never. We cannot conquer ten millions of people united in solid phalanx against us, powerfully aided by Northern sympathizers and European allies. We must have scouts, guides, spies, cooks, teamsters, diggers, and choppers from the blacks of the South, whether we allow them to fight for us or not, or we shall be baffled and repelled.

As one of the millions who would gladly have avoided this struggle at any sacrifice but that of principle and honor, but who now feel that the triumph of the Union is indispensable not only to the existence of our country but to the well-being of mankind, I entreat you to render a hearty and unequivocal obedience to the law of the land.

Yours,
HORACE GREELEY

Sources: New York Tribune, August 19, 1862. Harlan Hoyt Horner, *Lincoln and Greeley.* Urbana: University of Illinois Press, 1953; Westport, CT: Greenwood, 1971.

President Lincoln's Response to Horace Greeley (1862)

Executive Mansion, Washington, August 22, 1862.
To Hon. Horace Greeley:

DEAR SIR:
I have just read yours of the nineteenth, addressed to myself through the *New-York Tribune.* If there be in it any statements or assumptions of fact which I may know to be erroneous, I do not now and here controvert them. If there be in it any inferences which I may believe to be falsely drawn, I do not now and here argue against them. If there be perceptible in it an impatient and dictatorial tone, I waive it in deference to an old friend, whose heart I have always supposed to be right.

As to the policy I "seem to be pursuing," as you say, I have not meant to leave any one in doubt.

I would save the Union. I would save it the shortest way under the Constitution. The sooner the National authority can be restored, the nearer the Union will be "the Union as it was." If there be those who would not save the Union unless they could at the same time *save* Slavery, I do not agree with them. If there be those who would not save the Union unless they could at the same time *destroy* Slavery, I do not agree with them. My paramount object in this struggle *is* to save the Union, and is *not* either to save or destroy Slavery. If I could save the Union without freeing *any* slave, I would do it; and if I could save it by freeing *all* the slaves, I would do it; and if I could do it by freeing some and leaving others alone, I would also do that. What I do about Slavery and the colored race, I do because I believe it helps to save this Union; and what I forbear, I forbear because I do not believe it would help to save the Union. I shall do *less* whenever I shall believe what I am doing hurts the cause, and I shall do *more* whenever I shall believe doing more will help the cause. I shall try to correct errors when shown to be errors and I shall adopt new views so fast as they shall appear to be true views. I have here stated my purpose according to my view of *official* duty, and I intend no modification of my oft-expressed *personal* wish that all men, everywhere, could be free.

Yours,

A. LINCOLN.

Source: Christian Times and Illinois Baptist, September 3, 1862.

An Editorial on Emancipation in Suriname (1863)

On this first day of July, in this year of our Lord, One thousand eight hundred and sixty-three, Forty-Five Thousand slaves, in the colony of Surinam, and in the islands adjacent, will be free. With the last stroke of the midnight [chime], of this present month of June, their bondage ceases; the shackles fall from their limbs; they leap at once into freedom. God be praised for this addition to the free citizens of the World! For this further instalment on the enormous debt of right and justice civilization owes to the negro! For many years the slaves in the Dutch colonies have known of the efforts which were being made to ensure their freedom, and for some months now they have counted the days, the hours, the minutes, which intervened between them and liberty. Who can conceive, who shall attempt to describe the feelings of the people, in the certainty of approaching freedom? To-day a chat-

tel; a labour-machine; a thing without rights; without legal family tie or obligation; without progeny to call his own, although the parent of children; liable to be flogged, maimed, tortured, worked to the extreme of physical endurance, yet labouring for another's behoof; lying down as a beast of burden, rising to worse than a beast of burden's toil, because sensible of injustice, wrong, outrage: this all his life past; this yesterday; this to-day; this to-night! Then, suddenly, a man! Born to a new life; a life of hope, of responsibility, of self-knowledge, of self-respect; born anew to kindred, family, society; to full social manhood; to right, to justice—in a word, to freedom! Is there a father, is there a mother, blessed with offspring, who have seen apparently certain death, laying cold finger on a beloved little one; who have stood by the young sufferer's bed, watching with beating heart, convulsive sob and tearful eye, the departing life; are there such who cannot recal[l] the intense joy that swelled their bosom when the shadow of the destroyer passed away, and hope revived with a new-born life? Let such place themselves now side by side with the slave-mother and the slave-father, whose offspring, their own and not their own, momently liable to be stolen away, and therefore to be lost to them as though daily dying in fact, are suddenly restored to them in full, inalienable possession, and they may perhaps realize the exceeding great joy of the slaves, who will be at once free, at the 1st chime of midnight on this coming 30th of June and who, then, for the first time, may call their children their own.

Yet, between the man of now, this minute, and the chattel-thing of one moment ago, what essential difference exists? Only one second of time between the thing slave and the being man! Who created the distinction? Clearly he who abolishes it. It never existed, it never can exist in nature; and what is against nature is against God, and therefore sin in the highest degree. May His holy name be praised! Holland, fourth amongst the emancipating nations, has purged herself, at last, of this national iniquity. Welcome! Thrice welcome the omen! Alas, NINE MILLIONS OF THE OPPRESSED RACE yet remain in bondage! May the midnight chime of the 30th June be the first stroke of their dawn of freedom!

But is there not here visible work for the friends of negro freedom? Shall they desist from their labours, while so many millions of their fellow-creatures remain slaves—chattel slaves? Forbid it humanity! Forbid it religion! Let them take courage. The moral world, like the physical, does move. Looking at what has been already achieved, and at what is on the eve of accomplishment abroad, let the abolitionist Galileos of to-day exclaim, *e puer se muovo*, and take courage.

Source: *Anti-Slavery Reporter* (New Series), 2:7 (July 1, 1863).

Joaquim Nabuco on the Brazilian Abolitionist Movement (1883)

London, April 5th, 1883.
TO THE EDITOR OF *The Anti-Slavery Reporter.*

SIR,—
I wish, through your paper to record the last achievement of a Brazilian Abolitionist Society, the *Cearense Libertadora.* Owing chiefly to its indomitable energy, there are at last three districts in Brazil redeemed from Slavery, namely, those of Acarape, Pacatuba, and S. Francisco.

The genesis of the Abolitionist movement in Ceará, a Northern Province of the South American Empire, deserves to be known. It began with the spontaneous refusal of the *jangadeiros*, the raftsmen of the harbour of Fortalera to transport the Slaves sold from the shore to the steamer which was to carry them to the Slave markets of the South. The Underground Railway in the United States placed the runaway Slave on a free soil; the Ceará *jangadeiros*, moved by the same spirit, made a strike against the coast Slave-trade, which carried the provincial Slaves from their Northern home to hard labours and uncongenial surroundings of the Southern estates.

By so doing, those poor people, whose only possessions were their sailing rafts, gave a deadly blow to the mighty Slave-holding interest. They brought down, in fact, the price of Slaves in Ceará from £150 to £10, and furthermore their strike had such an electric effect all over the country that each Province decided to shut itself off by prohibitive import taxes from the wave of adventitious Slavery.

Once the value of a Slave so materially reduced, a movement was started to buy them off, in that way those of Acarape, Pacatuba and S. Francisco were ransomed. No doubt the whole of Ceará will follow, and Brazil, in a short time, by the initiative of a few men, will have at least one province of free soil.

I wish you would give me space enough to mention the officers of the *Cearense Libertadora* to whom every true Brazilian owes a debt of gratitude for their untiring efforts to redeem every Slave they possibly can. The following are a few names from a long list of public benefactors: J. CORDEIRO, J.C. DO AMARAL, DR. FREDERICO BORGES, A.G. DE MENEZES, A.D. MARTINS, JUN., J. TH. DE CASTRO.

The Emperor has subscribed £100 for the freedom of the Slaves of Acarape.

I beg leave to add that in Rio there is a movement on foot, at whose head are DR. NICOLAO MOREIRA, DR. VINCENTE DE SOUZA, SENOR J.F. CLAPP, DR. UBALDINO DO AMARAL, to clear, by redemption, the capital of the Empire from its black stain of Slavery. I hope some generous hearts will congregate, too, in order to promote by law the immediate enfranchisement of all Africans held in Slavery. Those wretched victims of the Slave-trade were all imported before the year 1853, that is to say, have been, at the least, thirty years in Slavery, and the most of them, I think nine tenths, are *legally* free.

I have the strongest belief that the national will of getting rid of a land and labour monopoly hostile to the interests of the country is daily gaining strength and will have, in a few years, coercive power enough to force itself on those who wish that the death of more than one million of persons of all ages still remaining in Slavery, shall be the natural end of an institution too anti-social, inhuman and backward to be charged for such a long period still to the moral account of an American country of eleven millions of free population.

I am, Sir, your obedient servant,
JOAQUIM NABUCO.

Source: *Anti-Slavery Reporter* (Series IV), 3 (April 1883).

Abolitionist Societies' Organizing Goals and Objectives

Abolitionist societies were formed to combat the twin evils of the slave trade and slavery itself. In taking up the antislavery banner, they also became institutions of societal change with an extended mission that they hoped to achieve.

An amorphous connection existed between the concepts of *abolition* and *emancipation,* blurring the boundaries and the ultimate goals of each. It was one task to call for the freedom of the enslaved, but it was quite another to monitor the quality of the freedom that ensued. Yet both notions were inextricably connected.

Institutional memory is an essential attribute of any organization, and it is especially important when the progress of a reform movement spans several generations. It is equally important to maintain a consistent level of sustained activism among members of a movement in which ultimate success might be deferred to points unknown and the level of commitment might wax and wane. The individuals who were inspired by the antislavery impulse realized the battle they had joined was one that was larger than themselves and one in which half-heartedness had no virtue. Dedication to the cause was key, and new generations of abolitionist supporters had to be drawn to the movement and inculcated with its values. These vagaries of time and circumstance made the work of attaining both abolition and emancipation all the more difficult.

It may be surprising to learn that many abolitionist organizations provided some of their most conscientious services in the decades *after* slavery was abolished in the transatlantic world. As societal realists who had been jaded by the erratic progress of antislavery efforts, many abolitionists recognized that only a sustained campaign aimed at monitoring governmental and societal commitment to abolition could guarantee that the blessings of liberty would indeed be provided to the former slaves. British abolitionists clearly understood this as they monitored the process of emancipation and campaigned against the apprenticeship system that was put into place when slavery was abolished throughout the British Empire in 1834. These vigilant observers were critical to the efficacy of the social and political change that antislavery agitation had helped to attain.

The founders of abolitionist societies also recognized the necessity of sustaining support for the reform impulse in a distant membership that might not be so closely connected to the heady activism that had initially inspired the organization. It was the role of these abolitionist societies to continue to educate—as well as to agitate—so that future generations of abolitionists might be drawn to the cause and motivated by the same social calling that had inspired others to the movement in previous years.

As institutions of the perpetual present, such organizations had to fashion a way of connecting past achievements with future obligations so that members would understand that the social debt had not yet been paid in full by the efforts of those who had come before. Organizations as far-reaching as the African Institution in Britain and the Spanish Ladies' Antislavery Society in Madrid outlined their goals and objectives, formulated mission statements, and generally informed each new generation of its responsibilities. The documents in this section reflect their intentions.

Abolitionist societies chartered themselves into institutions with clearly defined starting points but no predetermined end point at which the mission of abolitionism would be completed. In fact, some of the abolitionist societies that formed during the nineteenth century are still functioning today to maintain the charges that their forbears adopted. Even though all the nations of the world have outlawed slavery, unfree labor practices persist, and the varying degrees of freedom that are evident in some parts of the modern world suggest that the goal of achieving universal emancipation is far from complete.

The African Institution (1807)

Rules and Regulations, &c.

Chapter 1. Objects of the Institution. The general objects of the Institution are expressed in the following Resolutions adopted at the first meeting of this Society, on the 14th of April, 1807, viz.

1. That this Meeting is deeply impressed with a sense of the enormous wrongs which the natives of Africa have suffered in their intercourse with Europe; and from a desire to repair those wrongs as well as from general feelings of benevolence, is anxious to adopt such measures as are best calculated to promote their civilization and happiness.
2. That the approaching cessation of the Slave Trade hitherto carried on by Great Britain, America, and Denmark, will, in a considerable degree, remove the barrier which has so long obstructed the natural course of social improvement in Africa; and that the way will be thereby opened for introducing the comforts and arts of a more civilized state of society.
3. That the happiest effects may be reasonably anticipated from diffusing useful knowledge, and exciting industry among the inhabitants of Africa, and from obtaining and circulating throughout this country more ample and authentic information concerning the agricultural and commercial faculties of that vast Continent; and that through the judicious prosecution of these benevolent endeavours, we may ultimately look forward to the establishment, in the room of that traffic by which Africa has been so long degraded, of a legitimate and far more extended commerce, beneficial alike to the natives of Africa and to the manufacturers of Great Britain and Ireland.
4. That the present period is eminently fitted for prosecuting these benevolent designs; since the suspension, during the war, of that large share of the Slave Trade which has commonly been carried on by France, Spain, and Holland, will, when combined with the effect of the Abolition Laws of Great Britain, America, and Denmark, produce nearly the entire cessation of that traffic along a line of coast extending between two and three thousand miles in length, and thereby afford a peculiarly favourable opportunity for giving a new direction to the industry and commerce of Africa.
5. That for these purposes a Society be immediately formed, to be called THE AFRICAN INSTITUTION.

Source: Report of the Committee of the African Institution, Read to the General Meeting on the 15th of July, 1807, Together With Rules and Regulations Adopted for the Government of the Society. London: Ellerton and Henderson, 1811.

The German Society for the Abolition of Slavery (1848)

Prospectus of the Provisional Committee.

Convinced of the necessity of using our utmost efforts for the abolition of slavery, as the most dreadful injury ever inflicted upon man, and the source of unutterable misery to [the] missions of our fellow-creatures;

Persuaded that the present is a good opportunity for the German people to unite with other nations in endeavouring to exterminate this high-treason against the human race;

Impressed moreover with a conviction of the duty of compensating such Germans who are the possessors of slaves, for the loss they would sustain by abolition;

And having been repeatedly called by friends in the United States to assist in opposing the systems of slavery which exists there;

We, the undersigned, have constituted ourselves into a Provisional Committee, for the organization of a German Society for the Abolition of Slavery, and have resolved, from this time forth, to take all such steps as may be necessary for accomplishing the desired end.

(Signed)
GAGERN, (Minister of State.)
C. WELCKER, (Professor.)
C.F. HEYDER, (Banker.)
DR. F.W. CAROVÉ.
DR. H. KUNZEL.
DR. J.W. WOLF.
M. BECK.
F. HAAS.
G. FISCHER.

Source: Anti-Slavery Reporter (New Series), 3:28 (April 1, 1848).

The Spanish Ladies' Anti-Slavery Society (1871)

Madrid, 22nd March, 1871.

Utilising the right of Association we possess by law, and impelled by a sentiment purely Christian and humanitarian, we whose names are subscribed, constitute ourselves into the "Sociedad de Senoras, Protectoras de los Esclavos" [Society of Ladies, Protectresses of the Slaves]. We declare our work to be purely humanitarian, and completely detached from all political ideas, and we place ourselves under the shelter of the Gospel of the Redeemer of the World, He who shed his blood to redeem all men, without distinction of race or colour. We write as our maxim the fundamental law of his holy and civilising doctrines, "that we should love one another as God loves all men."

Because we are Christians we desire to comply with the sweet precept of our religion of love.

Because we are mothers, wives, and daughters, we desire to wipe away the tears of so many thousands of slave-mothers, wives, and daughters who weep in the greatest of misfortunes, for the forced absence of those whom God has made so dear to the heart of woman—the husband and the children.

Because we are Spaniards, we desire to contribute to rid our country of the stain which is impressed on its escutcheon by this horrible institution—a relic of the barbarity of past times, and to take, in the work of the redemption of the slave, the part that has fallen to woman in all countries where justice has triumphed and freedom been conceded. In inaugurating our work of Christian charity, we declare once for all, that our weakness is our strength, and that while loving the poor slave, and lamenting his terrible condition, we indulge no hate against those who enslave and ill-treat him, for our mission is one of peace and love. Our hearts only desire to feel for, and with tears to supplicate and beg for, compassion upon our unfortunate protegees, all the more unfortunate as they are enduring endless punishment for no faults of their own.

BASIS OF THE SOCIETY.

1. The Society of Ladies, Protectresses of the Slaves, is constituted in Madrid.
2. All ladies belong to this Society who desire to do so, and who, sympathising with the misfortunes of the slave, undertake to employ their legitimate influence in the hearts of their families, in favour of the Immediate Abolition of Slavery.
3. The ladies of this Society have no other mission or charge than that above mentioned.
4. The direction and conduct of the Society devolves on the "Junta Directiva," who are elected to-day.
5. The Junta Directiva may increase their members whenever they think proper.

President.—Faustina Saez de Melgar.
Vice-President.—Julia Jimenez de Moya.
Committee.
Aurora Calza lo de Pelayo.
Carmen Gonzales de Neda.
Florentina Decraene de Navarro.
María Francisca Gil de Garcia.
Gracia O. de Bustos.
Secretaries.
Angela Grassi.
María del Pilar Sinnués de Marco.
Micaela de Silva.
Blanca Gassó.

Source: Anti-Slavery Reporter, 17:5 (April 1, 1871).

The Constitution of the British and Foreign Anti-Slavery Society (1873)

I. That the name of this Society be, "THE BRITISH AND FOREIGN ANTI-SLAVERY SOCIETY."

II. That the objects of this Society be, THE UNIVERSAL EXTINCTION OF SLAVERY AND THE SLAVE-TRADE, AND THE PROTECTION OF THE RIGHTS AND INTERESTS OF THE ENFRANCHISED POPULATION IN THE BRITISH POSSESSIONS AND OF ALL PERSONS CAPTURED AS SLAVES.

III. That the following shall be the fundamental principles of the Society:—

That so long as Slavery exists, there is no reasonable prospect of the annihilation of the Slave-trade, and of extinguishing the sale and barter of human beings; that the extinction of Slavery and the Slave-trade will be attained most effectually by the employment of those means which are of a moral, religious, and pacific character; and that no measures be resorted to by this Society, in the prosecution of these objects, but such as are in entire accordance with these principles.

IV. That the following be among the means to be employed by this Society:—

1. To circulate, both at home and abroad, accurate information on the enormities of the slave-trade

and Slavery: to furnish evidence to the inhabitants of slaveholding countries, not only of the practicability, but of the pecuniary advantage of free labour; to diffuse authentic intelligence respecting the results of emancipation in Hayti, the British colonies, and elsewhere; to open a correspondence with Abolitionists in America, France, and other countries; and to encourage them in the prosecution of their objects by all methods consistent with the principles of this Society.

2. To recommend the use of free-grown produce (as far as practicable) in preference to slave-grown; and to promote the adoption of fiscal regulations in favour of free-labour.

3. To obtain the unequivocal recognition of the principle, that the slave, of whatever clime or colour, entering any portion of the British dominions, shall be free, the same as upon the shores of the United Kingdom; and to carry this principle into full and complete effect.

4. To recommend that every suitable opportunity be embraced for evincing, in our intercourse with slaveholders and their apologists, our abhorrence of the system which they uphold, and our sense of its utter incompatibility with the spirit of the Christian.

V. That every person who subscribes not less than Ten Shillings annually, or makes a donation of Five Pounds or upwards, shall be a member of this Society.

VI. That the Society be under the management of a Treasurer, a Secretary, and a Committee of not less than twenty-one persons, who shall be annually elected, and shall have power to fill up vacancies, and to add to their number.

VII. That there be held in London a General Meeting of the subscribers once in each year, at which a report of the proceedings, and a financial statement, shall be presented, and a Committee and Officers elected.

VIII. That the Committee have power to transact all business of the Society, in the intervals of the General Meeting, and to convene special general meetings of the Society when necessary.

IX. That it be recommended to the anti-slavery friends throughout the world to form Auxiliary Societies upon the principles of, and in connection with, this Society.

X. That Auxiliary Societies be empowered annually to appoint, and where such Auxiliaries are not formed the Committee shall have power annually to appoint, one or more corresponding members, who shall be at liberty to attend and vote at all meetings of the committee in London; and that the Committee shall also be authorized to appoint annually honorary corresponding members who shall have the same privileges.

XI. That the Committee do invite and encourage the formation of Ladies' Branch Associations, in furtherance of the objects of this Society.

Source: Anti-Slavery Reporter (Third Series), vol. 18 (1872–1873).

Congressional and Public Addresses, Speeches, and Proclamations

Language can be quite persuasive. Throughout history, individuals have used rhetoric to sway adherents to a cause and, on occasion, to move people to take direct action with respect to a position or point of view. Powerful speech can be used to support the forces of good or those of evil, and, not surprisingly, both proslavery and antislavery agitators employed it to express the righteousness of their cause.

Slavery was often used in a metaphorical sense by those who loved liberty, including slaveholders who decried any efforts to diminish their personal freedom to own slaves. The founders of the United States, in drafting the charter documents of the new nation, walked a tenuous line between slavery and freedom as they broke away from oppressive British rule and created a government in which the majority ruled, subsuming minority interests. Parsing the meaning of liberty in such times was challenging, as the semantic power and meaning of slavery and slavish impulses seemed ever present.

During the era of transatlantic slavery, many individuals—from social reformers to politicians and jurists—recognized the highly potent and dramatic effect of rhetoric in persuading individuals to think differently about the question of slavery. Both proslavery and antislavery supporters effectively used rational arguments to defend their positions. Each side made effective use of emotional appeals that were meant to incite an active response from their adherents.

As history proves, words had the power and potency to encourage rebellion and direct action on the part of slaves to effect their own freedom. Many proslavery supporters believed this was ultimately the goal of antislavery agitation and thus justified their efforts to stifle abolitionist discourse. They defended this suppression of free speech as necessary to preserve and protect community safety and standards against outside agitators who meant to challenge the legitimate activities of those who owned slaves. In similar fashion, potent language was used to persuade individuals to burn abolitionist pamphlets that were legally delivered through the U.S. mail and to threaten the life and safety of any who were suspected of harboring antislavery sentiment. Used in this way, rhetoric had the chilling effects of silencing debate and imposing ubiquitous order on a community—frightening outcomes that were incongruent with the high-minded principles traditionally associated with freedom-loving people.

Rhetoric also could be used to heal and bind the wounds of divisiveness. As President Abraham Lincoln called on citizens to summon "the better angels" of their character in his March 1861 inaugural address, reasoned arguments could be presented in such a way that antithesis might lead to catharsis, as bitter wounds gave way to a higher calling. Yet, in spite of these glimpses of what might be possible, the rhetoric of proslavery and antislavery thought was more often focused on the perpetuation of animus between polarized perspectives.

The strident voices documented in this section animated the discourse on slavery in the transatlantic world, as the merits and shortcomings of proslavery and antislavery thought were articulated and challenged by competing interests. Often lost in the confusion of debate and the multiplicity of voices was the truth—the sane, reasoned ground on which policies and proposals should be evaluated and considered.

In all the noise and confusion, the voices of the slaves themselves were seldom heard. They remained marginalized actors in the great morality play that would eventually determine their future.

Lord Dunmore's Proclamation (1775)

By His Excellency the Right Honorable JOHN Earl of DUNMORE, His MAJESTY'S Lieutenant and Governor-General of the Colony and Dominion of VIRGINIA, and Vice-Admiral of the same.

A PROCLAMATION.

As I have ever entertained Hopes, that an Accommodation might have taken Place between GREAT-BRITAIN and this Colony, without being compelled by my Duty to this most disagreeable but now absolutely necessary Step, rendered so by a Body of armed Men unlawfully assembled, firing on His MAJESTY'S Tenders, and the formation of an Army, and that Army now on their March to attack His MAJESTY'S Troops and destroy the well disposed Subjects of this Colony. To defeat such treasonable Purposes, and that all such Traitors, and their Abettors, may be brought to Justice, and that the Peace, and good Order of this Colony may be again restored, which the ordinary Course of the Civil Law is unable to effect; I have thought fit to issue this my Proclamation, hereby declaring, that until the aforesaid good Purposes can be obtained, I do in Virtue of the Power and Authority to ME given, by His MAJESTY, determine to execute Martial Law, and cause the same to be executed throughout this Colony: and to the end that Peace and good Order may the sooner be restored, I do require every Person capable of bearing Arms, to resort to His MAJESTY'S STANDARD, or be looked upon as Traitors to His MAJESTY'S Crown and Government, and thereby become liable to the Penalty the Law inflicts upon such Offences; such as forfeiture of Life, confiscation of Lands, &c. &c. And I do hereby further declare all indent[ur]ed Servants, Negroes, or others, (appertaining to Rebels,) free that are able and willing to bear Arms, they joining His MAJESTY'S Troops as soon as may be, for the more speedily reducing this Colony to a proper Sense of their Duty, to His MAJESTY'S Crown and Dignity. I do further order, and require, all His MAJESTY'S Leige Subjects, to retain their Quitrents, or any other Taxes due or that may become due, in their own Custody, till such Time as Peace may be again restored to this at present most unhappy Country, or demanded of them for their former salutary Purposes, by Officers properly authorised to receive the same.

GIVEN under my Hand on board the ship WILLIAM, off NORFOLK, the 7th Day of November, in the SIXTEENTH Year of His MAJESTY'S Reign.

DUNMORE.
(GOD save the KING.)

Source: John Earl of Dunmore, *By His Excellency the Right Honourable John Earl of Dunmore, His Majesty's Lieutenant and Governor-General of the Colony and Dominion of Virginia, and Vice-Admiral of the Same: A Proclamation {Declaring Martial Law, and to Cause the Same to be Executed Throughout This Colony}.* Williamsburg, Virginia, 1775.

David Walker Addresses Free Persons of Color (1828)

ADDRESS, Delivered before the General Colored Association at Boston, by David Walker

Mr. President,—

I cannot but congratulate you, together with my brethren on this highly interesting occasion, the first semi-annual meeting of this Society. When I reflect upon the many impediments through which we have had to conduct its affairs, and see, with emotions of delight, the present degree of eminency to which it has arisen, I cannot, sir, but be of the opinion, that an invisible arm must have been stretched out in our behalf. From the very second conference, which was by us convened, to agitate the proposition respecting this society, to its final consolidation, we were by some, opposed, with an avidity and zeal, which, had it been on the opposite side, would have done great honor to themselves. And, sir, but for the undeviating, and truly patriotic exertions of those who were favorable to the formation of this institution, it might have been this day, in a yet unorganized condition. Did I say in an unorganized condition? Yea, had our opponents their way, the very notion of such an institution might have been obliterated from our minds. How strange it is, to see men of sound sense, and of tolerably good judgment, act so diametrically in opposition to their interest; but I forbear making any further comments on this subject, and return to that for which we are convened.

First then, Mr. President, it is necessary to remark here, at once, that the primary object of this institution, is, to unite the colored population, so far, through the United States of America, as may be practicable and expedient; forming societies, opening, extending, and keeping up correspondences, and not withholding any thing which may have the least tendency to meliorate *our* miserable condition—with the restrictions, however, of not infringing on the articles of its constitution, or that of the United States of America. Now, that we are disunited, is a fact, that no one of common sense will deny; and, that the cause of which, is a powerful auxiliary in keeping us from rising to the scale of reasonable and thinking beings, none but those who delight in our degradation will attempt to contradict. Did I say those who delight in our degradation? Yea, sir, glory in keeping us ignorant and miserable, that we might be the better and the longer slaves. I was credibly informed by a gentleman of unquestionable veracity, that a slaveholder upon finding one of his young slaves with a small spelling book in his hand (not opened) fell upon and beat him almost to death, exclaiming, at the same time, to the child, you will acquire better learning than I or any of my family.

I appeal to every candid and unprejudiced mind, do not all such men glory in our miseries and degradations; and are there not millions whose chief glory centres in this horrid wickedness? Now, Mr. President, those are the very humane, philanthropic, and charitable men who proclaim to the world, that the blacks are such a poor, ignorant and degraded species of beings, that, were they set at liberty, they would die for the want of something to subsist upon, and in consequence of which, they are compelled to keep them in bondage, to do them good.

O Heaven! What will not avarice and the love of despotic sway cause men to do with their fellow creatures, when actually in their power? But, to return whence I digressed; it has been asked, in what way will the *General Colored Association* (or the Institution) unite the colored population, so far, in the United States as may be practicable and expedient? To which enquiry I answer, by asking the following: Do not two hundred and eighty years [of] very intolerable sufferings teach us the actual necessity of a general union among us? Do we not know indeed, the horrid dilemma into which we are, and from which, we must exert ourselves, to be extricated? Shall we keep slumbering on, with our arms completely folded up, exclaiming every now and then, against our miseries, yet never do the least thing to ameliorate our condition, or that of posterity? Shall we not, by such inactivity, leave, or farther entail a hereditary degradation on our children, but a little, if at all, inferior to that which our fathers, under all their comparative disadvantages and privations, left on us? In fine, shall we, while almost every other people under Heaven, are

making such mighty efforts to better their condition, go around from house to house, enquiring what good associations and societies are going to do [for] us? Ought we not to form ourselves into a general body, to protect, aid, and assist each other to the utmost of our power, with the beforementioned restrictions?

Yes, Mr. President, it is indispensably our duty to try every scheme that we think will have a tendency to facilitate our salvation, and leave the final result to that God, who holds the destinies of people in the hollow of his hand, and who ever has, and will, repay every nation according to its works.

Will any be so hardy as to say, or even to imagine, that we are incapable of effecting any object which may have a tendency to hasten our emancipation, in consequence of the prevalence of ignorance and poverty among us? That the major part of us are ignorant and poor, I am at this time unprepared to deny.—But shall this deter us from all lawful attempts to bring about the desired object? Nay, sir, it should rouse us to greater exertions; there ought to be a spirit of emulation and inquiry among us, a hungering and thirsting after religion; these are requisitions, which, if we ever be so happy as to acquire, will fit us, for all the departments of life; and, in my humble opinion, ultimately result in rescuing us from an oppression, unparalleled, I had almost said, in the annals of the world.

But some may even think that our white breathren and friends are making such mighty efforts, for the amelioration of our condition, that we may stand as neutral spectators of the work. That we have very good friends yea, very good, among that body, perhaps none but a few of those who have, ever read at all will deny; and that many of them have gone, and will go, all lengths for our good, is evident, from the very works of the great, the good, and the godlike Granville Sharpe [*sic*], Wilberforce, Lundy, and the truly patriotic and lamented Mr. Ashmun, late Colonial Agent of Liberia, who, with a zeal which was only equalled by the goodness of his heart, has lost his life in our cause, and a host of others too numerous to mention: a number of private gentlemen too, who, though they say but little, are nevertheless, busily engaged for good. Now, all of those great, and indeed, good friends whom God has given us I do humbly, and very gratefully acknowledge. But, that we should co-operate with them, as far as we are able by uniting and cultivating a spirit of friendship and of love among us, is obvious, from the very exhibition of our miseries, under which we groan.

Two millions and a half of colored people in these United States, more than five hundred thousand of whom are about two thirds of the way free. Now, I ask, if no more than these last were united (which they must be, or always live as enemies) and resolved to aid and assist each other to the utmost of their power, what mighty deeds could be done by them for the good of our cause?

But, Mr. President, instead of a general compliance with these requisitions, which have a natural tendency to raise us in the estimation of the world, we see, to our sorrow, in the very midst of us, a gang of villains, who, for the paltry sum of fifty or a hundred dollars, will kidnap and sell into perpetual slavery, their fellow creatures! And, too, of one of their fellow sufferers, whose miseries are a little more enhanced by the scourges of a tyrant, should abscond from his pretended owner, to take a little recreation, and unfortunately fall in their way, he is gone! Brethren and fellow sufferers, I ask you, in the name of God, and of Jesus Christ, shall we suffer such notorious villains to rest peaceably among us? Will they not take our wives and little ones, more particularly our *little ones*, when a convenient opportunity will admit and sell them for money to slave holders, who will doom them to *chains*, *handcuffs*, and even unto death? May God open our eyes on these children of the devil and enemies of all good!

But, sir, this wickedness is scarcely more infernal than that which was attempted a few months since, against the government of our brethren, the Haytians, by a consummate rogue, who ought to have, long since, been *haltered*, but who, I was recently informed, is nevertheless, received into company among some of our most respectable men, with a kind of brotherly affection which ought to be shown only to a gentleman of honor.

Now, Mr. President, all such mean, and more than disgraceful actions as these, are powerful auxiliaries, which work for our destruction, and which are abhorred in the sight of God and of good men.

But, sir, I cannot but bless God for the glorious anticipation of a not very distant period, when these things which now help to degrade us still no more be practised among the sons of Africa,—for, though this, and perhaps another, generation may not experience the promised blessings of Heaven, yet, the dejected, degraded, and now enslaved children of Africa will have, in spite of all their enemies, to take their stand among the nations of the earth. And, sir, I verily believe that God has something in reserve for us, which, when he shall have poured it out upon us, will repay us for all our suffering and miseries.

Source: Freedom's Journal, December 19, 1828.

Abolitionists Protest British Recognition of the Republic of Texas (1840)

At an adjourned meeting of the committee of the British and Foreign Anti-Slavery Society, held at 27, New Broad Street, London, on Wednesday the 2nd day of December, 1840; Jacob Post, Esq., in the chair—

It was unanimously resolved,

I. That, inasmuch as the system of slavery forms an integral part of the constitutional law of the new republic of Texas, this committee have heard with feelings of the deepest sorrow and humiliation, that Her Majesty's government have been induced to enter into a commercial treaty with its representative, by which act that republic has been introduced to the high distinction of a place amongst the great family of civilized nations; and that thus the moral dignity and national honour of this great country have been outraged, the dearest interests of multitudes of human beings—their liberty and happiness—trampled under foot, a fearful impulse given to slavery and the slave-trade, and the sacred cause of Christianity, civilization, and freedom immeasurably retarded.

II. That, in view of the great fact that the legislature of this country, stimulated by the Christian zeal of its people, has abolished for ever the guilty-traffic in human beings, and terminated the atrocious system of bondage which formerly existed in the British colonies; and that the government has perseveringly, if not hitherto successfully, sought the entire suppression of the foreign slave-trade, at an enormous cost of the national treasure and of human life; the committee cannot but express their great astonishment, as well as their profound regret, that Her Majesty's ministers should have entered into friendly relations with a people whose first act, after a successful but wholly unjustifiable revolt, was to engraft on their constitution the system of slavery, to create a slave trade between the United States and themselves, as well as for the utter expulsion of all free persons of African descent, and the final extirpation of the aboriginal tribes from the soil; and thus to violate every principle of humanity and justice, and to consolidate, extend, and perpetuate slavery and the slave-trade in a country, which, as part of the Mexican Empire, had been previously devoted to freedom.

III. That, therefore, this committee, as the organ of the anti-slavery principles and feelings of the country, feel bound to enter their solemn protest against the recognition of the independence of Texas as a most immoral and impolitic act—alike uncalled for by the justice or the exigency of the case—as fraught with the most injurious consequences to mankind, and as consequently deserving the unqualified reprobation of all good men.

(Signed,)
JACOB POST, Chairman.

Source: The British and Foreign Anti-Slavery Reporter, 1:26 (December 16, 1840).

Abraham Lincoln's "Spot Resolutions" (1847)

Presented to the United States House of Representatives, on December 22, 1847.

Whereas the President of the United States, in his message of May 11, 1846, has declared that "the Mexican Government not only refused to receive him, (the envoy of the United States,) or listen to his propositions, but, after a long-continued series of menaces, has at last invaded *our territory* and shed the blood of our fellow-citizens on our *own soil*":

And again, in his message of December 8, 1846, that "we had ample cause of war against Mexico long before the breaking out of hostilities; but even then we forbore to take redress into our own hands until Mexico herself became the aggressor, by invading *our soil* in hostile array, and shedding the blood of our citizens":

And yet again, in his message of December 7, 1847, that "the Mexican Government refused even to hear the terms of adjustment which he (our minister of peace) was authorized to propose, and finally, under wholly unjustifiable pretexts, involved the two countries in war, by invading the territory of the State of Texas, striking the first blow, and shedding the blood of our citizens on *our own soil.*"

And whereas this House is desirous to obtain a full knowledge of all the facts which go to establish whether the particular spot on which the blood of our citizens was so shed was or was not at that time *our own soil*: Therefore, *Resolved By the House of Representatives,* That the President of the United States be respectfully requested to inform this House—

1st. Whether the spot on which the blood of our citizens was shed, as in his messages declared, was or was not within the territory of Spain, at least after the treaty of 1819, until the Mexican revolution.

2d. Whether that spot is or is not within the territory which was wrested from Spain by the revolutionary Government of Mexico.

3d. Whether that spot is or is not within a settlement of people, which settlement has existed ever since long before the Texas revolution, and until its inhabitants fled before the approach of the United States army.

4th. Whether that settlement is or is not isolated from any and all other settlements by the Gulf and the Rio Grande on the south and west, and by wide uninhabited regions on the north and east.

5th. Whether the people of that settlement, or a majority of them, or any of them, have ever submitted themselves to the government or laws of Texas or the United States, by consent or compulsion, either by accepting office, or voting at elections, or paying tax, or serving on juries, or having process served upon them, or in any other way.

6th. Whether the people of that settlement did or did not flee from the approach of the United States army, leaving unprotected their homes and their growing crops, *before* the blood was shed, as in the messages stated; and whether the first blood, so shed, was or was not shed within the enclosure of one of the people who had thus fled from it.

7th. Whether our *citizens,* whose blood was shed, as in his message declared, were or were not, at that time, armed officers and soldiers, sent into that settlement by the military order of the President, through the Secretary of War.

8th. Whether the military force of the United States was or was not sent into that settlement after General Taylor had more than once intimated to the War Department that, in his opinion, no such movement was necessary to the defence or protection of Texas.

Source: U.S. House Journal, 30th Cong., 1st sess., December 22, 1847.

Frederick Douglass's What to the Slave Is the Fourth of July? (1852)

An address delivered in Rochester, New York, on 5 July 1852.

Fellow Citizens, I am not wanting in respect for the fathers of this republic. The signers of the Declaration of

Independence were brave men. They were great men, too—great enough to give frame to a great age. It does not often happen to a nation to raise, at one time, such a number of truly great men. The point from which I am compelled to view them is not, certainly, the most favorable; and yet I cannot contemplate their great deeds with less than admiration. They were statesmen, patriots and heroes, and for the good they did, and the principles they contended for, I will unite with you to honor their memory. . . .

Fellow-citizens, pardon me, allow me to ask, why am I called upon to speak here to-day? What have I, or those I represent, to do with your national independence? Are the great principles of political freedom and of natural justice, embodied in that Declaration of Independence, extended to us? and am I, therefore, called upon to bring our humble offering to the national altar, and to confess the benefits and express devout gratitude for the blessings resulting from your independence to us?

Would to God, both for your sakes and ours, that an affirmative answer could be truthfully returned to these questions! Then would my task be light, and my burden easy and delightful. For *who* is there so cold, that a nation's sympathy could not warm him? Who so obdurate and dead to the claims of gratitude, that would not thankfully acknowledge such priceless benefits? Who so stolid and selfish, that would not give his voice to swell the hallelujahs of a nation's jubilee, when the chains of servitude had been torn from his limbs? I am not that man. In a case like that, the dumb might eloquently speak, and the "lame man leap as an hart."

But such is not the state of the case. I say it with a sad sense of the disparity between us. I am not included within the pale of glorious anniversary! Your high independence only reveals the immeasurable distance between us. The blessings in which you, this day, rejoice, are not enjoyed in common. The rich inheritance of justice, liberty, prosperity and independence, bequeathed by your fathers, is shared by you, not by me. The sunlight that brought light and healing to you, has brought stripes and death to me. This Fourth [of] July is *yours,* not *mine. You* may rejoice, *I* must mourn. To drag a man in fetters into the grand illuminated temple of liberty, and call upon him to join you in joyous anthems, were inhuman mockery and sacrilegious irony. Do you mean, citizens, to mock me, by asking me to speak to-day? If so, there is a parallel to your conduct. And let me warn you that it is dangerous to copy the example of a nation whose crimes, towering up to heaven, were thrown down by the breath of the Almighty, burying that nation in irrevocable ruin! I can to-day take up the plaintive lament of a peeled and woe-smitten people!

"By the rivers of Babylon, there we sat down. Yea! we wept when we remembered Zion. We hanged our harps upon the willows in the midst thereof. For there, they that carried us away captive, required of us a song; and they who wasted us required of us mirth, saying, Sing us one of the songs of Zion. How can we sing the Lord's song in a strange land? If I forget thee, O Jerusalem, let my right hand forget her cunning. If I do not remember thee, let my tongue cleave to the roof of my mouth."

Fellow-citizens; above your national, tumultuous joy, I hear the mournful wail of millions! whose chains, heavy and grievous yesterday, are, to-day, rendered more intolerable by the jubilee shouts that reach them. If I do forget, if I do not faithfully remember those bleeding children of sorrow this day, "may my right hand forget her cunning, and may my tongue cleave to the roof of my mouth!" To forget them, to pass lightly over their wrongs, and to chime in with the popular theme, would be treason most scandalous and shocking, and would make me a reproach before God and the world. My subject, then fellow-citizens, is AMERICAN SLAVERY. I shall see, this day, and its popular characteristics, from the slave's point of view. Standing, there, identified with the American bondman, making his wrongs mine, I do not hesitate to declare, with all my soul, that the character and conduct of this nation never looked blacker to me than on this 4th of July! Whether we turn to the declarations of the past, or to the professions of the present, the conduct of the nation seems equally hideous and revolting. America is false to the past, false to the present, and solemnly binds herself to be false to the future. Standing with God and the crushed and bleeding slave on this occasion, I will, in the name of humanity which is outraged, in the name of liberty which is fettered, in the name of the constitution and the Bible, which are disregarded and trampled upon, dare to call in question and to denounce, with all the emphasis I can command, everything that serves to perpetuate slavery—the great sin and shame of America! "I will not equivocate; I will not excuse;" I will use the severest language I can command; and yet not one word shall escape me that any man, whose judgment is not blinded by prejudice, or who is not at heart a slaveholder, shall not confess to be right and just.

But I fancy I hear some one of my audience say, it is just in this circumstance that you and your brother abolitionists fail to make a favorable impression on the public mind. Would you argue more, and denounce less, would you persuade more, and rebuke less, your cause would be much more likely to succeed. But, I submit, where all is plain there is nothing to be argued. What point in the anti-slavery creed would you have me argue? On what branch of the subject do the people of this country need light? Must I undertake to prove that the slave is a man? That point is conceded already. Nobody doubts it. The slaveholders themselves acknowledge it in the enactment of laws for their government. They acknowledge it when they punish disobedience on the part of the slave. There are seventy-two crimes in the State of Virginia, which, if committed by a black man, (no matter how ignorant he be), subject him to the punishment of death; while only two of the same crimes will subject a white man to the like punishment. What is this but the acknowledgment that the slave is a moral, intellectual and responsible being? The manhood of the slave is conceded. It is admitted in the fact that Southern statute books are covered with enactments forbidding, under severe fines and penalties, the teaching of the slave to read or to write. When you can point to any such laws, in reference to the beasts of the field, then I may consent to argue the manhood of the slave. When the dogs in your streets, when the fowls of the air, when the cattle on your hills, when the fish of the sea, and the reptiles that crawl, shall be unable to distinguish the slave from a brute, *then* will I argue with you that the slave is a man!

For the present, it is enough to affirm the equal manhood of the negro race. Is it not astonishing that, while we are ploughing, planting and reaping, using all kinds of mechanical tools, erecting houses, constructing bridges, building ships, working in metals of brass, iron, copper, silver and gold; that, while we are reading, writing and ciphering, acting as clerks, merchants and secretaries, having among us lawyers, doctors, ministers, poets, authors, editors, orators and teachers; that, while we are engaged in all manner of enterprises common to other men, digging gold in California, capturing the whale in the Pacific, feeding sheep and cattle on the hill-side, living, moving, acting, thinking, planning, living in families as husbands, wives and children, and, above all, confessing and worshipping the Christian's God, and looking hopefully for life and immortality beyond the grave, we are called upon to prove that we are men!

Would you have me argue that man is entitled to liberty? that he is the rightful owner of his own body? You have already declared it. Must I argue the wrongfulness of slavery? Is that a question for Republicans? Is it to be settled by the rules of logic and argumentation, as a matter beset with great difficulty, involving a doubtful application of the principle of justice, hard to be understood? How should I look to-day, in the presence of Americans, dividing, and subdividing a discourse, to show that men have a natural right to freedom? speaking of it relatively and positively, negatively and affirmatively. To do so, would be to make myself ridiculous, and to offer an insult to your understanding. There is not a man beneath the canopy of heaven, that does not know that slavery is wrong for *him.*

What, am I to argue that it is wrong to make men brutes, to rob them of their liberty, to work them without wages, to keep them ignorant of their relations to their fellow men, to beat them with sticks, to flay their flesh with the lash, to load their limbs with irons, to hunt them with dogs, to sell them at auction, to sunder their families, to knock out their teeth, to burn their flesh, to starve them into obedience and submission to their masters? Must I argue that a system thus marked with blood, and stained with pollution, is *wrong?* No! I will not. I have better employment for my time and strength, than such arguments would imply.

What, then, remains to be argued? Is it that slavery is not divine; that God did not establish it; that our doctors of divinity are mistaken? There is blasphemy in the thought. That which is inhuman, cannot be divine! *Who* can reason on such a proposition? They that can, may; I cannot. The time for such argument is passed.

At a time like this, scorching irony, not convincing argument, is needed. O! had I the ability, and could I reach the nation's ear, I would, to-day, pour out a fiery stream of biting ridicule, blasting reproach, withering sarcasm, and stern rebuke. For it is not light that is needed, but fire; it is not the gentle shower, but thunder. We need the storm, the whirlwind, and the earthquake. The feeling of the nation must be quickened; the conscience of the nation must be roused; the propriety of the nation must be startled; the hypocrisy of the nation must be exposed; and its crimes against God and man must be proclaimed and denounced.

What, to the American slave, is your 4th of July? I answer: a day that reveals to him, more than all other days in the year, the gross injustice and cruelty to which he is the constant victim. To him, your celebration is a sham; your boasted liberty, an unholy license; your national greatness, swelling vanity; your sounds of rejoicing are empty and heartless; your denunciation of tyrants, brass fronted impudence; your shouts of liberty and equality, hollow mockery; your prayers and hymns, your sermons and thanksgivings, with all your religious parade, and solemnity, are, to him, mere bombast, fraud, deception, impiety, and hypocrisy—a thin veil to cover up crimes which would disgrace a nation of savages. There is not a nation on the earth guilty of practices more shocking and bloody than are the people of the United States, at this very hour.

Go where you may, search where you will, roam through all the monarchies and despotisms of the old world, travel through South America, search out every abuse, and when you have found the last, lay your facts by the side of the everyday practices of this nation, and you will say with me, that, for revolting barbarity and shameless hypocrisy, America reigns without a rival. . . .

Allow me to say, in conclusion, notwithstanding the dark picture I have this day presented of the state of the nation, I do not despair of this country. There are forces in operation, which must inevitably work the downfall of slavery. *"The arm of the Lord is not shortened,"* and the doom of slavery is certain. I, therefore, leave off where I began, with *hope*. While drawing encouragement from the Declaration of Independence, the great principles it contains, and the genius of American Institutions, my spirit is also cheered by the obvious tendencies of the age. Nations do not now stand in the same relation to each other that they did ages ago. No nation can now shut itself up from the surrounding world and trot round in the same old path of its fathers without interference. The time *was* when such could be done. Long established customs of hurtful character could formerly fence themselves in, and do their evil work with social impunity. Knowledge was then confined and enjoyed by the privileged few, and the multitude walked on in mental darkness. But a change has now come over the affairs of mankind. Walled cities and empires have become unfashionable. The arm of commerce has borne away the gates of the strong city. Intelligence is penetrating the darkest corners of the globe. It makes its pathway over and under the sea, as well as on the earth. Wind, steam, and lightning are its chartered agents. Oceans no longer divide, but link nations together. From Boston to London is now a holiday excursion. Space is comparatively annihilated.

Thoughts expressed on one side of the Atlantic are distinctly heard on the other.

The far off and almost fabulous Pacific rolls in grandeur at our feet. The Celestial Empire, the mystery of ages, is being solved. The fiat of the Almighty, *"Let there be Light,"* has not yet spent its force. No abuse, no outrage whether in taste, sport or avarice, can now hide itself from the all-pervading light. The iron shoe, and crippled foot of China must be seen, in contrast with nature. *Africa must rise and put on her yet unwoven garment. "Ethiopia shall stretch out her hand unto God."* In the fervent aspirations of William Lloyd Garrison, I say, and let every heart join in saying it:

God speed the year of jubilee
The wide world o'er!
When from their galling chains set free,
Th' oppress'd shall vilely bend the knee,
And wear the yoke of tyranny
Like brutes no more.
That year will come, and freedom's reign, To man
　　his plundered rights again
Restore.

God speed the day when human blood
Shall cease to flow!
In every clime be understood,
The claims of human brotherhood,
And each return for evil, good,
Not blow for blow;
That day will come all feuds to end,
And change into a faithful friend
Each foe.

God speed the hour, the glorious hour,
When none on earth Shall exercise a lordly power,
Nor in a tyrant's presence cower;
But to all manhood's stature tower,
By equal birth!
THAT HOUR WILL COME, to each, to all,
And from his prison-house, to thrall
Go forth.

Until that year, day, hour, arrive,
With head, and heart, and hand I'll strive,
To break the rod, and rend the gyve,
The spoiler of his prey deprive—
So witness Heaven!
And never from my chosen post,
Whate'er the peril or the cost,
Be driven.

Source: Frederick Douglass, "What to the Slave Is the Fourth of July," in *The Life and Writings of Frederick Douglass*, vol. II,

Pre-Civil War Decade, 1850–1860, ed. Philip S. Foner. New York: International Publishers, 1950.

Owen Lovejoy Speaks Out Against the Kansas-Nebraska Act (1855)

Delivered in the House of Representatives, Illinois Legislature, February 6, 1855.

On Joint Resolutions of Instruction to the Illinois Delegation in Congress to Restore the Missouri Compromise Line, &c.

There are several points involved in that preamble, and those resolutions. There is

1st. The question: What are the principles on which this government is based in their application to human slavery?

2nd. What has been the application of those principles? And what ought still to be the application of those principles, through the agency of the Federal Government, in regard to the extension of slavery?

3rd. What is the proper application of those principles, which underlie our government, to the question of admitting into the Union, States, the constitutions of which have not a prohibition of human slavery?

4th. What are the principles of the Constitution of the United States in regard to the subject of slavery, and especially in regard to the recapture or reclamation of persons who have escaped, owing service or labor under the law of the several states?

On these points, Mr. Speaker, I propose to make a few remarks: first, in regard to the question, what are the principles which underlie our government in regard to the question of human slavery?

These principles, Sir, as I understand them find an embodiment and annunciation in the instrument which the framers of the government, early in the struggle of the revolution, with their garments and hands moistened with the blood of that struggle;— the government which they drew up,

[Mr. L. was here interrupted by a message from the Governor to the House.]

I was about to remark Mr. Speaker that the principles which underlie our government found a suitable exposition in the Declaration of Independence.

I trust it will not be considered tedious or inappropriate in the House of Representatives, of a state that has always boasted of its unwavering, unterrified and pure democracy it will not, I say, be regarded out of place or considered tedious, if I repeat a few of the sentiments which are contained in that instrument. It announced them as we all know in the following manner.

"We hold these truths to be self evident, that all men are created free and equal, endowed by their Creator with certain inalienable rights." If you look into the Madison papers and find the original term in brackets you'll find the term included the word "inherent"—"inalienable rights, among which are life, liberty, and the pursuit of happiness." To protect these rights, governments are instituted among men, deriving all their just powers from the consent of the governed. When governments become subversive of these rights, it is the privilege—nay, the declaration goes beyond that, and asserts that is it the duty of the people to overthrow those governments and establish others, upon such principles, and in such forms as to secure these rights. Now, mark you, that was the first embodiment and national proclamation of the great principles of democracy, of human equality. The doctrine that had prevailed was the very reverse of this, the doctrine of the divine right of kings, nobles, lords and earls with a regular graduation on the descending scale till you reached the lowest strata, and there you found the common rabble, the serf, the helot, liegeman and slave.

Our forefathers, deriving their principles and spirit from the old puritan stock, which God selected from the choicest seed of the world, to plant a nation, here declared that these doctrines which had prevailed were untrue, that one man has not a right of a king, and another a peasant. Those long established dogmas, hoary with the powdered wigs of antiquity, were confronted with the great and glorious principle of true democracy that all men are created free and equal. It is the principle of a pure and genuine democracy, that the man whom God has made in his own image and who wears the lineaments of the divine character, has by virtue of a fee simple from the Creator, a title deed to these inherent rights, whether he wields a scepter or guides a plow, whether he was born in a palace or beneath a hedge, and that he possessed these rights of whatever clime, or nation, aye, or whatever color, they inure alike to the pauper whom giant famine lands upon our shores, to the most abject and lash tortured slave that groans in his brutism, and to the rich and princely.

These are the glorious principles which underlie our government; these are the principles of genuine Democracy to which I hold, and planting myself upon them, as upon an immovable rock, pour contempt upon that sham skin-deep democracy of the present day, which would convert our temple of freedom into a slave mart, and make it, like the money changers of old, a den of thieves and robbers.

There are the principles which underlie our government, the principles of Democracy; and I appeal to my democratic friends here if I do not state it truly. Democracy is the evangel of God, applied to civil affairs.

So it is obtained, and I subscribe to it. I subscribe to this article in the creed of genuine Democracy, that man is an immortal being, around whom, cluster those rights, and that they can never be justly, nay, without foul wrong, taken away from him.

These, sir, are the great principles which underlie our government, the principles which form the corner-stone upon which our republic is based—upon which the glorious superstructure, there is no man that can pray more fervently than I that it shall remain as imperishable as the eternal truths and principles upon which it has been reared—*esto perpetus.* Let it be permanent and perpetual, a glorious monument to the wisdom, foresight and patriotism of our fathers.

I now come, Sir, to the second point, the application of these principles—embodied in the Declaration of Independence, and which underlie our federal government—to the extension of slavery. What was the object of its organization! Was it organized to protect slavery in any way? Was this government organized in any wise to extend and propagate slavery! Never. Never, Sir. It is a perversion of the government to apply it to such a purpose, to the accomplishment of these objects.

I ask your attention, sir, to a familiar fact, that as far back as the year 1787, a point contemporaneous with that of the adoption of the Constitutions—that old Virginia, which has been styled the mother of Presidents under the leadership of Jefferson, proposed to cede a certain territory to the United States, making it an express condition of the cession, that slavery should never exist in all that territory, save in the punishment of crime, whereof the person shall be duly convicted:—

[Mr. L. was here interrupted again by a Senate message to the House.]

I was about remarking, Mr. Speaker, that the policy of the federal government, under the influence of the principles upon which that government was based—that the policy of the federal government, from the very outset of its organic existence, had been against the extension of human slavery; and so clearly defined was that policy of the government, and so universally adopted, that by a slave-holder himself, conjointly with a then leading slave-holding State, a proposition was made in the cession of the North-western Territory, that is as a condition of that cession that slavery never should exist throughout all that vast territory, embracing, as you know, what is now a cluster of magnificent States, among which is the Prairie State of Illinois, that is, as I believe, destined to be among the richest and proudest of them all. May she become the freest and most virtuous and intelligent. If we can only get if from under the dominion of the Nebraska democrats, it will be such a State, perhaps even in spite of that.

All this Territory, at that early period, was consecrated to freedom, and free men.—Mark you, Sir, this was all the Territory that then belonged to the United States.—The framers of the Constitution, the very founders of this Republic, imbued as the Preamble to the resolution asserts with the spirit of freedom, with which the very atmosphere was impregnated, utterly prohibited it within that region and forever consecrated it to freedom; and under the influences of that consecration, these States, these Empires have sprung up.

I cannot stop to institute a comparison between these States and an equal number of slave States. That ground has been traveled over, and you know the result.

I wish however, that it be remembered by every gentleman in the House, that from every inch of Territory that belonged to the United States in 1787, slavery, by an act of the Federal Government, was forever excluded.

A word to my friend from Shelby [Moulton], to whom I am indebted for many courtesies in giving me information, which my Legislative inexperience has made valuable. He says that the ordinance of 1787 has not been obeyed by the State of Illinois.—But he is mistaken. If the gentleman will turn to the Constitution of this State, he will find that slavery is forever prohibited here; and although our Statute book unhappily shows too many relics of Legislative barbarism, yet a process of expurgation has been initiated, which will ultimately purge away every vestige of this undemocratic class and caste legislation, as servile as it is unchristian.

There was indeed, a kind of slavery of a limited extent, but nobody seriously pretends that Illinois is a slave State, or ever has been a slave State in any proper sense or common acceptation of the term.

This then, was the policy of the Government at the early period of our history.—Now, we come down from 1787 to 1826—

[Mr. L. was here interrupted by another message from the Senate. After pausing awhile, he playfully remarked—"I administered an expurgative dose to the Senate library the other day and it would seem that the Senate must have found access to some ipecac in quantities larger than Homeopathic." (Laughter)]

I was about coming down to another period on the history of our Government—the facts connected with which have been made somewhat familiar to us by the recent discussion.

The main point I wish to keep in view is this, the cause, the policy of the general Government in the application of these great principles, to the question of extending human slavery; and being necessarily limited to time, I wish to come down at once on the period of 1820—the time that the State of Missouri was admitted into the Union as one of the United States. Hereto, substantially, the same principle has been carried out and applied as in the ordinance of 1787.

What was that Missouri Compromise, of which we hear so much and how has it been violated by the Wilmot Proviso as it is asserted to have been?

I will not go into the minutiae of the history of that Compromise, but the general fact is this, Missouri came and asked for admission into the Union—it's constitution had a clause allowing and protecting human slavery within the limits of the proposed State.—Objection was made against its admission into the Union with its constitution, recognizing and protecting slavery, [thus] its admission was refused.

Congress refused to admit Missouri for the reason that its constitution tolerated slavery and they were right, and if I had been there, and the matter had depended upon my vote, I would have voted against it to this day, and there is where I am opposed to the Missouri Compromise. Slave States, as such, have no more right to come into the Union, than would a company of buccaneers who should get possession of one of the Antilles and adopt the form of a republican Government. The simple question before this nation was "Shall Missouri be admitted into the Union?" Congress said no, we will not receive her, because she is a slave State.—

Then the slave holders began to play a game of scarecrow, which, shame to our want of nerve and backbone, they have frequently and too successfully acted over in grand tragic and comedy style since,

and cried out, "We will dissolve the Union." Here then, was the substance of the Compromise. The slaveholders said virtually to those who were opposed to the admission of Missouri, Now admit Missouri as a slave State, and then, in the bill admitting her, we will insert a clause forever prohibiting slavery in all the Territories north of the line of 36 degrees 20 min., this being the southern boundary of the State.

Now mark you sir and gentlemen of the house, it was not an agreement that slavery should be allowed in all the territories south of that line—nothing in it at all, direct or implied, that slavery might ever go south of that line, much less that such a line should be applied to territories that might subsequently be attained by purchase or otherwise.

In the first place it was all the territory we had not covered by territorial Government, save that which belonged to the Indian tribes. The bargain was, that slavery should be prohibited, nay, in the language of Thomas Benton, whom Democrats will regard as a good authority, abolished in all that territory, and its entrance there utterly prohibited, declaring that it should never defile that virgin soil with its loathsome presence. That is what they declared; this is the whole of the Compromise.

What do we complain of, what do we want! We complain that Senator Douglas in the Senate of [the] U[nited] States, claiming to represent the free people of this state moved, and with the help of his allies and his fellow slaveholders of the south, carried through a motion to repeal that clause that prohibited slavery in that territory; in other words, after having purchased a horse and given a note for it, at less than half its value, they wish to cheat us out of the payment of even that, in other words still, the consideration which the south received and which freedom received for admitting Missouri into the Union as a slaveholding state was, that slavery should be forever prohibited in this territory. They still hold their part of the bargain, and with brazen effrontery, seek to deprive us of the equivalent they were to give; that is the whole of it. They have repealed that prohibition, and now the resolution asks that that prohibition be restored, and that is what is involved in this controversy.

Somehow Douglas never urged the repeal of the Missouri Compromise; if he had, Missouri would have been put out of the Union. If you democratic allies of slavery propagandism won't pay the consideration that we were to receive, then I ask you to throw Missouri out of the Union, and then you have repealed the

Missouri Compromise, and not until then. No, that does not suit them. The democra[ts] have placed themselves in a false position, and I hope I shall convert them before I get through my speech. Yes, Sir, they repealed simply this clause prohibiting slavery. Now, if they will go back and repeal the whole Compromise, I do not care so much about it. We will refuse to admit it into the Union, with the savage and piratical provision in her constitution allowing slavery. Every principal of honor and every principal of common honesty requires the restoration of the prohibition or the exclusion of Missouri. Cancel the entire compact, or let it remain untouched. The morality of holding to their share of the spoils, while ours is wrested from us, does not find its level till you get into the region of swindlers and horse jockeys, and it would require a pretty hardened case, even from the latter gentry, to sell you sprained horse for a sound animal, and then steal him away. This is virtually what has been done by the repeal of the eighth section of the Act to which allusion has been made. This is just the position occupied by the Nebraska Democrats.

This is plain talk I know. [A voice—"It is a fact."] Yes, it is a fact, and the worst of it is I am going to prove it on you gentlemen, [Laughter and applause] the assertion won't hurt you but the established fact will.—

Nay, I am not fighting Senator Douglas particularly, he is a mere item or instrument that the slave power has used in the fraud, although it might not be untimely just now to bring Senator Shields upon the carpet, as we are about to elect a Senator. In extenuation of this crime, for so I choose to designate the transaction, it is pled that they had to obey instructions claiming the legislature had instructed our Senators to do as they have done in this regard. Let us see if this is so.

I will call the attention of the House to a few facts as far back as 1848 or 1849, at which time Senator Douglas declared the principle of the Missouri Compromise was canonized in the hearts of the American people, and that no ruthless hand could be found reckless enough to disturb it.

In 1851 were certain resolutions of instructions requiring our senators to vote for the repeal of the Missouri Compromise, so it is affirmed. This was in 1851. Mark the date. They passed the legislature but who knew it. A gentleman who represented districts in that session was asked if he knew of the passage of any such resolution. He said in reply that he did not recall passage of any such resolutions, but they were in the record.

And more than all Senator Douglas himself never dreamed of it. It never entered his mind that he had been instructed to go for the repeal of the Missouri Compromise. Rather, let us call things by their right names—the repeal of the clause in the acts, which prohibited slavery, but not the repeal of the Missouri Compromise. Senator Douglas did not know that he was instructed in January, February, March, and all the months of 1851 rolled away and he never thought of it. The sun of 1851 came and marked the days and months of that year, and he had not found it out. The same was true of 1853 in as much as the writers of the compromise of 1850 did not deem it necessary to disturb it.

Eighteen hundred and fifty four came and when the morning sun of the New Year arrived, shown in golden beauty upon the earth, Senator Douglas did not know. . . . About the first of January he announced his intention to disturb the Missouri Compromise.

Here are the facts. They cannot be gainsaid. They can be denied but they cannot be disproved. Subsequent to this, during an interval of fifteen days, there was sudden light broke into the mind of the senator. He learned all at once, that three years before, in 1851 he had been instructed to go for the repeal of the clause prohibiting slavery in the Missouri Compromise Act. Fifteen or forty days before, he declared he would not disturb that Compromise; but during this short interval; he had been enlightened, and his conscience began to hurt him because he had not obeyed those instructions.

Do you [Looking toward Mr. Martin] believe it? You like, 'that footed open dealing'? Confess the truth; and say that he has never thought of it until that time—that it was a dodge, a subterfuge, conjured up to cover his nefarious assault on human freedom. He was in favor of this restriction in 1848, 1849, 1850 and up to 1854, but during that fifteen days of remarkable illumination—whether it was the light of heaven or the fiery glare of some other place beneath, that flashed upon his mind, I will not say—a flood of light poured in upon his mind, a sense of unfulfilled obligations pressed upon his soul. The Whigs and abolitionists, so it is said, broke in upon the Compromise in advocating the Wilmot Proviso, and all at once our senator became very complacent, and so yielded to instructions. He concluded to give up the point and go against the Missouri Compromise. Where is my friend here, Mr. Richmond of Schuyler, that was so unterrified? Yes, that unterrified democrat, Stephen A. Douglas, yielded to Whig and abolition pressure, repealed an act that had been en-shrined in the hearts of the American people like the *penates* of the old Romans. Because the Whigs and abolitionists had in 1846 favored the Wilmot Pro-viso, the senator moved this repeal. Who believes that? No living man. See the sophistry of it? It is said by gentlemen on the floor here and I think by my friend from Shelby, Mr. Moulton, that the antislavery men were opposed to the Missouri Compromise line. And why? What evidence is there of it? Because they were in favor of the Wilmot Proviso.

[Mr. Moulton interrupting] I said the aboli-tionists first broke in upon the Missouri Compromise in 1848. They refused to stand by it, when Senator Douglas wanted to extend it to the Pacific—

[Mr. L.—quote] "Thereby hangs a tail." I thank the gentleman for the word. There was no guarantee, Sir, that the Missouri line should extend westward to the Pacific. What was the Missouri Compromise, I again ask—It was a prohibition of slavery in a given territory. It was substantially all the territory we had; and we prohibited slavery in it. I want the gentleman, the unterrified, to understand it, if it is possible for them to do so. We agreed to admit Missouri as a slave state, if slavery should be prohibited in the remaining part of the Louisiana Purchase. Beyond that, we had no territory at the time. We had no territory but the Northwest Territory in 1787, and slavery was ex-cluded from that by the act of cession and a clause in the ordinance of 1787. In 1820 we admitted Missouri and excluded slavery from all the territory we then had, save the Indian Territory. Meanwhile, in 1848 we had acquired new territory in our war with Mexico, and the slaveholders desired us to renew the bargain of 1820. The Missouri Compromise did not bind us to any such thing, neither by word nor by implication. We were under no obligation whatsoever to go for a similar line, extending to the Pacific Ocean. And now in 1848 the question came up—shall we apply the principles of prohibition to all this territory?—Territory that we had acquired. We said, "Yes." It was simply this: suppose you own a section of land and you own it in conjunction with another individual, and you agree that it shall be divided so and so and that a portion of it shall be cultivated, and another portion to be given to thistles and brambles [so it] shall run to waste. Afterwards you buy another section of land: does it follow that the same division is to take place? This is preposterous. The Missouri Compro-mise was a settlement as to the admission of Missouri and the prohibition of slavery in Kansas and Nebraska

and had no reference to territories afterwards ac-quired. I deny utterly and forever here and every-where, in the House and out of the House, by moon light and sunlight and gas light and star light, on the road, in the cars and in the mobank,—that we ever agreed or are under any obligation formal or by impli-cation to apply this dividing line to any new territory which we might acquire. That is a figment of the imagination. Such a claim is as unsubstantial and un-real as "the baseless fabric of a dream." We never agreed, and in the name of liberty, we never will agree to it. I desire that these two points be kept in mind— the admission of Missouri into the Union, and the prohibition of slavery in Kansas and Nebraska. This was the whole of it. The prohibition has been re-pealed, the barrier has been broken down, and slavery, as it were, invited in to take possession of that glori-ous and far-reaching territory, extending as it does, to forty-nine degrees north latitude, and stretching westward to the snowcapped summits of the Rocky Mountains. It is all broken down, sir, and slavery is in-vited to enter in, to take possession, to curse it with the blight and mildew of its presence. And the ruth-less hand that recklessly accomplished this impious demolition was that of Senator Douglas aided by the vote of Senator Shields, not under the instructions of the people of Illinois, but of the slaveholders. "But," says a Nebraska friend,—(I don't like to call you a democrat, for you don't deserve that title, we have got your principles, and would be glad to take possession of the name which you have desecrated)—"why we propose to leave it to the people of the territory there, we do not propose to interfere one way or another, but let the people do as they please." In reply to this, I say that according to our theory, and as our government has been administered from the very outset, the Con-gress of the United States is the government of the territories. The territories are under the exclusive ju-risdiction of the people of the United States, and I as one of the people have the right to a voice in this mat-ter just as much as though I lived upon the soil. They have no more right to the exclusive jurisdiction over that territory than one partner has to the exclusive control of the affairs of the company. The territory of the United States is different from the states, we have jurisdiction over it.

I have other objections to this "squatter sover-eignty" doctrine as it is preached. I do not admit that these "sovereigns" or any other sovereigns have any right to convert man into a chattel, into goods, into four-footed beasts. I tell you, gentlemen, they have no authority to do it. I do not believe such a transformation is right, whether expressed by the people of the territory, or by the state, or by the czar of Russia, and the one has the same right as the other—

No power on earth has the right to make a man a slave; in doing so, you trample upon the principles of the Declaration of Independence. They have no right to blot out his humanity and convert him into a thing and carry him to market, as they would a mere brute. I deny in the name of the great principles of the Revolution—in the name of a common God, and a common father, I deny this right to anybody and everybody. God made that man as he made you and me in his own image, and the sanction of his authority is around him. Sir, you had better take your foot from his neck, you might as well trample the Son of God. He is degraded, I know. He is often vicious, I grant it.—He is often ignorant, repulsive: I do not deny it, but he is still a man. With the germ of immortal existence buried beneath this outside rubbish, though defaced, crippled, coffined, and confined, there is the divine miniature, and you "squatter sovereigns," I repeat, had better take your feet from off him. If that is the case, some one may ask, why don't you go for abolishing slavery in the states? I do not go for it simply because I do not have the power. If I had the power, you could rely upon my doing. Had I the power, I would abolish serfdom in Russia. If I had the power, I would dot the European continent all over with republics. I have no power to enter the state of South Carolina and abolish slavery there by an act of Congress than I have to go into Brazil and abolish it there. But we have the power to do it in territories as they are under the exclusive jurisdiction of the people of the United States.

Now, Sir, I want these resolutions to pass. I want the resolution that require[s] our senators to use their best endeavors to rescue the prohibition of slavery in all our territories to pass. Nobody contends that the federal government has not a clear right to say to slavery that it shall never occupy one square foot of earth belonging to the United States. All must concede that they have the right to say to this system, so fraught with evil; thus far shall thou come and no farther; here let thy dark wave be stayed. I want to instruct Senator Douglas and Shields to vote for a bill applying the prohibition to Kansas and Nebraska and then extend it south and west till it guards as the cherubims guarded the paradise of God. Every inch of territory over which the stars and stripes, the glorious banner of my country, waves, the emblem of exclusive jurisdiction.

Now, gentlemen, will you not vote for these resolutions? Are they not right? Don't you believe it is the duty of our senator to vote for such a bill whether you be Whigs or Democrats? Ought it not really to be the policy to be adopted by the Government of the United States? That is one of the planks of the Republican Party. The party that has stepped forth like Minerva from the head of Jupiter, full grown and fully equipt for battle, and has already in deed gained no inconsiderable victories—and here is one old, fanatical abolitionist voting with the majority in the Illinois legislature.

[A voice—"Your allies deny that you are an abolitionist."]

If anyone denies I am an abolitionist he denies erroneously. I have no doubt what is the truth.

I am an abolitionist.
I glory in the name.
Though now by slavery's imminence hissed
And covered with shame,
It is a spell of light and power
The watch word of the free;
Who spares it in the trial hour,
A craven soul is he.
[Applause.]

Some of you may be enlightened as to what abolitionism is. My abolitionism is just what I state here. I do not acknowledge it to be all you may fancy it.—I can hardly refrain from a smile sometimes. Ask a simple act of justice for the poor Negro, that he may have the means of education, and up starts my friend here, and exclaims, "Oh! You want to bring them up on a social equality with the whites—you want to marry them, do you?" When I hear them and similar remarks on such occasions it reminds me of an anecdote related of Lady Wortley Montague and Fox. Fox: passing the evening at the home of the former had the misfortune to displease her ladyship, and she, rather petulant, retorted in language allowable at that age, that she didn't care three skips of a louse for him. Fox immediately wrote impromptu:

A lady hath told me, and in her own house,
She cares not for me three skips of a louse.
I forgive the dear creature of what she has said
For a woman still thinks of what runs in her head.
[Laughter and applause.]

It must be that this thing is running in the head of these gentlemen, this amalgamation idea, I mean. [Applause.]

I have digressed, as ministers sometimes will in their discourse. Where was I? Ah. I was speaking in regard to the platform of the Republican Party that, in one of our planks, made of live oak, and it in a craft that is going to run out every storm and already glides over the waters as gracefully as the barge of Cleopatra. Thus I may in one article of our creed that it is constitutional for the American people to prohibit slavery in the territory of the United States, and that it is a sacred obligation which they owe to their country, to the world and to their God to do it.

Another plank in our craft is this: the admission of no more slave states into the union. I would indeed be willing to leave it to any people, so far as the practical result is concurred, to say whether it should be a slave state. Sixty thousand people cannot be found on earth who will vote slavery into a territory, not contaminated with its presence. If you will keep it out until they have inhabitants enough to organize a state government, they will not introduce it.

As for the other plank, the Fugitive Slave Law, as it is called, I wish to remark, so far as the Fugitive Slave Law is concerned in the title, I do not think it is unconstitutional, because it uses in the title of the bill the language of the constitution. I shall in my remarks consider it not a law to return persons owing service of labor, but as a law for the recapture and return of fugitive slaves. I hold it to be in its practical workings, unconstitutional, and if you will bear with me a single moment, I want to take this ground that the constitution of the United States nowhere recognizes, much less guarantees the right of property in man. Now that is not abolition fanaticism, it is a clear legal truth, and a truth that will be admitted sooner or later, that the constitution of the United States recognizes no right of property in man. It says nothing about slavery, nothing in the letter and certainly nothing in the spirit.—It only speaks of persons held to service or labor under the law of the state: according to Madison's own expressed declaration, he would not recognize the idea of property in man. I have the Madison Papers here, and if any gentleman wishes to see them he can in these debates. Madison repudiated the idea of recognizing property in man, he would not use the word servant or servitude, lest it should be so construed, and instead of it, he would employ the terms "person" and "labor" or "service." And, sir, they did this intentionally, because they would not admit the idea of property in man. The interpretation that has been put upon the constitution making it guarantee slavery is traditional, and like most traditions,

false. It is not the idea of the language; it is not the spirit of the constitution of the United States. But someone will say it means something. I grant it, let us see what it does. . . .

[A voice from the opposition—"What did Jefferson say?"] He said, he trembled for his country when he remembered that God was just, and that his justice would not sleep forever, and that in the event of a servile war, there was no attribute of this just God that would take sides with us. He said that the little finger of American slavery was thicker than the loins of British slavery—this is what Jefferson said. Does the gentleman want any further quotations?

The constitution says, "any person held to service or labor—that is all the foundation that the act has: it is the basis of the fugitive slave law. Now I declare to you honestly, I am in favor of executing that clause of the constitution, but I believe the Fugitive Slave Law unconstitutional for several reasons.

In the first place, Congress has no business with the subject. And to express this power is an invasion of states' rights. It is the business of the states and not of the federal government to execute that clause. Read the fourth article of the Constitution. It defines the duties which the states owe to each other, and what they shall not do. . . . Any person charged with a felony or any other crime, who shall run from justice, shall be delivered to be moved to the state having jurisdiction of the crime.

Suppose a man commits murder in Missouri and escapes into Illinois, who delivers him up? The federal constitution—know the executive of the state. And so in regard to the next clause, where persons held to service or labor are to be delivered up—the conclusion in my own mind after examining this whole subject that it is the business of the state and not of the federal government to execute the clause under consideration. It is our business to take them up and send them back or rather to let them be taken back. But you return a slave under any circumstances. I would have a state law and extend to the latter this clause of the constitution, and with it before a jury you can prove that a man owes service or labor. I will be part of that jury to send him back. I will send back anyone who owes service or labor, whether it be an indentured apprentice, an immigrant pledged to work for his passage money, or the person who has bargained for so many—and dodged the contract. The slave does not owe service or labor under the law of the slave states and though it has been the wild vagaries of a fanatic now, it will yet be the established doctrine in the construction of the constitution, that the slave does not owe service or labor under the laws of the slave states. He is not held to service or labor by these laws. In Kentucky, for instance, he is made an article of property by the laws the same as a horse or an ox. The law places him as a piece of property at the feet of the master, and he whips the labor out of him if necessary. If the slave runs away in order to proclaim him, the master does not obtain a magistrate's warrant, he takes his dogs and finding him heads him back as he would his stray horse or ox. It would be a fine operation for a constable to take out a warrant from a justice of the peace and seizing the old brindle ox by the horn or the old gray mare by the mane, read his warrant and arrest them in the name of the Christian people of the palmetto State. Now a slave is no more held to service or labor by the laws of a slave state than the horse he drives or the plow he holds. The constitution of the United States was ordained to establish and secure the blessings of liberty to ourselves and our posterity. It was not ordained to hunt men and women, for this is to establish injustice and secure the cursor of slavery. No, Sir, it is not nominated in the bond: and I am like the disguised Portia pleading for the unfortunate merchant; if slavery, like the old Jew Shylock will have its pound of flesh, it shall not have a drop of blood. I will not yield one inch of slavery beyond what the Constitution demands. I am going on the very verge of the constitution against it as Franklin declared he would. I understand that it is a duty of the states to deliver up those who escape from justice. Let the state do this and take it out of the hands of the federal government.

I have many objections against the Fugitive Slave Law, mighty and insuperable. I object to it because, as I have said, it imposes upon us obligations that the constitution does not require. I object to it because it requires of us a repulsive and degrading service—that it requires of the north a duty—I will not dignify it by calling it a duty—it requires of us a service against which our nature, our humanity, with all our sense of justice and right revolts. Ask an honorable slaveholder if he will thus pursue a fugitive slave, and he will say no. They usually employ some drunken, degraded, vagabond, the very dregs of society—some miserable bloated retch to perform this drudgery for them, and when this scum reaches a free state, the law calls upon us, all of us, to transform ourselves into four footed beasts and chase down the fugitive. I repeat, it is degrading to us as American citizens, American free men, to do this. Sir, I have seen three fugitives within the last three months. One, I recollect, without the least trace of African descent—fair, graceful, and educated, and betrothed to the man of her choice, fleeing from a wretched libertine who had purchased her, and doomed her to a fate worse than death, asked me for shelter and protection.—

Now, what does your Fugitive Slave bill ask of me? It asks me to seize this young woman, to fetter and mangle her, and drag her back to the possession of that . . . Libertine. Do you want me to do it?

For American citizens who come down and transform themselves into hunters of men? I know of no such transformation. I have read the metamorphoses of Ovid, which teemed in his fertile imagination. There was the change of one of their deities into a beautiful animal; there was a change of a beautiful lady into a tree weeping blood; there was the change of a hunter into a deer, and devoured by his dogs; and there was the Cirecan transformation of men into swine. All these I have read of, but none of them so revolting as the transmogrifying as American citizen into a slave catcher. The only thing that resembles it, was the transformation of an archangel into a toad.

"I would rather be a dog and bay at the moon, I would a kitten and cry mew," before I would be such a citizen. My Nebraska friends, if you fancy this transformation, you may make the experiment, but I apprise you, if they get on the Underground Railroad, they are safe in spite of you.

I have but a word or two more in conclusion. I have traced the principles which underlie our government in their application to the extension of slavery; then, in the admission of new states and as found in the constitution in the application to the Fugitive Slave Law; in these in the main are the planks that go to make up the Republican platform. I want simply to express my confident belief that these principles will triumph—that they will prevail. I was struck with the thought in the discussion of a little railroad down south (mound city road). In regard to that railroad, gentlemen who discussed the matter had become "higher law" men, and they did not want to fight against providence. They did not wish to oppose nature. Now, gentlemen, you can fight against the elements, you can build cities upon quagmires—the magnificent city St. Petersburg is so founded and sits there queen of the north. Man can overcome the elements. Mind is continually gaining the mastery over matter. It tunnels the mountains, it makes a pathway under the river, and the lightning's even come and say "Here we are, ready to carry your message." But you cannot overcome God's truth. I was pleased with the ability and courtesy with which the young gentlemen conducted the discussion yesterday. Let me entreat them to disregard mere party ties, and consecrate themselves to a high and honorable ambition to serve their country and their race, then, gentlemen, looking back upon your lives, you can say—*eregi monumentum area perennius non omnis motar.*

> Fear not: scorn the worldling laughter;
> Thine ambition trample thou:
> Thou shall find a long hereafter
> To be more than tempts thee now.
> O let all that tempts within thee
> For the truth's sake go ahead
> Strike that every nerve and sinew
> Tell on ages tell for God.

Source: The Western Citizen, April 5, 1855.

Abraham Lincoln's "House Divided" Speech (1858)

Mr. President and Gentlemen of the Convention,

If we could first know *where* we are, and *whither* we are tending, we could then better judge *what* to do, and *how* to do it.

We are now far into the *fifth* year, since a policy was initiated, with the *avowed* object, and *confident* promise, of putting an end to slavery agitation.

Under the operation of that policy, that agitation has not only, *not ceased,* but has *constantly augmented.*

In *my* opinion, it will not cease, until a *crisis* shall have been reached, and passed.

"A house divided against itself cannot stand."

I believe this government cannot endure, permanently half *slave* and half *free.*

I do not expect the Union to be *dissolved*—I do not expect the house to *fall*—but I *do* expect it will cease to be divided.

It will become *all* one thing, or *all* the other.

Either the *opponents* of slavery, will arrest the further spread of it, and place it where the public mind shall rest in the belief that it is in course of ultimate extinction; or its *advocates* will push it forward, till it shall become alike lawful in all the States, old as well as *new*—North as well as *South.*

Have we no *tendency* to the latter condition?

Let any one who doubts, carefully contemplate that now almost complete legal combination—piece of machinery so to speak—compounded of the Nebraska doctrine, and the Dred Scott decision. Let him consider not only *what work* the machinery is adapted to do, and *how well* adapted; but also, let him study the *history* of its construction, and trace, if he can, or rather *fail,* if he can, to trace the evidences of design, and concert of action, among its chief bosses, from the beginning.

The new year of 1854 found slavery excluded from more than half the States by State Constitutions, and from most of the national territory by Congressional prohibition.

Four days later, commenced the struggle, which ended in repealing that Congressional prohibition.

This opened all the national territory to slavery; and was the first point gained.

But, so far, *Congress* only, had acted; and an *indorsement* by the people, *real* or apparent, was indispensable, to *save* the point already gained, and give chance for more.

This necessity had not been overlooked; but had been provided for, as well as might be, in the notable argument of *"squatter sovereignty,"* otherwise called *"sacred right of self government,"* which latter phrase, though expressive of the only rightful basis of any government, was so perverted in this attempted use of it as to amount to just this: That if any *one* man choose to enslave *another,* no *third* man shall be allowed to object.

That argument was incorporated into the Nebraska bill itself, in the language which follows: *"It being the true intent and meaning of this act not to legislate slavery into any Territory or state, not exclude it therefrom; but to leave the people thereof perfectly free to form and regulate their domestic institutions in their own way, subject only to the Constitution of the United States."*

Then opened the roar of loose declamation in favor of "Squatter Sovereignty," and "Sacred right of self government."

"But," said opposition members, "let us be more *specific*—let us *amend* the bill so as to expressly declare that the people of the territory *may* exclude slavery." "Not we," said the friends of the measure; and down they voted the amendment.

While the Nebraska bill was passing through congress, a *law case,* involving the question of a negroe's freedom, by reason of his owner having voluntarily taken him first into a free state and then a territory covered by the congressional prohibition, and held him as a slave, for a long time in each, was passing through the U. S. Circuit Court for the District of Missouri; and both Nebraska bill and law suit were brought to a decision in the same month of May, 1854. The negroe's name was "Dred Scott," which name now designates the decision finally made in the case.

Before the *then* next Presidential election, the law case came *to,* and was argued *in* the Supreme Court of the United States; but the *decision* of it was deferred until after the election. Still, *before* the election, Senator Trumbull, on the floor of the Senate, requests the leading advocate of the Nebraska bill to state *his opinion* whether the people of a territory can constitutionally exclude slavery from their limits; and the latter answers, "That is a question for the Supreme Court."

The election came. Mr. Buchanan was elected, and the indorsement, such as it was, secured. That was the *second* point gained. The indorsement, however, fell short of a clear popular majority by nearly four hundred thousand votes, and so, perhaps, was not overwhelmingly reliable and satisfactory.

The *outgoing* President, in his last annual message, as impressively as possible *echoed back* upon the people the *weight* and *authority* of the indorsement.

The Supreme Court met again; *did not* announce their decision, but ordered a re-argument.

The Presidential inauguration came, and still no decision of the court; but the *incoming* President, in his inaugural address, fervently exhorted the people to abide by the forthcoming decision, *whatever it might be.*

Then, in a few days, came the decision.

The reputed author of the Nebraska bill finds an early occasion to make a speech at this capitol indorsing the Dred Scott Decision, and vehemently denouncing all opposition to it.

The new President, too, seizes the early occasion of the Silliman letter to *indorse* and strongly *construe* that decision, and to express his *astonishment* that any different view had ever been entertained.

At length a squabble springs up between the President and the author of the Nebraska bill, on the *mere* question of *fact,* whether the Lecompton constitution was or was not, in any just sense, made by the people of Kansas; and in that squabble the latter declares that all he wants is a fair vote for the people, and that he *cares* not whether slavery be voted *down* or voted *up.* I do not understand his declaration that he cares not whether slavery be voted down or voted up, to be intended by him other than as an *apt definition* of the *policy* he would impress upon the public mind—the *principle* for which he declares he has suffered much, and is ready to suffer to the end.

And well may he cling to that principle. If he has any parental feeling, well may he cling to it. That principle, is the only *shred* left of his original Nebraska doctrine. Under the Dred Scott decision, "squatter sovereignty" squatted out of existence, tumbled down like temporary scaffolding—like the mould at the foundry served through one blast and fell back into loose sand—helped to carry an election, and then was kicked to the winds. His late *joint* struggle with the Republicans, against the Lecompton Constitution, involves nothing of the original Nebraska doctrine. That struggle was made on a point, the right of a people to make their own constitution, upon which he and the Republicans have never differed.

The several points of the Dred Scott decision, in connection with Senator Douglas' "care not" policy, constitute the piece of machinery, in its *present* state of advancement. This was the third point gained.

The *working* points of that machinery are:

First, that no negro slave, imported as such from Africa, and no descendant of such slave can ever be a *citizen* of any State, in the sense of that term as used in the Constitution of the United States.

This point is made in order to deprive the negro, in every possible event, of the benefit of this provision of the United States Constitution, which declares, that—

"The citizens of each State shall be entitled to all privileges and immunities of citizens in the several States."

Secondly, that "subject to the Constitution of the United States," neither *Congress* nor a *Territorial Legislature* can exclude slavery from any United States territory.

This point is made in order that individual men may *fill up* the territories with slaves, without danger of losing them as property, and thus to enhance the chances of *permanency* to the institution through all the future.

Thirdly, that whether the holding a negro in actual slavery in a free State, makes him free, as against the holder, the United States courts will not decide, but will leave to be decided by the courts of any slave State the negro may be forced into by the master.

This point is made, not to be pressed *immediately*; but, if acquiesced in for a while, and apparently *indorsed* by the people at an election, *then* to sustain the logical conclusion that what Dred Scott's master might lawfully do with Dred Scott, in the free State of Illinois, every other master may lawfully do with any other *one,* or one *thousand* slaves, in Illinois, or in any other free State.

Auxiliary to all this, and working hand in hand with it, the Nebraska doctrine, or what is left of it, is to *educate* and *mould* public opinion, at least *Northern* public opinion, to not *care* whether slavery is voted *down* or voted *up.*

This shows exactly where we now *are*; and *partially* also, whither we are tending.

It will throw additional light on the latter, to go back, and run the mind over the string of historical facts already stated. Several things will *now* appear less *dark* and *mysterious* than they did *when* they were transpiring. The people were to be left "perfectly free" "subject only to the Constitution." What the *Constitution* had to do with it, outsiders could not *then* see. Plainly enough *now,* it was an exactly fitted *niche,* for the Dred Scott decision to afterwards come in, and declare the *perfect freedom* of the people, to be just no freedom at all.

Why was the amendment, expressly declaring the right of the people to exclude slavery, voted down? Plainly enough *now,* the adoption of it, would have spoiled the niche for the Dred Scott decision.

Why was the court decision held up? Why, even a Senator's individual opinion withheld, till *after* the Presidential election? Plainly enough *now,* the speaking out *then* would have damaged the *"perfectly free"* argument upon which the election was to be carried.

Why the *outgoing* President's felicitation on the indorsement? Why the delay of a reargument? Why the incoming President's *advance* exhortation in favor of the decision?

These things *look* like the cautious *patting* and *petting* a spirited horse, preparatory to mounting him, when it is dreaded that he may give the rider a fall.

And why the hasty after indorsements of the decision by the President and others?

We can not absolutely *know* that all these exact adaptations are the result of preconcert. But when we see a lot of framed timbers, different portions of which we know have been gotten out at different times and places and by different workmen—Stephen, Franklin, Roger and James, for instance—and when we see these timbers joined together, and see they exactly make the frame of a house or a mill, all the tenons and mortices exactly fitting, and all the lengths and proportions of the different pieces exactly adapted to their respective places, and not a piece too many or too few—not omitting even scaffolding—or, if a single piece be lacking, we can see the place in the frame exactly fitted and prepared to yet bring such piece in—in *such* a case, we find it impossible to not *believe* that Stephen and Franklin and Roger and James all understood one another from the beginning, and all worked

upon a common *plan* or *draft* drawn up before the first lick was struck.

It should not be overlooked that, by the Nebraska bill, the people of a State as well as *Territory,* were to be left "perfectly free" "subject only to the Constitution."

Why mention a *State?* They were legislating for *territories,* and not *for* or *about* States. Certainly the people of a State *are* and *ought to be* subject to the Constitution of the United States; but why is mention of this *lugged* into this merely *territorial law?* Why are the people of a *territory* and the people of a *state* therein *lumped* together, and their relation to the Constitution therein treated as being *precisely* the same?

While the opinion of *the Court,* by Chief Justice Taney, in the Dred Scott case, and the separate opinions of all the concurring Judges, expressly declare that the Constitution of the United States neither permits Congress nor a Territorial legislature to exclude slavery from any United States territory, they all *omit* to declare whether or not the same Constitution permits a *state,* or the people of a State, to exclude it.

Possibly, this was a mere *omission;* but who can be *quite* sure, if McLean or Curtis had sought to get into the opinion a declaration of unlimited power in the people of a state to exclude slavery from their limits, just as Chase and Macy sought to get such declaration, in behalf of the people of a territory, into the Nebraska bill—I ask, who can be quite *sure* that it would not have been voted down, in the one case, as it had been in the other.

The nearest approach to the point of declaring the power of a State over slavery, is made by Judge Nelson. He approaches it more than once, using the precise idea, and *almost* the language too, of the Nebraska act. On one occasion his exact language is, "except in cases where the power is restrained by the Constitution of the United States, the law of the State is supreme over the subject of slavery within its jurisdiction."

In what *cases* the power of the *states is* so restrained by the U.S. Constitution, is left an *open* question, precisely as the same question, as to the restraint on the power of the *territories* was left open in the Nebraska act. Put *that* and *that* together, and we have another nice little niche, which we may, ere long, see filled with another Supreme Court decision, declaring that the Constitution of the United States does not permit a state to exclude slavery from its limits.

And this may especially be expected if the doctrine of "care not whether slavery be voted *down* or voted *up*," shall gain upon the public mind sufficiently to give promise that such a decision can be maintained when made.

Such a decision is all that slavery now lacks of being alike lawful in all the States.

Welcome or unwelcome, such decision *is* probably coming, and will soon be upon us, unless the power of the present political dynasty shall be met and overthrown.

We shall *lie down* pleasantly dreaming that the people of *Missouri* are on the verge of making their State *free*; and we shall *awake to the reality*, instead, that the *Supreme* Court has made *Illinois* a *slave* State.

To meet and overthrow the power of that dynasty, is the work now before all those who would prevent that consummation.

That is *what* we have to do.

But *how* can we best do it?

There are those who denounce us *openly* to their *own* friends, and yet whisper *us softly*, that *Senator Douglas* is the *aptest* instrument there is, with which to effect that object. *They* do *not* tell us, nor has *he* told us, that he *wishes* any such object to be effected. They wish us to *infer* all, from the facts, that he now has a little quarrel with the present head of the dynasty; and that he has regularly voted with us, on a single point, upon which, he and we, have never differed.

They remind us that *he* is a very *great man,* and that the largest of *us* are very small ones. Let this be granted. But "a *living dog* is better than a *dead lion*." Judge Douglas, if not a *dead* lion *for this work,* is at least a *caged* and *toothless* one. How can he oppose the advances of slavery? He don't *care* anything about it. His avowed *mission is impressing* the "public heart" to *care* nothing about it.

A leading Douglas Democratic newspaper thinks Douglas' superior talent will be needed to resist the revival of the African slave trade.

Does Douglas believe an effort to revive that trade is approaching? He has not said so. Does he really *think* so? But if it is, how can he resist it? For years he has labored to prove it is a *sacred right* of white men to take negro slaves into the new territories. Can he possibly show that it is *less* a sacred right to *buy* them where they can be bought cheapest? And, unquestionably they can be bought *cheaper in Africa* than in *Virginia.*

He has done all in his power to reduce the whole question of slavery to one of a mere *right of property*; and as such, how can *he* oppose the foreign slave trade—how can he refuse that trade in that "property" shall be "perfectly free"—unless he does it as a *protection* to the home production? And as the home *producers* will probably not *ask* the protection, he will be wholly without a ground of opposition.

Senator Douglas holds, we know, that a man may rightfully be *wiser to-day* than he was *yesterday*—that he may rightfully *change* when he finds himself wrong.

But, can we for that reason, run ahead, and *infer* that he *will* make any particular change, of which he, himself, has given no intimation? Can we *safely* base *our* action upon any such *vague* inference?

Now, as ever, I wish to not *misrepresent* Judge Douglas' *position*, question his *motives*, or do ought that can be personally offensive to him.

Whenever, *if ever,* he and we can come together on *principle* so that *our great cause* may have assistance from *his great ability,* I hope to have interposed no adventitious obstacle.

But clearly, he is not *now* with us—he does not *pretend* to be—he does not *promise* to ever be.

Our cause, then, must be intrusted to, and conducted by its own undoubted friends—those whose hands are free, whose hearts are in the work—who *do care* for the result.

Two years ago the Republicans of the nation mustered over thirteen hundred thousand strong.

We did this under the single impulse of resistance to a common danger, with every external circumstance against us.

Of *strange, discordant,* and even, *hostile* elements, we gathered from the four winds, and *formed* and fought the battle through, under the constant hot fire of a disciplined, proud, and pampered enemy.

Did we brave all *then,* to *falter* now?—*now*—when that same enemy is *wavering,* dissevered and belligerent?

The result is not doubtful. We shall not fail—if we stand firm, we shall not fail.

Wise councils may *accelerate* or *mistakes delay* it, but, sooner or later the victory is *sure* to come.

Source: Abraham Lincoln, "The House Divided Speech, June 16, 1858," in *Abraham Lincoln: A Documentary Portrait Through His Speeches and Writings,* ed. Don E. Fehrenbacher. Stanford, CA: Stanford University Press, 1964.

The Freeport Doctrine (1858)

Excerpt from the second of the Lincoln-Douglas debates, held August 27, 1858, in Freeport, Illinois {Mr. Lincoln has just spoken}.

DOUGLAS'S REPLY
Ladies and Gentlemen:

The silence with which you have listened to Mr. Lincoln during his hour is creditable to this vast audience, composed of men of various political parties. Nothing is more honorable to any large mass of people assembled for the purpose of a fair discussion, than that kind and respectful attention that is yielded not only to your political friends, but to those who are opposed to you in politics.

I am glad that at last I have brought Mr. Lincoln to the conclusion that he had better define his position on certain political questions to which I called his attention at Ottawa. He there showed no disposition, no inclination to answer them. I did not present idle questions for him to answer merely for my gratification. I laid the foundation for those interrogatories by showing that they constituted the platform of the party whose nominee he is for the Senate. I did not presume that I had the right to catechise him as I saw proper, unless I showed that his party, or a majority of it, stood upon the platform and were in favor of the propositions upon which my questions were based. I desired simply to know, inasmuch as he had been nominated as the first, last, and only choice of his party, whether he concurred in the platform which that party had adopted for its government. In a few moments I will proceed to review the answers which he has given to these interrogatories; but in order to relieve his anxiety I will first respond to these which he has presented to me. Mark you, he has not presented interrogatories which have ever received the sanction of the party with which I am acting, and hence he has no other foundation for them than his own curiosity. ["That's a fact."]

First, he desires to know if the people of Kansas shall form a constitution by means entirely proper and unobjectionable and ask admission into the Union as a state, before they have the requisite population for a member of Congress, whether I will vote for that admission. Well, now, I regret exceedingly that he did not answer that interrogatory himself before he put it to me, in order that we might understand, and not be left to infer, on which side he is. ["Good, good."] Mr. Trumbull, during the last session of Congress, voted from the beginning to the

end against the admission of Oregon, although a free state, because she had not the requisite population for a member of Congress. ["That's it."] Mr. Trumbull would not consent, under any circumstances, to let a state, free or slave, come into the Union until it had the requisite population. As Mr. Trumbull is in the field, fighting for Mr. Lincoln, I would like to have Mr. Lincoln answer his own question and tell me whether he is fighting Trumbull on that issue or not. ["Good, put it to him," and cheers.] But I will answer his question. In reference to Kansas; it is my opinion, that as she has population enough to constitute a slave state, she has people enough for a free state. [Cheers.] I will not make Kansas an exceptional case to the other states of the Union. ["Sound," and "hear, hear."] I hold it to be a sound rule of universal application to require a territory to contain the requisite population for a member of Congress, before it is admitted as a state into the Union. I made that proposition in the Senate in 1856, and I renewed it during the last session, in a bill providing that no territory of the United States should form a constitution and apply for admission until it had the requisite population. On another occasion I proposed that neither Kansas, [n]or any other territory, should be admitted until it had the requisite population. Congress did not adopt any of my propositions containing this general rule, but did make an exception of Kansas. I will stand by that exception. [Cheers.] Either Kansas must come in as a free state, with whatever population she may have, or the rule must be applied to all the other territories alike. [Cheers.] I therefore answer at once, that it having been decided that Kansas has people enough for a slave state, I hold that she has enough for a free state. ["Good," and applause.] I hope Mr. Lincoln is satisfied with my answer; ["he ought to be," and cheers,] and now I would like to get his answer to his own interrogatory—whether or not he will vote to admit Kansas before she has the requisite population. ["Hit him again."] I want to know whether he will vote to admit Oregon before that territory has the requisite population. Mr. Trumbull will not, and the same reason that commits Mr. Trumbull against the admission of Oregon, commits him against Kansas, even if she should apply for admission as a free state. ["You've got him," and cheers.] If there is any sincerity, any truth in the argument of Mr. Trumbull in the Senate against the admission of Oregon because she had not 93,420 people, although her population was larger than that of Kansas, he stands pledged against the admission of both Oregon and Kansas until they have 93,420 inhabitants. I would like Mr. Lincoln to answer this question. I would like him to take his own medicine. [Laughter.] If he differs with Mr. Trumbull, let him answer his argument against the admission of Oregon, instead of poking questions at me. ["Right, good, good," laughter and cheers.]

The next question propounded to me by Mr. Lincoln is, can the people of a territory in any lawful way against the wishes of any citizen of the United States exclude slavery from their limits prior to the formation of a state constitution? I answer emphatically, as Mr. Lincoln has heard me answer a hundred times from every stump in Illinois, that in my opinion the people of a territory can, by lawful means, exclude slavery from their limits prior to the formation of a state constitution. [Enthusiastic applause.] Mr. Lincoln knew that I had answered that question over and over again. He heard me argue the Nebraska Bill on that principle all over the State in 1854, in 1855 and in 1856, and he has no excuse for pretending to be in doubt as to my position on that question. It matters not what way the Supreme Court may hereafter decide as to the abstract question whether slavery may or may not go into a territory under the Constitution, the people have the lawful means to introduce it or exclude it as they please, for the reason that slavery cannot exist a day or an hour anywhere, unless it is supported by local police regulations. ["Right, right."] Those police regulations can only be established by the local legislature, and if the people are opposed to slavery they will elect representatives to that body who will by unfriendly legislation effectually prevent the introduction of it into their midst. If, on the contrary, they are for it, their legislation will favor its extension. Hence, no matter what the decision of the Supreme Court may be on that abstract question, still the right of the people to make a slave territory or a free territory is perfect and complete under the Nebraska Bill. I hope Mr. Lincoln deems my answer satisfactory on that point.

[Deacon Bross spoke.]

In this connection, I will notice the charge which he has introduced in relation to Mr. Chase's amendment. I thought that I had chased that amendment out of Mr. Lincoln's brain at Ottawa; [laughter] but it seems that still haunts his imagination, and he is not yet satisfied. I had supposed that he would be ashamed to press that question further. He is a lawyer, and has been a member of Congress, and has occupied his time and amused you by telling you about parliamentary proceedings. He ought to have known better than to try to palm off his miserable impositions upon this intelligent audience. ["Good," and cheers.] The Nebraska Bill provided that the legislative power, and authority of the said territory, should extend to all rightful subjects of legislation consistent with the organic act and the Constitution of the United States. It did not make any exception as to slavery, but gave all the power that it was possible for Congress to give, without violating the Constitution to the territorial legislature, with no exception or limitation on the subject of slavery at all. The language of that bill which I have quoted, gave the full power and the full authority over the subject of slavery, affirmatively and negatively, to introduce it or exclude it, so far as the Constitution of the United States would permit. What more could Mr. Chase give by his amendment? Nothing. He offered his amendment for the identical purpose for which Mr. Lincoln is using it, to enable demagogues in the country to try and deceive the people. ["Good, hit him again," and cheers.]

[Deacon Bross spoke.]

His amendment was to this effect. It provided that the legislature should have the power to exclude slavery: and General Cass suggested, "why not give the power to introduce as well as exclude?" The answer was, they have the power already in the bill to do both. Chase was afraid his amendment would be adopted if he put the alternative proposition and so make it fair both ways, but would not yield. He offered it for the purpose of having it rejected. He offered it, as he has himself avowed over and over again, simply to make capital out of it for the stump. He expected that it would be capital for small politicians in the country, and that they would make an effort to deceive the people with it, and he was not mistaken, for Lincoln is carrying out the plan admirably. ["Good, good."] Lincoln knows that the Nebraska Bill, without Chase's amendment, gave all the power which the Constitution would permit. Could Congress confer any more? ["No, no."] Could Congress go beyond the Constitution of the country? We gave all, a full grant, with no exception in regard to slavery one way or the other. We left that question as we left all others, to be decided by the people for themselves, just as they pleased. I will not occupy my time on this question. I have argued it before all over Illinois. I have argued it in this beautiful city of Freeport; I have argued it in the North, the South, the East and the West, avowing the same sentiments and the same principles. I have not been afraid to avow my sentiments up here for fear I would be trotted down into Egypt. [Cheers and laughter.]

The third question which Mr. Lincoln presented is, if the Supreme Court of the United States shall decide that a state of this Union cannot exclude slavery from its own limits, will I submit to it? I am amazed that Lincoln should ask such a question. ["A school boy knows better."] Yes, a school boy does know better. Mr. Lincoln's object is to cast an imputation upon the Supreme Court. He knows that there never was but one man in America, claiming any degree of intelligence or decency, who ever for a moment pretended such a thing. It is true that the Washington *Union*, in an article published on the 17th of last December, did put forth that doctrine, and I denounced the article on the floor of the Senate, in a speech which Mr. Lincoln now pretends was against the President. The *Union* had claimed that slavery had a right to go into the free states, and that any provision in the Constitution or laws of the free States to the contrary were null and void. I denounced it in the Senate, as I said before, and I was the first man who did. Lincoln's friends, Trumbull, and Seward, and Hale, and Wilson, and the whole Black Republican side of the Senate were silent. They left it to me to denounce it. [Cheers.] And what was the reply made to me on that occasion? Mr. Toombs, of Georgia, got up and undertook to lecture me on the ground that I ought not to have deemed the article worthy of notice, and ought not to have replied to it; that there was not one man, woman or child south of the Potomac, in any slave state, who did not repudiate any such pretension. Mr. Lincoln knows that that reply was made on the spot, and yet now he asks this question. He might as well ask me, suppose Mr. Lincoln should steal a horse would I sanction it; [Laughter.] and it would be as genteel in me to ask him, in the event he stole a horse, what ought to be done with him. He casts an imputation upon the Supreme Court of the United States by supposing that they would violate the Constitution of the United States. I tell him that such a thing is not possible. [Cheers.] It would be an act of moral treason that no man on the bench could ever descend to. Mr. Lincoln himself would never in his partisan feelings so far forget what was right as to be guilty of such an act. ["Good, good."]

The fourth question of Mr. Lincoln is, are you in favor of acquiring additional territory, in disregard as to how such acquisition may affect the Union on the slavery questions? This question is very ingeniously and cunningly put.

[Deacon Bross here spoke, *sotto voce,*—the reporter understanding him to say, "Now we've got him."]

The Black Republican creed lays it down expressly, that under no circumstances shall we acquire any more territory unless slavery is first prohibited in the country. I ask Mr. Lincoln whether he is in favor of that proposition. Are you [addressing Mr. Lincoln] opposed to the acquisition of any more territory, under any circumstances, unless slavery is prohibited in it? That he does not like to answer. When I ask him whether he stands up to that article in the platform of his party, he turns, Yankee-fashion, and without answering it, asks me whether I am in favor of acquiring territory without regard to how it may affect the Union on the slavery question. ["Good."] I answer that whenever it becomes necessary, in our growth and progress, to acquire more territory, that I am in favor of it, without reference to the question of slavery, and when we have acquired it, I will leave the people free to do as they please, either to make it slave or free territory, as they prefer. [Here Deacon Bross spoke; the reporter believes he said, "That's bold." It was said solemnly.] It is idle to tell me or you that we have territory enough. Our fathers supposed that we had enough when our territory extended to the Mississippi River, but a few years' growth and expansion satisfied them that we needed more, and the Louisiana territory, from the west branch of the Mississippi to the British possessions, was acquired. Then we acquired Oregon, then California and New Mexico. We have enough now for the present, but this is a young and a growing nation. It swarms as often as a hive of bees, and as new swarms are turned out each year, there must be hives in which they can gather and make their honey. ["Good."] In less than fifteen years, if the same progress that has distinguished this country for the last fifteen years continues, every foot of vacant land between this and the Pacific Ocean, owned by the United States, will be occupied. Will you not continue to increase at the end of fifteen years as well as now? I tell you, increase, and multiply, and expand, is the law of this nation's existence. ["Good."] You cannot limit this great Republic by mere boundary lines, saying, "thus far shalt thou go, and no further." Any one of you gentlemen might as well say to a son twelve years old that he is big enough, and must not grow any larger, and in order to prevent his growth put a hoop around him to keep him to his present size. What would be the result? Either the hoop must burst and be rent asunder, or the child must die. So it would be with this great nation. With our natural increase, growing with a rapidity unknown in any other part of the globe, with the tide of emigration that is fleeing from despotism in the old world to seek refuge in our own, there is a constant torrent pouring into this country that requires more land, more territory upon which to settle, and just as fast as our interests and our destiny require additional territory in the north, in the south, or on the islands of the ocean, I am for it, and when we acquire it will leave the people, according to the Nebraska Bill, free to do as they please on the subject of slavery and every other question. ["Good, good," "hurra for Douglas."]

I trust now that Mr. Lincoln will deem himself answered on his four points. He racked his brain so much in devising these four questions that he exhausted himself, and had not strength enough to invent the others. [Laughter.] As soon as he is able to hold a council with his advisers, Lovejoy, Farnsworth, and Fred. Douglass, he will frame and propound others. ["Good, good," &c. Renewed laughter, in which Mr. Lincoln feebly joined, saying that he hoped with their aid to get seven questions, the number asked him by Judge Douglas, and so make *conclusions* even.] You Black Republicans who say good, I have no doubt think that they are all good men. ["White, white."] I have reason to recollect that some people in this country think that Fred. Douglass is a very good man. The last time I came here to make a speech, while talking from the stand to you people of Freeport, as I am doing to-day, I saw a carriage and a magnificent one it was, drive up and take a position on the outside of the crowd; a beautiful young lady was sitting on the box seat, whilst Fred. Douglass and her mother reclined inside, and the owner of the carriage acted as driver. [Laughter, cheers, cries of "Right, what have you to say against it," &c.] I saw this in your own town. ["What of it."] All I have to say of it is this, that if you, Black Republicans, think that the negro ought to be on a social equality with your wives and daughters, and ride in a carriage with your wife, whilst you drive the team, you have perfect right to do so. ["Good, good," and cheers, mingled with hooting and cries of "white, white."] I am told that one of Fred. Douglass' kinsmen, another rich black negro, is now traveling in this part of the state

making speeches for his friend Lincoln as the champion of black men. ["White men, white men," and "what have you got to say against it," "that's right," &c.] All I have to say on that subject is, that those of you who believe that the negro is your equal and ought to be on an equality with you socially, politically, and legally, have a right to entertain those opinions, and of course will vote for Mr. Lincoln. ["Down with the negro," "no, no," &c.]

I have a word to say on Mr. Lincoln's answer to the interrogatories contained in my speech at Ottawa, and which he has pretended to reply to here to-day. Mr. Lincoln makes a great parade of the fact that I quoted a platform as having been adopted by the Black Republican party at Springfield in 1854, which, it turns out, was adopted at another place. Mr. Lincoln loses sight of the thing itself in his ecstacies over the mistake I made in stating the place where it was done. He thinks that that platform was not adopted on the right "spot."

When I put the direct questions to Mr. Lincoln to ascertain whether he now stands pledged to that creed—to the unconditional repeal of the fugitive slave law, a refusal to admit any more slave states into the Union even if the people want them, a determination to apply the Wilmot Proviso not only to all the territory we now have, but all that we may hereafter acquire, he refused to answer, and his followers say, in excuse, that the resolutions upon which I based my interrogatories were not adopted at the "*right spot.*" [Laughter and applause.] Lincoln and his political friends are great on "*spots.*" [Renewed laughter.] In Congress, as a representative of this state, he declared the Mexican war to be unjust and infamous, and would not support it, or acknowledge his own country to be right in the contest, because he said that American blood was not shed on American soil in the "*right spot.*" ["Lay on to him."] And now he cannot answer the questions I put to him at Ottawa because the resolutions I read were not adopted at the "*right spot.*" It may be possible that I was led into an error as to the *spot* on which the resolutions I then read were proclaimed, but I was not, and am not in error as to the fact of their forming the basis of the creed of the Republican party when that party was first organized. [Cheers.] I will state to you the evidence I had, and upon which I relied for my statement that the resolutions in question were adopted at Springfield on the 5th of October, 1854. Although I was aware that such resolutions had been passed in this district, and nearly all the northern congressional districts and county conventions, I had not noticed whether or not they had been adopted by any state convention. In 1856, a debate arose in Congress between Major Thomas L. Harris, of the Springfield district, and Mr. Norton, of the Joliet district, on political matters connected with our state, in the course of which Major Harris quoted those resolutions as having been passed by the first Republican State Convention that ever assembled in Illinois. I knew that Major Harris was remarkable for his accuracy, that he was a very conscientious and sincere man, and I also noticed that Norton did not question the accuracy of this statement. I therefore took it for granted that it was so, and the other day when I concluded to use the resolutions at Ottawa, I wrote to Charles H. Lanphier, editor of the *State Register*, at Springfield, calling his attention to them, telling him that I had been informed that Major Harris was lying sick at Springfield, and desiring him to call upon him and ascertain all the facts concerning the resolutions, the time and the place where they were adopted. In reply Mr. Lanphier sent me two copies of his paper, which I have here. The first is a copy of the *State Register*, published at Springfield, Mr. Lincoln's own town, on the 16th of October 1854, only eleven days after the adjournment of the convention, from which I desire to read the following:

> During the late discussions in this city, Lincoln made a speech, to which Judge Douglas replied. In Lincoln's speech he took the broad ground that, according to the Declaration of Independence, the whites and blacks are equal. From this he drew the conclusion, which he several times repeated, that the white man had no right to pass laws for the government of the black man without the nigger's consent. This speech of Lincoln's was heard and applauded by all the Abolitionists assembled in Springfield. So soon as Mr. Lincoln was done speaking, Mr. Codding arose and requested all the delegates to the Black Republican convention to withdraw into the senate chamber. They did so, and after long deliberation, they laid down the following abolition platform as the platform on which they stood. We call the particular attention of all our readers to it.

Then follows the identical platform, word for word, which I read at Ottawa. [Cheers.] Now, that was published in Mr. Lincoln's own town, eleven days

after the convention was held, and it has remained on record up to this day never contradicted.

When I quoted the resolutions at Ottawa and questioned Mr. Lincoln in relation to them, he said that his name was on the committee that reported them, but he did not serve, nor did he think he served, because he was, or thought he was, in Tazewell county at the time the convention was in session. He did not deny that the resolutions were passed by the Springfield convention. He did not know better, and evidently thought that they were, but afterward his friends declared that they had discovered that they varied in some respects from the resolutions passed by that convention. I have shown you that I had good evidence for believing that the resolutions had been passed at Springfield. Mr. Lincoln ought to have known better; but not a word is said about his ignorance on the subject, whilst I, notwithstanding the circumstances, am accused of forgery.

Now, I will show you that if I have made a mistake as to the place where these resolutions were adopted—and when I get down to Springfield I will investigate the matter and see whether or not I have—that the principles they enunciate were adopted as the Black Republican platform ["White, white."] in the various counties and congressional districts throughout the north end of the state in 1854. This platform was adopted in nearly every county that gave a Black Republican majority for the legislature in that year, and here is a man [pointing to Mr. Denio, who sat on the stand near Deacon Bross,] who knows as well as any living man that it was the creed of the Black Republican party at that time. I would be willing to call Denio as a witness, or any other honest man belonging to that party. I will now read the resolutions adopted at the Rockford Convention on the 30th of August, 1854, which nominated Washburne for Congress. You elected him on the following platform:

> *Resolved*, That the continued and increasing aggressions of slavery in our country are destructive of the best rights of a free people, and that such aggressions cannot be successfully resisted without the united political action of all good men.
>
> *Resolved*, That the citizens of the United States hold in their hands peaceful, constitutional, and efficient remedy against the encroachments of the slave power, the ballot box, and, if that remedy is boldly and wisely applied, the principles of liberty and eternal justice will be established.

Resolved, That we accept this issue forced upon us by the slave power, and, in defense of freedom, will co-operate and be known as Republicans, pledged to the accomplishment of the following purposes:

To bring the administration of the government back to the control of first principles; to restore Kansas and Nebraska to the position of free territories; to repeal and entirely abrogate the fugitive slave law; to restrict slavery to those states in which it exists; to prohibit the admission of any more slave states into the Union; to exclude slavery from all the territories over which the general government has exclusive jurisdiction, and to resist the acquisition of any more territories unless the introduction of slavery therein forever shall have been prohibited.

Resolved, That in furtherance of these principles we will use such constitutional and lawful means as shall seem best adapted to their accomplishment, and that we will support no man for office under the general or state government who is not positively committed to the support of these principles, and whose personal character and conduct is not a guaranty that he is reliable and shall abjure all party allegiance and ties.

Resolved, That we cordially invite persons of all former political parties whatever in favor of the object expressed in the above resolutions to unite with us in carrying them into effect.

[Senator Douglas was frequently interrupted in reading these resolutions by loud cries of "Good, good," "that's the doctrine," and vociferous applause.]

Well, you think that is a very good platform, do you not? ["Yes, yes, all right," and cheers.] If you do, if you approve it now, and think it is all right, you will not join with those men who say that I libel you by calling these your principles, will you? ["Good, good, hit him again," and great laughter and cheers.] Now, Mr. Lincoln complains; Mr. Lincoln charges that I did you and him injustice by saying that this was the platform of your party. [Renewed laughter.] I am told that Washburne made a speech in Galena last night in which he abused me awfully for bringing to light this platform, on which he was elected to Congress. He thought that you had forgotten it, as he and Mr. Lincoln desire to. [Laughter.] He did not deny but that you had adopted it, and that he had subscribed to and was pledged by it, but he did not

think it was fair to call it up and remind the people that it was their platform.

[Here Deacon Bross spoke.]

But I am glad to find you are more honest in your abolitionism than your leaders, by avowing that it is your platform, and right in your opinion. [Laughter, "you have them, good, good."]

In the adoption of that platform, you not only declared that you would resist the admission of any more slave states, and work for the repeal of the fugitive slave law, but you pledged yourselves not to vote for any man for state or federal offices who was not committed to these principles. ["Exactly so." "Exactly so!" Cheers.] You were thus committed. Similar resolutions to those were adopted in your county convention here, and now with your admissions that they are your platform and embody your sentiments now as they did then, what do you think of Mr. Lincoln, your candidate for the U.S. Senate, who is attempting to dodge the responsibility of this platform, because it was not adopted in the right spot. [Shouts of laughter, "hurra for Douglas," &c.] I thought that it was adopted in Springfield, but it turns out it was not, that it was adopted at Rockford and in the various counties which comprise this congressional district. When I get into the next district, I will show that the same platform was adopted there, and so on through the state, until I nail the responsibility of it upon the back of the Black Republican party throughout the state. ["White, white," three cheers for Douglas.]

[A voice—"Couldn't you modify and call it brown?" Laughter.]

[Mr. Douglas] Not a bit. I thought that you were becoming a little brown when your members in Congress voted for the Crittenden-Montgomery bill, but since you have backed out from that position and gone back to Abolitionism, you are black, and not brown. [Shouts of laughter, and a voice, "Can't you ask him another question?"]

Gentlemen, I have shown you what your platform was in 1854. You still adhere to it. The same platform was adopted by nearly all the counties where the Black Republican party had a majority in 1854. I wish now to call your attention to the action of your representatives in the legislature when they assembled together at Springfield. In the first place you must remember that this was the organization of a new party. It is so declared in the resolutions themselves, which say that you are going to dissolve all old party ties and call the new party Republican. The old Whig party was to have its throat cut from ear to ear, and the Democratic party was to be annihilated and blotted out of existence, whilst in lieu of these parties the Black Republican party was to be organized on this Abolition platform. You know who the chief leaders were in breaking up and destroying these two great parties. Lincoln on the one hand and Trumbull on the other, being disappointed politicians, [laughter,] and having retired or been driven to obscurity by an outraged constituency because of their political sins, formed a scheme to abolitionize the two parties and lead the Old Line Whigs and Old Line Democrats captive, bound hand and foot into the Abolition camp. Giddings, Chase, Fred. Douglass and Lovejoy were here to christen them whenever they were brought in. [Great laughter.] Lincoln went to work to dissolve the Old Line Whig party. Clay was dead, and although the sod was not yet green on his grave, this man undertook to bring into disrepute those great compromise measures of 1850, with which Clay and Webster were identified. Up to 1854 the old Whig party and the Democratic party had stood on a common platform so far as this slavery question was concerned. You Whigs and we Democrats differed about the bank, the tariff, distribution, the specie circular and the sub-treasury, but we agreed on this slavery question and the true mode of preserving the peace and harmony of the Union. The compromise measures of 1850 were introduced by Clay, were defended by Webster, and supported by Cass, and were approved by Fillmore, and sanctioned by the national men of both parties. They constituted a common plank upon which both Whigs and Democrats stood. In 1852 the Whig party, in its last national convention at Baltimore endorsed and approved these measures of Clay, and so did the national convention of the Democratic party held that same year. Thus the Old Line Whigs and the Old Line Democrats stood pledged to the great principle of self-government, which guaranties to the people of each territory the right to decide the slavery question for themselves. In 1854 after the death of Clay and Webster, Mr. Lincoln on the part of the Whigs undertook to abolitionize the Whig party, by dissolving it, transferring the members into the Abolition camp and making them train under Giddings, Fred. Douglass, Lovejoy, Chase, Farnsworth, and other Abolition leaders. Trumbull undertook to dissolve the Democratic party by taking old Democrats into the Abolition camp. Mr. Lincoln was aided in his efforts by many leading Whigs throughout the state, your member of Congress, Mr. Washburne, being one of the most active. ["Good fellow."] Trumbull was aided by many renegades from the Democratic party, among whom were John Wentworth, [laughter,] Tom Turner and others with whom you are familiar.

[Mr. Turner, who was one of the moderators, here interposed and said that he had drawn the resolutions which Senator Douglas had read.]

[Mr. Douglas] Yes, and Turner says that he drew these resolutions. ["Hurra' for Turner." "Hurra' for Douglas."] That is right, give Turner cheers for drawing the resolutions if you approve them. If he drew those resolutions he will not deny that they are the creed of the Black Republican party.

[Mr. Turner] "They are our creed exactly."

[Mr. Douglas] And yet Lincoln denies that he stands on them. ["Good, good," and laughter.] Mr. Turner says that the creed of the Black Republican party is the admission of no more slave states, and yet Mr. Lincoln declares that he would not like to be placed in a position where he would have to vote for them. All I have to say to friend Lincoln is, that I do not think there is much danger of his being placed in such a position. [More laughter.] As Mr. Lincoln would be very sorry to be placed in such an embarrassing position as to be obliged to vote on the admission of any more slave states, I propose, out of mere kindness, to relieve him from any such necessity. [Renewed laughter and cheers.]

When the bargain between Lincoln and Trumbull was completed for abolitionizing the Whig and Democratic parties, they "spread" over the state, Lincoln still pretending to be an Old Line Whig in order to "rope in" the Whigs, and Trumbull pretending to be as good a Democrat as he ever was in order to coax the Democrats over into the Abolition ranks. ["That's exactly what we want."] They played the part that "decoy ducks" play down on the Potomac River. In that part of the country they make artificial ducks and put them on the water in places where the wild ducks are to be found for the purpose of decoying them. Well, Lincoln and Trumbull played the part of these "decoy ducks" and deceived enough Old Line Whigs and Old Line Democrats to elect a Black Republican legislature. When that legislature met, the first thing it did was to elect a[s] Speaker of the House the very man who is now boasting that he wrote the Abolition platform on which Lincoln will not stand. ["Good," "hit him again," and cheers.] I want to know of Mr. Turner whether or not, when he was elected he was a good embodiment of Republican principles?

[Mr. Turner] "I hope I was then and am now."

[Mr. Douglas] He answers that he hopes he was then and is now. He wrote that Black Republican platform, and is satisfied with it now. ["Hurrah for Turner," "good," &c.] I admire and acknowledge Turner's honesty. Every man of you know that what he says about these resolutions being the platform of the Black Republican party is true, and you also know that each one of these men who are shuffling and trying to deny it are only trying to cheat the people out of their votes for the purpose of deceiving them still more after the election. ["Good," and cheers.] I propose to trace this thing a little further, in order that you can see what additional evidence there is to fasten this revolutionary platform upon the Black Republican party. When the Legislature assembled, there was an United States Senator to elect in the place of Gen. Shields, and before they proceeded to ballot, Lovejoy insisted on laying down certain principles by which to govern the party. It has been published to the world and satisfactorily proven that there was at the time the alliance was made between Trumbull and Lincoln to abolitionize the two parties, an agreement that Lincoln should take Shields' place in the United States Senate, and Trumbull should have mine so soon as they could conveniently get rid of me. When Lincoln was beaten for Shields' place in a manner I will refer to in a few minutes, he felt very sore and restive; his friends grumbled, and some of them came out and charged that the most infamous treachery had been practised against him; that the bargain was that Lincoln was to have had Shields' place, and Trumbull was to have waited for mine, but that Trumbull having the control of a few abolitionized Democrats, he prevented them from voting for Lincoln, thus keeping him within a few votes of an election until he succeeded in forcing the party to drop him and elect Trumbull. Well, Trumbull having cheated Lincoln, his friends made a fuss, and in order to keep them and Lincoln quiet, the party were obliged to come forward, in advance, at the last state election, and make a pledge that they would go for Lincoln and nobody else. Lincoln could not be silenced in any other way.

Now, there are a great many Black Republicans of you who do not know this thing was done. ["White, white," and great clamor.] I wish to remind you that while Mr. Lincoln was speaking there was not a Democrat vulgar and black-guard enough to interrupt him. [Great applause and cries of "hurrah for Douglas."] But I know that the shoe is pinching you. I am clinching Lincoln now and you are scared to death for the result. [Cheers.] I have seen this thing before. I have seen men make appointments for joint discussions, and the moment their man has been heard, try to interrupt and prevent a fair hearing of the other side. I have seen your mobs before, and defy your wrath. [Tremendous applause.] My friends, do not cheer, for I need my whole time. The object of the opposition is to occupy my attention in order to prevent me from giving the whole evidence and nailing this double dealing on the Black Republican party. As I have before said, Lovejoy demanded a declaration of principles on the part of the Black Republicans of the legislature before going into an election for United States Senator. He offered the following preamble and resolutions which I hold in my hand:

Whereas, human slavery is a violation of the principles of natural and revealed rights; and whereas, the fathers of the Revolution, fully imbued with the spirit of these principles, declared freedom to be the inalienable birthright of all men; and whereas, the preamble to the Constitution of the United States avers that that instrument was ordained to establish justice, and secure the blessings of liberty to ourselves and our posterity; and whereas, in furtherance of the above principles, slavery was forever prohibited in the old Northwest Territory, and more recently in all that territory lying west and north of the state of Missouri, by the act of the federal government; and whereas, the repeal of the prohibition last referred to, was contrary to the wishes of the people of Illinois, a violation of an implied compact, long deemed sacred by the citizens of the United States, and a wide departure from the uniform action of the general government in relation to the extension of slavery; therefore,

Resolved, by the House of Representatives, the Senate concurring therein, That our Senators in Congress be instructed, and our Representatives requested, to introduce, if not otherwise introduced, and to vote for a bill to restore such prohibition to the aforesaid territories, and also to extend a similar prohibition to all territory which now belongs to the United States, or which may hereafter come under their jurisdiction.

Resolved, That our Senators in Congress be instructed, and our Representatives requested, to vote against the admission of any state into the Union, the constitution of which does not prohibit slavery, whether the territory out of which such state may have been formed shall have been acquired by conquest, treaty, purchase, or from original territory of the United States.

Resolved, That our Senators in Congress be instructed and our Representatives requested to introduce and vote for a bill to repeal an act entitled "an act respecting fugitives from justice and persons escaping from the service of their masters"; and, failing in that, for such a modification of it as shall secure the right of *habeas corpus* and trial by jury before the regularly-constituted authorities of the state, to all persons claimed as owing service or labor.

[Cries of "good," "good," and cheers.] Yes, you say "good," "good," and I have no doubt you think so. Those resolutions were introduced by Mr. Lovejoy immediately preceding the election of Senator. They declared first, that the Wilmot Proviso must be applied to all territory north of 36 deg., 30 min. Secondly, that it must be applied to all territory south of 36 deg., 30 min. Thirdly, that it must be applied to all the territory now owned by the United States, and finally, that it must be applied to all territory hereafter to be acquired by the United States. The next resolution declares that no more slave states shall be admitted into this Union under any circumstances whatever, no matter whether they are formed out of territory now owned by us or that we may hereafter acquire, by treaty, by Congress, or in any manner whatever. [A voice—"That is right."] You say that is right. We will see in a moment. The next resolution demands the unconditional repeal of the fugitive slave law, although its unconditional repeal would leave no provision for carrying out that clause of the Constitution of the United States which guaranties the surrender of fugitives. If they could not get an unconditional repeal, they demanded that that law should be so modified as to make it as nearly useless as possible. Now I want to show you who voted for these resolutions. When the vote was taken on the first resolution it was decided in the affirmative—yeas 41, nays 32. You will find that this is a strict party vote, between the Democrats, on the one hand, and the Black Republicans, on the other. [Cries, of "white, white," and clamor.] I know your name, and always call things by their right name. The point I wish to call your attention to, is this: that these reso-

lutions were adopted on the 7th day of February, and that on the 8th they went into an election for a U.S. Senator, and that day every man who voted for these resolutions, with but two exceptions, voted for Lincoln for the U.S. Senate. [Cries of "good, good," and "give us their names."] I will read the names over to you if you want them, but I believe your object is to occupy my time. [Cries of "that is it."]

On the next resolution, the vote stood—yeas 33, nays 40, and on the third resolution—yeas 35, nays 47. I wish to impress it upon you, that every man who voted for those resolutions, with but two exceptions, voted on the next day for Lincoln, for U.S. Senator. Bear in mind that the members who thus voted for Lincoln were elected to the legislature, pledged to vote for no man for office under the state or federal government who was not committed to this Black Republican platform. [Cries of "white, white," and "good for you."] They were all so pledged. Mr. Turner, who stands by me, and who then represented you, and who says that he wrote those resolutions, voted for Lincoln, when he was pledged not to do so unless Lincoln was in favor of those resolutions. I now ask Mr. Turner, [turning to Turner] did you violate your pledge in voting for Mr. Lincoln, or did he commit himself to your platform before you cast your vote for him? [Mr. Lincoln here started forward, and grasping Mr. Turner, shook him nervously, and said, "Don't answer, Turner, you have no right to answer."]

I could go through the whole list of names here and show you that all the Black Republicans in the legislature, ["white, white,"] who voted for Mr. Lincoln, had voted on the day previous for these resolutions. For instance, here are the names of Sargent and Little, of Jo Daviess and Carroll; Thomas J. Turner, of Stephenson; Lawrence, of Boone and McHenry; Swan, of Lake; Pinckney, of Ogle county, and Lyman, of Winnebago. Thus you see every member from your congressional district voted for Mr. Lincoln, and they were pledged not to vote for him unless he was committed to the doctrine of no more slave states, the prohibition of slavery in the territories, and the repeal of the fugitive slave law. Mr. Lincoln tells you to-day that he is not pledged to any such doctrine. Either Mr. Lincoln was then committed to those propositions, or Mr. Turner violated his pledges to you when he voted for him. Either Lincoln was pledged to each one of those propositions, or else every Black Republican—[cries of "white, white,"]—representative from this congressional district violated his pledge of honor to his constituents by voting for him. I ask you which horn of the dilemma will you take? Will you hold Lincoln up to the platform of his party, or will you accuse every representative you had in the legislature of violating his pledge of honor to his constituents. [Voices—"we go for Turner," "we go for Lincoln," "hurrah for Douglas," "hurrah for Turner."] There is no escape for you. Either Mr. Lincoln was committed to those propositions, or your members violated their faith. Take either horn of the dilemma you choose. There is no dodging the question, I want Lincoln's answer. He says he was not pledged to repeal the fugitive slave law, that he does not quite like to do it; he will not introduce a law to repeal it, but thinks there ought to be some law; he does not tell what it ought to be; upon the whole, he is altogether undecided, and don't know what to think or do. That is the substance of his answer upon the repeal of the fugitive slave law. I put the question to him distinctly, whether he endorsed that part of the Black Republican platform which calls for the entire abrogation and repeal of the fugitive slave law. He answers no! that he does not endorse that, but he does not tell what he is for, or what he will vote for. His answer is, in fact, no answer at all. Why cannot he speak out and say what he is for and what he will do? [Cries of "that's right."]

In regard to there being no more slave states, he is not pledged to that. He would not like, he says, to be put in a position where he would have to vote one way or another upon that question. I pray you do not put him in a position that would embarrass him so much. [Laughter.] Gentlemen, if he goes to the Senate, he may be put in that position, and then which way will he vote?

[A voice—"How will you vote?"]

[Mr. Douglas] I will vote for the admission of just such a state as by the form of their constitution the people show they want; if they want slavery, they shall have it; if they prohibit slavery it shall be prohibited. They can form their institutions to please themselves, subject only to the Constitution; and I for one stand ready to receive them into the Union. ["Three cheers for Douglas."] Why cannot your Black Republican candidates talk out as plain as that when they are questioned? [Cries of "good, good."]

[Here Deacon Bross spoke.]

I do not want to cheat any man out of his vote. No man is deceived in regard to my principles if I have the power to express myself in terms explicit enough to convey my ideas.

Mr. Lincoln made a speech when he was nominated for the U.S. Senate which covers all these abolition platforms. He there lays down a proposition so broad in its Abolitionism as to cover the whole ground.

> In my opinion it [the slavery agitation] will not cease until a crisis shall have been reached and passed. "A house divided against itself cannot stand." I believe this government cannot endure permanently half slave and half free. I do not expect the house to fall—but I do expect it will cease to be divided. It will become all one thing or all the other. Either the opponents of slavery will arrest the further spread of it, and place it where the public mind shall rest in the belief that it is in the course of ultimate extinction, or its advocates will push it forward till it shall become alike lawful in all the States—old as well as new, North as well as South.

There you find that Mr. Lincoln lays down the doctrine that this Union cannot endure divided as our Fathers made it, with free and slave states. He says they must all become one thing, or all the other; that they must all be free or all slave, or else the Union cannot continue to exist. It being his opinion that to admit any more slave states, to continue to divide the Union into free and slave states, will dissolve it. I want to know of Mr. Lincoln whether he will vote for the admission of another slave state. [Cries of "Bring him out."]

He tells you the Union cannot exist unless the states are all free or all slave; he tells you that he is opposed to making them all slave, and hence he is for making them all free, in order that the Union may exist; and yet he will not say that he will not vote against another slave state, knowing that the Union must be dissolved if he votes for it. [Great laughter.] I ask you if that is fair dealing? The true intent and inevitable conclusion to be drawn from his first Springfield speech is, that he is opposed to the admission of any more slave states under any circumstance. If he is so opposed why not say so? If he believes this Union cannot endure divided into free and slave states, that they must all become free in order to save the Union, he is bound, as an honest man, to vote against any more slave states. If he believes it he is bound to do it. Show me that it is my duty in order to save the Union to do a particular act, and I will do it if the Constitution does not prohibit it. [Applause.] I am not for the dissolution of the Union under any circumstances. [Renewed applause.] I will pursue no course of conduct that will give just cause for the dissolution of the Union. The hope of the friends of freedom throughout the world rests upon the perpetuity of this Union. The down-trodden and oppressed people who are suffering under European despotism all look with hope and anxiety to the American Union as the only resting place and permanent home of freedom and self-government.

Mr. Lincoln says that he believes that this Union cannot continue to endure with slave states in it, and yet he will not tell you distinctly whether he will vote for or against the admission of any more slave states, but says he would not like to be put to the test. [Laughter.] I do not think he will be put to the test. [Renewed laughter.] I do not think that the people of Illinois desire a man to represent them who would not like to be put to the test on the performance of a high constitutional duty. [Cries of "good."] I will retire in shame from the Senate of the United States when I am not willing to be put to the test in the performance of my duty. I have been put to severe tests. ["That is so."] I have stood by my principles in fair weather and in foul, in the sunshine and in the rain. I have defended the great principles of self-government here among you when Northern sentiment ran in a torrent against me, [A voice—"that is so,"] and I have defended that same great principle when Southern sentiment came down like an avalanche upon me. I was not afraid of any test they put to me. I knew I was right—I knew my principles were sound—I knew that the people would see in the end that I had done right, and I knew that the God of Heaven would smile upon me if I was faithful in the performance of my duty. [Cries of "good," cheers and laughter.]

Mr. Lincoln makes a charge of corruption against the Supreme Court of the United States, and two Presidents of the United States, and attempts to bolster it up by saying that I did the same against the Washington *Union*. Suppose I did make that charge of corruption against the Washington *Union*, when it was true, does that justify him in making a false charge against me and others? That is the question I would put. He says that at the time the Nebraska Bill was introduced, and before it was passed there was a conspiracy between the Judges of the Supreme Court, President Pierce, President Buchanan and myself by that bill, and the decision of the court to break down the barrier and establish slavery all over the Union. Does he not know that that charge is historically false as against President Buchanan? He knows that Mr. Buchanan was at that time in England, representing

this country with distinguished ability at the Court of St. James, that he was there for a long time before and did not return for a year or more after. He knows that to be true, and that fact proves his charge to be false as against Mr. Buchanan. [Cheers.] Then again, I wish to call his attention to the fact that at the time the Nebraska Bill was passed the Dred Scott case was not before the Supreme Court at all; it was not upon the docket of the Supreme Court; it had not been brought there, and the Judges in all probability, knew nothing of it. Thus the history of the country proves the charge to be false as against them. As to President Pierce, his high character as a man of integrity and honor is enough to vindicate him from such a charge, [laughter and applause,] and as to myself, I pronounce the charge an infamous lie, whenever and wherever made, and by whomsoever made. I am willing that Mr. Lincoln should go and rake up every public act of mine, every measure I have introduced, report I have made, speech delivered, and criticise them, but when he charges upon me a corrupt conspiracy for the purpose of perverting the institutions of the country, I brand it as it deserves. I say the history of the country proves it to be false, and that it could not have been possible at the time. But now he tries to protect himself in this charge, because I made a charge against the Washington *Union*. My speech in the Senate against the Washington *Union* was made because it advocated a revolutionary doctrine, by declaring that the free states had not the right to prohibit slavery within their own limits. Because I made that charge against the Washington *Union*, Mr. Lincoln says it was a charge against Mr. Buchanan. Suppose it was; is Mr. Lincoln the peculiar defender of Mr. Buchanan? Is he so interested in the federal administration, and so bound to it, that he must jump to the rescue and defend it from every attack that I may make against it? [Great laughter and cheers.] I understand the whole thing. The Washington *Union*, under that most corrupt of all men, Cornelius Wendell, is advocating Mr. Lincoln's claim to the Senate. Wendell was the printer of the last Black Republican House of Representatives; he was a candidate before the present Democratic House, but was ignominiously kicked out, and then he took the money which he had made out of the public printing by means of the Black Republicans, bought the Washington *Union*, and is now publishing it in the name of the Democratic party, and advocating Mr. Lincoln's election to the Senate. Mr. Lincoln therefore considers an attack upon Wendell and his corrupt gang as a personal attack upon him. [Immense cheering and laughter.] This only proves what I have charged, that there is an alliance between Lincoln and his supporters, and the federal office-holders of this state, and presidential aspirants out of it, to break me down at home.

[A voice—"That is impossible," and cheering.]

Mr. Lincoln feels bound to come in to the rescue of the Washington *Union*. In that speech which I delivered in answer to the Washington *Union*, I made it distinctly against the *Union*, and against the *Union* alone. I did not choose to go beyond that. If I have occasion to attack the President's conduct, I will do it in language that will not be misunderstood. When I differed with the President, I spoke out so that you all heard me. ["That you did," and cheers.] That question passed away; it resulted in the triumph of my principle by allowing the people to do as they please, and there is an end of the controversy. ["Hear, hear."] Whenever the great principle of self-government— the right of the people to make their own constitution, and come into the Union with slavery, or without it, as they see proper—shall again arise, you will find me standing firm in defense of that principle, and fighting whoever fights it. ["Right, right." "Good, good," and cheers.] If Mr. Buchanan stands, as I doubt not he will, by the recommendation contained in his message, that hereafter all state constitutions ought to be submitted to the people before the admission of the state into the Union, he will find me standing by him firmly, shoulder to shoulder, in carrying it out. I know Mr. Lincoln's object, he wants to divide the Democratic party, in order that he may defeat me and get to the Senate.

LINCOLN'S REJOINDER

My friends,

It will readily occur to you that I cannot in half an hour notice all the things that so able a man as Judge Douglas can say in an hour and a half, and I hope, therefore, if there be any thing that he has said upon which you would like to hear something from me, but which I omit to comment upon, you will bear in mind that it would be expecting an impossibility for me to go over his whole ground. I can but take up some of the points that he has dwelt upon, and employ my half-hour specially on them.

The first thing I have to say to you is a word in regard to Judge Douglas' declaration about the "vulgarity and blackguardism" in the audience—that no such thing, as he says, was shown by any Democrat while I was speaking. Now, I only wish, by way of reply on this subject, to say that while *I* was speaking, *I* used no "vulgarity or blackguardism" toward any Democrat. [Great laughter and applause.]

Now, my friends, I come to all this long portion of the Judge's speech—perhaps half of it—which he has devoted to the various resolutions and platforms that have been adopted in the different counties in the different congressional districts, and in the Illinois legislature—which he supposes are at variance with the positions I have assumed before you to-day. It is true that many of these resolutions are at variance with the positions I have here assumed. All I have to ask is that we talk reasonably and rationally about it. I happen to know, the Judge's opinion to the contrary notwithstanding, that I have never tried to conceal my opinions, nor tried to deceive any one in reference to them. He may go and examine all the members who voted for me for United States Senator in 1855, after the election of 1854. They were pledged to certain things here at home, and were determined to have pledges from me, and if he will find any of these persons who will tell him any thing inconsistent with what I say now, I will resign, or rather retire from the race, and give him no more trouble. [Applause.]

The plain truth is this: At the introduction of the Nebraska policy, we believed there was a new era being introduced in the history of the Republic, which tended to the spread and perpetuation of slavery. But in our opposition to that measure we did not agree with one another in everything. The people in the north end of the state were for stronger measures of opposition than we of the central and southern portions of the state, but we were all opposed to the Nebraska doctrine. We had that one feeling and that one sentiment in common. You at the north end met in your conventions and passed your resolutions. We in the middle of the state and further south did not hold such conventions and pass the same resolutions, although we had in general a common view and a common sentiment. So that these meetings which the Judge has alluded to, and the resolutions he has read from were local, and did not spread over the whole state. We at last met together in 1856 from all parts of the state, and we agreed upon a common platform. You, who held more extreme notions, either yielded those notions, or if not wholly yielding them, agreed to yield them practically, for the sake of embodying the opposition to the measures which the opposite party were pushing forward at that time. We met you then, and if there was any thing yielded, it was for practical purposes. We agreed then upon a platform for the party throughout the entire state of Illinois, and now we are all bound as a party, *to that platform.* And I say here to you, if any one expects of me—in the case of my election—that I will do anything not signified by our Republican platform and my answers here to-day, I tell you very frankly that person will be deceived. I do not ask for the vote of any one who supposes that I have secret purposes or pledges that I dare not speak out. Cannot the Judge be satisfied? If he fears, in the unfortunate case of my election, [laughter] that my going to Washington will enable me to advocate sentiments contrary to those which I expressed when you voted for and elected me, I assure him that his fears are wholly needless and groundless. Is the Judge really afraid of any such thing? [Laughter.] I'll tell you what he is afraid of. *He is afraid we'll all pull together.* [Applause, and cries of "we will, we will."] This is what alarms him more than anything else. [Laughter.] For my part, I do hope that all of us, entertaining a common sentiment in opposition to what appears to us a design to nationalize and perpetuate slavery, will waive minor differences on questions which either belong to the dead past or the distant future, and all pull together in this struggle. What are your sentiments? ["We will, we will," and loud cheers.] If it be true, that on the ground which I occupy—ground which I occupy as frankly and boldly as Judge Douglas does his—my views, though partly coinciding with yours, are not as perfectly in accordance with your feelings as his are, I do say to you in all candor, Go for him and not for me. I hope to deal in all things fairly with Judge Douglas, and with the people of the state, in this contest. And if I should never be elected to any office, I trust I may go down with no stain of falsehood upon my reputation,—notwithstanding the hard opinions Judge Douglas chooses to entertain of me. [Laughter.]

The Judge has again addressed himself to the abolition tendencies of a speech of mine, made at Springfield in June last. I have so often tried to answer what he is always saying on that melancholy theme, that I almost turn with disgust from the discussion—from the repetition of an answer to it. I trust that nearly all of this intelligent audience have read that speech. ["We have; we have."] If you have, I may venture to leave it to you to inspect it closely, and see whether it contains any of those "bugaboos" which frighten Judge Douglas. [Laughter.]

The Judge complains that I did not fully answer his questions. If I have the sense to comprehend and answer those questions, I have done so fairly. If it can be pointed out to me how I can more fully and fairly answer him, I aver I have not the sense to see how it is to be done. He says I do not declare I would in any event vote for the admission of a slave state into the Union. If I have been fairly reported he will see that I did give an explicit answer to his interrogatories. I did not merely say that I would dislike to be put to the test; but I said clearly, if I were put to the test, and a territory from which slavery had been excluded should present herself with a state constitution sanctioning slavery—a most extraordinary thing and wholly unlikely to happen—I did not see how I could avoid voting for her admission. But he refuses to understand that I said so, and he wants this audience to understand that I did not say so. Yet it will be so reported in the printed speech that he cannot help seeing it.

He says if I should vote for the admission of a slave state I would be voting for a dissolution of the Union, because I hold that the Union cannot permanently exist half slave and half free. I repeat that I do not believe this government *can* endure permanently half slave and half free, yet I do not admit, nor does it at all follow, that the admission of a single slave state will permanently fix the character and establish this as a universal slave nation. The Judge is very happy indeed at working up these quibbles. [Laughter and cheers.] Before leaving the subject of answering questions I aver as my confident belief, when you come to see our speeches in print, that you will find every question which he has asked me more fairly and boldly and fully answered than he has answered those which I put to him. Is not that so? [Cries of "yes, yes."] The two speeches may be placed side by side; and I will venture to leave it to impartial judges whether his questions have not been more directly and circumstantially answered than mine.

Judge Douglas says he made a charge upon the editor of the Washington *Union, alone,* of entertaining a purpose to rob the states of their power to exclude slavery from their limits. I undertake to say, and I make the direct issue, that he did *not* make his charge against the editor of the *Union* alone. [Applause.] I will undertake to prove by the record here, that he made that charge against more and higher dignitaries than the editor of the Washington *Union.* [Applause.] I am quite aware that he was shirking and dodging around the form in which he put it, but I can make it manifest that he leveled his "fatal blow" against more persons than this Washington editor. Will he dodge it now by alleging that I am trying to defend Mr. Buchanan against the charge? Not at all. Am I not making the same charge myself? [Laughter and applause.] I am trying to show that you, Judge Douglas, are a witness on my side. [Renewed laughter.] I am not defending Buchanan, and I will tell Judge Douglas that in my opinion, when he made that charge, he had an eye farther North than he was to-day. [Cheers and laughter.] He was then fighting against people who called him a Black Republican and an Abolitionist. It is mixed all through his speech, and it is tolerably manifest that his eye was a great deal farther north than it is to-day. [Cheers and laughter.] The Judge says that though he made this charge, Toombs got up and declared there was not a man in the United States, except the editor of the *Union*, who was in favor of the doctrines put forth in that article. And thereupon, I understand that the Judge withdrew the charge. Although he had taken extracts from the newspaper, and then from the Lecompton constitution, to show the existence of a conspiracy to bring about a "fatal blow," by which the states were to be deprived of the right of excluding slavery, it all went to pot as soon as Toombs got up and told him it was not true. [Laughter.] It reminds me of the story that John Phoenix, the California railroad surveyor, tells. He says they started out from the Plaza to the Mission of Dolores. They had two ways of determining distances. One was by a chain and pins taken over the ground. The other was by a "go-it-ometer"—an invention of his own—a three-legged instrument, with which he computed a series of triangles between the points. At night he turned to the chain-man to ascertain what distance they had come, and found that by some mistake he had merely dragged the chain over the ground without keeping any record. By the "go-it-ometer" he found he had made ten miles. Being skeptical about this, he asked a drayman who was passing how far it was to the plaza. The drayman replied it was just half a mile, and the surveyor put it down in his book—just as Judge Douglas says, after he had made his calculations and computations, he took Toombs' statement. [Great laughter.] I have no doubt that after Judge Douglas had made his charge, he was as easily satisfied about its truth as the surveyor was of the drayman's statement of the distance to the Plaza. [Renewed laughter.] Yet it is a fact that the man who put forth all that matter which Douglas deemed a

"fatal blow" at state sovereignty, was elected by the Democrats as public printer.

Now, gentlemen, you may take Judge Douglas' speech of March 22d, 1858, beginning about the middle of page 21, and reading to the bottom of page 24, and you will find the evidence on which I say that he did not make his charge against the editor of the *Union* alone. I cannot stop to read it, but I will give it to the reporters. Judge Douglas said:

Mr. President, you here find several distinct propositions advanced boldly by the Washington *Union* editorially and apparently *authoritatively*, and every man who questions any of them is denounced as an absolutionist, a Free-Soiler, a fanatic. The propositions are, first, that the primary object of all government at its original institution is the protection of persons and property; second, that the Constitution of the United States declares that the citizens of each State shall be entitled to all the privileges and immunities of citizens in the several States; and that, therefore, thirdly, all State laws, whether organic or otherwise, which prohibit the citizens of one State from settling in another with their slave property, and especially declaring it forfeited, are direct violations of the original intention of the Government and Constitution of the United States; and fourth, that the emancipation of the slaves of the Northern States was a gross outrage on the rights of property, inasmuch as it was involuntarily done on the part of the owner.

Remember that this article was published in the *Union* on the 17th of November, and on the 18th appeared the first article giving the adhesion of the *Union* to the Lecompton Constitution. It was in these words:

"KANSAS AND HER CONSTITUTION.—The vexed question is settled. The problem is solved. The dead point of danger is passed. All serious trouble to Kansas affairs is over and gone."

And a column, nearly, of the same sort. Then, when you come to look into the Lecompton constitution, you find the same doctrine incorporated in it which was put forth editorially in the *Union*. What is it?

"ARTICLE 7. *Section* 1. The right of property is before and higher than any constitutional sanction; and the right of the owner of a slave to such slave and its increase is the same and as invariable as the right of the owner of any property whatever."

Then in the schedule is a provision that the constitution may be amended after 1864 by a two-thirds vote.

"But no alteration shall be made to affect the right of property in the ownership of slaves."

It will be seen by these clauses in the Lecompton constitution that they are identical in spirit with this *authoritative* article in the Washington *Union* of the day previous to its indorsement of this constitution.

When I saw that article in the *Union* of the 17th of November, followed by the glorification of the Lecompton Constitution on the 18th of November, and this clause in the Constitution asserting the doctrine that a State has no right to prohibit slavery within its limits, I saw that there was a *fatal blow* being struck at the sovereignty of the States of this Union.

Here he says, "Mr. President, you here find several distinct propositions advanced boldly, and apparently *authoritatively.*" By whose authority, Judge Douglas? [Great cheers and laughter.] Again, he says in another place, "It will be seen by these clauses in the Lecompton constitution, that they are identical in spirit with this *authoritative* article." *By whose authority?* [Renewed cheers.] Who do you mean to say authorized the publication of these articles? He knows that the Washington *Union* is considered the organ of the administration. *I* demand of Judge Douglas *by whose authority* he meant to say those articles were published, if not by the authority of the President of the United States and his Cabinet? I defy him to show whom he referred to, if not to these high functionaries in the federal government. More than this, he says the articles in that paper and the provisions of the Lecompton constitution are "identical," and being identical, he argues that the authors are co-operating and conspiring together. He does not use the word "conspiring," but what other construction can you put upon it? He winds up with this:

When I saw that article in the *Union* of the 17th of November, followed by the glorification of the Lecompton constitution on the 18th of November, and this clause in the constitution asserting the doctrine that a State has no right to prohibit slavery within its limits, I saw that

there was a *fatal blow* being struck at the sovereignty of the states of this Union.

I ask him if all this fuss was made over the editor of this newspaper. [Laughter.] It would be a terribly *"fatal blow"* indeed which a single man could strike, when no President, no Cabinet officer, no member of Congress, was giving strength and efficiency to the moment. Out of respect to Judge Douglas' good sense I must believe he didn't manufacture his idea of the "fatal" character of that blow out of such a miserable scapegrace as he represents that editor to be. But the Judge's eye is farther south now. [Laughter and cheers.] Then, it was very peculiarly and decidedly north. His hope rested on the idea of visiting the great "Black Republican" party, and making it the tail of his new kite. [Great laughter.] He knows he was then expecting from day to day to turn Republican and place himself at the head [of] our organization. He has found that these despised "Black Republicans" estimate him by a standard which he has taught them none too well. Hence he is crawling back into his old camp, and you will find him eventually installed in full fellowship among those whom he was then battling, and with whom he now pretends to be at such fearful variance. [Loud applause and cries of "go on, go on."] I cannot, gentlemen, my time has expired.

Source: Abraham Lincoln and Stephen A. Douglas, "The Freeport Debate," in *Created Equal? The Complete Lincoln-Douglas Debates of 1858,* ed. Paul M. Angle. Chicago: University of Chicago Press, 1958.

John Brown's Last Speech (1859)

November 2, 1859.

I have, may it please the Court, a few words to say. In the first place, I deny everything but what I have all along admitted,—the design on my part to free the slaves. I intended certainly to have made a clean thing of that matter, as I did last winter, when I went into Missouri and there took slaves without the snapping of a gun on either side, moved them through the country, and finally left them in Canada. I designed to have done the same thing again, on a larger scale. That was all I intended. I never did intend murder, or treason, or the destruction of property, or to excite or incite slaves to rebellion, or to make insurrection.

I have another objection; and that is, it is unjust that I should suffer such a penalty. Had I interfered in the manner which I admit, and which I admit has been fairly proved (for I admire the truthfulness and candor of the greater portion of the witnesses who have testified in this case),—had I so interfered in behalf of the rich, the powerful, the intelligent, the so-called great, or in behalf of any of their friends,—either father, mother brother, sister, wife, or children, or any of that class,—and suffered and sacrificed what I have in this interference, it would have been all right; and every man in this court would have deemed it an act worthy of reward rather than punishment.

This court acknowledges, as I suppose, the validity of the law of God. I see a book kissed here which I suppose to be the Bible, or at least the new Testament. That teaches me that all things whatsoever I would that men should do to me, I should do even so to them. It teaches me, further, to remember them that are in bonds, as bound with them. I endeavored to act up to that instruction. I say, I am yet too young to understand that God is any respecter of persons. I believe that to have interfered as I have done—as I have always freely admitted I have done—in behalf of His despised poor, was not wrong, but right. Now, if it is deemed necessary that I should forfeit my life for the furtherance of the ends of justice, and mingle my blood further with the blood of my children and with the blood of millions in this slave country whose rights are disregarded by wicked, cruel, and unjust enactments,—I submit; so let it be done!

Let me say one word further. I feel entirely satisfied with the treatment I have received in my trial. Considering all the circumstances, it has been more generous than I expected. But I feel no consciousness of guilt. I have stated from the first what was my intention, and what was not. I never had any design against the life of any person, nor any disposition to commit treason, or excite slaves to rebel, or make any general insurrection. I never encouraged any man to do so, but always discouraged any idea of that kind.

Let me say, also, a word in regard to the statements made by some of those connected with me. I hear it has been stated by some of them that I have induced them to join me. But the contrary is true. I do not say this to injure them, but as regretting their weakness. There is not one of them but joined me of his own expense. A number of them I never saw, and never had a word of conversation with, till the day they came to me; and that was for the purpose I have stated.

Now I have done.

Source: American State Trials, ed. J.D. Lawson, vol. VI. St. Louis, MO: Thomas Law Book Co., 1914–; repr. Buffalo, NY: W.S. Hein, 2000.

John C. Frémont's Proclamation on Slaves (1861)

Saint Louis, August 30, 1861.

PROCLAMATION.
HEADQUARTERS WESTERN DEPARTMENT.
Circumstances, in my judgment, of sufficient urgency render it necessary that the commanding general of this department should assume the administrative powers of the State. Its disorganized condition, the helplessness of the civil authority, the total insecurity of life, and the devastation of property by bands of murderers and marauders, who infest nearly every county of the State, and avail themselves of the public misfortunes and the vicinity of a hostile force to gratify private and neighborhood vengeance, and who find an enemy wherever they find plunder, finally demand the severest measures to repress the daily-increasing crimes and outrages which are driving off the inhabitants and ruining the State.

In this condition the public safety and the success of our arms require unity of purpose, without let or hinderance to the prompt administration of affairs. In order, therefore, to suppress disorder, to maintain as far as now practicable the public peace, and to give security and protection to the persons and property of loyal citizens, I do hereby extend and declare established martial law throughout the State of Missouri.

The lines of the army of occupation in this State are for the present declared to extend from Leavenworth, by way of the posts of Jefferson City, Rolla, and Ironton, to Cape Girardeau, on the Mississippi River.

All persons who shall be taken with arms in their hands within these lines shall be tried by court-martial, and if found guilty will be shot.

The property, real and personal, of all persons in the State of Missouri who shall take up arms against the United States, or who shall be directly proven to have taken an active part with their enemies in the field, is declared to be confiscated to the public use, and their slaves, if any they have, are hereby declared freemen.

All persons who shall be proven to have destroyed, after the publication of this order, railroad tracks, bridges, or telegraphs shall suffer the extreme penalty of the law.

All persons engaged in treasonable correspondence, in giving or procuring aid to the enemies of the United States, in fomenting tumults, in disturbing the public tranquillity by creating and circulating false reports or incendiary documents, are in their own interests warned that they are exposing themselves to sudden and severe punishment.

All persons who have been led away from their allegiance are required to return to their homes forthwith. Any such absence, without sufficient cause, will be held to be presumptive evidence against them.

The object of this declaration is to place in the hands of the military authorities the power to give instantaneous effect to existing laws, and to supply such deficiencies as the conditions of war demand. But this is not intended to suspend the ordinary tribunals of the country, where the law will be administered by the civil officers in the usual manner, and with their customary authority, while the same can be peaceably exercised.

The commanding general will labor vigilantly for the public welfare, and in his efforts for their safety hopes to obtain not only the acquiescence but the active support of the loyal people of the country.

J.C. FRÉMONT,
Major-General, Commanding.

Source: The War of the Rebellion: A Compilation of the Official Records of the Union and Confederate Armies, series I, vol. 3, Correspondence, Orders, and Returns, Relating Specially to Operations in Arkansas, the Indian Territory, Kansas, and Missouri, from May 10 to November 19, 1861. Washington, DC: U.S. Government Printing Office, 1881.

President Lincoln's Response to David Hunter's Proclamation Freeing Slaves (1862)

PROCLAMATION.

Whereas, there appears in the public prints what purports to be a proclamation of Major-General Hunter in the words and figures following, to wit:

Hilton Head, S.C., May 9, 1862.
HEADQUARTERS DEPARTMENT
OF THE SOUTH,
GENERAL ORDERS No. 11.
The three States of Georgia, Florida and South Carolina, comprising the Military Department of the South, having deliberately declared themselves no longer under the protection of the United States of America and having taken up arms against the said United States it becomes a military necessity to declare them under martial law. This was accordingly done on the 25th day of April, 1862. Slavery and martial law in a free

country are altogether incompatible; the persons in these three States—Georgia, Florida and South Carolina—heretofore held as slaves are therefore declared forever free.

DAVID HUNTER,
Major-General, Commanding.

And whereas, the same is producing some excitement and misunderstanding:

Therefore, I, Abraham Lincoln, President of the United States, proclaim and declare that the Government of the United States had no knowledge, information or belief of an intention on the part of General Hunter to issue such a proclamation nor has it yet any authentic information that the document is genuine. And further that neither General Hunter nor any other commander or person has been authorized by the Government of the United States to make proclamations declaring the slaves of any State free; and that the supposed proclamation now in question whether genuine or false is altogether void so far as respects such declaration.

I further make known that whether it be competent for me as Commander-in-Chief of the Army and Navy to declare the slaves of any State or States free, and whether at any time in any case it shall have become a necessity indispensable to the maintenance of the Government to exercise such supposed power are questions which under my responsibility I reserve to myself and which I cannot feel justified in leaving to the decision of commanders in the field. These are totally different questions from those of police regulations in armies and camps.

On the 6th day of March last by a special message I recommended to Congress the adoption of a joint resolution to be substantially as follows:

Resolved, That the United States ought to cooperate with any State which may adopt a gradual abolishment of slavery, giving to such State pecuniary aid to be used by such State in its discretion to compensate for the inconveniences public and private produced by such change of system.

The resolution in the language above quoted was adopted by large majorities in both branches of Congress and now stands an authentic, definite and solemn proposal of the nation to the States and people most immediately interested in the subject-matter. To the people of those States I now earnestly appeal; I do not argue, I beseech you to make the argument for yourselves; you cannot if you would be blind to the signs of the times; I beg of you a calm and an enlarged consideration of them, ranging if it may be far above personal and partisan politics. This proposal makes common cause for a common object casting no reproaches upon any; it acts not the Pharisee. The changes it contemplates would come gently as the dews of Heaven, not rending or wrecking anything. Will you not embrace it! So much good has not been done by one effort in all past time as in the Providence of God it is now your high privilege to do. May the vast future not have to lament that you have neglected it.

In witness whereof I have hereunto set my hand and caused the seal of the United States to be affixed.

Done at the city of Washington this nineteenth day of May, in the year of our Lord one thousand eight hundred and sixty-two, and of the Independence of the United States the eighty-sixth.

By the President,
ABRAHAM LINCOLN.

Secretary of State,
WILLIAM H. SEWARD.

Source: The War of the Rebellion: A Compilation of the Official Records of the Union and Confederate Armies, series II, vol. 1, *Miscellaneous Records Relating to the Negro in the Early Stage of the Rebellion.* Washington, DC: U.S. Government Printing Office, 1894.

Chronology

1510s

The Spanish begin importing African slaves into their Caribbean colonies.

1619

Slavery is introduced in British North America when the first African slaves arrive at Jamestown, Virginia.

1662

To define the status of slaves, Virginia passes a law making children born to enslaved mothers slaves from birth. Other colonies will adopt similar laws during the late seventeenth and early eighteenth centuries.

1672

King Charles II of England charters the Royal African Company, increasing the number of slaves imported to British North America.

1682

Slavery becomes legal in South Carolina.

1688

Pennsylvania Quakers issue the Germantown Protest, denouncing the practice of slavery in colonial Pennsylvania.

1696

In their yearly meeting, colonial American Quakers advise members against importing slaves.

1698

The Royal African Company loses its monopoly on the English slave trade.

1700

Rhode Island and Pennsylvania legally sanction slavery.

Massachusetts judge Samuel Sewall publishes *The Selling of Joseph*, the first antislavery tract in America.

1705

Virginia's Black Code restricts the mobility of slaves and penalizes miscegenation.

1712

A slave uprising in the city of New York results in the death of eight whites. Twenty-five slaves are convicted and sentenced to death.

Pennsylvania bans the further importation of slaves.

1717

Congregational clergyman Cotton Mather opens an evening school in Boston for slaves and American Indians.

1739

Three slave revolts take place in South Carolina. The most serious occurs in September along the Stono River, approximately 20 miles southwest of Charles Town. Involving as many as a hundred slaves, the Stono Rebellion is the largest slave uprising in the British colonies prior to the American Revolution.

The British sign a treaty with the maroons in Jamaica, ending eighty years of conflict.

1741

Pope Benedict XIV condemns the Brazilian slave trade.

1748

Enlightenment thinker Baron de Montesquieu publishes *The Spirit of Laws*, in which he defines slavery as "neither useful to the master nor the slave."

1749

Georgia repeals its prohibition on the importation of slaves.

1750

Almost all of the 236,000 blacks living in the thirteen British colonies are slaves.

1754

Philadelphia Quakers define slavery as a sin at their yearly meeting.

1765

The *Encyclopédie*, edited by Frenchmen Denis Diderot and Jean d'Alembert, defines liberty as a natural right.

1772

In the case of *Knowles v. Somersett*, British chief justice Lord Mansfield rules that slaves who set foot on English soil automatically become freedmen and cannot be forced to return to slave colonies.

In London, James Albert Ukawsaw Gronniosaw publishes the first English-language slave narrative, *A Narrative of the Most Remarkable Particulars in the Life of James Albert Ukawsaw Gronniosaw.*

1774

Philadelphia Quakers vote to adopt rules forbidding members to buy or sell slaves.

1775

The American Revolution begins. The earl of Dunmore, governor of Virginia, offers to free male slaves who join the British army in opposing the American rebels.

1776

Following protest by the Southern delegates to the Continental Congress, Thomas Jefferson's attack on the British Empire's role in the slave trade is stricken from the draft of the Declaration of Independence.

The Continental Congress passes a resolution calling for the end of slave importation to the United States.

Philadelphia Quakers' yearly meeting is closed to slave owners.

Slavery remains a legal institution in all thirteen of the newly established states.

1777

Slavery is prohibited in Vermont by the state constitution.

1780

Pennsylvania passes An Act for the Gradual Abolition of Slavery.

The Massachusetts state constitution declares that "all men are born free and equal, and have . . . the right of enjoying and defending their lives and liberties."

The French sign a treaty with maroons in the colony of Saint-Domingue.

1783

A Massachusetts Supreme Court ruling, *Commonwealth v. Jennison,* abolishes slavery in the state.

Maryland prohibits the slave trade.

With the end of the American Revolution and the departure of the British forces, approximately 15,000 Black Loyalists, who had fought on the side of the British, leave the United States.

1784

Connecticut and Rhode Island pass gradual abolition legislation.

The Pennsylvania Abolition Society is organized; within two years, the group will grow to more than eighty members. This society helps inspire the establishment of other antislavery organizations.

1785

The Society for Promoting the Manumission of Slaves is established in New York. Headed by John Jay and Alexander Hamilton, the organization purchases the freedom of persons held in bondage and founds the African Free School.

1787

The Northwest Ordinance bans slavery in all lands north of the Ohio River in the Northwest Territory (which will become the states of Ohio, Indiana, Illinois, Michigan, and Wisconsin).

The U.S. Constitution is framed, counting each slave as three-fifths of one free person in the appropriation of direct taxes and representation in Congress.

As the founder and first bishop of the African Methodist Episcopal Church, Richard Allen leads Philadelphia blacks to form their own congregation after being forced from a white church.

London abolitionists settle Sierra Leone, Africa, as a colony for freed slaves.

British abolitionists organize the Society for the Abolition of the Slave Trade.

1788

La Société des Amis des Noirs (Society of Friends of the Blacks) is founded in France.

1790

The Pennsylvania Quakers present the first emancipation petition to the U.S. Congress.

1791

The Haitian Revolution begins as Toussaint L'Ouverture leads a large-scale uprising of the colony's slaves against the French.

1793

The U.S. Congress enacts the first Fugitive Slave Law, which allows slave owners to cross state lines to recapture their slaves. In response, some Northern states pass personal liberty laws that grant alleged fugitives the right to habeas corpus and jury trials.

Eli Whitney's invention of the cotton gin leads to the rapid expansion of cotton cultivation in the U.S. South.

Upper Canada passes a gradual emancipation law. By 1800, legislation will limit slavery effectively elsewhere in Canada.

1794

Congress prohibits the slave trade to foreign ports and the outfitting of foreign slave trade vessels in U.S. ports, in an effort to prevent U.S. citizens from participating in the trade.

The French National Assembly abolishes the slave trade and ends slavery in all French colonies.

1799

New York State passes gradual abolition legislation.

1800

In August, white Virginians discover and suppress Gabriel Prosser's slave revolt in Henrico County, just outside of Richmond.

The U.S. Census lists some 893,000 slaves and 4.3 million whites.

1802

Slavery is prohibited in Ohio by the state constitution.

Napoleon Bonaparte reinstates slavery and the slave trade in the French colonies.

1803

South Carolina opens its port to South American slave traders.

Denmark ends its international slave trade.

1804

New Jersey passes gradual abolition legislation.

Ohio passes Black Laws that restrict the movement of free blacks.

Haitian independence is achieved.

1806

Virginia requires that all slaves who are emancipated after May 1 leave the state.

1807

Congress passes a law prohibiting the importation of slaves from Africa beginning on January 1, 1808, the earliest date allowed by the U.S. Constitution. The slave trade continues within and between states where slavery is still legal.

The British Parliament passes the Abolition of the Slave Trade Act, thus outlawing participation in the transatlantic slave trade by all British citizens.

1811

From January 8 to 10, a large slave revolt takes place near New Orleans, Louisiana.

Chile enacts a gradual emancipation law, which will end slavery in the country by 1823.

1813

Argentina begins a policy of gradual emancipation.

1816

Slavery is prohibited in Indiana by the state constitution.

The American Colonization Society is established to relocate African Americans to Africa as an alternative to emancipation within the United States.

Simón Bolívar and José Francisco de San Martín promise freedom to slaves who support the struggle for black liberation from Spain in the Spanish colonies of the Americas.

1817

Great Britain and Spain sign a treaty prohibiting the slave trade. Spain agrees to end the slave trade north of the equator immediately and south of the equator by 1820.

1818

Slavery is prohibited in Illinois by the state constitution.

1820

The Missouri Compromise admits Missouri into the Union as a slave state, but it prohibits slavery in all new states north of the 36°30' latitude, or the border of the Arkansas Territory (excluding Missouri).

1821

Abolitionist Benjamin Lundy founds the *Genius of Universal Emancipation*, a newspaper dedicated to describing the evils of slavery and advocating political pressure to bring an end to it.

Colombia, Ecuador, Peru, and Venezuela begin the process of gradual emancipation.

1822

The American Colonization Society settles its first colony at Monrovia (later Liberia) in West Africa. By 1867, the society has sent more than 13,000 emigrants to West Africa.

In May, Denmark Vesey's plot for slave rebellion, the largest and most complex in American history, is uncovered in Charleston, South Carolina. The conspiracy results in the arrest of more than a hundred individuals and the hanging of Vesey and thirty-five others.

1823

Thomas Clarkson, William Wilberforce, and others form the British Anti-Slavery Society, which campaigns for better conditions for slaves in the West Indies and for the gradual abolition of slavery there.

1824

Abolitionist Elizabeth Heyrick publishes the pamphlet *Immediate, Not Gradual Abolition* in Philadelphia and London.

Slavery is abolished in Central America.

1825

Frances Wright's *Plan for the Gradual Abolition of Slavery in the United States* is published in Baltimore.

Uruguay begins a process of gradual emancipation.

1826

Frances Wright establishes Nashoba, a utopian community near Memphis, Tennessee, with the goal of training blacks and providing for their eventual resettlement outside the United States.

1827

Freedom's Journal, the first newspaper owned and operated by African Americans in the United States, is published weekly in the city of New York.

Slavery ends in New York State.

1829

In September, free black David Walker publishes the militant antislavery publication *An Appeal to the Colored Citizens of the World*, advocating resistance by blacks to the institution of slavery.

Mexico abolishes slavery.

1831

In January, William Lloyd Garrison begins publication of *The Liberator* in Boston.

In August, slave preacher Nat Turner leads a slave rebellion in Southampton County, Virginia, in which at least fifty-five whites and at least a hundred blacks die. Turner is sentenced to death by hanging in November. In the aftermath of the rebellion, the Virginia legislature debates whether to maintain slavery within the state.

Shortly after Christmas, a slave rebellion led by itinerant preacher Samuel Sharpe in western Jamaica destroys $3.5 million in property and brings economic ruin to sugar planters on the island. The Great Jamaican Slave Revolt, as it comes to be known, will hasten Parliament's decision to mandate general emancipation in the British West Indies.

Bolivia begins a process of gradual emancipation.

1832

In January, William Lloyd Garrison establishes the New England Anti-Slavery Society to advocate the immediate abolition of slavery through nonviolence and to oppose the colonization of blacks.

Schoolteacher Prudence Crandall admits black children to her school in Canterbury, Connecticut, igniting a scandal. The school is later vandalized, and Crandall closes its doors.

1832–1834

Women-run antislavery societies begin to appear throughout New England, particularly in Massachusetts, Rhode Island, Connecticut, and New York.

Students at the Lane Theological Seminary leave the school after being ordered to cease debates with faculty on the subjects of colonization and abolition.

On August 29, 1833, the British Parliament passes the Abolition of Slavery Act (also known as the Emancipation Act); it becomes effective on August 1, 1834. The law effectively ends slavery in all British colonial possessions.

1833

In December, abolitionists Theodore Dwight Weld, Arthur Tappan, Lewis Tappan, and others establish the American Anti-Slavery Society in Philadelphia; it is the first national antislavery society in the United States. Under the leadership of William Lloyd Garrison, the society becomes known for its abolitionist tactics of moral suasion.

1835

Georgia enacts the death penalty for those who publish abolitionist tracts.

1836

Southerners in the U.S. Congress pass the Gag Rule, which prohibits the reading and circulation of antislavery petitions in Congress.

Sarah Grimké's *Epistle to the Clergy of the Southern States* is published in New York; Angelina Grimké's "Appeal to the Christian Women of the South" appears in the September issue of the *Anti-Slavery Examiner*. In December, the two sisters begin an abolitionist speaking tour.

1837

Catherine E. Beecher's *An Essay on Slavery and Abolitionism* is published in Philadelphia and Boston.

In May, the first Anti-Slavery Convention of American Women is held in New York.

In November, newspaper editor Elijah Lovejoy is murdered in Alton, Illinois, by a proslavery mob while defending his press.

1837–1838

Great Britain signs a series of treaties with other nations allowing its Royal Navy to search their ships for slaves.

1838

Black women of Philadelphia form the Female Vigilant Committee to support the efforts of the Underground Railroad, an informal network of abolitionists that helps runaway slaves reach freedom

In May, the Second Anti-Slavery Convention of American Women takes place in Philadelphia. When a proslavery mob attacks the gathering, Pennsylvania Hall burns.

1839

With the contributions of abolitionist sisters Angelina and Sarah Grimké, Theodore Dwight Weld publishes *American Slavery As It Is: Testimony of a Thousand Witnesses*.

Off the coast of Cuba, Africans led by Joseph Cinqué revolt on the Spanish slave ship *Amistad*, kill the captain, and seize the vessel. Two years later, the U.S. Supreme Court's decision in the *Amistad* case will determine that the Africans, who were illegally abducted from Sierra Leone, West Africa, cannot be held as slaves and have the right to return to their homeland.

The British and Foreign Anti-Slavery Society is founded in London with a commitment to abolishing slavery throughout the world.

The Boston Female Anti-Slavery Society publishes the first successful antislavery annual, *The Liberty Bell,* edited by Maria Weston Chapman. It is sold to raise funds to help support the abolitionist cause.

1840

Abby Kelley and Lydia Maria Child are elected as officers of the American Anti-Slavery Society.

Amid increased disagreement over its abolitionist strategy and Garrison's support of women's rights, the American Anti-Slavery Society splits. Dissenters, including Arthur and Lewis Tappan and Theodore Dwight Weld, form the American and Foreign Anti-Slavery Society.

The American Anti-Slavery Society begins publishing the *National Anti-Slavery Standard.*

The Liberty Party, dedicated to ending slavery in the United States through the political process, is formed. Ohio abolitionist James G. Birney runs for president on the party's platform.

The World Anti-Slavery Convention takes place in London. Convention organizers refuse to allow American female abolitionist delegates to participate in the proceedings.

Great Britain frees the slaves aboard the *Hermosa,* a slave-carrying vessel that had shipwrecked in the Bahamas.

1841

England, France, Russia, Prussia, and Austria sign the Quintuple Treaty, acknowledging the slave trade as piracy and allowing seafaring vessels to be searched in order to suppress the international slave trade.

1842

Slavery ends in Rhode Island.

The U.S. Supreme Court's decision in *Prigg v. Pennsylvania* upholds the Fugitive Slave Law of 1793 and rules that Pennsylvania's antikidnapping law is unconstitutional. The Court also declares that enforcement of the law is a federal responsibility in which the states are not required to participate, prompting Northern states to pass personal liberty laws that forbid state officials from cooperating in the return of fugitives.

Paraguay approves a gradual emancipation law.

1843

Great Britain and the United States agree to intercept slave-carrying ships along the West African coastline; this action is carried out using the vessels of the African Squadron.

Vermont and Massachusetts bar state officials from assisting efforts to remove fugitive slaves from these states.

1844

The Methodist Church of the United States divides over the question of whether a bishop can hold slaves. In response, white Southerners organize the Methodist Episcopal Church, South.

1845

Slavery ends in New Hampshire and Pennsylvania.

The annexation of Texas opens new areas of the United States to the expansion of slavery.

Under increased pressure from Northern abolitionists, the Gag Rule is repealed in the U.S. House of Representatives.

Frederick Douglass publishes his *Narrative of the Life of Frederick Douglass, An American Slave.* The first of three autobiographies that he will write, it is employed as antislavery propaganda and establishes Douglass as a pioneer of the slave narrative.

1846

In the U.S. House of Representatives, Congressman David Wilmot of Pennsylvania proposes to outlaw slavery in any territory acquired from Mexico as a result of the Mexican-American War. The Wilmot Proviso is ultimately defeated in the Senate.

1847

In Rochester, New York, Frederick Douglass and Martin Delany begin publishing their abolitionist newspaper, *The North Star.*

1848

Slavery ends in Connecticut.

Antislavery Barnburners in the Democratic Party join with the abolitionist Liberty Party to form the Free Soil Party.

France abolishes slavery in all of its colonies.

1850

As part of the Missouri Compromise of 1850, a more restrictive Fugitive Slave Law is passed, requiring citizens to assist in the recovery of runaway slaves and denying fugitives the right to a trial. Passage of the law results in increased abolitionist activity and marks the peak of the Underground Railroad system.

The Missouri Compromise admits California to the Union as a free state, establishes New Mexico and Utah as territories, and curtails the slave trade in the District of Columbia.

The Narrative of Sojourner Truth, memoirs of the abolitionist, women's rights advocate, and former slave, is published in Boston.

Brazil ends the importation of slaves.

1851

The British occupy the slaving port of Lagos, West Africa.

1852

Harriet Beecher Stowe publishes the antislavery novel *Uncle Tom's Cabin,* which sells more than 10,000 copies in its first week of publication.

Slavery ends in Colombia and Ecuador. All remaining slaves in those nations are emancipated.

1854

The Kansas-Nebraska Act repeals the Missouri Compromise and allows the people of Kansas and Nebraska to decide whether to allow slavery within their borders. In opposition to the expansion of slavery into the Western territories, antislavery activists, along with those who believe that the government should grant Western lands to settlers free of charge, form the Republican Party.

Slavery ends in Uruguay.

Peru abolishes slavery.

Argentina and Venezuela liberate all remaining slaves.

1855

Racial segregation is abolished in Massachusetts schools by state law.

1855–1856

A civil war, known as Bleeding Kansas, erupts in the Kansas Territory over the issue of slavery. By the end of 1856, 200 people in Kansas have been killed and $2 million in property has been damaged or destroyed.

1856

The Republican Party officially organizes as a national party and nominates John C. Frémont for president under the slogan "Free soil, free labor, free speech, free men, Frémont."

1857

The U.S. Supreme Court rules in *Dred Scott v. Sandford* that blacks are not citizens and that the U.S. Congress holds no power to exclude slavery from the territories.

1858

Accepting the Republican nomination for senator from Illinois, Abraham Lincoln states, "A house divided against itself cannot stand. I believe this government cannot endure permanently half slave and half free."

1859

In October, the radical abolitionist John Brown raids the federal arsenal at Harpers Ferry, Virginia, in order to seize arms and free Southern slaves. His plan is thwarted, and Brown is tried for treason, found guilty, and hanged in December—a martyr to the antislavery cause.

1860

In November, Abraham Lincoln is elected the sixteenth president of the United States on a Republican Party platform that opposes slavery in the territories. In December, South Carolina secedes from the Union, followed by six more Southern states—Mississippi, Florida, Alabama, Georgia, Louisiana, and Texas—between January and February 1861.

1861

The seven seceding Southern states write the Confederate Constitution, which emphasizes the autonomy of each state. Jefferson Davis is named provisional president of the Confederate States of America.

In April, the U.S. Civil War begins when Confederate forces attack Fort Sumter in Charleston Harbor, South Carolina.

Slavery ends in Bolivia.

1862

In April, the U.S. Congress agrees to cooperate with states that consent to a plan of gradual emancipation for their slaves. In the District of Columbia, compensated emancipation becomes law.

In July, the U.S. Congress passes the Militia Act, which permits the employment of blacks in "any military or naval service for which they may be found competent."

In September, President Abraham Lincoln issues the preliminary Emancipation Proclamation.

1862–1863

Peruvian "blackbirding" expeditions (forced labor recruitment) occur in the Pacific.

1863

In January, President Abraham Lincoln issues the Emancipation Proclamation, declaring that "all persons held as slaves" within the rebellious states "are, and henceforward shall be free." The proclamation announces the acceptance of black men into the Union army and navy.

In May, the War Department places control of black recruits under the U.S. Colored Troops. Within two months, more than thirty regiments are armed and in battle.

The Netherlands ends slavery in its colonies, with an apprenticeship period.

1865

In April, President Abraham Lincoln is assassinated. The U.S. Civil War comes to a close, as the remaining Confederate troops are defeated between the end of April and May.

The states ratify the Thirteenth Amendment, which abolishes slavery in the United States.

The U.S. Congress establishes the Bureau of Refugees, Freedmen and Abandoned Lands (commonly known as the Freedmen's Bureau) to educate and rehabilitate more than 4 million former slaves in the South and to ease their transition from slavery to freedom.

1867

The last slave ship from Africa arrives in Cuba.

The Reconstruction Acts send Union troops back to the South to protect the rights of freed slaves.

Congressman Thaddeus Stevens introduces a Reparations Bill in the U.S. House of Representatives, but the measure is not adopted.

1868

The states ratify the Fourteenth Amendment, which defines citizenship and guarantees the rights of all U.S. citizens.

1868–1878

The Ten Years' War begins the emancipation of slaves in Cuba.

1870

The states ratify the Fifteenth Amendment, which prohibits discrimination against U.S. citizens in voting on the basis of race.

The Moret Law begins the process of gradual emancipation in the Spanish colonies.

1871

Brazil initiates gradual emancipation with the passage of the *Lei do Ventre Libre* (Free Birth Law), which grants freedom to the unborn children of slave mothers.

1873

Zanzibar agrees to end the slave trade.

Slavery is abolished in Puerto Rico.

1877

Federal troops withdraw from the U.S. South, ending the period of Reconstruction.

1880

The Brazilian Anti-Slavery Society is founded.

Spain's Law of Patronato begins the abolition of slavery in Cuba.

1885

Brazil passes the Sexagenarian Law (also known as the Saraiva-Cotegipe Law), which frees all slaves at the age of sixty.

1886

The Spanish government decrees the complete abolition of African slavery in Cuba.

1888

Brazil abolishes slavery, breaking the last stronghold of slavery in the transatlantic world.

Bibliography

Abbott, Lyman. *Henry Ward Beecher.* Cambridge, MA: Riverside Press, 1904; Miami, FL: Mnemosyne, 1969.

Abdy, Edward S. *Journal of a Residence and Tour in the United States of North America, From April, 1833, to October, 1834.* 1835. New York: Negro Universities Press, 1969.

Abels, Jules. *Man on Fire: John Brown and the Cause of Liberty.* New York: Macmillan, 1971.

Abzug, Robert H. "The Influence of Garrisonian Abolitionists' Fear of Slave Violence on the Antislavery Argument, 1829–40." *Journal of Negro History* 55 (January 1970): 14–26.

———. *Passionate Liberator: Theodore Dwight Weld and the Dilemma of Reform.* New York: Oxford University Press, 1980.

Acholonu, Catherine Obianuju. *The Igbo Roots of Olaudah Equiano.* Owerri, Nigeria: AFA, 1989.

Ackerson, Wayne. *The African Institution (1807–1827) and the Antislavery Movement in Great Britain.* Lewiston, NY: Edwin Mellen, 2004.

Adams, James Truslow. "Disenfranchisement of Negroes in New England." *American Historical Review* 30 (April 1925): 543–47.

Adams, Jerome R. *Latin American Heroes: Liberators and Patriots from 1500 to the Present.* New York: Ballantine, 1991.

Adams, John Quincy. *The Diary of John Quincy Adams, 1794–1845: American Diplomacy, and Political, Social, and Intellectual Life, from Washington to Polk.* Ed. Allan Nevins. New York: F. Ungar, 1951.

———. *Memoirs of John Quincy Adams, Comprising Portions of His Diary From 1795 to 1848.* 12 vols. Ed. Charles Frances Adams. Philadelphia: J.B. Lippincott, 1874–1877.

Adams, John R. *Harriet Beecher Stowe.* Boston: Twayne, 1989.

Adams, Robert. "Nathaniel Peabody Rogers: 1794–1846." *New England Quarterly* 20 (September 1947): 365–76.

Adams, William E. *Memoirs of a Social Atom.* 1901. New York: Augustus M. Kelley, 1968.

Agnes, Peter W., Jr. "The Quork [*sic*] Walker Cases and the Abolition of Slavery in Massachusetts: A Reflection of Popular Sentiment or an Expression of Constitutional Law?" *Boston Bar Journal* 36 (March/April 1992): 8–14.

Ajayi, J.E. Ade. *A Patriot to the Core: Samuel Ajayi Crowther.* Ibadan, Nigeria: Anglican Diocese of Ibadan, 1992.

Albrecht-Carrié, René. *The Concert of Europe.* New York: Walker, 1968.

Alexander, A. John. "The Ideas of Lysander Spooner." *New England Quarterly* 23 (June 1950): 200–17.

Alexander, Ken, and Avis Glaze. *Towards Freedom: The African-Canadian Experience.* Toronto, Ontario, Canada: Umbrella, 1996.

Alexander, Robert J., ed. *Biographical Dictionary of Latin American and Caribbean Political Leaders.* New York: Greenwood, 1988.

Alilunas, Leo. "Fugitive Slave Cases in Ohio Prior to 1850." *Ohio Archaeological and Historical Quarterly* 49 (April 1940): 160–84.

Allen, James. *Without Sanctuary: Lynching Photography in America.* Santa Fe, NM: Twin Palms, 2000.

Alvis, John. "The Slavery Provisions of the U.S. Constitution: Means for Emancipation." *Political Science Reviewer* 17 (Spring 1987): 241–65.

Alvord, John. *Semi-Annual Reports of Schools for Freedmen, 1866–1870.* New York: AMS, 1980.

American Tract Society. "The Address of the Executive Committee." In *The America Tract Society Documents, 1824–1925.* New York: Arno, 1972.

———. *Brief History of the American Tract Society.* Boston: T.R. Marvin, 1857.

Anderson Imbert, Enrique. *Spanish-American Literature: A History.* Trans. John V. Falconieri. Detroit, MI: Wayne State University Press, 1963.

Anderson, James. *The Education of Blacks in the South, 1860–1935.* Chapel Hill: University of North Carolina Press, 1988.

Anderson, Osborne Perry. *A Voice From Harper's Ferry.* 1861. Atlanta, GA: World View, 1980.

Andrews, Charles C. *The History of the New-York African Free Schools.* 1830. New York: Negro Universities Press, 1969.

Andrews, George Reid. *The Afro-Argentines of Buenos Aires, 1800–1900.* Madison: University of Wisconsin Press, 1980.

———. "Black and White Workers: São Paulo, Brazil, 1888–1928." *Hispanic American Historical Review* 68 (August 1988): 491–524.

Andrews, Horace, Jr. "Kansas Crusade: Eli Thayer and the New England Emigrant Aid Society." *New England Quarterly* 35 (December 1962): 497–514.

Andrews, William L. *Critical Essays on W.E.B. Du Bois.* Boston: G.K. Hall, 1985.

———, ed. *North Carolina Slave Narratives: The Lives of Moses Roper, Lunsford Lane, Moses Grandy, and Thomas H. Jones.* Chapel Hill: University of North Carolina Press, 2003.

Andrews, William L., and Henry Louis Gates, Jr., eds. *Slave Narratives.* New York: Library of America, 2000.

Anstey, Roger. *The Atlantic Slave Trade and British Abolition, 1760–1810.* London: Macmillan, 1975.

Anthony, Katharine. *Susan B. Anthony: Her Personal History and Her Era.* Garden City, NY: Doubleday, 1954.

Aptheker, Herbert. *American Negro Slave Revolts.* New York: International Publishers, 1993.

———, ed. *A Documentary History of the Negro People in the United States.* Vol. 1, *From the Colonial Times Through the Civil War.* New York: Citadel, 1951.

———. *The Literary Legacy of W.E.B. Du Bois.* White Plains, NY: Kraus International, 1980.

———. "Militant Abolitionists." *Journal of Negro History* 26 (October 1941): 438–84.

———. "The Negro in the Abolitionist Movement." *Science and Society* 5 (1941): 2–23.

———. "The Quakers and Negro Slavery." *Journal of Negro History* 25 (July 1940): 331–62.

Arbena, Joseph L. "Politics or Principle? Rufus King and the Opposition to Slavery, 1785–1825." *Essex Institute Historical Collections* 101 (January 1965): 65–77.

Arkin, Marc M. "The Federalist Trope: Power and Passion in Abolitionist Rhetoric." *Journal of American History* 88 (June 2001): 75–98.

Arms, Goodsil Filley. *History of the William Taylor Self-Supporting Missions in South America.* New York: Methodist Book Concern, 1921.

Ashton, Owen R. *W.E. Adams—Chartist, Radical, and Journalist (1832–1906): An Honour to the Fourth Estate.* Whitley Bay, UK: Bewick, 1991.

Ashworth, John. "The Relationship Between Capitalism and Humanitarianism." *American Historical Review* 92 (October 1987): 797–829.

Asimov, Isaac. *Asimov's Biographical Encyclopedia of Science and Technology: The Living Stories of More Than 1,000 Great Scientists From the Age of Greece to the Space Age.* New York: Doubleday, 1964.

Athey, Stephanie, and Daniel Cooper Alarcón. "Oroonoko's Gendered Economies of Honor/Horror: Reframing Colonial Discourse Studies in the Americas." *American Literature* 65 (September 1993): 415–43.

Ausubel, Herman. *John Bright: Victorian Reformer.* New York: Wiley, 1966.

Avins, Alfred, comp. *The Reconstruction Amendments' Debates: The Legislative History and Contemporary Debates in Congress on the 13th, 14th, and 15th Amendments.* Richmond: Virginia Commission on Constitutional Government, 1967.

Ayres, Anne. *Life and Work of William Augustus Muhlenberg.* New York: Harper & Brothers, 1880.

Azavedo, Celia M. *Abolitionism in the United States and Brazil: A Comparative Perspective.* New York: Garland, 1995.

Bacon, Jacqueline. *The Humblest May Stand Forth: Rhetoric, Empowerment, and Abolition.* Columbia: University of South Carolina Press, 2002.

Bacon, Leonard. "Reminiscences of Joshua Leavitt." *The Independent,* February 13, 1873.

Bacon, Margaret Hope. *Abby Hopper Gibbons: Prison Reformer and Social Activist.* Albany: State University of New York Press, 2000.

———. *Sarah Mapps Douglass, Faithful Attender of Quaker Meeting: View from the Back Bench.* Philadelphia: Quaker Press, 2003.

———. *Valiant Friend: The Life of Lucretia Coffin Mott.* New York: Walker, 1980.

Baer, Helene G. "Mrs. Child and Miss Fuller." *New England Quarterly* 26 (June 1953): 249–55.

Baigent, Michael, Richard Leigh, and Henry Lincoln. *Holy Blood, Holy Grail.* New York: Delacorte, 2005.

Bailey, David T. *Shadow on the Church: Southwestern Evangelical Religion and the Issue of Slavery, 1783–1860.* Ithaca, NY: Cornell University Press, 1985.

Bailey, David Thomas. "A Divided Prism: Two Sources on Black Testimony on Slavery." *Journal of Southern History* 46 (August 1980): 381–404.

Bailey, Hugh. *Hinton Rowan Helper: Abolitionist and Racist.* Tuscaloosa: University of Alabama Press, 1965.

Bailey, William S. "Underground Railroad in Southern Chautauqua County." *New York History* 33 (January 1935): 53–63.

Bain, Alexander. *James Mill: A Biography.* London: Longman, Green, 1882; New York: Augustus M. Kelley, 1967.

Baker, Anthony A. "With One Voice: Wisconsin's Legislative Contribution to the National Slavery Debate—1848–1861." *Wisconsin Law Review* (May/June 1998): 777–90.

Baker, Eric W. *A Herald of the Evangelical Revival.* London: Epworth, 1948.

Baker, Frank. *John Wesley and the Church of England.* Nashville, TN: Abingdon, 1970.

Baker, Houston A., Jr. "The Black Man of Culture: W.E.B. Du Bois and *The Souls of Black Folk.*" In *Long Black Song: Essays in Black American Literature and Culture,* by Houston A. Baker, Jr. Charlottesville: University of Virginia Press, 1972.

Baker, Keith Michael. *Condorcet: From Natural Philosophy to Social Mathematics.* Chicago: University of Chicago Press, 1975.

Balazs, Marianne E. *Sheldon Peck.* New York: Whitney Museum of American Art, 1975.

Baldwin, Simeon E. *The Captives of the* Amistad. New Haven, CT: New Haven Colony Historical Society, 1886.

Bales, Kevin. *Disposable People: New Slavery in the Global Economy.* Berkeley: University of California Press, 1999.

Ball, Charles. *Slavery in the United States: A Narrative of the Life and Adventures of Charles Ball.* 1837. New York: Negro Universities Press, 1969.

Ballaster, Rosalind. "New Hystericism: Aphra Behn's *Oroonoko:* The Body, the Text and the Feminist Critic." In *New Feminist Discourses: Critical Essays on Theories and Texts,* ed. Isobel Armstrong. London: Routledge, 1992.

Bancroft, Frederic. *The Life of William H. Seward.* Gloucester, MA: P. Smith, 1967.

Banner, Lois W. *Elizabeth Cady Stanton: A Radical for Woman's Rights.* Boston: Little, Brown, 1980.

———. "Religion and Reform in the Early Republic: The Role of Youth." *American Quarterly* 22 (December 1971): 677–95.

———. "Religious Benevolence as Social Control: A Critique of an Interpretation." *Journal of American History* 60 (June 1973): 23–41.

Barbour, Hugh, ed. *Slavery and Theology: Writings of Seven Quaker Reformers, 1800–1870: Elias Hicks, Joseph John Gurney, Elizabeth Gurney Fry, Lucretia Coffin Mott, Levi Coffin, John Greenleaf Whittier, John Bright.* Dublin, IN: Prinit Press, 1985.

Barbour, Hugh, and J. William Frost. *The Quakers.* Westport, CT: Greenwood, 1988.

Barclay, Oliver. *Thomas Fowell Buxton and the Liberation of Slaves.* York, UK: William Sessions, 2001.

Bardolph, Richard. *The Civil Rights Record: Black Americans and the Law, 1849–1970.* New York: Crowell, 1970.

Barker, Anthony J. *Captain Charles Stuart, Anglo-American Abolitionist.* Baton Rouge: Louisiana State University Press, 1986.

———. "Captain Charles Stuart and the British and American Abolition Movements: 1830–34." *Slavery and Abolition* 1 (Fall 1980): 43–63.

Barman, Roderick J. *Princess Isabel of Brazil: Gender and Power in the Nineteenth Century.* Wilmington, DE: Scholarly Resources, 2002.

Barnes, Charles E. "Battle Creek as a Station on the Underground Railway." *Michigan Pioneer and Historical Society Collections* 38 (1912).

Barnes, Gilbert Hobbs. *The Antislavery Impulse, 1830–1844.* New York, London: D. Appleton-Century, 1933.

Barnett, Randy E. "Was Slavery Unconstitutional Before the Thirteenth Amendment? Lysander Spooner's Theory of Interpretation." *Pacific Law Review* 28 (Summer 1997): 977–1014.

Baros-Johnson, Irene. *The Just Demands of the Other: An Introduction to Samuel Joseph May.* Syracuse, NY: Syracuse University, Kellogg Project/Center for the Study of Citizenship, 1989.

Barry, Kathleen. *Susan B. Anthony: Biography of a Singular Feminist.* New York: New York University Press, 1988.

Bartell, C.J. *Castlereagh.* New York: Scribner's, 1966.

Bartlett, Irving H. *Wendell and Ann Phillips: The Community of Reform, 1840–1880.* New York: W.W. Norton, 1979.

———. "Wendell Phillips and the Eloquence of Abuse." *American Quarterly* 11 (Winter 1959): 509–20.

Bartour, Ron. "American Views on 'Biblical Slavery': 1835–1865: A Comparative Study." *Slavery and Abolition* 4 (May 1983): 41–63.

Basler, Roy Prentice, ed. *The Collected Works of Abraham Lincoln.* 9 vols. New Brunswick, NJ: Rutgers University Press, 1953–1955.

Bay, Mia. *The White Image in the Black Mind: African-American Ideas About White People, 1830–1925.* New York: Oxford University Press, 2000.

Beattie, James. *Elements of Moral Science.* 2 vols. 1790, 1793. London: Routledge/Thoemmes, 1996.

Beck, Warren A. "Lincoln and Negro Colonization." *Abraham Lincoln Quarterly* 6 (September 1959): 162–83.

Beckles, Hilary. *Black Rebellion in Barbados: The Struggle Against Slavery, 1627–1838.* Bridgetown, Barbados: Antilles, 1987.

Beecher, Edward. *Narrative of Riots at Alton.* New York: E.P. Dutton, 1965.

Behn, Aphra. *Oroonoko.* Ed. Joanna Lipking. New York: W.W. Norton, 1997.

Belaúnde, Víctor Andrés. *Bolívar and the Political Thought of the Spanish American Revolution.* Baltimore: Johns Hopkins University Press, 1938.

Belby, Henry. *Death Struggles of Slavery.* London: Hamilton, Adams, 1835.

Bell, Howard H. "The American Moral Reform Society, 1836–1841." *Journal of Negro Education* 27 (Winter 1958): 34–40.

———. "Expressions of Negro Militancy in the North, 1840–1860." *Journal of Negro History* 45 (January 1960): 11–20.

———. "Free Negroes of the North, 1830–1835: A Study in National Cooperation." *Journal of Negro Education* 26 (Fall 1957): 447–55.

———, ed. *Minutes of the Proceedings of the National Negro Conventions, 1830–1864.* New York: Arno, 1969.

———. "The National Negro Convention, 1848." *Ohio Historical Quarterly* 67 (October 1958): 357–68.

———. "National Negro Conventions of the Middle 1840s: Moral Suasion vs. Political Action." *Journal of Negro History* 42 (October 1957): 247–60.

———. "The Negro Convention Movement, 1830–1860: New Perspectives." *Negro History Bulletin* 14 (Fall 1951): 103–5, 114.

———. "The Negro Emigration Movement, 1849–1854: A Phase of Negro Nationalism." *Phylon* 20 (Summer 1959): 132–42.

———. "Negro Nationalism: A Factor in Emigration Projects, 1858–1861." *Journal of Negro History* 47 (January 1962): 42–53.

———. "Some Reform Interests of the Negro During the 1850s as Reflected in State Conventions." *Phylon* 21 (Summer 1960): 173–82.

Bellegarde-Smith, Patrick. *Haiti: The Breached Citadel.* Boulder, CO: Westview, 1990.

Bellot, Leland J. "Evangelicals and the Defense of Slavery in Britain's Old Colonial Empire." *Journal of Southern History* 37 (February 1971): 19–40.

Belz, Herman. "Henry Winter Davis and the Origins of Congressional Reconstruction." *Maryland Historical Magazine* 67 (Summer 1972): 129–43.

Bemis, Samuel Flagg. *John Quincy Adams and the Union.* New York: Alfred A. Knopf, 1956.

Bennett, Lerone. *Before the Mayflower: A History of Black America, 1619–1962.* Chicago: Johnson, 1961.

Bentlry, Nancy. "White Slaves: The Mulatto Hero in Antebellum Fiction." *American Literature* 65 (September 1993): 501–22.

Bergad, Laird W., Fe Iglesias García, and María del Carmen Barcia. *The Cuban Slave Market, 1790–1880.* New York: Cambridge University Press, 1995.

Berlin, Ira. *Many Thousands Gone: The First Two Centuries of Slavery in North America.* Cambridge, MA: Belknap Press, 1998.

Berlin, Ira, and Ronald Hoffman, eds. *Slavery and Freedom in the Age of the American Revolution.* Charlottesville: University of Virginia Press, 1983.

Bernard, Joel. "Authority, Autonomy, and Radical Commitment: Stephen and Abby Kelley Foster." *Proceedings of the American Antiquarian Society* 90 (1981): 347–86.

Bernstein, Iver. *The New York City Draft Riots: Their Significance for American Society and Politics in the Age of the Civil War.* New York: Oxford University Press, 1990.

Bertrand, Louis. *Lamartine.* Paris: A. Fayard, 1940.

Bethel, Elizabeth Rauh. *The Roots of African-American Identity: Memory and History in Free Antebellum Communities.* New York: St. Martin's, 1997.

Bethell, Leslie. *The Abolition of the Brazilian Slave Trade: Britain, Brazil and the Slave Trade Question, 1807–1869.* Cambridge, UK: Cambridge University Press, 1970.

Beveridge, Charles E., and Charles Capen McLaughlin, eds. *The Papers of Frederick Law Olmsted.* Vol. 2, *Slavery and the South, 1852–1857.* Baltimore: Johns Hopkins University Press, 1981.

Bibb, Henry. *Narrative of the Life and Adventures of Henry Bibb, An American Slave.* 1849. Madison: University of Wisconsin Press, 2001.

Bilby, Kenneth L., and Diana Baird N'Diaye. "Creativity and Resistance: Maroon Culture in the Americas." 1992 Smithsonian Festival of American Folklife, Smithsonian Institute, Washington, DC. http://www.folklife.si.edu/resources/maroon/presentation.htm.

Billington, Louis. "The Millerite Adventists in Great Britain, 1840–1850." In *The Disappointed: Millerism and Millenarianism in the Nineteenth Century,* ed. Ronald L. Numbers and Jonathan M. Butler. Bloomington: Indiana University Press, 1987.

Billington, Ray Allen. "James Forten, Forgotten Abolitionist." *Negro History Bulletin* 30 (November 1949): 31–36, 45.

———. *The Journal of Charlotte L. Forten: A Young Black Woman's Reactions to the White World of the Civil War Era.* New York: W.W. Norton, 1981.

Birney, Catherine H. *Sarah and Angelina Grimké: The First American Women Advocates of Abolition and Women's Rights.* New York: Haskell House, 1970.

Birney, James Gillespie. *Letters of James Gillespie Birney, 1831–1857.* 2 vols. Ed. Dwight L. Dumond. New York: D. Appleton-Century, 1938; Gloucester, MA: P. Smith, 1966.

Birney, William. *James G. Birney and His Times: The Genesis of the Republican Party with Some Account of Abolition Movements in the South Before 1828.* 1890. New York: Negro Universities Press, 1969.

Blackburn, Robin. *The Overthrow of Colonial Slavery, 1776–1848.* New York: Verso, 1988.

Blackett, R.J.M. "Fugitive Slaves in Britain: The Odyssey of William and Ellen Craft." *Journal of American Studies* 12 (1978): 41–62.

———. "In Search of International Support for African Colonization: Martin Delany's Visit to England, 1860." *Canadian Journal of History* 10 (1975): 307–24.

———. "Martin R. Delany and Robert Campbell: Black Americans in Search of an African Colony." *Journal of Negro History* 62 (January 1977): 1–25.

———. "William G. Allen: The Forgotten Professor." *Civil War History* 26 (March 1980): 38–52.

Blackstone, William. *Commentaries on the Laws of England: A Facsimile of the First Edition of 1765–1769.* 4 vols. Introduction by Stanley N. Katz. Chicago: University of Chicago Press, 1979.

Blanchard, Jonathan. *A Perfect State of Society.* Oberlin, OH: James Steele, 1839.

———. *Public Men and Public Institutions of the Church.* Cincinnati, OH: C. Clark, 1845.

———. *Sermons and Addresses.* Chicago: National Christian Association, 1892.

Blanchard, Jonathan, and Nathan L. Rice. *A Debate on Slavery: Held in Cincinnati, on the First, Second, Third, and Sixth Day of October, 1845, Upon the Question: Is Slave-Holding in Itself Sinful, and the Relation Between Master and Slave, a Sinful Relation?* Cincinnati, OH: William H. Moore, 1846; New York: Negro Universities Press, 1969.

Blassingame, John W. *The Slave Community: Plantation Life in the Antebellum South.* New York: Oxford University Press, 1979.

———, ed. *Slave Testimony: Two Centuries of Letters, Speeches, Interviews, and Autobiographies.* Baton Rouge: Louisiana State University Press, 1977.

Blassingame, John W., Mae Henderson, and Jessica M. Dunn. *Antislavery Newspapers and Periodicals.* 5 vols. Boston: G.K. Hall, 1980–1984.

Blatt, Martin H., Thomas J. Brown, and Donald Yacovne, eds. *Hope and Glory: Essays on the Legacy of the Fifty-Fourth Massachusetts Regiment.* Amherst: University of Massachusetts Press, 2001.

Blight, David W. "Frederick Douglass and the American Apocalypse." *Civil War History* 31 (December 1985): 309–28.

———. "In Search of Learning, Liberty, and Self-Definition: James McCune Smith and the Ordeal of the Antebellum Black Intellectual." *Afro-Americans in New York Life and History* 9 (July 1985): 7–25.

———. "The Martyrdom of Elijah P. Lovejoy." *American History* 12 (November 1977): 20–27.

———. "Perceptions of Southern Intransigence and the Rise of Radical Antislavery Thought." *Journal of the Early Republic* 3 (Summer 1983): 139–63.

Bloch, Herman D. "The New York Negro's Battle for Political Rights, 1777–1865." *International Review of Social History* 9 (1964): 65–80.

Blockson, Charles L. *The Underground Railroad: First-Person Narratives of Escapes to Freedom in the North.* New York: Prentice Hall, 1987.

Bloomer, Dexter C. *Life and Writings of Amelia Bloomer.* New York: Schocken, 1975.

Blue, Frederick J. *Charles Sumner and the Conscience of the North.* Arlington Heights, IL: Harlan Davidson, 1994.

———. *The Free Soilers: Third Party Politics, 1848–54.* Urbana: University of Illinois Press, 1973.

———. "James Monroe: Oberlin's Forgotten Abolitionist." *Civil War History* 35 (December 1989): 285–301.

———. "The Ohio Free Soilers and Problems of Factionalism." *Ohio History* 76 (Winter 1967): 17–32.

Blum, Jerome. *Noble Landowners and Agriculture in Austria, 1815–1848.* Baltimore: Johns Hopkins University Press, 1948.

Boadi-Siaw, S.Y. "Brazilian Returnees of West Africa." In *Global Dimensions of the African Diaspora,* ed. Joseph E. Harris. Washington, DC: Howard University Press, 1993.

Boase, Paul H. "Philip Gatch, Pioneer." *Bulletin of the Historical and Philosophical Society of Ohio* 13 (October 1955): 286–96.

Bogin, Ruth. "Sarah Parker Remond: Black Abolitionist from Salem." *Essex Institute Historical Collections* 110 (April 1974): 120–50.

Boison, Anton T. "Divided Protestantism in a Midwest County: A Study in the Natural History of Organized Religion." *Journal of Religion* 20 (October 1940): 359–81.

Bolden, Tonya. *Strong Men Keep Coming: The Book of African American Men.* New York: Wiley, 1999.

Bolívar, Simón. *The Liberator Simón Bolívar: Man and Image.* Ed. David Bushnell. New York: Alfred A. Knopf, 1970.

Bolland, O. Nigel. *The Politics of Labour in the Caribbean: The Social Origins of Authoritarianism and Democracy in the Labour Movement.* Kingston, Jamaica: Ian Randle, 2001.

Boller, Paul. "Washington, the Quakers and Slavery." *Journal of Negro History* 46 (April 1961): 83–88.

Bonafoux, Luis. *Betances.* San Juan, Puerto Rico: Instituto de Cultura Puertorriqueña, 1987.

Bond, Horace Mann. *Education for Freedom: A History of Lincoln University, Pennsylvania.* Oxford, PA: Lincoln University, 1976.

Bonetto, Gerald. "Tocqueville and American Slavery." *Canadian Review of American Studies* 15 (Summer 1984): 123–39.

Bontemps, Alex. *The Punished Self: Surviving Slavery in the Colonial South.* Ithaca, NY: Cornell University Press, 2001.

Bordewich, Fergus M. *Bound for Canaan: The Underground Railroad and the War for the Soul of America.* New York: Amistad, 2005.

Borome, Joseph A. "Henry Clay and James G. Birney." *Filson Club History Quarterly* 35 (April 1961): 122–24.

———. "Robert Purvis and His Early Challenge to American Racism." *Negro History Bulletin* 30 (May 1967): 8–10.

———. "Some Additional Light on Frederick Douglass." *Journal of Negro History* 38 (April 1953): 216–24.

———. "The Vigilant Committee of Philadelphia." *Pennsylvania Magazine of History and Biography* 92 (July 1968): 320–51.

Borrit, Gabor S. "The Voyage to the Colony of Lincolnia: The Sixteenth President, Black Colonization, and the Defense Mechanism of Avoidance." *The Historian* 37 (August 1975): 619–33.

Borzendowski, Janice, and Nathan Irvin Huggins. *John Russwurm.* New York: Chelsea House, 1989.

Botkin, Benjamin A., ed. *Lay My Burden Down: A Folk History of Slavery.* Chicago: University of Chicago Press, 1945.

Botting, Douglas. *Humboldt and the Cosmos.* New York: Harper & Row, 1973.

Bougenot, Louis. *Victor Schoelcher.* Paris: Nouvelle Revue, 1921.

Bourne, George. *A Condensed Anti-Slavery Bible Argument; by a Citizen of Virginia.* New York: S.W. Benedict, 1845.

Bourne, Theodore. "Rev. George Bourne: The Pioneer of American Anti-Slavery." *Methodist Quarterly Review* 64 (January 1882): 68–91.

Bowditch, Vincent Yardley, ed. *Life and Correspondence of Henry Ingersoll Bowditch.* Freeport, NY: Books for Libraries, 1970.

Bowen, David Warren. *Andrew Johnson and the Negro.* Knoxville: University of Tennessee Press, 1989.

Boyd, Melba Joyce. *Discarded Legacy: Politics and Poetics in the Life of Frances E.W. Harper.* Detroit, MI: Wayne State University Press, 1994.

Boyd, Willis D. "James Redpath and American Negro Colonization in Haiti, 1860–1862." *The Americas* 12 (October 1955): 169–82.

Boyer, Paul. *Urban Masses and Moral Order in America, 1820–1920.* Cambridge, MA: Harvard University Press, 1978.

Bradford, Sarah H. *Scenes in the Life of Harriet Tubman.* 1869. Salem, NH: Ayer, 1999.

Bradley, Richard L. "The Lutheran Church and Slavery." *Concordia Historical Institute Quarterly* 44 (February 1971): 32–41.

Braithwaite, William. *The Second Period of Quakerism.* 2nd ed. Cambridge, UK: Cambridge University Press, 1961.

Bramble, Linda. *Black Fugitive Slaves in Early Canada.* Saint Catharines, Ontario, Canada: Vanwell, 1988.

Brana-Shute, Gary, ed. *Resistance and Rebellion in Suriname: Old and New.* Studies in Third World Societies 43. Williamsburg, VA: College of William and Mary, 1990.

Brana-Shute, Rosemary. "Approaching Freedom: Slave Manumission in Suriname, 1760–1828." *Slavery and Abolition* 10 (December 1989): 41–63.

Breault, Judith Colucci. *The World of Emily Howland: Odyssey of a Humanitarian.* Millbrae, CA: Les Femmes, 1976.

Breiseth, Christopher N. "Lincoln and Frederick Douglass: Another Debate." *Illinois State Historical Society Journal* 68 (February 1975): 9–26.

Brereton, Bridget. "Review Essay: Abolition and Its Aftermath." *Slavery and Abolition* 7 (December 1986): 299–306.

Bretz, Julian P. "The Economic Background of the Liberty Party." *American Historical Review* 34 (January 1929): 250–64.

Breunig, Charles, and Mathew Levinger. *The Revolutionary Era, 1789–1850.* New York: W.W. Norton, 2002.

Brewer, William M. "Henry Highland Garnet." *Journal of Negro History* 13 (January 1928): 36–52.

———. "John Russwurm." *Journal of Negro History* 13 (October 1928): 413–22.

Briere, Jean-Francois. "Abbé Grégoire and Haitian Independence." *Research in African Literatures* 35 (Summer 2004): 34–43.

Briestman, Karen Williams. "Abolitionism and Wooden Nutmegs: Repealing the Gag Rule." *Black Law Journal* 8 (Winter 1983): 408–16.

Bright, John. *John Bright on America: The* Trent *Affair, Slavery and Secession, the Struggle in America, 1861–3.* New York, G.P. Putnam's Sons, 1891.

Britten, Emma Hardinge. *Modern American Spiritualism: A Twenty Years' Record of the Communion Between Earth and the World of Spirits.* New York: Emma Hardinge Britten, 1870.

Brodie, Fawn N. *Thaddeus Stevens, Scourge of the South.* New York: W.W. Norton, 1966.

Bromberg, Alan B. "John Mercer Langston: Black Congressman from the Old Dominion." *Virginia Cavalcade* 30 (Summer 1980): 60–67.

Brophy, Alfred L. "'Over and Above . . . There Broods a Portentous Shadow, the Shadow of the Law': Harriet Beecher Stowe's Critique of Slave Law in *Uncle Tom's Cabin.*" *Journal of Law and Religion* 13 (1996/1997): 406–512.

Brown, Gillian. *Domestic Individualism: Imagining Self in Nineteenth-Century America.* Berkeley: University of California Press, 1990.

Brown, Glenn. *History of the U.S. Capitol.* Washington, DC: U.S. Government Printing Office, 1900.

Brown, Henry. *A Narrative of the Anti-Masonic Excitement.* New York: Adams & McLeary, 1829.

Brown, Henry Box. *Narrative of the Life of Henry Box Brown, Written by Himself.* 1851. New York: Oxford University Press, 2002.

Brown, Ira V. "'Am I Not a Woman and a Sister?': The Anti-Slavery Conventions of American Women, 1837–1839." *Pennsylvania History* 50 (January 1983): 1–19.

———. "An Anti-Slavery Journey: Garrison and Douglass in Pennsylvania, 1847." *Pennsylvania History* 67 (January 2000): 532–50.

———. "Cradle of Feminism: The Female Anti-Slavery Society, 1833–1840." *Pennsylvania Magazine of History and Biography* 102 (April 1978): 143–66.

———. "Miller McKim and Pennsylvania Abolitionism." *Pennsylvania History* 30 (January 1963): 56–73.

———. "Racism and Sexism: The Case of Pennsylvania Hall." *Phylon* 37 (Second Quarter 1976): 126–36.

Brown, Laura. "The Romance of Empire: *Oroonoko* and the Trade in Slaves." In *The New Eighteenth Century,* ed. Felicity Nussbaum and Laura Brown. London: Methuen, 1987.

Brown, Lois. "Out of the Mouths of Babes: The Abolitionist Campaign of Susan Paul and the Juvenile Choir of Boston. *New England Quarterly* 75 (March 2002): 52–79.

Brown, Patrick T.J. "'To Defend Mr. Garrison': William Cooper Nell and the Personal Politics of Antislavery." *New England Quarterly* 70 (September 1997): 415–42.

Brown, Prince, Jr. *Runaway Enslaved Person Database (REPD).* Highland Heights: Institute for Freedom Studies, Northern Kentucky University, 2004.

Brown, Richard H. "The Missouri Crisis, Slavery, and the Politics of Jacksonianism." *South Atlantic Quarterly* 65 (Winter 1966): 55–72.

Brown, Sterling. *The Negro in American Fiction.* Port Washington, NY: Kennikat, 1937.

Brown, William Wells. *From Fugitive Slave to Free Man: The Autobiographies of William Wells Brown.* Ed. William L. Andrews. New York: New American Library, 1993.

Bruce, Henry Clay. *The New Man: Twenty-Nine Years a Slave, Twenty-Nine Years a Free Man.* 1895. Lincoln: University of Nebraska Press, 1996.

Bruns, Roger, ed. *Am I Not a Man and a Brother: The Anti-slavery Crusade of Revolutionary America, 1688–1788.* New York: Chelsea House, 1977.

Buckmaster, Henrietta. *Let My People Go: The Story of the Underground Railroad and the Growth of the Abolition Movement.* New York: Harper & Brothers, 1941; Columbia: University of South Carolina Press, 1992.

Buffum, Arnold. *Constitution of the New-England Anti-Slavery Society; With an Address to the Public.* Boston: Garrison and Knapp, 1832.

Buker, George E. *Blockaders, Refugees, and Contrabands: Civil War on Florida's Gulf Coast, 1861–1865.* Tuscaloosa: University of Alabama Press, 2004.

Buley, R. Carlyle. *The American Life Convention, 1906–1952: A Study in the History of Life Insurance.* New York: Appleton-Century-Crofts, 1953.

Bull, Josiah. *John Newton of Olney and St. Mary Woolnoth.* London: Religious Tract Society, 1869.

Burgan, Michael. *William Henry Seward: Senator and Statesman.* Philadelphia: Chelsea House, 2002.

Burke, Joseph C. "What Did the *Prigg* Decision Really Decide?" *Pennsylvania Magazine of History and Biography* 93 (January 1969): 73–85.

Burke, Ronald K. "The Anti-Slavery Activities of Samuel Ringgold Ward in New York State." *Afro-Americans in New York Life and History* 2 (1978): 17–28.

———. *Frederick Douglass: Crusading Orator for Human Rights.* New York: Garland, 1996.

———. *Samuel Ringgold Ward: Christian Abolitionist.* New York: Garland, 1995.

Burleigh, Charles Calistus. *The Genealogy of the Burley or Burleigh Family of America.* Portland, OR: B. Thurston, 1880.

———. *Slavery and the North.* New York: American Anti-Slavery Society, 1855; Westport, CT: Negro Universities Press, 1970.

Burn, William L. *Emancipation and Apprenticeship in the British West Indies.* London: Jonathan Cape, 1937.

Burns, E. Bradford. *A History of Brazil.* 3rd ed. New York: Columbia University Press, 1993.

Burroughs, Wilbur Greeley. "Oberlin's Part in the Slavery Conflict." *Ohio Archaeological and Historical Publications* 20 (1911): 269–334.

Bushnell, David. "The Independence of Spanish South America." In *The Cambridge History of Latin America,* vol. 3, ed. Leslie Bethell. Cambridge, UK: Cambridge University Press, 1984.

Butchart, Ronald E. "Caroline F. Putnam." In *Women Educators in the United States, 1820–1993: A Bio-Bibliographical Sourcebook,* ed. Maxine Seller. Westport, CT: Greenwood, 1994.

———. *Northern Schools, Southern Blacks, and Reconstruction: Freedmen's Education, 1862–1875.* Westport, CT: Greenwood, 1980.

Butler, Jon. *Awash in a Sea of Faith: Christianizing the American People.* Cambridge, MA: Harvard University Press, 1990.

Buxton, Thomas Fowell. *The African Slave Trade and Its Remedy.* London: Frank Cass, 1967.

Byerman, Keith E. *Seizing the Word: History, Art, and the Self in the Work of W.E.B. Du Bois.* Athens: University of Georgia Press, 1994.

Cable, Mary. *Black Odyssey: The Case of the Slave Ship* Amistad. New York: Viking, 1971.

Cadbury, Henry J. "An Early Quaker Anti-Slavery Statement." *Journal of Negro History* 22 (October 1937): 492–93.

———. "Another Early Quaker Anti-Slavery Statement." *Journal of Negro History* 27 (April 1942): 210–15.

———. "Negro Membership in the Society of Friends." *Journal of Negro History* 21 (April 1936): 151–213.

———. "Quaker Bibliographical Notes, II, Anti-Slavery Writings," *Bulletin of the Friends' Historical Association* 26 (1937).

Cadbury, William A. *Richard Tapper Cadbury, 1768–1860.* Birmingham, UK: William A. Cadbury, 1944.

Caldwell, Joshua W. *Sketches of the Bench and Bar of Tennessee.* Knoxville, TN: Ogden Brothers, 1898.

Call, Joseph L. "The Fourteenth Amendment and Its Skeptical Background." *Baylor Law Review* 13 (1961): 1–20.

Calligaro, Lee. "The Negro's Legal Status in Pre-Civil War New Jersey." *New Jersey History* 85 (Fall/Winter 1967): 167–80.

Cameron, W.J. *New Light on Aphra Behn: An Investigation Into the Facts and Fictions Surrounding Her Journey to Surinam in 1663, and Her Activities as a Spy in Flanders in 1666.* Auckland, New Zealand: University of Auckland, 1961.

Campbell, Mavis C. *The Maroons of Jamaica, 1655–1796: A History of Resistance, Collaboration, and Betrayal.* Granby, MA: Bergin & Garvey, 1988.

Campbell, Stanley W. *The Slave Catchers; Enforcement of the Fugitive Slave Law.* Chapel Hill: University of North Carolina Press, 1970.

Candler, John. *A Friendly Mission: John Candler's Letters From America, 1853–1854.* Indianapolis: Indiana Historical Society, 1951.

Cardoso, J.J. "Hinton Rowan Helper as a Racist in the Abolitionist Camp." *Journal of Negro History* 55 (October 1970): 323–30.

Careless, J.M.S. "Brown, George." In *The 1999 Canadian Encyclopedia: World Edition.* Toronto, Ontario, Canada: McClelland & Stewart, 1998.

Carey, Brycchan. *British Abolitionism and the Rhetoric of Sensibility: Writing, Sentiment, and Slavery, 1760–1807.* Basingstoke, UK: Palgrave Macmillan, 2005.

———. " 'The Extraordinary Negro': Ignatius Sancho, Joseph Jekyll, and the Problem of Biography." *British*

Journal for Eighteenth-Century Studies 26 (Spring 2003): 1–13.

Carl'ee, Roberta Baughman. *The Last Gladiator: Cassius M. Clay.* Berea, KY: Kentucke Imprints, 1979.

Carpenter, John A. *Sword and Olive Branch: Oliver Otis Howard.* Pittsburgh: University of Pittsburgh Press, 1964.

Carretta, Vincent, ed. *The Letters of the Late Ignatius Sancho, An African.* New York: Penguin, 1998.

Carrington, Selwyn H.H. *The Sugar Industry and the Abolition of the Slave Trade, 1775–1810.* Gainesville: University Press of Florida, 2002.

Carrithers, M., Steven Collins, and Steven Lukes, eds. *The Category of the Person: Anthropology, Philosophy, History.* Cambridge, UK: Cambridge University Press, 1985.

Carroll, Bret E. Review of *The Religious World of Antislavery Women: Spirituality in the Lives of Five Abolitionist Lecturers,* by Anna M. Speicher. *Journal of American History* 88 (December 2001): 1068–69.

Carroll, Joseph Cephas. *Slave Insurrections in the United States, 1800–1865.* 1938. New York: Negro Universities Press, 1968.

Carroll, Kenneth. "George Fox on Slavery." *Quaker History* 86 (Fall 1997): 16–25.

———. "Maryland Quakers and Slavery." *Maryland Historical Magazine* 45 (September 1950): 215–25.

———. "Religious Influences on the Manumission of Slaves in Caroline, Dorchester, and Talbot Counties." *Maryland Historical Magazine* 56 (June 1961): 176–97.

Carter, Dan T. *When the War Was Over: The Failure of Self-Reconstruction in the South, 1865–1867.* Baton Rouge: Louisiana State University Press, 1985.

Carter, George W. "The Booth War in Ripon." *Proceedings of the State Historical Society of Wisconsin,* 1902, 161–72.

Cassady, Marsh. "William W. Brown." *American History* 30 (February 1996): 16–18.

Castel, Albert. *The Presidency of Andrew Johnson.* Lawrence: Regents Press of Kansas, 1979.

Castellanos, Jorge, and Isabel Castellanos. *Cultura afrocubana* [Afro-Cuban Culture]. 4 vols. Miami, FL: Ediciones Universales, 1988–1994.

Castro Alves, Antônio de. *The Major Abolitionist Poems.* Ed. and trans. Amy A. Peterson. New York: Garland, 1990.

Cave, Alfred A. "The Case of Calvin Colton: White Racism in Northern Antislavery Thought." *New York Historical Society Quarterly* 53 (1969): 215–28.

Central Negro Emancipation Committee. *The British Emancipator.* 61 vols. London: J. Haddon, 1837–1840.

Ceplair, Larry. "Mattie Griffith Browne: A Kentucky Abolitionist." *Filson Club History Quarterly* 68 (April 1994): 2–19.

———, ed. *The Public Years of Sarah and Angelina Grimké.* New York: Columbia University Press, 1989.

Chace, Elizabeth Buffum. *Two Quaker Sisters.* New York: Liveright, 1937.

Chaffin, Tom. *Pathfinder: John Charles Frémont and the Course of American Empire.* New York: Hill and Wang, 2002.

Chalmers, David Mark. *Hooded Americanism: The History of the Ku Klux Klan.* 3rd ed. Durham, NC: Duke University Press, 1987.

Chamberlain, Joshua Lawrence, ed. *Universities and Their Sons: History, Influence and Characteristics of American Universities, With Biographical Sketches and Portraits of Alumni and Recipients of Honorary Degrees.* Boston: R. Herndon, 1898–1900.

Chang-Rodríguez, Eugenio. *Latinoamérica: Su civilización y su cultura* [Latin America: Its Civilization and Culture]. 3rd ed. Boston: Heinle & Heinle, 1999.

Chapman, Abraham. *Steal Away: Stories of the Runaway Slaves.* New York: Praeger, 1971.

Chapman, John Jay. *William Lloyd Garrison.* Boston: Atlantic Monthly Press, 1921.

Cheek, William F. "John Mercer Langston: Black Protest Leader and Abolitionist." *Civil War History* 16 (June 1970): 101–20.

———. "A Negro Runs for Congress: John Mercer Langston and the Virginia Campaign of 1888." *Journal of Negro History* 52 (January 1967): 14–34.

Cheek, William F., and Aimee Lee Cheek. *John Mercer Langston and the Fight for Black Freedom, 1829–1865.* Urbana: University of Illinois Press, 1989.

Cheever, H.T., ed. *Memorabilia of George B. Cheever, D.D., Late Pastor of the church of the Puritans, Union Square, New York, and of His Wife.* New York: Wiley, 1890.

Child, Alfred T., Jr. "Prudence Crandall and the Canterbury Experiment." *Bulletin of the Friends' Historical Association* 22 (Spring 1933): 35–55.

Child, Lydia Maria. *An Appeal in Favor of That Class of Americans Called Africans.* Ed. Carolyn L. Karcher. Amherst: University of Massachusetts Press, 1996.

———. *Lydia Maria Child: Selected Letters, 1817–1880.* Ed. Milton Meltzer, Patricia G. Holland, and Francine Krasno. Amherst: University of Massachusetts Press, 1982.

Christiano, David. "Synod and Slavery." *New Jersey History* 90 (Spring 1972): 27–42.

Cimprich, John. "The Beginning of the Black Suffrage Movement in Tennessee, 1864–65." *Journal of Negro History* 65 (Summer 1980): 185–95.

———. "Military Governor Johnson and Tennessee Blacks, 1862–65." *Tennessee Historical Quarterly* 39 (1980): 459–70.

Clark, John Ruskin. *Joseph Priestley: A Comet in the System.* Northumberland, PA: Friends of Joseph Priestley House, 1994.

Clarke, John H. *William Styron's Nat Turner: Ten Black Writers Respond.* Boston: Beacon, 1968.

Clarkson, Thomas. *History of the Rise, Progress, and Accomplishment of the Abolition of the African Slave-Trade by the British Parliament.* 2 vols. 1808. London: Frank Cass, 1968.

Clay, Cassius Marcellus. *The Life of Cassius Marcellus Clay.* Cincinnati, OH: J.F. Brennan, 1886.

Clay, Mary B. "Biography of Cassius M. Clay: Written by His Daughter." Pts. 1 and 2. *Filson Club History Quarterly* 46 (April 1972): 123–46; 46 (July 1972): 254–87.

Clephane, Walter C. "Lewis Clephane: A Pioneer Washington Republican." *Columbia Historical Society Records* 21 (1918): 263–77.

Cleven, N.A.N. "Some Plans for Colonizing Liberated Negro Slaves in Hispanic America." *Journal of Negro History* 9 (January 1926): 35–49.

Clifford, Deborah Pickman. *Crusader for Freedom: A Life of Lydia Maria Child.* Boston: Beacon, 1992.

———. *Mine Eyes Have Seen the Glory: A Biography of Julia Ward Howe.* Boston: Little, Brown, 1979.

Clinton, Catherine. *Fanny Kemble's Civil Wars.* New York: Oxford University Press, 2000.

———, ed. *Fanny Kemble's Journals.* Cambridge, MA: Harvard University Press, 2000.

Clive, John Leonard. *Macaulay: The Shaping of the Historian.* New York: Alfred A. Knopf, 1973.

Coates, Tim, ed. *King Guezo of Dahomey, 1850–52: The Abolition of the Slave Trade on the West Coast of Africa.* London: Her Majesty's Stationery Office, 2001.

Cobb, W. Montague. "Martin Robinson Delany, 1812–1855." *Journal of the National Medical Association* 44 (May 1952).

Cochran, William Cox. *The Western Reserve and the Fugitive Slave Law: A Prelude to Civil War.* Cleveland, OH: Western Reserve Historical Society, 1920.

Coffin, Levi. *Reminiscences of Levi Coffin, the Reputed President of the Underground Railroad.* Chicago: Robert Clark, 1880.

Cogan, Frances B. *All American Girl: The Ideal of Real Womanhood in Mid-Nineteenth-Century America.* Athens: University of Georgia Press, 1989.

Cohen, David, and Jack Greene. *Neither Slave nor Free: The Freedman of African Descent in the Slave Societies of the New World.* Baltimore: Johns Hopkins University Press, 1972.

Cohen, William. "Thomas Jefferson and the Problem of Slavery." *Journal of American History* 56 (December 1969): 503–26.

Cohn, Avern. "Constitutional Interpretation and Judicial Treatment of Blacks in Michigan Before 1870." *Detroit College of Law Review* (Winter 1986): 1121–30.

Colburn, David R., and Jane L. Landers. *The African American Heritage of Florida.* Gainesville: University Press of Florida, 1995.

Cole, Charles C., Jr. "Horace Bushnell and the Slavery Question." *New England Quarterly* 23 (March 1950): 19–30.

Coleman, J. Winston, Jr. "Delia Webster and Calvin Fairbanks: Underground Railroad Agents." *Filson Club History Quarterly* 17 (July 1943): 129–42.

———. "Henry Clay, Kentucky, and Liberia." *Kentucky State Historical Society Register* 45 (October 1947): 309–22.

———. "The Kentucky Colonization Society." *Kentucky State Historical Society Register* 39 (October 1941).

Collison, Gary. *Shadrach Minkins: From Fugitive Slave to Citizen.* Cambridge, MA: Harvard University Press, 1997.

Commanger, Henry Steele. "Constitutional History and Higher Law." *Pennsylvania Magazine of History and Biography* 62 (January 1938): 20–40.

Conniff, Michael L., and Thomas J. Davis. *Africans in the Americas: A History of the Black Diaspora.* New York: St. Martin's, 1994.

Connor, Elizabeth. *Methodist Trail Blazer: Philip Gatch, 1751–1834, His Life in Maryland, Virginia, and Ohio.* Cincinnati, OH: Creative Publishers, 1970.

Conrad, Robert E. *Children of God's Fire: A Documentary History of Black Slavery in Brazil.* Princeton, NJ: Princeton University Press, 1983.

———. *The Destruction of Brazilian Slavery, 1850–1888.* Berkeley: University of California Press, 1972; 2nd ed., Malabar, FL: Krieger, 1993.

Cook, Adrian. *The Armies of the Streets: The New York City Draft Riots of 1863.* Lexington: University Press of Kentucky, 1974.

Cooke, J.W. "Freedom in the Thoughts of Frederick Douglass, 1845–1860." *Negro History Bulletin* 32 (February 1969): 6–10.

Cooley, Verna. "Illinois and the Underground Railroad to Canada." *Transactions of the Illinois State Historical Society* 23 (1917): 76–98.

Cooper, Anna Julia. *The Voice of Anna Julia Cooper: Including "A Voice from the South" and Other Important Essays, Papers, and Letters.* Ed. Charles Lemert and Esme Bhan. Lanham, MD: Rowman & Littlefield, 1998.

Cooper, Barbara. *Marriage in Maradi: Gender and Culture in a Hausa Society in Niger, 1900–1989.* Portsmouth, NH: Heinemann, 1997.

Cooper, Frederick. "Elevating the Race: The Social Thought of Black Leaders, 1827–1850." *American Quarterly* 24 (December 1972): 604–25.

Cornelius, Janet Duitsman. *"When I Can Read My Title Clear": Literacy, Slavery, and Religion in the Antebellum South.* Columbia: University of South Carolina Press, 1991.

Corwin, Arthur F. *Spain and the Abolition of Slavery in Cuba, 1817–1886.* Austin: University of Texas Press, 1967.

Corwin, Edwin S. "The 'Higher Law' Background of American Constitutional Law." Pts. 1 and 2. *Harvard Law Review* 42 (December 1928): 149–83; 42 (January 1929): 365–409.

Costa, Emilia Viotti da. *Crowns of Glory, Tears of Blood: The Demerara Slave Rebellion of 1823.* New York: Oxford University Press, 1994.

Coupland, Reginald. *The British Anti-Slavery Movement.* 2nd ed. New York: Barnes & Noble, 1964.

———. *Wilberforce: A Narrative.* New York: Negro Universities Press, 1968.

Cover, Robert. *Justice Accused: Antislavery and the Judicial Process.* New Haven, CT: Yale University Press, 1975.

Covey, Herbert C., and Paul T. Lockman, Jr. "Narrative References to Older African Americans Living Under Slavery." *Social Science Journal* 33 (1996): 23–37.

Covington, James W. *The Seminoles of Florida.* Gainesville: University Press of Florida, 1993.

Cox, Joseph Mason Andrew. *Great Black Men of Masonry.* Bronx, NY: Blue Diamond, 1982

Cox, LaWanda. *Lincoln and Black Freedom: A Study in Presidential Leadership.* Columbia: University of South Carolina Press, 1981.

Craig, Gerald M. *Upper Canada: The Formative Years, 1784–1841.* Toronto, Ontario, Canada: McClelland and Stewart, 1963.

Cramer, Clarence Henley. *Open Shelves and Open Minds: A History of the Cleveland Public Library.* Cleveland, OH: Press of Case Western Reserve University, 1972.

Craton, Michael. *Empire, Enslavement, and Freedom in the Caribbean.* Princeton, NJ: Markus Wiener, 1997.

———. *Sinews of Empire: A Short History of British Slavery.* Garden City, NY: Anchor, 1974.

———. *Testing the Chains: Resistance to Slavery in the British West Indies.* Ithaca, NY: Cornell University Press, 1982.

Crockett, Walter Hill. *Vermont: The Green Mountain State.* 5 vols. New York: Century History, 1921.

Cronyn, Benjamin. *A Charge Delivered to the Clergy of the Diocese of Huron, in St. Paul's Cathedral, London, Canada West, at His Primary Visitation, in June, 1859. By . . . Lord Bishop of Huron.* Toronto, Ontario, Canada: Rowsell and Ellis, 1859.

Crowther, Samuel Ajayi. "A Second Narrative of Samuel Ajayi Crowther's Early Life." Ed. A.F. Walls. *Bulletin of the Society for African Church History* 2 (1965): 5–14.

Cugoano, Quobna Ottobah. *Thoughts and Sentiments on the Evils of Slavery and Other Writings.* 1787, 1791. Ed. Vincent Carretta. New York: Penguin, 1999.

Cunha, Euclides da. *Os Sertões* [Rebellion in the Backlands]. 1902. Chicago: University of Chicago Press, 1944.

Curry, Richard O. "The Abolitionists and Reconstruction: A Critical Reappraisal." *Journal of Southern History* 54 (November 1968): 529–32.

———. "Note on the Motives of Three Radical Republicans [With Text of Letters]." *Journal of Negro History* 47 (October 1962): 273–77.

———. "The Political War Against Slavery." *Reviews in American History* 4 (December 1976): 546–50.

———. "Romantic Radicalism in Antebellum America." *Reviews in American History* 1 (December 1973): 524–30.

Curry, Richard O., and Lawrence B. Goodheart. "'Knives in their Heads': Passionate Self-Analysis and the Search for Identity in American Abolitionism." *Canadian Review of American Studies* 14 (Winter 1983): 401–14.

Curti, Merle. "Non-Resistance in New England." *New England Quarterly* 2 (January 1929): 34–57.

Curtin, Philip D. *The Atlantic Slave Trade: A Census.* Madison: University of Wisconsin Press, 1969.

———. *Economic Change in Precolonial Africa: Senegambia in the Era of the Slave Trade.* Madison: University of Wisconsin Press, 1975.

Curtis, Michael Kent. "The Curious History of Attempts to Suppress Antislavery Speech, Press, and Petitions in 1835–37." *Northwestern University Law Review* (Spring 1995): 785–870.

———. "The 1859 Crisis Over Hinton Helper's Book, *The Impending Crisis:* Free Speech, Slavery, and Some Light on the Meaning of the First Section of the Fourteenth Amendment." *Chicago-Kent Law Review* 68 (Summer 1993): 1113–77.

———. "The 1837 Killing of Elijah Lovejoy by an Anti-Abolition Mob: Free Speech, Republican Government, and the Privileges of American Citizens." *UCLA Law Review* 44 (April 1997): 1109–84.

———. *No State Shall Abridge: The Fourteenth Amendment and the Bill of Rights.* Durham, NC: Duke University Press, 1986.

Cushing, John D. "The Cushing Court and the Abolition of Slavery in Massachusetts: More Notes on the 'Quock Walker Case.'" *American Journal of Legal History* 5 (April 1961): 118–19.

Custer, Lawrence B. "Bushrod Washington and John Marshall: A Preliminary Inquiry." *American Journal of Legal History* 4 (January 1960): 34–48.

Cutler, William G. *History of the State of Kansas.* Chicago: A.T. Andreas, 1883.

Daniel, W. Harrison. "Virginia Baptists and the Negro in the Early Republic." *Virginia Magazine of History and Biography* 80 (January 1972): 60–69.

Daumas, Maurice. *Arago.* Paris: Gallimard, 1943.

David, Deirdre. *Intellectual Women and Victorian Patriarchy.* Ithaca, NY: Cornell University Press, 1987.

Davidson, Basil. *The African Slave Trade: Pre-Colonial History, 1450–1850.* Boston: Little, Brown, 1961.

Davies, Edward. *The Bishop of Africa; the Life of William Taylor, With an Account of the Congo Country and Mission.* Reading, MA: Holiness Book Concern, 1885.

Davis, Charles T., and Henry Louis Gates, Jr., eds. *The Slave's Narrative.* New York: Oxford University Press, 1985.

Davis, Cynthia J. "Speaking the Body's Pain: Harriet Wilson's *Our Nig.*" *African American Review* 27 (Fall 1993): 391–404.

Davis, David Brion. "The Emergence of Immediatism in British and American Antislavery Thought." *Mississippi Valley Historical Review* 49 (September 1962): 209–30.

———. *From Homicide to Slavery: Studies in American Culture.* New York: Oxford University Press, 1986.

———. "New Side-Lights on Early Anti-Slavery Radicalism." *William and Mary Quarterly,* 3rd ser., 28 (October 1971): 585–94.

———. *The Problem of Slavery in the Age of Revolution, 1770–1823.* Ithaca, NY: Cornell University Press, 1975; New York: Oxford University Press, 1999.

———. *The Problem of Slavery in Western Culture.* Ithaca, NY: Cornell University Press, 1966.

———. "Reflections on Abolitionism and Ideological Hegemony." *American Historical Review* 92 (October 1987): 787–812.

———. "Slavery and the Post-World War II Historians." *Daedalus* 103 (Spring 1974): 1–16.

Davis, Henry Winter. *The War of Ormuzd and Ahriman in the Nineteenth Century.* Baltimore: J.S. Waters, 1852.

Davis, Hugh H. "The Failure of Political Abolitionism." *Connecticut Review* 6 (April 1973): 76–86.

DeBoer, Clara Merritt. *Be Jubilant My Feet: African American Abolitionists in the American Missionary Association, 1839–1861.* New York: Garland, 1994.

"The Declaration of the Rights of Man and of the Citizen." In *The Great Documents of Western Civilization,* ed. Milton Viorst. New York: Barnes & Noble, 1965.

Delany, Martin R. *The Condition, Elevation, Emigration, and Destiny of the Colored People of the United States, Politically Considered.* 1852. New York: Arno, 1968.

———. "Official Report of the Niger River Valley Exploring Party." In *Search for a Place,* ed. Howard Bell. Ann Arbor: University of Michigan Press, 1969.

Demos, John. "The Antislavery Movement and the Problem of Violent 'Means.'" *New England Quarterly* 37 (December 1964): 501–26.

Dent, John Charles. *The Last Forty Years: Canada Since the Union of 1841.* 2 vols. Toronto, Ontario, Canada: G. Virtue, 1881.

Denton, Charles R. "The Unitarian Church and 'Kansas Territory,' 1854–1861." *Kansas Historical Quarterly* 30 (Autumn 1964): 307–38.

Derby, James Cephas. *Fifty Years Among Authors, Books and Publishers.* New York: G.W. Carleton, 1884.

Derry, John W. *Castlereagh.* New York: St. Martin's, 1976.

———. *Charles James Fox.* New York: St. Martin's, 1972.

Detweiler, Philip F. "Congressional Debate on Slavery and the Declaration of Independence, 1819–1821." *American Historical Review* 63 (April 1958): 598–616.

Dew, Thomas R. *Review of the Debate in the Virginia Legislature of 1831–1832.* Westport, CT: Negro Universities Press, 1970.

Dexter, Franklin Bowditch. *Biographical Sketches of the Graduates of Yale College.* Vol. 6. New York: Holt, 1912.

Diaz, Ada Suárez. *El Doctor Ramón Emeterio Betances y la abolición de la esclavitud* [Dr. Ramón Emeterio Betances and the Abolition of Slavery]. San Juan, Puerto Rico: Instituto de Cultura Puertorriqueña, 1980.

Dick, Robert C. "Negro Oratory in the Antislavery Societies, 1830–1860." *Western Speech* 28 (Winter 1964): 5–14.

———. "Rhetoric of Ante-Bellum Black Separatism." *Negro History Bulletin* 34 (October 1971): 133–37.

Dickson, Bruce D., Jr. "National Identity and African American Colonization, 1773–1817." *The Historian* 58 (Autumn 1995): 15–28.

Diedrich, Maria. *Love Across Color Lines: Ottilie Assing and Frederick Douglass.* New York: Hill and Wang, 1999.

Dillon, Merton L. "The Abolitionists: A Decade of Historiography, 1959–1969." *Journal of Southern History* 26 (November 1969): 500–522.

———. *Benjamin Lundy and the Struggle for Negro Freedom.* Urbana: University of Illinois Press, 1966.

———. "Elizabeth Chandler and the Spread of Antislavery Sentiment to Michigan." *Michigan History* 39 (December 1955): 481–95.

———. "The Failure of the American Abolitionists." *Journal of Southern History* 25 (March 1959): 159–77.

———. "Three Southern Antislavery Editors: The Myth of the Southern Antislavery Movement." *East Tennessee Historical Society's Publications* 42 (1970): 47–56.

Diouf, Sylviane A. *Servants of Allah: African Muslims Enslaved in the Americas.* New York: New York University Press, 1998.

Dixon, Christopher. "'A True Manly Life': Abolitionism and the Masculine Ideal." *Mid-America: An Historical Review* 77 (Fall 1995): 213–36.

Doherty, Robert W. "Social Bases for the Presbyterian Schism of 1837–1838: The Philadelphia Case." *Journal of Social History* 2 (Fall 1968): 69–79.

———. "Status Anxiety and American Reform: Some Alternatives." *American Quarterly* 19 (Summer 1967): 329–37.

Donald, David. "Reply to R.A. Skotheim, 'A Note on the Historical Method.'" *Journal of Southern History* 26 (February 1960).

Donald, David H. *Charles Sumner and the Coming of the Civil War.* New York: Alfred A. Knopf, 1960.

———. *Charles Sumner and the Rights of Man.* New York: Alfred A. Knopf, 1970.

———. *Lincoln.* New York: Simon & Schuster, 1995.

Donnan, Elizabeth. *Documents Illustrative of the History of the Slave Trade to America.* New York: Octagon, 1965.

Dookhan, Isaac. *A History of the Virgin Islands of the United States.* 1974. Kingston, Jamaica: Canoe, 2002.

Dorigny, Marcel, ed. *The Abolitions of Slavery: From Léger Félcité Sonthonax to Victor Schoelcher, 1793, 1794, 1848.* Paris: Berghahn, 2003.

Dormon, John H. "The Persistent Specter: Slave Rebellion in Territorial Louisiana." *Louisiana History* 18 (1977): 389–404.

Dorsey, Joseph C. *Slave Traffic in the Age of Abolition: Puerto Rico, West Africa, and the Non-Hispanic Caribbean.* Gainesville: University Press of Florida, 2003.

Dorsey, Peter A. "De-Authorizing Slavery: Realism in Stowe's *Uncle Tom's Cabin* and Brown's *Clotel.*" *Emerson Society Quarterly* 41:4 (1995): 256–88.

Douglass, Frederick. "Oration, Delivered in Corinthian Hall, Rochester, July 5, 1852." In *Black Writers of Amer-*

ica, ed. Richard Barksdale and Keneth Kinnamon. New York: Macmillan, 1972.

Douglass, William. *Annals of St. Thomas' Church.* Philadelphia: King and Baird, 1862.

Douty, Esther M. *Forten the Sailmaker: Pioneer Champion of Negro Rights.* Chicago: Rand McNally, 1968.

Dowd, Jerome. "The African Slave Trade." *Journal of Negro History* 2 (January 1917): 1–20.

Downs, Robert Bingham. *Horace Mann: Champion of Public Schools.* New York: Twayne, 1974.

Doyle, William. *The Oxford History of the French Revolution.* New York: Oxford University Press, 1989.

Drake, Richard B. "Freedmen's Aid Societies and Sectional Compromise." *Journal of Southern History* 29 (May 1963): 175–86.

Drake, Thomas E. *Quakers and Slavery in America.* New Haven, CT: Yale University Press. 1950.

———. "Thomas Garrett, Quaker Abolitionist." In *Friends in Wilmington, 1738–1938,* ed. Edward P. Bartlett. Wilmington, OH: Clinton County Historical Society, 1938.

Drayton, Daniel. *Personal Memoir of Daniel Drayton, for Four Years and Four Months a Prisoner (for Charity's Sake) in Washington Jail, Including a Narrative of the Voyage and Capture of the Schooner Pearl.* New York: Negro Universities Press, 1969.

Drescher, Seymour. "British Way, French Way: Opinion Building and Revolution in the Second French Slave Emancipation." *American Historical Review* 96 (June 1991): 709–34.

———. *From Slavery to Freedom: Comparative Studies in the Rise and Fall of Atlantic Slavery.* London: Macmillan, 1999.

Drinkwater, John. *Charles James Fox.* London: Ernest Benn, 1928.

Duberman, Martin. "The Abolitionists and Psychology." *Journal of Negro History* 47 (July 1962): 183–91.

———, ed. *The Anti-Slavery Vanguard: New Essays on the Abolitionists.* Princeton, NJ: Princeton University Press, 1965.

Du Bois, W.E.B. *The Souls of Black Folks.* Chicago: A.C. McClurg, 1903; ed. David Wright and Robert Williams, New York: Bedford/St. Martin's, 1997.

Duffy, Maureen. *The Passionate Shepherdess: Aphra Behn, 1640–89.* London: Jonathan Cape, 1977.

Dulles, Foster Rhea. *Prelude to World Power: American Diplomatic History, 1860–1900.* New York: Macmillan, 1965.

Dumond, Dwight Lowell. *Antislavery: The Crusade for Freedom in America.* Ann Arbor: University of Michigan Press, 1961.

———. "The Fourteenth Amendment in Historical Perspective." *Michigan Alumni Quarterly Review,* Autumn 1957, 55–64.

———. "Race Prejudice and Abolition, New Views on the Antislavery Movement." *Michigan Alumni Quarterly Review* 41 (April 1935): 377–85.

Dunbar-Nelson, Alice. "Lincoln and Douglass." *Negro History Bulletin* 23 (February 1960): 98, 119.

Duncan, Russell. *Where Death and Glory Meet: Colonel Robert Gould Shaw and the Fifty-Fourth Massachusetts Infantry.* Athens: University of Georgia Press, 1999.

Duncan, Troy, and Chris Dixon. "Denouncing the Brotherhood of Thieves: Stephen Symonds Foster and the Abolitionist Critique." *Civil War History* 47 (June 2001): 97–117.

Dunn, Martin E., ed. *The Black Press, 1827–1890: The Quest for National Identity.* New York: Putnam, 1971.

Dunne, Gerald T. "Bushrod Washington and the Mount Vernon Slaves." *Supreme Court Historical Society Yearbook* (1980): 25–29.

Dyer, Brainerd. "The Persistence of the Ideas of Negro Colonization." *Pacific Historical Review* 12 (March 1943): 53–66.

Dyson, Zita. "Gerrit Smith's Effort in Behalf of Negroes in New York." *Journal of Negro History* 3 (October 1918): 354–59.

Early, Gerald, ed. *Lure and Loathing: Essays on Race, Identity, and the Ambivalence of Assimilation.* New York: A. Lane/Penguin, 1993.

Eaton, Clement. "A Dangerous Pamphlet in the Old South." *Journal of Southern History* 2 (August 1936): 323–44.

Eaton, John. *Grant, Lincoln, and the Freedmen: Reminiscences of the Civil War, With Special Reference to the Work for the Contrabands and Freedmen of the Mississippi Valley.* New York: Longman, Green, 1907.

Edgell, David P. *William Ellery Channing: An Intellectual Portrait.* Westport, CT: Greenwood, 1983.

Edwards, Lester C. *The Life of Sam Houston.* New York: J.C. Derby, 1855.

Edwards, Linda McMurray. *To Keep the Waters Troubled: The Life of Ida B. Wells.* New York: Oxford University Press, 1998.

Edwards, Paul, and James Walvin, eds. *Black Personalities in the Era of the Slave Trade.* London: Macmillan, 1983.

Edwards, Samuel. *Rebel! A Biography of Tom Paine.* New York: Praeger, 1974.

Egerton, Douglas R. "Averting a Crisis: The Proslavery Critique of the American Colonization Society." *Civil War History* 43 (June 1997): 142–56.

———. *Gabriel's Rebellion: The Virginia Slave Conspiracies of 1800 and 1802.* Chapel Hill: University of North Carolina Press, 1993.

———. *He Shall Go Out Free: The Lives of Denmark Vesey.* Lanham, MD: Rowman & Littlefield, 2004.

———. "'Its Origin Is Not a Little Curious': A New Look at the American Colonization Society." *Journal of the Early Republic* 5 (Winter 1985): 463–80.

Ehrlich, Walter. *They Have No Rights: Dred Scott's Struggle for Freedom.* Westport, CT: Greenwood, 1979.

Elbert, Sarah, ed. *The American Prejudice Against Color: William G. Allen, Mary King, Louisa May Alcott.* Boston: Northeastern University Press, 2002.

Ellis, Markman. *The Politics of Sensibility: Race, Gender, and Commerce in the Sentimental Novel.* New York: Cambridge University Press, 1996.

Ellis, Richard, and Adam Wildavasky. "A Cultural Analysis of the Role of Abolitionists in the Coming of the Civil War." *Comparative Studies in Society and History* 32 (January 1990): 89–116.

Ellsworth, Clayton Sumner. "The American Churches and the Mexican War." *American Historical Review* 45 (January 1940): 301–26.

Eltis, David. *Economic Growth and the Ending of the Transatlantic Slave Trade.* New York: Oxford University Press, 1987.

Embree, Elihu. *The Emancipator.* Jonesborough, TN: Embreeville, 1995.

Embree, Elijah Hoss. *Elihu Embree, Abolitionist.* Nashville, TN: Vanderbilt Southern History Society, 1897.

Emmer, Pieter C. "Between Slavery and Freedom: The Period of Apprenticeship in Suriname (Dutch Guiana), 1863–1873." *Slavery and Abolition* 14 (April 1993): 87–113.

———. "The Price of Freedom: The Constraints of Change in Post-Emancipation America." In *The Meaning of Freedom: Economics, Politics, and Culture After Slavery,* ed. Frank McGlynn and Seymour Drescher. Pittsburgh: University of Pittsburgh Press, 1992.

Endres, Kathleen. "Jane Grey Swisshelm: 19th Century Journalist and Feminist." *Journalism History* 2 (Winter 1975–1976): 126–32.

English, Philip Wesley. *John G. Fee: Kentucky Spokesman for Abolition and Reform.* Lanham, MD: University Press of America, 1986.

Equiano, Olaudah. *The Interesting Narrative of the Life of Olaudah Equiano.* 1789. Ed. Robert J. Allison. Boston: Bedford, 1995.

Erdem, Y. Hakan. *Slavery in the Ottoman Empire and Its Demise, 1800–1909.* Basingstoke, UK: Palgrave Macmillan, 1996.

Erickson, Leonard. "Politics and Repeal of Ohio's Black Laws, 1837–1849." *Ohio History* 82 (Summer/Fall 1973): 154–75.

Ernst, Daniel R. "Legal Positivism, Abolitionist Litigation, and the New Jersey Slave Cases of 1845." *Law and History Review* 4 (Fall 1986): 337–65.

Escott, Paul D., David R. Goldfield, Sally G. McMillen, and Elizabeth Hayes Turner, eds. *Major Problems in the History of the American South.* Vol. II, *The New South.* 2nd ed. Boston: Houghton Mifflin, 1999.

Essig, James David. "The Lord's Free Man: Charles G. Finney and His Abolitionism." *Civil War History* 24 (March 1978): 25–45.

Estrade, Paul. "Betances, el jíbaro más indócil de Puerto Rico." *Casa de las Amÿricas* 226 (2002): 40–47.

———. "El abolicionismo radical de Ramón Emeterio Betances" [The Radical Abolitionism of Ramón Emeterio Betances]. *Anuario de Estudios Americanos* 43 (1986): 275–94.

Etcheson, Nicole. "Black Slavery, White Liberty." *North and South* 3 (September 2000): 42–58.

Evans, Mathilda W. "Elihu Embree, Quaker Abolitionist, and Some of His Co-Workers." *Bulletin of the Friends' Historical Association* 21 (1922).

Everts, Louis H. *History of Connecticut Valley in Massachusetts, With Illustrations and Biographical Sketches of Some of Its Prominent Men and Pioneers.* Philadelphia: Louis H. Everts, 1879.

Ewy, Marvin. "The United States Army in the Kansas Border Troubles, 1855–1856." *Kansas Historical Quarterly* 32 (Winter 1966): 385–400.

Eyck, Erich. *Pitt Versus Fox: Father and Son, 1735–1806.* Trans. Eric Northcott. London: G. Bell & Sons, 1950.

Faber, David A. "Justice Bushrod Washington and the Age of Discovery in American Law." *West Virginia Law Review* 102 (Summer 2000): 735–807.

Fabi, Giulia. "The Unguarded Expressions of the Feelings of the Negroes: Gender, Slave Resistance, and William Wells Brown's Revisions of *Clotel.*" *African American Review* 27 (Winter 1993): 639–54.

Fabre, Genevieve. "African-American Commemorative Celebrations in the Nineteenth Century." In *History and Memory in African-American Culture,* ed. Genevieve Fabre and Robert O'Meally. New York: Oxford University Press, 1994.

Fahrney, Ralph R. *Horace Greeley and the Tribune in the Civil War.* 1936. New York: Da Capo, 1970.

Fairbanks, Calvin. *Rev. Calvin Fairbanks During Slavery Times: How He "Fought the Good Fight" to Prepare the Way.* Chicago: R.R. McCabe, 1890.

Fairbanks, Edward T. *Town of St. Johnsbury: A Review of One Hundred Twenty-Five Years to the Anniversary Pageant 1912.* St. Johnsbury, VT: Cowles, 1914.

Fanuzzi, Robert. *Abolition's Public Sphere.* Minneapolis: University of Minnesota Press, 2003.

Faria, A. *Luiz Gama.* Rio de Janeiro, Brazil: Academia Brasileira de Letras, 1927.

Farley, Ena L. "Methodists and Baptists on the Issue of Black Equality in New York, 1865 to 1868." *Journal of Negro History* 61 (October 1976): 374–92.

Farrell, John. "Schemes for the Transplanting of Refugee American Negroes From Upper Canada in the 1840s." *Ontario History* 52 (December 1960): 245–50.

Farrison, William Edward. "A Flight Across Ohio: The Escape of William Wells Brown From Slavery." *Ohio State Historical Quarterly* 11 (July 1952): 273–83.

————. "Phylon Profiles, XVI: William Wells Brown." *Phylon* 9 (First Quarter 1948): 13–33.

————. *William Wells Brown: Author and Reformer.* Chicago: University of Chicago Press, 1969.

————. "William Wells Brown, Social Reformer." *Journal of Negro Education* 5 (December/March 1949): 29–49.

————. "William Wells Brown in Buffalo." *Journal of Negro History* 60 (October 1954): 299–314.

Fee, John G. *Autobiography of John G. Fee.* Chicago: National Christian Association, 1891.

Fehrenbacher, Don E. *Constitutions and Constitutionalism in the Slaveholding South.* Athens: University of Georgia Press, 1989.

————. *The* Dred Scott *Case: Its Significance in American Law and Politics.* New York: Oxford University Press, 1978.

————. *Sectional Crisis and Southern Constitutionalism.* Baton Rouge: Louisiana State University Press, 1980.

————. *The Slaveholding Republic: An Account of the United States Government's Relations to Slavery.* New York: Oxford University Press, 2001.

————. *Slavery, Law, and Politics: The* Dred Scott *Case in Historical Perspective.* New York: Oxford University Press, 1981.

————. *The South and Three Sectional Crises.* Baton Rouge: Louisiana State University Press, 1980.

Feller, Daniel. "Benjamin Tappan: The Making of a Democrat." In *The Pursuit of Public Power: Political Culture in Ohio, 1787–1861,* ed. Jeffrey P. Brown and Andrew R.L. Cayton. Kent, OH: Kent State University Press, 1994.

————. "A Brother in Arms: Benjamin Tappan and the Antislavery Democracy." *Journal of American History* 88 (June 2001): 48–74.

Fellman, Michael. "Rehearsal for the Civil War: Antislavery and Proslavery at the Fighting Point in Kansas, 1854–1856." In *Antislavery Reconsidered: New Perspectives on the Abolitionists,* ed. Lewis Perry and Michael Fellman. Baton Rouge: Louisiana State University Press, 1979.

————. "Theodore Parker and the Abolitionist Role in the 1850s." *Journal of American History* 61 (December 1974): 666–84.

Ferguson, Margaret. "Juggling the Categories of Race, Class and Gender: Aphra Behn's *Oroonoko.*" *Women's Studies* 19 (1991): 159–81.

Ferguson, Robert A. "Story and Transcription in the Trial of John Brown." *Yale Journal of Law and Humanities* 6 (Winter 1994): 37–73.

Ferrero, Guglielmo. *The Reconstruction of Europe: Talleyrand and the Congress of Vienna, 1814–1815.* Toronto, Ontario, Canada: W.W. Norton, 1963.

Fessenden, Francis. *Life and Public Services of William Pitt Fessenden.* 2 vols. Boston: Houghton Mifflin, 1907.

Fick, Carolyn. "Emancipation in Haiti: From Plantation Labour to Peasant Proprietorship." *Slavery and Abolition* 21 (August 2000): 11–40.

Field, Phyllis F. "Republicans and Black Suffrage in New York State: The Grass Roots Response." *Civil War History* 21 (June 1975): 136–47.

Fields, Annie Adams. "Days With Mrs. Stowe." *Atlantic Monthly,* August 1896, 145–56.

Fields, Barbara J. "Who Freed the Slaves?" In *The Civil War: An Illustrated History,* ed. Geoffrey C. Ward, Rick Burns, and Ken Burns. New York: Alfred A. Knopf, 1990.

Filler, Louis. *The Crusade Against Slavery, 1830–1860.* New York: Harper & Row, 1960.

————. "Nonviolence and Abolition." *University Review* 30 (Spring 1964): 172–78.

————. "Parker Pillsbury: An Anti-Slavery Apostle." *New England Quarterly* 19 (September 1946): 315–37.

————, ed. *Wendell Phillips on Civil Rights and Freedom.* 2nd ed. Lanham, MD: University Press of America, 1982.

Findley, Paul. *A. Lincoln: the Crucible of Congress.* New York: Crown, 1979.

Finkelman, Paul. "The *Dred Scott* Case, Slavery, and the Politics of Law." *Hamline Law Review* 20 (Fall 1996): 1–42.

————. "Evading the Ordinance: The Persistence of Bondage in Indiana and Illinois." *Journal of the Early Republic* 9 (Spring 1989): 21–52.

————. "Fugitive Slaves, Midwestern Racial Tolerance, and the Value of Justice Delayed." *Iowa Law Review* 78 (October 1992): 89–114.

————, ed. *His Soul Goes Marching On: Responses to John Brown and the Harpers Ferry Raid.* Charlottesville: University of Virginia Press, 1995.

————. "The Kidnapping of John Davis and the Adoption of the Fugitive Slave Law of 1793." *Journal of Southern History* 56 (August 1990): 397–422.

————. "Legal Ethics and Fugitive Slaves: The Anthony Burns Case, Judge Loring, and Abolitionist Attorneys." *Cardozo Law Review* 17 (May 1996): 1793–1858.

————. "Prelude to the Fourteenth Amendment: Black Legal Rights in the Antebellum North." *Rutgers Law Review* 17 (Spring/Summer 1986): 415–82.

————. "*Prigg v. Pennsylvania* and Northern State Courts: Anti-Slavery Use of a Pro-Slavery Decision." *Civil War History* 25 (March 1979): 5–35.

————. "The Protection of Black Rights in Seward's New York." *Civil War History* 34 (September 1988): 125–58.

————. "Slavery and the 'More Perfect Union' and the Prairie State." *Illinois Historical Journal* 80 (Winter 1987): 248–69.

————. "Slavery and the Northwest Ordinance: A Study in Ambiguity." *Journal of the Early Republic* 6 (Winter 1986): 343–70.

————. "Sorting Out *Prigg v. Pennsylvania.*" *Rutgers Law Journal* 24 (Spring 1993): 605–65.

————. "State Constitutional Protections of Liberty and the Antebellum New Jersey Supreme Court: Chief Justice

Hornblower and the Fugitive Slave Law of 1793." *Rutgers Law Review* 23 (Summer 1992): 753–87.

———. "Story Telling on the Supreme Court: *Prigg v. Pennsylvania* and Justice Joseph Story's Judicial Nationalism." *Supreme Court Review* (1994): 247–94.

———. "What Did the *Dred Scott* Case Really Decide?" *Reviews in American History* 7 (September 1979): 368–74.

Finney, Charles Grandison. *Memoirs of Charles G. Finney, Written by Himself.* 1876. New York: AMS, 1973.

Finnie, Gordon E. "The Antislavery Movement in the Upper South Before 1840." *Journal of Southern History* 35 (August 1969): 319–42.

Fisch, Audrey. *American Slaves in Victorian England: Abolition in Popular Literature and Culture.* New York: Cambridge University Press, 2000.

Fishback, Mason McCloud. "Illinois Legislation on Slavery and Free Negroes, 1818." *Transactions of the Illinois State Historical Society* 9 (1904): 414–32.

Fishel, Leslie H., Jr. "Wisconsin and Negro Suffrage." *Wisconsin Magazine of History* 46 (Spring 1963): 180–96.

Fisher, Miles Mark. "Friends of Humanity: A Quaker Anti-Slavery Influence." *Church History* 4:3 (September 1935): 187–202.

Fisher, S.J. "Reminiscences of Jane Grey Swisshelm." *Western Pennsylvania Historical Magazine* 4 (July 1921): 165–74.

Fisher, William Harvey. *The Invisible Empire: A Bibliography of the Ku Klux Klan.* Metuchen, NJ: Scarecrow, 1980.

Fishkin, Shelly Fisher, and Carla L. Peterson. "'We Hold These Truths to Be Self-Evident': The Rhetoric of Frederick Douglass' Journalism." In *Frederick Douglass: New Literary and Historical Essays,* ed. Eric J. Sundquist. Cambridge, MA: Cambridge University Press, 1990.

Fishman, George. "New Jersey's Abolition Voice and the Negro." *Negro History Bulletin* 31 (May 1968): 18–19.

Fitzgerald, Michael W. "Abbott, Cotton and Capital: Boston Businessmen and Antislavery Reform." *Journal of Mississippi History* 54 (November 1992): 388.

Fladeland, Betty. *Abolitionist and Working-Class Problems in the Age of Industrialization.* Baton Rouge: Louisiana State University Press, 1984.

———. "Abolitionist Pressures on the Concert of Europe, 1814–1822." *Journal of Modern History* 38 (December 1966): 355–73.

———. "Abolitionists v. Revisionists: The Historiographical Cold War of the 1930s and 1940s." *Journal of the Early Republic* 6 (Spring 1986): 1–21.

———. "Birney, James Gillespie." In *American National Biography,* ed. John A. Garraty and Mark C. Carnes. New York: Oxford University Press, 1999.

———. "Compensated Emancipation: A Rejected Alternative." *Journal of Southern History* 42 (May 1976): 169–86.

———. *James Gillespie Birney: Slaveholder to Abolitionist.* Ithaca, NY: Cornell University Press, 1955.

———. *Men and Brothers: Anglo-American Antislavery Co-operation.* Urbana: University of Illinois Press, 1972.

———. "'Our Cause Being One and the Same': Abolitionists and Chartism." In *Slavery and British Society, 1776–1846,* ed. James Walvin. Baton Rouge: Louisiana State University Press, 1982.

———. "Who Were the Abolitionists?" *Journal of Negro History* 49 (April 1964): 99–115.

Fleischner, Jennifer. *Mrs. Lincoln and Mrs. Keckley: The Remarkable Story of the Friendship Between a First Lady and a Former Slave.* New York: Broadway, 2003.

Fleming, Walter L. *Documentary History of Reconstruction: Political, Military, Social, Religious, Educational and Industrial, 1865 to the Present Time.* 2 vols. Cleveland, OH: A.H. Clark, 1906.

Fletcher, F.T.H. "Montesquieu's Influence on Anti-Slavery Opinion in England." *Journal of Negro History* 18 (October 1933): 414–26.

Fletcher, Robert Samuel. *A History of Oberlin College from Its Foundation Through the Civil War.* Oberlin, OH: Oberlin College, 1943.

Floyd, Barry. *Jamaica: An Island Microcosm.* New York: St. Martin's, 1979.

Fogarty, Anne. "Looks That Kill: Violence and Representation in Aphra Behn's *Oroonoko.*" In *The Discourse of Slavery: Aphra Behn to Toni Morrison,* ed. Carl Plasa and Betty J. Ring. London: Routledge, 1994.

Foner, Eric. *Free Soil, Free Labor, Free Men: The Ideology of the Republican Party Before the Civil War.* New York: Oxford University Press, 1970.

———. *Nat Turner.* Englewood Cliffs, NJ: Prentice Hall, 1971.

———. *Nothing but Freedom: Emancipation and Its Legacy.* Baton Rouge: Louisiana State University Press, 1983.

———. *Politics and Ideology in the Age of the Civil War.* New York: Oxford University Press, 1980.

———. "Politics and Prejudice: The Free Soil Party and the Negro, 1849–1852." *Journal of Negro History* 50 (October 1965): 239–56.

———. "Racial Attitudes of the New York Free Soilers." *New York History* 46 (October 1965): 311–29.

———. *Reconstruction: America's Unfinished Revolution.* New York: Harper & Row, 1988.

———. "The Wilmot Proviso Revisited." *Journal of American History* 61 (September 1969): 269–79.

Foner, Philip S. *Life and Writings of Frederick Douglass.* 5 vols. New York: International Publishers, 1950.

Foner, Philip S., and George E. Walker, eds. *Proceedings of the Black State Conventions, 1840–1865.* Vol. 1, *New York, Pennsylvania, Indiana, Michigan, Ohio.* Philadelphia: Temple University Press, 1969.

Foot, Michael, and Isaac Kramnick, eds. *The Thomas Paine Reader.* London: Penguin, 1987.

Foote, Henry S. *The Bench and Bar of the South and Southwest.* St. Louis, MO: Soule, Thomas, and Wentworth, 1876.

Forbes, Robert Pierce. "Slavery and the Meaning of America, 1819–1837." Ph.D. diss., Yale University, 1994.

Ford, Charles Howard. *Hannah More.* New York: Peter Lang, 1996.

Formisano, Ronald P. "Edge of Caste: Colored Suffrage in Michigan, 1827–1861." *Michigan History* 56 (Spring 1972): 19–40.

———. "Political Character, Antipartyism and the Second Party System." *American Quarterly* 21 (Winter 1969): 683–709.

Forte, David F. "Spiritual Equality, the Black Codes and the Americanization of the Freedmen." *Loyola Law Review* 43 (Winter 1998): 569–611.

Fortenbaugh, Robert. "American Lutheran Synods and Slavery, 1830–1860." *Journal of Religion* 13 (January 1933): 72–92.

Fortescue, William. *Alphonse de Lamartine: A Political Biography.* New York: St. Martin's, 1983.

Foster, Charles I. "The Colonization of Free Negroes in Liberia, 1816–1835." *Journal of Negro History* 38 (January 1953): 41–66.

Fowler, P.H. *Historical Sketch of Presbyterianism Within the Bounds of the Synod of Central New York.* Utica, NY: Curtiss & Childs, 1877.

Fox, Dixon Ryan. "The Negro Vote in Old New York." *Political Science Quarterly* 32 (June 1917): 252–75.

Fox, George. *The Autobiography of George Fox.* Grand Rapids, MI: Christian Classics Ethereal Library, 2000.

Franklin, Cathy Rogers. "James Gillespie Birney: The Revival Spirit, and *The Philanthropist.*" *American Journalism* 17 (2000): 31–51.

Franklin, John Hope. *The Emancipation Proclamation.* Wheeling, IL: Harlan Davidson, 1995.

Franklin, John Hope, and Loren Schweninger. *Runaway Slaves: Rebels on the Plantation.* New York: Oxford University Press, 1999.

Frasure, C.M. "Charles Sumner and the Rights of the Negro." *Journal of Negro History* 13 (April 1928): 1–24.

Freehling, Alison Goodyear. *Drift Toward Dissolution: The Virginia Slavery Debate of 1831–1832.* Baton Rouge: Louisiana State University Press, 1982.

Freehling, William W. "The Founding Fathers and Slavery." *American Historical Review* 77 (February 1972): 81–93.

———. *The Road to Disunion: Secessionists at Bay, 1776–1854.* New York: Oxford University Press, 1991.

French, David. "Elizur Wright, Jr., and the Emergence of Anti-Colonization Sentiments on the Connecticut Western Reserve." *Ohio History* 85 (Winter 1976): 49–66.

French, Scot. *The Rebellious Slave: Nat Turner in American Memory.* Boston: Houghton Mifflin, 2003.

Frey, John Andrew. *A Victor Hugo Encyclopedia.* Westport, CT: Greenwood, 1999.

Friedman, Dorothy Sterling. *Freedom Train: The Story of Harriet Tubman.* Garden City, NY: Doubleday, 1954.

Friedman, Lawrence J. "Abolitionist Historiography 1965–1979: An Assessment." *Reviews in American History* 8 (June 1980): 200–205.

———. "Abolitionists Versus Historians." *Reviews in American History* 5 (September 1977): 342–47.

———. "Antebellum Abolitionism and the Problem of Violent Means." *Psychohistory Review* 9 (Fall 1980): 23–58.

———. "Confidence and Pertinacity in Evangelical Abolitionism: Lewis Tappan's Circle." *American Quarterly* 31 (Spring 1979): 81–106.

———. "The Gerrit Smith Circle: Abolitionism in the Burned-Over District." *Civil War History* 26 (March 1980): 18–38.

———. *Gregarious Saints: Self and Community in American Abolitionism, 1830–1870.* New York: Cambridge University Press, 1982.

———. "'Historical Topics Sometimes Run Dry': The State of Abolitionist Studies." *The Historian* 43 (February 1981): 177–94.

Friedman, Lawrence M. *A History of American Law.* New York: Simon & Schuster, 1973.

Friis, Hermann R. "Baron Alexander von Humboldt's Visit to Washington." *Records of the Columbia Historical Society* 44 (1963): 1–35.

Frost, J. William. "The Origins of the Quaker Crusade Against Slavery: A Review of Recent Literature." *Quaker History* 67 (1978): 42–58.

Frothingham, Octavius Brooks. *Gerrit Smith: A Biography.* New York: G.P. Putnam's Sons, 1909.

Fryer, Mary Beacock, and Christopher Dracott. *John Graves Simcoe, 1752–1806: A Biography.* Toronto, Ontario, Canada: Dundurn, 1998.

Fryer, Peter. *Staying Power: A History of Black People in Britain.* London: Pluto, 1984.

Fuess, Claude. "Daniel Webster and the Abolitionists." *Proceedings of the Massachusetts Historical Society* 64 (1932): 29–42.

Fuller, Edmund. *Prudence Crandall: An Incident of Racism in Nineteenth-Century Connecticut.* Middletown, CT: Wesleyan University Press, 1971.

Furer, Howard B. *The Germans in America, 1607–1970: A Chronology and Fact Book.* Dobbs Ferry, NY: Oceana, 1973.

Furneaux, Robin. *William Wilberforce.* London: Hamish Hamilton, 1974.

Futhey, J. Smith, and Gilbert Cope. *History of Chester County, Pennsylvania, With Genealogical and Biographical Sketches.* Philadelphia: Louis H. Everts, 1881.

Fyfe, Christopher. *A History of Sierra Leone.* New York: Oxford University Press, 1962.

Galpin, W. Freeman. "Samuel Joseph May: God's Chore Boy." *New York History* 21 (April 1946): 144–46.

Gama, Luis. *Trovas Burlescas* [Burlesque Ballads]. São Paolo, Brazil: Editora Três, 1974.

Gamble, Douglas A. "Garrison Abolitionism in the West: Some Suggestions for Study." *Civil War History* 18 (March 1977): 52–68.

————. "Joshua Giddings and the Ohio Abolitionists: A Study in Radical Politics." *Ohio History* 29 (November 1979): 36–56.

Gara, Larry. "Antislavery Congressmen, 1848–1856: Their Contribution to the Abolitionist Cause." *Civil War History* 32 (September 1986): 197–207.

————. "The Fugitive Slave Law: A Double Paradox." *Civil War History* 10 (September 1964): 229–40.

————. "A Glorious Time: The 1874 Abolitionist Reunion in Chicago." *Illinois State Historical Society Journal* 65 (Autumn 1972).

————. "Horace Mann: Anti-Slavery Congressman." *The Historian* 32 (November 1969): 19–33.

————. *The Liberty Line: The Legend of the Underground Railroad.* Louisville: University Press of Kentucky, 1996.

————. "The Professional Fugitive in the Abolition Movement." *Wisconsin Magazine of History* 48 (Spring 1965): 196–204.

————. "Propaganda Uses of the Underground Railway." *Mid-America: An Historical Review* 34 (July 1952): 155–71.

————. "Slavery and the Slave Power: A Crucial Distinction." *Civil War History* 15 (March 1969): 5–18.

————. "The Underground Railway: A Reevaluation." *Ohio Historical Quarterly* 69 (July 1960): 334–39.

————. "'The Underground Railway': Legend or Reality?" *Proceedings of the American Philosophical Society* 105 (1961): 334–39.

Garfield, Deborah M., and Rafia Zafar, eds. *Harriet Jacobs and* Incidents in the Life of a Slave Girl: *New Critical Essays.* New York: Cambridge University Press, 1996.

Garnet, Henry Highland. "An Address to the Slaves of the United States of America." In *The Norton Anthology of African American Literature,* ed. Henry Louis Gates, Jr., and Nellie Y. McKay. New York: W.W. Norton, 1997.

————. "A Memorial Discourse Delivered in the Hall of the House of Representatives, February 12, 1865." In *Black Writers of America,* ed. Richard Barksdale and Keneth Kinnamon. New York: Macmillan, 1972.

————. *Walker's Appeal, With a Brief Sketch of His Life.* New York: J.H. Tobitt, 1848.

Garnett, J.M. *Biographical Sketches of Hon. Charles Fenton Mercer.* Richmond, VA: Whittet and Shepperson, 1911.

Garrison, Wendell Phillips, and Francis Jackson Garrison. *William Lloyd Garrison, 1805–1879; The Story of His Life Told by His Children.* 4 vols. New York: Century, 1885–1889.

Garrison, William Lloyd. *The Letters of William Lloyd Garrison.* Ed. Walter M. Merrill. Cambridge, MA: Belknap Press, 1971.

————. *Thoughts on African Colonization.* 1832. Introduction by William Loren Katz. New York: Arno, 1968.

Gaspar, David Barry, and David Patrick Geggus, eds. *A Turbulent Time: The French Revolution and the Greater Caribbean.* Bloomington: Indiana University Press, 1997.

Gatell, Frank Otto. "Conscience and Judgment: The Bolt of Massachusetts Conscience Whigs." *The Historian* 27 (November 1958): 18–45.

Gates, Henry Louis, Jr. *The Trials of Phillis Wheatley: America's First Black Poet and Her Encounters With the Founding Fathers.* New York: Basic Civitas, 2003.

Gaustad, Edwin Scott. *The Great Awakening in New England.* New York: Harper, 1957.

Gavronsky, Serge. *The French Liberal Opposition and the American Civil War.* New York: Humanities, 1968.

Gay, Arthur Royall. "The Clapham Sect." Master's thesis, University of Chicago, 1917.

Geffen, Elizabeth M. "William Henry Furness, Philadelphia Antislavery Preacher." *Pennsylvania Magazine of History and Biography* 82 (July 1958): 259–92.

Geggus, David, ed. *The Impact of the Haitian Slave Revolt in the Atlantic World.* Columbia: University of South Carolina Press, 2001.

Gellman, David. "Pirates, Sugar, Debtors, and Slaves: Political Economy and the Case for Gradual Abolition in New York." *Slavery and Abolition* 22 (August 2001): 51–68.

————. "Race, the Public Sphere, and Abolition in Late Eighteenth-Century New York. *Journal of the Early Republic* 20 (Winter 2000): 607–36.

Genovese, Eugene. *From Rebellion to Revolution: Afro-American Slave Revolts in the Making of the Modern World.* Baton Rouge: Louisiana State University Press, 1979; New York: Vintage Books, 1981.

————. "Slavery in the Legal History of the South and the Nation." *Texas Law Review* 59 (May 1981): 969–98.

Gershman, Sally. "Alexis de Tocqueville and Slavery." *French Historical Studies* 9 (Spring 1976): 467–84.

Gershoni, Yekutiel. *Black Colonialism: The Americo-Liberian Scramble for the Hinterland.* Boulder, CO: Westview, 1985.

Gerteis, Louis S. *From Contraband to Freedman: Federal Policy Toward Southern Blacks, 1861–1865.* Westport, CT: Greenwood, 1973.

————. "Slavery and Hard Times: Morality and Utility in American Antislavery Reform." *Civil War History* 29 (December 1983): 316–31.

Gerzina, Gretchen. *Black London: Life Before Emancipation.* New Brunswick, NJ: Rutgers University Press, 1995.

Gewertz, Ken. "Professor Brought Christmas Tree to New England." *Harvard University Gazette,* December 1996, 24.

Gibbs, F.W. *Joseph Priestley: Revolutions of the Eighteenth Century.* Garden City, NY: Doubleday, 1967.

Gibbs, Howard A., and John Keep. *Blandford: An Early History; and, Selected Collection of Blandford Poems.* Blandford, MA: Blandford Historical Society, 1976.

Gibbs, Mifflin Wistar. *Shadow and Light: An Autobiography With Reminiscences of the Last and Present Century.* Lincoln: University of Nebraska Press, 1995.

Gibson, Robert A. "A Deferred Dream: The Proposal for a Negro College in New Haven, 1831." *New Haven Colony Historical Society Journal* 37:2 (1991): 22–29.

Giddings, Paula. *When and Where I Enter: The Impact of Black Women on Race and Sex in America.* New York: William Morrow, 1996.

Gienapp, William E. "Salmon P. Chase, Nativism, and the Formation of the Republican Party in Ohio." *Ohio History* 93 (Spring 1984): 5–39.

Gilje, Paul A. *Rioting in America.* Bloomington: Indiana University Press, 1996.

Gillispie, Charles Coulston. *Dictionary of Scientific Biography.* 16 vols. New York: Scribner's, 1970–1980.

Ginzberg, Lori. "'Moral Suasion Is Moral Balderdash': Women, Politics, and Social Activism in the 1850s." *Journal of American History* 73 (December 1986): 601–22.

———. *Women in Antebellum Reform.* Wheeling, IL: Harlan Davidson, 2000.

Glatthaar, Joseph T. *Forged in Battle: The Civil War Alliance of Black Soldiers and White Officers.* New York: Free Press, 1990; Baton Rouge: Louisiana State University Press, 2000.

Glenn, Myra C. "Northern Opposition to Mid-Nineteenth Century Abolitionism: The Case of Thomas K. Beecher." *Mid-America: An Historical Review* 72 (October 1990): 191–211.

Goings, Charles Buxton. *David Wilmot, Free-Soiler: A Biography of the Great Advocate of the Wilmot Proviso.* Gloucester, MA: P. Smith, 1966.

Goldberg, Isaac. *Brazilian Literature.* New York: Alfred A. Knopf, 1922.

Goldin, Claudia Dale. "The Economics of Emancipation." *Journal of Economic History* 33 (March 1973): 66–85.

Gómez-Gil, Orlando, ed. *Literatura Hispanoamericana. Antología crítica* [Hispanic American Literature: A Critical Anthology]. 2 vols. New York: Holt, Rinehart and Winston, 1972.

Goodell, William. *Slavery and Anti-Slavery: A History of the Great Struggle in Both Hemispheres.* 1852. New York: Augustus M. Kelley, 1970.

Goodheart, Lawrence B. *Abolitionist, Actuary, Atheist: Elizur Wright and the Reform Impulse.* Kent, OH: Kent State University Press, 1990.

———. "Childrearing, Conscience and Conversion to Abolitionism: The Example of Elizur Wright, Jr." *Psychohistory Review* 12 (1984): 24–33.

———. "'Chronicles of Kidnapping in New York': Resistance to the Fugitive Slave Law, 1834–1835." *Afro-Americans in New York Life and History* 8 (January 1984): 7–15.

Goodman, Paul. "The Manual Labor Movement and the Origins of Abolitionism." *Journal of the Early Republic* 13 (Fall 1983): 355–88.

———. *Of One Blood: Abolitionism and the Origins of Racial Equality.* Berkeley: University of California Press, 1998.

Goody, Jack. "Writing, Religion, and Revolt in Bahía." *Visible Language* 20 (Summer 1986): 318–43.

Gordon, Anne, ed. *The Selected Papers of Elizabeth Cady Stanton and Susan B. Anthony.* Vol. 2, *Against the Aristocracy of Sex, 1866 to 1873.* New Brunswick, NJ: Rutgers University Press, 2000.

Goreau, Angeline. *Reconstructing Aphra: A Social Biography of Aphra Behn.* New York: Dial, 1980.

Goslinga, Cornelis C. *The Dutch in the Caribbean and in Surinam, 1791/5–1942.* Assen, Netherlands: Van Gorcum, 1990.

Gossett, Thomas F. Uncle Tom's Cabin *and American Culture.* Dallas, TX: Southern Methodist University Press, 1965.

Gottschalk, Louis. *Lafayette and the Close of the American Revolution.* Chicago: University of Chicago Press, 1942.

Gottschalk, Louis, and Margaret Maddox. *Lafayette in the French Revolution.* 2 vols. Chicago: University of Chicago Press, 1969, 1973.

Goveia, Elsa V. *Amelioration and Emancipation in the British Caribbean.* St. Augustine, Trinidad: University of the West Indies, 1977.

Gragg, Larry. "A Heavenly Visitation: Larry Gragg Recounts the Reasons for a Visit of the Quaker George Fox to Barbados in 1671, and the Significance of His Presence There." *History Today* 52 (February 2002): 46–51.

———. "The Making of an Abolitionist: Benjamin Lay on Barbados, 1718–1720." *Journal of the Barbados Museum and Historical Society* 47 (2001): 166–84.

Graham, Howard Jay. "The Early Antislavery Background of the Fourteenth Amendment." *Wisconsin Law Review* (May 1950): 479–507.

———. "The Early Background of the Fourteenth Amendment, II: Systemization, 1835–1837." *Wisconsin Law Review* (July 1950): 610–61.

Graham, Jenny. *Revolutionary in Exile: The Emigration of Joseph Priestley to America, 1794–1804.* Philadelphia: American Philosophical Society, 1995.

Graham, Maryemma. *The Complete Works of Frances E.W. Harper.* Oxford, UK: Oxford University Press, 1988.

Grandy, Moses. *Narrative of the Life of Moses Grandy; Late a Slave in the United States of America.* 1843. Chapel Hill: Academic Affairs Library, University of North Carolina, 1996.

Grant, Mary Hetherington. *Private Woman, Public Person: An Account of the Life of Julia Ward Howe From 1819–1868.* Brooklyn, NY: Carlson, 1994.

Gravely, William B. "The Dialectic of Double-Consciousness in Black Freedom Celebrations, 1808–1863." *Journal of Negro History* 67 (Winter 1982): 302–17.

———. "Early Methodism and Slavery: The Roots of a Tradition." *Wesleyan Quarterly Review* 2 (May 1965): 301–15.

————. *Gilbert Haven, Methodist Abolitionist; A Study in Race, Religion, and Reform, 1850–1880.* Nashville, TN: Abington, 1973.

————. "Methodist Preachers, Slavery, and Caste: Types of Social Concern in Antebellum America." *Duke Divinity School Review* 34 (Autumn 1969): 209–29.

Gray, David L. *Inside Prince Hall.* Lancaster, VA: Anchor Communications, 2004.

Gray, Myra Gladys. "Archibald W. Campbell—Party Builder." *West Virginia History* 7 (April 1946): 221–37.

Gray, Thomas R., ed. *The Confessions of Nat Turner, the Leader of the Late Insurrection in Southampton, Virginia.* Baltimore: T.R. Gray, 1831.

Greeley, Horace. *Recollections of a Busy Life.* 1868. Port Washington, NY: Kennikat, 1971.

Green, Fletcher M. "Northern Missionary Activities in the South, 1846–1861." *Journal of Southern History* 21 (May 1955): 147–72.

Green, Michael. "The Expansion of European Colonization to the Mississippi Valley, 1780–1880." In *The Cambridge History of the Native Peoples of the Americas,* ed. Bruce G. Trigger and Wilcomb E. Washburn. Cambridge, UK: Cambridge University Press, 1996.

Green, William A. *British Slave Emancipation: The Sugar Colonies and the Great Experiment, 1830–1865.* Oxford, UK: Clarendon, 1976.

Greenberg, Kenneth S. *The Confessions of Nat Turner and Related Documents.* Boston: St. Martin's, 1996.

Greene, Anne. "Haiti: Historical Setting." In *Dominican Republic and Haiti: Country Studies,* ed. Helen Chapin Metz. Washington, DC: Federal Research Division, Library of Congress, 2001.

Greer, Germaine. *The Uncollected Verse of Aphra Behn.* Essex, UK: Stump Cross, 1989.

Grégoire, Henri. *On the Cultural Achievements of Negroes.* Trans. Thomas Cassirer and Jean-Francois Briere. Amherst: University of Massachusetts Press, 1996.

Gregory, James P. "The Question of Slavery in the Kentucky Constitutional Convention of 1849." *Filson Club History Quarterly* 23 (April 1949): 89–110.

Griffin, Clifford S. "The Abolitionists and the Benevolent Societies, 1831–1861." *Journal of Negro History* 44 (July 1959): 195–216.

————. "Religious Benevolence as Social Control, 1815–1860." *Mississippi Valley Historical Review* 44 (December 1957): 423–44.

Griffin, J. David. "Historians and the Sixth Article of the Ordinance of 1787." *Ohio History* 78 (Autumn 1969): 252–60.

Griffith, Elisabeth. *In Her Own Right: The Life of Elizabeth Cady Stanton.* New York: Oxford University Press, 1984.

Griggs, Earl Leslie. *Thomas Clarkson, the Friend of Slaves.* 1936. Westport, CT: Negro Universities Press, 1970.

Grim, Paul R. "The Rev. John Rankin, Early Abolitionist." *Ohio State Archaeological and Historical Quarterly* 46 (May 1937): 215–56.

Grimshaw, William H. *Official History of Freemasonry Among the Colored People in North America.* New York: Negro Universities Press, 1969.

Grimsted, David. *American Mobbing, 1828–1861: Toward Civil War.* New York: Oxford University Press, 1998.

————. "Rioting in Its Jacksonian Setting." *American Historical Review* 77 (April 1972): 361–97.

Grinnell, Josiah Bushnell. *Men and Events of Forty Years: Autobiographical Reminiscences of an Active Career From 1850 to 1890.* Boston: D. Lothrop, 1891.

Griswold, Charles L. *Adam Smith and the Virtues of Enlightenment.* Cambridge, UK: Cambridge University Press, 1999.

Gross, Bella. "Freedom's Journal and the Rights of All." *Journal of Negro History* 27 (July 1932): 241–86.

————. "Life and Times of Theodore S. Wright, 1797–1847." *Negro History Bulletin* 3 (June 1940): 133–38.

Grossman, Lawrence. "George T. Downing and Segregation of Rhode Island Public Schools, 1855–1866." *Rhode Island History* 36 (November 1977): 99–105.

Grover, Kathryn. *The Fugitive's Gibraltar: Escaping Slaves and Abolitionism in New Bedford, Massachusetts.* Amherst: University of Massachusetts Press, 2001.

Guelzo, Allen C. *Lincoln's Emancipation Proclamation: The End of Slavery in America.* New York: Simon & Schuster, 2004.

Gurko, Miriam. *The Ladies of Seneca Falls: The Birth of the Women's Movement.* New York: Schocken, 1976.

Haberly, David T. *Three Sad Races: Racial Identity and National Consciousness in Brazilian Literature.* Cambridge, UK: Cambridge University Press, 1983.

Hagan, Horace H. "Ableman vs. Booth." *American Bar Association Journal* 17 (January 1931): 1–20.

Hale, Frank W. "Frederick Douglass: Antislavery Crusader and Lecturer." *Journal of Human Relations* 14 (First Quarter 1966).

Haliburton, Gordon McKay. "The Nova Scotia Settlers of 1792." *Sierra Leone Studies* NS:9 (1957): 16–25.

Hall, Catherine. *Civilising Subjects: Colony and Metropole in the English Imagination, 1830–1867.* Chicago: University of Chicago Press, 2002.

Hall, Neville. "Heegaard, Anna—Enigma." In *Bondmen and Freedmen in the Danish West Indies,* ed. George Tyson. St. Thomas: Virgin Islands Humanities Council, 1996.

————. *Slave Society in the Danish West Indies: St. Thomas, St. John, and St. Croix.* Ed. B.W. Higman. Baltimore: Johns Hopkins University Press, 1992.

Hallowell, Anna D. "Lydia Maria Child." *Medford Historical Review* 3 (July 1900).

Hamer, Philip M. "Great Britain, the United States, and the Negro Seamen's Acts, 1822–1848." *Journal of Southern History* 1 (February 1935): 3–28.

Hamilton, James Cleland. "John Brown in Canada." *Canadian Magazine,* December 1894, 133–34.

Hamilton, Thomas, and Robert Hamilton, eds. *The Weekly Anglo-African Magazine*. New York: Thomas Hamilton, 1859–1865.

Hamilton, William. *Address to the Fourth Annual Convention of the People of Color of the United States*. New York: S.W. Benedict & Co., 1834.

Hamlin, Charles E. *The Life and Times of Hannibal Hamlin*. Cambridge, MA: Riverside Press, 1899.

Hamm, Thomas D. *God's Government Begun: The Society for Universal Inquiry and Reform, 1842–1846*. Bloomington: Indiana University Press, 1995.

Hamm, Thomas D., David Ditter, Chenda Fruchter, Ann Giordano, Janice Matthews, and Ellen Swain. "Moral Choices: Two Indiana Quaker Communities and the Abolitionist Movement." *Indiana Magazine of History* 87 (June 1991): 117–54.

Hammett, Theodore M. "Two Mobs of Jacksonian Boston: Ideology and Interest." *Journal of American History* 42 (March 1976): 845–68.

Hammond, John L. "Revival Religion and Antislavery Politics." *American Sociological Review* 39 (April 1974): 175–86.

Hancock, Harold B. "Mary Ann Shadd: Negro Editor, Educator, and Lawyer." *Delaware History* 15 (April 1973): 187–94.

———. "Not Quite Men: The Free Negroes in Delaware in the 1830s." *Civil War History* 17 (December 1970): 320–31.

Hansen, Debra Gold. *Strained Sisterhood: Gender and Class in the Boston Female Anti-Slavery Society*. Amherst: University of Massachusetts Press, 1993.

Hardman, Keith J. *Charles Grandison Finney, 1792–1875: Revivalist and Reformer*. Syracuse, NY: Syracuse University Press, 1987.

Hargrave, Francis. *An Argument in the Case of James Sommersett, a Negro, Lately Determined by the Court of King's Bench: Wherein It Is Attempted to Demonstrate the Present Unlawfulness of Domestic Slavery in England; To Which Is Prefixed a State of the Case*. London: W. Otridge, 1772.

Harlan, Louis R. *Booker T. Washington: The Making of a Black Leader, 1856–1901*. New York: Oxford University Press, 1972.

———. *Booker T. Washington: The Wizard of Tuskegee, 1901–1915*. New York: Oxford University Press, 1983.

Harlow, Ralph V. *Gerrit Smith: Philanthropist and Reformer*. New York: Henry Holt, 1939.

———. "Gerrit Smith and the Free Church Movement." *New York History* 18 (July 1937).

———. "The Rise and Fall of the Kansas Aid Movement." *American Historical Review* 41 (October 1935): 1–25.

Harper, Frances E.W. *Iola Leroy*. Boston: Beacon, 1999.

Harrell, David E., Jr. "The Sectional Origins of the Churches of Christ." *Journal of Southern History* 30 (August 1964): 261–77.

Harris, Donald R. "The Gradual Separation of Southern and Northern Baptists, 1845–1907." *Foundations* 7 (April 1964): 130–44.

Harris, Franklin Steward. *The Sugar-Beet in America*. New York: Macmillan, 1919.

Harris, Leslie M. *In the Shadow of Slavery: African Americans in New York City, 1626–1863*. Chicago: University of Chicago Press, 2003.

Harris, Robert L., Jr. "H. Ford Douglas: Afro-American Antislavery Emigrationist." *Journal of Negro History* 62 (July 1977): 217–34.

Harris, Sheldon. *Paul Cuffe: Black America and the African Return*. New York: Simon & Schuster, 1972.

Harrison, Lowell H. "The Anti-Slavery Career of Cassius M. Clay." *Register of the Kentucky Historical Society* 59 (October 1961): 259–317.

———. "Cassius M. Clay and the *True American*." *Filson Club History Quarterly* 22 (January 1948): 30–49.

Harrison, Richard S. "Irish Quaker Perspective on the Antislavery Movement." *Journal of the Friends Historical Society* 56 (Spring 1991): 107–25.

Harrold, Stanley C., Jr. *American Abolitionists*. New York: Longman, 2001.

———. "Bailey, Gamaliel." In *American National Biography*, ed. John A. Garraty and Mark C. Carnes. New York: Oxford University Press, 1999.

———. "Cassius M. Clay on Slavery and Race: A Reinterpretation." *Slavery and Abolition* 9 (May 1988): 42–56.

———. "Forging an Antislavery Instrument: Gamaliel Bailey and the Formation of the Ohio Liberty Party." *Old Northwest* 2 (December 1976): 371–87.

———. *Gamaliel Bailey and Antislavery Union*. Kent, OH: Kent State University Press, 1986.

———. "The Intersectional Relationship Between Cassius M. Clay and the Garrisonian Abolitionists." *Civil War History* 35 (June 1989): 101–19.

———. "John Brown's Forerunners: Slave Rescue Attempts and the Abolitionists, 1841–1851." *Radical History Review* 55 (Winter 1992): 89–112.

———. "The Perspective of a Cincinnati Abolitionist: Gamaliel Bailey on Social Reform in America." *Bulletin of the Cincinnati Historical Society* 35 (Fall 1977): 173–90.

———. *The Rise of Aggressive Abolitionism: Addresses to the Slaves*. Lexington: University Press of Kentucky, 2004.

———. "The Southern Strategy of the Liberty Party." *Ohio History* 87 (Winter 1978): 21–36.

———. *Subversives: Antislavery Community in Washington, D.C., 1828–1865*. Baton Rouge: Louisiana State University Press, 2003.

Hartman, Saidiya V. *Scenes of Subjection: Terror, Slavery, and Self-Making in Nineteenth-Century America*. New York: Oxford University Press, 1997.

Harwood, Thomas F. "British Evangelical Abolitionism and American Churches in the 1830s." *Journal of Southern History* 28 (August 1962): 287–306.

————. "Prejudice and Antislavery: The Colloquy Between William Ellery Channing and Edward Strutt Abdy, 1834." *American Quarterly* 18 (Winter 1966): 697–700.

Haskell, Thomas L. "Capitalism and the Origins of the Humanitarian Sensibility: Part 1." *American Historical Review* 90 (April 1985): 339–61.

————. "Capitalism and the Origins of the Humanitarian Sensibility: Part 2." *American Historical Review* 90 (June 1985): 457–566.

————. "Convention and Hegemonic Interest in the Debate over Antislavery: A Reply to Davis and Ashworth." *American Historical Review* 92 (October 1987): 829–78.

Hassett, Constance W. "Siblings and Antislavery: The Literary and Political Relations of Harriet Martineau, James Martineau, and Maria Weston Chapman." *Signs* 21 (Winter 1996): 374–409.

Hauerwas, Stanley. *In Good Company: The Church as Polis.* Notre Dame, IN: University of Notre Dame Press, 1995.

Havas, John M. "Commerce and Calvinism: The *Journal of Commerce, 1827–65.*" *Journalism Quarterly* 38 (Winter 1961): 84–86.

Haven, Gilbert. *National Sermons: Sermons, Speeches and Letters on Slavery and Its War; From the Passage of the Fugitive Slave Bill to the Election of President Grant.* Boston: Lee and Shepard, 1869.

Hawke, David Freeman. *Benjamin Rush: Revolutionary Gadfly.* Indianapolis, IN: Bobbs-Merrill, 1971.

Hayward, Jack, ed. *Out of Slavery: Abolition and After.* London: Frank Cass, 1985.

Hearn, Chester G. *When the Devil Came Down to Dixie: Ben Butler in New Orleans.* Baton Rouge: Louisiana State University Press, 1997.

Heckman, Oliver S. "The Presbyterian Church in the United States of America and Southern Reconstruction, 1860–1880." *North Carolina Historical Review* 20 (July 1943): 219–37.

Hedrick, Joan D., ed. *The Oxford Harriet Beecher Stowe Reader.* New York: Oxford University Press, 1999.

————. "'Peaceable Fruits': The Ministry of Harriet Beecher Stowe." *American Quarterly* 40 (September 1988): 307–22.

Heidler, David S., and Jeanne T. Heidler. *Old Hickory's War: Andrew Jackson and the Quest for Empire.* Baton Rouge: Louisiana State University Press, 2003.

Heinl, Robert Debs, Jr., and Nancy Gordon Heinl. *Written in Blood: The Story of the Haitian People, 1492–1995.* 2nd ed. Lanham, MD: University Press of America, 1996.

Helg, Aline. "The Limits of Equality: Free People of Colour and Slaves During the First Independence of Cartagena, Colombia, 1810–1815." *Slavery and Abolition* 20 (August 1999): 1–30.

————. *Our Rightful Share: The Afro-Cuban Struggle for Equality, 1886–1912.* Chapel Hill: University of North Carolina Press, 1995.

Hembree, Michael F. "The Question of 'Begging': Fugitive Slave Relief in Canada, 1830–1865." *Civil War History* 37 (December 1991): 314–27.

Hendrick, George, and Willene Hendrick, eds. *Fleeing for Freedom: Stories of the Underground Railroad, as Told by Levi Coffin and William Still.* Chicago: Ivan R. Dee, 2004.

Henig, Gerald S. *Henry Winter Davis: Antebellum and Civil War Congressman From Maryland.* New York: Twayne, 1973.

————. "The Jacksonian Attitude Toward Abolitionism in the 1830s." *Tennessee Historical Quarterly* 28 (1969): 42–56.

Henson, Josiah. *An Autobiography of the Reverend Josiah Henson.* Introduction by Robin W. Winks. Reading, MA: Addison-Wesley, 1969.

Herndl, Diane Price. *Invalid Women: Figuring Feminine Illness in American Fiction and Culture 1840–1940.* Chapel Hill: University of North Carolina Press, 1993.

————. "The Invisible (Invalid) Woman: African-American Women, Illness, and Nineteenth-Century Narrative." *Women's Studies* 24 (September 1995) 553–72.

Herriott, F.I. "The German Conference in the Deutsches Haus, Chicago, May 14–15, 1860." *Transactions of the Illinois State Historical Society* 35 (1928): 101–91.

Hersh, Blanch Glassman. *The Slavery of Sex: Feminist-Abolitionists in America.* Urbana: University of Illinois, 1978.

Heuman, Gad J. *The Killing Time: The Morant Bay Rebellion in Jamaica.* Knoxville: University of Tennessee Press, 1994.

————, ed. *Out of the House of Bondage: Runaways, Resistance, and Maroonage in Africa and the New World.* London: Frank Cass, 1982.

Hewitt, Nancy A. "Feminist Friends: Agrarian Quakers and the Emergence of Women's Rights in America." *Feminist Studies* 12 (Spring 1986): 27–49.

————. "Incidents in the Life of a Slave Girl." In *Handbook of American Women's History,* ed. Angela Howard Zophy and Frances M. Kavenik. New York: Garland, 1990.

————. *Women's Activism and Social Change: Rochester, New York, 1822–1872.* Ithaca, NY: Cornell University Press, 1984.

Heyrman, Christine L. *Southern Cross: The Beginnings of the Bible Belt.* New York: Alfred A. Knopf, 1997.

Hicklin, Patricia. "Gentle Agitator: Samuel M. Janney and the Antislavery Movement in Virginia, 1842–1851." *Journal of Southern History* 37 (May 1971): 159–90.

————. "John C. Underwood and the Anti-Slavery Movement in Virginia, 1847–1860." *Virginia Magazine of History and Biography* 73 (April 1965): 156–68.

Hicks, Peter P. *To Awaken My Afflicted Brethren: David Walker and the Problem of Antebellum Slave Resistance.* University Park: Pennsylvania State University Press, 1997.

Higginbotham, A. Leon, Jr. *In the Matter of Color: The Colonial Period.* New York: Oxford University Press, 1978.

———. *Shades of Freedom: Racial Politics and Presumptions of the American Legal Process.* New York: Oxford University Press, 1996.

Higginson, Thomas Wentworth. "Eccentricities of Reformers." In *Contemporaries,* by Thomas Wentworth Higginson. Boston: Houghton Mifflin, 1900.

Highfield, Arnold, ed. *Emancipation in the U.S. Virgin Islands: 150 Years of Freedom.* Saint Croix: Virgin Islands Emancipation Commission/Virgin Islands Humanities Council, 1998.

Higman, B.W. "Remembering Slavery: The Rise, Decline, and Revival of Emancipation Day in the English Speaking Caribbean." *Slavery and Abolition* 19:1 (1998): 90–105.

———. *Slave Population and Economy in Jamaica, 1807–1834.* Kingston, Jamaica: The Press, University of the West Indies, 1995.

———. *Slave Populations of the British Caribbean, 1807–1834.* Baltimore: Johns Hopkins University Press, 1984.

Hildreth, Richard. *Despotism in America: An Inquiry Into the Nature, Results, and Legal Basis of the Slave-Holding System in the United States.* New York: John P. Jewett, 1854; New York: Negro Universities Press, 1968.

Hill, Daniel G. "Black History in Early Toronto." *Polyphony,* Summer 1984, 28–30.

———. *The Freedom Seekers: Blacks in Early Canada.* Agincourt, Ontario, Canada: Society of Canada, 1981.

Hill, John E. *Revolutionary Values for a New Millennium: John Adams, Adam Smith, and Social Virtue.* Lanham, MD: Lexington, 2000.

Hill, Patricia Liggins. "Henry Highland Garnet." In *Call and Response: The Riverside Anthology of the African American Literary Tradition,* ed. Patricia Liggins Hill, et al. Boston: Houghton Mifflin, 1998.

Hindmarsh, D. Bruce. *John Newton and the English Evangelical Tradition.* Oxford, UK: Clarendon, 1996.

Hine, Orlo Daniel. *Early Lebanon: An Historical Address.* Hartford, CT: Press of the Case, 1880.

Hinton, Richard J. *John Brown and His Men' With Some Account of the Roads They Traveled to Reach Harper's Ferry.* New York: Funk & Wagnalls, 1894.

———, ed. *Richard Realf's Free-State Poems; With Personal Lyrics Written in Kansas.* Topeka, KS: Crane, 1900.

———. "Wendell Phillips: A Reminiscent Study." *Arena,* July 1895, 220–35.

Hintzen, Percy C. "L'Ouverture, Toussaint." In *Encyclopedia of Latin American Politics,* ed. Diana Alexander Kapiszewski and Alexander Kazan. Westport, CT: Oryx, 2002.

Hirsch, Leo H., Jr. "New York and the Negro From 1783 to 1865." *Journal of Negro History* 16 (October 1931): 383–423.

Hite, Roger W. "Voice of a Fugitive: Henry Bibb and Ante-Bellum Black Separatism." *Journal of Black Studies* 4 (March 1974): 272–73.

Hoare, Prince, ed. *Memoirs of Granville Sharp, Esq.* London: H. Colburn, 1820.

Hobart, John Henry. *The Correspondence of John Henry Hobart.* 6 vols. New York, 1911–1912.

Hobhouse, Stephen. *Joseph Sturge: His Life and Work.* London: J.M. Dent & Sons, 1919.

Hodgson, Robert, ed. *The Works of the Right Reverend Beilby Porteus, D.D. Late Bishop of London: with His Life.* 6 vols. London: T. Cadell, 1823.

Hoecker-Drysdale, Susan. *Harriet Martineau: First Woman Sociologist.* New York: Berg, 1992.

Hoefte, Rosemarijn. "Free Blacks and Coloureds in Plantation Suriname." *Slavery and Abolition* 17 (April 1996): 102–29.

Hoffert, Sylvia D. *Jane Grey Swisshelm: An Unconventional Life, 1815–1884.* Chapel Hill: University of North Carolina Press, 2004.

———. "Jane Grey Swisshelm, Elizabeth Keckley, and the Significance of Race Consciousness in American Women's History." *Journal of Women's History* 13 (Autumn 2001): 8–33.

Hoganson, Kristin. "Garrisonian Abolitionists and the Rhetoric of Gender, 1850–1860." *American Quarterly* 45 (December 1993): 558–95.

Holbraad, Carsten. *The Concert of Europe: A Study in German and British International Theory, 1815–1914.* London: Longman, 1970.

Holden-Smith, Barbara. "Lords of Lash, Loom, and Law: Justice, Story, Slavery and *Prigg v. Pennsylvania.*" *Cornell Law Review* 78 (September 1993): 1086–1151.

Holland, Rupert Sargent, ed. *Letters and Diary of Laura M. Towne: Written From the Sea Islands of South Carolina: 1862–1884.* New York: Negro Universities Press, 1969.

Holley, Sallie. *A Life for Liberty: Anti-Slavery and Other Letters of Sallie Holley.* Ed. John White Chadwick. New York: Negro Universities Press, 1969.

Hollins, Dennis Charles. "A Black Voice of Antebellum Ohio: A Rhetorical Analysis of *The Palladium of Liberty.*" Ph.D. diss., Ohio State University, 1978.

Holt, Michael F. "Antislavery and the Law: The Story of a Reciprocal Relationship." *Reviews in American History* 6 (December 1978): 512–17.

Holt, Thomas C. *The Problem of Freedom: Race, Labor, and Politics in Jamaica and Britain, 1832–1938.* Baltimore: Johns Hopkins University Press, 1992.

———. "Review Essay: Explaining Abolition." *Journal of Social History* 24 (Winter 1990): 371–78.

Holt, Thomas C., and Elsa Barkley Brown, eds. *Major Problems in African-American History.* Vol. 2, *From Freedom to "Freedom Now," 1865–1990s.* Boston: Houghton Mifflin, 2000.

Holtzman, Clara Cornelia. "Frances Dana Gage." Master's thesis, Ohio State University, 1931.

Holzman, Robert S. *Stormy Ben Butler.* New York: Macmillan, 1954.

Hoogbergen, Wim. *The Boni Maroon Wars in Suriname.* Leiden, Netherlands: Brill, 1990.

Hope, Vincent M. 1989. *Virtue by Consensus: The Moral Philosophy of Hutcheson, Hume, and Adam Smith.* New York: Oxford University Press, 1989.

Hopkins, Samuel. *A Dialogue Concerning the Slavery of the Africans.* New York: Arno, 1969.

——. *The Works of Samuel Hopkins.* New York: Garland, 1987.

Horton, James Oliver. "Generations of Protest: Black Families and Social Reform in Ante-Bellum Boston." *New England Quarterly* 49 (June 1976): 242–56.

Horton, James Oliver, and Lois E. Horton. *In Hope of Liberty: Culture, Community, and Protest Among Northern Free Blacks, 1700–1860.* New York: Oxford University Press, 1997.

Horton, Lois E. "Community Organization and Social Activism: Black Boston and the Antislavery Movement." *Sociological Inquiry* 55 (Spring 1985): 182–99.

Host, John Arthur. "Owen Lovejoy, Illinois Abolitionist." Master's thesis, University of Illinois at Urbana, 1951.

Howard, Victor B. "Cassius M. Clay and the Origins of the Republican Party." *Filson Club History Quarterly* 45 (January 1971): 49–71.

——. "The 1856 Election in Ohio: Moral Issues in Politics." *Ohio History* 80 (Winter 1971): 135–57.

——. *Evangelical War Against Slavery and Caste: The Life and Times of James G. Fee.* Selinsgrove, PA: Susquehanna University Press, 1996.

——. "James Madison Pendleton: A Southern Crusader Against Slavery." *Register of the Kentucky Historical Society* 74 (July 1976): 192–215.

——. "Kentucky Presbyterians in 1849: Slavery and the Kentucky Constitution." *Register of the Kentucky Historical Society* 73 (July 1975).

——. "Presbyterians, the Kansas-Nebraska Act, and the Election of 1856." *Journal of Presbyterian History* 49 (Summer 1971): 133–57.

——. "The Southern Aid Society and the Slavery Controversy." *Church History* 41 (June 1972): 208–24.

Howard-Duff, Ian. "D.F.J. Arago, 1786–1853." *Journal of the British Astronomical Association* 97 (1986): 26–29.

Howe, Daniel Walker. "The Evangelical Movement and Political Culture in the North During the Second Party System." *Journal of American History* 77 (March 1991): 1216–39.

Howe, Julia Ward. *Memoir of Dr. Samuel Gridley Howe.* Boston: Albert J. Wright, 1876.

Howe, Samuel Gridley. *Letters and Journals of Samuel Gridley Howe.* 2 vols. Ed. Laura A. Richards. Boston: D. Estes, 1906–1909.

Howell, Raymond. *The Royal Navy and the Slave Trade.* New York: St. Martin's, 1987.

Howse, Ernest Marshall. *Saints in Politics: The "Clapham Sect" and the Growth of Freedom.* London: Allen & Unwin, 1971.

Hubbell, John. "The National Free Soil Convention of '48." Paper presented to the Buffalo Historical Society, January 7, 1878.

Hubert, Miriam Blanton. *Story and Verse for Children.* 3rd ed. New York: Macmillan, 1965.

Huddle, Mark Andrew. "North Carolina's Forgotten Abolitionist: The American Missionary Association Correspondence of Daniel Wilson." *North Carolina Historical Review* 72 (October 1995): 416–55.

Huggins, Nathan Irvin. *Black Odyssey: The Afro-American Ordeal in Slavery.* New York: Pantheon, 1977.

Hunt, Gaillard. *William Thornton and Negro Colonization.* Worcester, MA: American Antiquarian Society, 1921.

Hunt, Lynn, ed. and trans. *The French Revolution and Human Rights: A Brief Documentary History.* New York: Bedford/St. Martin's, 1996.

Hunter, Heidi, ed. *Rereading Aphra Behn: History, Theory, and Criticism.* Charlottesville: University of Virginia Press, 1993.

Huntington, Pope Catlin. *The True History of William Morgan.* New York: M.W. Hazen, 1886.

Huston, James L. "The Experiential Basis of the Northern Antislavery Impulse." *Journal of Southern History* 56 (November 1990): 609–40.

Hutton, Frankie G. *The Early Black Press in America, 1827 to 1860.* Westport, CT: Greenwood, 1993.

Hyman, Harold Melvin, ed. *The Radical Republicans and Reconstruction, 1861–1870.* Indianapolis, IN: Bobbs-Merrill, 1967.

Ignatiev, Noel. *How the Irish Became White.* New York: Routledge, 1995.

Ingle, H. Larry. *First Among Friends: George Fox and the Creation of Quakerism.* New York: Oxford University Press, 1994.

Inikori, Joseph E., ed. *Forced Migration: The Impact of the Export Slave Trade on African Societies.* London: Hutchinson, 1982.

Inikori, Joseph E., and Stanley L. Engerman, eds. *The Atlantic Slave Trade: Effects on Economies, Societies, and Peoples in Africa, the Americas, and Europe.* Durham, NC: Duke University Press, 1992.

Innes, C.L. *A History of Black and Asian Writing in Britain, 1700–2000.* Cambridge, UK: Cambridge University Press, 2002.

Inscoe, John C. "Olmsted in Appalachia: A Connecticut Yankee Encounters Slavery and Racism in the Southern Highlands." *Slavery and Abolition* 9 (September 1988): 171–82.

Isely, Jeter Allen. *Horace Greeley and the Republican Party, 1853–1861: A Study of the New York Tribune.* New York: Octagon, 1965.

Isely, William H. "The Sharps Rifle Episode in Kansas History." *American Historical Review* 12 (April 1907): 546–66.

Jackson, Luther P. "The Educational Efforts of the Freedmen's Bureau and Freedmen's Aid Societies in South Carolina, 1862–1872." *Journal of Negro History* 8 (January 1923): 1–40.

Jacob, J.R. "La Roy Sunderland: The Alienation of an Abolitionist." *Journal of American Studies* 6 (April 1972): 1–17.

Jacobs, David M., ed. *Antebellum Black Newspapers.* Westport, CT: Greenwood, 1997.

———. "David Walker: Boston Race Leader, 1825–1830." *Essex Institute Historical Collections* 107 (January 1971): 94–107.

Jacobs, Donald M. "David Walker: Boston Race Leader, 1825–1830." *Essex Institute Historical Collections* 107 (January 1971): 94–107.

———. "The Nineteenth Century Struggle Over Segregated Education in the Boston Schools." *Journal of Negro Education* 39 (Winter 1970): 76–85.

———. "William Lloyd Garrison's *Liberator* and Boston's Blacks, 1830–1865." *New England Quarterly* 44 (June 1971): 259–77.

Jacobs, Harriet. *Incidents in the Life of a Slave Girl, as Written by Herself.* Ed. Henry Louis Gates, Jr. New York: Oxford University Press, 1988; ed. Jean Fagan Yellin, Cambridge, MA: Harvard University Press, 2000.

James, C.L.R. *The Black Jacobins: Toussaint L'Ouverture and the Saint-Domingue Revolution.* New York: Vintage Books, 1989.

James, Edward T., and Janet W. James, eds. *Notable American Women 1607–1950: A Biographical Dictionary.* Boston: Harvard University Press, 1974.

James, M.G. "The Clapham Sect: Its History and Influence." Ph.D. diss., University of Oxford, 1950.

Jarvis, Charles A. "Admission to Abolitionism: The Case of John Greenleaf Whittier." *Journal of the Early Republic* 4 (Summer 1984): 161–76.

Jeffery, Julie Roy. *The Great Silent Army of Abolitionism: Ordinary Women in the Antislavery Movement.* Chapel Hill: University of North Carolina Press, 1998.

———. "Permeable Boundaries: Abolitionist Women and Separate Spheres." *Journal of the Early Republic* 21 (Spring 2001): 79–93.

Jekyll, Joseph. "The Life of Ignatius Sancho." In *Letters of the Late Ignatius Sancho, An African,* ed. Vincent Carretta. New York: Penguin, 1998.

Jenkins, William Sumner. *Pro-Slavery Thought in the Old South.* 1935. Chapel Hill: University of North Carolina Press, 1960.

Jennings, Judith. *The Business of Abolishing the Slave Trade, 1783–1807.* London: Frank Cass, 1997.

Jennings, Lawrence C. *French Anti-Slavery: The Movement for the Abolition of Slavery in France, 1802–1848.* Cambridge, UK: Cambridge University Press, 2000.

Jensen, Peter. *From Serfdom to Fireburn and Strike: The History of Black Labor in the Danish West Indies 1848–1916.* St. Croix, Virgin Islands: Antilles, 1998.

Jentz, John B. "The Antislavery Constituency in Jacksonian New York City." *Civil War History* 27 (June 1981): 101–22.

Jewett, Frederic Clarke. *History and Genealogy of the Jewett's of America.* 2 vols. New York: Grafton, 1908.

Johnson, Allen. "The Constitutionality of the Fugitive Slave Acts." *Yale Law Journal* 31 (December 1921): 161–82.

Johnson, Clifton H. "Abolitionist Missionary Activities in North Carolina." *North Carolina Historical Review* 40 (July 1963): 295–320.

———. "Mary Shadd Cary: Crusader for the Freedom of Man." *The Crisis: A Record of the Darker Races* 78 (April/May 1971): 89–90.

Johnson, David W. "Freesoilers for God: Kansas Newspaper Editors and the Antislavery Crusade." *Kansas History* 2 (Summer 1979): 74–85.

Johnson, J.H., Fleming Bates, William Count, Nathan L. Wums, and John Chamberlayn. "Antislavery Petitions Presented to the Virginia Legislature by Citizens of Various Counties." *Journal of Negro History* 12 (October 1927): 670–91.

Johnson, J.K. *Becoming Prominent: Regional Leadership in Upper Canada, 1791–1841.* Kingston, Ontario, Canada: McGill-Queen's University Press, 1989.

Johnson, Michael P. "Denmark Vesey and His Co-Conspirators." *William and Mary Quarterly,* 3rd ser., 58 (October 2001): 915–76.

Johnson, Reinhold O. "The Liberty Party in Massachusetts, 1840–1848: Antislavery Third Party Politics in the Bay State." *Civil War History* 28 (1982): 237–65.

———. "The Liberty Party in New Hampshire, 1840–1848: Antislavery Politics in the Granite State." *Historical New Hampshire* 33 (Summer 1978): 123–59.

———. "The Liberty Party in Vermont, 1840–1848: The Forgotten Abolitionists." *Vermont History* 47 (Fall 1979): 258–75.

Jones, Howard. *Mutiny on the Amistad: The Saga of a Slave Revolt and Its Impact on American Abolition, Law, and Diplomacy.* New York: Oxford University Press, 1987.

Jones, Jacqueline. *Soldiers of Light and Love: Northern Teachers and Georgia Blacks, 1865–1873.* Chapel Hill: University of North Carolina Press, 1980.

Jones, Matt B. *Vermont in the Making, 1750–1777.* Hamden, CT: Archon, 1968.

Jones, R.M. "Laborers of David Sands." In *Journal of the Life and Gospel Labours of David Sands, With Extracts From His Correspondence,* by David Sands. London: C. Gilpin, 1848.

Jones, Rufus M. *The Quakers in the American Colonies.* London: Macmillan, 1911.

Jordan, John W., ed. *Colonial Families of Philadelphia.* 2 vols. New York: Lewis, 1911.

Julian, George W. "The Genesis of Modern Abolitionism." *International Review* 12 (June 1882): 533–55.

———. "The Strength and Weakness of the Slave Power—The Duty of Anti-Slavery Men." In *Speeches on Political Questions,* by George Washington Julian. 1872. Westport, CT: Negro Universities Press, 1970.

Kachun, Mitch. *Festivals of Freedom: Memory and Meaning in African American Emancipation Celebrations, 1808–1915.* Amherst: University of Massachusetts Press, 2003.

Kadish, Doris Y., and Françoise Massardier-Kenney, eds. *Translating Slavery: Gender and Race in French Women's Writing, 1783–1823.* Kent, OH: Kent State University Press, 1994.

Kaplan, Amy. "Nation, Region, and Empire." In *The Columbia History of the American Novel,* ed. Cathy N. Davidson. New York: Columbia University Press, 1991.

Karcher, Carolyn L. "Censorship, American Style: The Case of Lydia Maria Child." *Studies in the American Renaissance* 9 (1986): 287–303.

———. *The First Woman in the Republic: A Cultural Biography of Lydia Maria Child.* Durham, NC: Duke University Press, 1994.

———. "From Pacifism to Armed Struggle: Lydia Maria Child's 'The Kansas Emigrants' and Antislavery Ideology in the 1850s." *Emerson Society Quarterly* 34 (Fall 1988): 141–58.

———. "Rape, Murder, and Revenge in 'Slavery's Pleasant Homes': Lydia Maria Child's Antislavery Fiction and the Limits of Genre." *Woman's Studies International Forum* 9 (1986): 323–32.

Kashatus, William C. *Just Over the Line: Chester County and the Underground Railroad.* West Chester, PA: Chester County Historical Society, 2002.

Kates, Don B. "Abolition, Deportation, Integration: Attitudes Toward Slavery in the Early Republic." *Journal of Negro History* 53 (January 1968): 33–47.

Katz, William Loren. "The Black/White Fight Against Slavery and for Women's Rights in America." *Freedomways* 16 (1976): 230–36.

Keagy, Walter R. "The Lane Seminary Rebellion." *Bulletin of the Historical and Philosophical Society of Ohio* 9 (April 1951): 141–60.

Keane, John. *Tom Paine: A Political Life.* New York: Grove, 2003.

Kearns, Frances E. "Margaret Fuller and the Abolition Movement." *Journal of the History of Ideas* 25 (January 1964): 120–27.

Keckley, Elizabeth. *Behind the Scenes; Thirty Years a Slave and Four Years in the White House.* 1868. New York: Arno, 1968.

Keith, Jean S. "Joseph Rogers Underwood, Friend of African Colonization." *Filson Club History Quarterly* 22 (April 1948): 117–32.

Kemble, Frances Anne. *Journal of a Residence on a Georgian Plantation in 1838–1839.* 1863. Ed. John A. Scott. Athens: University of Georgia Press, 1984.

Kennedy, James H. "Luiz Gama: Pioneer of Abolition in Brazil." *Journal of Negro History* 59 (July 1974): 255–67.

Kennedy, Lionel H., and Thomas Parker, eds. "An Official Report of the Trials of Sundry Negroes, Charged with an Attempt to Raise an Insurrection in the State of South Carolina." In *The Trial Record of Denmark Vesey,* introduction by John Oliver Killens. Boston: Beacon, 1970.

Kennedy, Melvin D., ed. *Lafayette and Slavery: From His Letters to Thomas Clarkson and Granville Sharp.* Eaton, PA: American Friends of Lafayette, 1950.

Kennon, Donald R. "'An Apple of Discord': The Woman Question at the World's Anti-Slavery Convention of 1840." *Slavery and Abolition* 5 (Winter 1984): 244–76.

Kent, Raymond K. "African Revolt in Bahía." *Journal of Social History* 3 (Summer 1970): 334–56.

Kerber, Linda K. "The Abolitionist Perception of the Indian." *Journal of American History* 62 (September 1975): 271–95.

———. "Abolitionists and Amalgamators: The New York City Race Riots of 1834." *New York History* 58 (January 1967): 28–39.

Kerr, Andrea. *Lucy Stone: Speaking Out for Equality.* New Brunswick, NJ: Rutgers University Press, 1992.

Kerrigan, Colm. "Irish Temperance and U.S. Anti-Slavery: Father Mathew and the Abolitionists." *History Workshop Journal* 31 (1991): 105–19.

Kielstra, Paul Michael. *The Politics of Slave Trade Suppression in Britain and France, 1814–1818.* London: Macmillan, 2000.

Kilby, Clyde S. *Minority of One.* Grand Rapids, MI: Eerdmans, 1959.

Kilian, Crawford. *Go Do Some Great Thing: The Black Pioneers of British Columbia.* Vancouver, British Columbia, Canada: Douglas & McIntyre, 1978.

King, Reyahn, ed. *Ignatius Sancho: An African Man of Letters.* London: National Portrait Gallery, 1997.

King, Stewart R. *Blue Coat or Powdered Wig: Free People of Color in Pre-Revolutionary Saint Domingue.* Athens: University of Georgia Press, 2001.

Kinoy, Arthur. "The Constitutional Right to Negro Freedom." *Rutgers Law Review* 21 (1967): 387–441.

———. "The Constitutional Right to Negro Freedom Revisited: Some First Thoughts on *Jones v. Alfred H. Mayer Company.*" *Rutgers Law Review* 22 (1968): 537–52.

Kirk-Green, A.H.M. "America in the Niger Valley: A Colonization Centenary." *Phylon* 23 (1962): 225–39.

Kirkham, E. Bruce. *The Building of Uncle Tom's Cabin.* Knoxville: University of Tennessee Press, 1977.

Klein, Herbert S. *African Slavery in Latin America and the Caribbean.* New York: Oxford University Press, 1986.

———. *The Atlantic Slave Trade.* Cambridge, UK: Cambridge University Press, 1999.

Klein, Martin A. *Historical Dictionary of Slavery and Abolition.* Lanham, MD: Scarecrow Press, 2002.

Klein, Martin A., and Paul Lovejoy. "Slavery in West Africa." In *The Uncommon Market: Essays in the Economic History of the Atlantic Slave Trade,* ed. Henry Gemery and Jan Hogendorn. New York: Academic Press, 1979.

Klement, Frank. "Jane Grey Swisshelm." *Abraham Lincoln Quarterly* 6 (December 1950): 227–38.

Klingberg, Frank J. *The Anti-Slavery Movement in England: A Study in English Humanitarianism.* New Haven, CT: Yale University Press, 1926.

———. "Harriet Beecher Stowe and Social Reform in England." *American Historical Review* 43 (April 1938): 542–52.

———. "The S.P.G. Program for Negroes in Colonial New York." *Historical Magazine of the Protestant Episcopal Church* 8 (1939): 306–71.

Klots, Steve. *Richard Allen: Religious Leader and Social Activist.* New York: Chelsea House, 1991.

Knee, Stuart E. "John Brown and the Abolitionist Ministry." *Negro History Bulletin* 45 (April/June 1982): 36–37, 42.

———. "The Quaker Petition of 1791: A Challenge to Democracy in Early America." *Slavery and Abolition* 6 (September 1985): 151–59.

Knight, Franklin W. *The Caribbean: The Genesis of a Fragmented Nationalism.* New York: Oxford University Press, 1990.

———. *Slave Society in Cuba During the Nineteenth Century.* Madison: University of Wisconsin Press, 1970.

Knight, Stephen. *The Brotherhood: The Explosive Exposé of the Secret World of the Freemasons.* New York: HarperCollins, 1985.

Kohler, Max J. "The Jews and the Anti-Slavery Movement." *Publications of the American Jewish Historical Society* 5 (1897): 137–55.

Korngold, Ralph. *Thaddeus Stevens: A Being Darkly Wise and Rudely Great.* New York: Harcourt, Brace, 1955.

Kraditor, Aileen S. "The Abolitionists Rehabilitated." *Studies on the Left* 5 (Spring 1965): 103–6.

———. "American Radical Historians on Their Heritage." *Past and Present* 56 (1972): 136–53.

———. *Means and Ends in American Abolitionism: Garrison and His Critics on Strategy and Tactics, 1834–1850.* New York: Pantheon, 1969.

———. "A Note on Elkins and the Abolitionists." *Civil War History* 13 (1967): 330–39.

Kramer, Lloyd. *Lafayette in Two Worlds: Public Cultures and Personal Identities in an Age of Revolution.* Chapel Hill: University of North Carolina Press, 1996.

Kraut, Alan M., and Phyllis F. Field. "Politics Versus Principles: The Partisan Response to 'Bible Politics' in New York State." *Civil War History* 25 (June 1979): 101–18.

Kraybill, Donald B., and Carl D. Bowman. *On the Backroad to Heaven: Old Order Hutterites, Mennonites, Amish, and Brethren.* Baltimore: Johns Hopkins University Press, 2001.

Kriegel, Abraham. "A Converging of Ethics: Saints and Whigs in British Antislavery." *Journal of British Studies* 26 (October 1987): 423–50.

Krigger, Marilyn. "Emancipation and the New Social Order: Views From the Upper Class." In *Emancipation in the U.S. Virgin Islands 150 Years of Freedom,* ed. Arnold Highfield. St. Croix: Virgin Islands Humanities Council, 1998.

Kuethe, Allan J. *Cuba, 1753–1815: Crown, Military, and Society.* Knoxville: University of Tennessee Press, 1986.

Kuhl, Irving Stoddard. "Presbyterian Attitudes Toward Slavery." *Church History* 7 (June 1938): 101–14.

Kuhns, Frederick. "Slavery and Missions in the Old Northwest." *Journal of the Presbyterian Historical Society* 24 (December 1946): 205–22.

Kunitz, Stanley J., ed. *British Authors of the Nineteenth Century.* New York: H.W. Wilson, 1936.

Kurtz, Michael J. Kurtz. "Emancipation in the Federal City." *Civil War History* 24 (1978): 250–67.

Kutler, Stanley I., ed. *The* Dred Scott *Decision: Law or Politics?* Boston: Houghton Mifflin, 1967.

Lamb, Robert Paul. "James G. Birney and the Road to Abolitionism." *Alabama Review* 48 (April 1994): 83–143.

Landon, Fred. "Canadian Negroes and the John Brown Raid." *Journal of Negro History* 6 (April 1921): 174–82.

———. "The Fugitive Slave in Canada." *University Magazine* 18 (Summer 1919).

———. "Fugitive Slaves in London, Ontario, Before 1860." *London and Middlesex Historical Society Transactions* 10 (1919).

———. "Henry Bibb: A Colonizer." *Journal of Negro History* 5 (October 1920): 437–47.

———. "The Negro Migration to Canada After the Passing of the Fugitive Slave Act." *Journal of Negro History* 5 (January 1920): 22–36.

———. "When Uncle Tom's Cabin Came to Canada." *Ontario History* 44 (1952): 1–5.

———. "Wilberforce, an Experiment in the Colonization of Freed Negroes in Upper Canada." *Transactions of the Royal Society of Canada* 31 (1937).

Landry, Donna. *The Muses of Resistance: Laboring-Class Women's Poetry in Britain, 1739–1796.* Cambridge, UK: Cambridge University Press, 1990.

Lane, Margaret. *Frances Wright and the "Great Experiment."* Totowa, NJ: Rowman & Littlefield, 1972.

Lange, Pamela Larson. "Owen Lovejoy Versus the Town of Princeton." Master's thesis, Western Illinois University, 1984.

Langston, John M. *From the Virginia Plantation to the National Capitol.* 1894. New York: Johnson Reprint, 1968.

Lapp, Rudolph M. *Blacks in Gold Rush California.* New Haven, CT: Yale University Press, 1977.

Lapsansky, Emma Jones. "Feminism, Freedom and Community: Charlotte Forten and Women Activists in Nineteenth-Century Philadelphia." *Pennsylvania Magazine of History and Biography* 113 (January 1989): 3–19.

———. "'Since They Got Those Separate Churches': Afro-Americans and Racism in Jacksonian Philadelphia." *American Quarterly* 32 (Spring 1980): 54–78.

Lascelles, Edward Charles Ponsonby. *Granville Sharp and the Freedom of Slaves in England.* New York: Negro Universities Press, 1969.

Laumer, Frank. *Dade's Last Command.* Gainesville: University Press of Florida, 1995.

Law, Howard. "'Self-Reliance Is the True Road to Independence': Ideology and the Ex-Slaves in Buxton and Chatham." *Ontario History* 74 (June 1985): 107–21.

Lawaetz, Herman. *Peter von Scholten.* Trans. Anne-Luise Knudsen. 1940. Herning, Denmark: Paul Kristensen, 1999.

Lawson, Ellen N., and Marlene Merrill. "The Antebellum 'Talented Thousandth': Black College Students at Oberlin Before the Civil War." *Journal of Negro Education* 52 (Spring 1983): 142–55.

Ledbetter, Patsy S., and Billy Ledbetter. "The Agitator and the Intellectuals: William Lloyd Garrison and the New England Transcendentalists." *Mid-America: An Historical Review* 62 (October 1980): 173–85.

LeDuc, Thomas H. "Grahamites and Garrisonites." *New York History* 20 (April 1939): 189–91.

Lee, R. Edward. "Madison Washington, Slave Mutineer." *Blackfax* (Winter/Spring 1998): 8.

Lemann, Nicholas. *Redemption: The Last Battle of the Civil War.* New York: Farrar, Straus and Giroux, 2006.

Lemons, J. Stanley, and Michael A. McKenna. "Re-Enfranchment of Rhode Island Negroes." *Rhode Island History* 30 (Winter 1971): 3–13.

Leopold, Richard William. *Robert Dale Owen: A Biography.* Cambridge, MA: Harvard University Press, 1940.

Lerner, Gerda. *The Feminist Thought of Sarah Grimké.* New York: Oxford University Press, 1983.

———. "The Grimké Sisters and the Struggle Against Race Prejudice." *Journal of Negro History* 48 (October 1963): 277–91.

———. *The Grimké Sisters from South Carolina: Pioneers for Woman's Rights and Abolition.* New York: Schocken, 1983; Chapel Hill: University of North Carolina Press, 2004.

———. *The Grimké Sisters From South Carolina: Rebels Against Slavery.* Boston: Houghton Mifflin, 1967.

Lesick, Lawrence. *The Lane Rebels: Evangelicalism and Antislavery in Antebellum America.* Metuchen, NJ: Scarecrow, 1980.

Leslie, William R. "The Constitutional Significance of Indiana's Statute of 1824 on Fugitives From Labor." *Journal of Southern History* 13 (August 1947): 338–53.

———. "The Pennsylvania Fugitive Slave Act of 1826." *Journal of Southern History* 18 (November 1952): 428–45.

———. "A Study in the Origins of Interstate Rendition: The Big Beaver Creek Murders." *American Historical Review* 57 (October 1951): 63–76.

Lester, C. Edwards. *The Life and Voyages of Americus Vespucius.* New Haven, CT: H. Mansfield, 1852.

Levernier, James A. "Phillis Wheatley and the New England Clergy." *Early American Literature* 26 (March 1991): 21–38.

Levesque, George A. "Boston's Black Brahmin: Dr. John S. Rock." *Civil War History* 26 (December 1980): 326–46.

———. "Inherent Reformers—Inherited Orthodoxy: Black Baptists in Boston, 1800–1873." *Journal of Negro History* 60 (October 1975): 491–525.

Levi, Kate Everest. "The Wisconsin Press and Slavery." *Wisconsin Magazine of History* 9 (June 1925): 423–34.

Levine, Robert M. *Vale of Tears: Revisiting the Canudos Massacre in Northeastern Brazil, 1893–1897.* Berkeley: University of California Press, 1995.

Levine, Robert S., ed. *Martin R. Delany: A Documentary Reader.* Chapel Hill: University of North Carolina Press, 2003.

Levinson, Sandra. "Talking About Cuban Culture: A Reporter's Notebook." In *The Cuba Reader: The Making of A Revolutionary Society,* ed. Philip Brenner, William M. Leogrande, Donna Rich, and Daniel Siegel. New York: Grove, 1989.

Levstik, Frank R. "Jenkins, David." In *American National Biography,* ed. John A. Garraty and Mark C. Carnes. New York: Oxford University Press, 1999.

Levy, David W. "Racial Stereotypes in Antislavery Fiction." *Phylon* 31 (Fall 1970): 265–79.

Levy, Leonard W. "Sims' Case: The Fugitive Slave Case in Boston in 1851." *Journal of Negro History* 35 (January 1950): 49–74.

Levy, Leonard W., and Harlan B. Phillips. "The *Roberts* Case: Source of the 'Separate but Equal' Doctrine." *American Historical Review* 56 (April 1951): 510–18.

Levy, Ronald. "Bishop Hopkins and the Dilemma of Slavery." *Pennsylvania Magazine of History and Biography* 91 (January 1967): 56–71.

Lewis, Bernard. *Race and Slavery in the Middle East.* Oxford, UK: Oxford University Press, 1990.

Lewit, Robert T. "Indian Missions and Antislavery Sentiment: A Conflict of Evangelical and Humanitarian Ideals." *Mississippi Valley Historical Review* 50 (June 1963): 39–55.

Libby, Jean. *Black Voices From Harpers Ferry; Osborne Anderson and the John Brown Raid.* Palo Alto, CA: Libby, 1979.

Liechty, Daniel. *Early Anabaptist Spirituality: Selected Writings.* New York: Paulist Press, 1994.

Lightner, D.L. "The Interstate Slave-Trade in Antislavery Politics." *Civil War History* 36 (1990): 119–36.

Lilly, Stephen R. *Fighters Against American Slavery.* San Diego, CA: Lucent, 1999.

Linden, Glenn. "A Note on Negro Suffrage and Republican Politics." *Journal of Southern History* 36 (August 1970): 411–20.

Lindhorst, Marie J. "Sarah Mapps Douglass: The Emergence of an African American Educator/Activist in Nineteenth Century Philadelphia." Ph.D. diss., Pennsylvania State University, 1995.

Lindsay, Julian Ira. *Tradition Looks Forward; The University of Vermont: A History, 1791–1904.* Burlington: University of Vermont Press, 1954.

Lindsey, Howard O. *A History of Black America.* Secaucus, NJ: Chartwell, 1994.

Linebaugh, Paul. "A Little Jubilee? The Literacy of Robert Wedderburn in 1817." In *Protest and Survival: The Historical Experience, Essays for E.P. Thompson,* ed. John Rule and Robert Malcolmson. London: Merlin, 1993.

Linebaugh, Paul, and Marcus Rediker. *The Many-Headed Hydra: Sailors, Slaves, Commoners, and the Hidden History of the Revolutionary Atlantic.* Boston: Beacon, 2000.

Link, Edith Murr. *The Emancipation of the Austrian Peasant, 1740–1798.* New York: Columbia University Press, 1949.

Link, Frederick M. *Aphra Behn.* New York: Twayne, 1968.

Litwack, Leon F. "The Abolitionist Dilemma: The Antislavery Movement and the Northern Negro." *New England Quarterly* 34 (March 1961): 50–73.

Lloyd, Christopher. *The Navy and the Slave Trade: The Suppression of the African Slave Trade in the Nineteenth Century.* London: Longman, Green, 1949; London: Frank Cass, 1968.

Locke, Mary Stoughton. *Anti-Slavery in America from the Introduction of African Slaves to the Prohibition of the Slave-Trade (1619–1808).* Boston: Ginn, 1901.

Lockhart, J.G. *The Peacemakers, 1814–1815.* Freeport, NY: Books for Libraries, 1968.

Lockhart, James, and Stuart B. Schwartz. *Early Latin America: A History of Colonial Spanish America and Brazil.* Cambridge, UK: Cambridge University Press, 1983.

Lofton, John. *Insurrection in South Carolina: The Turbulent World of Denmark Vesey.* Yellow Springs, OH: Antioch, 1964.

Lofton, William H. "Abolition and Labor." *Journal of Negro History* 33 (October 1949): 249–83.

Logan, Rayford W., and Michael R. Winston, eds. *Dictionary of American Negro Biography.* New York: W.W. Norton, 1982.

LoGerfo, James W. "Sir William Dolben and 'The Causes of Humanity': The Passage of the Slave Trade Regulation Act of 1788." *Eighteenth-Century Studies* 6 (1973): 431–51.

Loggins, Vernon. *The Negro Author: His Development in America.* New York: Columbia University Press, 1931.

Lohmann, Christoph. *Radical Passion: Ottilie Assing's Reports From America and Letters to Frederick Douglass.* New York: Peter Lang, 1999.

Lombard, Charles M. *Lamartine.* New York: Twayne, 1973.

London Friends Institute. *Biographical Catalogue, Being an Account of the Lives of Friends and Others Whose Portraits Are in the London Friends' Institute.* London: London Friends Institute, 1888.

Long, Byron R. "Joshua Reed Giddings: A Champion of Political Freedom." *Ohio Archaeological and Historical Publications* 28 (January 1919): 1–47.

Longford, Elizabeth. *Wellington.* London: Weidenfield, 1992.

Lonsdale, Roger. *Eighteenth-Century Woman Poets.* New York: Oxford University Press, 1989.

Lorimer, Douglas A. "The Role of Anti-Slavery Sentiment in English Reactions to the American Civil War." *Historical Journal* 19 (June 1976): 405–20.

Lovejoy, David S. "Samuel Hopkins: Religion, Slavery, and the Revolution." *New England Quarterly* 40 (June 1967): 227–43.

Lovejoy, Paul E., and A.S. Kanya-Forstner, eds. *Slavery and Its Abolition in French West Africa: The Official Reports of G. Poulet, E. Roume, and G. Deherme.* Madison: University of Wisconsin–Madison, African Studies Program, 1994.

Loveland, Anne C. "Evangelicalism and Immediate Emancipation in American Antislavery Thought." *Journal of Southern History* 32 (May 1966): 172–88.

Lowance, Mason. *Against Slavery: An Abolitionist Reader.* New York: Penguin, 2000.

Ludlum, David M. *Social Ferment in Vermont.* New York: Columbia University Press, 1939.

Ludlum, Robert P. "The Antislavery 'Gag-Rule': History and Argument." *Journal of Negro History* 26 (April 1941): 203–43.

———. "Joshua Giddings, Radical." *Mississippi Valley Historical Review* 23 (June 1936): 49–60.

Lumpkin, Katherine Du Pre. *The Emancipation of Angelina Grimké.* Chapel Hill: University of North Carolina Press, 1974.

———. "The General Plan Was Freedom: A Negro Secret Order on the Underground Railroad." *Phylon* 28 (Spring 1967): 63–77.

Lumsden, Joy. "'A Brave and Loyal People': The Role of the Maroons in the Morant Bay Rebellion in 1865." In *Working Slavery, Pricing Freedom: Perspectives from the Caribbean, Africa, and the African Diaspora,* ed. Verene A. Shepherd. New York: Palgrave, 2002.

Luna, Luiz. *O Negro na Luta contra a Escravidão.* Rio de Janeiro, Brazil: Editora Livraria Catédra, 1967.

Luthin, Reinhard. "Salmon P. Chase's Political Career Before the Civil War." *Mississippi Valley Historical Review* 29 (March 1943): 517–40.

Lutz, Alma. *Crusade for Freedom: The Women of the Antislavery Movement.* Boston: Beacon, 1968.

Lynd, Staughton. "The Compromise of 1787." *Political Science Quarterly* 81 (June 1966): 225–50.

———. "Rethinking Slavery and Reconstruction." *Journal of Negro History* 50 (July 1965): 198–209.

Lyons, Adelaide A. "Religious Defense of Slavery in the North." *Trinity College Historical Society Historical Papers* 13 (1919): 5–34.

Lyons, John F. "The Attitude of Presbyterianism in Ohio, Indiana, and Illinois Toward Slavery, 1825–1861." *Journal of Presbyterian History* 11 (ca. 1920–1923).

Mabee, Carlton. *Black Freedom: The Nonviolent Abolitionists From 1830 Through the Civil War.* New York: Macmillan, 1970.

———. "A Negro Boycott to Integrate Boston Schools." *New England Quarterly* 41 (September 1968): 341–61.

Mabee, Carlton, with Susan Mabee Newhouse. *Sojourner Truth: Slave, Prophet, Legend.* New York: New York University Press, 1995.

MacDonald, Cheryl. "Mary Ann Shadd in Canada: Last Stop on the Underground Railroad." *The Beaver* 70 (February/March 1990): 32–38.

Macdougall, Donald V. "Habeus Corpus, Extradition and the Fugitive Slave in Canada." *Slavery and Abolition* 7 (September 1986): 118–28.

Macintyre, Angus D. *The Liberator: Daniel O'Connell and the Irish Party, 1830–1847.* New York: Macmillan, 1965.

Mackenzie, P.R. *Inter-Religious Encounters in Nigeria: S.A. Crowther's Attitude to African Traditional Religion and Islam.* Leicester, UK: Leicester University Press, 1976.

MacLean, Nancy. *Behind the Mask of Chivalry: The Making of the Second Ku Klux Klan.* New York: Oxford University Press, 1995.

Maclear, J.F. "The Evangelical Alliance and the Antislavery Crusade." *Huntington Library Quarterly* 42 (Spring 1979): 141–64.

MacLeod, Duncan. "From Gradualism to Immediatism: Another Look." *Slavery and Abolition* 3 (September 1982): 140–52.

———. *Slavery, Race, and the American Revolution.* Cambridge, UK: Cambridge University Press, 1974.

MacLeod, Murdo J. "Haiti." In *Encyclopedia of Latin American History and Culture,* vol. 3, ed. Barbara A. Tenenbaum. New York: Scribner's, 1996.

MacMaster, Richard K. "Arthur Lee's 'Address on Slavery': An Aspect of Virginia's Struggle to End the Slave Trade, 1765–1774." *Virginia Magazine of History and Biography* 80 (April 1972): 141–53.

———. "Henry Highland Garnet and the African Civilization Society." *Journal of Presbyterian History* 48 (Summer 1970).

Macmillan, Mona. *The Land of Look Behind: A Study of Jamaica.* London: Faber and Faber, 1957.

Madron, Thomas J. "John Wesley on Race: A Christian View of Equality." *Methodist History,* New Series, 2 (July 1964): 24–34.

Magdol, Edward. *Owen Lovejoy: Abolitionist in Congress.* New Brunswick, NJ: Rutgers University Press, 1967.

Magee, Michael. "Emerson's Emancipation Proclamations." *Raritan* 20 (2001): 96–116.

Maginnes, David R. "The Case of the Court House Rioters in the Rendition of Fugitive Slave Anthony Burns, 1854." *Journal of Negro History* 56 (January 1971): 31–43.

Maier, Pauline. *American Scripture: Making the Declaration of Independence.* New York: Alfred A. Knopf, 1997.

Maltz, Earl M. *Civil Rights, the Constitution, and Congress, 1863–1869.* Lawrence: University Press of Kansas, 1990.

Malvin, John. *North Into Freedom: The Autobiography of John Malvin, Free Negro, 1795–1880.* Ed. Allan Peskin. Kent, OH: Kent State University Press, 1988.

Mangione, Jerre. *The Dream and the Deal: The Federal Writers' Project, 1935–1943.* Boston: Little, Brown, 1972.

Mann, Charles Wesley. "The Chicago Common Council and the Fugitive Slave Law of 1850." *Proceedings of the Chicago Historical Society* 2 (1903–1905): 55–86.

Mann, Horace. "Speech Delivered in the House of Representatives, February 15, 1850." In *Slavery: Letters and Speeches,* by Horace Mann. Boston: B.B. Mussey, 1851.

Manzano, Juan Francisco. *Autobiografía de un esclavo* [Autobiography of a Slave]. Ed. Ivan A. Schulman. Madrid, Spain: Ediciones Guadarrama, 1976.

Marcus, Robert D. "Wendell Phillips and American Institutions." *Journal of American History* 56 (June 1969): 41–48.

Marrero, Leví. Prologue to *Cultura afrocubana,* Vol. 2., *El negro en Cuba, 1845–1959,* ed. Jorge Castellanos and Isabel Castellanos. Miami, FL: Ediciones Universales, 1990.

Marshall, Curtis. "Eleutherian College." *Indiana History Bulletin* 25 (November 1948): 200–203.

Marshall, Schuyler C. "The Free Democratic Convention of 1852." *Pennsylvania History* 22 (January 1955): 146–67.

Martin, Asa Earl. "Anti-Slavery Activities of the Methodist Episcopal Church in Tennessee." *Tennessee Historical Magazine* 2 (June 1916).

———. "Pioneer Anti-Slavery Press." *Mississippi Valley Historical Review* 2 (March 1916): 509–22.

Martin, Bernard. *John Newton: A Biography.* London: Heinemann, 1950.

Martin, James Joseph. *Men Against the State: The Expositors of Individualist Anarchism in America, 1827–1908.* De Kalb, IL: Adrian Allen, 1953.

Martin, Thomas P. "Some International Aspects of the Anti-Slavery Movement, 1818–1823." *Journal of Economic and Business History* 1 (November 1928): 137–48.

———. "The Upper Mississippi Valley in Anglo-American Anti-Slavery and Free Trade Relations: 1837–1842." *Mississippi Valley Historical Review* 15 (September 1928): 204–20.

Martineau, Harriet. *Harriet Martineau's Autobiography.* Ed. Maria Weston Chapman. Boston: James R. Osgood, 1877.

Martínez-Fernández, Luis, D.H. Figueredo, Louis A. Perez, Jr., and Luis González, eds. *Encyclopedia of Cuba*. Vol. 1, *People, History, Culture*. Westport, CT: Greenwood, 2003.

Martins, Heitor. *Luis Gama e a consciência negra na literatura Afro-Ásia no. 17*. Bahía, Brazil: Centro de estudos Afro-Orientais, 1996.

Mason, Julian D. *The Poems of Phillis Wheatley*. Chapel Hill: University of North Carolina Press, 1989.

Mason, Vroman. "The Fugitive Slave Law in Wisconsin, With Reference to Nullification Sentiment." *Proceedings of the State Historical Society of Wisconsin*, 1895, 117–44.

Massey, William. *A History of England, During the Reign of George the Third*. 4 vols. London: J.W. Parker, 1855–1863.

Mathews, Donald G. "The Abolitionists on Slavery: The Critique Behind the Social Movement." *Journal of Southern History* 33 (May 1967): 163–82.

———. "Methodist Mission to the Slaves, 1829–1844." *Journal of American History* 51 (March 1965): 615–31.

———. "The Methodist Schism of 1844 and the Popularization of Antislavery Sentiment." *Mid-America: An Historical Review* 51 (January 1968): 3–23.

Mathieson, William Law. *British Slave Emancipation, 1838–1849*. New York: Octagon, 1967.

———. *British Slavery and Its Abolition, 1823–1838*. London: Longman, Green, 1932.

———. *Great Britain and the Slave Trade, 1839–1865*. New York: Octagon, 1967.

Matlack, Lucius C. *The History of American Slavery and Methodism from 1780 to 1849, and History of the Wesleyan Methodist Connection of America*. Freeport, NY: Books for Libraries, 1849.

———. *The Life of Rev. Orange Scott: Compiled From His Personal Narrative, Correspondence, and Other Authentic Sources of Information, in Two Parts*. New York: C. Prindle and L.C. Matlack, 1847.

May, Philip S. "Zephaniah Kingsley, Nonconformist (1765–1843)." *Florida Historical Quarterly* 23 (1945): 145–59.

Mayer, Henry. *All on Fire: William Lloyd Garrison and the Abolition of Slavery*. New York: St. Martin's, 1998.

———. "All on Fire: William Lloyd Garrison and the Abolition of Slavery." *New England Quarterly* 73 (June 2000): 335–36.

Maynard, Douglas H. "The World's Anti-Slavery Convention of 1840." *Mississippi Valley Historical Review* 47 (December 1969): 452–71.

Mayo, Anthony R. "Charles Lewis Reason." *Negro History Bulletin* 5 (June 1942): 212–15.

McBride, David. "Black Protest Against Racial Politics: Gardner, Hinton and Their Memorial of 1838." *Pennsylvania History* 46 (April 1979): 149–62.

McBride, Dwight A. *Impossible Witnesses: Truth, Abolitionism, and Slave Testimony*. New York: New York University Press, 2001.

McCague, James. *The Second Rebellion: The Story of the New York City Draft Riots of 1863*. New York: Dial, 1968.

McCalla, Douglas. *Planting the Province: The Economic History of Upper Canada, 1784–1870*. Toronto, Ontario, Canada: University of Toronto Press, 1993.

McCalman, Ian, ed. *The Horrors of Slavery and Other Writings by Robert Wedderburn*. Edinburgh, UK: Edinburgh University Press, 1991.

McCarron, Anna. "The Trial of Prudence Crandall for the Crime of Educating Negroes in Connecticut." *Connecticut Magazine* 12 (1908): 225–32.

McCarthy, Charles. "The Antimasonic Party: A Study of Political Antimasonry in the United States, 1827–1840." In *Annual Report of the American Historical Association for the Year 1902*. Washington, DC: Government Printing Office, 1903.

McClendon, R. Earl. "The *Amistad* Claims: Inconsistencies of Policies." *Political Science Review* 48 (September 1933): 386–412.

McCluskey, Neil Gerard. *Public Schools and Moral Education: The Influence of Horace Mann, William Torrey Harris, and John Dewey*. New York: Columbia University Press, 1958.

McCormack, Thomas J., ed. *Memoirs of Gustave Koerner, 1809–1896: Life Sketches Written at the Suggestion of His Children*. Cedar Rapids, IA: Torch, 1909.

McCormick, Richard P. "William Whipper: Moral Reformer." *Pennsylvania History* 43 (January 1976): 23–48.

McDaid, W. "Kinsley S. Bingham and the Republican Ideology of Antislavery." *Michigan Historical Review* 16 (1990): 42–73.

McDonald, John J. "Emerson and John Brown." *New England Magazine* 44 (1971): 385–86.

McDowell, Tremaine. "Webster's Words on Abolitionists." *New England Quarterly* 7 (June 1934): 315.

McElroy, James L. "Social Control and Romantic Reform in Antebellum America: The Case of Rochester, New York." *New York History* 58 (January 1977): 17–46.

McFaul, John M. "Expediency vs. Morality: Jacksonian Politics and Slavery." *Journal of American History* 62 (June 1975): 24–39.

McFeely, William S. *Frederick Douglass*. New York: W.W. Norton, 1991.

———. *Yankee Stepfather: General O.O. Howard and the Freedmen*. New Haven, CT: Yale University Press, 1968.

McGlone, Robert. "Forgotten Surrender: John Brown's Raid and the Cult of Martial Values." *Civil War History* 40 (September 1994): 185–201.

———. "Rescripting a Troubled Past: John Brown's Family and the Harpers Ferry Conspiracy." *Journal of American History* 75 (March 1989): 1179–1200.

McGowan, James A. *Station Master on the Underground Railroad: The Life and Letters of Thomas Garrett*. Moylan, PA: Whimsie Press, 1977; rev. ed., Jefferson, NC: McFarland, 2005.

McInerney, Daniel J. "'A Faith for Freedom': The Political Gospel of Abolition. *Journal of the Early Republic* 11 (Fall 1991): 371–93.

———. "'A State of Commerce': Market Power and Slave Power in Abolitionist Political Economy." *Civil War History* 37 (1991): 101–19.

McKissack, Patricia, and Frederick McKissack. *The Civil Rights Movement in America: From 1865 to the Present.* 2nd ed. Chicago: Children's, 1991.

McKitrick, Eric L. *Andrew Johnson and Reconstruction.* New York: Oxford University Press, 1988.

McKivigan, John R., ed. *Abolitionism and American Politics and Government.* New York: Garland, 1999.

———. *Abolitionism and American Reform.* New York: Garland, 1999.

———. *Abolitionism and American Religion.* New York: Garland, 1999.

———. *Abolitionism and Issues of Race and Gender.* New York: Garland, 1999.

———. "The American Baptist Free Mission Society: Abolitionist Reaction to the 1845 Baptist Schism." *Foundations* 21 (October/December 1978): 340–55.

———. "The Antislavery "Comeouter Sects': A Neglected Dimension of the Abolitionist Movement." *Civil War History* 26 (June 1980): 142–60.

———. "The Christian Anti-Slavery Conventions of the Northwest." *Old Northwest* 5 (October/December 1979): 345–66.

———. "'The Gospel Will Burst the Bonds of the Slave': The Abolitionists' Bibles for Slaves Campaign." *Negro History Bulletin* 45 (July/September 1982): 62–64, 77.

———. "James Redpath, John Brown, and Abolitionist Advocacy of Slave Insurrection." *Civil War History* 37 (December 1991): 293–313.

———. "Prisoner of Conscience: George Gordon and the Fugitive Slave Law." *Journal of Presbyterian History* 60 (Winter 1982): 336–54.

———. *The War Against Proslavery Religion: Abolitionism and the Northern Churches, 1830–1865.* Ithaca, NY: Cornell University Press, 1984.

McKivigan, John R., and Madeleine L. McKivigan. "'He Stands Like Jupiter': The Autobiography of Gerrit Smith." *New York History* 65 (April 1984): 189–200.

McKivigan, John R., and Jason H. Silverman. "Monarchial Liberty and Republican Slavery: West Indies Emancipation Celebrations in Upstate New York and Canada West." *Afro-Americans in New York Life and History* 10 (January 1986): 7–18.

McLaughlin, William G. "Pietism and the American Character." *American Quarterly* 17 (Summer 1965): 163–86.

McLaughlin, William G., and Winthrop D. Jordan. "Baptists Face the Barbarities of Slavery in 1710." *Journal of Southern History* 29 (November 1963): 495–97.

McManus, Edgar J. "Antislavery Legislation in New York." *Journal of Negro History* 46 (October 1961): 208–16.

McPherson, James M. "Abolitionist and Negro Opposition to Colonization During the Civil War." *Phylon* 26 (Winter 1965): 391–99.

———. "Abolitionists, Woman Suffrage, and the Negro, 1863–1869." *Mid-America: An Historical Review* 47 (January 1965): 40–47.

———. "Abolitionists and the Civil Rights Act of 1875." *Journal of American History* 52 (December 1965): 493–510.

———. "The Fight Against the Gag Rule: Joshua Leavitt and Antislavery Insurgency in the Whig Party, 1839–1842." *Journal of Negro History* 48 (July 1963): 177–95.

———. "Grant or Greeley? The Abolitionist Dilemma in the Election of 1872." *American Historical Review* 71 (October 1965): 43–61.

———. *The Negro's Civil War: How American Negroes Felt and Acted During the War for the Union.* Urbana: University of Illinois Press, 1965.

———. *The Struggle for Equality: Abolitionists and the Negro in the Civil War and Reconstruction.* Princeton, NJ: Princeton University Press, 1964.

———. "Who Freed the Slaves?" *Proceedings of the American Philosophical Society* 139 (March 1995): 1–10.

McQueen, Keven. *Cassius M. Clay: Freedom's Champion.* Paducah, KY: Turner, 2001.

McQueeny, Mary Beth. "Simeon Jocelyn, New Haven Reformer." *New Haven Colony Historical Society Journal* 19 (September 1970): 63–68.

McReynolds, Edwin C. *The Seminoles.* Norman: University of Oklahoma Press, 1988.

Meaders, Daniel. *Dead or Alive: Fugitive Slaves and White Indentured Servants Before 1830.* New York: Garland, 1993.

———, ed. *Kidnappers in Philadelphia: Isaac Hopper's Tales of Oppression, 1780–1843.* New York: Garland, 1994.

Medoff, Jeslyn. "The Daughters of Behn and the Problem of Reputation." In *Women, Writing, History: 1640–1740,* ed. Isobel Grundy and Susan Wiseman. Athens: University of Georgia Press, 1992.

Mehlinger, Louis R. "The Attitude of the Free Negro Toward African Colonization." *Journal of Negro History* 1 (June 1916): 276–301.

Meier, August. *Negro Thought in America, 1880–1915: Racial Ideologies in the Age of Booker T. Washington.* Ann Arbor: University of Michigan Press, 1963.

Meigs, Henry Benjamin. *Record of the Descendants of Vincent Meigs.* Baltimore: J.S. Bridges, 1901.

Melder, Keith E. "Forerunners of Freedom: The Grimké Sisters in Massachusetts, 1837–38." *Essex Institute Historical Collections* 103 (July 1976): 223–49.

Melish, Joanne Pope. *Disowning Slavery: Gradual Emancipation and "Race" in New England, 1780–1860.* Ithaca, NY: Cornell University Press, 1998.

Mellafe, Rolando. *Negro Slavery in Latin America.* Berkeley: University of California Press, 1975.

Meltzer, Milton. *Slavery: A World History.* New York: Da Capo, 1993.

Meltzer, Milton, and Patricia G. Holland, eds. *Collected Correspondence of Lydia Maria Child, 1817–1880.* Millwood, NY: Kraus Microfilm, 1980.

———, eds. *Lydia Maria Child: Selected Letters, 1817–1880.* Amherst: University of Massachusetts Press, 1982.

Melzer, Sara, and Leslie W. Rabine, eds. *Rebel Daughters: Women and the French Revolution.* New York: Oxford University Press, 1991.

Mendelsohn, Jack. *Channing, The Reluctant Radical: A Biography.* Westport, CT: Greenwood, 1980.

Mendelson, Wallace. "Dred Scott's Case—Reconsidered." *Minnesota Law Review* 38 (1953): 16–28.

Mennucci, Sud. *O precursor do Abolicionismo no Brasil (Luiz Gama).* São Paolo, Brazil: Companhia Editora Nacional, 1938.

Mercer, Charles E. *Statue of Liberty.* New York: G.P. Putman's Sons, 1985.

Merideth, Robert. "A Conservative Abolitionist at Alton: Edward Beecher's Narrative." Pts. 1 and 2. *Journal of Presbyterian History* 42 (March 1964): 39–53; 42 (June 1964): 92–103.

Merkel, Benjamin G. "The Abolition Aspects of Missouri's Antislavery Controversy, 1819–1865." *Missouri Historical Review* 44 (April 1950): 232–54.

Merrill, Louis Taylor. "The English Campaign for Abolition of the Slave Trade." *Journal of Negro History* 30 (October 1945): 382–99.

Merrill, Walter M. *Against Wind and Tide: A Biography of William Lloyd Garrison.* Cambridge, MA: Harvard University Press, 1963.

———, ed. *The Letters of William Lloyd Garrison.* 6 vols. Cambridge, MA: Belknap Press, 1971–1981.

———. "Prologue to Reform—Garrison's Early Career." *Essex Institute Historical Collections* 92 (April 1956): 153–70.

Messerli, Jonathan. *Horace Mann: A Biography.* New York: Alfred A. Knopf, 1972.

Middleton, Stephen. "Antislavery Litigation in Ohio—The Case-Trowbridge Letters." *Mid-America: An Historical Review* 70 (October 1988): 105–24.

Miers, Suzanne. *Britain and the Ending of the Slave Trade.* London: Longman, 1975; New York: Africana, 1975.

Miers, Suzanne, and Igor Kopytoff, eds. *Slavery in Africa: Historical and Anthropological Perspective.* Madison: University of Wisconsin Press, 1977.

Mill, John Stuart. *Collected Works of John Stuart Mill.* 33 vols. Ed. John M. Robson. Toronto, Ontario, Canada: University of Toronto Press, 1963–1991.

———. *On Liberty; With "The Subjection of Women" and Chapters on Socialism.* Ed. Stefan Collini. Cambridge, UK: Cambridge University Press, 1989.

Millar, David, et al., eds. *Chambers Concise Dictionary of Scientists.* Cambridge, UK: Chambers Cambridge, 1989.

Miller, Floyd J. "The Father of Black Nationalism." *Civil War History* 17 (December 1971): 310–19.

———. *The Search for Black Nationality: Black Emigration and Colonization, 1787–1863.* Urbana: University of Illinois Press, 1975.

Miller, Keith D. "Frederick Douglass, Martin Luther King Jr., and Malcolm X Interpret the Declaration of Independence." In *The Declaration of Independence: Origins and Impact,* ed. Scott Douglas Gerber. Washington, DC: CQ, 2002.

Miller, Perry. "John Greenleaf Whittier: The Conscience in Poetry." *Harvard Review* 2 (Winter/Spring 1964): 31–38.

Miller, Ruth. "Henry Highland Garnet." In *Black American Literature 1760–Present,* ed. Ruth Miller. Beverly Hills, CA: Glencoe, 1971.

Miller, William Lee. *Arguing About Slavery: The Great Battle in the United States Congress.* New York: Alfred A. Knopf, 1995.

Mills, Bruce. *Cultural Reformations: Lydia Maria Child and the Literature of Reform.* Athens: University of Georgia Press, 1994.

Mintz, Sidney W. *Caribbean Transformations.* Chicago: Aldine, 1974.

Mitchell, Betty L. "Realities not Shadows: Franklin Benjamin Sanborn, the Early Years." *Civil War History* 20 (June 1974): 105–17.

Mock, Stanley Upton. *The Morgan Episode in American Free Masonry.* East Aurora, NY: Roycrofters, 1930.

Mohler, Mark. "The Episcopal Church and National Reconciliation, 1865." *Political Science Quarterly* 41 (December 1926): 567–95.

Money, Charles H. "Fugitive Slave Law of 1850 in Indiana." Pts. 1 and 2. *Indiana Magazine of History* 17 (June 1921): 167–88; 17 (September 1921): 257–97.

Montesquieu, Charles de Secondat, Baron de. *The Spirit of the Laws.* 1900. Trans. Thomas Nugent. New York: Hafner Library of Classics, 1949.

Moody, Marjory M. "The Evolution of Emerson as an Abolitionist." *American Literature* 17 (March 1945): 1–21.

Moody, R.E. "The First Year of the Emigrant Aid Company." *New England Quarterly* 4 (January 1931): 148–55.

Moore, Edmund A. "Robt. J. Breckinridge and the Slavery Aspect of the Presbyterian Schism." *Church History* 4 (December 1935): 282–94.

Moore, Glover. *The Missouri Controversy, 1819–1821.* Lexington: University Press of Kentucky, 1953.

Moore, John Trotwood. *Tennessee, the Volunteer State: 1769–1923.* Chicago: S.J. Clarke, 1923.

Moorhead, James H. "Social Reform and the Divided Conscience of Antebellum Protestantism." *Church History* 48 (December 1979): 416–30.

Morgan, Edmund S. "Slavery and Freedom: The American Paradox." *Journal of American History* 59 (June 1972): 5–29.

Morison, Samuel Eliot, and Henry Steele Commager. *The Growth of the American Republic.* 2 vols. New York: Oxford University Press, 1942.

Morris, Celia. *Fanny Wright: Rebel in America.* Cambridge, MA: Harvard University Press, 1984.

Morris, Robert C. *Reading, 'Riting, and Reconstruction: The Education of Freedmen in the South, 1861–1870.* Chicago: University of Chicago Press, 1981.

Morris, Thomas D. *Free Men All: The Personal Liberty Laws of the North, 1780–1861.* Baltimore: Johns Hopkins University Press, 1974.

Morrison, Chaplain W. *Democratic Politics and Sectionalism: The Wilmot Proviso Controversy.* Chapel Hill: University of North Carolina Press, 1967.

Morrison, Howard A. "Gentlemen of Proper Understanding: A Closer Look at Utica's Anti-Abolitionist Mob." *New York History* 62 (January 1978): 61–82.

Morrison, Toni. *Beloved.* New York: Alfred A. Knopf, 1987.

Morriss, Thomas D. *Free Men All: The Personal Liberty Laws of the North, 1780–1861.* Baltimore: Johns Hopkins University Press, 1974.

Morrow, R.L. "The Liberty Party in Vermont." *New England Quarterly* 2 (April 1929): 165–78.

Morrow, Ralph E. "The Proslavery Argument Revisited." *Mississippi Valley Historical Review* 47 (June 1961): 79–93.

Moses, Wilson Jeremiah. *Alexander Crummell: A Study of Civilization and Discontent.* New York: Oxford University Press, 1989.

———, ed. *Destiny and Race: Selected Writings of Alexander Crummell, 1840–1898.* Amherst: University Press of Massachusetts, 1992.

Muelder, Hermann R. *Fighters for Freedom; The History of Anti-Slavery Activities of Men and Women Associated with Knox College.* New York: Columbia University Press, 1959.

Mullin, Michael. *Africa in America: Slave Acculturation and Resistance in the American South and the Caribbean, 1736–1831.* Chicago: University of Chicago Press, 1992.

Mulvey, Christopher. "The Fugitive Self and the New World of the North: William Wells Brown's Discovery of America." In *The Black Columbiad: Defining Moments in African American Literature and Culture,* ed. Werner Sollors and Maria Diedrich. Cambridge, MA: Harvard University Press, 1994.

Munsterberg, Margaret. "The Weston Sisters and the Boston Controversy." *Boston Public Library Quarterly* 10 (January 1958): 38–50.

———. "The Weston Sisters and the 'Boston Mob.'" *Boston Public Library Quarterly* 9 (October 1958): 183–94.

Murphy, Robert J. "Catholic Church in the United States During the Civil War Period, 1852–1866." *American Catholic Historical Society of Philadelphia Records* 39 (December 1928): 272–346.

Murray, Alexander L. "The Extradition of Fugitive Slaves from Canada: A Re-Evaluation." *Canadian Historical Review* 43 (December 1962): 298–314.

———. "The *Provincial Freeman:* A New Source for the History of the Negro in Canada and the United States." *Journal of Negro History* 44 (April 1959): 123–35.

Muthu, Sankar. *Enlightenment Against Empire.* Princeton, NJ: Princeton University Press, 2003.

Myers, John L. "Organization of the "Seventy': To Arouse the North Against Slavery." *Mid-America: An Historical Review* 48 (1966): 29–46.

Nabuco, Carolina. *The Life of Joaquim Nabuco.* Palo Alto, CA: Stanford University Press, 1950.

Nabuco, Joaquim. *Abolitionism: The Brazilian Anti-Slavery Struggle.* Ed. and trans. Robert Conrad. Urbana: University of Illinois Press, 1977.

Nadelhaft, Jerome. "The Somersett Case and Slavery: Myth, Reality, and Repercussions." *Journal of Negro History* 51 (July 1966): 193–208.

Nash, Gary B. *Forging Freedom: The Formation of Philadelphia's Black Community, 1720–1840.* Cambridge, MA: Harvard University Press, 1988.

Nash, Roderick W. "The Christiana Riot: An Evaluation of its National Significance." *Journal of the Lancaster County Historical Society* 64 (1961): 66–91.

———. "William Parker and the Christiana Riot." *Journal of Negro History* 46 (January 1961): 24–31.

Nason, Elias. *Discourse on the Life and Character of Governor Andrew.* Boston, 1868.

National Anti-Slavery Standard. In *The Black Experience in America: Negro Periodicals in the United States, 1840–1860,* Series I. Westport, CT: Negro Universities Press, 1970.

Nederveen Pieterse, Jan. *White on Black: Images of Africans and Blacks in Western Popular Culture.* New Haven, CT: Yale University Press, 1992.

Nell, William C. *The Colored Patriots of the American Revolution.* 1855. New York: Arno, 1968.

Nelson, O.N. *History of the Scandinavians in the United States.* Minneapolis: O.N. Nelson, 1904.

Nelson, William E. "The Impact of the Antislavery Movement Upon Styles of Judicial Reasoning in Nineteenth Century America." *Harvard Law Review* 87 (January 1975): 513–66.

Nevins, Allan. *Frémont: Pathmarker of the West.* Lincoln: University of Nebraska Press, 1992.

Newbould, Ian. *Whiggery and Reform, 1830–41: The Politics of Government.* Palo Alto, CA: Stanford University Press, 1990.

Newman, Richard S. "Creating Free Spaces: Blacks and Abolitionist Activism in Pennsylvania Courts During the Early Republic." *Proteus* 19 (2002): 25–29.

———. *The Transformation of American Abolitionism: Fighting Slavery in the Early Republic.* Chapel Hill: University of North Carolina Press, 2002.

Newton, John. *Out of the Depths: An Autobiography.* New Canaan, CT: Keats, 1981.

NgCheong-Lum, Roseline. *Haiti.* New York: Marshall Cavendish, 1995.

Nichols, Charles H., Jr. "The Origins of *Uncle Tom's Cabin.*" *Phylon* 19 (Third Quarter 1958): 328–34.

———. "Who Read the Slaves Narratives?" *Phylon* 20 (Second Quarter 1959): 149–62.

Nies, Judith. *Seven Women: Portraits from the Radical Tradition.* New York: Penguin, 1977.

Nock, David A. "The Social Effects of Missionary Education: A Victorian Case Study." In *Reading, Writing, and Riches: Education and the Socio-Economic Order in North America,* ed. Randle W. Nelsen and David A. Nock. Toronto, Ontario: Between the Lines, 1978.

Nogee, Joseph L. "The *Prigg* Case and Fugitive Slavery 1842–1850." *Journal of Negro History* 39 (April 1954): 185–205.

Noonan, John T. *The Antelope: The Ordeal of the Recaptured Africans in the Administrations of James Monroe and John Quincy Adams.* Berkeley: University of California Press, 1977.

Northup, Solomon. *Twelve Years a Slave.* 1853. Ed. Sue Eakin and Joseph Logsdon. Baton Rouge: Louisiana State University Press, 1968.

Norton, L. Wesley. "The Methodist Episcopal Church in Michigan and the Politics of Slavery, 1850–1860." *Michigan History* 48 (September 1964): 193–213.

Norwood, John Nelson. *The Schism in the Methodist Episcopal Church, 1844: A Study of Slavery and Ecclesiastical Politics.* Alfred, NY: Alfred University Press, 1923.

Nuermberger, Ruth Ketring. *The Free Produce Movement: A Quaker Protest Against Slavery.* New York: AMS, 1970.

Nye, Russel B. *Fettered Freedom: Civil Liberties and the Slavery Controversy, 1830–1860.* East Lansing: Michigan State College Press, 1949.

———. "The Slave Power Conspiracy, 1830–1860." *Science and Society* 10 (Summer 1946): 262–74.

———. *William Lloyd Garrison and the Humanitarian Reformers.* Boston: Little, Brown, 1955.

Oaks, Dallin H. "Habeus Corpus in the States: 1776–1865." *University of Chicago Law Review* 32 (Winter 1965): 243–88.

Oates, Stephen B. *The Fires of Jubilee: Nat Turner's Fierce Rebellion.* New York: Harper & Row, 1990.

———. "John Brown and His Judges: A Critique of the Historical Literature." *Civil War History* 17 (March 1971): 5–23.

———. *To Purge This Land With Blood: A Biography of John Brown.* New York: Harper & Row, 1970.

———. *With Malice Toward None: A Life of Abraham Lincoln.* New York: Harper & Row, 1977.

O'Brien, William. "Did the *Jennison* Case Outlaw Slavery in Massachusetts?" *William and Mary Quarterly,* 3rd ser., 17 (April 1961): 219–41.

Ohio Anti-Slavery Society. *Narrative of the Late Riotous Proceedings Against the Liberty of the Press, in Cincinnati: With Remarks and Historical Notices, Relating to Emancipation; Addressed to the People of Ohio.* Cincinnati: Ohio Anti-Slavery Society, 1836.

Okihiro, Gary Y., ed. *In Resistance: Studies in African, Caribbean, and Afro-American History.* Amherst: University of Massachusetts Press, 1986.

Oldfield, John R. *Alexander Crummell (1819–1898) and the Creation of an African-American Church in Liberia.* New York: Edwin Mellon, 1990.

———. "Anti-Slavery Sentiment in Children's Literature, 1750–1850." *Slavery and Abolition* 10 (May 1989): 44–59.

———. *Popular Politics and British Anti-Slavery: The Mobilization of Public Opinion Against the Slave Trade, 1787–1807.* New York: St. Martin's, 1995.

Oldham, Ellen M. "Irish Support of the Abolitionist Movement." *Boston Public Library Quarterly* 10 (October 1958): 175–87.

Oldham, James. "New Light on Mansfield and Slavery." *Journal of British Studies* 27 (1988): 45–68.

Olmsted, Frederick Law. *A Journey in the Seaboard Slave States; With Remarks on Their Economy.* 1856. Chapel Hill: University of North Carolina Press, 2001.

Olwig, Karen. *Cultural Adaptation and Resistance on St. John: Three Centuries of Afro-Caribbean Life.* Gainesville: University Press of Florida, 1984.

Oostindie, Gert, ed. *Fifty Years Later: Antislavery, Capitalism and Modernity in the Dutch Orbit.* Pittsburgh: University of Pittsburgh Press, 1996.

Osagie, Iyunolu F. *The Amistad Revolt: Memory, Slavery, and the Politics of Identity in the United States and Sierra Leone.* Athens: University of Georgia Press, 2000.

Osofsky, Gilbert. "Abolitionism, Irish Immigrants, and the Dilemmas of Romantic Nationalism." *American Historical Review* 80 (October 1985): 889–912.

Ostander, Gillman. "Emerson, Thoreau and John Brown." *Mississippi Valley Historical Review* 34 (March 1955): 713–26.

Osthaus, Carl. *Freedmen, Philanthropy, and Fraud: A History of the Freedman's Savings Bank.* Urbana: University of Illinois Press, 1976.

Oubre, Claude F. *Forty Acres and a Mule: The Freedmen's Bureau and Black Land Ownership.* Baton Rouge: Louisiana State University Press, 1978.

Owen, Robert Dale. *Threading My Way: Twenty-Seven Years of Autobiography.* 1874. New York: Augustus M. Kelley, 1967.

Owen, T.M. "An Alabama Protest Against Abolitionism." *Gulf States Historical Magazine* 2 (July 1903): 30–41.

Packe, Michael Saint John. *The Life of John Stuart Mill.* New York: Macmillan, 1954.

Padgett, Chris. "Hearing the Antislavery Rank-and-File: The Wesleyan Methodist Schism of 1843." *Journal of the Early Republic* 12 (Spring 1992): 63–84.

Page, Jesse. *The Black Bishop.* London: Hodder and Stoughton, 1908.

Paine, Thomas. *The Complete Writings of Thomas Paine.* Ed. Philip S. Foner. New York: Citadel, 1945.

Painter, Nell Irvin. *Sojourner Truth: A Life, a Symbol.* New York: W.W. Norton, 1996.

———. "Sojourner Truth in Life and Memory: Writing the Biography of an American Exotic." *Gender and History* 2 (Spring 1990): 3–16.

Palmer, Beverly Wilson, ed. *The Selected Letters of Charles Sumner.* 2 vols. Boston: Northeastern University Press, 1990.

Palmer, Beverly Wilson, and Holly Byers Ochoa, eds. *The Selected Papers of Thaddeus Stevens.* 2 vols. Pittsburgh: University of Pittsburgh Press, 1997.

Palmer, Erwin. "A Partnership in the Abolition Movement." *University of Rochester Library Bulletin* 26 (1970/1971): 1–19.

Paludan, Phillip Shaw. *The Presidency of Abraham Lincoln.* Lawrence: University Press of Kansas, 1994.

Pangle, Thomas. *Montesquieu's Philosophy of Liberalism: A Commentary on "The Spirit of the Laws."* Chicago: University of Chicago Press, 1973.

Paquette, Robert. *Sugar Is Made With Blood: The Conspiracy of La Escalera and the Conflict Between Empires Over Slavery in Cuba.* Middletown, CT: Wesleyan University Press, 1988.

Parham, William H., and Jeremiah Brown, eds. *An Official History of the Most Worshipful Grand Lodge, Free and Accepted Masons for the State of Ohio.* 1906. Ohio Historical Society, Columbus.

Parish, Peter J. "Ethics and Economics: Slavery and Antislavery Re-Examined." *Georgia Historical Quarterly* 75 (Spring 1991): 43–75.

Parker, Harold M., Jr. "The Urban Failure of the New School Presbyterian Church." *Social Science Journal* 14 (January 1977): 139–48.

Parker, Jane M. *Rochester: A Story Historical.* Rochester, NY: Scrantom, Westmore, 1884.

Parrish, Jenni. "The Booth Cases: Final Step to the Civil War." *Willamette Law Review* 29 (Spring 1993): 237–78.

Patterson, Orlando. *Slavery and Social Death: A Comparative Study.* Cambridge, MA: Harvard University Press, 1985.

Pattock, Florence Bangert. "Cassius M. Clay's Mission to Russia." *Filson Club History Quarterly* 43 (October 1969): 325–44.

Paul, John Haywood. *The Soul Digger; or, Life and Times of William Taylor.* Upland, IN: Taylor University Press, 1928.

Payne, Charles E. *Josiah Bushnell Grinnell.* Iowa City: State Historical Society of Iowa, 1938.

Payne, Walter A. "Lincoln's Caribbean Colonization Plan." *Pacific Historian* 7 (May 1963): 65–72.

Pearson, Edward, ed. *Designs Against Charleston: The Trial Record of the Denmark Vesey Slave Conspiracy of 1822.* Chapel Hill: University of North Carolina Press, 1999.

Pease, Jane H., and William H. Pease. "The Abolitionist Dilemma: The Antislavery Movement and the Northern Negro." *American Quarterly* 42 (Winter 1965): 682–95.

———. "Anti-Slavery Ambivalence: Immediatism, Expediency, Race." *American Quarterly* 17 (Winter 1965): 682–95.

———. "Black Power—The Debate in 1840." *Phylon* 19 (Spring 1968): 19–26.

———. *Black Utopia: Negro Communal Experiments in America.* Madison: University of Wisconsin Press, 1963.

———. "Boston Garrisonians and the Problem of Frederick Douglass." *Canadian Journal of History* 2 (September 1967): 29–48.

———. *Bound With Them in Chains: A Biographical Story of the Antislavery Movement.* Westport, CT: Greenwood, 1972.

———. "Confrontation and Abolition in the 1850s." *Journal of American History* 58 (March 1972): 923–37.

———. "Ends, Means, and Attitudes: Black-White Conflict in the Antislavery Movement." *Civil War History* 18 (June 1972): 117–28.

———. "Freedom and Peace: A Nineteenth Century Dilemma." *Midwest Quarterly* 9 (October 1967): 23–42.

———. *The Fugitive Slave Law and Anthony Burns: A Problem in Law Enforcement.* Philadelphia: J.B. Lippincott, 1975.

———. "Negro Conventions and the Problem of Black Leadership." *Journal of Black Studies* 2 (September 1971): 29–44.

———. "Opposition to the Founding of the Elgin Settlement." *Canadian Historical Review* 38 (September 1957): 202–18.

———. "Uncle Tom and Clayton: Fact, Fiction and Mystery." *Ontario History* 2 (1958): 61–73.

Pease, William H. "Three Years Among the Freedmen: William C. Gannett and the Port Royal Experiment." *Journal of Negro History* 42 (April 1957): 98–117.

Peck, Thomas Bellows. *William Slade of Windsor, Conn., and His Descendants.* Keene, NH: Sentinel, 1910.

Peleg, W. Chandler. *Memoir of Governor Andrew, With Personal Reminiscences.* Boston: Roberts Brothers, 1880.

Pemberton, Doris Hollis. *Juneteenth at Comanche Crossing.* Austin, TX: Eakin, 1983.

Pendleton, Othniel A., Jr. "Slavery and the Evangelical Churches." *Journal of Presbyterian History* 25 (September 1947): 153–74.

Pennington, J.W.C. *The Fugitive Blacksmith; or, Events in the History of James W.C. Pennington.* 1850. Westport, CT: Negro Universities Press, 1971.

Pérez, Louis A., Jr. *Cuba Between Empires, 1878–1902.* Pittsburgh: University of Pittsburgh Press, 1983.

———. *Cuba: Between Reform and Revolution.* 3rd ed. New York: Oxford University Press, 2006.

Perkal, M. Leon. "American Abolition Society: A Viable Alternative to the Republican Party?" *Journal of Negro History* 65 (Winter 1980): 57–71.

————. "William Goodell: Radical Abolitionist." *Centerpoint* 2 (Spring 1977): 17–25.

Perlman, Daniel. "Organizations of the Free Negro in New York City, 1800–1860." *Journal of Negro History* 56 (July 1971): 181–97.

Perry, Lewis. "Adin Ballou's Hopedale Community and the Theology of Antislavery." *Church History* (September 1970): 372–90.

————. *Childhood, Marriage, and Reform: Henry Clarke Wright, 1797–1870.* Chicago: University of Chicago Press, 1980.

————. "The Panorama and the Mills: A Review of Letters of John Greenleaf Whittier." *Civil War History* 22 (September 1976).

————. "Psychology and the Abolitionists: Reflections on Martin Duberman and the Neo-Abolitionism of the 1960s." *Reviews in American History* 2 (September 1974): 318–22.

————. *Radical Abolitionism: Anarchy and the Government of God in Antislavery Thought.* Ithaca, NY: Cornell University Press, 1973; Knoxville: University of Tennessee Press, 1995.

————. "Up From Antislavery." *Reviews in American History* 4 (September 1976): 403–8.

————. "Versions of Anarchism in the Antislavery Movement." *American Quarterly* 22 (Winter 1968): 768–82.

————. " 'We Have Had Conversation in the World': The Abolitionists and Spontaneity." *Canadian Review of American Studies* 6 (Spring 1975): 3–26.

Perry, Lewis, and Michael Fellman, eds. *Antislavery Reconsidered: New Perspectives on the Abolitionists.* Baton Rouge: Louisiana State University Press, 1979.

Perry, P.B. "Before the *North Star*: Frederick Douglass' Early Journalistic Career." *Phylon* 35 (March 1974): 96–107.

Pescatello, Ann M. "Prêto Power, Brazilian Style: Modes of Re-Actions to Slavery in the Nineteenth Century." In *Old Roots in New Lands: Historical and Anthropological Perspectives on Black Experiences in the Americas,* ed. Ann M. Pescatello. Westport, CT: Greenwood, 1977.

Peters, James S. *The Spirit of David Walker: The Obscure Hero.* Lanham, MD: University Press of America, 2002.

Peterson, Dale. "Notes From the Underworld: Dostoyevsky, Du Bois, and the Discovery of Ethnic Soul." *Massachusetts Review* 35 (Summer 1994): 225–47.

Peterson, John. *Province of Freedom: A History of Sierra Leone.* London: Faber, 1969.

Peterson, Merrill D. *John Brown: The Legend Revisited.* Charlottesville: University of Virginia Press, 2002.

Petry, Ann. *Harriet Tubman: Conductor on the Underground Railroad.* New York: Thomas Y. Crowell, 1955.

Phelps, Amos A. *Lectures on Slavery and Its Remedy.* Boston: New England Anti-Slavery Society, 1834.

Phillips, Daniel L. *Griswold—A History; Being a History of the Town of Griswold, Connecticut.* New Haven, CT: Tuttle, Morehouse & Taylor, 1929.

Phillips, Paul. *The Controversialist: An Intellectual Life of Goldwin Smith.* Westport, CT: Praeger, 2002.

Phipps, William E. *Amazing Grace in John Newton: Slave-Ship Captain, Hymnwriter, and Abolitionist.* Macon, GA: Mercer University Press, 2001.

Pickard, John B. "John Greenleaf Whittier and the Abolitionist Schism of 1840." *New England Quarterly* 37 (June 1964): 250–54.

Pickard, Kate E.R. *The Kidnapped and the Ransomed: The Narrative of Peter and Vera Still After Forty Years of Slavery.* 1856. Lincoln: University of Nebraska Press, 1995.

Pierson, Michael D. "Between Antislavery and Abolition: The Politics and Rhetoric of Jane Grey Swisshelm." *Pennsylvania History* 60 (July 1993): 305–19.

Pillsbury, Parker. *Acts of the Anti-Slavery Apostles.* Concord, NH: Clague, Wegman, Schlicht, 1883.

Planck, George R. "Abraham Lincoln and Black Colonization: Theory and Practice." *Lincoln Herald* 72 (Summer 1970): 61–77.

Plasa, Carl, and Betty J. Ring, eds. *The Discourse of Slavery: Aphra Behn to Toni Morrison.* New York: Routledge, 1994.

Pope, Charles Henry, and Katharine Peabody Loring. *Loring Genealogy.* Cambridge, MA: Murray and Emery, 1917.

Popkin, Jeremy D., and Richard H. Popkin, eds. *The Abbé Grégoire and His World.* Dordrecht, Netherlands: Kluwer Academic, 2000.

Porter, Dorothy. "David Ruggles: An Apostle of Human Rights." *Journal of Negro History* 28 (January 1943): 23–50.

————. "Organized Educational Activities of Negro Literary Societies." *Journal of Negro Education* 5 (October 1936): 555–76.

————. "Sarah Parker Remond: Abolitionist and Physician." *Journal of Negro History* 20 (July 1935): 287–93.

Posey, Walter B. "The Slavery Question in the Presbyterian Church in the Old Southwest." *Journal of Southern History* 15 (August 1949): 311–24.

Post, Marie Caroline de Trobriand. *The Post Family.* New York: Sterling Potter, 1905.

Postma, Johannes. *The Dutch in the Atlantic Slave Trade.* New York: Cambridge University Press, 1990.

Potter, David Morris. *The Impending Crisis, 1848–1861.* Comp. and ed. Don E. Fehrenbacher. New York: Harper & Row, 1976.

Power, Richard L. "A Crusade to Extend Yankee Culture, 1820–1865." *New England Quarterly* 13 (December 1940): 638–53.

Prentice, George. *The Life of Gilbert Haven.* New York: Phillips and Hunt, 1883.

Prentiss, George Lewis. *The Union Theological Seminary in the City of New York: Historical and Biographical Sketches of its First Fifty Years.* New York: A.D.F. Randolph, 1889.

Preston, Dickson J. *Young Frederick Douglass: The Maryland Years.* Baltimore: Johns Hopkins University Press, 1980.

Preston, Emmett D. "The Fugitive Slave Acts in Ohio." *Journal of Negro History* 27 (October 1943): 422–78.

Price, Edward. "The Black Voting Rights Issue in Pennsylvania, 1780–1900." *Pennsylvania Magazine of History and Biography* 100 (July 1976): 356–73.

Price, Edwin H. "The Election of 1848 in Ohio." *Ohio Archaeological and Historical Quarterly* 36 (1927): 297–309.

Price, Richard. *Maroon Societies: Rebel Slave Communities in the Americas.* Baltimore: Johns Hopkins University Press, 1996.

———. "Maroons: Rebel Slaves in the Americas." 1992 Smithsonian Festival of American Folklife, Smithsonian Institute, Washington, DC. http://www.folklife.si.edu/resources/maroon/educational_guide/23.htm.

Pride, Armistead, and Clint Wilson. *A History of the Black Press.* Washington, DC: Howard University Press, 1997.

Prince, Benjamin Franklin. "The Rescue Case of 1857." *Ohio Archaeological and Historical Publications* 16 (January 1907): 292–309.

Proctor, Candice. *Women, Equality, and the French Revolution.* Westport, CT: Greenwood, 1990.

Pudney, John. *John Wesley and His World.* New York: Scribner's, 1978.

Pulis, John W., ed. *Moving On: Black Loyalists in the Afro-Atlantic World.* New York: Garland, 1997.

Purifoy, Lewis B. "The Methodist Anti-Slavery Tradition, 1784–1844." *Methodist History* 4 (July 1966): 3–16.

Putney, Martha. "The Slave Trade in French Diplomacy From 1814 to 1815." *Journal of Negro History* 60 (July 1975): 411–27.

Quarles, Benjamin. *Allies for Freedom: Blacks and John Brown.* New York: Oxford University Press, 1974.

———. *Black Abolitionists.* New York: Oxford University Press, 1969.

———. "The Breach Between Douglass and Garrison." *Journal of Negro History* 23 (January 1938): 144–51.

———. "Douglass and the Compromise of 1850." *Negro History Bulletin* 14 (October 1950): 19–21, 24.

———. "Douglass' Mind in the Making." *Phylon* 6 (First Quarter 1945): 5–12.

———. "Frederick Douglass and the Women's Rights Movement." *Journal of Negro History* 25 (January 1940): 35–44.

———. "John Brown Writes to Blacks." *Kansas Historical Quarterly* 41 (Winter 1975): 454–67.

———. "Letters From Negro Leaders to Gerrit Smith." *Journal of Negro History* 27 (October 1942): 432–53.

———. *Lincoln and the Negro.* New York: Oxford University Press, 1962.

———. "Ministers Without Portfolio." *Journal of Negro History* 39 (January 1954).

———. *The Negro in the American Revolution.* Chapel Hill: University of North Carolina Press, 1961.

———. *The Negro in the Civil War.* Boston: Little, Brown, 1953.

———. "The Revolutionary War as a Black Declaration of Independence." In *Slavery and Freedom in the Age of the American Revolution,* ed. Ira Berlin and Ronald Hoffman. Charlottesville: University of Virginia Press, 1983.

———. "Sources of Abolitionist Income." *Mississippi Valley Historical Review* 32 (June 1945): 63–76.

Quinney, Valerie. "Decisions on Slavery, the Slave Trade and Civil Rights for Negroes in the Early French Revolution." *Canadian Journal of History* 17 (1982): 447–67.

Quirin, James A. " 'Her Sons and Daughters Are Ever on the Altar': Fisk University and Missionaries to Africa, 1866–1937." *Tennessee Historical Quarterly* 60 (Spring 2001): 16–37.

Quist, John W. " 'The Great Majority of Our Subscribers Are Farmers': The Michigan Abolitionist Constituency of the 1840s." *Journal of the Early Republic* 14 (Autumn 1994): 325–58.

Raboteau, Albert J. *Slave Religion: The "Invisible Institution" in the Antebellum South.* Oxford, UK: Oxford University Press, 1978.

Rael, Patrick. *Black Identity and Black Protest in the Antebellum North.* Chapel Hill: University of North Carolina Press, 2002.

Raffo, Steven M. *A Biography of Oliver Johnson, Abolitionist and Reformer, 1809–1889.* Lewiston, NY: Edwin Mellen, 2002.

Raines, Edgar F., Jr. "The American Missionary Association in Southern Illinois, 1856–1862: A Case Study in the Abolition Movement." *Illinois State Historical Society Journal* 65 (Autumn 1972): 246–68.

Rammelkamp, C.H. "Illinois College and the Antislavery Movement." *Illinois State Historical Society Proceedings* (1908): 192–203.

———. "The Reverberations of the Slavery Conflict in a Pioneer College." *Mississippi Valley Historical Review* 14 (March 1928): 447–61.

Rampersad, Arnold. *The Art and Imagination of W.E.B. Du Bois.* New York: Schocken, 1990.

Ramsay, James. "An Essay on the Treatment and Conversion of African Slaves in the British Sugar Colonies." In *Slavery, Abolition and Emancipation: Writings in the British Romantic Period,* ed. Peter J. Kitson and Debbie Lee. London: Pickering & Chatto, 1999.

Randall, J.G. *Civil War and Reconstruction.* Boston: D.C. Heath, 1953.

Ratcliffe, Donald J. "The Autobiography of Benjamin Tappan." *Ohio Historical Quarterly* 85 (Spring 1976): 109–57.

Ratner, Lorman. "Northern Concern for Social Order as a Cause for Rejecting Anti-Slavery." *The Historian* 27 (November 1965): 1–18.

Rattermann, Heinrich Armenius. *Johann Bernhard Stallo: German-American Philosopher, Jurist, and Statesman.* Cincinnati, OH: Verlag des Verfassers, 1902.

Rawick, George P., ed. *The American Slave: A Composite Autobiography.* Westport, CT: Greenwood, 1972–1979.

Ray, Perley Orman. *Repeal of the Missouri Compromise, Its Origin and Authorship.* Cleveland, OH: Arthur H. Clark, 1909.

Rayback, Joseph G. "The American Workingman and the Anti-Slavery Crusade." *Journal of Economic History* 3 (November 1943): 152–63.

———. *Free Soil: The Election of 1848.* Lexington: University Press of Kentucky, 1971.

———. "The Liberty Party Leaders in Ohio Exponents of Antislavery Coalition." *Ohio Archaeological and Historical Quarterly* 57 (April 1948): 165–78.

Realf, Richard. *Guesses at the Beautiful.* London: Longman, 1852.

Reckerd, Mary. "The Jamaican Slave Rebellion of 1831." *Past and Present* 40 (July 1969): 108–25.

Redkey, Edwin S. *Black Exodus: Black Nationalist and Back-to-Africa Movements, 1890–1910.* New Haven, CT: Yale University Press, 1969.

Reed, Harry A. "The Slave as Abolitionist: Henry Highland Garnet's Address to the Slaves of the United States of America." *Centennial Review* 20 (1976): 385–94.

Reesink, Edwin. "'Til the End of Time': The Differential Attraction of the 'Regime of Salvation' and the 'Entheotopia' of Canudos." *Journal of Millennial Studies* 2 (Winter 2000): 1–18.

Reid, C.S. *Samuel Sharpe: From Slave to National Hero.* Kingston, Jamaica: Bustamante Institute for Public and International Affairs, 1988.

Reidell, Heidi. "The Maroon Culture of Endurance." *Americas* (English ed.) 42 (January/February 1990): 46–49.

Reilly, Edward C. "Politico-Economic Considerations in the Western Reserve's Early Slavery Controversy." *Ohio Archaeological and Historical Quarterly* 52 (1943): 141–57.

Reis, Jaime. *Abolition and the Economics of Slaveholding in North East Brazil.* Glasgow, UK: Institute of Latin American Studies, 1974.

Reis, João José. *Slave Rebellion in Brazil: The Muslim Uprising of 1835 in Bahía.* Trans. Arthur Brakel. Baltimore: Johns Hopkins University Press, 1993.

Resnick, Daniel P. "The Société des Amis des Noirs and the Abolition of Slavery." *French Historical Studies* 7 (Autumn 1972): 558–69.

Reyes, Félix Ojeda. *Peregrinos de la libertad* [Pilgrims of Liberty]. Río Piedras, Puerto Rico: Instituto de Estudios del Caribe, Editorial de la Universidad de Puerto Rico, 1992.

Rhodes, John Ford. *History of the United States From the Compromise of 1850.* New York: Harper, 1895.

Riach, Douglas C. "Richard Davis Webb and Antislavery in Ireland." In *Antislavery Reconsidered: New Perspectives on the Abolitionists,* ed. Lewis Perry and Michael Fellman. Baton Rouge: Louisiana State University Press, 1979.

Rice, C. Duncan. "'Humanity Sold for Sugar!' The British Abolitionist Response to Free Trade in Slave-Grown Sugar." *Historical Journal* 13 (September 1970): 402–18.

———. *The Scots Abolitionist: 1833–1861.* Baton Rouge: Louisiana State University Press, 1981.

Richards, David A.J. "Abolitionist Feminism, Moral Slavery, and the Constitution: 'On the Same Platform of Human Rights.'" *Cardozo Law Review* 18 (November 1996): 767–843.

———. "Abolitionist Political and Constitutional Theory and the Reconstruction Amendments." *Loyola of Los Angeles Law Review* 25 (June 1992): 1187–1205.

———. *Conscience and the Constitution: History, Theory, and Law of the Reconstruction Amendments.* Princeton, NJ: Princeton University Press, 1993.

———. "Public Reason and Abolitionist Dissent." *Chicago-Kent Law Review* 69 (Summer 1994): 787–842.

Richards, Leonard L. *Gentlemen of Property and Standing: Anti-Abolition Mobs in Jacksonian America.* New York: Oxford University Press, 1970.

Richardson, H. Edward. *Cassius Marcellus Clay: Firebrand of Freedom.* Lexington: University Press of Kentucky, 1976.

Richardson, Joe M. "The American Missionary Association and Black Education in Missouri." *Missouri Historical Review* 69 (July 1974): 433–48.

———. *Christian Reconstruction: The American Missionary Association and Southern Blacks, 1861–1890.* Athens: University of Georgia Press, 1986.

———. "The Failure of the American Missionary Association to Expand Congregationalism among Southern Blacks." *Southern Studies* 18 (Spring 1979): 51–73.

Richardson, Patrick. *Empire and Slavery.* London: Longman, Green, 1968.

Riddell, William Renwick. *The Life of John Graves Simcoe: First Lieutenant-Governor of the Province of Upper Canada, 1792–96.* Toronto, Ontario, Canada: McClelland and Stewart, 1926.

Riddle, A.G. "The Rise of Anti-Slavery Sentiment on the Western Reserve." *Magazine of Western History* 6 (June 1887).

Riddle, Donald W. *Congressman Abraham Lincoln.* Urbana: University of Illinois Press, 1957.

Riddleberger, Patrick W. "George W. Julian: Abolitionist Land Reformer." *Agricultural History* 29 (July 1955): 108–36.

———. *George Washington Julian, Radical Republican: A Study in Nineteenth-Century Politics and Reform.* Indianapolis: Indiana Historical Bureau, 1966.

———. "The Making of a Political Abolitionist: George W. Julian and the Free Soilers, 1848." *Indiana Magazine of History* 51 (September 1955): 222–36.

———. "The Radicals' Abandonment of the Negro During Reconstruction." *Journal of Negro History* 45 (April 1960): 88–102.

Riga, Peter J. "American Crisis Over Slavery: An Example of the Relationship Between Legality and Morality." *American Journal of Jurisprudence* 26 (1981): 80–111.

Rigsby, Gregory U. *Alexander Crummell: Pioneer in Nineteenth-Century Pan-African Thought.* Westport, CT: Greenwood, 1987.

Ripley, C. Peter, et al., eds. *The Black Abolitionist Papers.* 5 vols. Chapel Hill: University of North Carolina Press, 1985–1992.

Rivers, Larry Eugene. *Slavery in Florida: Territorial Days to Emancipation.* Gainesville: University Press of Florida, 2000.

Roach, George W. "The Presidential Campaign of 1844 in New York State." *New York History* 19 (April 1938): 153–72.

Robboy, Stanley J., and Anita W. Robboy. "Lewis Hayden: From Fugitive Slave to Statesman." *New England Quarterly* 46 (December 1973): 591–613.

Robert, Joseph C. *The Road From Monticello: A Study of the Virginia Slavery Debate of 1832.* New York: AMS, 1970.

Robert, Stanley J., and Anita W. Robert. "Lewis Hayden: From Fugitive Slave to Statesman." *New England Quarterly* 46 (December 1973): 591–613.

Robertson, James I., Jr. "The Book That Enraged the South." *Civil War Times Illustrated* 7 (September 1969): 20–22.

Robertson, James Rood. *A Kentuckian at the Court of the Tsars: The Ministry of Cassius Marcellus Clay to Russia, 1861–1862 and 1863–1864.* Berea, KY: Berea College Press, 1935.

Robertson, Stacey M. *Parker Pillsbury: Radical Abolitionist, Male Feminist.* Ithaca, NY: Cornell University Press, 2000.

Robinson, Charles. *The Kansas Conflict.* New York: Harper & Brothers, 1892.

Robinson, David, ed. *William Ellery Channing: Selected Writings.* New York: Paulist Press, 1985.

Robinson, Roger J., and William Forbes. *An Account of the Life and Writings of James Beattie.* 2 vols. 1806. London: Routledge/Thoemmes, 1996.

Robinson, William H. *From Log Cabin to the Pulpit; Or, Fifteen Years in Slavery.* Eau Claire, WI: W.H. Robinson, 1913.

Rockwood, George I. "George Barrell Cheever, Protagonist of Abolition; Religious Emotionalism the Underlying Factor in the Cause of the Civil War." *Proceedings of the American Antiquarian Society* 46 (1936): 83–113.

Roediger, David R. *Towards the Abolition of Whiteness: Essays on Race, Politics, and Working Class History.* New York: Verso, 1994.

Roessler, Shirley Elson. *Out of the Shadows: Women and Politics in the French Revolution 1789–95.* New York: Peter Lang, 1996.

Rogers, Nathaniel P. *A Collection From the Miscellaneous Writings of Nathaniel Peabody Rogers.* 2nd ed. Ed. John Pierpoint. Manchester, NH: W.H. Fisk, 1849.

Rohne, John Magnus. *Norwegian American Lutheranism Up to 1872.* New York: Macmillan, 1926.

Rohrbach, Augusta. "Review of *All on Fire: William Lloyd Garrison and the Abolition of Slavery,* by Henry Mayer." *New England Quarterly* 73 (June 2000): 335–36.

———. "'Truth Stronger and Stranger Than Fiction': Re-examining William Lloyd Garrison's *Liberator.*" *American Literature* 73 (December 2001): 727–55.

Rohrs, Richard C. "Antislavery Politics and the Pearl Incident of 1848." *The Historian* 56 (Summer 1994): 711–24.

Rolle, Andrew. *John Charles Frémont: Character as Destiny.* Norman: University of Oklahoma Press, 1991.

Roper, Donald M. "In Quest of Judicial Objectivity: The Marshall Court and the Legitimization of Slavery." *Stanford Law Review* 21 (February 1969): 532–40.

Roper, Moses. *A Narrative of the Adventures and Escape of Moses Roper, From American Slavery.* London, 1837.

Rose, Willie Lee. *Rehearsal for Reconstruction: The Port Royal Experiment.* Indianapolis, IN: Bobbs-Merrill, 1964; Athens: University of Georgia Press, 1999.

Rosen, Bruce. "Abolition and Colonization, the Years of Conflict: 1829–1834." *Phylon* 33 (June 1972): 177–92.

Rosenberg, Norman L. "Personal Liberty Laws and the Sectional Crisis, 1850–1861." *Civil War History* 17 (March 1971): 25–45.

Rosenburg, John S. "Towards a New Civil War Revisionism." *American Scholar* 38 (Spring 1969): 250–73.

Roth, Randolph A. "The First Radical Abolitionists: The Reverend James Milligan and the Reformed Presbyterians of Vermont." *New England Quarterly* 55 (December 1982): 540–63.

Rousseau, Jean-Jacques. *Discourse on the Origin of Inequality.* 1754. Trans. Henry J. Tozzer, ed. Lester G. Crocker. New York: Simon & Schuster, 1967.

———. *The Social Contract.* 1762. Trans. and ed. Lester G. Crocker. New York: Simon & Schuster, 1967.

Rout, Leslie B., Jr. *The African Experience in Spanish America, 1502 to the Present Day.* Cambridge, UK: Cambridge University Press, 1976.

Rowe, David L. "Elon Galusha and the Millerite Movement." *Foundations* 18 (July/September 1975): 252–60.

Rowland, Peter. *The Life and Times of Thomas Day, 1748–1789: English Philanthropist and Author; Virtue Almost Personified.* Lewiston, NY: Edwin Mellen, 1996.

Rowntree, C. Brightwen. "Benjamin Lay." *Journal of the Friends' Historical Society* 33 (1936): 3–13.

Rozett, John M. "Racism and Republican Emergence in Illinois, 1848–1860: A Reevaluation of Republican Negrophobia." *Civil War History* 22 (June 1976): 101–15.

Ruchames, Louis. "The Abolitionists and the Jews." *Publications of the American Jewish Historical Society* 42 (1952): 131–55.

———, ed. *The Letters of William Lloyd Garrison.* Vol. 2., *A House Dividing Against Itself, 1836–1840.* Cambridge, MA: Belknap Press, 1971.

———. "Race, Marriage and Abolition in Massachusetts." *Journal of Negro History* 40 (July 1955): 250–73.

———. "William Lloyd Garrison and the Negro Franchise." *Journal of Negro History* 50 (January 1965): 37–49.

Ruchin, Judith P. "The Abolition of Colored Schools in Rochester, New York: 1832–1856." *New York History* 51 (July 1970): 376–93.

Rugoff, Milton. *The Beechers: An American Family in the Nineteenth Century.* New York: Harper & Row, 1981.

Runcie, John. "'Hunting the Nigs' in Philadelphia: The Race Riot of August, 1842." *Pennsylvania History* 39 (April 1972): 187–218.

Rush, Benjamin. *An Address to the Inhabitants of the British Settlements on the Slavery of the Negroes in America.* Philadelphia: John Dunlap, 1773; New York: Arno, 1969.

Rush, N. Orwin. "Lucretia Mott and the Philadelphia Antislavery Fairs." *Bulletin of the Friends' Historical Association* 35 (1946): 69–75.

Ryan, Halford R. *Henry Ward Beecher: Peripatetic Preacher.* New York: Greenwood, 1990.

Sagarin, Mary. *John Brown Russwurm; The Story of Freedom's Journal, Freedom's Journey.* New York: Lothrop, Lee & Shepard, 1970.

Salisbury, Cynthia. *Phillis Wheatley: Legendary African-American Poet.* Berkeley Heights, CA: Enslow, 2001.

Salitan, Lucille, and Eve Lewis Perera, eds. *Virtuous Lives: Four Quaker Sisters Remember Family Life, Abolitionism, and Women's Suffrage.* New York: Continuum, 1994.

Salomon, Ronald. "Being Good: An Abolitionist Family Attempts to Live Up to Its Own Standards." *Vermont History* 69, Supplement (2001): 32–47.

Sam, Dicky [pseud.]. *Liverpool and Slavery.* Newcastle upon Tyne, UK: Frank Graham, 1969.

Sanborn, Franklin Benjamin. "Benjamin Lundy." *Friends' Intelligencier and Journal,* May 18, 1889.

———. *Dr. S.G. Howe, the Philanthropist.* New York: Funk & Wagnalls, 1891.

———. "The Great Agitation." *Cosmopolitan Magazine* 7 (May 1889): 52–58.

Sanchez-Eppler, Karen. "Bodily Bonds: The Intersecting Rhetoric of Feminism and Abolition." *Representations* 24 (Fall 1988): 34–43.

———. *Touching Liberty: Abolition, Feminism, and the Politics of the Body.* Berkeley: University of California Press, 1993.

Sanders, Carl. *History of the Supreme Court of the United States: The Taney Period, 1836–1864.* New York: Macmillan, 1974.

Sanders, Valerie. *Harriet Martineau: Selected Letters.* Oxford, UK: Clarendon, 1990.

Sandiford, Ralph. *A Brief Examination of the Practice of the Times, by the Foregoing and Present Dispensation, Etc.* Philadelphia: Benjamin Franklin, 1729.

Savage, W.S. "Abolitionist Literature in the Mails, 1835–1836." *Journal of Negro History* 13 (April 1928): 150–85.

Schafer, Joseph. "Stormy Days in Court—The *Booth* Case." *Wisconsin Magazine of History* 20 (September 1936): 89–110.

Schafer, Judith Kelleher. *Becoming Free, Remaining Free: Manumission and Enslavement in New Orleans, 1846–1862.* Baton Rouge: Louisiana State University Press, 2003.

Schama, Simon. *Rough Crossings: Britain, the Slaves, and the American Revolution.* New York: Ecco, 2006.

Schechter, Patricia Ann. *Ida B. Wells-Barnett and American Reform, 1880–1930.* Chapel Hill: University of North Carolina Press, 2001.

Scheips, Paul J. "Lincoln and the Chiriqui Colonization Project." *Journal of Negro History* 38 (October 1952): 418–53.

Schick, Tom. *Behold the Promised Land: A History of Afro-American Settler Society in Nineteenth-Century Liberia.* Baltimore: Johns Hopkins University Press, 1977.

Schlesinger, Arthur M., ed. *The Cotton Kingdom: A Traveler's Observations on Cotton and Slavery in the American Slave States.* New York: Da Capo, 1996.

Schmidhauser, John R. "Judicial Behavior and the Sectional Crisis of 1837–1860." *Journal of Politics* 23 (November 1961): 615–41.

Schmidt, Nelly. *Victor Schoelcher et l'abolition de l'esclavage* [Victor Schoelcher and the Abolition of Slavery]. Paris: Fayard, 1994.

Schmidt-Nowara, Christopher. *Empire and Antislavery: Spain, Cuba, and Puerto Rico, 1833–1874.* Pittsburgh: University of Pittsburgh Press, 1999.

Schnell, Kempes Y. "Anti-Slavery Influence on the Status of Slaves in a Free State." *Journal of Negro History* 50 (October 1965): 257–73.

Schor, Joel. "The Rivalry Between Frederick Douglass and Henry Highland Garnet." *Journal of Negro History* 64 (Winter 1969): 30–38.

Schriver, Edward O. "Antislavery: The Free Soil and Free Democratic Parties in Maine, 1848–1855." *New England Quarterly* 42 (March 1969): 82–94.

———. "Black Politics Without Blacks: Maine, 1841–1848." *Phylon* 31 (Summer 1970): 194–201.

Schuler, Monica. "Ethnic Slave Rebellions in the Caribbean and the Guianas." *Journal of Social History* 3 (Summer 1970): 374–85.

Schurz, Carl. *Reminiscences of Carl Schurz.* 3 vols. New York: McClure, 1907–1908.

Schwartz, Harold. "The Controversial *Dred Scott* Decision." *Mississippi Valley Historical Review* 54 (April 1960): 262–73.

———. "Fugitive Slave Days in Boston." *New England Quarterly* 27 (June 1954): 191–211.

Schwartz, Rosalie. *Across the Rio to Freedom: U.S. Negroes in Mexico.* El Paso: Texas Western, 1975.

Schwartz, Stuart B. *Slaves, Peasants, and Rebels.* Urbana: University of Illinois Press, 1992.

————. *Sugar Plantations in the Formation of Brazilian Society: Bahía, 1550–1835.* Cambridge, UK: Cambridge University Press, 1985.

Schwarz, Philip. "Gabriel's Challenge: Slaves and Crime in Late Eighteenth-Century Virginia." *Virginia Magazine of History and Biography* 90 (July 1982): 283–87.

Scobie, Edward. *Black Britannia: A History of Blacks in Britain.* Chicago: Johnson, 1972.

Scott, Anne. *Hannah More: The First Victorian.* Oxford, UK: Oxford University Press, 2003.

Scott, Otto J. *The Secret Six: John Brown and the Abolitionist Movement.* New York: Times Books, 1979.

Scott, Rebecca. *The Abolition of Slavery and the Aftermath of Emancipation in Brazil.* Durham, NC: Duke University Press, 1988.

————. "Defining the Boundaries of Freedom in the World of Cane: Cuba, Brazil, and Louisiana After Emancipation." *American Historical Review* 99 (February 1994): 70–102.

————. *Slave Emancipation in Cuba: The Transition to Free Labor, 1860–1899.* Princeton, NJ: Princeton University Press, 1985.

Scott, Rebecca, and Michael Zeuske. "Property in Writing, Property on the Ground: Pigs, Horses, Land, and Citizenship in the Aftermath of Slavery, Cuba, 1880–1909." *Comparative Studies in Society and History* 44 (October 2002): 669–99.

Sears, Richard D. *Day of Small Things: Abolitionists in the Midst of Slavery, Berea, Kentucky, 1854–1864.* Lanham, MD: University Press of America, 1986.

————. "John G. Fee, Camp Nelson, and Kentucky Blacks." *Register of the Kentucky Historical Society* 85 (Winter 1987): 29–45.

————. *The Kentucky Abolitionist in the Midst of Slavery 1854–1864: Exiles For Freedom.* Lewiston, NY: Edwin Mellen, 1993.

————. *"Practical Recognition of the Brotherhood of Man": John G. Fee and the Camp Nelson Experience.* Berea, KY: Berea College Press, 1986.

Seeber, Edward Derbyshire. *Anti-Slavery Opinion in France During the Second Half of the Eighteenth Century.* Baltimore: Johns Hopkins University Press, 1937.

Sehr, Timothy J. "Leonard Bacon and the Myth of the Good Slaveholder." *New England Quarterly* 49 (June 1976): 194–213.

Semmel, Bernard. *Jamaican Blood and Victorian Conscience: The Governor Eyre Controversy.* Boston: Houghton Mifflin, 1962.

SenGupta, Gunja. "'A Model New England State': Northeastern Antislavery in Territorial Kansas, 1854–1860." *Civil War History* 39 (March 1993): 31–46.

————. "Servants for Freedom: Christian Abolitionists in Territorial Kansas, 1854–1858." *Kansas History* 16 (Fall 1993): 200–213.

Sernett, Milton C. "The Efficacy of Religious Participation in the National Debates Over Abolitionism and Abortion." *Journal of Religion* 64 (April 1984): 205–20.

————. "First Honor: Oneida Institute's Role in the Fight Against Racism and Slavery." *New York History* 66 (April 1985): 197–209.

————. *North Star Country: Upstate New York and the Crusade for African American Freedom.* Syracuse, NY: Syracuse University Press, 2002.

Sevitsh, Benjamin. "The Well-Planned Riot of October 21, 1835: Utica's Answer to Abolitionism." *New York History* 50 (July 1969): 251–63.

Sewell, Richard H. *Ballots for Freedom: Anti-Slavery Politics in the United States, 1837–1860.* New York: Oxford University Press, 1976.

————. "John P. Hale and the Liberty Party, 1847–1848." *New England Quarterly* 37 (June 1964): 200–233.

Shanks, Caroline L. "The Biblical Antislavery Argument of the Decade, 1830–1840." *Journal of Negro History* 16 (April 1931): 132–57.

Shapiro, Mary J., and Huck Scarry. *How They Built the Statue of Liberty.* New York: Random House, 1985.

Shapiro, Samuel. "The Rendition of Anthony Burns." *Journal of Negro History* 44 (January 1959): 34–51.

Shaw, Benjamin. "Owen Lovejoy, Constitutional Abolitionists and the Republican Party." *Transactions of the McLean County Historical Society* 3 (1900): 59–73.

Shay, Frank. *Judge Lynch: His First Hundred Years.* New York: Biblo and Tannen, 1969.

Sheeler, J. Reuben. "The Struggle of the Negro in Ohio for Freedom." *Journal of Negro History* 31 (April 1946): 208–26.

Sheller, Mimi. *Democracy After Slavery: Black Publics and Peasant Radicalism in Haiti and Jamaica.* Gainesville: University Press of Florida, 2000.

Shepherd, Verene, ed. *Slavery Without Sugar: Diversity in Caribbean Economy and Society Since the Seventeenth Century.* Gainesville: University Press of Florida, 2002.

Shepherd, Verene, and Ahmed Reid. "Rebel Voices: Testimonies From the 1831–32 Emancipation War in Jamaica." *Jamaica Journal* 27 (May 2004): 54–63.

Shepperson, George A. "Frederick Douglass and Scotland." *Journal of Negro History* 38 (July 1953): 307–21.

————. "The Free Church and American Slavery," *Scottish Historical Review* 30 (October 1951): 126–43.

————. "Harriet Beecher Stowe and Scotland, 1852–1853." *Scottish Historical Review* 32 (1953): 40–46.

————. "Thomas Chalmers, the Free Church of Scotland, and the South." *Journal of Southern History* 17 (November 1951): 517–37.

Sheridan, Richard B. "Slavery and Antislavery Literature." *Books and Libraries at the University of Kansas* 2 (May 1963).

Sherman, Joan R. "James Monroe Whitfield, Poet and Emigrationist: A Voice of Protest and Despair." *Journal of Negro History* 57 (April 1972): 169–76.

Sherman, Michael, ed. *A More Perfect Union: Vermont Becomes a State, 1777–1816.* Montpelier: Vermont Historical Society, 1991.

Sherrard, Owen Aubrey. *Freedom From Fear; The Slave and His Emancipation.* New York: St. Martin's, 1959.

Sherrill, P.M. "The Quakers and the North Carolina Manumission Society." *Trinity College Historical Society Historical Papers,* Ser. 10, 1914, 32–51.

Sherwood, Henry Noble. "The Formation of the American Colonization Society." *Journal of Negro History* 2 (July 1917): 209–28.

———. "Paul Cuffe and His Contributions to the American Colonization Society." *Proceedings of the Mississippi Valley Historical Association* 6 (1912/1913): 370–402.

Shick, Tom W. *Behold the Promised Land: A History of Afro-American Settler Society in Nineteenth-Century Liberia.* Baltimore: Johns Hopkins University Press, 1980.

Shiffrin, Steven H. "The Rhetoric of Black Violence in the Antebellum Period: Henry Highland Garnet." *Journal of Black Studies* 2 (September 1971): 45–56.

Shippee, Lester B. "Jane Grey Swisshelm: Agitator." *Mississippi Valley Historical Review* 7 (December 1920): 206–27.

Shively, Charles, ed. *The Collected Works of Lysander Spooner.* Weston, MA: M & S, 1971.

Short K.R.M. "Jamaican Christian Missions and the Great Slave Rebellion of 1831–2." *Journal of Ecclesiastical History* 27 (1976): 57–72.

Short, Kenneth R. "New York Central College: A Baptist Experiment in Integrated Education, 1848–1861." *Foundations* 5 (July 1962): 250–56.

Shortreed, Margaret. "The Antislavery Radicals: From Crusade to Revolution, 1840–1868." *Past and Present* 16 (November 1959): 65–87.

Shortridge, Ray M. "Voting for Minor Parties in the Antebellum Midwest." *Indiana Magazine of History* 74 (June 1978): 117–34.

Shyllon, Folarin O. *Black Slaves in Britain.* London: Oxford University Press, 1974.

———. *James Ramsay: The Unknown Abolitionist.* Edinburgh, UK: Canongate, 1977.

Sidbury, James. *Ploughshares into Swords: Race, Rebellion, and Identity in Gabriel's Virginia, 1730–1810.* New York: Cambridge University Press, 1997.

Siebert, Wilbur H. "A Quaker Section of the Underground Railroad in Northern Ohio." *Ohio State Archaeological and Historical Quarterly* 39 (July 1930): 479–502.

———. *The Underground Railroad From Slavery to Freedom.* New York: Macmillan, 1898; New York: Arno, 1968.

Siegel, Carolyn Lee. *Cassius Marcellus Clay: The Man Behind the Legend.* Berea, KY: Kentucke Imprints, 1988.

Sigerman, Harriet. *Elizabeth Cady Stanton: The Right Is Ours.* New York: Oxford University Press, 2001.

Silbey, Joel H. "Sentiment in Iowa, 1838–1861." *Iowa Journal of History* 55 (1957): 289–318.

Silva, J. Romão da. *Luis Gama e suas Poesias satiricas.* 2nd ed. Rio de Janeiro, Brazil: Livraria Editora Catédra, 1981.

Silverman, Jason H. "The American Fugitive in Canada: Myths and Realities." *Southern Studies* 39 (Fall 1980): 215–27.

———. " 'In Isles Beyond the Main': Abraham Lincoln's Philosophy on Black Colonization." *Lincoln Herald* 80 (Fall 1978): 115–22.

———. "Kentucky, Canada, and Extradition: The Jesse Happy Case." *Filson Club History Quarterly* 54 (January 1980): 50–60.

———. *Unwelcome Guests: Canada West's Response to American Fugitive Slaves, 1800–1865.* Millwood, NY: Associated Faculty, 1985.

———. " 'We Shall Be Heard!': The Development of the Fugitive Slave Press in Canada." *Canadian Historical Review* 65 (March 1984): 54–69.

Silverman, Jason H., and Donna J. Gillie. " 'The Pursuit of Knowledge Under Difficulties': Education and the Fugitive Slave in Canada." *Ontario History* 74 (June 1982): 95–112.

Silverman, Susan S., and Lois A. Walker, eds. *A Documented History of Gullah Jack Pritchard and the Denmark Vesey Slave Insurrection of 1822.* Lewiston, NY: Edwin Mellen, 2000.

Simmons, William J. *Men of Mark: Eminent, Progressive, and Rising.* 1887. Chicago: Johnson, 1970.

Simms, Henry H. "A Critical Analysis of Abolition Literature, 1830–1840." *Journal of Southern History* 6 (August 1940): 368–82.

Simpson, Henry. *Lives of Eminent Philadelphians, Now Deceased.* Philadelphia: W. Brotherhead, 1859

Simpson, Lewis P. "Slavery and the Cultural Imperialism of New England." *Southern Review* 25 (January 1989): 1–29.

Singleton, Gregory H. "Protestant Voluntary Organizations and the Shaping of Victorian America." *American Quarterly* 27 (December 1975): 549–60.

Skidmore, Thomas E. *Brazil: Five Centuries of Change.* New York: Oxford University Press, 1999.

Skotheim, Robert Allen. "A Note on Historical Method: David Donald's 'Toward a Reconsideration of Abolitionists.' " *Journal of Southern History* 25 (August 1959): 356–65.

Small, Edwin, and Miriam Small. "Prudence Crandall, Champion of Negro Education." *New England Quarterly* 18 (December 1941): 506–39.

Smedley, R.C. *History of the Underground Railroad in Chester and the Neighboring Counties of Pennsylvania.* New York: Arno, 1969.

Smiley, David L. *The Lion of Whitehall: The Life of Cassius Marcellus Clay of Kentucky.* Madison: University of Wisconsin Press, 1962.

Smith, George H., ed. *The Lysander Spooner Reader.* San Francisco: Fox and Wilkes, 1992.

Smith, George Winston. "Ante-Bellum Attempts of Northern Business Interests to 'Redeem' the Upper South." *Journal of Southern History* 11 (May 1945): 177–213.

Smith, James H., and Hume H. Cale. *History of Livingston County, New York.* Syracuse, NY: Mason, 1881.

Smith, James M. "The 'Separate but Equal' Doctrine: An Abolitionist Discusses Racial Segregation and Educational Policy During the Civil War." *Journal of Negro History* 41 (April 1956): 138–47.

Smith, James Wesley. *Sojourners in Search of Freedom: The Settlement of Liberia by Black Americans.* Lanham, MD: University Press of America, 1987.

Smith, John David, ed. *Black Soldiers in Blue: African American Troops in the Civil War Era.* Chapel Hill: University of North Carolina Press, 2003.

Smith, Robert P. "William Cooper Nell: Crusading Black Abolitionist." *Journal of Negro History* 55 (July 1970): 182–99.

Smith, Theodore C. "The Free Soil Party in Wisconsin." *Proceedings of the State Historical Society of Wisconsin,* 1894, 97–162.

Smith, Theophus H. *Conjuring Culture: Biblical Formations of Black America.* Oxford, UK: Oxford University Press, 1994.

Smith, Valerie. *Self-Discovery and Authority in Afro-American Narrative.* Cambridge, MA: Harvard University Press, 1987.

Smythe, Hugh H., and Martin S. Price. "The American Jew and Negro Slavery." *Midwest Journal* 7 (1956): 315–19.

Soapes, Thomas F. "The Federal Writers' Project Slave Interviews: Useful Data or Misleading Source." *Oral History Review* 2 (1977): 33–38.

Sobel, Mechal. *The World They Made Together: Black and White Values in Eighteenth-Century Virginia.* Princeton, NJ: Princeton University Press, 1987.

Soderlund, Jean R. *Quakers and Slavery: A Divided Spirit.* Princeton, NJ: Princeton University Press, 1985.

Sokolow, Jayme A. "Henry Clarke Wright: Antebellum Crusader." *Essex Institute Historical Collections* 3 (April 1975): 122–37.

———. "Revolution and Reform: The Antebellum Jewish Abolitionists." *Journal of Ethnic Studies* 9 (Spring 1981): 27–41.

Sorin, Gerald. *Abolitionism: A New Perspective.* New York: Praeger, 1972.

Sorisio, Carolyn. "Unmasking the Genteel Performer: Elizabeth Keckley's *Behind the Scenes* and the Politics of Public Wrath." *African American Review* 34 (Spring 2000): 19–38.

Southall, Eugene Portlette. "Arthur Tappan and the Anti-slavery Movement." *Journal of Negro History* 15 (April 1930): 162–98.

Sowle, Patrick. "The North Carolina Manumission Society, 1816–1834." *North Carolina Historical Review* 42 (Winter 1965): 47–69.

Sox, David. *John Woolman: Quintessential Quaker, 1720–1772.* Richmond, IN: Friends United Press, 1999.

Spector, Robert M. "The Quock Walker Cases (1781–83): Slavery, Its Abolition, and Negro Citizenship in Early Massachusetts." *Journal of Negro History* 53 (January 1968): 12–32.

Speer, Michael. "Autobiography of Adam Lowry Rankin." *Ohio History* 79 (Winter 1970): 18–55.

Spevack, Edmund. *Charles Follen's Search for Nationality and Freedom: Germany and America, 1796–1840.* Cambridge, MA: Harvard University Press, 1997.

Spindel, Donna J. "Assessing Memory: Twentieth-Century Slave Narratives Reconsidered." *Journal of Interdisciplinary History* 27 (1996): 247–61.

Spindler, George Washington. *Karl Follen: A Biographical Study.* Chicago, 1917.

Spitzer, Leo. *Lives in Between: The Experience of Marginality in a Century of Emancipation.* New York: Hill and Wang, 1999.

Sprading, Charles T. *Liberty and the Great Libertarians: An Anthology on Liberty, A Hand-Book of Freedom.* New York: Arno, 1972.

Sprague, Stuart Seely, ed. *His Promised Land: The Autobiography of John P. Parker, Former Slave and Conductor on the Underground Railroad.* New York: W.W. Norton, 1996.

Sprague, William. *Vicente Guerrero, Mexican Liberator: A Study in Patriotism.* Chicago: R.R. Donnelley, 1939.

Spring, L.W. *Kansas: The Prelude to the War for the Union.* Boston: Houghton Mifflin, 1890.

Staiger, C. Bruce. "Abolitionism and the Presbyterian Schism of 1837–1838." *Mississippi Valley Historical Review* 36 (December 1949): 391–414.

Stampp, Kenneth M. "The Fate of the Southern Anti-Slavery Movement." *Journal of Negro History* 28 (January 1943): 10–22.

———. *The Peculiar Institution: Slavery in the Ante-Bellum South.* New York: Random House, 1956.

Stange, Douglas C. "Abolitionism as Maleficence: Southern Unitarians Versus 'Puritan Fanaticism'—1831–1860." *Harvard Library Bulletin* 26 (1978): 146–71.

———. "Abolitionism as Treason: The Unitarian Elite Defends Law, Order, and the Union." *Harvard Library Bulletin* 28 (1980): 152–70.

———. "A Compassionate Mother to Her Poor Negro Slaves: The Lutheran Church and Negro Slavery in Early America." *Phylon* 29 (Fall 1968): 272–81.

———. "Document: Bishop Alexander Payne's Protestation of American Slavery." *Journal of Negro History* 52 (January 1967): 59–64.

———. "From Treason to Antislavery Patriotism: Unitarian Conservatives and the Fugitive Slave Law." *Harvard Library Bulletin* 25 (1977): 466–88.

———. "Lutheran Involvement in the American Colonization Society." *Mid-America: An Historical Review* 49 (1969): 171–82.

Stanley, John L. "Majority Tyranny in Tocqueville's America: The Failure of Negro Suffrage in 1846." *Political Science Quarterly* 84 (September 1969): 412–35.

Stanton, Elizabeth Cady. *Eighty Years and More; Reminiscences, 1815–1897.* 1898. New York: Schocken, 1971.

Stanton, William A. *A Record Genealogical, Biographical, Statistical of Thomas Stanton of Connecticut, and His Descendants, 1635–1891.* Albany, NY: Joel Munsell's Sons, 1891.

Staudenraus, P.J. *The African Colonization Movement, 1816–1865.* New York: Columbia University Press, 1961; New York: Octagon, 1980.

Stauffer, John. *The Black Hearts of Men: Radical Abolitionists and the Transformation of Race.* Cambridge, MA: Harvard University Press, 2001.

Stearn, Bertha-Monica. "Reform Periodicals and Female Reformers, 1830–1860." *American Historical Review* 37 (July 1932): 678–99.

Stearns, Frank Preston. "John Brown and His Eastern Friends." *New England Magazine* 42 (July 1910): 589–99.

———. *The Life and Public Services of George Luther Stearns.* Philadelphia: J.B. Lippincott, 1907.

Steelman, Joseph F. "Daniel Reeves Goodloe: A Perplexed Abolitionist During Reconstruction." *East Carolina College Publications in History* 2 (1965): 66–90.

Steely, Will Frank. "William Shreve Bailey, Kentucky Abolitionist." *Filson Club History Quarterly* 31 (July 1957): 274–81.

Stein, Robert Louis. *Léger Félicité Sonthonax: The Lost Sentinel of the Republic.* Rutherford, NJ: Fairleigh Dickinson University Press, 1985.

Steiner, Bernard C. *Life of Henry Winter Davis.* Baltimore: John Murphy, 1916.

Stephen, James. *Essays in Ecclesiastical Biography.* London: Longman, Green, 1907.

———. *The Slavery of the British West India Colonies, Delineated as It Exists Both in Law and Practice, and Compared With the Slavery of Other Countries, Ancient and Modern.* 2 vols. London: J. Butterworth and Son, 1824–1830.

———. *War in Disguise; or, The Frauds of the Neutral Flags.* 2nd ed. London: C. Whittingham, 1805.

Sterling, Dorothy. *Ahead of Her Time: Abby Kelley and the Politics of Anti-Slavery.* New York: W.W. Norton, 1991.

———, ed. *Speak Out in Thunder Tones: Letters and Other Writings by Black Northerners, 1787–1865.* Garden City, NY: Doubleday, 1973; New York: Da Capo, 1998.

Stern, Julia. "Excavating Genre in *Our Nig.*" *American Literature* 67 (September 1995): 439–64.

Stern, Madeleine B. "Trial of Anthony Burns." *Proceedings of the Massachusetts Historical Society* 44 (1910/1911): 322–34.

Stevens, Elizabeth C. *Elizabeth Buffum Chace and Lillie Chace Wyman: A Century of Abolitionist, Suffragist, and Worker's Rights' Activism.* Jefferson, NC: McFarland, 2003.

Stevenson, Brenda, ed. *The Journals of Charlotte Forten Grimké.* New York: Oxford University Press, 1988.

Steward, Austin. *Twenty-Two Years a Slave and Forty Years a Freeman.* 1857. Syracuse, NY: Syracuse University Press, 2002.

Steward, T.G. "The Banishment of the People of Color from Cincinnati." *Journal of Negro History* 8 (July 1923): 331–32.

Stewart, James Brewer. "The Aims and Impact of Garrisonian Abolitionism, 1840–1860." *Civil War History* 15 (September 1969): 197–209.

———. "Evangelicalism and the Radical Strain in Southern Antislavery Thought During the 1820s." *Journal of Southern History* 39 (August 1973): 379–96.

———. *Holy Warriors: The Abolitionists and American Slavery.* New York: Hill and Wang, 1996.

———. *Joshua R. Giddings and the Tactics of Radical Politics.* Cleveland, OH: Press of Case Western Reserve University, 1970.

———. "Peaceful Hopes and Violent Experiences: The Evolution of Reforming and Radical Abolitionism, 1831–1837." *Civil War History* 17 (December 1971): 293–309.

———. "Politics and Beliefs in Abolitionism: Stanley Elkins' Concept of Anti-institutionalism and Recent Interpretations of American Antislavery." *South Atlantic Quarterly* (Winter 1976): 74–97.

———. *Wendell Phillips: Liberty's Hero.* Baton Rouge: Louisiana State University Press, 1986.

———. *William Lloyd Garrison and the Challenge of Emancipation.* Arlington Heights, IL: Harlan Davidson, 1992.

Still, William. *The Underground Railroad.* 1872. Chicago: Johnson, 1970; Medford, NJ: Plexus, 2005.

Stimson, John Ward. "An Overlooked American Shelley." *The Arena,* July 1903, 15–26.

Stinchcombe, Arthur L. *Sugar Island Slavery in the Age of Enlightenment: The Political Economy of the Caribbean World.* Princeton, NJ: Princeton University Press, 1995.

Stirn, James R. "Urgent Gradualism: The Case of the American Union for Relief and Improvement of the Colored Race." *Civil War History* 25 (December 1979): 309–28.

Stouffer, Allen P. "Michael Willis and the British Roots of Canadian Antislavery." *Slavery and Abolition* 8 (December 1987): 294–312.

Stover, Kenneth. "Maverick at Bay: Ben Wade's Senate Re-Election Campaign." *Civil War History* 12 (1966): 23–42.

Stowe, Charles Edward. *The Life of Harriet Beecher Stowe.* New York: Houghton Mifflin, 1889.

Stowe, Harriet Beecher. *Men of Our Times; or, Leading Patriots of the Day.* New York: J.D. Denison, 1868.

———. *Uncle Tom's Cabin.* 1852. Boston: Houghton Mifflin, 1951.

Strange, Douglas Charles. *British Unitarians Against American Slavery.* Cranbury, NJ: Associated University Presses, 1984.

Strangis, Joel. *Lewis Hayden and the War Against Slavery.* North Haven, CT: Linnett, 1999.

Streifford, David M. "The American Colonization Society: An Application of Republican Ideology to Early Antebellum Reform." *Journal of Southern History* (May 1979): 201–20.

Strong, Donald. *Perfectionist Politics: Abolitionism and the Religious Tensions of American Democracy.* Syracuse, NY: Syracuse University Press, 2000.

Strong, Robert A. "Alexis de Tocqueville and the Abolition of Slavery." *Slavery and Abolition* (September 1987): 204–15.

Strong, Sydney. "The Exodus of Students from Lane Seminary." *Ohio Church History Society Papers* 4 (1893): 1–16.

Stuart, Charles. *A Memoir of Granville Sharp.* New York: American Anti-Slavery Society, 1836.

Stutler, Boyd B. "John Brown's Constitution." *Lincoln Herald* 50–51 (1948/1949): 17–25.

Sumler-Harris, Janice. "The Forten-Purvis Women of Philadelphia and the American Anti-Slavery Crusade." *Journal of Negro History* 66 (Winter 1981/1982): 281–88.

Sundquist, Eric J., ed. *New Essays on* Uncle Tom's Cabin. Cambridge, UK, and New York: Cambridge University Press, 1986.

Sussmann, Charlotte. "The Other Problem With Women: Reproduction and Slave Culture in Aphra Behn's *Oroonoko.*" In *Rereading Aphra Behn: History, Theory, and Criticism,* ed. Heidi Hutner. Charlottesville: University of Virginia Press, 1993.

Sweet, Leonard I. "The Fourth of July and Black Americans in the Nineteenth Century: Northern Leadership Opinion within the Context of the Black Experience." *Journal of Negro History* 61 (July 1976): 256–76.

Sweet, William W. "Some Religious Aspects of the Kansas Struggle." *Journal of Religion* 7 (October 1927): 578–95.

Swift, David. "O! This Heartless Prejudice." *Wesleyan* 67 (Spring 1984): 13–17.

Swift, Samuel. *History of the Town of Middlebury.* Middlebury, VT: A.H. Copeland, 1859.

Swint, Henry L., ed. *Dear Ones at Home: Letters From Contraband Camps.* Nashville, TN: Vanderbilt University Press, 1966.

Swisher, Carl. *History of the Supreme Court of the United States: The Taney Period, 1836–1864.* New York: Macmillan, 1974.

Swisshelm, Jane Grey Cannon. *Crusader and Feminist: Letters of Jane Grey Swisshelm, 1858–1865.* Ed. Arthur J. Larsen. St. Paul: Minnesota Historical Society, 1934.

———. *Half a Century.* 2nd ed. New York: Source Book, 1970.

Tanner, Edwin Platt. "Gerrit Smith, An Interpretation." *New York Historical Society Quarterly* 5 (January 1924): 21–39.

Tap, Bruce. *Over Lincoln's Shoulder: The Committee on the Conduct of the War.* Lawrence: University Press of Kansas, 1998.

Tapié, Victor Lucien. *Joaquim Nabuco, 1849–1910.* Trans. Jacob Bean. Paris: UNESCO, 1949.

Tappan, Lewis. *The Life of Arthur Tappan.* 1870. Westport, CT: Negro Universities Press, 1970.

Tate, W. Carrington. "Gabriel's Insurrection." *Henrico County Historical Society Magazine* 3 (Fall 1979): 13–15.

Taylor, Clare. *British and American Abolitionists: An Episode in Transatlantic Understanding.* Edinburgh, UK: Edinburgh University Press, 1974.

———. *Women of the Anti-Slavery Movement: The Weston Sisters.* New York: St. Martin's, 1995.

Taylor, John M. *William Henry Seward: The Definitive Biography of Abraham Lincoln's Controversial Secretary of State.* New York: HarperCollins, 1991.

Taylor, Richard S. "Beyond Immediate Emancipation: Jonathan Blanchard, Abolitionism, and the Emergence of American Fundamentalism." *Civil War History* 27 (September 1981): 260–74.

———. "Seeking the Kingdom: A Study in the Career of Jonathan Blanchard, 1811–1892." Ph.D. diss., Northern Illinois University, 1977.

Taylor, Yuval, ed. *I Was Born a Slave: An Anthology of Classic Slave Narratives.* Chicago: Lawrence Hill, 1999.

Temperley, Howard. *British Antislavery, 1833–1870.* London: Longman, 1972.

tenBroek, Jacobus. "Thirteenth Amendment to the Constitution of the United States: Consummation to Abolition and Key to the Fourteenth Amendment." *California Law Review* 39 (1951): 171–203.

Tennant, Bob. "Sentiment, Politics, and Empire: A Study of Beilby Porteus's Anti-Slavery Sermon." In *Discourses of Slavery and Abolition: Britain and Its Colonies, 1760–1838,* ed. Brycchan Carey, Markman Ellis, and Sara Salih. Basingstoke, UK: Palgrave Macmillan, 2004.

Terra, Helmut de. *Humboldt: The Life and Times of Alexander von Humboldt, 1769–1859.* New York: Alfred A. Knopf, 1955.

Thomas, Allan C. "The Attitude of the Society of Friends Toward Slavery in the Seventeenth and Eighteenth Centuries." *Papers of the American Society of Church History* 8 (1897): 263–99.

Thomas, Benjamin P. *Theodore Weld: Crusader for Freedom.* New Brunswick, NJ: Rutgers University Press, 1950.

Thomas, Hugh. *The Slave Trade.* New York: Simon & Schuster, 1997.

Thomas, John L. "Romantic Reform in America, 1815–1865." *American Quarterly* 17 (Winter 1965): 656–81.

Thomas, Lamont. *Paul Cuffe: Black Entrepreneur and Pan-Africanist.* Urbana: University of Illinois Press, 1988.

Thomas, R. Dew. *Review of the Debate in the Virginia Legislature of 1831 and 1832.* Westport, CT: Negro Universities Press, 1970.

Thompson, Carol. "Women and the Anti-Slavery Movement." *Current History* 70 (May 1976): 198–201.

Thompson, J. Earl. "Abolitionism and Theological Education at Andover." *New England Quarterly* 47 (June 1974): 238–61.

———. "Lyman Beecher's Long Road to Conservative Abolitionism." *Church History* 42 (March 1973): 89–109.

Thompson, Lawrence R. "The Printing and Publishing Activities of the American Tract Society from 1825 to 1850." *Papers of the Bibliographical Society of America* 35 (1941): 81–114.

Thompson, Priscilla. "Harriet Tubman, Thomas Garrett, and the Underground Railroad." *Delaware History* 22 (September 1986): 1–21.

Thompson, Ralph. *American Literary Annuals and Gift Books, 1825–1865.* 1936. Hamden, CT: Archon, 1967.

———. "The *Liberty Bell* and Other Anti-Slavery Gift Books." *New England Quarterly* 7 (January 1934): 154–68.

Thornton, John K. "African Dimensions of the Stono Rebellion." *American Historical Review* 96 (October 1991): 1101–13.

Tiainen-Anttila, Kaija. *The Problem of Humanity: The Blacks in the European Enlightenment.* Helsinki: Finnish Historical Society, 1994.

Tiffany, Nina Moore. "Stories of the Fugitive Slaves, I: The Escape of William and Ellen Craft." *New England Magazine* 1 (1890): 524–31.

Tillery, Tyrone. "The Inevitability of the Douglass-Garrison Conflict." *Phylon* 37 (June 1976): 137–49.

Tise, Edward. "The Interregional Appeal of Proslavery Thought: An Ideological Profile of the Antebellum American Clergy." *Plantation Society in the Americas* 1 (February 1979): 63–72.

Tocqueville, Alexis de. *Democracy in America.* 2 vols. New York: Alfred A. Knopf, 1945.

Todd, Janet ed. *Aphra Behn Studies.* Cambridge, UK: Cambridge University Press, 1996.

Tolbert, Noble. "Daniel Worth: Tar Heel Abolitionist." *North Carolina Historical Review* 39 (Summer 1962): 284–404.

Toledano, Ehud. *The Ottoman Slave Trade and Its Suppression, 1840–1890.* Princeton, NJ: Princeton University Press, 1982.

Tomich, Dale. "The Wealth of Empire: Francisco Arango y Parreño, Political Economy, and the Second Slavery in Cuba." *Comparative Studies in Society and History* 45 (January 2003): 4–28.

Tompkins, Jane. *Sensational Designs: The Cultural Work of American Fiction, 1790–1860.* New York: Oxford University Press, 1985.

Toplin, Robert Brent. *The Abolition of Slavery in Brazil.* New York: Atheneum, 1972.

———. "Peter Still Versus the Peculiar Institution." *Civil War History* 13 (December 1967): 340–49.

Tragle, Henry Irving, ed. *The Southampton Slave Revolt of 1831: A Compilation of Source Material.* Amherst: University of Massachusetts Press, 1971.

Trefousse, Hans L. *Andrew Johnson: A Biography.* New York: W.W. Norton, 1989.

———. *Benjamin F. Wade: Radical Republican From Ohio.* New York: Twayne, 1963.

———. "The Motivation of a Radical Republican: Benjamin F. Wade." *Ohio History* 73 (1964): 63–74.

———. *The Radical Republicans: Lincoln's Vanguard for Racial Justice.* New York: Alfred A. Knopf, 1969.

———. *Thaddeus Stevens: Nineteenth-Century Egalitarian.* Chapel Hill: University of North Carolina Press, 1997.

Trelease, Allen W. *White Terror: The Ku Klux Klan Conspiracy and Southern Reconstruction.* Baton Rouge: Louisiana State University Press, 1971, 1995.

Trendel, Robert. "William Jay and the International Peace Movement." *Peace and Change* 2 (Fall 1974): 17–23.

Trudeau, Noah A. *Like Men of War: Black Troops in the Civil War, 1862–1865.* Boston: Little, Brown, 1998.

Trumbull, John. *Autobiography, Reminiscences and Letters of John Trumbull, From 1756 to 1841.* New York: Wiley and Putnam, 1841.

Truth, Sojourner. *Narrative of Sojourner Truth: A Bondswoman of Olden Time.* Ed. Olive Gilbert. New York: Oxford University Press, 1991.

Tuckerman, Bayard. *William Jay and the Constitutional Movement for the Abolition of Slavery.* 1893. New York: Negro Universities Press, 1969.

Tulchinsky, Gerald. "Goldwin Smith: Victorian Liberal Anti-Semite." In *Antisemitism in Canada: History and Interpretation,* ed. Alan Davies. Waterloo, Ontario, Canada: Wilfrid Laurier University Press, 1992.

Tulloch, Headley. *Black Canadians: A Long Line of Fighters.* Toronto, Ontario, Canada: NC, 1975.

Turley, D. *The Culture of English Antislavery, 1780–1860.* London: Routledge, 1991.

Turner, Lorenzo D. "Antislavery Sentiment in Literature: The Second Period of Militant Abolitionism, 1850–1861." *Journal of Negro History* 14 (October 1929): 440–75.

Turner, Mary. *Slaves and Missionaries: The Disintegration of Jamaican Slave Society, 1787–1834.* Urbana: University of Illinois Press, 1982.

Tushnet, Mark V. *The American Law of Slavery, 1810–1860: Considerations of Humanity and Interest.* Princeton, NJ: Princeton University Press, 1981.

Tyrrell, Alex. *Joseph Sturge and the Moral Radical Party in Early Victorian Britain.* London: Christopher Helm, 1987.

Tyson, George, ed. *Bondmen and Freedmen in the Danish West Indies.* Saint Thomas: Virgin Islands Humanities Council, 1996.

———. "'Our Side': Caribbean Immigrant Labourers and the Transition to Free Labour on St. Croix, 1849–1879." In *Small Islands, Large Questions: Society, Culture, and Resistance in the Post-Emancipation Caribbean,* ed. Karen Fog Olwig. London: Frank Cass, 1995.

Ullman, Victor. *Martin R. Delany: The Beginnings of Black Nationalism.* Boston: Beacon, 1971.

U.S. Congress. *Biographical Directory of the American Congress, 1774–1971.* Washington, DC: Government Printing Office, 1971.

———. "Report of the Decisions of the Commissioner of Claims under the Convention of February 8, 1833, Between the United States and Great Britain, Transmitted to the Senate by the President of the United States, August 11, 1856." Senate Executive Doc. 103, 34th Cong., 1st sess. Washington, DC: Nicholson, 1856.

Usrey, Mirian L. "Charles Lenox Remond: Garrison's Ebony Echo at the World's Anti-Slavery Convention 1840." *Essex Institute Historical Collections* 106 (April 1970): 112–25.

Utley, Robert M. "General O.O. Howard." *New Mexico Historical Review* 62 (Spring 1987): 55–63.

Uya, Okon Edet. *From Slavery to Public Service: Robert Smalls, 1839–1915.* New York: Oxford University Press, 1971.

Van Broeckhoven, Deborah B. "'A Determination to Labor': Female Antislavery Activity in Rhode Island." *Rhode Island History* 44 (May 1985): 35–45.

Van Deburg, William L. "William Lloyd Garrison and the 'Pro-Slavery Priesthood': The Changing Beliefs of an Evangelical Reformer." *Journal of the American Academy of Religion* 43 (June 1975): 224–37.

Van den Berghe, Pierre L. *Race and Racism: A Comparative Perspective.* New York: Wiley, 1967.

Van Deusen, Glyndon G. *Horace Greeley: Nineteenth-Century Crusader.* New York: Hill and Wang, 1953.

Van Wagenen, Avis S. *Genealogy and Memoirs of Charles and Nathaniel Stearns, and Their Descendants.* Syracuse, NY: Courier, 1901.

Van Zelm, Antoinette. "Virginia Women as Public Citizens: Emancipation Day Celebrations and Lost Cause Commemorations, 1863–1890." In *Negotiating Boundaries of Southern Womanhood: Dealing With the Powers That Be,* ed. Janet L. Coryell, et al. Columbia: University of Missouri Press, 2000.

Vaughan, Alden T. "The Origins Debate: Slavery and Racism in Seventeenth-Century Virginia." *Virginia Magazine of History and Biography* 97 (July 1989): 311–54.

Vaux, Roberts. *Memoirs of the Lives of Benjamin Lay and Ralph Sandiford.* Philadelphia: Solomon W. Conrad, 1815.

Venet, Wendy Hamand. *Neither Ballots nor Bullets: Women Abolitionists and the Civil War.* Charlottesville: University of Virginia Press, 1991.

Ver Nooy, Amy Pearce. "The Anti-Slavery Movement in Dutchess County, 1835–1850." *Dutchess County Historical Society Year Book* 28 (1943): 57–66.

Vibert, Faith. "The Society for the Propagation of the Gospel in Foreign Parts: Its Work for the Negroes in North America Before 1763." *Journal of Negro History* 18 (April 1933): 171–212.

Villard, Oswald Garrison. "Wendell Phillips After Fifty Years." *American Mercury* (January 1935): 89–99.

Vincent, Theodore G. *The Legacy of Vicente Guerrero: Mexico's First Black Indian President.* Gainesville: University Press of Florida, 2001.

Volpe, Vernon L. *Forlorn Hope of Freedom: The Liberty Party in the Old Northwest, 1838–1848.* Kent, OH: Kent State University Press, 1990.

Von Scholten, Peter. "Letter of December 22, 1849." In *Emancipation in the U.S. Virgin Islands: 150 Years of Freedom,* ed. Arnold Highfield. Saint Croix: Virgin Islands Emancipation Commission/Virgin Islands Humanities Council, 1998.

Vorenberg, Michael. *Final Freedom: The Civil War, the Abolition of Slavery, and the Thirteenth Amendment.* Cambridge, UK: Cambridge University Press, 2001.

Wade, Richard C. "The Negro in Cincinnati 1800–1830." *Journal of Negro History* 39 (January 1954): 43–57.

Wagenknecht, Edward. *Harriet Beecher Stowe: The Known and the Unknown.* New York: Oxford University Press, 1965.

Waldrep, Christopher. *The Many Faces of Judge Lynch: Extralegal Violence and Punishment in America.* New York: Palgrave, 2002.

Waldron, Mary. *Lactilla, Milkwoman of Clifton: The Life and Writings of Ann Yearsley, 1753–1806.* Athens: University of Georgia Press, 1996.

Walker, Clarence E. *A Rock in a Weary Land: The African Methodist Episcopal Church During the Civil War and Reconstruction.* Baton Rouge: Louisiana State University Press, 1982.

Walker, Peter F. *Moral Choices: Memory, Desire, and Imagination in Nineteenth-Century American Abolition.* Baton Rouge: Louisiana State University Press, 1978.

Walker, Sheila. "The Feast of Good Death: An Afro-Catholic Emancipation Celebration in Brazil." *Sage: A Scholarly Journal on Black Women* 3:2 (1986): 27–31.

Walkes, Joseph A., Jr. *A Prince Hall Masonic Quiz Book.* Rev. ed. Richmond, VA: Macoy, 1989.

Wallace, Elizabeth. *Goldwin Smith: Victorian Liberal.* Toronto, Ontario, Canada: University of Toronto Press, 1957.

Walls, Andrew F. *The Missionary Movement in Christian History: Studies in the Transmission of Faith.* Edinburgh, UK: T&T Clark, 1996.

———. *The Nineteenth Century Missionary Task and Continental Europe.* Cambridge, MA: North Atlantic Missiology Project, 1996.

Walsh, Oonah. *Ireland Abroad: Politics and Professions in the Nineteenth Century.* Portland, OR: Four Courts, 2003.

Walters, Ronald. "The Erotic South: Civilization and Sexuality in American Abolitionism." *American Quarterly* 25 (May 1973): 177–202.

———. "The Family and Ante-Bellum Reform: An Interpretation." *Societas* 4 (Summer 1973): 221–32.

Walvin, James. *Black Ivory: A History of British Slavery.* London: HarperCollins, 1992.

———. *England, Slaves, and Freedom, 1776–1838.* Jackson: University Press of Mississippi, 1986.

———. *Making the Black Atlantic: Britain and the African Diaspora.* New York: Cassell, 2000.

———. *Slavery and British Society, 1776–1846.* Baton Rouge: Louisiana State University Press, 1982.

Ward, Samuel Ringgold. *Autobiography of a Fugitive Negro: His Anti-Slavery Labours in the United States, Canada and England.* 1855. Chicago: Johnson, 1970.

Ward, William. *The Royal Navy and the Slavers.* New York: Pantheon, 1969.

Warner, Oliver. *William Wilberforce and His Times.* London: B.T. Batsford, 1962.

Warner, Robert A. "Amos Gerry Beman 1812–1894: A Memoir on a Forgotten Leader." *Journal of Negro History* 22 (April 1937): 200–221.

———. *New Haven Negroes: A Social History.* New Haven, CT: Yale University Press, 1940.

Washington, Booker T. *Frederick Douglass.* 1907. New York: Haskell House, 1968.

Watkins, Richard H. "Baptists of the North and Slavery, 1856–1860." *Foundations* 13 (October/December 1970): 317–33.

Watt, James. "James Ramsay, 1733–1789: Naval Surgeon, Naval Chaplain and Morning Star of the Anti-Slavery Movement." *Mariner's Mirror* 81 (May 1995): 156–70.

Way, R.B. "Was the Fugitive Slave Clause of the Constitution Necessary?" *Iowa Journal of History and Politics* 5 (July 1907): 326–36.

Webber, Thomas L. *Deep Like Rivers: Education in the Slave Quarter Community, 1831–1865.* New York: W.W. Norton, 1978.

Webster, Charles K. *The Congress of Vienna, 1814–1815.* New York: Barnes and Noble, 1963.

———. *The Foreign Policy of Castlereagh, 1815–1822.* London: G. Bell & Sons, 1925, 1931.

Wedgwood, Julia. *The Personal Life of Josiah Wedgwood the Potter.* Ed. C.M. Herford. London: Macmillan, 1915.

Weeks, Stephen B. "Anti-Slavery Sentiment in the South." *Southern Historical Association Publications* 2 (1898): 87–130.

Weisenburger, Steven. *Modern Medea: A Family Story of Slavery and Child-Murder From the Old South.* New York: Hill and Wang, 1998.

Weisman, Stephen M. "Frederick Douglass, Portrait of a Black Militant: A Study in the Family Romance." *Psychoanalytic Study of the Child* 25 (1975): 725–51.

Weiss, John, ed. *The Life and Correspondence of Theodore Parker.* 2 vols. New York: D. Appleton, 1864.

Weland, Gerald. *O.O. Howard: Union General.* Jefferson, NC: McFarland, 1995.

Welborn, Max. "Victor Schoelcher's Views on Race and Slavery." Ph.D. diss., Ohio State University, 1965.

Weld, Theodore Dwight. *The Bible Against Slavery; or, an Inquiry Into the Genius of the Mosaic System, and the Teachings of the Old Testament on the Subject of Human Rights.* 1837. Pittsburgh: United Presbyterian Board of Publication, 1864; Detroit, MI: Negro History, 1970.

Wells, Ida B. *Crusade for Justice: The Autobiography of Ida B. Wells.* Ed. Alfreda M. Duster. Chicago: University of Chicago Press, 1991.

Werlich, Robert. *"Beast" Butler: Biography of Union Major General Benjamin Franklin Butler.* Washington, DC: Quaker Press, 1962.

Wesley, Charles H. "Lincoln's Plan for Colonizing Emancipated Negroes." *Journal of Negro History* 4 (January 1919): 7–21.

———. "The Negro in the Organization of Abolition." *Phylon* 2 (Third Quarter 1941): 223–35.

———. "Negro Suffrage in the Period of Constitution-Making, 1787–1865." *Journal of Negro History* 32 (April 1947): 143–68.

———. "The Negroes of New York in the Emancipation Movement." *Journal of Negro History* 24 (January 1939): 65–103.

———. "The Negro's Struggle for Freedom in Its Birthplace." *Journal of Negro History* 30 (January 1945): 62–81.

———. "The Participation of Negroes in Anti-Slavery Political Parties." *Journal of Negro History* 29 (January 1944): 32–74.

———. *Richard Allen: An Apostle of Freedom.* Ed. James L. Conyers, Jr. Trenton, NJ: Africa World Press, 2000.

West, Robert C. *Colonial Placer Mining in Colombia.* Baton Rouge: Louisiana State University Press, 1952.

West, Robin. "Toward an Abolitionist Interpretation of the Fourteenth Amendment." *West Virginia Law Review* 94 (Fall 1991): 111–55.

Wheatley, Phillis. *The Collected Works of Phillis Wheatley.* Ed. John C. Fields. New York: Oxford University Press, 1988.

White, Arthur O. "The Black Movement Against Jim-Crow Education in Buffalo, New York, 1800–1900." *Phylon* 30 (December 1969): 375–93.

———. "The Black Movement Against Jim-Crow Education in Lockport, New York, 1800–1900." *New York History* 50 (July 1969): 265–82.

White, Barbara A. "*Our Nig* and the She-Devil: New Information about Harriet Wilson and the 'Bellmont Family.'" *American Literature* 65 (March 1993): 19–52.

White, Dana F., and Victor A. Kramer. *Olmsted South: Old South Critic/New South Planner.* Westport, CT: Greenwood, 1979.

White, David O. "The Crandall School and the Degree of Influence by Garrison and the Abolitionists Upon It." *Connecticut Historical Society Bulletin* 43 (October 1978).

———. "The Fugitive Blacksmith of Hartford: James W.C. Pennington." *Connecticut Historical Society Bulletin* 49 (Winter 1984): 4–29.

White, Marie S. "The Methodist Antislavery Struggle in the Land of Lincoln." *Methodist History* 10 (July 1972): 33–52.

Whitman, Karen. "Re-Evaluating John Brown's Raid at Harpers Ferry." *West Virginia History* 34 (October 1972): 46–84.

Whitman, T. Stephen. *The Price of Freedom: Slavery and Manumission in Baltimore and Early National Maryland.* Lexington: University Press of Kentucky, 1997.

Whittier, John Greenleaf. "The Antislavery Convention of 1833." *Atlantic Monthly* 33 (February 1874): 169.

———. *Essays and Pamphlets on Antislavery.* Westport, CT: Negro Universities Press, 1970.

———. *The Letters of John Greenleaf Whittier.* Ed. John B. Pickard. Cambridge, MA: Harvard University Press, 1975.

Wiecek, William M. "Abolitionist Constitutional Theory." *Society* 24 (November/December 1986): 60–62.

———. "Slavery and Abolition Before the United States Supreme Court, 1820–1860." *Journal of American History* 65 (June 1978): 34–59.

———. *The Sources of Antislavery Constitutionalism in America, 1760–1848.* Ithaca, NY: Cornell University Press, 1977.

———. "The Statutory Law of Slavery and Race in the Thirteen Mainland Colonies of British America." *William and Mary Quarterly,* 3rd ser., 34 (April 1977): 258–80.

Wiggins, William H., Jr. "Juneteenth: Tracking the Progress of an Emancipation Celebration." *American Visions* 8 (June/July 1993): 28–31.

———. "'Lift Every Voice': A Study of Afro-American Emancipation Celebrations." *Journal of Asian and African Studies* 9 (1974): 180–91.

———. *O Freedom! Afro-American Emancipation Celebrations.* Knoxville: University of Tennessee Press, 1987.

Wiggins, William H., and Douglas DeNatale, eds. *Jubilation! African American Celebrations in the Southeast.* Columbia: McKissick Museum, University of South Carolina, 1993.

Wilder, D.W. *Annals of Kansas.* Topeka, KS: G.W. Martin, 1875.

Wilkinson, Norman B. "The Philadelphia Free Produce Attack Upon Slavery." *Pennsylvania Magazine of History and Biography* 66 (July 1942): 294–313.

Williams, Cecil. "Whittier's Relation to Garrison and the 'Liberator.'" *New England Quarterly* 25 (June 1952): 248–55.

Williams, David Alan. "William Lloyd Garrison, the Historians, and the Abolitionist Movement." *Essex Institute Historical Collections* 98 (April 1962): 84–99.

Williams, David H. *The American Almanac: A Repository of Useful Knowledge, for the Year 1840.* Boston: David H. Williams, 1839.

Williams, Eric. "The British West Indian Slave Trade after Its Abolition in 1807." *Journal of Negro History* 27 (April 1942): 175–91.

———. *From Columbus to Castro: The History of the Caribbean, 1492–1969.* New York: Vintage Books, 1984.

Williams, Heather Andrea. *Self-Taught: African American Education in Slavery and Freedom.* Chapel Hill: University of North Carolina Press, 2005.

Williams, Irene E. "The Operation of the Fugitive Slave Law in Western Pennsylvania From 1850 to 1860." *Western Pennsylvania Historical Magazine* 4 (January 1921): 150–61.

Williams, L.A. "Northern Intellectual Reaction to the Policy of Emancipation." *Journal of Negro History* 46 (July 1961): 174–88.

Williams, Sandra Boyd. "The Indiana Supreme Court and the Struggle Against Slavery." *Indiana Law Review* 30 (Winter 1997): 305–17.

Williams, William H. *Slavery and Freedom in Delaware, 1639–1865.* Wilmington, DE: Scholarly Resources, 1996.

Willmore, Gayraud S. *Black Religion and Black Radicalism.* Garden City, NY: Doubleday, 1972.

Wills, Garry. *Inventing America: Jefferson's Declaration of Independence.* New York: Vintage Books, 1979.

Wills, William. *A History of the Law, the Courts, and the Lawyers of Maine, From Its First Colonization to the Early Part of the Present Century.* Portland, ME: Bailey and Noyes, 1863.

Wilmshurst, Walter Leslie. *The Meaning of Masonry.* 6th ed. London: J.M. Watkins, 1947.

Wilson, Carol. *Freedom at Risk: The Kidnapping of Free Blacks in America, 1780–1865.* Lexington: University Press of Kentucky, 1994.

Wilson, Charles Morrow. *The Dred Scott Decision.* Philadelphia: Auerbach, 1973.

Wilson, Ellen Gibson. *John Clarkson and the African Adventure.* London: Macmillan, 1980.

———. *The Loyal Blacks.* New York: Capricorn, 1976.

———. *Thomas Clarkson: A Biography.* 2nd ed. New York: William Sessions, 1996.

Wilson, Harriet E. *Our Nig; or Sketches from the Life of a Free Black.* 1859. Ed. Henry Louis Gates, Jr. New York: Vintage Books, 1983.

Wilson, Henry, and Samuel Hunt. *History of the Rise and Fall of the Slave Power in America.* 3 vols. Boston: J.R. Osgood, 1872.

Wilson, Janet. "The Early Anti-Slavery Propaganda." Pts. 1 and 2. *Bulletin of the Boston Public Library* 19

(November 1944): 343–60; 19 (December 1944): 393–405.

Wilson, Keith P. *Campfires of Freedom: The Camp Life of Black Soldiers During the Civil War.* Kent, OH: Kent State University Press, 2002.

Wilson, Major L. "The Free Soil Concept of Progress and the Irrepressible Conflict." *American Quarterly* 22 (1970): 769–90.

———. *The Presidency of Martin Van Buren.* Lawrence: University of Kansas, 1984.

Winch, Julie, ed. *The Elite of Our People: Joseph Willson's Sketches of Black Upper-Class Life in Antebellum Philadelphia.* University Park: Pennsylvania State University Press, 2000.

———. *A Gentleman of Color: The Life of James Forten.* New York: Oxford University Press, 2002.

———. "Philadelphia and the Other Underground Railroad." *Pennsylvania Magazine of History and Biography* 61 (January 1987): 3–25.

———. *Philadelphia's Black Elite: Activism, Accommodation, and Struggle for Autonomy, 1787–1848.* Philadelphia: Temple University Press, 1988.

Windley, Lathan A. *Runaway Slave Advertisements: A Documentary History from the 1730s to 1790.* Westport, CT: Greenwood, 1983.

Winks, Robin W. *Blacks in Canada: A History.* New Haven, CT: Yale University Press, 1971.

———. "The Making of a Fugitive Slave Narrative: Josiah Henson and Uncle Tom—A Case Study." In *The Slave's Narrative,* ed. Charles T. Davis and Henry Louis Gates, Jr. Oxford, UK: Oxford University Press, 1985.

Winnerstein, John R. "Parke Godwin, Utopian Socialism, and the Politics of Antislavery." *New York History Society Quarterly* 9 (July/October 1976): 107–27.

Wittaker, Cynthia. "The White Negro: A Comparison of Russian and American Abolition Movements." *North Dakota Quarterly* 33 (1965): 32–37.

Wixom, Robert. *Benjamin Lundy (1789–1839): The Pioneer Quaker Abolitionist.* Columbia: University of Missouri Press, 1971.

Wolseley, Roland. *The Black Press, U.S.A.* Ames: Iowa State University Press, 1990.

Wood, Forest G. *The Arrogance of Faith: Christianity and Race in America from the Colonial Era to the Twentieth Century.* Boston: Northeastern University Press, 1990.

Wood, Gary V. *Heir to the Fathers: John Quincy Adams and the Spirit of Constitutional Government.* Lanham, MD: Lexington, 2004.

Wood, Peter. *Black Majority: Negroes in Colonial South Carolina From 1670 Through the Stono Rebellion.* New York: Alfred A. Knopf, 1974.

Woodhull, Ronald H. "Whittier on Abolition—a Letter to Emerson." *Essex Institute Historical Collections* 9 (1957).

Woodson, Carter G. "Anthony Benezet." *Journal of Negro History* 2 (January 1917): 37–50.

———. *The Education of the Negro Prior to 1861.* Salem, NH: Ayer, 1986.

Woodward, C. Vann. "The Antislavery Myth." *American Scholar* 31 (Spring 1962): 312–23.

Woolf, Virginia. "Aphra Behn." In *Women and Writing,* ed. Michèle Barrett. New York: Harcourt Brace Jovanovich, 1979.

Woolman, John. *The Journal and Major Essays of John Woolman.* Ed. Phillips P. Moulton. New York: Oxford University Press, 1971.

Work, Monroe N. "Life of Charles B. Ray." *Journal of Negro History* 4 (October 1919): 361–71.

Wormer, William Frederic. "The Columbia Race Riots." *Lancaster County Historical Society Papers* 26 (October 1922): 175–87.

Wormley, G.S. "Prudence Crandall." *Journal of Negro History* 8 (January 1923): 72–80.

Wright, Elizur. "The Father of the Liberty Party." *The Independent,* January 30, 1873.

Wright, Josephine R.B., ed. *Ignatius Sancho (1729–1780), An Early African Composer in England: The Collected Editions of His Music in Facsimile.* New York: Garland, 1981.

Wright, Marion T. "A Dramatic Historical Event: Negro Suffrage in New Jersey, 1776–1875." *Journal of Negro History* 33 (April 1948): 168–71.

Wright, Philip. *Knibb "The Notorious": Slaves' Missionary, 1803–1845.* London: Sidgwick and Jackson, 1973.

Wright, William E. *Serf, Seigneur, and Sovereign: Agrarian Reform in Eighteenth-Century Bohemia.* Minneapolis: University of Minnesota Press, 1966.

Wyatt-Brown, Bertram. "Abolitionism: Its Meaning for Contemporary American Reform." *Midwest Quarterly* 8 (October 1966): 41–55.

———. "The Abolitionists' Postal Campaign of 1835." *Journal of Negro History* 50 (October 1965): 227–38.

———. "John Brown, Weathermen, and the Psychology of Antinomian Violence." *Soundings* 58 (1975): 417–40.

———. *Lewis Tappan and the Evangelical War Against Slavery.* Cleveland, OH: Press of Case Western Reserve University, 1969.

———. "The New Left and the Abolitionists: Romantic Radicalism in America." *Soundings* 54 (Summer 1971): 147–63.

———. "New Leftists and Abolitionists: A Comparison of American Radical Styles." *Wisconsin Magazine of History* 53 (Summer 1970): 256–68.

———. "Prelude to Abolitionism: Sabbatarian Politics and the Rise of the Second Party System." *Journal of American History* 58 (September 1971): 316–41.

———. *Southern Honor: Ethics and Behavior in the Old South.* New York: Oxford University Press, 1982.

———. "Stanley Elkins' Slavery: The Antislavery Interpretation Re-Examined." *American Quarterly* 25 (May 1973): 154–76.

———. "Three Generations of Yankee Parenthood: The Tappan Family, a Case Study of Antebellum Nature." *Illinois Quarterly* 38 (Fall 1975): 12–28.

———. "William Lloyd Garrison and Antislavery Unity: A Reappraisal." *Civil War History* 13 (March 1967): 5–24.

Wyly-Jones, Susan. "The 1835 Anti-Abolition Meetings in the South: A New Look at the Controversy Over the Abolition Postal Campaign." *Civil War History* 47:4 (2001): 289–309.

Wyman, Lillie Buffum Chace. "Reminiscences of Two Abolitionists." *New England Magazine,* January 1903.

Yacovone, Donald. "Samuel Joseph May, Antebellum Reform, and the Problem of Patricide." *Perspectives in American History* 2 (1985): 99–124.

———. *Samuel Joseph May and the Dilemma of the Liberal Persuasion, 1797–1871.* Philadelphia: Temple University Press, 1991.

Yale, Allen. "Ingenious and Enterprising Mechanics: A Case Study of Industrialization in Rural Vermont, 1815–1900." Ph.D. diss., University of Connecticut, 1995.

Yanuck, Julius. "The Garner Fugitive Slave Case." *Mississippi Valley Historical Review* 40 (June 1953): 47–66.

Yee, Shirley. *Black Women Abolitionists: A Study in Activism, 1828–1860.* Knoxville: University of Tennessee Press, 1994.

Yellin, Jean Fagan. *Harriet Jacobs: A Life.* New York: Basic Civitas, 2004.

———. *Women and Sisters: The Anti-Slavery Feminists in American Culture.* New Haven, CT: Yale University Press, 1992.

Yellin, Jean Fagan, and John C. Van Horne, eds. *The Abolitionist Sisterhood: Women's Political Culture in Antebellum America.* Ithaca, NY: Cornell University Press, 1994.

Yetman, Norman. "The Background of the Slave Narrative Collection." *American Quarterly* 19 (Fall 1967): 534–53.

———. "Ex-Slave Interviews and the Historiography of Slavery." *American Quarterly* 36 (Summer 1984): 181–210.

———. *Voices From Slavery: 100 Authentic Slave Narratives.* Mineola, NY: Dover, 2000.

Zanger, Jules. "The 'Tragic Octroon' in Pre-Civil War Fiction." *American Quarterly* 18 (Spring 1966): 63–70.

Zangrando, Robert L. *The NAACP Crusade Against Lynching, 1909–1950.* Philadelphia: Temple University Press, 1980.

Zembola, Zamba. *The Life and Adventures of Zamba, an African Negro King; and His Experience of Slavery in South Carolina.* 1847. Corrected and arranged by Peter Neilson. Freeport, NY: Books for Libraries, 1970.

Zeuyner, John. "A Note on Martin Delany's *Blake,* and Black Militancy." *Phylon* 32 (Spring 1971): 98–105.

Zilversmit, Arthur. *The First Emancipation.* Chicago: University of Chicago Press, 1967.

———. "Quok [*sic*] Walker, Mumbet, and the Abolition of Slavery in Massachusetts." *William and Mary Quarterly,* 3rd ser., 25 (October 1968): 614–24.

Zipf, Karen. " 'Among These American Heathens': Congregationalist Missionaries and African American Evangelicals During Reconstruction." *North Carolina Historical Review* 74 (April 1997): 111–34.

Zoellner, Robert H. "Negro Colonization: The Climate of Opinion Surrounding Lincoln." *Mid-America: An Historical Review* 42 (July 1960): 141–45.

Zorbaugh, Charles L. "From Lane to Oberlin—An Exodus Extraordinary." *Ohio Presbyterian Historical Society Proceedings* 2 (June 1940): 30–47.

Zorn, Roman J. "Criminal Extradition Menaces the Canadian Haven for Fugitive Slaves 1841–1861." *Canadian Historical Review* 38 (December 1957): 284–94.

———. "The New England Anti-Slavery Society: Pioneer Abolitionist Organization." *Journal of Negro History* 43 (July 1957): 157–76.

Index